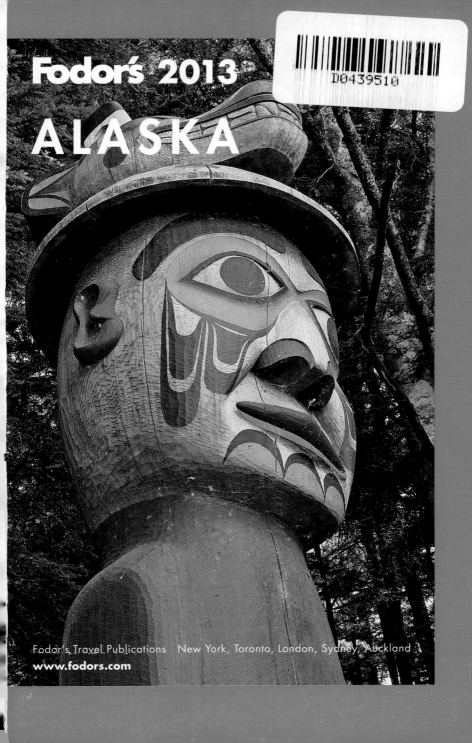

Fodor's 2013
ALASKA

Fodor's Travel Publications   New York, Toronto, London, Sydney, Auckland
www.fodors.com

FODOR'S ALASKA 2013
Editorial Contributors: Bethany Beckerlegge, Debbie Harmsen, Amanda R. Theunissen

Writers: Teeka Ballas, Linda Coffman, Amy Fletcher, Sarah Henning, Lisa Hupp, E. Readicker-Henderson, Jessica Rohe
Editor: Salwa Jabado

Production Editor: Jennifer DePrima
Maps & Illustrations: Mark Stroud and David Lindroth, *cartographers;* Rebecca Baer, *map editor;* William Wu, *information graphics*
Design: Fabrizio La Rocca, *creative director;* Tina Malaney, Chie Ushio, Jessica Ramirez, *designers;* Melanie Marin, *associate director of photography;* Jennifer Romains, *photo research*
Cover photos: front: (Brown bear fishing for spawning salmon at Geographic Harbor): Paul Souders/Corbis. Back: (from left to right): Ron Sanford/iStockphoto; Manamana/Shutterstock; Alaska Bounty. Spine: Darryl Brooks/iStockphoto.
Production Manager: Angela L. McLean

ISBN 978–0–87637–126–8

ISSN 0271–2776

SPECIAL SALES
This book is available at special discounts for bulk purchases for sales promotions or premiums. Special editions, including personalized covers, excerpts of existing books, and corporate imprints, can be created in large quantities for special needs. For more information, write to Special Markets/Premium Sales, 1745 Broadway, MD 3-1, New York, NY 10019, or e-mail specialmarkets@randomhouse.com.

AN IMPORTANT TIP & AN INVITATION
Although all prices, opening times, and other details in this book are based on information supplied to us at press time, changes occur all the time in the travel world, and Fodor's cannot accept responsibility for facts that become outdated or for inadvertent errors or omissions. So **always confirm information when it matters,** especially if you're making a detour to visit a specific place. Your experiences—positive and negative—matter to us. If we have missed or misstated something, **please write to us.** Share your opinion instantly through our online feedback center at fodors.com/contact-us.

PRINTED IN COLOMBIA

10 9 8 7 6 5 4 3 2 1

CONTENTS

MAPS

ABOUT THIS GUIDE

Fodor's Ratings

Everything in this guide is worth doing—we don't cover what isn't—but exceptional sights, hotels, and restaurants are recognized with additional accolades. **Fodor's** Choice★ indicates our top recommendations; ★ highlights places we deem highly recommended; and **Best Bets** call attention to notable hotels and restaurants in various categories. Care to nominate a new place? Visit Fodors.com/contact-us.

Trip Costs

We list prices wherever possible to help you budget well. Hotel and restaurant price categories from $ to $$$$ are noted alongside each recommendation. For hotels, we include the lowest cost of a standard double room in high season. For restaurants, we cite the average price of a main course at dinner or, if dinner isn't served, at lunch. For attractions, we always list adult admission fees; discounts are usually available for children, students, and senior citizens.

Hotels

Our local writers vet every hotel to recommend the best overnights in each price category, from budget to expensive. Unless otherwise specified, you can expect private bath, phone, and TV in your room. For expanded hotel reviews, facilities, and deals visit Fodors.com.

TripAdvisor

Our expert hotel picks are reinforced by high ratings on TripAdvisor. Look for representative quotes in this guide, and the latest TripAdvisor ratings and feedback at Fodors.com.

Restaurants

Unless we state otherwise, restaurants are open for lunch and dinner daily. We mention dress code only when there's a specific

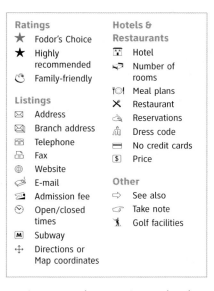

Ratings	Hotels & Restaurants
★ Fodor's Choice	🏨 Hotel
★ Highly recommended	↴ Number of rooms
☺ Family-friendly	❍ Meal plans
Listings	✕ Restaurant
✉ Address	⎘ Reservations
✉ Branch address	🏛 Dress code
☎ Telephone	⊟ No credit cards
🖨 Fax	$ Price
⊕ Website	**Other**
✎ E-mail	⇨ See also
🎫 Admission fee	☞ Take note
⊙ Open/closed times	🏌 Golf facilities
Ⓜ Subway	
✛ Directions or Map coordinates	

requirement and reservations only when they're essential or not accepted. To make restaurant reservations, visit Fodors.com.

Credit Cards

The hotels and restaurants in this guide typically accept credit cards. If not, we'll say so.

1

Experience
Alaska

WHAT'S WHERE

Numbers refer to chapter numbers.

4 Southeast Alaska. Southeast Alaska (or "the Panhandle") includes the Inside Passage. Here you'll find Juneau, the state capital, and Sitka, the former Russian hub. Haines and Skagway are the only towns along the water route that have roads to "the Outside." A boat trip through the Alaska Chilkat Eagle Preserve will take you into wilderness that draws about 4,000 eagles to the area. Along this passage, fjords snake between the mountains, timbered slopes plunge to rocky shores, and marine life abounds.

5 Anchorage. With nearly half the state's population, Anchorage is Alaska's biggest city and a good jumping-off point for visitors. The restaurants, art and history museums, copious espresso stands, and performing arts have earned the city the sobriquet "Seattle of the North." Alaskans often deride the place as "Los Anchorage," but the occasional moose ambling down a street hints at the nearby wilderness.

6 South Central Alaska. South Central offers great fishing, hiking, rafting, and wildlife viewing. Visit Seward and Homer on the Kenai

Peninsula. Kodiak, in the Gulf of Alaska, is known for its green-carpeted mountains and brown bears. Charter outfits take you to remote wilderness spots. The summer crowds can be daunting, but a little research will take you to areas of true wilderness.

7 Denali National Park. Home to Mt. McKinley—the highest peak in North America—Denali National Park and Preserve comprises 6 million acres of Alaska's best wildlife, scenery, and adventures.

8 The Interior. Bound by the Brooks Range to the north and the Alaska Range to the south, the Interior is home to Denali National Park and Preserve. The region's major city is Fairbanks (gateway to the towns of the Arctic), the Bering Coast, and Canada's Yukon Territory.

9 The Bush. Many call the Bush the "real Alaska." Inupiaq people share the tundra with the Prudhoe Bay oil fields. Brown bears roam Katmai National Park. Volcanoes shake the Alaska Peninsula. Prospectors still pan for gold in Nome. Except for the Dalton Highway and a few short roads near Nome, the region is essentially roadless. Traveling here requires planning; the reward is true adventure.

ALASKA TODAY

Politics

Alaska's politics and policies seem as wild as its vast, untamed acres. This is partly due to the fact that the largest state in the nation comes with a seemingly limitless supply of natural resources, and with them come conflict and controversy. Alaska's politics are thus saddled with numerous fiscal and environmental responsibilities, none of which are easily met. As a state that is often overlooked in the political media, it caught the public eye in 2008 when then-governor Sarah Palin was tapped to be the running mate for presidential candidate John McCain. Since then, Alaska has stayed in the limelight.

Gas and mining corporations have enormous influence on public policy in Alaska, but not without rivalry from environmentalists and subsistence advocates. There are ongoing and highly publicized battles over the proposed Pebble Mine project and the Donlin Gold Mine. If built, they could be the largest copper and gold mines in the world. Supporters claim they will bring much-needed jobs to local Native populations. Opponents say they will irrevocably pollute the lakes, rivers, and surrounding terrain (not to mention, near Pebble Mine project, swaths of Bristol Bay), destroying the fishing industry and other subsistence ways of life on which local populations rely.

Rapidly gaining national attention is the Arctic National Wildlife Refuge (ANWR), 19.2 million roadless acres supporting 45 species of land and marine mammals, 36 species of fish, and 180 species of birds. ANWR is in the northeast corner of the state and has been dubbed the Last Great Wilderness. The only way to get there is by bush plane. Area 1002, 1.5 million acres along the refuge's coastal plain, has long been a subject of controversy, as it is thought to contain a large supply of oil.

From the Iditarod to cabin building, everything in Alaska is steeped in politics. This is inevitable, as there are more politicians per capita than police officers.

Economics

More than 75% of Alaska's revenue is derived from oil extraction. The state is also the nation's leader in commercial fishing, but ranks dead last in number of farms and farm products. There is very little manufacturing in the state. Thus the cost of manufactured goods, produce, and other foodstuffs is considerably higher than in other states.

Because Alaska is predominantly composed of rural villages, thousands of miles from any distribution center, the cost of living is relatively high. In Barrow, for instance, one can expect to pay $10 for a gallon of milk.

The Permanent Fund Dividend (PFD) is a sacred check that Alaskans receive once a year, and for many in the Bush it can be a lifesaver. In 1977 the fund was created to receive 25% of Alaska's oil royalty income. It was designed to maintain a state income even after the reserves had been tapped out. Residents receive a check every October in amounts that vary from year to year, but are in the ballpark of $1,200. For many who live in the Bush, this stipend helps heat their homes in the winter. Every bit helps; rural and remote Alaska has seen heating fuel go as high as $10 per gallon.

Global Warming

In Alaska few people disagree that the glaciers and permafrost are melting; it's just a fact. It is what to do about it that has politicians and constituents bickering.

Regardless of political persuasion, however, things are changing in Alaska. Icebergs are melting, and unfortunately for polar bears, that's where they live. In 2008 the Interior Department put polar bears on the protected species list, but some environmentalists believe that without addressing the causes of global warming the designation will do little to help. The polar bear is currently listed as threatened, not endangered.

As ocean temperatures rise, new migrations are starting to take effect. One unfortunate one, however, is the steady northward migration of the Humboldt giant squid. It is a voracious predator that travels in packs and is starting to be found as far north as Sitka. This could pose a serious threat to the salmon population and the fishing industry in general.

Warmer temperatures also mean new economic opportunities. As the Arctic ice melts, the region is becoming more accessible, which means there is greater possibility for more oil and gas exploration.

Many indigenous tribes in the Arctic region have begun to adapt to the changes. Their hunting patterns have adjusted to new migration times and routes. Unfortunately permafrost, the frozen ground they live upon, is also melting. Towns and villages are sinking, and the cost of relocation could rise into the billions of dollars. Permafrost that once held the coastline together is disappearing, and groups like the Army Corps of Engineers are scrambling to save villages from falling off into the ocean.

The Arts

Visitors are often surprised to find that Alaska is filled with extraordinarily talented contemporary artists. Not only do some of the world's foremost artists,

writers, and photographers reside in Alaska, there is equal talent found among those whose work never sees the Outside. For many Alaskans the long, dark winter is a great time to hunker down, season their craft, and prepare to sell their wares in the summer at galleries, museums, and theaters all over the state. In summer, weekend outdoor markets are also a great place to find local and Native talent. Look for the Made in Alaska sticker or the silver hand symbol for authenticity.

Sports

In a state full of renegades and thrill seekers, it is no wonder that the biggest sporting event of the year occasionally requires a racer to permanently relinquish feeling in a finger or a foot. The Iditarod Trail Sled Dog Race, a 1,150-mile-long trek, is by far the most popular sporting event in Alaska. It began in 1973 in homage to the brave souls who ventured to Nome in 1925 to take medicine to villagers struck with one of the worst outbreaks of diphtheria ever recorded. Nowadays, more than 100 racers and their packs of canines converge on the ice and snow on the first Saturday in March to race from Anchorage to Nome. In 2012, 25-year-old Dallas Seavey became the youngest dog musher to win the Iditarod, besting both his father and grandfather. The sport is not without controversy; mushers have come under scrutiny, since several groups have made allegations of animal cruelty.

Although Alaskans from all over the state are passionate about their dog mushers, the most popular team sport is hockey. College hockey is big news, as are the Alaska Aces, the state minor-league team that feeds into the NHL's St. Louis Blues.

ALASKA
TOP ATTRACTIONS

Katmai National Park

(A) When people come to Alaska they want to see bears. Yet most visitors never get a glimpse (bears prefer their privacy). However, at Katmai National Park, which boasts the world's largest brown bear population, you're almost guaranteed a photograph of bears doing bear things. Just remember, their teeth and claws are mighty sharp.

Alaska Native Heritage Center

(B) There are more than 200 Native tribal entities in Alaska. At the Heritage Center, experience the lifestyles and traditions of these Native cultures through art and artifact displays and activities like blanket tossing, parka sewing, and drumming.

Mt. McKinley

(C) There are a dozen places between Anchorage and Fairbanks that boast the best viewing of Mt. McKinley (which most Alaskans refer to by its original name, Denali). At 20,320 feet, McKinley is the highest peak in North America, and most places within 100 miles can be good viewing areas. It is so large it creates its own weather patterns, and when the skies are otherwise clear, the mountain may be completely obscured. Try not to be too disappointed if you don't see it; just know you've been in the company of greatness.

Denali National Park

(D) Denali National Park is one of the most popular destinations in the state. It is a spectacular region that can be experienced by saddle safari, bus trip, hike, raft, or flightseeing tour. The first 15 miles of the park road are paved, but after that visitors must ride on a bus or get off and see Denali on foot. No matter which adventure you choose, Denali is truly a wonderful experience.

The Aurora Borealis

(E) The most popular attraction in the wintertime doesn't charge admission or have set viewing times. The northern lights seem to appear without rhyme or reason. There is a science to it, but explanations are still hotly debated by meteorologists, astronomers, and pretty-color enthusiasts. Seeing the northern lights generally requires there be no nearby city light, very little moonlight, the cold fall and winter months, and a lot of luck. Chena Hot Springs outside Fairbanks keep the hopeful warm while they watch the skies.

Mendenhall Glacier
(F) Alaska's capital, Juneau, is surrounded by ice and water and can be reached only by boat or plane. The best way to understand this is to fly over the ice fields just outside the city and visit the Mendenhall Glacier. Only 13 miles from downtown Juneau, this gargantuan glacier is right outside the city in plain view. It's 12 miles long—nearly the same distance as between it and downtown Juneau.

The Inside Passage
(G) If you don't arrive in Alaska by cruise ship, make a point of taking a ferry trip along the longest, deepest fjord in North America. Depending on which ferry you take, the trip from Juneau to Skagway can be two or six hours long. In summer the tall peaks surrounding the boats release hundreds of waterfalls from snow and glacial melt. You might see pods of orcas, humpbacks, and dolphins.

Mt. Marathon Race
(H) On July 4, the scenic small town of Seward hosts the Mt. Marathon Race. This race is 1½ miles straight up and 1½ miles straight down the mountain. It began with a bet between two sourdoughs in 1915, and now the celebration turns a town of 2,000 into a city of 40,000 overnight. It's a great way to participate in Alaskan life, and you don't even have to race.

TOP EXPERIENCES

Net a Fish

Summertime in Alaska means fishing season for most. Although there are many types of fish Alaskans stock their freezers with, salmon is by far the most common. That's because it's easy to catch and you don't have to organize a boat or a plane to fish for it. There are thousands of Alaskan anglers, but en masse, dipnetting is the most popular way to catch salmon. Dipnetting is the act of putting on neoprene waders, walking out until the water is nearly chest high, and holding a large net on a 5- to 10-foot pole in front of you until a salmon swims into it. It doesn't take long. It hardly seems sporting, but there is something truly amazing about standing in the water of the Kenai alongside thousands of other Alaskans, watching gulls dive, sea otters bob their heads, and salmon leap up into the sky.

Drive the Alcan

When driving the Alaska Highway, or Alcan, you quickly realize that "rural" means something entirely different in Alaska. (While we're on the subject, so does "remote"; here the word refers to areas with no road access.) You will drive through regions, villages, and towns that are nearly 1,000 miles from the nearest city. Inhabitants have never seen anything that even slightly resembles a shopping mall or fast-food stand. Gas stations can be 75 to 150 miles apart, and mechanics rarer than a wolverine sighting. The Alcan is the true Alaskan experience. Driving 1,000 miles on a long, potholed stretch of highway can put things into perspective. It is also a great way to be guaranteed wildlife sightings.

Sleep on a Deserted Island

Gustavus is the gateway to Glacier Bay, the place that the father of the national parks system, John Muir, called "unspeakably pure and sublime" in 1879. It is considered by many to be 70 miles of the finest sea kayaking in the world. The first 24 square miles comprise the Beardslee Islands, a complex system for kayakers who glide atop flat water between tides, enveloped in silence except for the sound of water slapping paddles, the soft spray from a nearby porpoise, and the howl of a wolf in the distance. And you'll likely be enjoying these sights with no other travelers nearby. Still, kayaking in this region presents challenges. There is a lively population of moose and bears on the islands, so it is imperative to choose wisely when setting up camp. Most visitors kayak only to the top of the Beardslees, which can take three to five days round-trip.

Safari through the Last Great Wilderness

The Arctic National Wildlife Refuge (ANWR) is 19.2 million acres of untamed land in the northeastern corner of Alaska. This is where there is still a sense of the unknown, where mountain peaks are unnamed and valleys are yet to be explored. There are no shops and no roads. The only way to get to ANWR is by small bush plane. You can be dropped off by air taxi, or you can arrange a guided group tour. The refuge is a great place to hunt, hike, camp, paddle, or climb in solitude. Fewer than 1,000 people visit this region every year, but tours must be booked months, if not a year, in advance. Even Alaskans dream of getting to this place someday.

Bed, Breakfast, and Snowmachine

Everywhere there is snow there seems to be a bitter rivalry between snowmachiners (aka snowmobilers) and skiers. If you're looking to have the perfect snowmachine experience without enmity or opposition, the best way to do it is to find one of the many rural wilderness lodges around Alaska that offer snowmachine rentals and tours. Yentna Station Roadhouse and Alaska Snow Safaris are just two of the many stellar rural establishments that are a day's drive or a short bush flight away. It's a great adrenaline rush to speed over frozen lakes and untouched powder with a motorized sled beneath you and wind in your face.

Ski under the Stars

There is something about the incongruous number of hours of sunlight and darkness Alaska gets that makes Alaskans yearn to break the rules of time. When you arrive in Alaska you may feel inclined to do the same. In many parts of the state bars still stay open all night long, fishermen can be sitting on the ice all hours of the night, and some people ski best when the witching hour strikes. At Alyeska Ski Resort in Girdwood, skiers can take the lift and bite the powder under the stars. On weekends this popular ski resort offers night skiing, and afterward, in the bar, rewards its visitors with live, high-energy, danceable music. This provides a good look at local Alaskan culture, as it caters to tourists and residents alike.

Hike the Chilkoot Trail

In the 1890s, during the gold rush, more than 20,000 stampeders disembarked from their steamships in Skagway, Alaska, and hiked the 35 miles of the Chilkoot Trail, just to get back into a boat and travel the remaining 600 miles to Dawson City (where the gold was). It took approximately three months to hike the trail back then. Their packs were heavy, their shoes were hard, and they had to hike the trail several times in order to get all of their possessions over the pass. These days, hiking history buffs can retrace the stampeders' steps in three to five days, with the help of lighter gear and equipment.

Drink Like an Alaskan

Every state in the nation has a list of attributed symbols: the state bird, flag, flower, song—and in Alaska there is the state drink. It's called the Duck Fart. It is quintessentially Alaskan, as it manages to weed out the meek and shy just by its name alone. It's comprised of Kahlúa, Bailey's Irish Cream, and Crown Royal. No need to be timid when it comes to ordering this drink; locals drink it, too. Once you've had a Duck Fart, you can honestly say you've experienced Alaska like an Alaskan.

Halibut Cove

Sometimes the best thing to do is nothing at all. Halibut Cove is a gorgeous little piece of euphoria-inducing land tucked into a corner of Kachemak Bay State Park, Alaska's first state park. It's a town of only 22 year-round residents, but there are two fantastic lodges and several others across the bay that offer the same thing: a peaceful look at the gorgeous scenery. Halibut Cove has no stores, but does offer a handful of art galleries, a post office (only open on mail-boat days), a high-end restaurant, and a floating espresso bar. There are plenty of outdoor activities, but there's not much else to do there, which is a good thing.

QUINTESSENTIAL ALASKA

Sourdough

Sourdough bread, pastries, and pancakes are a local tradition, dating back to the gold-rush days. Prospectors and pioneers carried a stash of sourdough starter so they could always whip up a batch of dough in short order. The experienced miners and those who survived the harsh winter became known as sourdoughs, a title that later came to define old-timers—anyone who had lived in Alaska at least 20 years—but there seems to be some debate over that now; some will swear it's defined by five consecutive winters in Alaska. Either way, newcomers and those still working to earn the title are referred to as Cheechakos, which is Chinook for "newcomer." After you return from your outdoor adventure, indulge your cravings with the best of Alaskan culinary delights. Start with sourdough pancakes for breakfast; for lunch, go for smoked salmon spread on sourdough bread; top it off with a dinner of fresh halibut and wild-berry cobbler. Then you can consider yourself an honorary Alaskan sourdough.

Fishing

Subsistence is a very important way of life, not only for Alaskans living in remote parts of the state, but for urban dwellers as well; moose, reindeer, halibut, and salmon are common meals. Salmon fishing is best in the summer months, and Alaskans all over the state take to their boats on rivers and shorelines to catch their year's supply. Though many people stock their freezers with fillets, many more pull out their smokers. Smoked salmon is not like lox; it is steeped first in brine and a variety of different spices or sugars. It comes out as a moist, oily jerky and is either air packed or jarred and can be found in shops everywhere.

In Alaska, you don't have to do everything Alaskans do, but knowing what is important and predominant in the lives of Alaskans will certainly enhance and enrich your experience.

Native Arts

Alaska's rich Native culture is reflected in its abundance of craft traditions, from totem poles to intricate baskets and detailed carvings. Many of the Native crafts you'll see across the state are result of generations of traditions passed down among tribes; the craft process is usually labor intensive, using local resources such as rye grasses or fragrant cedar trees. Each of Alaska's Native groups is noted for particular skills and visual-art styles. Inuit art includes ivory carvings, spirit masks, dance fans, baleen baskets, and jewelry. Also be on the lookout for mukluks (seal- or reindeer-skin boots). The Tlingit peoples of Southeast Alaska are known for their totem poles, as well as for baskets and hats woven from spruce root and cedar bark. Tsimshian Indians also work with spruce root and cedar bark, and Haida Indians are noted basket makers and carvers. Athabascans specialize in birch-bark creations, decorated fur garments, and beadwork. The Aleut, a maritime people dwelling in the southwest reaches of the state, make grass basketry that is considered among the best in the world. ⇨ *For tips about buying an authentic item, check out Native Handicrafts in Chapter 8.*

Alaska Native culture is also evident in music and dance. It may seem simple when you first experience it, but the mukluks, *kuspuks* (Yup'ik overshirts), robes, and headdresses worn are embedded with rich stories and symbolism, and each region's dance and music varies. You may hear young men cry out during a song—listen carefully: they are imitating the sound of the seal, the walrus, or the whale.

ALASKA'S HISTORY

The First People

No one knows when humans first began living in the northwest corner of the North American continent, and it is still a subject of great controversy and debate. One popular theory is that 12,000 years ago humans followed the eastern migration of Ice Age mammals over the Bering Land Bridge, a 600-mile-wide stretch of land that connected present-day Alaska to Siberia. To date, the oldest human remains found in Alaska are 11,500 years old, the second-oldest Ice Age remains to be found in the world. Found in Central Alaska near the Tanana River, the remains of a three-year-old girl are thought to possibly be that of an Athabascan ancestor.

No matter when humans first arrived, by 1750 there were 57,300 Native peoples living in Russian Alaska, including Aleuts, Alutiiqs, Yup'iks, Inupiats, Athabascan, Tlingit, and Haida. Today there are more than 100,000 American Indians and Alaska Natives living in Alaska.

Russians in Alaska

Alaska was a late bloomer on the world scene. It wasn't until 1741 that Danish navigator Vitus Bering, under Russian rule, made the Alaska region known to the world. Bering died before he could ever explore the continent or return to Russia.

Politically speaking, Russia imposed itself on Alaska in varying degrees. It was the arrival of the *promyshlenniki,* or fur hunters, that had the biggest impact on the Native cultures. By most accounts, the hunters were illiterate, quarrelsome, hard drinking, and virtually out of control. They penetrated the Aleutian Chain and made themselves masters of the islands and their inhabitants, the Aleuts. Several

times the Natives revolted; their attempts were squelched, and they were brutalized.

By 1790 the small fur traders were replaced by large Russian companies. Siberian fur trader Aleksandr Andreyevich Baranov became manager of a fur-trading company and director of a settlement on Kodiak Island in 1791. He essentially governed all Russian activities in North America until 1818, when he was ordered back to Russia. Word was spreading to the Russian government that foreigners, particularly Americans, were gaining a disproportionate share of the Alaskan market. The Russian Navy was ordered to assume control of Alaska, and by 1821 it had barred all foreign ships from entering Alaskan waters. Russia created new policies forbidding any trade with non-Russians and requiring that the colonies be supplied solely by Russian ships.

The 1853 Crimean War between Imperial Russia and Britain and France put a great financial burden on Russia. It fiscally behooved the country to sell Russian Alaska. In 1867, under a treaty signed by U.S. Secretary of State William H. Seward, Alaska was sold to the United States for $7.2 million. On October 18, 1867, the territory officially changed hands. Newspapers around the nation hailed the purchase of Alaska as "Seward's Folly." Within 30 years, however, one of the biggest gold strikes in the world would bring hundreds of thousands of people to this U.S. territory.

The Gold Rush

The great Klondike gold discoveries of 1896 gained national (and worldwide) attention. Due to the depression of 1893, the need for food, money, and hope sparked a gold fever unmatched in history. Men and women alike clamored for information about Alaska, not realizing that the Klondike was in the Yukon Territory of Canada. Perhaps if they'd known their geography Alaska would never have become the state that it is now.

The most popular route for the gold stampeders was to go entirely by water. It wasn't cheaper, but it was far easier than taking the inland route. They would start in either San Francisco or Seattle, buy passage on a steamship, and disembark more than 1,000 nautical miles later in Skagway, Alaska. No gold was in Skagway, but overnight it became a city of 20,000 miners. Gold-seekers used it as a place to negotiate and get ready for the only part of their journey that would be traversed on foot. The Chilkoot Trail was 35 challenging miles that were too rugged for pack horses. The hardest part of the journey was the climb to the summit, Chilkoot Pass. This climb was known as the Golden Staircase, a 45-degree-angle hike of nearly .75 miles. Chilkoot Pass was the gateway to Canada and the point at which the Canadian government required each person entering the territory to have at least a year's supply (approximately 1 ton) of food. This is partially why it took most stampeders one to three months to complete this 35-mile stretch. At the base of the Golden Staircase, stampeders had everything they were taking over the pass weighed, and were charged $1 per pound. Once into Canada, they built boats and floated the remaining 600 miles to Dawson City, where the gold rush was taking place. By 1899 the Yukon Gold Rush was over, however, and the population of Skagway shrank dramatically.

Alaska experienced its own gold strike in Nome, on the Seward Peninsula, in 1898. The fever didn't actually hit until 1900, but because it did, gold mining all over Alaska began to get national attention.

World War II

In 1942, after the United States entered the war, the War Production Board deemed gold mining nonessential to the war effort, and forced gold mining all over the country to come to a halt. Despite the closing of mines, World War II was financially beneficial to parts of Alaska. Numerous bases and ports were strategically built around the state, and the Alaska Highway was created to help deliver supplies to them.

The only time Alaska had any direct involvement with the war was in June 1942, when the Japanese attacked Attu and Kiska islands in the Aleutian Chain. The attack has been recorded in history as an "incident," but it had a great impact on many lives; a few hundred casualties occurred due to friendly fire. Nearly a thousand inhabitants were relocated and many died in the process.

Statehood

On January 3, 1959, "Seward's Folly" became the 49th state in the nation—more than 100 years after Seward first visited. Soon, a mass of investors, bold entrepreneurs, tourists, and land grabbers began to arrive. It's still a new state, far from direct scrutiny by the rest of the nation. With a constantly growing, competitive industry of oil and other natural resources, Alaska has made an identity for itself that resembles that of no other state in the nation. It boasts the second-highest production of gas and oil in the country, is twice the size of the second-largest state, and has millions of lakes, minimal pollution, and endless possibilities.

ALASKA OUTDOOR ADVENTURES

BICYCLING

People come from all over the world to bike down the Alcan Highway, but it's not the only route to bicycle in Alaska. Short- and long-distance cycling are possible all over the state.

As with any adventure to be had in Alaska, what you wear can define the quality of your experience. Always bring along rain gear appropriate for bicycling and wear clothing that wicks.

Safety

There are countless trails for road and mountain bikes all over the state. The paved-road system is straightforward, and traffic is usually light. However, road shoulders can be narrow, and people drive fast in rural areas. Unpaved highways are bikeable but tougher going.

Because winter can be a little rough on the roads and trails, tires have a tendency to acquire flats. Always carry a kit in case you should need to fix your flats a few times along the way—and be sure to learn how to use it before you head out.

Best Rides

Anchorage. Anchorage has an excellent bike-trail system. Biking the city is a good way to appreciate its setting as a metropolis perched on the edge of vast wilderness—but beware the occasional furry creature sharing the bike trail with you. There are four paved greenbelt trails; the 11-mile Tony Knowles Coastal Trail is the most popular. Alaska Bike Rentals (⊕ *www.alaska-bike-rentals.com*) in downtown Anchorage also offers shuttle rides to Flattop, a great place to hike and bike. *See Ch. 5.*

Denali National Park and Preserve. Take your mountain bike on the Alaska Railroad and bike Denali. Although the park road is largely unpaved, it has a good dirt surface and only light traffic, making it a peaceful and joyful ride. *See Ch. 7.*

Kluane Chilkat International Bike Relay. For more than 20 years, in the month of June, bicyclists from all over have come to relay the 150-mile-long route from Haines Junction in the Yukon Territory to Haines, Alaska. This stretch of highway is breathtaking, sometimes literally. You can do all eight legs of the trip yourself, hook up with a team, or create your own. Many teams get dressed up for the event in wacky attire, while others take the race quite seriously. To find a team, register to ride, or find a place to rent a bike, check the KCIBR website (⊕ *www. kcibr.org*). *See Ch. 4.*

The Interior. Fairbanks has miles of scenic bike paths along the Chena River. Most roads have wide shoulders and those incredible Alaska views. Trails used in winter by mushers, snowmachiners, and cross-country skiers are taken over by bikers when the snow melts. *See Ch. 8.*

Seward Highway. Riding from Indian (10 miles south of Anchorage) to Girdwood is a stunning way to experience what is considered one of the most beautiful drives in the country. This 14-mile paved bike path follows the highway, occasionally cutting into the woods and along the backs of creeks and lakes. *See Ch. 6.*

Southeast Alaska and the Ferry System. You can bring your bike on Alaska's ferry system for an extra charge. Use it to explore Southeast's charming communities and surrounding forests. If you don't have a bike to tote along, you'll find most towns offer bike rentals as well as guided rides down scenic highways and over hardy trails. *See Ch. 4.*

HIKING

Whether you're an avid expert or amateur hiker, you'll find amazing hikes in Alaska that vary from rolling woodland strolls to serious overnight adventures. There is no place in Alaska where you won't find someplace to hike—even the big city of Anchorage has greenbelts laden with trails, and sits at the doorstep of the Chugach Mountain Range. Regardless of what type of hike you take, urban or remote, always be bear and moose savvy. Keep your eyes and ears alert.

Safety

There are several hazards to hiking, but a little preparedness goes a long way. Know your limits, and make sure the terrain you are about to embark on does not exceed your abilities. Check the elevation change on a trail before you set out—a 1-mile trail might be more difficult than you expect. Always pack extra water, and make sure someone knows where you're going and when to expect your return. Employ the buddy system if you can. If you must hike alone, make sure there are other hikers on the trail the day you go, and leave a note on the dashboard of your car to let authorities and park rangers know your route and the day you left.

What to Wear

For most day hikes, you'll need good hiking shoes, gators, a rain jacket (and possibly rain pants), wool socks, and a shirt that wicks. You'll also want to take along: mosquito repellent, hiking poles, layered clothes and fleeces that wick, a water bottle or CamelBak, extra food (it's best to store food in your day pack and not on your body), bear mace, and hiking poles. Check out local secondhand stores or gear swaps in the area if you're traveling long enough, or go online to find local groups who lend gear or know where to get affordable options.

Best Hikes

Chilkoot Trail, Skagway. Beginning in Dyea, just outside Skagway, this 33-mile trail traverses the historic gold-rush route of the 1890s, and ends in British Columbia. In its entirety, this trail is a moderate-to-difficult hike, and takes two to three days one way; you can catch the train back. If you want a less difficult daylong jaunt and perhaps a raft trip back, outfitters in Skagway can set you up. *See Ch. 4.*

Harding Icefield Trail, Kenai Fjords National Park, Seward. This trail, located near Seward's Exit Glacier (a 120-mile drive from Anchorage), is about 8.2 miles round trip with a 3,000-foot change in elevation, and affords one of the best glacier-overlook views in the state. It's a strenuous hike, slightly more challenging in areas where the snow hasn't melted off the upper reaches (even as late as July), but doable by most—and immensely rewarding. The ice field is tough to photograph, but your mind's eye will carry a fantastic panorama for years to come. *See Ch. 6.*

Eagle River Valley Trails, Eagle River Nature Center. Hiking in the Eagle River Valley is a gorgeous experience, and even more convenient due to the variety of short loops available in the same vicinity. Crow Pass in particular affords great views, wonderful scenery, and a high chance of spotting local wildlife. You can hike just a portion of Crow Pass, or you can hike all the way to Raven Glacier, and on in to Girdwood. But be prepared: it's a two- to three-day trip. *See Ch. 6.*

KAYAKING

Kayaks have the great advantage of portability. More stable than canoes, they also give you a feel for the water and a view from water level. Oceangoing kayakers will find plenty of offshore Alaska adventures, especially in the protected waters of the Southeast, Prince William Sound, and Kenai Fjords National Park. The variety of Alaska marine life that you can view from a sea kayak is astonishing. It's possible to see whales, seals, sea lions, and sea otters, as well as bird species too numerous to list. Although caution is required when dealing with large stretches of open water, the truly Alaskan experience of self-propelled boating in a pristine ocean environment can be a life-changing thrill.

The best part about kayaking is that it puts you in touch with the biggest domain around—Alaska's fresh- and saltwater scenery. It's also relatively easy to pick up, but Alaska's waters should not be taken for granted. Be sure to go with a guide or take a survival class so you know how to pull yourself out of the icy waters, should your kayak tip over.

When to Go

The best time to kayak in Alaska is at the peak of summer, from June through August. During these months there's a higher likelihood of sunshine, and it's also the best time for aquatic-wildlife viewing.

Best Places to Paddle

Glacier Bay National Park. This park, 60 miles northwest of Juneau, is 70 miles long and surrounded by mountains—spectacularly glaciated mountains, no less. It's a wild, undeveloped country with an air of mystery. The best way to experience Glacier Bay is by boat, and a kayak is one of the best boats to captain in the narrow, remote passageways in the park. *See Ch. 4.*

Kelowna Lake. You can rent a kayak at Kelowna Lake (approximately 35 minutes north of Anchorage) for a few bucks, spend the day on the water, then pack it back into town with a slight sunburn and a full soul.

Kenai Peninsula. Seward is the unofficial capital of kayaking in Alaska. The home of an annual kayaking symposium that draws novices and pros from all over Alaska, it's also the gateway to some of the most incredible ocean kayaking in the world, with the Kenai Fjords, Aialik Bay, and Resurrection Bay. Because the Kenai Peninsula is so renowned for its kayaking, just about every street corner has a reliable kayaking outfitter on it. *See Ch. 6.*

Lake Bernard. The best way to access this lake is with one of the outfitters in Skagway. They'll take you by bus or train up to the border, where you can dip your kayak into the water and propel yourself through the truly unique terrain known as Tormented Valley. This waterway was part of the stampeders' journey to Dawson city during the 1890s. *See Ch. 4.*

Prince William Sound. In just an afternoon kayaking here, you can find fabulous hidden coves, calving glaciers, and spectacular views of flora and fauna. The sound has truly magical destinations only accessible by kayak. *See Ch. 6.*

MOUNTAINS AND GLACIERS

Alaska has roughly 100,000 glaciers and ice fields covering more than 29,000 square miles, and 17 of the 20 highest mountains in the United States. Most of these awe-inspiring sights are in remote and inaccessible regions. However, some are accessible by road, or by hiking or kayaking out to them. Flight companies all over the state offer aerial views—and some will even land to allow you to hike or dog sled.

Glaciers, although seemingly still, are constantly in motion, whereas ice fields are constrained by mountain peaks and plateaus. Both are comprised of thousands of feet of compacted snow and ice. They are cold and very slick, and their deep crevasses can be deadly.

Be glacier wise: use crampons for walking, and dress for below-freezing temperatures.

Best Mountains and Glaciers

Exit Glacier, Seward. You can take a short, easy walk to view this glacier, or if you're in the mood for a challenge, hike the steep trail onto the enormous Harding Icefield. Scan the nearby cliffs for mountain goats and watch for bears. *See Ch. 6.*

Flattop Mountain, Anchorage. Drive to the Glen Alps parking lot in Chugach State Park, pay the $5 parking fee, and take the short walk west to a scenic overlook: on a clear day, the view sweeps from Denali south along the Alaska Range past several active volcanoes on the other side of Cook Inlet. Follow the hikers to the top of the mountain for even more stunning scenery, or take the Powerline Trail for day hike up to the pass for a great vista view. *See Ch. 6.*

Glacier Bay National Park, Gustavus. Whether you view this natural wonder by air, boat, or on foot, Glacier Bay is well worth the effort and expense it takes to get there. If you opt to go by boat, you have a strong chance of witnessing calving glaciers. *See Ch. 4.*

Mendenhall Glacier, Juneau. This drive-up glacier comes complete with visitor center, educational exhibits, nature trails, and, when the cruise ships are in town, lots of bused-in tourists. Don't let the crush of visitors dissuade you from stopping by, though—it's a great resource for learning about glacier dynamics and the natural forces that have shaped Alaska. *See Ch. 4.*

Mt. McKinley, Talkeetna. For the ultimate mountain sightseeing adventure, take a flight from Talkeetna and land on a glacier on Mt. McKinley. If you arrive in early summer, you can fly onto the Kahiltna Glacier, where teams attempting to summit the mountain gather. *See Ch. 6.*

Mt. Roberts, Juneau. The tram takes you up the mountain and, if the weather cooperates, offers great views of the area. It's another cruise-ship favorite, but at least you can have a quick beer as you soak in the scenery. *See Ch. 4.*

Portage Glacier, Anchorage. This glacier has been receding rapidly, but you can ride the tour boat *Ptarmigan* across the lake to view its face. Keep an eye out for office-building–size chunks of ice falling into the water. *See Ch. 6.*

Spencer Glacier, Grandview. The glacier is visible from the tracks, but it's also a whistle-stop on the Alaska Railroad. In this spot only accessible by train, you can hike, camp, or take a rafting or afternoon kayaking trip around immense icebergs, right up to the face of the glacier. But don't get too close! Calving ice can be deadly.

WILDLIFE VIEWING

Whether you're looking for ice worms, songbirds, or giant moose or caribou, Alaska's wilderness is vast, and viewing wildlife requires knowledge, planning, and preparation. Alaska has several state-run viewing programs at wildlife preserves and in other tourist areas that enable visitors to see the state's creatures in their natural world. Depending on your preference, the Alaska Department of Fish and Game (⊕ *adfg.alaska. gov*) offers a comprehensive "Watchable Wildlife Program" that provides information on viewing locations across the state based on species, location, and best areas for viewing.

When to go

Wildlife is abundant in Alaska year-round—the key is to understand how migration, breeding, and hibernation affect the wildlife you want to see. In the spring, birds and waterfowl emerge and migration north intensifies—bears emerge from dens, caribou, Dall sheep, and mountain goats return to more observable locations. Spring is also the best time to view marine mammals such as walrus, seals, and bowhead whales. In the summer months, bears and other wildlife concentrate on streams where salmon spawn, providing a prime time for easy viewing along riverbanks, lakefronts, and even at times from the side of the road next to your car. Summer also means the best time to visit seabird colonies.

Especially in South Central, moose can be seen year-round. However, it's important to understand the nature of the beast. It's never a good idea to get too close to a moose; they can be deadly. Especially stay far away from the cows in the spring, when they are giving birth and toting around their young; they are very protective. Mating season is in the fall, and that's when it's best to give the bulls a lot of space: they get a tad aggressive.

Best Wildlife-viewing Areas

Anchorage. From mid-July through August visitors can view beluga whales south of Anchorage along the Turnagain Arm— look for the white finless backs breaking the surface of the water below. Also along the highway, Windy Point is a great place to pull over and see the Dall sheep hoofing it over the rugged mountainside. *See Ch. 5.*

Denali National Park. Seeing wildlife in Alaska is never a given. Often it takes patience and luck combined. Denali National Park covers diverse terrain that lends itself to a wide array of wildlife from grizzly bears to moose. *See Ch. 7.*

Kenai National Wildlife Refuge. For **land-based wildlife**, the Kenai National Wildlife Refuge is a great, central, and easily accessible choice. The Refuge was established in 1907 to protect moose populations, Dall sheep, mountain goats, wolves, bald eagles, and both brown and black bears. At nearly 2 million acres, the refuge is comprised of diverse habitats that contain species including the regular suspects (bears, moose, eagles) as well as many others (wolves, coyotes, shrews, voles, muskrats, caribou, marmots, lynx, wolverines, martens, and more). *See Ch. 6.*

South Central or Southeast Alaska. Humpback whales can be viewed in the summer months between Homer and Kodiak. Find a whale-watching tour in South Central or Southeast Alaska and enjoy with your fellow boaters as the whales fluke and glide. *See Ch. 6.*

IF YOU LIKE

Creature Comforts

Alaska isn't only tundra hiking, grizzly-bear watching, and salmon fishing. It's possible to spend your vacation pampering yourself, enjoying a nice glass of wine and excellent food, and still experience outdoor adventures.

Alaska's Capital Inn, Juneau. Luxury meets gold-rush history in this gracious hilltop bed-and-breakfast with upscale services and period furnishings from the early 1900s. *See Ch 4.*

Chena Hot Springs Resort, Chena Hot Springs. Here you can spend the day enjoying a wide range of outdoor activities, followed by a long soak in the hot springs topped off by an exceptional dinner. *See Ch. 8.*

Hotel Alyeska, Girdwood. An hour south of Anchorage, this luxurious hotel offers plenty of opportunities for spoiling yourself silly. The crown jewel of the resort is the Seven Glaciers Restaurant, a seven-minute tram ride up Mt. Alyeska. There you can enjoy the stunning view of the valley and the namesake glaciers. *See Ch. 5.*

Kachemak Bay Wilderness Lodge, Homer. Across Kachemak Bay from Homer, and accessible by boat or floatplane, you can fill your days hiking, fishing, boating, and sightseeing, followed by delicious seafood dinners. *See Ch. 6.*

Kenai Princess Wilderness Lodge, Cooper Landing. Charming bungalows with fireplaces and vaulted ceilings make up this sprawling complex on a bluff overlooking the Kenai River. *See Ch. 6.*

Pearson's Pond Luxury Inn and Adventure Spa, Juneau. Yoga in the morning; wine and cheese in the evening; whirlpool tubs with rain showers; private balconies; and a well-stocked breakfast nook—luxurious amenities define this B&B on a small pond near Mendenhall Glacier. *See Ch. 4.*

Small-town Life

Alaska's entire population is barely more than 700,000 people, and almost half of that population calls Anchorage home. Scrolling down the list of Alaska cities, by the time you get to Sitka, the third-largest town, you're looking at a population of fewer than 9,000 souls. Nearly 60% of Alaskans reside in small towns.

There's a considerable variety of small-town experiences available in Alaska, such as that in **Kotzebue,** the regional hub for northwest Alaska and Alaska's largest Eskimo community. Perched on the shore of Kotzebue Sound, the town strikes a fine mix of Native and contemporary-American cultures. Be forewarned: landing at the one-runway airport is . . . interesting.

The towns of **Haines** and **Skagway** are a mere 17 miles apart as the eagle flies, but they're light-years apart in their ambience. Haines has chosen to limit cruise-ship visitation to a mere fraction of what Skagway sees. The result is a laid-back, small-town feeling in Haines, where you can enjoy fantastic views of Portage Cove, fishing, and a yearly migration of eagles visiting the late run of succulent chum salmon. Skagway has embraced its gold-rush history, with plenty of restored false-front stores and historic memorabilia.

In the towns of **Kenai** and **Soldotna,** about 150 miles southwest of Anchorage, commercial fishing boats fill the harbor at the mouth of the Kenai River, and Kenai's onion-dome Russian Orthodox Church accents the old town's skyline. During the salmon dipnetting season in July, you can watch Alaskans stocking up for the coming winter.

GREAT ITINERARIES

Alaska is a vast and wild state. It's twice the size of Texas, has 17 of the country's 20 highest peaks, a longer coastline than all U.S. states combined, and a glacier the size of Switzerland. Transportation here is tricky. Much of the state, including Juneau, the state capital, is not connected to the outside via roads. The only way to get there is by boat or plane. Careful planning is paramount, especially in regard to travel times—distances between towns and parks can be daunting.

Lay of the Land

Alaska can be roughly divided into four regions: Southeast and the Inside Passage, South Central, the Interior, and the Bush.

Southeast Alaska and the Inside Passage. Southeast Alaska is largely along the northernmost end of the famous Inside Passage, a winding, 25,500-mile-long waterway that begins in the Puget Sound in Washington State, runs up the Canadian Coast, and ends in Glacier Bay. The Alaska portion is 500 miles from north to south and 100 miles from east to west, with thousands of islands, coves, and bays to explore. Around 80% of visitors experience Alaska's glaciers and spectacular wilderness by cruising through the Inside Passage. If this is the type of trip you're looking for, check out Alaska by Cruise Ship (⇨ *Chapter 2)* or check out our *Alaska Ports of Call* guide. This region (the Panhandle) is almost entirely comprised of the Tongass National Forest— the largest national forest in the country, and the largest intact temperate rain forest in the world. It's green, lush, and filled with glaciers, waterways, islands, and wildlife. Given the rugged, mountainous nature of this province, none of the communities here, except for Hyder, Skagway, and Haines, have road connections to the outside world—the only way to get in and out of town is via planes and boats.

South Central Alaska. This region hugs the Gulf of Alaska and is the most populated area in the state, thanks to Anchorage. Here you'll find mountain ranges, active volcanoes, rugged coasts, thick forests, and glacier-fed rivers. From Anchorage it's not difficult to hop on a train to the Interior and visit Denali National Park and the famous Mt. McKinley, the highest peak in North America. Kenai Peninsula and the Copper River Delta are where you'll have the iconic salmon-fishing experience.

The Interior. The Interior holds North America's highest peak, 20,320-foot Mt. McKinley and Denali National Park. Its vast forests of birch and spruce are warm in the summer and bitterly cold in the winter, though the long winter nights do feature dazzling displays of the aurora borealis (northern lights). Fairbanks is the region's largest city. When gold prospectors and missionaries settled there at the end of the 19th century, it was already surrounded by long-established Alaska Native villages.

The Bush (Western and Northern Alaska). Come here to experience the seemingly flat, endless wilderness—the beauty of infinite tundra spotted with herds of caribou and musk oxen. Witness the brown bears of Katmai Island, the extraordinary birders' paradise on the Probilof Islands, gold panning in Nome, and the notorious Dalton Highway—the only thoroughfare in the region. Even further north in arctic Alaska, caribou and polar bears share the northern third of the state with oil companies and just a few thousand souls. Because there are virtually no roads to the towns and villages in the Bush, planning

The Interior

CANADA
UNITED STATES

RUSSIA
U.S.

Nome

The
Bush

Fairbanks

Denali National
Park & Reserve

South
Central
Alaska

Mt. McKinley

Anchorage

KENAI
PENINSULA

Gulf of Alaska

Inside
Passage

PACIFIC OCEAN

transportation and lodging in advance is imperative. If you'd like to get out into the wilderness here, we highly recommend a tour. It's far less stressful and much safer.

Timing

Planning a trip to Alaska is a daunting task, especially given the sheer size of the state and dearth of roads. It's best to embrace a "less is more" philosophy and stick to a single region or combine sites in adjacent regions. If you're taking a cruise, assume it will take at least a week. Inside Passage routes start in Seattle or Vancouver, with ports of call in Ketchikan, Juneau, and Skagway or Sitka, and stops in either Glacier Bay or Hubbard Glacier. If you want to visit the Interior via rail or car, allot at least 7–10 days. Most of the must-seeattractions are at least 100 miles apart, so you'll need to factor in transportation time. If you prefer to stick to the

coast and hop from city to city using ferries, give yourself at least a week or two.

Itineraries

The following itineraries only cover a small slice of this massive state. They focus on the Southeast, South Central, and Denali National Park, and can be combined with one another, or tacked on at the end of a weeklong Inside Passage cruise. We give the minimum amount of time for each destination, but we highly recommend adding days to these itineraries if your vacation allows it.

Peak Season: May to September

Temperatures hover around 60°F and prices are at their peak. Many lodges, especially those close to national parks, book up months in advance.

GREAT ITINERARIES

SOUTHEAST ALASKA

THE BEST OF THE INSIDE PASSAGE, 7 DAYS

The Inside Passage is the second-longest and -deepest fjord in the world, and a ride on the ferry up the Passage during summer months offers up fantastic views of waterfalls and sharp peaks cascading into the ocean; it can be a great way to spot orcas and humpback whales.

The Inside Passage is also known as Lynn Canal, but this is a misnomer: a canal is a man-made channel and the Passage is glacially carved fjord.

Day 1: Juneau

Kick off your journey in **Juneau** (p. 160), where you'll have to arrive by plane or boat, as there aren't any roads to the outside. Stay at **Alaska's Capital Inn** (p. 172), a bed-and-breakfast far away from the cruise-ship traffic. Be sure to book in advance, as this place is popular with returning visitors.

Once you're settled into your quarters, take a trip to the **Shrine of St. Therese** (p. 177). You can spend a good portion of the day on this tiny island, accessible by a pedestrian causeway. Afterward, head into downtown Juneau and peruse the shops and galleries, many of which specialize in original local art.

Finish the day with dinner at the bar in the **Westmark Baranof Hotel** (p. 173); it serves the same menu as the hotel's well-regarded Gold Room Restaurant.

Day 2: Mendenhall Glacier
(Excursion will take approximately five hours)

One of Juneau's most popular attractions, **Mendenhall Glacier** (p. 177) is nestled right up against the town. Whether you arrive by boat or plane, you're sure not to miss it as you approach the capital city. The glacier sits at the back of the icy blue Mendenhall Lake. **Alaska Boat and Kayak Rental** (p. 166) offers shuttle service from downtown Juneau, as well as kayak rentals. Kayak across the lake and up close to icebergs that have calved off the glacier, or hit the trails and hike up to the waterfalls.

Grab lunch before checking out of the inn. Board an afternoon or early-evening flight to Gustavus on **Wings of Alaska** (⊕ *www. wingsofalaska.com*).

Days 3 and 4: Glacier Bay National Park
(25 minutes by plane from Juneau; 4½ hours by ferry)

Located at the northern tip of the Inside Passage, **Glacier Bay National Park** (p. 179) is one of the country's most awe-inspiring national treasures. Stay at the **Glacier Bay Lodge** (p.187), the only accommodation located inside the park. The lodge can arrange a daylong boat excursion that will take you past hundreds of lush green islands and straight up to the calving glaciers. Some excursions allow you to disembark and kayak around the glaciers for a couple of hours.

Or take a kayaking adventure like none you've ever had before. Experienced guides can be hired for multiday excursions that paddle all the way to the calving glaciers. Regardless of how far you paddle, the experience is incredibly rewarding. Though the lodge does rent solo kayaks, unless you are a very experienced sea kayaker, we recommend taking a tour.

Whichever way you decide to explore the park, you'll find great comfort in the hot meals and comfy beds at the end of the day.

If you're only spending one night at the park, get up early on the day of your departure and set out on any one of a number of great hikes that begin at the lodge. If you have time, consider tacking on a few extra days.

Day 5: Return to Juneau
(4½ hours by ferry from Glacier Bay)

The ferry departs Gustavus at different times depending on the day of the week, but it's usually before 3 pm.

Stay at the **Alaskan Hotel** (p. 162), right in the heart of downtown. The location offers quick access to nature trails, the beach, and to the Douglas Island walkway. If you get back from Gustavus in time, try to catch a show at **Perseverance Theatre** (p. 174) on Douglas Island, a quick boat ride from Juneau. This theater is renowned for its great set designs and talented casts.

Day 6: Take a Hike

On your last day in Juneau, get out and see some of the countryside. One of the locals' favorite hikes is **Perseverance Trail** (p. 164). To get here, follow Gold Street until it turns into 8th Street. Follow 8th until it dead-ends on Basin Road. Take a left and keep walking until you get to the trail. This 3-mile one-way trail takes

WHAT TO PACK

The summertime weather in Southeast can fluctuate dramatically throughout the day: wet-weather gear is essential, and you might experience sleet and snow on a July afternoon that started out sunny and 75°F. The better you're prepared for extreme weather (mentally and physically), the better your experience will be. For every outing, be sure to dress in layers, carry a backpack with bug repellent, wool socks, a hat, and waterproof jacket and pants. Cotton doesn't dry quickly, especially jeans; wool, or clothing that wicks away moisture, is much more comfortable. Any good outdoor-sportswear store can set you up.

about three to four hours to hike. In its past life, this was Alaska's first road.

After your hike, grab lunch at any of the many eateries around downtown Juneau. Then immerse yourself in Alaska's history at the **Alaska State Museum** (p. 161). Sample some of the locally brewed beer at **Hangar on the Warf** (p. 170), or take one last stroll along the waterfront.

Day 7: Take Off for Home

Head off to the airport for your flight back.

GREAT ITINERARIES

SOUTHEAST ALASKA

A DIFFERENT VANTAGE OF THE INSIDE PASSAGE, 7 DAYS

Hands down, the best way to experience the Inside Passage is by boat. For visitors and locals, the ferry is the number one choice for traversing the fjord; it's economical, relaxing, and offers tremendous views. To optimize your time and cover more distance, fly some legs of the trip. Don't worry, this won't compromise your sightseeing: a bird's-eye view from your plane window is breathtaking, and not to be missed.

Days 1 and 2: Ketchikan

Fly directly into **Ketchikan** (p. 111) and stay at the **Black Bear Inn** (p. 123), an elegant, affordable, waterfront B&B. It's highly regarded, so be sure to book well in advance.

Get settled in and take a day trip on a catamaran by **Alaska Travel Adventure** (p. 118) to the awe-inspiring **Misty Fiords National Monument** (p. 126). The Ketchikan area is known for its salmon fishing, so if you're interested in catching your own dinner, book a day trip that includes fishing and license.

On your second day, acquaint yourself with the beautiful town of Ketchikan. This charming town is known for its contemporary and traditional art. Spend a few hours walking through the town's two famous totem pole parks, **Totem Bight** (p.119) and **Saxman Totem Pole Park** (p. 119). Stop in at the **Soho Coho Gallery** (p. 125), owned by well-known Alaskan artist Ray Troll, where you'll find an array of original, Alaska-made collectibles. And don't miss the Ketchikan **Arts and Humanities Council's Main Street Gallery** (p. 125).

Day 3: Wrangell
(6 hours by ferry from Ketchikan)

Wrangell is less touristy than many of the towns along the Inside Passage. It's an excellent place to get away from the hectic cruise-ship foot traffic and the T-shirt and knickknack shops that go along with it. Book your room at the **Stikine Inn** (p. 139) downtown and try to get one of the rooms with views of the water.

After you've unloaded at your hotel, take a stroll through the galleries and shops featuring wares by local artists and artisans. Grab lunch and walk down to the **Petroglyph Beach State Historic Park** (p. 135) and see ancient art chiseled on the rocks. No one knows who created these carvings or how long ago; they're curious, original, and intriguing.

For the latter part of the afternoon, take a jet-boat ride with **Breakaway Adventures** (p. 137) and soak in the nearby Chief Shakes Hot Springs.

Day 4: Petersburg
(3-hour ferry ride from Wrangell)

Petersburg's Scandinavian heritage is evident from the moment you arrive. The Norwegian-style homes and boat docks set it apart from other Alaskan towns. Book a room in **Scandia House** (p. 144) and then spend the day glacier viewing and whale-watching with **Kaleidoscope Cruises** (p. 141). Just 25 miles outside of town is **LeConte Glacier** (p. 140), the continent's southernmost tidewater glacier and Petersburg's biggest draw.

Day 5: Juneau
(8-hour ferry ride from Petersburg)

Most of the ferries from Petersburg to Juneau depart in the wee hours. You can book a cabin, or do as most Alaskans do, and just curl up with your blanket on a deck chair under the heat lamps.

Once you're in Juneau, check into your room at **Alaska's Capital Inn** (p. 172). Grab breakfast at **Heritage Coffee Company** (p. 170) and then take a helicopter ride on **Temsco Helicopters** (p. 168) to the Juneau Icefields. Spend an exciting afternoon dogsledding across the ice like the great Iditarod mushers do.

Once you're back in town, grab the bus to the **Gold Creek Salmon Bake** (p. 170) for dinner. If you'd like to walk off the meal, hike up to the remains of the old Wagner Gold Mine and do a little gold panning of your own.

Day 6: Haines
(4½-hour ferry ride from Juneau)

Check into **Hotel Halsingland** (p. 194), the old Victorian officers' bunkers of Ft. Seward, then head over to the **Mountain Market** (p. 193). This popular hangout is a health-food market–deli–coffee shop. Grab some things for a packed lunch, then rent a bike from **Sockeye Cycle** (p. 192) and spend an afternoon on the well-groomed trails that meander through the rain forest.

ALONG THE ALASKA MARINE HIGHWAY

The Inside Passage is part of the Alaska Marine Highway, and for most towns and villages along the fjord, this aquatic highway is a lifeline to the outside world. Hop on a ferry and share the waterway with barges delivering mail, produce, fuel, and other essentials. Food often begins its journey far south, in Bellingham, Washington, which explains the mediocre quality of produce here, and shipping expenses help account for the high costs.

Get back to your hotel in time to take the Twilight Bear Viewing Trip or Valley of the Eagles Nature Tour (3–4 hours) with **Alaska Nature Tours** (p. 192). Afterward, have a libation at the **Fogcutter Bar** (p. 194) and rub elbows with the locals. Don't lose track of time, though: Southeast bars have a tendency to stay open until the wee hours of morning, and you'll need to catch the ferry or flight back to Juneau the next day for your trip home.

Day 7: Head Home
Travel back to Juneau and depart for home.

GREAT ITINERARIES

SOUTH CENTRAL AND THE INTERIOR

DISCOVERING ANCHORAGE AND DENALI, 8 DAYS

Like all of Alaska, the South Central region is very spread out and the topography is incredibly diverse. But unlike in other regions, there are loads of ways to get around, and each mode of transport offers a different kind of experience.

Day 1: Arrive in Anchorage

As soon as you land in Anchorage, you'll probably want to rent a car in preparation for an early departure the next day. Decompress after your flight at the tasteful **Copper Whale Inn** (p. 242); it's a stone's throw from the **Tony Knowles Coastal Trail** (p. 220) and its great eateries and shops. For a leisurely stroll, walk along the Coastal Trail to Westchester Lagoon, or hike the entire 9 miles past Earthquake Park to Kincaid Park.

For dinner, **Simon & Seafort's** (p. 237) is within walking distance from the inn and has great food and a fantastic view across the water to Mt. Susitna (the "Sleeping Lady"). **Humpy's Great Alaskan Ale House** (p. 249) is a fun bar with live music and surprisingly good pub grub.

Day 2: Kayaking in Whittier
(1½-hour drive from Anchorage)

Hunker down to an early breakfast at the inn, and then go pick up some picnic fixings for your day trip. Drive down the scenic Seward Highway and turn off toward **Whittier** (p. 276). Before reaching Whittier, pull over at the **Portage Glacier** (p. 273) turnoff, where you can see the glacier and the iceberg-filled lake right from your car. Continue on to the **Anton Anderson Memorial Tunnel** (p. 277)—the longest highway tunnel in North America that's shared with trains.

Kayaking on the **Prince William Sound** (p. 267) is wonderful, and the knowledgeable guides at **Alaska Sea Kayakers** (p. 278) provide the gear and know-how to make it an experience of a lifetime.

At the end of the day, head back to Anchorage and return the car. Have dinner at the **Snow Goose** (p. 237); be sure to request a table on the outdoor deck overlooking the bay. If you're not too tired, check out the nightlife at **Crush Wine and Bistro** (p. 232) and **Bernie's Bungalow Lounge** (p. 247).

Day 3: Talkeetna
(7-hour train trip from Anchorage)

Board the morning train with **Alaska Railroad** (p. 214) and enjoy the seven-hour scenic ride to Talkeetna, a small Alaska town where artists, pilots, and mountaineers congregate. It's where climbers preparing to ascend Mt. McKinley hang out before they're flown to base camp. Book a room at the **Talkeetna Alaskan Lodge** (p. 331) and take a chartered flight over the summit (weather permitting) with **Talkeetna Aero Services** (p. 330). Spend the rest of the afternoon walking on a glacier.

Take a before- or after-dinner stroll through this tiny town, and check out the artwork that residents create during the quiet, cold winter months. **Talkeetna Roadhouse** (p. 331) is a nice dinner option and a good place to soak in the bustling summer scene.

Denali
National Park
(Mt. McKinley)

Denali and
North Face Lodge

Talkeetna

Anchorage

Portage
Glacier

Whittier

Prince William
Sound

Days 4, 5, and 6: Denali National Park
(5-hour train trip from Talkeetna)

The 30-year family-owned-and-operated **Camp Denali and North Face Lodge** (p. 363) offers three-, four-, or seven-night stays. A shuttle will pick you up at the train station and deliver you to a rustic wilderness lodge, deep within Denali National Park. Knowledgeable naturalists offer daily guided outings; evening programs focus on the natural and cultural history of Denali.

Denali National Park (p. 338) is a 6-million acre Arctic wonderland that teems with wildlife. On any given day you may see grizzlies, wolves, caribou, and moose. The weather around Mt. McKinley is fickle, so there's never a guarantee of seeing the mountain's peaks, though that hardly matters as you explore the glaciers, forests, and candy-colored tundra. On day two in the park, take advantage of the lodge's outstanding, off-trail, wildlife-watching expedition. Fill the rest of your time here with canoeing on Wonder Lake, biking, or a flightseeing tour around the mountain.

MIGHTY MT. MCKINLEY

Mt. McKinley has the highest peak in North America and it is an awesome sight—if you can see it. In the summer months, the 20,320-foot peak has its own weather system. It can be sunny and warm down below, but it might be shrouded in cloud cover at the summit. It's often easier to see it from Anchorage, 140 miles away. Though the views may be blocked, it's still worth trying to catch a glimpse up close.

Day 7: Anchorage
(8-hour train trip from Denali)

Take the afternoon train back to Anchorage and arrive in time for a late dinner. Check into one of our recommended hotels, and get ready for your flight the next day.

Day 8: Fly Home

Pack your bags and check out of the hotel. It's time to go to the airport and fly home.

GREAT ITINERARIES

SOUTH CENTRAL

INTO THE WILDERNESS— EXPERIENCING WRANGELL–ST. ELIAS, 9 DAYS

This itinerary is a great way to see an impressive amount of South Central, but it needs to be well planned and executed with relative precision, as much of this trip is dependent on the departure times for trains and ferries. One mistake and your itinerary can change dramatically—which doesn't mean a ruined vacation, just not the one you'd planned on.

Day 1: Anchorage

For this trip, you'll overnight in Anchorage and catch the train out early the next morning. Make the most of your time here by booking a room at the **Hotel Captain Cook** (p. 243). Put on your hiking shoes and grab the **Flattop Mountain Shuttle** (p. 270). This popular trailhead is at the edge of the city, where the Chugach Mountain Range begins. The hour-long hike to the top can be strenuous. From the summit you can see the entire city of Anchorage, the bay, and, on a clear day, you can see the Alaska Mountain Range and even Mt. McKinley. Should you opt to only explore the easier portion of the trail, you won't be denied excellent views. If you still have energy after Flattop, explore the Powerline Trail; it's the left-hand path at the trailhead. These trails are used year-round for hiking in the summer and snowshoeing, skiing, and snowmobiling in the winter. You'll understand why Anchoragites refer to their city as a great base camp.

After an afternoon of hiking in Anchorage's backyard, **Orso** (p. 233) is a nice option for dinner.

Day 2: Seward
(4-hour train ride from Anchorage)

The train ride to Seward offers stunning views that motorists miss. Once here, get situated at **Hotel Edgewater** (p. 294).

Seward is renowned for its tremendous sea kayaking. Book a day trip with **Sunny Cove Sea Kayaking** (⊕ www.sunnycove. com). The experienced guides here can take you past pods of orcas, sea otters, and groups of seals. Afterward, dine at the locals' favorite hangout, **Railway Cantina** (p. 296), and then catch a little nightlife at **Yukon Bar**, a popular spot with live music and tons of local flavor.

Day 3: Valdez
(3-hour bus ride from Seward; 6-hour ferry trip from Whittier)

Book an early-morning bus to **Whittier** (p. 276). Connect immediately with the ferry for a six-hour trip to Valdez. Know that as the weather gets colder, ferries run less frequently, so be sure to plan ahead.

Arrange a room in Valdez's **Mountain Sky Hotel and Suites** (p. 282) and rent a car with **Valdez U Drive** (⊕ valdezudrive. com); be sure to request an SUV or a high-clearance vehicle for the drive to McCarthy, just outside of Wrangell–St. Elias National Park. If you arrived late and want to linger in Valdez, spend the next day with **H2O guides** (p. 281) on a day trip to Worthington Glacier State Park. Dine at **MacMurray's Alaska Halibut House** (p. 282), and be sure to try the fresh catch.

Days 4–7: Wrangell–St. Elias National Park and Preserve
(5-hour drive from Valdez)

You've got some driving to do and one of the most gorgeous mountains in the state to see, so you'll want to get an early start. On the road, take care to fill the gas tank at every opportunity; gas stations here are few and far between. Summer is the only time that road construction can get done, so be prepared for delays.

Arrange your accommodations with **Kennicott Glacier Lodge** (p. 336). After you've arrived, and if you've still got some energy, the lodge can help you book a tour of the mining ghost towns of Kennicott and McCarthy to explore the abandoned mines. The menu at the lodge is terrific, so you'll definitely want to take your meals there.

In the days to follow, get out and enjoy the park. Contact **St. Elias Alpine Guides** (p. 335) for an excursion into the heart of the preserve. The front desk at the Lodge can also arrange glacier trekking, flightseeing, rafting, and alpine hiking. And the kitchen will pack you a picnic lunch to take with you.

Day 8: Whittier and Anchorage Connections
(6 hours by ferry from Valdez to Whittier; 2-hour train ride from Whittier to Anchorage)

It's another early-morning departure. Take your car back and catch the 7 am ferry to Whittier. There are snacks available on the ferry, but once you get to Whittier, try the pizza at **Varly's Ice Cream and Pizza** (p. 279). You'll only have a couple of hours to spare before you catch the train to Anchorage, but Whittier is small and easy to explore.

Once you're in Anchorage, if you're flying out the next day, book your stay at the **Millenium Anchorage Hotel** (p. 246), near the airport and right on the shore of Lake Spenard. Take a cab to **Club Paris** (p. 247)—it's a blast from the past and serves the best steak in the state. If you have the energy, catch a live theater show at **Cyrano's Playhouse** (p. 253) or live music at **Tap Root** (p. 249).

Day 9: Head Home

Say goodbye to Alaska and head for home.

LET THE JOURNEY BEGIN

Getting to your destination is as much a part of the Last Frontier experience as being there. Whether traveling by sea, air, or land, keep your eyes open in Alaska: the only thing you can expect is the unexpected. Whales suddenly breach beside ferries; Mt. McKinley peeks through train windows; moose amble along scenic roadways; and the tundra spreads out beneath bush planes.

ON THE WATER

About 50% of visitors choose to cruise Alaska, but for a real adventure, travel Alaska Marine Highway System ferries. Either way, you'll see glaciers, forests, and maybe a whale or two.

The ferry system operates year-round and has two different routes: Bellingham, Washington to Skagway mimics the most popular cruise ship itinerary; the second route runs from Homer to the Aleutian Chain and Dutch Harbor.

Unlike cruise ships, which follow set itineraries, ferries come and go frequently for added flexibility. Consider, though, that they can arrive at inconvenient times whereas cruises dock for daytrips.

At first glance, the $363 one-way ticket from Bellingham to Skagway is a dream compared to the bare minimum $700 for a cruise ship berth. Add a cabin or bring a vehicle and the price can double or triple—and food isn't included. If you go without amenities, need to bring a car, or want flexibility, the ferry price is right; for those on a budget, an all-inclusive cruise may work better. The AlaskaPass can mitigate ferry costs if adding rail or car travel to a trip. (⇨ *Travel Smart Alaska*)

Ferries might not be as luxurious as cruise ships, but they're comfortable. Each has an observation lounge, and cafeterias serve inexpensive meals. Most cabins have private washrooms. Daring passengers sleep outside on cots beneath the heat lamps free of charge. ■**TIP**→ The schedule comes out in January or February, and cabins fill up almost instantly for summer trips; advance booking is essential.

Ferry travel is, with a few exceptions, slow: maximum speed is 16.5 knots, compared with 21 knots or better for a cruise ship. Taking your time has its advantages, though; you'll take in the scenery with the locals who add their own color to the mix.

CONTACTS Alaska Marine Highway (☎ *907/ 465–3941* or *800/642–0066* ⊕ *www.ferry- alaska.com*). Pick up tickets at your starting point or have them mailed to you. Alaska- Pass (☎ *206/463–6550* or *800/248–7598* ⊕ *www.alaskapass.com*).

(left) The White Pass Yukon Route Railroad from Skagway on historic steam Engine 73;
(top right) Passenger stands at stern of Alaska Sate Ferry sailing along Inside Passage under light of midnight sun

ON THE PATH, OR OFF

These maps illustrate major ferry landings, scenic roads, and main rail lines. Beyond Southeast, South Central, and Interior Alaska, you're in the Bush—remote and accessible largely by small plane.

ROADS

With mountains, marine vistas, and miles of open tundra you'll be hard-pressed to find a drive in Alaska that isn't scenic, and not just because there are so few to find. There's always the potential for wildlife encounters, so be alert to something furry darting—or strolling, in the case of moose—out of the roadside brush.

Every year, tourists bring home on the road in RVs. Campgrounds can accommodate trailers, but only private RV parks have hookups. Most drives connect South Central and the Interior, but the Dalton takes adventurers almost to the Arctic Ocean.

RAILROADS

On Alaska's rails you'll ride history. Relive the Gold Rush on Southeast's only railroad, the cliff-hugging White Pass & Yukon Route, the same trail followed by prospectors.

In South Central, one of the best ways to see Alaska's myriad landscapes is to take the Alaska Railroad from Anchorage to Denali National Park. Don't forget to look for Mt. McKinley; while it's the highest peak in North America, it's frequently hidden in clouds.

PLANES

Bush planes are inextricably part of the Alaskan landscape. To get to that remote wilderness lodge or fly-fishing location, there's often no other choice. The flight you take to a native village off the road system is also a trip on that community's lifeline to the rest of the world.

FERRIES

The thin strip of land and hodgepodge of islands that make up Southeast Alaska are best explored by ships or ferries. If you want to see Southeast, the only way to do it is by boat or plane. Even the state capital, Juneau, is only reached by sea or air.

The Kenai Peninsula and the Aleutian Islands are also popular ship or ferry destinations. If you choose to travel by ferry rather than cruise ship, there won't be endless shipboard entertainment, but on some vessels, forest service naturalists will provide a running commentary on the sights you pass.

Expedition Cruise in Glacier Bay

IN THE SKIES

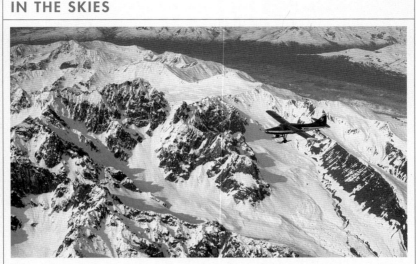

No roads, rails, or even airstrips? No problem. Bush planes are meant to go beyond the trappings of civilization, and pilots deftly land on riverbanks, fields, even water. Lake Hood, outside of Anchorage, is the world's busiest port for seaplanes (and a great place from which to charter a direct flight to remote wilderness spots). One in 78 residents here is a pilot—the most per capita in the U.S.

Bush planes aren't for everyone, though. Extremely nervous fliers should consider how to cope with the effects of updrafts, downdrafts, and even breezes—not to mention the sharp, steeply banked turns pilots make to view wildlife or scenery.

GETTING THERE. Because of the Alaska bypass-mail program (rural towns receive mail and goods at parcel-post rates through regional air carriers), there are more pre-scheduled flights to hidden-away villages than you might think. Flights travel from Anchorage and Fairbanks to regional hubs like Bethel, Nome, Kotzebue, Dillingham, and Kodiak; you'll likely transfer at least once (sometimes the following day) to get elsewhere.

If you're on a tight schedule or headed to a location without mail service, charter an air taxi. When arranging a flight, ask for and check references, and inquire about insurance coverage and safety records—any hesitation to fully address your concerns is a sign to move on.

PACK RIGHT. As for what to wear, *always* carry rain gear. If traveling by float-plane, you can buy, borrow, or rent hip waders. Pack in small, soft-sided bags; gear gets stashed in a plane's nooks and crannies. Finally, don't schedule a small-plane pickup for the same day you're flying out of Alaska—weather can delay flights for days.

CONTACTS Commuter lines include Arctic Circle Air (⊕ *www.arcticcircleair.com*) and Era Alaska (⊕ *www.flyera.com*). For a list if Alaska air taxis, see ⊕ *www.flyalaska.com*. The National Transportation Safety Board keeps a database (⊕ *www.ntsb.gov/ntsb/query.asp*) of air taxi safety records.

(top) de Havilland Turbine Otter on skis near Alaska Range

ALONG THE RAILS

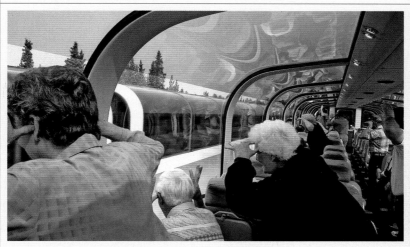

Sit back and relax as the train chugs along and the panorama of alpine meadows, snowcapped peaks, and taiga forests unfolds. There's not a bad seat in the house!

Alaska Railroad trains run between Seward and Fairbanks via Anchorage. The *Coastal Classic* goes from Seward to Anchorage in about 4 hours. The *Denali Star* makes the Anchorage to Fairbanks trip in 12 hours. Standard railroad-coach passengers have access to dining cars, lounges, and dome cars (with windows to the ceiling). One-way, peak-season tickets range from $70 to $320, depending on the route and seating class. Service is less expensive but limited off-season.

Princess Tours and Gray Line of Alaska run luxury class service in cars connected to Alaska Railroad trains between Anchorage and Fairbanks. Day- and multiday trips are available.

MOOSE SPOTTING. Conductors may encourage you to give a "moose salute" to passing trains (see photo.) Hold your hands up as though you're being held at gunpoint, and touch your thumbs to your temples to create moose antlers. It's a fun way to say hi to your fellow travelers.

RIDE HISTORY. Since 1923, Alaskans have been flagging down the *Hurricane Turn* much like you'd hail a taxi. One of the last flag-stop trains in America, it still makes unscheduled stops to transport locals to remote cabins in the Interior.

HOW TO HAIL A TRAIN

■ Stand 25 feet from the tracks and wave a large, white cloth above your head.
■ The conductor will acknowledge you by blowing the train whistle.
■ When the train stops and the conductor opens the door (and not before), proceed toward the train.
■ Hop aboard with fellow homesteaders, hikers, and anglers.

CONTACTS Alaska Railroad Corporation (☎ *907/265–2494* or *800/544–0552* ⊕ *www. akrr.com*). Gray Line of Alaska (☎ *206/281– 3535* or *888/452–737* ⊕ *www.graylinealaska. com*). Princess Tours (☎ 800/774–6237 ⊕ www.princess.com).

(top) Friendly moosing—Seymour Levy, Fodors.com photo-contest winner

ON THE ROAD

Alaska's highways may only reach a fraction of the state, but they get high marks for natural beauty, cultural and historic significance, and recreational opportunites. Here are our top picks.

SEWARD HIGHWAY
(127 mi, Anchorage to Seward)
Region: South Central (⇨ Ch. 6)
Points of Interest: This All-American Highway (the highest designation for a National Scenic Byway) shoulders Turnagain Arm and Chugach National Forest. Dall sheep roam the mountainsides, and beluga whales swim Cook Inlet. Just north of Seward is the easily accessible Exit Glacier.

GLENN HIGHWAY
(328 mi, Anchorage to Glennallen, Gakona Junction to Tok)
Region: South Central (⇨ Ch. 6)

Points of Interest: Chugach and Talkeetna mountains, Matanuska-Susitna Valley. At Mile 50, stop at the Musk Ox Farm to learn about the animal's rare underwool (*qiviut*); head to Matanuska Glacier at Mile 101.

GEORGE PARKS HIGHWAY
(358 mi, Wasilla to Fairbanks)
Regions: South Central and Interior (⇨ Chs. 6 & 7)
Points of Interest: Enter Denali National Park & Preserve at Mile 237. At the Mile 135 turnout get an exceptional view of Mt. McKinley and access Denali State Park.

RICHARDSON HIGHWAY
(364 mi, Fairbanks to Valdez)
Regions: South Central and Interior (⇨ Chs. 6 & 7)
Points of Interest: Wrangell–St. Elias National Park and Preserve. Mile 28 provides an eyeful of Worthington Glacier near Thompson Pass. See the tumbling waterfalls and rock walls of Keystone Canyon, 15 mi north of Valdez.

DALTON HIGHWAY
(414 mi, starting 84 miles north of Fairbanks near Livengood to Deadhorse)
Regions: Interior and the Bush (⇨ Chs. 7 & 8)
Points of Interest: Watch for caribou ducking under the above-ground portion of the Trans-Alaska Pipeline. Don't get so distracted you that miss Coldfoot—your last chance to get supplies before trekking the last 234 mi to Deadhorse.

FOR MORE INFO

The Milepost (⊕ *http://milepost.com*), an extensive guide to Alaska's roadways, is an absolute must. At the end of this book, you'll find safety tips and road rules in *Travel Smart Alaska*.

(top) Taylor Highway—Som Vembar, Fodors.com photo-contest participant

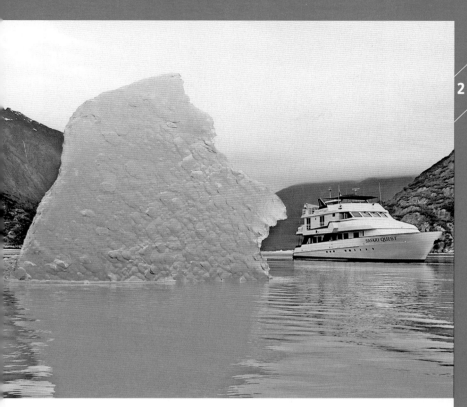

Alaska By Cruise Ship

WORD OF MOUTH

"Part II of our trip was the *Island Princess* 7-day one-way cruise from Vancouver to Anchorage. The mini-suite was much larger than we expected, with plenty of room for everything. The food was delicious. The views in Glacier Bay and College Fjord were outstanding (2400 pictures later)."

—musictub

By Linda Coffman

Alaska is one of cruising's showcase destinations. Itineraries give passengers more choices than ever before—from traditional loop cruises of the Inside Passage, round-trips from Vancouver or Seattle, to one-way Inside Passage–Gulf of Alaska cruises.

Though Alaska cruises have generally attracted an older-passenger demographic, more young people and families are setting sail for the 49th state and children are a common sight aboard ship. Cruise lines have responded with youth programs and shore excursions with appeal for youngsters and their parents. Shore excursions have become more active, too, often incorporating activities families can enjoy together, such as bicycling, kayaking, and hiking. Many lines also offer pre- or postcruise land tours as an optional package trip, and onboard entertainment and learning programs are extensive. Most also hire Alaska Native speakers, naturalists, or local personalities to lead discussions stimulated by the local environment.

Cruise ships may seem like floating resorts, but you can't check out and go elsewhere if you don't like your ship. The one you choose will be your home—it determines the type of accommodations you have, what kind of food you eat, what style of entertainment you see, and even the destinations you visit. If you don't enjoy your ship, you probably won't enjoy your cruise. That is why the most important choice you'll make when booking a cruise is the combined selection of cruise line and cruise ship.

CRUISING IN ALASKA

Which cruise is right for you depends on numerous factors, notably your budget, the size and style of ship you choose, and the itinerary.

CRUISE ITINERARIES

Cruise ships typically follow one of two itineraries in Alaska: round-trip Inside Passage loops and one-way Inside Passage–Gulf of Alaska cruises. Itineraries are usually seven days, though some lines offer longer trips. ■ TIP→ Keep in mind that the landscape along the Inside Passage changes dramatically over the course of the summer cruise season. In May and June, you'll see snowcapped mountains and dramatic waterfalls from snowmelt cascading down the cliff faces, but by July and August most of the snow and some waterfalls will be gone.

The most popular Alaskan ports of call are Haines, Juneau, Skagway, Ketchikan, and Sitka. Lesser-known ports in British Columbia, such as Victoria and the charming fishing port of Prince Rupert, have begun to see more cruise traffic.

Small ships typically sail within Alaska, setting sail from Juneau or other Alaskan ports, stopping at the popular ports as well as smaller, less visited villages. Some expedition vessels focus on remote beaches and fjords, with few, if any, port calls.

ROUND-TRIP INSIDE PASSAGE LOOPS

A seven-day cruise typically starts and finishes in Vancouver, British Columbia, or Seattle, Washington. The first and last days are spent at sea, traveling to and from Alaska along the mountainous coast of British Columbia. Once in Alaska waters, most ships call at a different port on each of four days, and reserve one day for cruising in or near Glacier Bay National Park or another glacier-rich fjord.

ONE-WAY INSIDE PASSAGE–GULF OF ALASKA ITINERARIES

These cruises depart from Vancouver, Seattle, or, occasionally, San Francisco or Los Angeles, and finish at Seward or Whittier, the seaports for Anchorage (or vice versa). They're a good choice if you want to explore Alaska by land, either before or after your cruise. For this itinerary, you'll need to fly into and out of different cities (into Vancouver and out of Anchorage, for example), which can be pricier than round-trip airfare to and from the same city.

SMALL-SHIP ALASKA-ONLY ITINERARIES

Most small ships and yachts home port in Juneau or other Alaskan ports and offer a variety of one-way and round-trip cruises entirely within Alaska. A typical small-ship cruise is a seven-day, one-way or round-trip from Juneau, stopping at several Inside Passage ports—including smaller ports skipped by large cruise ships.

SMALL-SHIP INSIDE PASSAGE REPOSITIONING CRUISES

Alaska's small cruise ships and yachts are based in Juneau or other Alaskan ports throughout the summer. In September they sail back to their winter homes in the Pacific Northwest; in May they return to Alaska via the Inside Passage. These repositioning trips are usually about 11 or more days and are often heavily discounted, because they take place during the shoulder season.

OTHER ITINERARIES

Although mainstream lines stick to the popular seven-day Alaskan itineraries, some smaller excursion lines add more exotic options. For example, you may find an occasional voyage across the Bering Sea to Japan and Asia. You can also create your own itinerary by taking an Alaska Marine Highway System ferry to ports of your choosing.

FERRY TRAVEL

The cruise-ship season is over by October, but for independent, off-season ferry travel November is the best month. After the stormy month of October, it's still relatively warm on the Inside Passage (temperatures will average about 40°F), and it's a good month for wildlife-watching. In particular, humpback whales are abundant off Sitka, and bald eagles congregate by the thousands near Haines.

> **TIP**
>
> Although most other kinds of travel are booked over the Internet nowadays, cruises are a different story. Your best bet is still to work with a travel agent who specializes in cruises. Agents with strong relationships with the lines have a much better chance of getting you the cabin you want, and possibly even extras.

PRE- AND POST-CRUISE ITINERARIES

LAND TOURS

Most cruise lines offer the option of independent, hosted, or fully escorted land tours before or after your cruise. Independent tours give you a preplanned itinerary with confirmed hotel and transportation arrangements, but you're free to follow your interests in each town. Hosted tours are similar, but tour-company representatives are available along the route for assistance. On fully escorted tours you travel with a group, led by a tour director. Activities are preplanned (and typically prepaid), so you have a good idea of how much your trip will cost (not counting meals and incidentals) before departure. Most lines offer cruise tour itineraries that include a ride aboard the Alaska Railroad.

Running between Anchorage, Denali National Park, and Fairbanks are Holland America Line's *McKinley Explorer,* Princess Tours' *Denali Express* and *McKinley Express,* and Royal Caribbean's *Wilderness Express,* which offer unobstructed views of the passing terrain and wildlife from private glass-domed railcars. Princess Cruises and Holland America Line have the most extensive Alaska cruise tours, owning and operating their own coaches, railcars, and lodges.

In addition to rail trips to Denali, Holland America offers tours into the Yukon, as well as river cruises on the Yukon River. Princess's cruise tours include trips to the Yukon and the Kenai Peninsula. Both lines offer land excursions across the Arctic Circle to Prudhoe Bay. Several cruise lines also offer pre- and postcruise tours of the Canadian Rockies. Of the traditional cruise-ship fleets, Carnival Cruise Lines, Norwegian Cruise Line, and Disney Cruise Line do not currently offer cruise-tour packages in Alaska. Many cruise lines also offer pre- or postcruise hotel and sightseeing packages in Vancouver, Seattle, or Anchorage lasting one to three days.

Cruise ships offer passengers panoramic views of Inside Passage glaciers.

SMALL SHIP LINES
Most small-ship lines offer hotel add-ons, but not land tours.

DO-IT-YOURSELF LAND ITINERARY
While there's much to be said for the cruise lines' traditional pre- or postcruise train or motor coach add-on trips to Denali National Park (namely the ease and lower cost as compared to a DIY trip with comparable amenities), it's worth considering breaking from the pack to customize the experience. Passengers generally begin or end their cruise in Anchorage, the most practical port city to use as a base for exploring Alaska. Before or after the cruise you may want to spend a few days in Anchorage to visit the Anchorage Museum of History and Art and the Alaska Native Heritage Center to expand your knowledge of Alaska's history and cultures. Then rent a car in Anchorage and drive to Denali—this is an especially good idea for photography buffs who will want to stop along the way and shoot to their heart's content.

DAY 1: DRIVE TO DENALI
Make a day of the drive with some interesting detours along the way, including Eklutna Village Historical Park and Eklutna Lake, and Talkeetna. EarthSong Lodge in Healy is our choice of tranquil accommodations, with a staff naturalist and its own sled-dog kennels on-site. The cabins are 17 miles outside the park entrance, but well worth the daily drive. After checking into the cabin (reserve well in advance), drive 25 minutes to the visitor center to acquaint yourself with the park, gather maps, and buy your park pass, which is good for seven days.

CLOSE UP

Choosing Your Cruise Cabin

2

INSIDE CABINS
An inside cabin is just that: a stateroom that's inside the ship with no window. These are always the least expensive cabins and are ideal for passengers who would rather spend on excursions than on upgraded accommodations. Inside cabins are generally as spacious as outside cabins, and decor and amenities are similar. Many ships locate cabins accommodating three or more passengers on the inside. ■TIP→ For passengers who want a very dark room for sleeping, an inside cabin is ideal.

OUTSIDE CABINS
Outside cabins have either a picture window or porthole. To give the illusion of more space, these cabins might rely on the generous use of mirrors. Outside cabins are the better choice for those prone to motion sickness.■TIP→ Check to make

sure your view of the sea is not obstructed by a lifeboat. The ship's deck plan will help you figure it out.

BALCONY CABINS
A balcony—or veranda—cabin is an outside cabin with floor-to-ceiling glass doors that open onto a private deck. Balconies are sometimes cut out of the cabin's square footage (depending on the ship). ■TIP→ If you have small children, a veranda cabin isn't the best choice. Accidents can happen, even on balconies with solid barriers beneath the railing.

SUITES
Suites are the most lavish accommodations. Although they're always larger than regular cabins, they don't always have separate rooms for sleeping. The most expansive (and expensive) have large living rooms and separate bedrooms and may also have huge private outdoor sundecks with hot tubs and dining areas.

DAY 2: GET ON THE BUS
You can't drive inside the park and, once you see some of the roads, you'll be glad to leave the driving to the National Park Service, which runs a number of different types of buses in the park. Although you could take a guided tour bus, the more personalized approach is via shuttle buses that allow you to get on and off at any stop to explore as much or as little as you choose. If you're in the mood for trekking, take a bus all the way to Wonder Lake at Mile 85 where there's a 5-mile round-trip hike to McKinley River. When you are ready to leave, simply wave down any green shuttle bus for a pickup. You may have to wait up to an hour for a ride, so bring water, snacks, clothing layers, and bug spray. Exploring Denali by bus is a wonderful experience, but not always comfortable.

DAY 3: EXPLORE DENALI
Today, fly up for a hike in the backcountry on a heli-hiking tour of Denali. The guided trips offer the thrill of a helicopter flight and the chance to experience the absolute quiet and beauty of backcountry Alaska. If you're not in a hiking mood, book just a flightseeing trip. Back on the ground, drive to Healy for a late lunch and time your arrival at EarthSong for a sled dog presentation.

DAY 4: RANGER DAY

The Park Service offers programs for every activity level, including sled dog demonstrations, trail walks, and off-trail Discovery Hikes. After your final day in Denali, spend another night or drive back to Anchorage by the light of the midnight sun.

WHEN TO GO

Cruise season runs from mid-May to late September. The most popular sailing dates are from late June through August, when warm days are apt to be most plentiful. In spring, wildflowers are abundant, and you'll likely see more wildlife along the shore because the animals haven't yet migrated to higher elevations. May and June are traditionally drier than July and August. Alaska's early fall brings the splendor of autumn hues and the first snowfalls in the mountains. Animals return to low ground, and shorter days bring the possibility of seeing the northern lights. Daytime temperatures in May, June, and September are in the 50s and 60s. July and August averages are in the 60s and 70s, with occasional days in the 80s. Cruising in the low and shoulder seasons provides other advantages besides discounted fares: availability of ships and particular cabins is greater, and ports are almost completely free of tourists.

BOOKING YOUR CRUISE

As a rule, the majority of cruisers plan their trips four to six months ahead of time. It follows then, that a four- to six-month window should give you the pick of sailing dates, ships, itineraries, cabins, and flights to the port city. If you're looking for a standard itinerary and aren't choosy about the vessel or dates, you could wait for a last-minute discount, but they are harder to find than in the past.

If particular shore excursions are important to you, consider booking them when you book your cruise to avoid disappointment later.

CRUISE COSTS

Average fares for Alaskan itineraries vary dramatically depending on when you sail, which ship and grade of cabin you choose, and when you book. Published rates are highest during June, July, and August; you'll pay less, and have more space on ship and ashore, if you sail in May or September.

Whenever you choose to sail, remember that the brochure price is the highest fare the line can charge for a given cruise. Most lines offer early-booking discounts. Although these vary tremendously, many lines will offer at least 10% off if you book ahead of time, usually by the end of January for a summer cruise. Sometimes you can book a discounted last-minute cruise if the ship hasn't filled all its cabins, but you won't get your pick of ships, cabins, or sailing dates. However, since most cruise lines will, if asked, refund the difference in fare if it drops after you've paid your deposit and before you make your final payment, there's little advantage in last-minute booking.

CLOSE UP

Before You Book

If you've decided to use a travel agent, ask yourself these 10 simple questions, and you'll be better prepared to help the agent do his or her job.

1. Who will be going on the cruise?

2. What can you afford to spend for the entire trip?

3. Where would you like to go?

4. How much vacation time do you have?

5. When can you get away?

6. What are your interests?

7. Do you prefer a casual or structured vacation?

8. What kind of accommodations do you want?

9. What are your dining preferences?

10. How will you get to the embarkation port?

2

SOLO TRAVELERS

Single cabins for solo travelers are nonexistent on most ships; taking a double cabin can cost as much as twice the advertised per-person rates (which are based on two people sharing a room). Some cruise lines will find roommates of the same sex for singles so that each can travel at the regular per-person rate.

EXTRAS

Cruise fares typically include accommodation, onboard meals and snacks, and most onboard activities. Not normally included are airfare, shore excursions, tips, soft drinks, alcoholic drinks, or spa treatments. Port fees, fuel surcharges, and sales taxes are generally added to your fare at booking.

PLANNING

What to Wear: When preparing for your Alaska cruise, remember this first rule of Alaskan thumb: be an onion. Never leave the ship without dressing in layers. Your first layer should be thin and airy so that if it gets warm your skin can breathe. Every layer over that, however, should aim to keep you warm and

> **TIP**
>
> Notify the cruise line of any dietary restrictions when booking your cruise, and follow up on the arrangements a couple of months before embarking.

dry. In Alaska it is quite common for a hot and sunny day to abruptly change. For onboard dress, follow your cruise line's suggestions regarding what to bring for the evening or two you might need to wear something formal to dinner.

What to Pack: Don't forget your valid passport; American and Canadian citizens are now required to provide proof of citizenship regardless of whether their Alaska cruise is crossing international boundaries. Although disposable and small digital cameras are very handy for candid shots, they are not much good for catching wildlife from afar. A good zoom lens can be heavy, but can make all the difference. Even if you have a quality camera, pack binoculars for everyone. Be sure to take bug spray during the summer months, as the mosquitoes are large, plentiful, and fierce.

Getting to the Port: Most cruise-ship passengers fly to their port of embarkation. If you book your cruise far enough in advance, you'll be given the opportunity to purchase an air-and-sea package, which can save you money on your flight. With this option a uniformed cruise-line agent will meet you at the airport to smooth your way to the pier. Without the package you can still access the cruise's transfer service, but it might cost more than a cab or shuttle.

Boarding: The lines at check-in can be long (up to an hour of wait time) if you are boarding a large cruise ship. You'll be issued a boarding card that doubles as your stateroom key and shipboard charge card. Either before you enter the check-in area or before proceeding to the ship, you and your hand luggage will pass through a security checkpoint. Once you're on board, you'll produce your boarding card once more before heading to your cabin. On a small-ship cruise, embarkation is much more relaxed and relatively line-free.

Restaurant Seating: Restaurant seating is a major consideration for most cruisers as they choose which line they'll travel with. Some cruise ships have traditional assigned dinner seatings, where you will choose between early or late seating and be assigned a table for the entire trip. Early seating is generally scheduled between 6 and 6:30 pm, while late seating can begin from 8:15 to 8:45 pm. Families with young children or older passengers often choose an early seating. Early diners are not encouraged to linger too long as the dining room needs to be prepared for the late seating, which is viewed by some passengers as more romantic and less rushed. Some lines offer open seating; you'll dine whenever you want within service hours and sit wherever you please. Still other cruise lines strike a balance of options with alternatives like à la carte restaurants and casual dinner menus in the buffet facilities.

Paying for Things on Board: Because cashless society prevails on cruise ships, during check-in an imprint is made of your credit card or you place a cash deposit for use against your onboard charges. Most onboard expenditures are charged to your shipboard account (via a swipe of your key card) with your signature as verification, with the exception of some casino gaming.

You'll get an itemized bill listing your purchases at the end of the voyage, and any discrepancies can be discussed at the purser's desk. To save time, check the balance of your shipboard account before the last day by requesting an interim printout of your bill from the purser to insure accuracy. On some ships you can even access your account on your stateroom television.

Will I Get Seasick? Many first-time passengers are anxious about whether they'll be stricken by seasickness, but there is no way to tell until you actually sail. Modern vessels are equipped with stabilizers that eliminate much of the motion responsible for seasickness. On an Alaska

ON-BOARD EXTRAS

As you budget for your trip, keep these likely additional costs in mind.

Cocktails: $5.75–$9

Wine by the glass: $6–$9

Beer: $5–$6

Bottled water: $2.50–$4

Specialty ice cream and coffee: $4–$6

Laundry: $1–$10 per piece (where self-launder facilities are unavailable)

Spa treatments: $100–$175

Salon services: $30–$100

Casino Gambling: 5¢ to $10 for slot machines; $5 and up for table games

Bingo: $5–$10 per card for multiple games in each session

cruise you will spend most of your time in calm, sheltered waters, so unless your cruise includes time out in the open sea (say, between San Francisco and Vancouver) you may not even feel the ship's movement—particularly if your ship is a megaliner. You may feel slightly more movement on a small ship, but not by much as these ships ply remote bays and coves that are even more sheltered than those traveled by regular cruise ships.

If you have a history of seasickness, don't book an inside cabin. For the terminally seasick, it will begin to resemble a moveable coffin in short order. If you do become seasick, you can use common drugs such as Dramamine and Bonine. Some people find anti-seasickness wristbands helpful; these apply gentle pressure to the wrist in lieu of drugs. Worn behind the ear, the Transderm Scop patch dispenses a continuous metered dose of medication, which is absorbed into the skin and enters the bloodstream. Apply the patch four hours before sailing and it will continue to be effective for three days.

KEEPING IN TOUCH

Rates for your in-room direct-dial phone vary from $5 to as much as $15 *per minute*; most passengers reserve it for emergency use only. Some cruise ships are wired to act as cell towers, so depending on your provider and roaming charges, you might be able to somewhat-affordably use your device throughout your trip uninterrupted (though we encourage you not to—you're on vacation!). In addition to the 75¢–$1 per minute Internet fee, you might also need to pay a onetime connection charge, and the connection might be maddeningly slow. For each port, we list a less expensive Internet option or two.

OTHER CONSIDERATIONS

Children's programs: Virtually every line has children's programs and Disney Cruise Line's entry into Alaska gives parents a superior option; however, high-end lines generally only offer supervised programs when enough children are aboard to warrant them or during school holidays.

SMALL-SHIP CRUISES

We cover the most recognized small-ship lines sailing in Alaska, but that is by no means exhaustive. Every cruise at **Lindblad Expeditions** (⊕ www.expeditions.com) is educational, focusing on soft adventure and environmentally conscientious travel through ecologically sensitive regions of Alaska. Since 2004 the line has partnered with *National Geographic* to enhance the experience by including *National Geographic* experts and photographers on board. The ships of Lindblad Expeditions spend time looking for wildlife, exploring out-of-the-way inlets, and making Zodiac landings at isolated beaches. Other great small ships sailing the Inside Passage include Fantasy Cruises' *Island Spirit* (⊕ www.smallalaskaship.com), owned and operated by Captain Jeff Behrens. Captain Behrens is committed to rapport-building with and respect for the area's smallest communities; as a result, 32-passenger *Island Spirit* can make off-the-beaten-path port calls like Tenakee Springs (⊕ www.tenakeespringsak.com), Five Finger Lighthouse (⊕ www.5fingerlighthouse.com), and Baranof Warm Springs, in addition to scenic anchorages like Ford's Terror that only small ships can access. Charters and photography-focused cruises are also available.

Alaska Sea Adventures (⊕ www.yachtalaska.com)focuses on charters and single-theme cruises on wildlife photography, birding, research, archaeology, whale migration, or fish spawning. Its two ships, *Northern Song* and *Alaska Legend*, can accommodate up to 8 passengers each.

Small ships are less likely to offer kids' programs; however, some do schedule a few family-friendly sailings. Check whether the available shore excursions include activities that will appeal to kids.

Dining: Some cruise lines offer traditional assigned dining, meaning you will dine each evening at the same table with the same companions. Others offer open seating, allowing you to dine whenever and with whomever you like; still others offer a choice between the two systems. Most traditional cruise ships have at least one restaurant in addition to the main dining room; some have more. Most ships offer vegetarian and heart-healthy or low-carb options.

Ports of call: You'll want to know where and when you will be stopping. Will there be enough time in port to do what you want to do there? Will it be the right time of day for your chosen activity? Will you tender to shore by boat or moor up at the dock? This is important, as tendering can take some time away from your port visit.

Onboard activities: Your cruise will likely include one or two full days at sea. Think about how you'd like to fill the time. Do you want great workout facilities or a spa? What about educational opportunities or shopping? If seeing Alaska itself is your priority, choose a ship with lots of outdoor *and* indoor viewing space.

ABOUT THE SHIPS

CRUISE SHIPS

Large cruise lines account for the majority of passengers sailing to Alaska. These typically have large cruise ships in their fleets with plentiful deck space and, often, a promenade deck that allows you to stroll the ship's perimeter. In the newest vessels, traditional meets trendy with resort-style innovations; however, they still feature cruise-ship classics, like afternoon tea and complimentary room service. The smallest cruise ships carry as few as 400 passengers, while the biggest can accommodate between 1,500 and 3,000 passengers—enough people to outnumber the residents of many Alaskan port towns. Large ships are a good choice if you're looking for nonstop activity and lots of options; they're especially appealing for groups and families with older kids. If you prefer a gentler pace and a chance to get to know your shipmates, try a smaller ship.

SMALL SHIPS

Compact expedition-type vessels bring you right up to the shoreline to skirt the face of a glacier and pull through narrow channels where big ships don't fit. These cruises focus on Alaska, and you'll see more wildlife and call into smaller ports, as well as some of the better-known towns. Enrichment talks—conducted by naturalists, Native Alaskans, and other experts in the state's natural history and Native cultures—are the norm. Cabins on expedition ships can be tiny, usually with no phone or TV, and bathrooms are often no bigger than cubbyholes. The dining room and lounge are usually the only public areas on these vessels; however, some are luxurious with cushy cabins, comfy lounges and libraries, and hot tubs. You won't find much nightlife aboard, but what you trade for space and onboard diversions is a unique and unforgettable glimpse of Alaska.

Many small ships are based in Juneau or another Alaska port and sail entirely within Alaska. Twice annually, some offer an Inside Passage cruise as the ships reposition to and from their winter homes elsewhere.

Small-ship cruising can be pricey, as fares tend to be inclusive (except for airfare), but have few onboard charges, and, given the size of ship and style of cruise, fewer opportunities to spend on board.

CRUISE SHIPS AT A GLANCE

Cruise Lines/Ships	Cabins	Double Occupancy	Decks	Restaurants	In-Cabin VCR/DVD Players	Wi-Fi	Pools	Hot Tubs	Bars	Cinema	Library	Showrooms	Children's Program	Dance Clubs
AMERICAN CRUISE LINE														
American Spirit	48	100	4	1	DVD	yes	no	no	1	no	yes	no	no	no
AMERICAN SAFARI LINE														
Safari Endeavour	43	86	4	1	DVD	no	no	2	2	no	yes	no	no	no
Safari Explorer	18	36	3	1	DVD	no	no	1	1	no	yes	no	no	no
Safari Quest	11	21	4	1	DVD	no	no	1	1	no	yes	no	no	no
CARNIVAL CRUISE LINES														
Carnival Miracle	1062	2124	12	3	VCR (some)	yes	3	4	7	no	yes	1	ages 2-17	2
CELEBRITY CRUISES														
Celebrity Solstice	1425	2850	13	7	DVD (some)	yes	3	6	11	no	yes	1	ages 3-17	1
Celebrity Millennium	975	1950	11	3	VCR (some) DVD (some)	yes	3	6	7	yes	yes	1	ages 3-17	1
Celebrity Century	875	1750	10	4	VCR (some)	yes	2	5	7	yes	yes	1	ages 3-17	1
DISNEY CRUISE LINE														
Disney Wonder	877	1754	11	5	DVD (some)	yes	3	4	6	yes	no	2	ages 3-17	2
HOLLAND AMERICA LINE														
Amsterdam	690	1380	9	3	DVD	yes	2	2	6	yes	yes	1	ages 3-17	1
Zuiderdam/Oosterdam/Westerdam	958	1916	11	3	DVD	yes	2	5	9	yes	yes	1	ages 3-17	2
Volendam/Zaandam	716	1432	10	3	DVD	yes	2	2	6	yes	yes	1	ages 3-17	1
Statendam	675	1350	10	3	DVD	yes	2	2	9	yes	yes	1	ages 3-17	1

Ship														
INNERSEAS DISCOVERIES														
Wilderness Adventurer	30	60	3	1	DVD	no	no	1	1	no	no	no	no	no
Wilderness Discoverer	38	76	3	1	DVD	no	no	2	1	no	no	no	no	no
Wilderness Explorer	38	76	3	1	DVD	no	no	1	1	no	no	no	no	no
Lindblad Expeditions														
National Geographic Sea Bird/Sea Lion	31	62	3	1	no	no	no	no	1	no	yes	no	no	no
NORWEGIAN CRUISE LINE														
Norwegian Pearl	1197	2394	15	10	DVD (some)	yes	2	6	9	yes	yes	1	ages 2-17	2
Norwegian Jewel	1188	2376	15	10	DVD (some)	yes	2	6	9	yes	yes	1	ages 2-17	2
Norwegian Sun	968	1936	11	7	DVD (some)	yes	2	5	8	no	yes	1	ages 2-17	1
OCEANIA CRUISES														
Regatta	342	684	9	2	DVD (some)	yes	1	3	4	no	yes	1	no	1
PRINCESS CRUISES														
Coral/Island Princess	985	1970	11	4	DVD (some)	yes	3	5	7	yes	yes	2	ages 3-17	2
Diamond/Sapphire Princess	1337	2670	13	7	DVD (some)	yes	4	8	11	no	yes	2	ages 3-17	2
Grand/Golden/Star Princess	1300	2600	14	6	DVD (some)	yes	4	9	9	no	yes	2	ages 3-17	2
REGENT SEVEN SEAS CRUISES														
Seven Seas Navigator	245	490	8	2	DVD	yes	1	1	4	no	yes	1	ages 5-17	1
ROYAL CARIBBEAN INTL														
Radiance of the Seas	1071	2139	12	8	VCR (some) DVD (some)	yes	2	3	11	yes	yes	1	ages 3-17	1
Rhapsody of the Seas	1020	1998	11	6	VCR (some) DVD (some)	yes	2	6	8	no	yes	1	ages 3-17	1
SILVERSEA CRUISES														
Silver Shadow	191	382	7	3	DVD	yes	1	2	3	no	yes	1	no	1

All large ships on this list have in-cabin safes, in-cabin refrigerators in most categories, laundry service, hair salons, gyms and fitness classes, spas, saunas, steam rooms or thermal suites (for which there is a charge), casinos, dance clubs, and showrooms; many ships have dry-cleaning service.

LARGE CRUISE LINES

SHIP	EMBARKATION PORT	DURATION IN NIGHTS	ITINERARY AND PORTS OF CALL
CARNIVAL CRUISE LINES			
Carnival Miracle	Seattle	7	Round-trip: Juneau, Skagway, Ketchikan, Victoria, BC, Sawyer Glacier
CELEBRITY CRUISES			
Celebrity Solstice	Seattle	7	Round-trip: Ketchikan, Juneau, Skagway, Victoria, BC, Sawyer Glacier
Celebrity Century	Vancouver	7	Round-trip: Ketchikan, Juneau, Icy Strait Point, Hubbard Glacier
Celebrity Millennium	Vancouver	7	Northbound: Skagway, Juneau, Ketchikan, Icy Strait Point, Hubbard Glacier
	Seward	7	Southbound: Skagway, Juneau, Ketchikan, Icy Strait Point, Hubbard Glacier
DISNEY CRUISE LINE			
Disney Wonder	Vancouver	7	Round-trip: Ketchikan, Juneau, Skagway, Sawyer Glacier
HOLLAND AMERICA LINE			
Amsterdam	Vancouver	7	Round-trip: Ketchikan, Juneau, Skagway, Glacier Bay or Sawyer Glacier
Oosterdam	Seattle	7	Round-trip: Juneau, Sitka, Ketchikan, Victoria, BC, Sawyer Glacier
Statendam	Vancouver	7	Northbound: Skagway, Juneau, Ketchikan, Glacier Bay
	Seward	7	Southbound: Haines, Juneau, Ketchikan, Glacier Bay
Volendam	Vancouver	7	Round-trip: Skagway, Juneau, Ketchikan, Sawyer Glacier, Glacier Bay
Westerdam	Seattle	7	Round-trip: Juneau, Sitka, Ketchikan, Victoria, BC, Glacier Bay
Zaandam	Vancouver	7	Northbound: Juneau, Skagway, Ketchikan, Glacier Bay
	Seward	7	Southbound: Juneau, Haines, Ketchikan, Glacier Bay
Zuiderdam	Vancouver	7	Round-trip: Skagway, Juneau, Ketchikan, Sawyer Glacier, Glacier Bay
NORWEGIAN CRUISE LINE			
Norwegian Pearl	Seattle	7	Round-trip: Juneau, Skagway, Ketchikan, Victoria, BC, Glacier Bay
Norwegian Jewel	Seattle	7	Round-trip: Juneau, Skagway, Ketchikan, Victoria, BC, Sawyer Glacier
Norwegian Sun	Whittier	7	Southbound: Hubbard Glacier, Icy Strait Point, Juneau, Skagway, Ketchikan, Vancouver, BC
	Vancouver	7	Northbound: Ketchikan, Juneau, Skagway, Glacier Bay, Hubbard Glacier, Whittier
OCEANIA CRUISES			
Regatta	San Francisco	9	Northbound: Astoria, OR, Ketchikan, Juneau, Sitka, Hubbard Glacier, Vancouver, BC
	Vancouver	7	Round-trip: Ketchikan, Juneau, Sitka, Wrangell, Sawyer Glacier
	Vancouver	10	Southbound: Sitka, Juneau, Skagway, Hoonah, Ketchikan, Hubbard Glacier, Seattle
	Seattle	7	Northbound: Sitka, Ketchikan, Wrangell or Prince Rupert, BC, Sawyer Glacier, Vancouver, BC
	Seattle	10	Round-trip: Ketchikan, Skagway, Juneau, Hoonah, Sitka, Victoria, BC, Hubbard or Sawyer Glacier
	Vancouver	10	Ketchikan, Juneau, Sitka, Hubbard Glacier, Victoria, BC, Astoria, OR, San Francisco

PRINCESS CRUISES

Coral Princess	Vancouver	7	Northbound: Ketchikan, Juneau, Skagway, Glacier Bay, College Fjord
	Whittier	7	Southbound: Ketchikan, Juneau, Skagway, Glacier Bay, Hubbard Glacier
Diamond Princess	Vancouver	7	Northbound: Ketchikan, Juneau, Skagway, Glacier Bay, College Fjord
	Whittier	7	Southbound: Ketchikan, Juneau, Skagway, Glacier Bay, Hubbard Glacier
Golden Princess	Seattle	7	Round-trip: Juneau, Skagway, Ketchikan, Victoria, BC, Sawyer Glacier
Grand Princess	San Francisco	10	Round-trip: Juneau, Skagway, Ketchikan, Victoria, BC, Sawyer Glacier or Glacier Bay; some sailings substitute Haines, Sitka, or Icy Strait Point
Island Princess	Vancouver	7	Northbound: Ketchikan, Juneau, Skagway, Glacier Bay, College Fjord
	Whittier	7	Southbound: Ketchikan, Juneau, Skagway, Glacier Bay, Hubbard Glacier
Sapphire Princess	Vancouver	7	Northbound: Juneau, Skagway, Ketchikan, Glacier Bay, College Fjord
	Whittier	7	Southbound: Juneau, Skagway, Ketchikan, Glacier Bay, Hubbard Glacier
Star Princess	Seattle	7	Round-trip: Juneau, Skagway, Ketchikan, Victoria, BC, Glacier Bay

REGENT SEVEN SEAS CRUISES

Seven Seas Navigator	Vancouver	7	Northbound: Sitka, Juneau, Skagway, Ketchikan, Hubbard Glacier, Sawyer Glacier, Seward
	Seward	7	Southbound: Sitka, Juneau, Skagway, Ketchikan, Hubbard Glacier, Sawyer Glacier, Vancouver, BC
	Vancouver	7	Round-trip: Wrangell, Sawyer Glacier, Juneau, Skagway, Ketchikan
	San Francisco	12	Northbound: Astoria, OR, Ketchikan, Juneau, Skagway, Sitka, Hubbard Glacier, Victoria, BC, Vancouver, BC
	Vancouver	12	Southbound: Sitka, Icy Strait Point, Ketchikan, Juneau, Skagway, Hubbard Glacier, Victoria BC, Astoria, OR, San Francisco

ROYAL CARIBBEAN INTERNATIONAL

Radiance of the Seas	Vancouver	7	Northbound: Ketchikan, Juneau, Skagway, Icy Strait Point, Hubbard Glacier
	Seward	7	Southbound: Ketchikan, Juneau, Skagway, Icy Strait Point, Hubbard Glacier
Rhapsody of the Seas	Seattle	7	Round-trip: Juneau, Skagway, Victoria, BC, Sawyer Glacier

SILVERSEA CRUISES

Silver Shadow	Vancouver	10	Round-trip: Skagway, Juneau, Sitka, Ketchikan, Sawyer Glacier, Prince Rupert, BC, Victoria, BC
	Vancouver	11	Round-trip: Skagway, Juneau, Sitka, Ketchikan, Wrangell, Sawyer Glacier, Prince Rupert, BC, Victoria, BC
	Vancouver	7	Northbound: Ketchikan, Juneau, Skagway, Sitka, Sawyer Glacier, Hubbard Glacier
	Seward	7	Southbound: Ketchikan, Juneau, Skagway, Sitka, Sawyer Glacier, Hubbard Glacier
	Anchorage	10	Southbound: College Fjord, Valdez, Hubbard Glacier, Skagway, Juneau, Sitka, Sawyer Glacier, Ketchikan, Vancouver, BC

SMALL CRUISE-SHIP LINES

SHIP	EMBARKATION PORT	DURATION IN NIGHTS	ITINERARY AND PORTS OF CALL
AMERICAN CRUISE LINES			
American Spirit	Juneau	7	Round-trip: Skagway, Glacier Bay, Icy Strait Point, Sitka, Petersburg, Dawes Glacier
	Seattle	11	Northbound: Anacortes, WA, Friday Harbor, WA, Ketchikan, Wrangell, Petersburg, Tracy Arm, Angoon, Icy Strait Point, Juneau
	Juneau	11	Southbound: Ketchikan, Wrangell, Petersburg, Tracy Arm, Angoon, Icy Strait Point, Anacortes, WA, Friday Harbor, WA, Seattle
AMERICAN SAFARI LINE			
Safari Endeavour, Safari Explorer, Safari Quest	Juneau	7	Round-trip: Glacier Bay (2 or 3 days), Icy Strait, Baranof Island, Endicott Arm
Safari Endeavour, Safari Explorer	Ketchikan	7	Northbound: Tongass National Forest, Klawock Native Village, Frederick Sound, Chatham Strait, Brothers Islands, Endicott Arm, Juneau
	Juneau	7	Southbound: Tracy Arm, Baird Glacier, Thomas Bay, Wrangell, Yes Bay, Misty Fjords, Ketchikan
Safari Endeavour, Safari Explorer, Safari Quest	Seattle	14	Northbound: Friday Harbor, San Juan Islands, Misty Fjords, Ketchikan, El Capitan, Klawock Native Village, Chatham Strait, Frederick Sound, Brothers Islands, Endicott Arm, Juneau
	Juneau	14	Southbound: Sawyer Glacier, Thomas Bay, Baird Glacier, Wrangell, Yes Bay, Misty Fjords, Ketchikan, San Juan Islands, Friday Harbor, Seattle
INNERSEA DISCOVERIES			
Wilderness Adventurer, Wilderness Discoverer, Wilderness Explorer	Ketchikan	7	Northbound: Tongass National Forest, Klawock Native Village, Frederick Sound, Chatham Strait, Brothers Islands, Endicott Arm, Juneau
Wilderness Explorer	Juneau	7	Southbound: Tracy Arm, Baird Glacier, Thomas Bay, Wrangell, Yes Bay, Misty Fjords, Ketchikan
	Sitka	7	Northbound: Peril Strait, Chichagof Island, Icy Strait, Glacier Bay (3 days), Juneau
	Juneau	7	Southbound: Glacier Bay (3 days) Icy Strait, Chichagof Island, Peril Strait, Sitka
Wilderness Adventurer, Wilderness Discoverer	Juneau	14	Round-trip: Tracy Arm, Thomas Bay, Baird Glacier, Wrangell, Yes Bay, Misty Fjords, Ketchikan, El Capitan, Klawock Native Village, Chatham Strait, Frederick Sound, Brothers Islands, Endicott Arm
Wilderness Adventurer, Wilderness Explorer	Seattle	14	Northbound: Friday Harbor, San Juan Islands, Misty Fjords, Ketchikan, El Capitan, Klawock Native Village, Chatham Strait, Frederick Sound, Brothers Islands, Endicott Arm, Juneau
Wilderness Adventurer, Wilderness Discoverer, Wilderness Explorer	Juneau	14	Southbound: Sawyer Glacier, Thomas Bay, Baird Glacier, Wrangell, Yes Bay, Misty Fjords, Ketchikan, San Juan Islands, Friday Harbor, Seattle

The Alaska Wilderness

BIODIVERSITY AND OUTDOOR ADVENTURE IN THE LAST GREAT PLACE

WORD OF MOUTH

"I think whatever you end up doing, do try to take at least one bush plane ride somewhere. I think the highlight for my parents was landing on a glacier on Denali."

—Spirobulldog

If Alaska were a country, it would be the seventh largest, just behind Australia but way ahead of India. And the state is as diverse as it is vast, with more than 5,000 miles of coast, myriad mountain ranges, alpine valleys, salmon-rich rivers, clear lakes, blue glaciers, temperate rain forests, and sweeping tundra. The Alaska wilderness is clearly *the* place for unforgettable outdoor adventures.

While Minnesota was busy bragging about 10,000 lakes, Alaska stopped counting after 2 million. Four great mountain ranges—the St. Elias, Alaska, Brooks, and Chugach—and more than 30 lesser chains sweep through the state. The St. Elias mountains form the world's highest coastal range. The Alaska Range contains North America's highest peak: Mt. McKinley—or Denali, as Alaskans call it—at 20,320 feet. The Brooks Range roughly follows the Arctic Circle, and the Chugach arcs through the state's most populous region along the South Central coast.

Alaska flora and fauna is just as varied. Along the northern coast polar bears take to the ice to hunt seals. Seventy-foot-long whales swim slowly past the grassy islands of the Aleutians. Voles weighing not much more than a postcard hide in the Southeastern rain forest. The sky is filled with nearly 500 species of birds, including the largest population of bald eagles anywhere. And among all those mountains lie North America's two largest national forests with more than 30 kinds of berries for the grizzly bears, which can grow to 11 feet tall and weigh more than a thousand pounds.

Indeed, this state has more parks, wilderness areas, and wildlife refuges than all the others combined. You can travel here for a lifetime and still find surprises, so the first step in planning any visit is determining which Alaska flora and fauna interest you most. Understanding the various ecozones; learning about the wildlife-viewing opportunities they hold; and finding the best activities, tours, and guides in each will go a long way toward creating a memorable outdoor adventure. Pick as much territory as time allows, and get ready for the last great place.

RAIN FOREST

The largest chunk of intact rain forest in North America lies in Alaska, scattered across hundreds of islands of the Southeast panhandle. This area—stretching from south of Ketchikan up to Skagway and mostly set aside as the Tongass National Forest—is a rich, dripping landscape of forested mountains coming straight out of the sea.

WORD OF MOUTH

"Misty Fiords by float plane is very different [from Kenai Fjords National Park], all green. With independent [guides], you may have the opportunity to land and get off the plane. This isn't available with ship contracted flights."

—BudgetQueen

The spaces between the trees are filled with devil's club, shelf fungus, dozens of kinds of ferns and moss and lichens, and enough berries—salmonberries, blueberries, huckleberries, raspberries, crowberries, and more than a dozen other kinds—to explain the common sight of the deep impression of a bear's footprint in the ground.

But it's water that truly defines the region: the 100 inches or more of rain that fall on most parts of it, feeding streams that lace through the forest canopy, bringing salmon and everything that hunts salmon, from seals to bald eagles. Even the trees along streambeds get a large percentage of their nutrients from bits of salmon left after everyone is done eating, water dripping from branches and needles and leaves speeding the decay.

Throughout the forest, decay is vital, because there is almost no soil in the Tongass—a couple of inches at best. New life sprouts on fallen trees, called "nursery logs," and often a couple of dozen species of plant grow on a spruce knocked down by spring storms; adult trees grow oddly shaped near their base, evidence of the nursery tree they once grew on.

And the Tongass isn't the only rain forest in Alaska; much of the Chugach National Forest, as well as most of the coastline from Valdez to Seward and beyond, is also rain forest.

Under the canopy, ravens yell, bears amble from berry bush to berry bush, Sitka black-tailed deer flit through the thick underbrush like ghosts. The rain forest is a riot of life, the best of what water, time, and photosynthesis can build.

SAFETY TIP

■ Although Devil's Club is commonly used for medicinal tea by Southeast Natives, it's also the region's only dangerous plant: the spines covering the plant's branches and undersides of the leaves can break off and dig into the skin of passing animals and hikers, where they can fester and infect.

■ Look out for tall plants with five-lobed leaves 6 inches across. It grows in large patches or solitarily in well-drained areas.

FLORA

Southeast's rain forest is one of the most diverse territories in the world: from towering old-growth to dozens of species of moss, all glistening with rainfall.

SALMONBERRY *(RUBUS SPECTABILIS)*
The salmonberry canes, on which the leaves and fruits grow, may reach 7 feet tall; they grow in dense thickets. The juicy raspberry-like fruits may be either orange or red at maturity; the time of ripening is late June through August. The favorite fruit of Alaska's bears.

SITKA SPRUCE *(PICEA SITCHENSIS)*
Alaska's state tree grows 150–225 feet high, up to 8 feet in diameter, and can live 500–700 years, although few make it that long. A combination of storms and very shallow soil tend to knock down most spruce within a couple of hundred years. The leaves are dark-green needles, about an inch long, pointing up, and they cover all the branches. At the top of the tree, light orange-brown cones develop. Spruce buds were used by early mariners for making beer, and Sitka spruce wood, now mostly used for making guitars, has always been one of the great treasures of the forest: the Russians used it for the beams and decks of ships built in their Sitka boat works, and for house building. During World War II, it was used for airplanes—the British made two fighter planes from Sitka spruce, and it's the namesake wood of Howard Hughes's Spruce Goose.

WESTERN HEMLOCK *(TSUGA HETEROPHYLLA)*
Western hemlocks grow to a maximum of about 150 feet, and they're thin, with a large tree only about 4 feet in diameter. Maximum lifespan is about 500 years, but few make it that long. The leaves are wider and lighter green than spruce leaves, pointing down, and the cones are a darker brown. Bark is a gray-brown. Western hemlock loves to come back in clear-cut areas, a fact that has changed the natural balance in some logged parts of Southeast Alaska.

WESTERN RED CEDAR *(THUJA PLICATA)*
Western red cedar covers a wider range, from sea level to about 3,000 feet in elevation. The leaves are much like those of the yellow cedar, but more yellow-green in color. The cones are oval, as opposed to the round yellow cedar cones. Red cedar was the treasure species for Southeast Natives, who used it for everything from house building to making clothes.

Sitka Spruce

Western Hemlock

Western Red Cedar

Salmonberry

FAUNA

Making their home in the spaces between the trees of the rain forest are bears, moose, wolves, and deer. Watch estuaries for seals, streams for salmon, and keep an eye on the sky for eagles, ravens, crows, and herons.

BALD EAGLE *(HALIAEETUS LEUCOCEPHALUS)*
With a wingspan of 6 to 8 feet and weighing as much as 20 pounds, these grand Alaska residents are primarily fish eaters, but they will also eat birds or small mammals. As young birds, they're all brown, with the characteristic white head developing in adulthood. The world's largest gathering of bald eagles occurs in Southeast Alaska each winter, along the Chilkat River near Haines. Bald eagles build the biggest bird nests in the world, weighing up to 1,000 pounds.

Black Bear

BLACK BEAR *(URSUS AMERICANUS)*
Black bears are found on nearly every large island in the Southeast, throughout South Central Alaska, and in coastal mainland areas. They average 5 feet in length and weigh from 150 to 400 pounds. A good-size black bear is often mistaken for a brown bear because black bears are not necessarily black: they range from black to very light brown. Black bears have a life expectancy in the wild of about 25 years.

Brown Bear

BROWN BEAR *(URSUS ARCTOS)*
Brown bears, or grizzlies, are rarer and considerably larger than their black cousins. In Southeast's rain forest, browns are most often seen on Admiralty Island, where they outnumber the human population; near Wrangell; and on Baranof, Chichagof, and Kruzof islands. Southeast's brown bears run 7 to 9 feet, with males ranging from 400 to 1,100 pounds; if they live in a place with a rich fish run, they can grow to 1,500 pounds. Brown bears range in color from a dark brown to blond. The easiest way to distinguish them is by the hump on their back, just behind the head. They have a life expectancy of about 20 years in the wild.

Sitka Blacktailed Deer

SITKA BLACKTAILED DEER *(ODOCOILEUS HEMIONUS SITKENSIS)*
The Panhandle's rain forest is the primary home of this deer, though it has been transplanted to Prince William Sound and Kodiak. Dark gray in winter and reddish brown in summer, it's smaller but stockier than the whitetails found in the Lower 48. The deer stay at lower elevations during the winter, then move up to alpine meadows in summer.

Bald Eagle

EXPERIENCING A RAIN FOREST

Sitka Blacktailed Deer are common throughout Alaska's rain forests.

Any trip into Southeast Alaska puts you in the rain forest. Even in a landscape this beautiful there are some highlights.

ANIMAL WATCHING

At **Pack Creek** on Admiralty Island, brown bears fish for spawning salmon. To get here, you can fly by air charter or take a boat from Juneau. Another option is near Wrangell; **Anan Bear Reserve** is at one of the few streams in the world where black and brown bears share the waters, fishing at the same time.

BY SEA

The Alaska Marine Highway runs ships to every major town—and many of the smaller ones—in Southeast Alaska. The local equivalent of a bus service, AMH ships go into small channels, offering views of rain-forest slopes, forays into quiet bays and inlets, and perhaps the best look at how the landscape was carved by glaciers.

FLIGHTSEEING

Misty Fiords National Monument, south of Ketchikan, is one of the most beautiful areas of drowned fjords and pristine rain-forest habitat in the Southeast. Covering more than 3,500 square miles, Misty Fiords is the Southeast's most popular flightseeing destination (though the monument is also laced with hiking trails and is perfect for kayaks).

HIKING

The Tongass has hundreds of miles of hiking trails, from short loops to ambitious multiday expeditions. Rain gear and a proper understanding of bear safety are essential. Hiking gives you a chance to have the forest to yourself, and lets you appreciate its intricacies, from tiny lichen to the towering canopy. This might just be the best way to understand the rain forest.

TOP GUIDES

BEAR-VIEWING

All of the Anan Wildlife Observatory–authorized guide companies we recommend (⇨ *see Ch. 4, Southeast)* are excellent, but a standout is **Alaska Vistas** (☏ *907/874–3006 or 866/874–3006* ⊕ *www.alaskavistas.com*). Based out of Wrangell, Alaska Vistas offers highly accommodating trip-planning services, and its guides' enthusiasm and respect for the bear experience makes your trip unforgettable. You can also choose from jet-boat tours up the Stikine, kayaking and canoe trips, and guided hikes, all of which come with that special Alaska Vistas touch.

A brown bear and cubs

NATURAL HISTORY

An excellent guide to the rain forest of the Southeast can be found quite easily and with minimal expense (once you get yourself to Juneau, that is): the docents at **Glacier Gardens** (✉ *7600 Glacier Hwy.* ☏ *907/790–3377* ⊕ *www.glaciergardens.com*) are Native Alaskans and will teach you more about the local forest than you're going to learn anywhere else.

HIKING

If you have any inclination to go hiking, try to fit it in with **Packer Expeditions** (☏ *907/983–3005 or 907/983–2544* ⊕ *www.packerexpeditions.com*), out of

Bald eagle

Skagway. It offers trips on the famous Chilkoot Trail as well as on local trails popular with the area's residents, both human and ursine. Packer Expeditions also offers many ways to combine rain-forest hiking with other modes of locomotion, such as a helicopter ride, or a ride on the White Pass & Yukon Route Railroad (either one way or, for accessing more remote trailheads, round-trip). It's a good choice if you're eager to combine rain-forest and glacier ecozone experiences; one trip offers a hike up to the Laughton Glacier, and a different itinerary will bring you there partially by train and leave time for hiking on the glacier itself.

If you have sufficient bear-safety experience and wilderness knowledge, the **Alaska Travel Industry Association** (⊕ *www.travelalaska.com*), or ATIA, provides fantastic guidance on exploring the rain forests of Southeast.

INTERIOR FORESTS

Rain forests dominate the southern coast of Alaska; but move inland, and a different kind of forest appears. Much of the interior is covered by thick spruce and birch forests, trees that can grow in harsher conditions—temperatures in the middle of the state can hit 100°F in summer and −50°F in the winter—than their coastal counterparts.

WORD OF MOUTH

"The drive down south towards Homer is beautiful going thru Turnagain Arm. As we got closer to Homer we saw several moose feeding on the side of the road so keep your eyes open."

—Calypso45

The soil is usually deeper here, but as much as 75% of the region that this taiga, or boreal forest, covers may have patches of permafrost—soil that never thaws. The plants also have to cope with a very short growing season; in most areas, the entire season from beginning to end spans no more than four months.

The interior forest is dominated by conifers—spruce, pine, fir—but also has plenty of broadleaf trees, such as birch and aspen. Fires are a regular occurrence throughout the region, usually caused by lightning strikes, and they can quickly burn out thousands of acres. Although

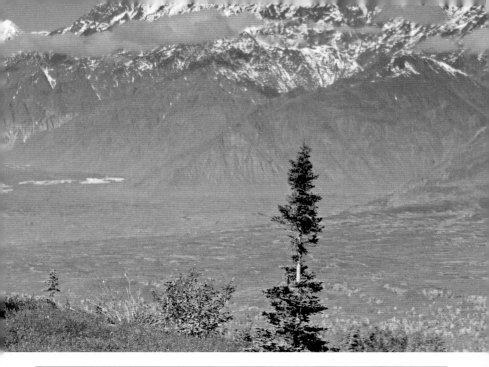

this may seem alarming (and no doubt is to anyone whose home is near a burning forest), these fires are actually beneficial to the long-term health of the forest. They serve to clear out dead trees and underbrush, and also open up the canopy to allow for new growth.

Taking advantage of the resources within these forests is a wide variety of animals, from bears and moose all the way down to the tiny vole. Like the trees, these animals have to know how to survive in dramatic temperature changes; come winter, many hibernate, but others find ways to scrape for food beneath the snow and ice. Still others rely on migration to stay warm; perhaps as many as 300 bird species spend part of the year in the forests, but only a couple of dozen have found ways to winter here.

Covering the vast, broad center of Alaska, the interior forests cover as much as 80,000,000 acres; include the parts of the state where the forests are patchier, and you get up to 220,000,000 acres of interior forest—an area bigger than Texas and Oklahoma combined. These forests are the heart of Alaska.

SAFETY TIP

■ So much of Alaska's interior forests are roadless wilderness that rivers often serve as the best avenues for exploring them. However, rivers can be dangerous. River difficulty is ranked Class I through Class IV; only very experienced river runners should attempt anything above Class II on their own. If you're traveling with a guide, research their safety record before you sign up.

FLORA

Alaska's interior forests aren't as biologically rich as those in some areas of the state, but what they lack in diversity, they more than make up for in beauty and sheer vastness.

ALASKAN PAPER BIRCH *(BETULA NEOALASKANA)*

A near relative of the more common paper birch *(Betula papyrifera)* and once commonly used by Natives for making birch-bark canoes, the Alaska subspecies grows up to 45 feet tall. It's noted for having a narrow trunk and leaves about 3 inches long. The bark is dark red-brown when the tree is young, and turns a delicate white or pinkish as the tree ages; like that of its relative, the bark peels off in layers, although not quite as well as does the paper birch. In Alaska, the Alaskan paper birch grows in bogs and on poorly drained soils, and is commonly mixed in with black spruce trees. It's one of the iconic features of the landscape of the Interior, often the subject of art from the region.

Alaskan Paper Birch

ALDER *(ALNUS)*

Common throughout central Alaska, alders range from trees (such as the Sitka alder, one of the first species to come back in a disturbed area, such as after a fire or intensive logging) to bushes (like the mountain alder, which grows along streams and in other areas with wet soil). Mountain alder, despite being classified as generally shrublike, can actually grow up to 30 feet high, with thin trunks of about 6 inches in diameter. Sitka alder can grow to about the same height, but with a slightly thicker trunk. Both types have saw-toothed leaves with parallel veins and smooth gray bark. It's difficult to tell them apart when they're young.

Tall fireweed

TALL FIREWEED *(EPILOBIUM ANGUSTIFOLIUM)*

The fireweed is among the first plants to reinhabit areas that have been burned out by wildfire, and in the proper conditions it grows well. Found throughout much of Alaska, it's a beautiful plant, with fuchsia flowers that bloom from the bottom to the top of stalks; it's said that the final opening of flowers is a sign that winter is only weeks away. Spring fireweed shoots can be eaten raw or steamed, and its blossoms can be added to salads. A related species is dwarf fireweed *(Epilobium latifolium)*, which is also known as "river beauty" and tends to be shorter and bushier.

Alder

FAUNA

With all that space, there's plenty of space for animals. From the rarely seen wolverine to the very common moose, the heart of the state has room for everything.

COMMON RAVEN *(CORVUS CORAX)*

A popular character in Alaska Native stories, the raven is both creator and trickster. Entirely black, with a wedge-shape tail and a heavy bill that helps distinguish it from crows, the raven is Alaska's most widespread avian resident. Ravens are also the smartest bird in the sky; scientists have shown that they are capable of abstract reasoning and teaching other ravens their tricks. They're among the most articulate of birds, with more than 50 calls of their own, plus the ability to mimic almost any sound they hear.

LYNX *(LYNX CANADENSIS)*

The lynx is the only wild cat to inhabit Alaska. It's a secretive animal that depends on stealth and quickness. It may kill birds, squirrels, and mice, but the cat's primary prey is the snowshoe hare *(Lepus americanus),* particularly in winter; its population numbers closely follow those of the hare's boom–bust cycles.

MOOSE *(ALCES ALCES GIGAS)*

The moose is the largest member of the deer family; the biggest bulls stand 7 feet tall at the shoulders and weigh up to 1,600 pounds. Bulls enter the rut in September, the most dominant engaging in brutal fights. Females give birth to calves in late May and early June. Though most commonly residents of woodlands, some moose live in or just outside Alaska's cities.

WOLF *(CANIS LUPUS)*

The largest and most majestic of the Far North's wild canines, wolves roam throughout Alaska. They form close-knit family packs, which may range from a few animals to more than 30. Packs hunt small mammals, birds, caribou, moose, and Dall sheep. They communicate through body language, barks, and howls.

WOLVERINE *(GULO GULO)*

Consider yourself lucky if you see a wolverine, because they are among the most secretive animals of the North. They are also fierce predators, with enormous strength and endurance. Denali biologists once reported seeing a wolverine drag a Dall sheep carcass more than 2 miles; they can run 40 mph through snow. Though they look like very small bears, wolverines are in fact the largest members of the weasel family.

Lynx

Wolverine

Moose

Wolf

EXPERIENCING INTERIOR FORESTS

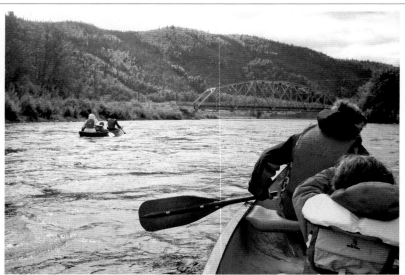

By river or by train, it's hard to find an unimpressive vista in Alaska's interior forests.

The interior forests are big enough you could spend years exploring and never see the same area twice. Or you could just go for a nice day hike. Whatever adventure you're after, you'll find it here.

CANOEING AND KAYAKING

It can be a lot easier to see the forest from a river than from the inside. Alaska's premier long canoe trip is along the Yukon River, starting across the Canadian border in Dawson City and taking out at Eagle. A wilder option is white-water kayaking the Fortymile, from Chicken, though this is definitely not for the faint of heart. Another popular float trip is one that takes you down the Nenana, through Fairbanks. Guides are available on all these rivers and more; no one unfamiliar with Alaskan conditions should try these trips alone under any circumstances.

DOG SLED

For those hardy enough to come to Alaska in winter, dog-sled tours offer the most classic way to see the state: behind a pack of howling dogs who are having the time of their lives, running as fast as they can. Trips range from short runs through forest loop trails to multiday adventures, and all you need are warm clothes and the ability to hang on tight.

HIKING

Nearly every town in the central forests has hiking trails lacing the woods around it. Especially popular are Angel Rock, Granite Tors, and Ester Dome hikes, all near Fairbanks. For something longer, try the Kesugi Ridge Trail, near Talkeetna; it's a two- to four-day alpine traverse along a beautiful ridgeline with possible views of Denali if the weather's right.

TOP GUIDES

HIKING

For a backcountry hiking experience in Wrangell–St. Elias National Park, contact **St. Elias Alpine Guides** (☎ *888/933–5427* ⊕ *www.steliasguides.com*), based in McCarthy. The guides here will facilitate anything from a few hours in the woods to a monthlong foray into the wilderness. This is the only company contracted by the Park Service to run tours of historic Kennicott buildings (⇨ *see Kennicott in Ch 6, South Central)*; if you have any interest in Alaska's history, it's a very compelling way to get out into the country.

RIVER SPORTS

St. Elias Alpine Guides also leads rafting trips through its river-travel-focused division, **Copper Oar** (☎ *800/523–4453* ⊕ *www.copperoar.com*). Also based in McCarthy, it will outfit and guide you along pristine waters into the heart of the wilderness.

Fishing trips are a great way to get out on the water, too. The Kenai Peninsula might be the best spot to combine fishing with boreal forest scenery. **Hi-Lo Charters** (⊕ *www.hilofishing.com*), in the town of Kenai, runs fishing trips from its home base on the Russian River; this fishing lodge scores high in all the important ways—excellent service, knowledgeable

Moose enjoy a view from the water, too.

guides, comfortable quarters—but the custom-built, sheltered, outdoor grilling area is a great perk.

Out of Fairbanks, a simple but highly educational and entertaining way to experience the surrounding landscape is to simply take a ride on the *Riverboat Discovery*. Onboard naturalists are enthusiastic and highly knowledgeable. If you prefer to go it alone, **Alaska Outdoor Rentals and Guides** (✉ *Pioneer Park Boat Dock, along Chena River next to Peger Rd.* ☎ *907/457–2453* ⊕ *www.2paddle1.com*) can rent you gear and facilitate drop-offs and pick-ups along the lower Chena River in Fairbanks or other local waterways.

DOG-SLED TOURS

Sun Dog Express Dog Sled Tours (☎ *907/479–6983* ⊕ *www.mosquitonet.com/~sleddog*), out of Fairbanks, runs winter and summer tours (weather permitting), and can accommodate whatever level of involvement you're looking for—from simple demonstrations to a full-tilt three-day mushing camp. Another great winter option in the Fairbanks area is **Chena Dog Sled Tours** (☎ *907/488–5845* ⊕ *www.ptialaska.net/~sleddogs*), out of Two Rivers (near Chena Hot Springs).

Racing sled dogs

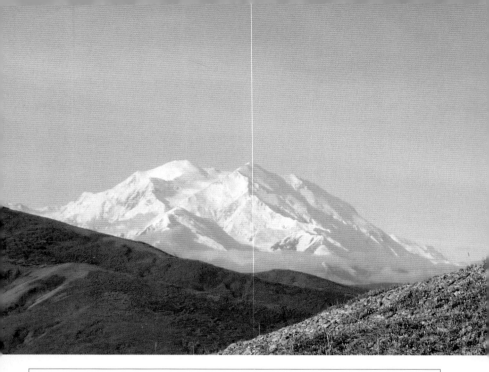

TUNDRA

At first glance the tundra might not look like very much: a low carpet plants, few more than shoelace high. But take a closer look and you'll realize you're encountering an ecozone every bit as fascinating and diverse as the showier forests, glaciers, and intertidal zones elsewhere in the state.

Tundra stretches throughout the Bush in Alaska, with patches as far south as Denali National Park. Characterized by dwarf shrubs, sedges, grasses, mosses, and lichen, tundra occurs in places where the temperatures are low (so it makes sense for plants to hug the ground) and the growing season is short—some prime tundra spots might not get more than a few weeks of summer.

Arctic tundra has roughly 1,700 species of plants growing in it; a single square foot of tundra might contain several dozen species, from saxifrage to bear berry to arctic rose. It does make for a hard place for most animals to build homes; mammals that depend on the tundra tend to cover a fair chunk of territory in their search for food, be they musk ox, lemmings, or caribou.

Throughout most of the tundra zone in Alaska the ground beneath is permafrost—permanently frozen soil—and too hard for many plants to put down deep roots. Permafrost happens when the average temperature of an area is below freezing, and it comes in both continuous—an entire region's soil encased in ice at a more or less uniform depth—and discontinuous— where some places get warm enough to thaw.

Tundra is extremely fragile; the short growing season means even the slightest damage can take years to recover from. Footprints across tundra might not fade for decades. But at the same time, tundra is extremely resilient, able to thrive in the most extreme conditions, regrow after a herd of 100,000 caribou have crossed over it, nibbling, and emerge ready again to help feed the millions of birds who depend on tundra areas as part of their migration route. The closer you look, the more you'll find in the tundra.

FLORA

The tundra is a close-up territory: the longer and closer you look, the more you'll see. Take it on its own terms and you'll find a whole world to discover.

BLUEBERRY *(VACCINIUM)*

A favorite of berry pickers, blueberries are found throughout Alaska, except for the farthest northern reaches of the Arctic. They come in a variety of forms, including head-high forest bushes and sprawling tundra mats. Pink, bell-shape flowers bloom in spring, and dark-blue to almost-black fruits begin to ripen in July or August, depending on the locale. But the tastiest are the tundra blueberries, which almost carpet the ground in some places; this is the true flavor of the midnight sun, and you'll want to factor in time on any hikes for plenty of berry-eating breaks.

REINDEER LICHEN *(CLADONIA RANGIFERINA)*

A slow-growing white lichen that grows in shapes somewhat reminiscent of reindeer antlers, or a small sea coral, reindeer lichen come up in a tangle of branches. Another reason for its name: it is a favored food of both reindeer and caribou (it's sometimes called caribou moss). It's also used traditionally in medicinal teas and in poultices for arthritis; nutritionally there's not much to be gained from eating it, but if you did it would feel sort of like chewing soft toothpicks.

SAXIFRAGE *(SAXIFRAGA RAZSHIVINII)*

One of the most characteristic plants of the tundra, able to grow in even the thinnest soil (the name translates to "stone breaker"), saxifrage is close to the ground, tends to grow in a kind of rosette shape, and sends up small, five-petaled flowers, which are usually white, but may also be red or yellow. Saxifrage is one of the first bits of color that show up on the tundra in spring, making it a particular favorite of many who live up here during the (very long, very cold) winters.

WILLOW *(SALIX)*

An estimated three dozen species of willow grow in Alaska. Some, like the felt-leaf willow *(Salix alaxensis)*, may reach tree size; others form thickets. In the tundra, what you'll find are others, like the Arctic willow *(Salix arctica)*, that hug the ground; a plant an inch tall might be 100 years old. Whatever the size, willows produce soft "catkins" (pussy willows), which are actually columns of densely packed flowers without petals.

Willow

Blueberry

Saxifrage

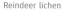

Reindeer lichen

FAUNA

The tundra is perfect for animal spotting.

ARCTIC GROUND SQUIRREL *(SPERMOPHILUS PAR-RYII)*

These yellowish-brown, gray-flecked rodents are among Alaska's most common and widespread mammals. Ground squirrels are known for their loud, persistent chatter. They are easiest to spot standing above their tundra den sites, watching for grizzlies, golden eagles, weasels, and anything else after the average 2,000 calories an arctic ground squirrel provides.

Musk Ox

CARIBOU *(RANGIFER TARANDUS)*

Sometimes called the "nomads of the north," caribou are long-distance wandering mammals. The Western Arctic Caribou Herd numbers nearly 500,000, while the Porcupine Caribou Herd has ranged between 70,000 and 180,000 over the past decades. They are the only members of the deer family in which both sexes grow antlers. Caribou might migrate over hundreds of miles between summer and winter grounds, a feat eased by the tendon in their ankle that snaps the foot back into place with each step with an audible click.

Sandhill crane

MUSK OX *(OVIBOS MOSCHATUS)*

The musk ox is an Ice Age relic that survived partly because of a defensive tactic: they stand side by side and form rings to fend off predators such as grizzlies and wolves. Unfortunately, that tactic didn't work very well against humans armed with guns. Alaska's last native musk oxen were killed in 1865. Musk oxen from Greenland were reintroduced here in 1930; they now reside on Nunivak Island, the North Slope of the Brooks Range, and in the Interior. The animal's most notable feature is its long guard hairs, which form "skirts" that nearly reach the ground. Inupiats called the musk ox *oomingmak*, meaning "bearded one." Beneath those coarser hairs is fine underfur called *qiviut*, which can be woven into incredibly soft, warm clothing.

Arctic Ground Squirrel

SANDHILL CRANE *(GRUS CANADENSIS)*

The sandhill's call has been described as "something between a French horn and a squeaky barn door." Though some dispute that description, most agree that the crane's calls have a prehistoric sound. Scientists say the species has changed little in the 9 million years since its earliest recorded fossils. Sandhills are the tallest birds in Alaska; their wingspan reaches up to 7 feet. The gray plumage of adults is set off by a bright red crown.

Caribou

EXPERIENCING ALASKA'S TUNDRA

If you keep your eyes open, you might spot musk oxen grazing on the tundra.

Get out and spend some time in this landscape and discover just how big the world of the tundra really is.

DRIVE (OR BE DRIVEN)

With a road system that leads into nearly uninhabited parts of Alaska, Nome offers the perfect jumping-off point for tundra fans. It's also the only town in Alaska where you are likely to spot musk oxen within a few miles of buildings. You can do this on your own, but many people prefer the extra knowledge gained by doing this with a guide. Hiring a guide also supports the local economy and helps promote preservation of Native knowledge.

HIKE

The easiest place to go for a tundra hike is in Denali National Park: away from the mountains, the park contains huge swatches of tundra, where you might also see bears, moose, and caribou.

The best time is in early autumn, when the colors start to change; that's when "the ground looks like a giant bowl of Captain Crunch." However, so long as you're properly equipped against mosquitoes, summer (when visitors are most likely to be here) is also a fine time to explore the tundra on foot.

RAFT

Several of Alaska's great arctic rivers cut through tundra: the Hulahula heads north through the Alaska National Wildlife Refuge, the largest patch of undisturbed land left in the United States. Another good option is the Kongakut, which rises in the Brooks Range and then flows towards the arctic plain where the caribou calve. Either river offers a week or more of the ultimate wilderness experience.

TOP GUIDES

DRIVE OR HIKE

A trip with **Nome Discovery Tours** (☎ *907/443–2814*) is maybe one of the most memorable experiences you could have in Alaska's tundra. Touted as Alaska's best tour guide by many who have had the pleasure of being shown around the tundra by him, former Broadway showman Richard Beneville has lived in the Far North for over 20 years and has developed an intimate knowledge of the land and its history. One tour includes Safety Sound, a tidal wetland about 30 miles out of Nome that has some fantastic birding. Another includes a tundra walk on which Richard serves as tundra-savvy interpreter.

Autumn on the tundra is a riot of color.

The best guide companies to the remotest places in Alaska tend to be owned and operated by those who have lived here for a while, and **Kuskokwim Wilderness Adventures** (☎ *907/543–3900* ⊕ *www.kuskofish.com*) is no exception. Local expert Jim McDonald does much of the guiding for this family-owned operation. Several birding and fishing tours are available. Spend a weekend fishing at its Kisaralik Camp, 80 miles north of town by riverboat—it's a great way to spend several days on some of the remotest tundra in the world without forgoing modern conveniences, like a shower.

Spring is the best time to see baby animals.

TOUR BUS

Not everyone will have the time to get out to the far Northwest; luckily, there's tundra to be found much closer to one of the main attractions in Alaska: Denali National Park. Take any of the guided bus tours in Denali (except for the shortest which doesn't get out of the forest). Since you're on a bus, you don't get the full benefit of seeing it up close and personal except for photo stops, but it's still a lot of reward for very little effort.

RAFT

Like the forests of the interior of the state, the tundra is a great place for a rafting trip. **Arctic Treks** (☎ *907/455–6522* ⊕ *www.arctictreksadventures.com*) runs top-notch rafting trips (and also hiking, bird-watching, and photography tours) to the Brooks Range, Arctic National Wildlife Refuge, and Gates of the Arctic National Park, among other locations. It's been in operation for over 30 years, and guides have deep knowledge of the tundra and its wildlife.

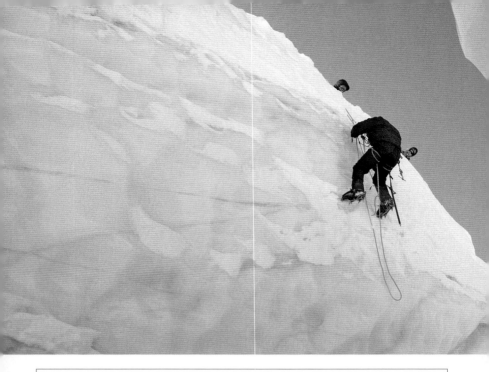

ICE

Ice is its own ecosystem in Alaska, and a vital one, as well as being the part of the state's environment that is at the most risk. Ice covers roughly 5% of Alaska—from the southernmost tidewater glacier at LeConte, through the Juneau Icefields, past Glacier Bay, and up to the Malaspina Glacier, the largest nonpolar glacier in the world.

Glaciers form when more snow falls than melts. If this keeps up year after year, the new snow presses down on the old snow, compacting it, turning it to ice. And after a time it all grows heavy enough to start moving, flowing with the landscape and the call of gravity.

Historically, nothing has shaped Alaska more than ice. A quick look at the mountains in Southeast Alaska offers ready proof: mountains under about 3,500 feet are rounded; those above, sharp and jagged. Why? Because during the last ice age, that's the height at which the glaciers came through, smoothing everything.

But it's not just that glaciers carve the landscape. They also rejuvenate it; a walk toward a glacial face is like walking backwards in time. Glaciers leave behind them the ultimate clean slate, a chance for nature to move back in and regrow from scratch.

Glacial winds, known as katabatic winds, carry seeds for hundreds of miles, allowing plant species to spread; the freshwater held in Alaska's ice feeds countless rivers, streams, and lakes, supporting everything from the incredibly delicate freshwater snails of the Brooks Range to the spawning grounds of the biggest king salmon.

And it's all under threat. Over the past decades nearly every glacier in Alaska has gotten smaller. Glaciers that used to be easily visible—Worthington, Exit, Portage—have almost disappeared from sight. Estimates are that Alaska has nearly 100,000 glaciers, but that number will likely change in the future.

SAFETY TIP

■ Glacier terrain includes a mix of ice, rock debris, and often-deep surface snow; sometimes frigid pools of meltwater collect on the surface. Watch out for glacier crevasses; sometimes hidden by snow, these cracks in the ice may present life-threatening traps. Glacier travel should be attempted only after you've been properly trained. If you haven't been taught proper glacial travel and crevasse-rescue techniques, hire a backcountry guide to provide the necessary gear and expertise.

FLORA

As a general rule, plants don't grow on ice, but Ruth Glacier has a fully mature forest growing on it. Still, for the most part, about the only life found on the ice might be some bacteria and algae, and a few lichen growing on rocks the ice is carrying along. The interest lies at the face of the glacier, and in the progression of plants leading away from it.

ALGAE

At least seven species of algae have been found on Alaska's glaciers. The most common include *Chlamydomonas nivalis*, technically classified as a green algae, which stains snow atop glaciers red when they bloom; and *Ancylonema nordenskioldii*, which is another green algae, and is perhaps the most common algae found on ice. Again, like the bacteria and the fungus, unless you know what you're looking for, you won't see much.

Lichen

BACTERIA

A close look on Alaska's glaciers might uncover some *Rhodobacteracae*, some *Polaronomas*, and *Variovorax*, and a few dozen more species of bacteria. For most people, all of these are going to either be invisible, or look like small smudges on the ice.

LICHEN

A bit more showy than the bacteria, lichen tend to grow near glacial faces; in fact, tracking lichen in moraines is a way scientists date glacial movement. A combination of a fungus and a bacteria, lichen are among the first noticeable things to grow near a glacier. Lichen get their nutrition from air and water, digging rootlike structures called rhizomes into the rocks where they grow, eventually breaking them down and turning them into soil. Favored among glacier scientists are *Rhizocarpon geographicum* (green and blotchy); but you'll also spot some that look like burned ash, some that look like branches, and, if the air is really clear, some that are orange. In all, Alaska has more than a thousand species of lichen, and hundreds can show up around glaciers.

Algae

SPRUCE FOREST (THE RUTH GLACIER EXCEPTION)

Although most of what grows on glaciers is nearly invisible, there is one exception. At the end of Ruth Glacier, which flows off Mt. McKinley, is a forest, growing atop the ice. Not the best place to be a tree: as the glacier moves (at a rate of about 3 feet a day), the trees at the edge get pitched into the river below.

Spruce Forest

3

FAUNA

Most animals can't live on the ice—there's nothing to eat. But living near the ice has some distinct advantages.

HARBOR SEAL *(PHOCA VITULINA)*

Ice broken off the face of tidewater glaciers is a favorite place for seals to pup, to sunbathe, and most of all, to stay safe from orcas on the prowl. All those berg shapes confuse the orca's sonar, making it a perfect place to be a seal. In Southeast Alaska, the easiest place to see them, they will be harbor seals, which grow to about 180 pounds. They're covered with short hair, and are usually colored either with a dark background and light rings, or light sides and a belly with dark splotches. They can dive to 600 feet and stay down for more than 20 minutes, their heart rate slowing to 15–20 beats per minute, about a fourth of their heart rate when at the surface. The easiest way to tell a seal from a sea lion is by the ears: seals have no external ear structure.

ICE WORM *(MESENCHYTRAEUS)*

Robert Service described this animal in his poem "Ballad of the Ice Worm Cocktail," where he wrote that they are "indigo of snout./And as no nourishment they find, to keep themselves alive/They masticate each other's tails, till just the Tough survive./Yet on this stern and Spartan fare so rapidly they grow,/That some attain six inches by the melting of the snow." He was very wrong. Pin-size, usually blue, black, or brown, and hard for even scientists to find, ice worms come to glacial surfaces only in morning and evening; they can actually melt at temperatures just a few degrees above freezing.

ORCA *(ORCINUS ORCA)*

Maybe the harbor seals are hiding from the orcas, but that doesn't mean the orcas don't view the ice edge as an open refrigerator door. Orcas, or killer whales—a term that has fallen out of favor with the politically (and taxonomically, as the scientific name translates to "one from the realms of the dead") correct, as they are neither killers per se nor, since they're really the largest member of the porpoise family—whales—can be more than 30 feet long, and the dorsal fin on a male can be as much as 6 feet high. At birth, orcas weigh roughly 400 pounds. A full-grown orca can weigh as much as 9 tons, and can swim 34 miles per hour; they can live as long as 80 years. Watch for the tall fin, the distinctive black-and-white markings, and size—Dall's porpoises are also black and white, but are smaller than a newborn orca.

Ice worm

Harbor Seal

Orca

EXPERIENCING ALASKA'S ICE

In Chatham Straight, be sure to glass the landscape to your west—Baranof Island's misty rainforest appearance belies the fact that it's home to more glaciers than any other island in the world.

What most people want to see in Alaska is a glacier. Luckily, there are plenty of them to explore.

FLIGHTSEEING

In the Southeast, helicopter tours to **Mendenhall Glacier**, an 85-mile-long, 45-mile-wide sheet of ice, just the tiniest finger of the 1,500-square-mile Juneau Icefields, provide fantastic views; most tours land on the ice for an up-close look. In South Central, trips over Ruth Glacier toward Mt. McKinley offer the best ice views.

HIKING

The **Matanuska Glacier**, at Mile 103 off the Glenn Highway (about a 90-minute drive northeast of Anchorage) is not only Alaska's biggest nonpolar glacier, but also one of the easiest to get to, with readily accessible ice; however, the inexperienced should not consider going far without professional guides.

KAYAKING

Some outfitters offer kayaking near glaciers and icebergs. The experience can be transformative. It can also be extremely dangerous; bergs can roll over and glaciers can calve at any moment. Be sure to go with an experienced guide and do exactly as he or she instructs.

SAILING

Glacier Bay is where most people get on boats to see calving glaciers (when big chunks of ice fall into the sea). Other options include Tracy Arm, near Juneau (smaller, but more dramatic); LeConte Glacier, between Wrangell and Skagway; or glacier cruises from Valdez and Seward. You're hard-pressed to find a cruise in the Southeast that doesn't put you within sight of a glacier. It can be dangerous to get too close to a glacier when cruising; you never know when it will calve and create a nasty wave before you can sail to safety.

TOP GUIDES

GLACIER CRUISES

Glacier-viewing cruises are extremely popular in Alaska, particularly in Prince William Sound. Of the plethora of operators these stand out for their commitment to good environmental stewardship, charismatic guides, and customer service.

Major Marine Tours (☎ *907/274–7300 or 800/764–7300* ⊕ *www.majormarine. com*), out of Whittier, runs excellent glacier-viewing tours into Prince William Sound. They visit at least two tidewater glaciers on each sailing and have an itinerary that is kind to those who are nervous about seasickness.

Kenai Fjords Tours provides a comfortable boat, a whole lot of glaciers, and excellent wildlife-watching along the way. You can see rain forest, mountains, glaciers, and the sea all at once. The route out for all trips to Kenai Fjords covers some open ocean that can be very rough at times; take the necessary seasickness precautions beforehand regardless of the weather.

From Southeast, **Adventure Bound Alaska** (☎ *907/463–2509 or 800/228–3875* ⊕ *www.adventureboundalaska.com*) will get you up close to the glacier in Tracy Arm, one of the most actively calving glaciers in Alaska.

Cruise ship in Seward harbor, Alaska

Sitting Pretty on Ruth Glacier

If you have limited time, consider **26 Glacier Cruise** (☎ *907/276–8023 or 800/544–0529* ⊕ *www.phillipscruises. com*), which travels 135 miles in 5 hours. You'll head out of Whittier and see 26 glaciers from a comfortable reserved-seating catamaran. This is another smooth-ride standout; even those who are always seasick will be pleasantly surprised.

FLIGHTSEEING

Air Excursions (☎ *800/354–2479, 907/697–2375 outside Alaska* ⊕ *www. airexcursions.com*) and **Wings of Alaska** (☎ *907/789–0790* ⊕ *www.wingsofalaska.com*) are top choices for glacier flights. Both have offices throughout the Southeast and can create custom flights. **ERA Aviation of Era Alaska** (⊕ *www. eraalaska.com*) can fly you via helicopter from Juneau or Skagway to various places, the cheapest and quickest (but no less dazzling) of which is the trip to Mendenhall Glacier.

KAYAKING

Tongass Kayak Adventures (⊕ *www.tongasskayak.com*), out of Petersburg, leads kayaking trips to the icebergs of nearby LeConte Glacier, among many other worthwhile adventures.

THE MOUNTAINS

An awful lot of Alaska lies a considerable way above sea level. The state is covered with mountains, from the relatively small peaks of Southeast Alaska—only a few much above 4,000 feet—to the highest point in North America, Mt. McKinley, at 20,320 feet above sea level.

The state's mainland is divided by mountains: the Chugach range along the South Central coastline; the Alaska Range, which includes Mt. McKinley, close to the center of the state; and the Brooks Range, which divides the interior from the arctic coast. On the eastern edge of the state lies the Wrangell Range, which, with the St. Elias mountains north of Glacier Bay and stretching into Canada, offers more unexplored high peaks than any other area in the hemisphere. Lesser ranges include the Ogilvie, Kuskokwim, and Talkeetna mountains, as well as the Aleutian Range, which never gets very high, but offers dramatic views from the storm-tossed sea.

The higher the peak, the less that grows on it, but along the way to the top, mountains provide rich biodiversity, from the trees on their lower slopes to the alpine meadows along the way to the peak. The mountains also influence everything around them, creating weather patterns that spread out across the state; the main reason why so few people ever see the peak of Mt. McKinley is because the mountain makes weather, and the weather that mountains like most is clouds.

In the Coast Mountains in Southeast, the effect of altitude on weather is particularly dramatic: the east sides of the mountains are relatively dry (for a rain forest), getting only 100 or so inches of rain a year; some spots on the west sides of the mountains get as much as 300 inches of rain.

Once above the alpine meadow level, not a whole lot grows or lives in the mountains, but mountains have shaped everything in Alaska, from Native culture to wildlife migrations. They're the birthplace of glaciers and the last truly unexplored edge of the state.

SAFETY TIP

■ For many visitors the mountains here beg to be skied. However, unless you are knowledgeable about avalanche dangers, the best strategy is to hire a guide when exploring Alaska's backcountry on skis. Be sure your guide has had avalanche-awareness training. Conditions can change quickly, especially in mountainous areas, and what begins as an easy cross-country ski trip can suddenly become a survival saga if you're not prepared.

FLORA

Each mountain is its own complete ecosystem; what you'll find depends on altitude, on exposure, on what other mountains are nearby.

ALPINE FIR *(ABIES LASIOCARPA)*

The alpine fir is a fairly large tree growing up to 150 feet tall, although more commonly around 60 feet, with a trunk around 3 feet in diameter. Branches are covered with needles about an inch long. Like ideal Christmas trees, the crown is very narrow, often only a single spike. Bark on young trees is smooth and gray, but roughens as the tree ages.

AVENS *(DRYAS)*

The avens is a low, evergreen, flowering plant (technically a subshrub) common in high alpine meadows, most frequently found in areas that were once glaciated. Usually growing in patches, avens have small leaves, and produce eight-lobed flowers with a yellow center. Avens is considered to be a member of the rose family.

CHOCOLATE LILY *(FRITILLARIA LANCEOLATA)*

A high-alpine-meadow plant, the chocolate lily grows up to 4 feet high, with one to five rich, brown flowers coming off the central stalk. Leaves are broad and flat, shaped like spearheads. The chocolate lily usually blooms from mid-June to mid-July, and is characterized by a smell that is very distinctive; nicknames for the chocolate lily include outhouse lily, skunk lily, and dirty diaper.

VALERIAN *(VALERIANA SITCHENSIS)*

One of the most common alpine flowers in Alaska, valerian grows on stems that range from about a foot to 4 feet long. Leaves grow in pairs, leading up to beautiful flower clusters of white, five-lobed flowers with long stamens shooting above the petals. Valerian has a sweet smell to it, and can be used for helping ease insomnia. While not native to Alaska, it's become an important part of the Alaskan landscape.

Avens

Alpine fir

Chocolate lily

Valerian

FAUNA

Dall Sheep

For many animals, up is the way to go to be safe from most predators. Changing altitude is also like changing seasons—up leads to cooler weather.

DALL SHEEP *(OVIS DALLI DALLI)*

One of four wild sheep to inhabit North America, the white Dall is the only one to reside within Alaska. Residents of high alpine areas, the sheep live in mountain chains from the St. Elias Range to the Brooks Range. Though both sexes grow horns, those of females are short spikes, while males grow grand curls that are status symbols displayed during mating season.

GOLDEN EAGLE *(AQUILA CHRYSAETOS)*

The bald eagle is mostly a coastal species in Alaska; golden eagles prefer the interior, especially around Denali and the Brooks Range. Characterized by the golden feathers on their head and neck, golden eagles have wingspans of 6 to 7 feet, and can weigh up to 12 pounds, with females much larger than males. They feed on squirrels, hares, and small birds, but they've also been known to occasionally attack larger animals, such as Dall sheep lambs. A single eagle might hunt over a territory of more than 60 square miles.

Mountain goat

MARMOT *(MARMOTA BROWERI)*

Alaska's biggest rodent, marmots are common in the Brooks Range, where they live communally in scree where they can hide easily from predators. Browsing on pretty much anything that grows at that altitude, a marmot can grow to 2 feet in length and weigh 8 pounds or more.

MOUNTAIN GOAT *(OREAMNOS AMERICANUS)*

Living on the high peaks, favoring rocky areas so steep that any predator would slip and fall, mountain goats live in the arc of coastal mountains from roughly Anchorage all the way down through the Panhandle. An adult male goat weighs 250–350 pounds, with females running about 40% smaller. Goats can live up to 18 years, although 12 is the high end of average. They feed on the high alpine plants—grasses, herbs, shrubs—and then in winter will eat whatever is available, favoring blueberry plants, hemlock, and lichens.

Marmot

Golden eagle

EXPERIENCING THE MOUNTAINS

No runway? No problem: bush planes can land anywhere from alpine meadows to snow-covered glaciers.

Alaska has more big mountains than the rest of the country combined.

FLIGHTSEEING

Unless you feel like spending a month or so climbing, the best way to see Alaska's peaks is by plane, and the best place to do that is in Denali. Flightseeing trips leave from Talkeetna; the best travel up Ruth Glacier, into the Great Gorge—an area of dramatic rock and ice—and up around the summit of Mt. McKinley. Although summit is often hidden in clouds, it's still the best ride in Alaska.

HORSEBACK

Encompassing more than 13 million acres of mountains, glaciers, and remote river valleys, **Wrangell–St. Elias National Park and Preserve** is wild and raw with so many big mountains that a lot of them don't even have names. There's no better way to absorb the enormity and natural beauty of this region than on horseback. Centuries-old game trails and networks blazed and maintained by contemporary outfitters wind through lowland spruce forests and into wide-open high-country tundra. From there, horses can take you almost anywhere, over treeless ridgelines and to sheltered campsites on the shores of scenic tarns.

SKIING

Alyeska Resort, located 40 miles south of Anchorage in Girdwood, is Alaska's largest and best-known downhill ski resort. A new high-speed quad lift gets you up the mountain. The resort encompasses 1,000 acres of terrain for all skill levels. Ski rentals are available at the resort. Local ski and snowboard guides teach classes and offer helicopter-ski and -snowboard treks into more remote sites in the nearby Chugach and Kenai ranges. You probably won't see much wildlife, but you'll see a lot of mountain.

TOP GUIDES

FLIGHTSEEING

There's no question that the top mountain-oriented activity in Alaska for most visitors is flightseeing in Denali National Park. One of the top companies to go with is **K2 Aviation**, out of Talkeetna. It provides thoroughly narrated tours that vary by length and route; we highly recommend going on the longest (and thus most expensive) one you can afford. Most people agree that the flight that takes you up over the top of McKinley itself is the best (you guessed it: it's also the priciest).

K2 Aviation is owned by **Rust's Flying Service** (☎ *907/243–1595 or 800/544–2299* ⊕ *www.flyrusts.com*), based in Anchorage, so even if you can't make it up to Talkeetna by land, Rust's can help you arrange a tour from your Anchorage base. If you prefer not to head north, you can take a trip out to the Brooks Range and the mountainous Harding Icefield and Kenai Fjords National Park, among other places.

HIKING

If you're fit and want to immerse yourself in the mountains, consider a trip with **Arctic Treks** (☎ *907/455–6502* ⊕ *www.arctictreksadventures.com*), based in Fairbanks. You don't need experience in the backcountry to go on

Watch for golden eagles in the mountains.

Alyeska Resort, Girdwood

the trips, and the company is very highly recommended.

HORSEBACK

Horseback riding is the unsung hero of mountain travel in Alaska; in the warmer months, there's hardly a more pleasant way to travel. **Chena Hot Springs Resort** (☎ *907/451–8104* ⊕ *www.chenahotsprings.com*), east of Fairbanks, can take you out on guided horse treks out on the trails and up into the mountains. If you won't have time to travel to the Fairbanks area, consider a guided ride with **Alaska Excursions** (☎ *907/983–4444* ⊕ *www.alaskaexcursions.com*), based in Skagway; guides lead very good tours in a more conveniently located mountain landscape.

MOUNTAINEERING

While serious climbing isn't for everyone, if you're fit and not afraid of heights, Alaska is both a top destination for the pros and a great place for those interested in the sport to try their hand. **Alaska Mountain Guides** (☎ *907/766–3366 or 800/766–3396* ⊕ *www.alaskamountainguides.com*) has offices all over the state and is especially strong in the area of helping first-timers feel comfortable with the sometimes vertigo-inducing sport.

3

THE SEA

The most philosophically accurate maps of Alaska are perhaps the nautical charts: they show the sea, in great detail, and only sketch in a few features on land. Anybody who has done much travel in Alaska understands why. Travel on land is arduous. Travel in a boat, unless the weather gets you, is sheer joy.

WORD OF MOUTH

"We did whale-watching out of Juneau, saw humpback whales doing 'bubble net feeding.' It was amazing—the highlight of the trip."

—sunbum1944

Alaska's coastline—longer than that of the rest of the United States combined—and adjacent waters range from the deep and smooth inlets and bays of Southeast Alaska to the huge, shallow, and wild waters of the Bering Sea.

The ocean influences almost everything in Alaska, from how people live to the weather they encounter. Fishing has always been one of the state's biggest industries since the Russians who settled here introduced the concept, and fish and other sea creatures had been important sources of food and materials for coastal communities for thousands and thousands of years before that (in fact, they still are).

And the health of the sea influences not just the adjacent coastal areas but fishing returns hundreds and hundreds of miles inland; if not enough salmon survive in the sea long enough to make it back to the mouth of their home river, it follows that a reduced amount will make it up the length of those rivers to spawn. Subsistence hunters deep in the Brooks Range can face hardship, as well as bears who depend on spawned-out salmon for much of their diet.

Perhaps even more compelling a reason to travel here: the sea is simply where some of Alaska's most beautiful, graceful, dramatic animals spend their time. Whether it's rafts of birds covering a dozen acres of sea off the Aleutians, or the slow arc of a whale's back in Southeast, the sea is the center of Alaska's life. However you travel through it, doing so with a knowledgeable guide who can help you better understand what you encounter will increase your enjoyment exponentially.

SAFETY TIP

■ If you're going to get out onto the water by self-propelled means—a kayak, canoe, or raft—go with a guide; a reputable one will ensure weather and tide conditions align in the chosen paddling spot for the smoothest ride possible (or roughest-while-still-safe, in the case of rafting).

■ Only consider going it alone if you have serious endurance-paddling experience under your belt and know what information to gather and what equipment to bring to avoid a dangerous situation.

FLORA

Most people go to the beach looking for animals, but there's no shortage of things for plant lovers to see, either. Some of the state's most weird and wonderful living organisms can be found here.

BULL KELP *(NEREOCYSTIS)*

Probably the most common seaweed found on Alaska's beaches, bull kelp is dull brown and has a bulb at one end of its otherwise long, whiplike structure. That's right: snap it just so and it will crack like a whip. Or you can cut the bulb in half and blow the whole thing like a trumpet. One of the fastest growing plants in nature, most strands of bull kelp are around 8 to 15 feet long. If you're kayaking and are feeling puckish, it's generally safe to pick a little (just make sure it looks healthy) and nibble it right there. Some people also bring it home and fry it or put it in a salad.

EELGRASS *(ZOSTERA MARINA)*

Common all along the Alaskan coast, eelgrass can grow up to 6 feet (although it usually doesn't in the short Alaska growing season). Thin, brown, and with roots that are covered with fine hairs, it's a perfect place for spawning herring to lay their eggs. The largest patch of eelgrass in the world is in Bristol Bay, off the west coast of the state (the patch is in Izembek Lagoon and stretches across roughly 34,000 hectares at last measure).

HORSETAIL *(EQUISETUM ARVENSE)*

One of the first plants to come up on beaches and along glacial moraines, horsetails look just like their name, if horses had bushy green tails with segments kind of like bamboo. They might grow to a couple of feet tall, and can have a cone, sort of like a pinecone, for spores. Traditionally, it's used for bladder or kidney problems, and it can also serve as a good natural solution for certain soil moisture imbalances.

SALIX

Salix include willows and several hundred other species of trees. However, along Alaskan beaches, what you are most likely to see are *Salix hookeriana,* or Dune willows, which can have yellow, green, or brown flowers. They like to grow on wet soil and in coastal meadows, often right near spots you might be near while fishing, wildlife-watching, cruising, or kayaking.

Bull kelp

Salix

Horsetail

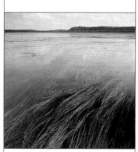
Eelgrass

FAUNA

Alaska's seas are among the biologically richest in the world—which is why the whales all come here to eat. For things with fins and flippers, this is paradise.

HORNED PUFFIN *(FRATERCULA CORNICULATA)*
Named for the black, fleshy projections above each eye, horned puffins spend most of their lives on water, coming to land only for nesting. They are expert swimmers, using their wings to "fly" underwater and their webbed feet as rudders. Horned puffins have large orange-red and yellow bills.

HUMPBACK WHALE *(MEGAPTERA NOVAEANGLIAE)*
Humpbacks are most commonly seen in the Southeast. Humpback whales grow to 50 feet, but most are closer to 40, weighing up to 80,000 pounds. They are distinguished by the way they swim and their shape at the waterline: their back forms a right angle as they dive. Whales do not generally show their tails above water unless they are sounding or diving deep. Baleen whales, humpbacks feed on krill and plankton, using the baleen to filter their food from the sea water. Most of Alaska's humpbacks winter in Hawaii, but there are a couple of small year-round populations, most notably near Sitka.

SALMON
Alaska has five species of salmon: pink (humpie), chum (dog), coho (silver), sockeye (red), and the king, or Chinook. All salmon share the trait of returning to the waters in which they were born to spawn and die. During the summer months this means rivers are clogged with dying fish, and a lot of very happy bears.

SEA OTTER *(ENHYDRA LUTRIS)*
Sea otters don't have blubber; instead, air trapped in their dense fur keeps their skin dry. Beneath their outer hairs, the underfur ranges in density from 170,000 to 1 million hairs per square inch. Not surprisingly, the otter spends much of every day grooming. Otters also eat about 14 crabs a day, or a quarter of their body weight.

STELLER SEA LION *(EUMETOPIAS JUBATUS)*
Its ability—and tendency—to roar is what gives the sea lion its name. Because they can rotate their rear flippers and lift their bellies off the ground, sea lions can get around on land much more easily than seals can. They are also much larger, the males reaching up to 9 feet and weighing up to 1,500 pounds. They feed primarily on fish, but will also eat sea otters and seals.

Humpback Whale

3

Salmon

Horned Puffin

Sea otter

EXPERIENCING THE SEA

Whale-watching trips are one of the most rewarding ways to experience the waters of Alaska.

To really see the sea, you're going to need a boat.

INSIDE PASSAGE AMH FERRY

The Alaska Marine Highway runs ferries from Bellingham, Washington, to as far out as Dutch Harbor, in the Aleutians. But there are also some island areas, where the land meets the sea, that offer a great chance for spotting wildlife.

WILDLIFE-WATCHING CRUISE

The best whale-watching is in Southeast Alaska: a lot of humpbacks hang out close to Juneau, making it the easiest place to start from. Frederick Sound is famous for its huge humpback population, as is Icy Strait, near the entrance to Glacier Bay.

Glacier Bay itself is one of the richest marine environments in the state, with humpbacks, orcas, seals, porpoises, and more.

TRIP TO REMOTE PACIFIC ISLANDS

For migratory birds and Northern Pacific seals, the place to go is the Pribilof Islands. Approximately 200 species of birds have been sighted on the twin islands of St. Peter and St. Paul, out in the middle of the Bering Sea, but you will almost certainly need to be part of a guided tour to get there. The Pribilofs are also home to the world's largest population of fur seals.

AMH FERRY TO THE ALEUTIANS

A little more accessible, the Aleutians—particularly Dutch Harbor—are also spots for adding to the life list, since many vagrants appear. Take the Alaska Marine Highway from Kodiak for the three-day run to Dutch. Along the way, you'll likely see humpbacks, fin whales, orcas, and more puffins, murres, and auklets than you knew the planet could hold.

TOP GUIDES

WILDLIFE-WATCHING EXCURSIONS

If you have the opportunity to travel to Sitka, **Otter Quest** is a great guide company for spotting not just otters but the whole spectrum of wildlife.

Believe it or not, there's an excellent snorkel outfitter in Ketchikan that facilitates trips most experienced snorkelers give an enthusiastic two thumbs up to. **Snorkel Alaska** (⊠ *S. Tongass Hwy. and Roosevelt Dr.*☎ *907/247–7783* ⊕ *www.snorkelalaska.com*) will provide a wet suit for protection against the water temperatures; you'll likely get an upclose view of such fascinating tidal sea creatures as giant sunflower stars, bright blood stars, and sea cucumbers.

If you want to get down to water level but aren't so keen on outright submersion, **Southeast Sea Kayaks** (☎ *907/225–1258 or 800/287–1607* ⊕ *www.kayakketchikan.com*) specializes in day trips that still take you to some of the remotest inlets in Southeast.

Orca Enterprises (with Captain Larry) (☎ *907/789–6801 or 888/733–6722* ⊕ *www.alaskawhalewatching.com*), out of Juneau, is a favorite Southeast whale-watching guide company; Captain Larry notes his whale-spotting success rate is 99.9% during the summer months. His success rate is due in part

Sea otter floating in Tutka Bay, Kenai Peninsula

to the speediness of his boat; he's able to cover more ground than some of the larger vessels.

If you've only got a few hours, **Weather Permitting Alaska** (☎ *907/209–4221* ⊕ *www.weatherpermittingalaska.com*) can get you out and back in about four hours. The ship is luxury-level with delicious food served, a plus.

WILDLIFE TOURS FARTHER AFIELD

If you can afford the trip out in terms of time and money, and if you have even a slight interest in birds, travel to the Pribilofs with **Wilderness Birding Adventures**. The guides with Wilderness Birding lead trips here regularly and have in-depth knowledge about the many different ways birds and other animals come from across the sea to breed here. Because of the wildlife that comes here, it's one of the most unique seascapes you could hope to experience in the state. Wilderness Birding also runs trips to other parts of the state; among other combinations, you could match a tour to the Pribilofs with another trip to the Brooks Range to immerse yourself in the mountains.

Steller Sea Lions

Southeast Alaska

INCLUDING KETCHIKAN, JUNEAU, HAINES, SITKA, AND SKAGWAY

WORD OF MOUTH

"We hiked to the tongue of the Mendenhall Glacier to find this roaring waterfall crashing into the bay. It gave us a perspective on man's insignificance next to Mother Nature."
—Chris Marlow, Photo Contest Winner

WELCOME TO SOUTHEAST ALASKA

TOP REASONS TO GO

★ **Native art and culture:** Ancestral home of the Tlingit, Haida, and Tsimshian, Southeast is dedicated to preserving Native heritage. Native crafts include totem poles and masks.

★ **Rivers of ice:** Visitors relish the opportunity to walk on Southeast's accessible glaciers or to admire them on flightseeing or kayak trips.

★ **Tongass National Forest:** America's largest national forest is home to bears, bald eagles, Sitka black-tailed deer, wolves, and marine mammals.

★ **Fishing nirvana:** Southeast is an angler's paradise. The region's healthy populations of salmon and halibut—as well as the wealth of charter boats and fishing lodges—make this a premier fishing destination.

★ **Taking the ferry:** The Alaska Marine Highway is the primary means of transportation here. It's a low-cost, high-adventure alternative to cruising, and an easy way to spend time talking to Alaskans.

1 **Ketchikan and Vicinity.** The self-proclaimed "Salmon Capital of the World," Ketchikan is the doorway to Southeast. Be sure to check out the area's charter-fishing opportunities and wealth of local art. Ketchikan is a jumping-off point for Misty Fiords National Monument and visits to the Indian community of Metlakatla.

2 **Wrangell and Petersburg.** These towns provide access to the magnificent Stikine River. Wrangell, which welcomes some of the smaller cruise ships, is the primary hub for those who want to travel to the Anan Bear & Wildlife Observatory to see both brown and black bears fishing for salmon. Petersburg has a vibrant fishing community and stellar access to fishing, whale-watching, and hiking.

3 **Sitka.** With its mixed history of Tlingit, Russian, and American rule, Sitka is home to a lively community, an excellent park system (including Sitka National Historical Park), and outdoor activities. It's a must-see for anyone traveling in Southeast and a must-paddle for kayakers of all experience levels.

4 **Juneau and Vicinity.** Cruise passengers flock by the hundreds of thousands to take in the state capital's historic charm, artsy community, and natural beauty, including world-famous Mendenhall Glacier. But with a number of hotels and B&Bs, Juneau also welcomes independent travelers. The city is also the access point for surrounding attractions, including Admiralty Island National Monument, home to Southeast's largest population of brown bears.

5 **Glacier Bay National Park and Preserve.** Southeast's signature attraction, Glacier Bay is home to the continent's largest collection of tidewater glaciers, which make for incredible viewing. The park's remote, undeveloped location—Gustavus, the closest town, isn't really a town at all—ensures that travelers in search of quiet repose will not be disappointed.

GETTING ORIENTED

As remote as it is, Southeast Alaska shares a few traits with heavily populated regions. It has skyscrapers (the towering peaks of the Coast Range), traffic jams (try to swim through a salmon creek in midsummer), and sprawl (the rain forests cover hundreds of thousands of acres). The area's settlements offer plenty of attractions, from Skagway's flashy gold-rush delights to Glacier Bay's isolated fjords.

4

6 Haines and Skagway. The northern outposts of the Inside Passage, these two towns seem to have it all. Haines, on stunning Chilkat Peninsula, is home to fishermen, helicopter-skiing guides, and eagle aficionados who flock to the nearby Chilkat Bald Eagle Preserve. Just down the road from Klukwan, a village 22 miles outside of Haines, visitors can learn about Tlingit culture. Skagway has gorgeous scenery, an incredible railway, and a boisterous gold-rush history.

0 ——— 50 miles
0 ——— 75 km

Updated by
Amy Fletcher

Southeast Alaska stretches down from the rest of the state like the tail of a kite. It is a world of soaring glaciers, steep-shouldered islands, cliff-rimmed fjords, and snowcapped peaks. Glacier Bay National Park and Preserve, one of the region's most prized attractions, is home to the largest concentration of coastal glaciers on earth.

Lush stands of spruce, hemlock, and cedar blanket thousands of islands. The region's myriad bays, coves, lakes, and swift, icy rivers provide some of the continent's best fishing grounds. Many of Southeast Alaska's wildest and most pristine landscapes are within Tongass National Forest, composed of nearly 17 million acres—almost three-quarters of the Panhandle's land.

Southeast lacks only one thing: connecting roads. The lack of pavement between the area's communities presents obvious challenges to four-wheeled transport. The isolation and the wet weather keep people from moving in; otherwise Southeast Alaska would probably be as densely populated as Seattle. To help remedy the transportation question, Alaskans created the Alaska Marine Highway System, a network of passenger and vehicle ferries, some of which have staterooms, observation decks, video theaters, arcades, cafeterias, cocktail lounges, and heated, glass-enclosed solariums.

Southeast's natural beauty and abundance of wildlife have made it one of the world's fastest-growing cruise destinations. About 25 big cruise ships ply the Inside Passage—once the traditional route to the Klondike goldfields and today the centerpiece of many Alaska cruises—during the height of summer. A number of smaller ships—some locally owned—also cruise through. Regular air service to Southeast is available from the Lower 48 states and other parts of Alaska.

Three groups of Native peoples inhabit Southeast coastal region: the Tlingit (*klink*-it), Haida, and Tsimshian (*sim*-shee-ann). Because their cultures were once in danger of being lost, there's an ever-growing focus in Southeast on preserving Native traditions and teaching visitors about their history. Efforts are underway in many towns to teach the often tricky-to-master Native languages in schools and through other programs. Visitors to Southeast benefit from these programs, since local teens often work as guides at cultural institutions. The Tlingit, Haida, and Tsimshian, like their coastal neighbors in British Columbia, have rich traditions of totemic art, including carved poles, masks, baskets, and ceremonial objects. At villages like Klukwan, outside of Haines, there's been a push to help residents learn these art forms and keep them alive for generations to come.

Residents—some from other states, some who can trace their ancestors back to the gold-rush days, and some whose ancestors came over the Bering Land Bridge from Asia thousands of years ago—are an adventurous bunch. The rough-and-tumble spirit of Southeast often combines with a worldly sophistication: those who fish for a living might also be artists, Forest Service workers may run a bed-and-breakfast on the side, and homemakers may be Native dance performers.

4

Southeast Panhandle stretches some 500 miles from Yakutat at its northernmost point to Ketchikan and Metlakatla at its southern end. At its widest point, the region measures only 140 miles, and in the upper Panhandle just south of Yakutat, at 30 miles across, it's downright skinny by Alaska standards. Most of the Panhandle consists of a sliver of mainland buffered on the west by islands and on the east by the imposing peaks of the Coast Mountains.

Those numerous coastal islands—more than 1,000 throughout the Inside Passage—collectively constitute the Alexander Archipelago. Most of them present mountainous terrain with lush covers of timber, though large clear-cuts are also common. Most communities are on islands rather than on the mainland. The principal exceptions are Juneau, Haines, and Skagway, plus the hamlets of Gustavus and Hyder. Island outposts include Ketchikan, Wrangell, Petersburg, Sitka, and the villages of Craig, Pelican, Metlakatla, Kake, Angoon, and Hoonah. Bordering Alaska just east of the Panhandle lies the Canadian province of British Columbia.

PLANNING

WHEN TO GO

The best time to visit is from May through September, when weather is mildest, rain is less frequent, daylight hours are longest, wildlife is most abundant, and festivals and visitor-oriented activities are in full swing. But remember: Southeast sits in a rain forest, so rain can rule the day. There's a reason why XtraTuf waterproof boots are nicknamed "Southeast sneakers." Summertime high temperatures hover around the low to mid-60s, with far warmer days interspersed throughout. Shoulder-season temperatures are cooler, and the region is less crowded. Bring rain gear, layered clothing, sturdy footwear, a hat, and binoculars.

Allow yourself at least a week here. Plenty of adventures await ambitious independent travelers who plan ahead and ride state ferries.

If strolling through downtown shopping districts and museum-hopping is your idea of a perfect afternoon, journey to Ketchikan, Juneau,

Skagway, Sitka, or Petersburg. For a wilderness experience in a peaceful, remote location, consider booking a multiple-night stay at one of Southeast's remote fly-in lodges.

GETTING HERE AND AROUND

AIR TRAVEL

Southeast Alaska is best explored by ship or plane.

Alaska Airlines. Alaska Airlines operates several flights daily from Seattle and other Pacific Coast and Southwestern cities to Ketchikan, Wrangell, Petersburg, Sitka, Glacier Bay, and Juneau. The carrier also connects Juneau to the northern Alaska cities of Yakutat, Cordova, Anchorage, Fairbanks, Nome, Kotzebue, and Prudhoe Bay. ☎ 800/252–7522 ⊕ www.alaskaair.com.

Unless your destination is Haines, Skagway, or Hyder, forget about driving to Southeast. Cars don't do much for travelers, as roads typically run just a few miles out from towns and villages, then dead-end. Many people elect to transport their vehicles (and themselves) via the ferries of the Alaska Marine Highway System. Serious cyclists bring their bikes along. Visitor information centers are generally open mid-May through August, daily 8 to 5, with additional hours when cruise ships are in port; between September and mid-May they're typically open weekdays 8 to 5.

FLIGHTSEEING

There's no better way to view Southeast's twisting channels, towering mountains, and gleaming glaciers than from one of the region's many small-aircraft flights.

At least four services offer daily flights between Southeast's larger towns—Juneau, Haines, Skagway, Ketchikan, Sitka, Petersburg, and Wrangell—in addition to the bevy of helicopter flightseeing services that specialize in short, scenic flights. Tops among the fixed-wing carriers are **Air Excursions** (☎ 800/354–2479 ⊕ www.airexcursions.com) and **Wings of Alaska** (☎ 907/789–0790 ⊕ www.wingsofalaska.com), both of which offer connecting flights and scenic air tours of Southeast landmarks.

Flying between destinations in Southeast—while significantly more expensive—is an experience you won't forget. If your itinerary includes an extra day or two in Southeast (particularly in Juneau), consider spending a day flying to and from a neighboring community. Round-trip tickets from Juneau to Skagway, for instance, start at around $250, as compared to approximately $170 for a one-hour flightseeing trip in and around Juneau.

A host of floatplane services offer access to remote cabins and remote freshwater fishing destinations. Check out **Southeast Aviation** (☎ 888/359–6478 ⊕ www.flymisty.com) for flight details.

CRUISE AND FERRY TRAVEL

Southeast Alaska includes a number of popular ports of call for cruise ships (⇨ *Chapter 3, Alaska by Cruise Ship*). For those looking to avoid cruise travel or for more flexibility, the **Alaska Marine Highway** (☎ 907/465–3941 or 800/642–0066 ⊕ www.ferryalaska.com) allows you to construct an itinerary that is all your own; it's quite popular with

BEST BETS FOR DIFFERENT TRAVELERS

For cruise travelers:

■ Get up close and personal with the sea life in Ketchikan with Snorkel Alaska

■ Kayak across Mendenhall Lake at the beginning or end of your cruise

For those traveling with kids:

■ Take the tram up Mt. Roberts in Juneau

■ Explore Skagway's Klondike Gold Rush National Historical Park

■ Dog sled on Denver Glacier, outside Skagway, or Juneau's Mendenhall Glacier

For travelers interested in luxury, but who still want an authentic Alaska experience:

■ Stay in McFarland's Floatel: all the seclusion of a beachfront cabin, plus the security of a main resort building floating right in the bay

■ Fly out to Waterfall Resort, out of Ketchikan, one of the most luxurious remote fishing lodges in the state

For those who want to see wildlife up close in their natural habitat:

■ Visit Anan Wildlife Observatory, which many argue is the best bear-viewing spot in the state—in terms of both proximity and quantity

4

budget-conscious, adventurous visitors. Ferry ports of call and landings in Southeast include Yakutat, Skagway, Haines, Pelican, Gustavus, Juneau, Hoonah, Tenakee, Angoon, Sitka, Kake, Petersburg, Wrangell, Ketchikan, and Metlakatla.

HEALTH AND SAFETY

Southeast is, as we've mentioned, wet. Make sure you bring raingear. No sense catching cold on vacation. Also, if you're new to catching seafood, consider hiring a guide to help you find the safest spots—Alaska's waters are powerful. Also, don't rent a boat and go out solo—even in a skiff—if you don't have boating experience. Shifts in weather, tides, and lots of other factors can turn a pleasant kayaking experience into something far less fun.

MONEY MATTERS

While most towns—especially the cruise ship-heavy towns—are loaded with ATMs, it doesn't hurt to have some cash in your wallet, especially if you're visiting some of the smaller towns of Prince of Wales Island.

RESTAURANTS

From scallops to king salmon, fresh seafood dominates menus in Southeast. Juneau, Sitka, and Ketchikan all have a variety of ethnic eateries, along with notable gourmet restaurants. Many towns also have good greasy spoons or roadhouses where you can get a serving of local gossip along with your breakfast or slice of pie. *Prices in the reviews are the average cost of a main course at dinner or, if dinner is not served, at lunch.*

HOTELS

Lodging choices along the Inside Passage range from remote Forest Service cabins to top-end hotels. In general, the latter are a pricey option, but rates drop in the off-season (mid-September to mid-May). Budget travelers will find hostels in many of the larger towns. Fine hotels are found in Ketchikan and Juneau, and luxurious fishing lodges attract anglers on Prince of Wales Island and in other places in Southeast. Bed-and-breakfasts are also popular in the Inside Passage. *Prices in the reviews are the lowest cost of a standard double room in high season.*

CABINS

U.S. Forest Service Cabins. Tongass National Forest has more than 150 rustic sites with cabins. The cabins make for a charming and cheap escape (up to $45 per night per cabin). Popular with local Alaskans and return visitors, many cabins book up long before summer arrives. ■ TIP→ Reserve in person, by mail, or online with the National Recreation Reservation System; in some cases nominal service fees may be charged for cancellations. If you haven't arranged a cabin before hitting town, check at the local Forest Service office; there's a good chance of finding something, although it may not be in one of the most popular locations. Still, every view in Alaska is great. Most are reached by floatplane or boat, but some are accessible by road. They offer bunks for six to eight occupants, tables, stoves, and outdoor privies—but no electricity or running water. You provide your own sleeping bag, food, and cooking utensils. Bedside reading in most cabins includes a diary kept by visitors—add your own adventure. ☎ 877/444–6777 reservations ⊕ www. recreation.gov.

But the U.S. Forest Service isn't the only cabin rental game in Southeast. **Alaska State Parks.** Near Ketchikan and Juneau, Alaska State Parks has a small number of cabins. Again, reservations can be made up to six months in advance. Cabins vary in size, with sleeping capacity ranging from 3 to 10 people. For more information or to reserve a cabin online, contact the Department of Natural Resources Public Information Center in Anchorage. ⊕ www.dnr.alaska.gov/parks/cabins/index.htm.

EQUIPMENT RENTAL

A few local outfitters rent cabin supplies, including cooking utensils, to travelers. Annahootz Alaskan Adventures in Sitka can outfit you with cabin supplies from lighters and matches to pots and pans. Alaska Wilderness Outfitting in Ketchikan rents cabin supplies like cooking utensils, Coleman stoves, coolers, knives, and hot pads.

Contacts Annahootz Alaskan Adventures ⊠ Sitka ☎ 907/747–2608 ⊕ www. annahootz.com/gear.php. **Alaska Wilderness Outfitting** ⊠ 3857 Fairview Ave., Ketchikan ☎ 907/225–7335 ⊕ www.latitude56.com/camping/index.html.

KETCHIKAN

Ketchikan is famous for its colorful totem poles, rainy skies, steep-as-San Francisco streets, and lush island setting. Some 13,500 people call the town home, and, in the summer, cruise ships crowd the shoreline, floatplanes depart noisily for Misty Fiords National Monument, and salmon-laden commercial fishing boats motor through Tongass Narrows. In the last decade Ketchikan's rowdy, blue-collar heritage of logging and fishing has been softened by the loss of many timber-industry jobs and the dramatic rise of cruise-ship tourism. With some effort, though, visitors can still glimpse the rugged frontier spirit that once permeated this hardscrabble cannery town. Art lovers should beeline for this town. Ketchikan's arts community is very active. Travelers in search of the perfect piece of Alaska art will find an incredible range of pieces to choose from.

WET YET WONDERFUL

Southeast has its drawbacks. For one thing, it rains a lot (though, really, that's to be expected in a rain forest). If you plan to spend a week or more, be prepared for showers during at least a few of those days. Hard-core Southeast residents just throw on slickers and rubber boots and shrug it off (leave your umbrella behind if you don't want to be pegged as a tourist). Their attitude is philosophical: without the rain, there would be no forests, no lakes, no streams running with salmon and trout, and no healthy populations of brown and black bears, moose, deer, mountain goats, and wolves.

The town is at the foot of 3,000-foot Deer Mountain, near the southeast corner of Revillagigedo (locals shorten it to Revilla) Island. Prior to the arrival of white miners and fishermen in 1885, the Tlingit used the site at the mouth of Ketchikan Creek as a summer fish camp. Gold discoveries just before the turn of the 20th century brought more immigrants, and valuable timber and commercial fishing resources spurred new industries. By the 1930s the town bragged that it was the "salmon-canning capital of the world." You will still find some of Southeast's best salmon fishing around here.

This town is the first bite of Alaska that many travelers taste. Despite its imposing backdrop, hillside homes, and many staircases, Ketchikan is relatively easy to walk through. Favorite downtown stops include the Spruce Mill Development shops and Creek Street. A bit farther away you'll find the Totem Heritage Center and Deer Mountain Tribal Hatchery. Out of town (but included on most bus tours) are two long-time favorites: Totem Bight State Historical Park and Saxman Native Village Totem Pole Park.

GETTING HERE AND AROUND

Ketchikan is a regular stop on cruise-ship and ferry routes, but Alaska Airlines also flies in from Seattle and other Pacific Northwest locations. If you're traveling out of the town on the highway in either direction, you won't go far before you run out of road. The North Tongass Highway ends about 18 miles from downtown, at Settler's

Cove Campground. The South Tongass Highway terminates at a power plant about 13 miles from town. Side roads soon end at campgrounds and at trailheads, viewing points, lakes, boat-launching ramps, and private property.

Ketchikan has three bus routes that serve the city and outlying areas. In addition, during the cruise-ship season (May to September) there is a local shuttle bus operating a circular route from Berth 4 and including stops at Eagle Park, Southeast Discovery Center, Creek Street, Totem Heritage Center, Deer Mountain Tribal Hatchery, and Ketchikan Historic Museum. The shuttle service is free.

Arriving at the airport, visitors can take the local Gateway Borough Ferry ($5). This is a vehicle and walk-on ferry that crosses the Tongass Passage, taking about 10 minutes. Ketchikan also has a water taxi that runs from the airport and will drop off visitors at the various marinas or piers along the waterfront (cost varies).

ESSENTIALS

Medical Assistance Ketchikan General Hospital ⊠ *3100 Tongass Ave.* ☎ *907/225–5171* ⊕ *www.peacehealth.org/ketchikan.*

Pharmacies Downtown Drugstore ⊠ *300 Front St.* ☎ *907/225–3144.* **Island Pharmacy** ⊠ *3526 Tongass Ave.* ☎ *907/225–6186.*

ALASKA TRAVEL SPECIALISTS

Viking Travel, Inc. This reservations service can help you with your Alaska Marine Highway trip or other Alaska vacation plans. The agency has special airfares that are booked in conjunction with ferry itineraries. ✉ *101 N. Nordic Dr., Petersburg* ☎ *907/772–3818, 800/327–2571* ⊕ *www.alaskaferry.com.*

Alaska Bound. Tour specialist Alaska Bound helps travelers choose the perfect small- or large-ship cruise through the Inside Passage. ☎ *231/439–3000, 888/252–7527* ⊕ *www.alaskabound.com.*

Alaska Tour & Travel. You can get customized tour packages to the Fairbanks area as well as through South Central and Southeast Alaska, and to most of the major national parks with Alaska Tour & Travel. ✉ *9170 Jewel Lake Rd., Suite 202,*

Anchorage ☎ *907/245–0200, 800/208–0200* ⊕ *www.alaskatravel. com.*

Alaska Tours. This organization helps individuals and groups plan Alaska trips from the Southeast to the Northwest (and everything in between). ✉ *600 Barrow St., Anchorage* ☎ *907/277–3000, 866/317– 3325* ⊕ *www.alaskatours.com.*

Mountain Travel Sobek. Adventure-seeking travelers looking for a Southeast-based tour company should consider one of the oldest outfits in the state, Alaska Discovery, a subsidiary of Mountain Travel Sobek. The adventure-travel company organizes several tours throughout Southeast, as well as in the rest of the state. ☎ *888/831–7526* ⊕ *www. mtsobek.com.*

Visitor Information Ketchikan Visitors Bureau ✉ *131 Front St.* ☎ *907/225– 6166, 800/770–3300* ⊕ *www.visit-ketchikan.com.* **Southeast Alaska Discovery Center** ✉ *50 Main St.* ☎ *907/228–6220* ⊕ *www.fs.fed.us/r10/tongass/districts/ discoverycenter.* **U.S. Forest Service** ✉ *648 Mission St.* ☎ *907/225–3101* ⊕ *www.fs.fed.us/r10/tongass.*

EXPLORING

TOP ATTRACTIONS

★ **Creek Street.** This was once Ketchikan's infamous red-light district. During Prohibition, Creek Street was home to numerous speakeasies, and in the early 1900s more than 30 houses of prostitution operated here. Today the small, colorful houses, built on stilts over the creek waters, have been restored as trendy shops.

Salmon ladder. Get out your camera and set it for high speed at the fish ladder, a series of pools arranged like steps that allow fish to travel upstream around a dam or falls. When the salmon start running from June onward, thousands of fish leap the falls (or take the easier fish-ladder route). They spawn in Ketchikan Creek's waters farther upstream. Many can also be seen in the creek's eddies above and below the falls. The falls, fish ladder, and a large carving of a jumping salmon are just off Park Avenue on Married Man's Trail. The trail was once used by

TAKE THE FERRY

The **Alaska Marine Highway System** operates stateroom-equipped vehicle and passenger ferries from Bellingham, Washington, and from Prince Rupert, British Columbia. Popular among budget-minded travelers, and those seeking an alternative to cruise-ship travel, the Alaska Marine Highway allows passengers to create their own itineraries. In Southeast Alaska the vessels call at Metlakatla, Ketchikan, Wrangell, Petersburg, Kake, Sitka, Angoon, Tenakee, Hoonah, Juneau, Gustavus, Pelican, Haines, Skagway, and Yakutat—though it's possible to take the ferry all the way to South Central and southwestern Alaska.

■TIP➜ In summer, staterooms on the ferries are sold out before sailing time; reserve months in advance. There are common areas on the ferries where you can throw a sleeping bag or sit in a recliner seat. If you are planning to take a car on the ferry, early reservations for vehicle space are also highly recommended. This is particularly true for recreational vehicles. Ferry travel is also an ideal way for bicyclists to hop from town to town. There is a fee of $15 to $50 (depending on your route) to bring a bicycle aboard. A separate ferry, operated by the Inter-Island Ferry Authority, runs between Ketchikan and Hollis (on Prince of Wales Island).

Information **Alaska Marine Highway.** Alaska Marine Highway central reservations office ⊠ *6858 Glacier Hwy., Juneau* ☎ *907/465–3941, 800/642–0066* ⊕ *www.dot.state. ak.us/amhs.* **B.C. Ferries** ⊠ *1112 Fort St., Victoria, British Columbia, Canada* ☎ *250/386–3431, 888/223–3779* ⊕ *www.bcferries. com.* **Inter-Island Ferry Authority** ☎ *907/225–4848, 866/308–4848* ⊕ *www.interislandferry.com.*

married men for discreet access to the red-light district on Creek Street. ⊠ *Married Man's Trail off Park Ave.*

Ⓢ **Southeast Alaska Discovery Center.** This impressive public lands interpre-
★ tive center features exhibits—including one on the rain forest—that focus on the resources, Native cultures, and ecosystems of Southeast Alaska. The U.S. Forest Service and other federal agencies provide information on Alaska's public lands, and a large gift shop sells natural-history books, maps, and videos about the sights in Ketchikan and Southeast. America the Beautiful–National Park and Federal Recreational Land Passes are accepted and sold. ⊠ *50 Main St.* ☎ *907/228–6220* ⊕ *www.fs.fed.us/r10/tongass/districts/discoverycenter* ➪*$5 May–Sept., free Oct.–Apr.* ☉ *May–Sept., weekdays 8–5, weekends 8–4; Oct.–Apr., Thurs.–Sun. 10–4.*

★ **Totem Heritage Center.** Gathered from uninhabited Tlingit and Haida village sites, many of the authentic Native totems in this rare collection are well over a century old—a rare age for cedar carvings, which are frequently lost to decay in Southeast's exceedingly wet climate. The center also features guided tours and displays crafts of the Tlingit, Haida, and Tsimshian cultures. Outside are several more poles carved in the three decades since this center opened. The center offers an annual series of classes, workshops, and seminars related to Northwest

CLOSE UP

The Aquaculture Debate

Five species of wild Pacific salmon are found in Alaska waters. All are anadromous (they spend part or all of their adult lives in salt water but depart to freshwater streams and rivers to spawn), and all five species have at least two common names: pink (humpback) salmon, chum (dog) salmon, coho (silver) salmon, sockeye (red) salmon, and Chinook (king) salmon. The smallest of these five, the pink salmon, has an average weight of only about 3 or 4 pounds, while king salmon can often tip the scales at more than 25 pounds. King salmon is generally considered the most flavorful, but sockeye and coho are also very highly regarded. Pinks and chum salmon are the mainstay of canneries.

After spending a year or more in the ocean (the length of time varies among the species), Pacific salmon return to their native streams to spawn and die. The annual summertime return of adult salmon is a major event in Alaska, both for the animals (including bears) that depend on this bounty, and for thousands of commercial fishers and sport anglers.

Alaska has long been famous for its seafood, and one of the first acts following statehood in 1959 was to protect fisheries from overharvesting. Today the stocks of salmon and other fish remain healthy, and careful management ensures that they will remain so in the future. In the 1980s and 1990s, aquaculture—fish farming—grew into an enormous international business, particularly in Norway, Chile, the United Kingdom, and British Columbia. Leery of the consequences to wild salmon, Alaska has never allowed any salmon aquaculture.

Pen-raised fish are affordable, available year-round, and of a consistent quality, but controversy surrounds the practice of fish farming. Many people believe it has a disastrous impact on the environment, citing such issues as disease; pollution from the waste of huge concentrations of fish; and the harvesting of non-native species, such as Atlantic salmon.

On the other side of the debate, there are those who believe that fish farming is helping to protect the earth's valuable—and decreasing—populations of salmon. Proponents of fish farms point out that the practice also offers revenue and more jobs. Offshore fish farming in the United States is a highly incendiary topic of debate; those supporting it believe that if the farms are placed in deep ocean pockets, the pollution from and medication given to the pen-raised fish will be scattered better by strong currents. Many environmentalists beg to differ, hoping to establish stringent guidelines before opening the ocean to fish-farming corporations.

One Alaska bumper sticker says: "Friends don't let friends eat farmed salmon." Just across the border, in British Columbia, many people find employment as fish-farm workers. No matter which side you agree with in the aquaculture debate, be sure to enjoy a plate of delicious wild salmon during your visit to Alaska—with luck, it could be a fish you've hooked yourself!

—Don Pitcher

Coastal Native art and culture. ⊠ *601 Deermount St.* ☎ *907/225–5900* ⊕ *www.city.ketchikan.ak.us/departments/museums/totem.html* ⊟ *$5* ⊙ *May–Sept., daily 8–5; Oct.–Apr., weekdays 1–5.*

WORD OF MOUTH

"Ketchikan is a very pretty little town w/ a lovely harbor view. We booked a private floatplane tour here and loved it." —Luv2travel15

WORTH NOTING

Cape Fox Lodge. For the town's best harbor views and one of Southeast Alaska's most luxurious lobbies, walk to the top of steep Venetia Avenue or take the funicular ($2) up from Creek Street. Don't miss the totems and other artwork created by master carvers Nathan Jackson and Lee Wallace. ⊠ *800 Venetia Way* ☎ *907/225–8001, 866/225–8001* ⊕ *www.capefoxlodge.com.*

City Park. The Deer Mountain Tribal Hatchery and Eagle Center leads into this small but charming park, which has picnic tables, a fountain, and paved paths. Ketchikan Creek runs through it. ⊠ *Park and Fair Sts.*

Creek Street Footbridge. Stand over Ketchikan Creek for good salmon viewing when the fish are running. In summer you can see impressive runs of coho, king, pink, and chum salmon, along with smaller numbers of steelhead and rainbow trout heading upstream to spawn. ■TIP➜ Keep your eyes peeled for sea lions snacking on the incoming fish.

Deer Mountain Tribal Hatchery and Eagle Center. Tens of thousands of king and coho salmon are raised at this hatchery on Ketchikan Creek owned by the Ketchikan Indian Community. Midsummer visitors can view natural spawning in the creek by pink salmon and steelhead trout as well as workers collecting and fertilizing the salmon eggs for the hatchery. Visitors to the Eagle Center can get a close-up view of eagles, great horned owls, red-tailed hawks, a falcon, and one turkey vulture. ⊠ *1158 Salmon Rd.* ☎ *907/228–5530, 800/252–5158* ⊕ *www.dmthec.org* ⊟ *$12 for hatchery and eagle compound admission* ⊙ *Early May–Sept., daily 8–4:30.*

Dolly's House Museum & Gift Shop. Formerly owned by the inimitable Dolly Arthur, this steep-roofed home once housed Creek Street's most famous brothel. The house has been preserved as a museum, complete with furnishings, beds, and a short history of the life and times of Ketchikan's best-known madam. ⊠ *24 Creek St.* ☎ *907/225–6329 (summer only)* ⊕ *www.dollyshouse.com* ⊟ *$5* ⊙ *Daily 8–4 when cruise ships are in port; closed in winter.*

Grant Street Trestle. At one time virtually all of Ketchikan's walkways and streets were made from wooden trestles, but now only one of these handsome wooden streets remains, constructed in 1908.

St. John's Church. Built in 1903, this church is the oldest remaining house of worship in Ketchikan. Its interior is formed from red cedar cut in the Native-operated sawmill in nearby Saxman. When cruise ships are in town, a docent is at the church to answer questions. There is a small gift shop. ⊠ *503 Mission St.* ☎ *907/225–3680* ⊕ *www.stjohnsketchikan.com.*

Salmon Landing Marketplace. Modeled after 1920s-style cannery architecture, this 6½-acre waterfront complex—much of it built out over the waters of Tongass Narrows—features five buildings filled with a mix of retail stores, souvenir shops, galleries, and restaurants. Cruise ships moor just a few steps away, filling the shops with tourists all summer long. ⊠ *Mill and Front Sts.*

Thomas Street and Marina. From this street you can see Thomas Basin, the most accessible of Ketchikan's four harbors and home port to pleasure and commercial fishing boats. Old buildings, including the maroon-fronted Potlatch Bar, sit atop pilings, and you can walk out to the breakwater for a better view of busy Tongass Narrows. ⊠ *Thomas St.*

Tongass Historical Museum. Native artifacts and pioneer relics revisit the mining and fishing eras at this museum in the same building as the library. Exhibits include a big, brilliantly polished lens from Tree Point Lighthouse, well-presented Native tools and artwork, and photography collections. Other exhibits rotate, but always include Tlingit items. ⊠ *629 Dock St.* ☎ *907/225–5600* 🖅 *$2* ◷ *May–Sept., daily 8–5; Oct.–Apr., Tues.–Fri. 1–5, Sat. 10–4.*

4

Whale Park. This small park on a traffic island across from St. John's Church is the site of the Chief Kyan Totem Pole, now in its third incarnation. The current replica was erected in 1993. The original was carved in the 1890s, but over the decades it deteriorated and it was replaced in the 1960s. The 1960s version is housed in the Totem Heritage Center. ⊠ *Park Ave. and Mission St.*

OUTDOOR ACTIVITIES AND GUIDED TOURS

CANOPY TOURS

Alaska Canopy Adventures. Often associated with rain forests of the tropical sort, canopy tours are Ketchikan's fastest-growing outdoor activity. Featuring a series of zip-lines, aerial boardwalks, and suspension bridges, canopy tours provide an up-close view of the coastal forests. At Alaska Canopy Adventures—a course at the Alaska Rainforest Sanctuary, 8.4 miles south of town—the longest of the tour's eight zip-lines stretches more than 800 feet, and whisks you along some 130 feet off the ground. Book online or with your cruise line. ⊠ *116 Wood Rd.* ☎ *907/225–5503* ⊕ *www.alaskacanopy.com.*

Southeast Exposure. A rain-forest zip-line and ropes course is offered through Southeast Exposure, a well-known kayaking outfit in the area. ⊠ *37 Potter Rd.* ☎ *907/225–8829* ⊕ *www.southeastexposure.com.*

DRIVING TOURS

Adventure Kart Expedition. There's no faster route to feeling like a kid on a first go-kart outing than spending a few hours in one of Adventure Kart Expedition's cool little off-road vehicles. After choosing a helmet, you'll get a quick lesson in the how-tos of driving one of the vehicles. Then you, and the people in the lineup of ATVs you'll race along with, will put pedal to metal (literally) as you zip down old backcountry timber trails. Wear old clothes: there's no way you're coming back from this one clean. Depending on the weather, the trails will either be dusty or mud-filled; but they're always fun. ⊠ *Whipple Creek* ☎ *907/617–6551* ⊕ *www.adventurekarts.com.*

FISHING

Ketchikan Visitors Bureau. Sportfishing for salmon and trout is excellent in the Ketchikan area, in both saltwater and freshwater lakes and streams. As a result, a plethora of local boat owners offer charter and guide services. Contact the Ketchikan Visitors Bureau for information on guide services and locations. ⊠ *131 Front Street* ☎ *907/225–6166, 800/770–3300* ⊕ *www.visit-ketchikan.com.*

HARBOR AND AIR TOURS

Alaska Travel Adventures. The company's backcountry Jeep trips are fun, as are the 20-person canoe outings perfect for people just dipping their toe into (very) soft adventure travel. ☎ *800/323–5757, 907/247–5295 outside Alaska* ⊕ *www. bestofalaskatravel.com.*

Allen Marine Tours. One of Southeast's largest and best-known tour operators, Allen Marine Tours leads Misty Fiords National Monument catamaran tours throughout the summer. The company also offers combo motorcoach and walking tours of Ketchikan sites that end with a water-jet-powered cruise into the Tongass Narrows. ⊠ *5 Salmon Landing* ☎ *907/225–8100, 877/686–8100* ⊕ *www.allenmarinetours.com.*

Southeast Aviation. If you want to head out on a floatplane to see the environs, contact Southeast Aviation. It offers tours of the glaciers and mountains of Misty Fiords National Monument, bear viewing, and charters. ⊠ *1249 Tongass Ave.* ☎ *907/225–2900, 888/359–6478* ⊕ *www.southeastaviation.com.*

HIKING

Deer Mountain. Get details on hiking around Ketchikan from the Southeast Alaska Discovery Center and Ketchikan Visitors Bureau (⇨ *Exploring, above*). The 3-mile trail from downtown to the 3,000-foot summit of Deer Mountain will repay your efforts with a spectacular panorama of the city below and the wilderness behind. The trail officially begins at the corner of Nordstrom Drive and Ketchikan Lake Road, but consider starting on the paved, 1.5-mile scenic walk on the corner of Fair and Deermount streets. Pass through dense forests before emerging into the alpine country. A shelter cabin near the summit provides a place to warm up. ⊠ *Fair and Deermount Sts.*

Ward Lake Recreation Area. About 6 miles north of town, Ward Lake Recreation Area has hikes next to lakes and streams and beneath towering spruce and hemlock trees; it also has several covered picnic spots and a pleasant campground. An easy 1.3-mile nature trail circles the lake,

CLOSE UP

Ketchikan's Totem Pole Parks

For the most part, the totem poles in Ketchikan's two biggest totem pole parks are replicas of those brought in from outlying villages as part of a federal project during the late 1930s.

Totem Bight State Historical Park. Totem Bight State Historical Park has many totem poles and a hand-hewn Native tribal house; it sits on a scenic spit of land facing the waters of Tongass Narrows. The clan house is open daily in summer. About a quarter of the Ketchikan bus tours include Totem Bight. ⊠ *N. Tongass Hwy., approx. 10 miles north of town* ☎ *907/247–8574* ☜ *Free* ⊙ *Dawn–dusk.*

Saxman Totem Park. A 2.5-mile paved walking path–bike trail parallels the road from Ketchikan to Saxman Native Village, named for a missionary who helped Native Alaskans settle here before 1900. A totem park dominates the center of Saxman, with poles that represent a wide range of human and animal-inspired figures, including bears, ravens, whales, and eagles. There is a $3 charge to enter.

Saxman's Beaver Clan tribal house is said to be the largest in Alaska. Carvers create totem poles and totemic art objects in the adjacent carver's shed. You can get to the park on foot or by taxi, bicycle, or city bus. You can visit the totem park on your own, but to visit the tribal house and theater you must take a tour. Tickets are sold at the gift shop across from the totems. Call ahead for tour schedules. ⊠ *S. Tongass Hwy., 2 miles south of town* ☎ *907/225–4421.*

which is popular for steelhead and salmon fishing. **Ward Creek Trail** begins from the lake and follows the creek 2.5 miles, with shoreside paths to creek-side platforms. The trail is hard-packed gravel, and is wide and gentle enough for wheelchairs. More ambitious hikers head up the 2-mile **Perseverance Trail,** a challenging set of steps and boardwalk that takes hikers through the open muskeg (peat bog) to a small lake. ⊠ *Ward Lake* ☎ *907/225–2148.*

LOCAL INTEREST

Cape Fox Tours. A Native-owned company, Cape Fox Tours leads tours of Saxman Totem Park and the historic George Inlet Cannery. You can book the cannery tour through your cruise line, and most of the other tours either through your cruise line or at the Ketchikan Visitors Bureau. ⊠ *300 Spruce Mill Way* ☎ *907/225–4846* ⊕ *www.capefoxtours.com.*

SEA KAYAKING

Southeast Exposure. Southeast Exposure offers a 3½-hour guided Eagle Islands sea-kayak tour and a 4½-hour Tatoosh Islands sea-kayak tour in Behm Canal. ⊠ *37 Potter Rd.* ☎ *907/225–8829* ⊕ *www.southeastexposure.com.*

Southeast Sea Kayaks. This company leads kayak tours of Ketchikan and Misty Fiords, and offers kayak lessons and rentals. It specializes in remote day trips and guided multinight trips to Misty Fiords. Travelers with just one day to spend on a Ketchikan adventure should consider the combination tour of kayaking through Orcas Cove and flightseeing Misty Fiord National Monument. It's hard to beat a day that includes a

WALKING AROUND KETCHIKAN

This walk originates at the helpful **Ketchikan Visitors Bureau** on Front Street. Just a few steps up Mill Street is the **Salmon Landing Marketplace**, filled with shops and restaurants. Next door, learn about Southeast Alaska's wild places at the **Southeast Alaska Discovery Center**. Farther up Mill Street, past minuscule **Whale Park** with its Chief Kyan totem pole, you can follow Stedman Street across the bridge to **Thomas Street**, which overlooks one of Ketchikan's four harbors. Following Deermont Street uphill for several blocks, you'll come across the **Totem Heritage Center** and its collection of ancient totem poles. A footbridge takes you to **Deer Mountain Tribal Hatchery and Eagle Center**, where you can see young salmon and rehabilitated bald eagles, and **City Park**. From here, Park Avenue runs parallel to Ketchikan Creek, heading downhill to the fish ladder and the salmon carving next to the **Falls at Salmon Falls**

Resort. Glance uphill from the falls to see historic **Grant Street Trestle**, where the road becomes a steep plank bridge supported on pilings. It's about a 10-minute walk down Park Avenue from the hatchery.

From the fish ladder, a boardwalk path follows Ketchikan Creek and leads to trendy **Creek Street**. For a good side trip, take the short funicular ($2) to **Cape Fox Lodge** to get a great view of the harbor. Back on the Creek Street boardwalk is former brothel **Dolly's House**. If you retrace your steps up the boardwalk and cross the **Creek Street Footbridge**, you may see salmon during summertime runs. Just in front of you is the Chief Johnson Totem Pole, near the **Tongass Historical Museum**, with interesting relics from the early days of mining and fishing. A left turn onto Bawden Street will take you past historic **St. John's Church**.

transfer from a boat to a floatplane. ✉ *3 Salmon Landing* ☎ *907/225–1258, 800/287–1607* ⊕ *www.kayakketchikan.com.*

SNORKELING

Snorkel Alaska. While signing up to go snorkeling in Alaska may seem like little more than a novelty, it takes just a few seconds in the waters off Ketchikan to understand that you're about to have an incredibly special experience. (Don't worry, you'll be given a wet suit to keep you warm.) Experienced guides provide both novice and experienced snorkelers the necessary information to quickly become comfortable and begin underwater gazing at giant sunflower stars, bright blood stars, sea cucumbers, and more. ✉ *S. Tongass Hwy. and Roosevelt Dr.* ☎ *907/247–7783* ⊕ *www.snorkelalaska.com.*

WHERE TO EAT

$$$ ✕ **Annabelle's Famous Keg and Chowder House.** Nestled into the ground
AMERICAN   floor of the historic Gilmore Hotel, this unpretentious Victorian-style restaurant serves a hearty array of seafood and pastas, including several kinds of chowder and steamer clams. Prime rib on Friday and

Saturday evenings is a favorite, and the lounge with a jukebox adds a friendly vibe. ⑤ *Average main: $20* ✉ *326 Front St.* ☎ *907/225–6009* ⊕ *www.gilmorehotel.com/anna belles.htm.*

$$$
SEAFOOD
★
✕ **Bar Harbor Restaurant.** Though a quick glance at the menu doesn't give the impression that one of Southeast's, if not Alaska's, more inventive chefs owns Bar Harbor, that is indeed the case. Even South-

east standards like fried halibut and chips are a notch better here. The chef brought all he learned at culinary school back to Ketchikan, and visitors and locals are the better for it. His joy in cooking comes through in every bite of his food. The tiny blue-and-white house on the waterfront makes for a cozy spot to dine, but if you can, try to get a seat on the back deck. Oh, and, inside or out: get the Gorgonzola fries. ⑤ *Average main: $22* ✉ *2813 Tongass Ave.* ☎ *907/225–2813* ⊕ *www.barharborrestaurantketchikan.com* ⌁ *Reservations essential.*

$
ASIAN
✕ **Diaz Café.** Take a break from salmon saturation at this Old Town Ketchikan spot. On historic Stedman Street, Diaz Café serves hearty Filipino cuisine that's a favorite of locals and, especially, of cruise ship staffers hungry for a taste of home. Budget-wary travelers take heart: you don't have to spend much at Diaz to get a really filling meal. And the place is a wonderful time warp; it's straight back to the linoleum-and-tile 1950s inside. ⑤ *Average main: $8* ✉ *335 Stedman St.* ☎ *907/225–2257.*

$$
MEXICAN
✕ **Ocean View Restaurante.** This locals' favorite eatery has burgers, steaks, pasta, pizzas, and seafood. They're all fine, but the main draws are authentic and very filling south-of-the-border dishes prepared under the direction of the Mexican-American owners. Three tables in the back have nice views of the Tongass Narrows. ⑤ *Average main: $12* ✉ *1831 Tongass Ave.* ☎ *907/225–7566.*

WHERE TO STAY

For expanded hotel reviews, visit Fodors.com.

$$
B&B/INN
⌂ **Black Bear Inn.** This isn't a typical B&B; it is, within minutes, your new home. **Pros:** kitchen fully stocked for breakfast and all-day snacks; a phenomenal backyard space. **Cons:** outside of downtown, so a car is helpful, though local buses and taxis can fill in. **TripAdvisor:** "perfect end to an Alaskan adventure," "a place to call your own," "amazing view from the hot tub." ⑤ *Rooms from: $165* ✉ *5528 N. Tongass Hwy.* ☎ *907/225–4343* ⊕ *www.stayinalaska.com* ⌁ *4 rooms, 1 apartment, 1 cabin.*

$$$
HOTEL
⌂ **Cape Fox Lodge.** With scenic views of the town and Thomas Basin from 135 feet above Creek Street, Cape Fox Lodge's setting is cozy yet luxurious. **Pros:** complimentary Wi-Fi; on-site artwork by master carvers. **Cons:** rooms are rather plain; hotel has a bit of a conference

property feel. **TripAdvisor:** "a lovely place to stay," "plush and cozy," "beautiful views." $ *Rooms from: $215* ✉ *800 Venetia Way* ☎ *907/225–8001, 866/225–8001 reservations* ⊕ *www.capefoxlodge. com* ⤵ *72 rooms, 2 suites* ❐ *No meals.*

$$ 🛏 **Inn at Creek Street & New York Hotel.**
HOTEL More than a century old, this quaint hotel is the site one of the nicest eateries in Ketchikan, now run by Ketchikan Coffee Company. **Pros:** loft suites have jetted tubs; rooms have Wi-Fi; standard rooms are reasonably priced. **Cons:** café hours limited Sunday through Thursday. **TripAdvisor:** "well run," "quirky but cool," "fun family vacation." $ *Rooms from: $139* ✉ *207 Stedman St.* ☎ *907/225–0246, 866/225–0246 outside Alaska* ⊕ *www.the newyorkhotel.com* ⤵ *8 rooms, 8 suites.*

$$$ 🛏 **The Landing.** Near the ferry terminal, this Best Western property is
HOTEL named for the state ferry landing directly across the road. **Pros:** free shuttle; near airport. **Cons:** somewhat overpriced given its location and amenities; room decor has little personality. **TripAdvisor:** "great staff," "great hotel for business and pleasure," "so happy to be here." $ *Rooms from: $186* ✉ *3434 Tongass Ave.* ☎ *907/225–5166, 800/428–8304* ⊕ *www.landinghotel.com* ⤵ *107 rooms, 21 suites.*

$$$ 🛏 **The Narrows Inn.** Three miles from the center of town and ¼ mile
HOTEL north of the airport parking lot, the Narrows is a modern lodge, where rustic wood trim enlivens the small rooms with simple furniture. **Pros:** great views of Tongass in selected rooms; complimentary continental breakfast; freezer available for fish storage. **Cons:** inconvenient location; not all rooms have good views. **TripAdvisor:** "great property," "you are treated like family," "most pleasant accommodation." $ *Rooms from: $155* ✉ *4871 N. Tongass* ☎ *907/247–2600, 888/686–2600* ⊕ *www. narrowsinn.com* ⤵ *44 rooms, 3 suites* ❐ *Breakfast.*

> ## B&B RESERVATIONS
>
> Bed-and-breakfasts are exceedingly popular in the Inside Passage, and for good reason. Dozens of regional B&Bs are excellent alternatives to local hotels; they also provide the opportunity to meet fellow travelers, dig into a homemade breakfast (such as smoked-salmon omelets or authentic sourdough pancakes), and learn about the area from local business owners.
>
> **Local Agents** Alaska Travelers Accommodations ⊕ *www. alaskatravelers.com.* Ketchikan Reservation Service ✉ *412 D-1 Loop Rd.* ⊕ *www.ketchikan-lodging.com.*

NIGHTLIFE

BARS

Ketchikan has quieted down in recent years as the economy shifted from logging to tourism, but it remains something of a party town, especially when crews stumble off fishing boats with cash in hand. You won't have any trouble finding something going on at several downtown bars.

First City Saloon. With live music throughout the summer, First City Saloon is the main dance spot. ✉ *830 Water St.* ☎ *907/225–1494.*

Ketchikan. "On a cool spring day, after walking on glaciers and seeing so much wildlife in the Tundra and sea coast, Ketchikan is comfortable and warm." —Sandy Cook, Fodors.com photo contest participant

Potlatch Bar. The Potlatch Bar delivers up music on weekends as well. ✉ *126 Thomas St.* ☎ *907/225–4855.*

SHOPPING

ART GALLERIES

Main Street Gallery. Run by the Ketchikan Area Arts and Humanities Council, the gallery hosts 11 exhibits per year, showcasing established local artists as well as rising national stars. The light and cheery gallery is well worth a visit as you stroll around town, especially if you're itching to discover a new-to-you favorite artist. ✉ *330 Main St.* ☎ *907/225–2211* ⊕ *www.ketchikanarts.org/main-street-gallery* ☉ *Weekdays 9–5, Sat. 11–3; closed every Sun. and last Sat. of each month.*

Scanlon Gallery. In business since 1972, Scanlon Gallery carries prints from a number of well-known Alaska artists, including Byron Birdsall, John Fehringer, Barbara Lavallee, Rie Muñoz, and Jon Van Zyle. ✉ *318 Mission St.* ☎ *907/247–4730, 888/228–4730* ⊕ *www.scanlongallery.com.*

Soho Coho Art Gallery. Design, art, clothing, and collectibles converge in the stylish Soho Coho Art Gallery, where you'll find an eclectic collection of art and T-shirts featuring the work of owner Ray Troll—best known for his wacky fish art—and other Southeast Alaska artists. ✉ *5 Creek St.* ☎ *907/225–5954, 800/888–4070* ⊕ *store.trollart.com.*

BOOKS

Parnassus Books. Upstairs from the Soho Coho Art Gallery, Parnassus Books is a book lover's bookstore, with creaky floors, cozy quarters, many Alaskan titles, and a knowledgeable staff. ⊠ *5 Creek St.* ☎ *907/225–7690* ⊕ *www.ketchikanbooks.com.*

SIDE TRIPS FROM KETCHIKAN

MISTY FIORDS NATIONAL MONUMENT

40 miles east of Ketchikan by air.

Misty Fiords National Monument. Just east of Ketchikan, Misty Fiords National Monument is a wilderness of cliff-faced fjords (or fiords, if you follow the monument's spelling), mountains, and islands with spectacular coastal scenery, wildlife, and recreation. Small boats provide views of breathtaking vistas. Travel on these waters can be an almost mystical experience, with the green forests reflected in the waters of the monument's many fjords. You may find yourself in the company of a whale, see a bear fishing for salmon along the shore, or even pull in your own salmon for an evening meal. ■ **TIP**→ Note that the name Misty refers to the weather you're likely to encounter.

Alaska Travel Adventures. Most visitors to Misty Fiords arrive on day trips via floatplane from Ketchikan or on board catamarans run by Alaska Travel Adventures. ☎ *800/323–5757, 907/247–5295 outside Alaska* ⊕ *www.bestofalaskatravel.com.*

Allen Marine Tours. This company offers tours of Misty Fiords. ☎ *907/225–8100, 877/686–8100* ⊕ *www.allenmarinetours.com.*

METLAKATLA

12 miles south of Ketchikan.

The village of Metlakatla—the name translates roughly as "saltwater passage"—is on Annette Island, just a dozen miles by sea from busy Ketchikan but a world away culturally. A visit to this quiet community offers visitors a chance to learn about life in a small Inside Passage Native community.

In most Southeast Native villages the people are Tlingit or Haida in heritage. Metlakatla is the exception, as most folks are Tsimshian. They moved to the island from British Columbia in 1887, led by William Duncan, an Anglican missionary from England. The town grew rapidly and soon contained dozens of buildings on a grid of streets, including a cannery, a sawmill, and a church that could seat 1,000 people. Congress declared Annette Island a federal Indian reservation in 1891, and it remains the only reservation in Alaska today. Father Duncan continued to control life in Metlakatla for decades, until the government finally stepped in shortly before his death in 1918.

During World War II the U.S. Army built a major air base 7 miles from Metlakatla that included observation towers for Japanese subs, airplane

BARANOF
ISLAND

Frederick Sound

Kake

A L E X A N D E R

Chatham Strait

KUIU
ISLAND

Gulf of Alaska

A R C H I P E L A G O

Point
Baker

Stikine River

Petersburg
see detail
map

Wrangell
see detail
map

BRITISH
COLUMBIA

Coffman
Cove

Prince of
Wales ♦
Island

Thorne Bay

Klawock

Craig

Hollis

Hydaburg

REVILLAGIGEDO
ISLAND

Misty Fiords
National
Monument
♦

Hyder

Stewart

Ketchikan
see detail
map

Metlakatla

ANNETTE
ISLAND

0   50 miles

0   50 kilometers

ALASKA
BRITISH COLUMBIA

Alaska Marine Hwy.

QUEEN CHARLOTTE
ISLAND

TO BELLINGHAM, WA

Prince Rupert

hangars, gun emplacements, and housing for 10,000 soldiers. After the war it served as Ketchikan's airport for many years, but today the long runways are virtually abandoned save for a few private flights.

GETTING HERE AND AROUND

The **Alaska Marine Highway System** offers daily ferry service from Ketchikan to Metlakatla and back. If you prefer to arrive from above, **ProMech Air** has scheduled floatplane flights between Ketchikan and outlying communities including Metlakatla and Prince of Wales Island. Run by the Metlakatla community, **Metlakatla Tours** leads local tours that include visits to Duncan Cottage, the cannery, and the longhouse, along with a Tsimshian dance performance. Local taxis can take you to other sights around the island, including Yellow Hill and the old Air Force base.

ESSENTIALS

Airplane Contact **Pacific Airways** ☎ 907/225–3500, 877/360–3500 ⊕ www.flypacificairways.com. **ProMech Air** ☎ 907/225–3845, 800/860–3845 ⊕ www.promechair.com.

Ferry Contact **Alaska Marine Highway System** ☎ 907/465–3941, 800/642–0066 ⊕ www.dot.state.ak.us/amhs.

Tour Information **Metlakatla Tours** ☎ 907/886–8687 ⊕ www.metlakatla.com.

EXPLORING

Longhouse. Father Duncan worked hard to eliminate traditional Tsimshian beliefs and dances, but today the people of Metlakatla have resurrected their past; they perform old dances in traditional regalia. The best place to catch these performances is at the traditional

longhouse (known as *Le Sha'as* in the Tsimshian dialect), which faces Metlakatla's boat harbor. Three totem poles stand on the back side of the building, and the front is covered with a Tsimshian design. Inside are displays of native crafts and a model of the fish traps that were once common throughout the Inside Passage. Native dance groups perform here on Wednesday and Friday in summer. Just next to the longhouse is an **Artists' Village,** where booths display locally made arts and crafts. The village and longhouse open when groups and tours are present.

William Duncan Memorial Church. Metlakatla's religious heritage still shows today. The clapboard William Duncan Memorial Church, topped with two steeples, burned in 1948 but was rebuilt several years later. It is one of nine churches in tiny Metlakatla. **Father Duncan's Cottage** is maintained to appear exactly as it would have in 1891, and includes original furnishings, personal items, and a collection of turn-of-the-20th-century music boxes. ⊠ *Corner of 4th Ave. and Church St.* ☎ *907/886–8687* ⊕ *www.metlakatla.com* ✉ *$2* �
 Weekdays 8:30–12:30, or when cruise ships are in port.

Yellow Hill. Two miles from town is a boardwalk path that leads up the 540-foot Yellow Hill. Distinctive yellow sandstone rocks and panoramic vistas make this a worthwhile detour on clear days.

WHERE TO STAY

For expanded hotel reviews, visit Fodors.com.

$
RENTAL
Metlakatla Inn. This two-story building, decorated with Native art, offers standard motel accommodations with private decks off the upstairs rooms. **Pros:** property has recently been renovated; car rental available on-site. **Cons:** guests share the same phone line; property lacks charm. **TripAdvisor:** "great place to stay," "very nice and cozy," "what Metlakatla is like." ⑤ *Rooms from: $99* ⊠ *3rd Ave. and Lower Milton St.* ☎ *907/886–3456* ⊕ *www.metlakatlainn.com* ➥ *9 rooms, 2 apartments* ⑩ *No meals.*

$
B&B/INN
Tuck'em Inn. This family-run lodging occupies two separate downtown houses. **Pros:** convenient location; breakfast included. **Cons:** some rooms share bathrooms; rooms don't have much personality. ⑤ *Rooms from: $99* ⊠ *Hillcrest Rd. and Western Ave.* ☎ *907/886–1074* ⊕ *www.alaskanow.com/tuckem-inn* ➥ *6 rooms* ⑩ *Breakfast.*

HYDER

90 miles northeast of Ketchikan.
The tiny, nondescript town of Hyder sits at the head of narrow Portland Canal, a 70-mile-long fjord northeast of Ketchikan. The fjord marks the border between Canada and the United States, and Hyder sits just 2 miles from the larger town of Stewart, British Columbia. ■ TIP→ It's also one of the few Southeast settlements accessible by paved road.

The 1898 discovery of gold and silver in the surrounding mountains brought a flood of miners to the Hyder area, and the town eventually became a major shipping port. Mining remained important for decades, but a devastating 1948 fire destroyed much of the town, which had been built on pilings over the water. A small amount of mining still takes place here, but the beauty of the area, while not any more interesting than Ketchikan, attracts a respectable number of tourists. Today Hyder calls itself "the friendliest ghost town in Alaska," a claim that may be based more on marketing than reality.

HYDER TIPS

The somewhat lackluster town of Hyder is small and has only a handful of tourist-oriented businesses, a post office, and a library. Nearby Stewart has slightly more to offer, including a museum, hotels, restaurants, and camping. You will need to check in at Canadian customs (open 24 hours) before crossing the border from Hyder into Stewart, a process that has unfortunately become more difficult. Canadian money is primarily used in Hyder, but greenbacks are certainly accepted.

GETTING HERE AND AROUND
From Stewart, in Canada, Highway 37A continues over spectacular Bear Pass to Hyder and connects the town with the rest of Canada. **Taquan Air** has year-round service between Ketchikan and Hyder every Monday and Thursday.

ESSENTIALS
Airplane Contact Taquan Air ⊠ 4085 Tongass Ave., Ketchikan ☎ 907/225–8800, 800/770–8800 ⊕ www.taquanair.com.

Visitor and Tour Information Stewart-Hyder Chamber of Commerce ☎ 250/636–9224, 888/366–5999 ⊕ www.stewart-hyder.com.

EXPLORING
Bear Glacier. Twenty-five miles east of Stewart on Highway 37A is the imposing Bear Glacier. The glacier sits across a small lake that is often crowded with icebergs.

Fish Creek Wildlife Observation Site. Six miles north of Hyder on Salmon River Road is the Fish Creek Wildlife Observation Site. From late July to early September, a large run of salmon attracts black and brown bears, which, in turn, attract more than a few photographers. The creek produces some of the largest chum salmon anywhere.

Glacier Inn. Getting "Hyderized" (which involves drinking and drinking-related silliness) is a term that you will hear upon arrival in the area.

You can get Hyderized at Glacier Inn, where the walls are papered with thousands of signed bills. The tradition supposedly began when prospectors would tack a dollar bill on the wall in case they were broke when they returned. ⊠ *Main St.* ☎ *250/636–9248.*

Salmon Glacier. A dirt road from Hyder into Canada leads 17 miles to remote Salmon Glacier, one of the few glaciers accessible by road in Southeast Alaska.

Stewart Historical Society Museum. Housed in the town's former fire hall, the Stewart Historical Society Museum contains wildlife displays and exhibits on the region's mining history. Pop-culture buffs will enjoy movie props from films made in the area, including *Insomnia*. ⊠ *603 Columbia St., Stewart, British Columbia, Canada* ☎ *250/636–2568* ⊕ *www.stewart-hyder.com/community.html* ⌨ *$5* ⊙ *May, June, and Sept., weekends 10–6; July and Aug., daily 10–6.*

WHERE TO EAT AND STAY
For expanded hotel reviews, visit Fodors.com.

$$ ⊺ **Ripley Creek Inn.** Stewart's best lodging option covers five historic
HOTEL   downtown buildings. **Pros:** nice decks and views from rooms. **Cons:** somewhat noisy; not much to do in immediate area. **TripAdvisor:** "nice rooms with unique views," "a place you'll never forget," "comfortable and quirky." ⑤ *Rooms from: $95* ⊠ *306 5th Ave., Stewart, British Columbia, Canada* ☎ *250/636–2344* ⊕ *www.ripleycreekinn.com* ⤴ *32 rooms* ⍾ *No meals.*

PRINCE OF WALES ISLAND

43 miles northwest of Ketchikan.

Prince of Wales Island stretches more than 130 miles from north to south, making it the largest island in Southeast Alaska. Only two other American islands—Kodiak in Alaska and Hawaii in the Hawaiian chain—are larger. Prince of Wales (or "P.O.W." as locals call it) has a diversity of landforms, a plethora of wildlife, and exceptional sportfishing, especially for steelhead, salmon, and trout anglers, with the Karta and Thorne rivers among the favorites.

The island has long been a major source of timber, both from Tongass National Forest lands and those owned by Native corporations. While much of the Native land has been cut over, environmental restrictions on public lands have greatly reduced logging activity. The island's economy is now supported by small-scale logging operations, tourism, and commercial fishing.

Approximately 5,500 people live full-time on Prince of Wales Island, scattered in small villages and towns. A network of 1,500 miles of roads—nearly all built to access clear-cuts—crisscrosses the island, providing connections to even the smallest settlements.

GETTING HERE AND AROUND
The **Inter-Island Ferry Authority** operates a daily vehicle and passenger ferry between Ketchikan and Prince of Wales Island. The ferry terminal is in the tiny settlement of Hollis, 31 miles from Craig on a paved road.

Paved roads link Craig and Hollis. The relative abundance of roads, combined with ferry and air access from Ketchikan, makes it easy to explore this island. It's a shame that more people don't do so.

ESSENTIALS

Ferry Information Inter-Island Ferry Authority ☎ *907/530–4848 or 866/308–4848* ⊕ *www.interislandferry.com.*

Visitor Information Prince of Wales Chamber of Commerce ☎ *907/775–2626* ⊕ *www.princeofwalescoc.org.*

EXPLORING

Craig. The primary commercial center for Prince of Wales is Craig, on the island's western shore. This town of 1,200 retains a hard-edged aura fast disappearing in many Inside Passage towns, where tourism now holds sway. Although sightseeing attractions are slim, the town exudes a frontier spirit, and its small-boat harbors buzz with activity. ⊠ *Craig.*

El Capitan Cave. A number of large natural caverns pockmark northern Prince of Wales Island. The best known of these, El Capitan Cave, has one of the deepest pits in the United States and is open to the public. Paleontologists have found a wealth of black bear, brown bear, and other mammal fossils in the cave's 13,000 feet of passageways, including some that date back more than 12,000 years. The Forest Service leads free El Capitan tours several times a week in summer. Tours take about two hours. It takes some work to get to the mouth of the cave but, if you're up for a 1,100-foot hike up a 367-step stairway, it's well worth the effort. The rangers don't rush and give visitors plenty of time to catch their breath along the way by discussing the intensely lush forest that surrounds the cave area. Reservations are required at least two days in advance, and no children under age seven are permitted. Bring a flashlight and wear hiking boots or rubber boots. A light jacket is also helpful, as the cave gets quite cool. ⊠ *Mile 51 along North Prince of Wales Rd., Prince of Wales Island* ☎ *907/828–3304.*

Hydaburg. The Haida village of Hydaburg, approximately 40 miles south of Klawock (via chip-sealed road), lies along scenic Sukkwan Strait. A small collection of **totem poles** occupies the center of this Haida settlement, the only one in Alaska. Originally from British Columbia's Queen Charlotte Island, the Haida settled here around 1700. ⊠ *Hydaburg.*

Klawock. A half-dozen miles from Craig is the Tlingit village of Klawock, with a sawmill, cannery, hatchery, and the island's only airport. The town is best known for its striking totem poles in **Totem Park.** Several of these colorful poles were moved here in the 1930s; others are more recent carvings. You can watch carvers restoring old totems at the carving shed, across the road from the grocery store.

Along the bay you'll find **St. John's by the Sea Catholic Church,** with stained-glass windows picturing Native Alaskans. ⊠ *Klawock* ☎ *907/755–2345.*

Prince of Wales Hatchery. Klawock is also home to Prince of Wales Hatchery, one of the state's most effective hatcheries. It's open for summertime tours ($2) and it also has a small visitor center with an aquarium full of young coho salmon. ✉ *Craig* ☎ *907/755–2231* ⊕ *www.powha.org* ⊙ *Weekdays 8:30-4:30.*

WHERE TO STAY

For expanded hotel reviews, visit Fodors.com.

$
B&B/INN

⊡ **Inn of the Little Blue Heron.** With sweeping water views, cozy rooms, and outdoor decks tailored for simultaneous coffee drinking and wildlife viewing, the Little Blue Heron is a favorite among regular visitors to Craig. **Pros:** both locations offer wireless Internet; can rent out whole inn or suite for large groups. **Cons:** rooms at the South Cove location are small. ⑤ *Rooms from: $79* ✉ *406 9th St. and 403 Beach Rd., Craig* ☎ *907/826–3608* ⊕ *www.littleblueheroninn.com* ↘ *6 rooms, 1 suite* ⑩ *Breakfast.*

$$$$
B&B/INN

⊡ **McFarland's Floatel.** At this quiet resort 2 miles across the bay from the logging town of Thorne Bay on the eastern side of Prince of Wales, each of the four beachfront log cabins sleeps up to six people and includes a loft, woodstove, full kitchen, and private bath. **Pros:** nightly rate covers up to four guests; quiet setting. **Cons:** restaurant is open only to hotel guests; location is remote. ⑤ *Rooms from: $295* ☎ *907/828–3335, 888/828–3335* ⊕ *www.mcfarlandsfloatel.com* ↘ *4 cabins* ⊙ *Closed Oct.–mid-Apr.*

$$$$
B&B/INN

⊡ **Rock Haven.** A few minutes' boat ride from the shores of the fishing-centric Coffman Cove, Rock Haven is instant peace and relaxation. **Pros:** stunning setting; owners clearly enjoy running a lodge; lodge pets are a friendly bunch. **Cons:** there's no way to just pop out for a quick bite to eat; even if the property weren't a boat ride from Coffman Cove, the town doesn't offer much in the way of restaurants; you need to be handy with a skiff if you want to motor out to the lodge on your own—there are some widowmaker rocks in the water. ⑤ *Rooms from: $2890* ✉ *Across bay, Coffman Cove* ☎ *907/329–2003* ⊕ *www.rockhavenalaska.com* ↘ *3 rooms, 1 one-bedroom apartment with kitchenette.*

$
HOTEL

⊡ **Ruth Ann's Hotel.** Victorian-style furnishings and details flavor this tasteful gingerbread hotel. **Pros:** honeymoon suite is perfect for romantic travelers. **Cons:** rooms are up the hill and not on the water. **TripAdvisor:** "lovely accommodations," "very cozy," "honeymoon suite is to die for." ⑤ *Rooms from: $2890* ✉ *505 Water St., Craig* ☎ *907/826–3378* ↘ *17 rooms, 1 suite* ⊙ *Restaurant closed Jan.*

$$$$
ALL-INCLUSIVE

⊡ **Shelter Cove Lodge.** Tall windows front the water at this modern lodge along the South Boat Harbor in Craig. **Pros:** price is all-inclusive; lodge was renovated in 2008. **Cons:** expensive rate in comparison to similar properties; no elevator. ⑤ *Rooms from: $2475* ✉ *703 Hamilton Dr., Craig* ☎ *907/826–2939, 888/826–3474* ⊕ *www.sheltercovelodge.com* ↘ *10 rooms* ⊙ *Restaurant closed Sept.–May* ⑩ *All-inclusive.*

$$$$
RESORT
Fodor's Choice
★

⊡ **Waterfall Resort.** At this upscale fishing lodge guests can choose from several accommodation styles, eat bountiful meals with all the trimmings, and fish from custom-built 25-foot cabin cruisers under the care of expert fishing guides. **Pros:** plenty of saltwater fishing; opportunity to spot wildlife. **Cons:** most kitchens in the condos aren't used, since meals are provided by the resort; remote location. **TripAdvisor:** "a pure Alaskan fishing experience," "I always hate to leave," "awesome location." ⑤ *Rooms from: $3975* ☎ *907/225–9461, 800/544–5125* ⊕ *www.waterfallresort.com* ↘ *10 lodge rooms, 4 suites, 4 condos, 26 cabins* ☾ *Closed Sept.–late May* �🍴 *All meals.*

WRANGELL

87 miles north of Ketchikan.

A small, unassuming timber and fishing community, Wrangell sits on the northern tip of Wrangell Island, near the mouth of the fast-flowing Stikine River—North America's largest undammed river. The Stikine plays a large role in the life of many Wrangell residents, including those who grew up homesteading on the islands that pepper the area. Trips on the river with local guides are highly recommended as they provide, basically, an insider's guide to the Stikine and a very Alaskan way of life. Like much of Southeast, Wrangell has suffered in recent years from a declining resource-based economy. But locals are working to build tourism in the town. Bearfest, which started in 2010, celebrates Wrangell's proximity to Anan Creek, where you can get a close-up view of both brown and black bears.

Wrangell has flown three different national flags in its time. Russia established Redoubt St. Dionysius here in 1834. Five years later Great Britain's Hudson's Bay Company leased the southern Alaska coastline, renaming the settlement Ft. Stikine. It was rechristened Wrangell when the Americans took over in 1867; the name came from Baron Ferdinand Petrovich von Wrangel, governor of the Russian-American Company.

The rough-around-the-edges town is off the track of the larger cruise ships, so it does not get the same seasonal traffic that Ketchikan and Juneau do. Hence, it is nearly devoid of the souvenir shops that dominate so many other nearby downtown areas. But the gift shops and art galleries that are here do sell locally created work, and the town is very welcoming to visitors; independent travelers would do well to add a stop in Wrangell to their Southeast wanderings.

GETTING HERE AND AROUND

Although you probably won't get to Wrangell on a cruise ship (though some small ship lines do sail here), ferries connect the town to other Southeast Alaska ports via the **Alaska Marine Highway.** The town is fairly compact, and most sights are within walking distance of the city dock or ferry terminal. Alaska Airlines provides two daily jet stops connecting from Seattle and Juneau.

ESSENTIALS

Ferry Contact Alaska Marine Highway System ☎ *907/465–3941, 800/642–0066* ⊕ *www.dot.state.ak.us/amhs.*

Medical Center Wrangell Medical Center ✉ *310 Bennett St.* ☎ *907/874–7000* ⊕ *www.wrangellmedicalcenter.com.*

Pharmacy Stikine Drug ✉ *202 Front St.* ☎ *907/874–3422* ⊕ *www. stikinedrug.com.*

Visitor Information **Wrangell Visitor Center** ✉ *296 Campbell Dr., in Nolan Center* ☎ *907/874–2829, 800/367–9745* ⊕ *www.wrangellalaska.org.*

EXPLORING

TOP ATTRACTIONS

★ **Nolan Center.** Wrangell's museum moved into a building that acts as a
☺ centerpiece for cultural life in Wrangell. Exhibits provide a window
on the region's rich history. Featured pieces include the oldest known
Tlingit house posts dating from the late 18th century, decorative posts
from Chief Shakes's clan house, petroglyphs, century-old spruce-root
and cedar-bark baskets, masks, gold-rush memorabilia, and a fascinating photo collection. If you're spending any time in town, don't pass
this up. ✉ *296 Campell Dr.* ☎ *907/874–3770* ⊕ *www.wrangell.com/cc/
welcome-nolan-center* ⊗ *May–Sept., Tues.–Sat. 10–5, and when ferry
or cruise ships are in port; Oct.–Apr., Tues.–Sat. 1–5.*

   Civic Center. Also in the building are the town's Civic Center, a
200-seat movie theater–performance space–convention center, and
the **Wrangell Visitor Center.** The latter is staffed when the museum is
open, and has details on local adventure options. ✉ *293 Campbell Dr.*
☎ *907/874–2829, 800/367–9745* ⊕ *www.wrangellalaska.org*

WALKING AROUND WRANGELL

Bone up on local history and biology at the **Wrangell Museum in the Nolan Center**, which houses informative and surprisingly entertaining exhibits, a well-stocked gift shop, and a helpful visitor center. Farther along Front Street, check out **Kik-setti Totem Park** before turning onto Shakes Street to see the town's prized attraction, **Chief Shakes Island.** You may want to spend time here just soaking in the harbor view and examining the old totem poles. **Chief Shakes's grave site** is on the hill overlooking Wrangell Harbor. Get here from Chief Shakes Island by turning right on Case Avenue. From the grave site, head up Church Street to the **Irene Ingle Public Library.** About 0.6 miles north of the ferry terminal along Evergreen Avenue you'll find **Petroglyph Beach,** where ancient etchings are visible along the shore. Be prepared to leave the observation deck behind: most of the best petroglyphs are scattered across the rocky beach. For a woodsy hike, climb **Mt. Dewey,** the hill right behind town. Farther afield (5 miles south of town) is the fun hike to **Rainbow Falls.**

It is a 1.5-mile walk between Petroglyph Beach and Chief Shakes Island, so you should plan at least three hours to complete the walk and sightseeing around town.

Petroglyph Beach State Historic Park. Scattered among other rocks at this public beach are three dozen or more large stones bearing designs and pictures chiseled by unknown ancient artists. No one knows why the rocks at this curious site were etched the way they were, or even exactly how old these etchings are. You can access the beach via a boardwalk, where you'll find signs describing the site along with carved replicas of the petroglyphs. Most of the petroglyphs are to the right between the viewing deck and a large outcropping of rock in the tidal beach area. Because the original petroglyphs can be damaged by physical contact, only photographs are permitted. But you are welcome to use the replicas to make a rubbing from rice paper and charcoal or crayons (available in local stores). ⊠ *0.6 mile north of ferry terminal off Evergreen Ave.*

WORTH NOTING

Chief Shakes's Grave Site. Buried here is Shakes V, who led the local Tlingit during the first half of the 19th century. A white picket fence surrounds the grave, and two killer-whale totem poles mark his resting spot overlooking the harbor. Find the grave on Case Avenue. ⊠ *Case Ave.*

Irene Ingle Public Library. The library, behind the post office, has two ancient petroglyphs out front and is home to a large collection of Alaskan books, computers with free Internet access, and a helpful staff. ⊠ *124 2nd St.* ☎ *907/874-3535* ⊕ *www.wrangell.com/library.*

Kik-setti Totem Park. You'll find several recently carved totem poles at this pocket-size park with Alaska greenery. ⊠ *Front St.*

Mt. Dewey. Despite the name, this landmark is more a hill than a peak. Still, it's a steep 15-minute climb up the John Muir Trail from town to the top through a second-growth forest. The trail begins from 3rd Street behind the high school, and an observation platform on top provides

WORTH THE DETOUR

Fodor's Choice ★ Anan Creek Wildlife Observatory. About 30 miles southeast of Wrangell in the Tongass National Forest, Anan is one of Alaska's premier black- and brown-bear–viewing areas. Each summer, from early July to late August, as many as 30 to 40 bears gather at this Southeast stream to feed on huge runs of pink salmon. On an average visit of about three hours you might spot bears while strolling the ½-mile viewing boardwalk. Once on the platform, you will likely see many bears at the same time. There is a photo blind accessible from the viewing platform. Five people at a time can use the photo blind for 30-minute intervals, which provides photo opportunities of bears at less than 11 yards. The photo blind provides stream-level photo-ops of bears catching salmon. Forest Service interpreters are on hand to answer questions. The site is accessible only by boat or floatplane. From July 5 to August 25 you must have a pass to visit Anan; the U.S. Forest Service places a limit on the number of people who can visit the site each day. Unless you have experience navigating the Stikine by boat and in walking through bear country, it's highly recommended that you go to Anan with a local guide. The guide companies provide passes to Anan for their guests. ☎ 907/874–2323.

The following Wrangell-based guide companies are all authorized to run trips to Anan.

Alaska Charters and Adventures ☎ 888/993–2750 ⊕ www.alaskaupclose.com.

Alaska Vistas ✉ Box 2245 ☎ 907/874–3006, 888/874–3006 ⊕ www.alaskavistas.com.

Alaska Waters ✉ 7 Stikine Ave. ☎ 907/874–2378, 800/347–4462 ⊕ www.alaskawaters.com.

Tongass National Forest Wrangell Ranger District. For additional details, contact the Tongass National Forest Wrangell Ranger District. ✉ 525 Bennett St. ☎ 907/874–2323 ⊕ www.fs.fed.us/r10/tongass.

a viewpoint for protected waterways and islands named from its Russian history, including Zarembo, Vank, and Woronkofski. The trail is named for naturalist John Muir, who, in 1879, made his way up the trail and built a campfire. Locals didn't realize there was anybody up on Mt. Dewey and the campfire light caused quite a commotion below. .

Rainbow Falls. The trail to this scenic waterfall starts across the road from Shoemaker Bay, 5 miles south of Wrangell. A ¾-mile trail climbs uphill through the rain forest, with long stretches of boardwalk steps, ending at an overlook just below the falls. Hikers with more stamina can continue another 3 miles and 1,500 vertical feet to Shoemaker Bay Overlook.

OUTDOOR ACTIVITIES AND GUIDED TOURS

AIR CHARTER

Sunrise Aviation. This charter-only air carrier flies to the Anan Creek Wildlife Observatory, LeConte Glacier, and Forest Service cabins. ☎ *907/874–2319, 800/874–2311* ⊕ *www.sunriseflights.com.*

BICYCLING

A waterfront trail connects Wrangell with Shoemaker Bay Recreation Area, 4½ miles south of town. The trail is mainly flat; more adventurous souls can brave the dozens of miles of logging roads that crisscross the island.

BOATING

Alaska Peak & Seas. Mark Galla of Alaska Peak & Seas guides wildlife trips, Stikine jet-boat tours, and boat trips to surrounding areas. ☎ *907/874–2454* ⊕ *www.wedoalaska.com.*

Alaska Vistas and Stikine Wilderness Adventures. Take jet-boat trips to Anan Creek Wildlife Observatory that depart from Wrangell, plus a variety of guided sea-kayak adventures and rafting trips. Alaska Vistas and Stikine Wilderness Adventures also offers custom tours and itinerary planning. ☎ *907/874–3006, 866/874–3006* ⊕ *www.alaskavistas.com.*

Breakaway Adventures. This outfitter leads a variety of jet-boat trips, including a tour to Chief Shakes Glacier and the nearby hot springs. You can catch one of its water taxis to Petersburg or Prince of Wales Island. ☎ *907/874–2488, 888/385–2488* ⊕ *www.breakawayadventures.com.*

FISHING

Wrangell Visitor Center. Numerous companies schedule salmon- and trout-fishing excursions ranging in length from an afternoon to a week. Contact the Wrangell Visitor Center for information on guide services and locations. ✉ *293 Campbell Dr.* ☎ *800/367–9745* ⊕ *www.wrangellalaska.org.*

GOLF

Muskeg Meadows Golf Course. Muskeg Meadows Golf Course, Southeast Alaska's first USGA regulation links, is a well-maintained, 2,950-yard 9-hole course with a driving range. Situated in a wooded area ½ mile from town, the course is easily accessible, and golf clubs and pull carts can be rented on-site. The course is, most likely, one of the only ones in the world with a "Ravens Rule," which states that "a ball stolen by a raven may be replaced, with no penalty, provided there is a witness." ☎ *907/874–4653* ⊕ *www.wrangellalaskagolf.com.*

NATURAL HISTORY

Alaska Charters and Adventures. Wildlife viewing, bear photography trips, fishing, glacier tours, and a Stikine River jet-boat wilderness tour are offered by Alaska Charters and Adventures. ☎ *888/993–2750* ⊕ *www.alaskaupclose.com.*

Alaska Vistas. This company does regular float trips on the Stikine, which rises in British Columbia and flows through the edges of the Stikine Icefield. This historic river, once an alternate route to the goldfields, is like nothing else in the state. ☎ *907/874–3006, 866/874–3006* ⊕ *www. alaskavistas.com.*

WHERE TO EAT

$ ✕ **Diamond C Cafe.** The big breakfasts at the Diamond C are just part of
CAFÉ the attraction. The café also serves as the gathering place for a group
of local guys and, really, it's fun to just sit back and listen. As you dig
into the breakfast hash and other goodies, though, there's a chance
you'll only have eyes for your plate. ⑤ *Average main: $7* ✉ *223 Front
St.* ☎ *907/874–3677* ☻ *No dinner.*

$$ ✕ **Stikine Inn Restaurant.** With views overlooking the water, the restaurant
AMERICAN at the Stikine Inn is, easily, the prettiest place to dine in town. Consid-
ering the sparse number of restaurants in town, the Stikine could just
serve a get-by menu, but the restaurant's salads, pizzas, burgers, and
hearty soups go far beyond—it serves seriously tasty dishes. Portions
tend to be oversized, especially on the dessert front. Consider splitting
that dessert you eyeballed on the menu with at least one other person (if
not two). The Stikine also has a full bar and serves good coffee drinks.
⑤ *Average main: $15* ✉ *107 Stikine Ave.* ☎ *907/874–4388* ⊕ *www.
stikineinn.com/dining.html.*

$$ ✕ **Zak's Cafe.** Though Zak's has a no-frills look about it, it's worth a visit
AMERICAN (especially since there aren't a huge number of dining choices in town).
The restaurant serves good food at reasonable prices. Check out the
day's specials or try the steaks, chicken, seafood, and salads. At lunch
the menu includes burgers, sandwiches, fish-and-chips, and wraps.
⑤ *Average main: $16* ✉ *314 Front St.* ☎ *907/874–3355* ☻ *Closed Sun.*

WHERE TO STAY

For expanded hotel reviews, visit Fodors.com.

$ ⛲ **Alaskan Sourdough Lodge.** Formerly Bruce Harding's Old Sourdough
B&B/INN Lodge, this rambling inn on the south side of the harbor, five blocks
from downtown, began life as a construction camp, and traces of its
rough-hewn origins remain today. **Pros:** excellent home-style dining;
continental breakfast included with room rate. **Cons:** tight hallways
and sparse furnishings; pets are not allowed. **TripAdvisor:** "a pleasant surprise," "comfortable friendliness," "a great Alaskan adventure." ⑤ *Rooms from: $114* ✉ *1104 Peninsula St.* ☎ *907/874–3613,
800/874–3613* ⊕ *www.akgetaway.com/HardingsLodge* ⤴ *15 rooms,
1 suite* ❍| *Breakfast.*

$$ ⛲ **Grand View Bed & Breakfast.** Two miles from town—perhaps within
B&B/INN walking distance for avid pedestrians—this unassuming beachfront
home provides spectacular views across Zimovia Strait. **Pros:** expert
sightseeing tours provided by owners; visitors get the inside scoop
from a true local; complimentary Wi-Fi. **Cons:** 2 miles from town;
credit cards accepted only during tourist season. **TripAdvisor:** "won-
derful accommodation," "the perfect spot," "like being with fam-
ily." ⑤ *Rooms from: $115* ✉ *Mile 2, Zimovia Hwy.* ☎ *907/874–3225*
⊕ *www.grandviewbnb.com* ⤴ *3 rooms* ❍| *Breakfast.*

$ ☷ **Rooney's Roost Bed & Breakfast.**
B&B/INN   This century-old home—easily Wrangell's most charming digs—is just a block from downtown. **Pros:** large, delicious breakfast; owned by a local who grew up in Wrangell. **Cons:** with just four rooms, you should book early. **TripAdvisor:** "a lovely place to stay," "excellent breakfast," "very pleasant." Ⓢ *Rooms from: $115* ✉ *206 McKinnon St.* ☎ *907/874–2026* ⊕ *www.rooneysroost.com* ⤳ *4 rooms* ⦿ *Breakfast.*

FOR STARTERS

"Sourdough" is a nickname for a longtime resident of Alaska. Prospectors who trekked here in search of gold often carried sourdough starter for pancakes and bread. To this day, you'll find sourdough goods on hundreds of menus throughout the state.

4

$ ☷ **Shakes Slough Cabins.** If you're a hot springs or hot tub enthusi-
RENTAL   ast, these Forest Service cabins on the Stikine River, accessible from Wrangell, are worth checking out. **Pros:** open-air hot tub; stunningly beautiful and remote location. **Cons:** cabins have no electricity or water; hard to get to if you don't hire a local boat guide to bring you to the cabins; popular with locals and return visitors, and tend to fill in advance. Ⓢ *Rooms from: $25* ✉ *Forest Service, 525 Bennett St.* ☎ *907/874–2323, 877/444–6777 National Recreation Reservation Service* ⊕ *www.recreation.gov* ⤳ *2 cabins.*

$$ ☷ **Stikine Inn.** After some down years, Wrangell's largest inn is on the
B&B/INN   upswing; the rooms and lobby have been remodeled, and the Stikine Inn's in-house restaurant and wine bar may be the best in town. **Pros:** scenic waterfront location; good restaurant; 100% smoke-free. **Cons:** decor won't win any design awards. **TripAdvisor:** "best location in town," "comfortable and friendly," "good food." Ⓢ *Rooms from: $139* ✉ *107 Stikine Ave.* ☎ *907/874–3388, 888/874–3388* ⊕ *www.stikineinn. com* ⤳ *34 rooms, 3 suites.*

SHOPPING

Garnet Ledge. Garnet Ledge, a rocky ledge at the mouth of the Stikine River, is the source for garnets sold by local children for 25¢ to $50. The site was deeded to the Boy Scouts in 1962 and to the Presbyterian Church in Wrangell in 2006, so only children can collect these colorful but imperfect stones, the largest of which are an inch across. You can purchase garnets at a few covered shelters near the city dock when cruise ships are in, at the Wrangell Museum, or at the ferry terminal when a ferry is in port.

Brenda Schwartz-Yeager. Local artist Brenda Schwartz-Yeager creates watercolor scenes of the Alaskan coast on navigational charts of the region. Schwartz-Yeager, who grew up in Wrangell, is also a boat captain and local guide who, with her husband, owns Alaska Charters and Adventures. ✉ *7 Front St.* ☎ *907/874–3508* ⊕ *www.marineartist.com.*

PETERSBURG

22 miles north of Wrangell.

Getting to Petersburg is an experience, whether you take the "high road" by air or the "low road" by sea. Alaska Airlines claims one of the shortest jet flights in the world, from takeoff at Wrangell to landing at Petersburg. The schedule calls for 20 minutes of flying, but it's usually more like 15. At sea level only ferries and smaller cruisers can squeak through Wrangell Narrows with the aid of more than 50 buoys and range markers along the 22-mile waterway, which takes almost four hours. But the inaccessibility of Petersburg is also part of its charm: you'll never be overwhelmed here by hordes of cruise passengers; only smaller ships can reach the town.

The Scandinavian heritage is gradually being submerged by the larger American culture, but you can occasionally hear Norwegian spoken, especially during the Little Norway Festival, held here each year on the weekend closest to May 17 (Norwegian Constitution Day). If you're in town during the festival, be sure to take part in one of the fish feeds that highlight Syttende Mai (aka the Norwegian Constitution Day) celebration. You won't find better folk dancing and beer-batter halibut outside Norway.

One of the most pleasant things to do in Petersburg is to roam among the fishing vessels tied up dockside in the town's expanding harbor. This is one of Alaska's busiest, most prosperous fishing communities, with an enormous variety of seacraft. You'll see small trollers, big halibut vessels, and sleek pleasure craft. By watching shrimp, salmon, or halibut catches being brought ashore (though be prepared for the pungent aroma), you can get a real appreciation for this industry.

On clear days Petersburg's scenery is second to none. Across Frederick Sound the sawlike peaks of the Stikine Ice Cap scrape clouds from the sky, looking every bit as malevolent as their monikers suggest. (Some of the most wickedly named summits include Devil's Thumb, Kate's Needle, and Witches Tits.) **LeConte Glacier,** Petersburg's biggest draw, lies at the foot of the ice cap, about 25 miles east of town. Accessible only by water or air, the LeConte is the continent's southernmost tidewater glacier and one of its most active, often calving off so many icebergs that the tidewater bay at its face is carpeted shore to shore with floating bergs.

Although Petersburg is nice to explore, commercial fishing is more important than tourism—in other words, you'll find more hardware stores than jewel merchants. But that's also a big part of its charm. The main attractions are the town's Norwegian heritage, its vibrant community, and its magnificent mountain-backed setting. The country around Petersburg provides an array of outdoor fun, from whale-watching and glacier-gazing to hiking and fishing.

GETTING HERE AND AROUND

Once you arrive in Petersburg by ferry on the **Alaska Marine Highway** or by airplane, a host of outdoor activities await you. **Kaleidoscope Cruises** conducts whale-watching and glacier-ecology boat tours led by a

Petersburg

KEY

Tourist information

TO ↗
SANDY BEACH

Wrangell Narrows

Nordic Dr.

Dolphin St.

Excel St.

Fram St.

Gjoa St.

Haugen Dr.

Harbor
Way

Floatplane
Base ◆

Sing Lee
Alley

Ferry
Terminal

Nordic Dr.

Mitkof Hwy.

TO CRYSTAL LAKE HATCHERY,
BLIND SLOUGH RECREATION AREA &
FALL'S CREEK FISH LADDER

0   1/4 mile

0   1/4 kilometer

professional naturalist, and **Tongass Kayak Adventures** leads day and overnight tours to the icebergs in LeConte Glacier Bay and to see the whales of Frederick Sound. You can also see the Stikine River and LeConte Glacier from above on a flightseeing tour with the locally popular air-taxi operator **Pacific Wings** or rent a boat at **Scandia House** or **Jensen's Boat Rentals.** For help finding more tours of the environs, contact travel agency **Viking Travel** or the **Petersburg Visitor Information Center.**

ESSENTIALS

Ferry Contact Alaska Marine Highway System ☎ *907/465–3941, 800/642–0066* ⊕ *www.dot.state.ak.us/amhs.*

Medical Assistance Petersburg Medical Center ✉ *103 Fram St.* ☎ *907/772–4291* ⊕ *www.pmc-health.com.*

Pharmacy Rexall Drugs ✉ *215 N. Nordic Dr.* ☎ *907/772–3265* ⊕ *www. petersburgrexall.com.*

Tour Information Jensen's Boat Rentals ☎ *907/772–4635* ⊕ *www. jensensboatrentals.com.* **Kaleidoscope Cruises** ☎ *907/772–3736, 800/868–4373* ⊕ *www.petersburglodgingandtours.com.* **Pacific Wings** ✉ *1500 Haugen Dr.* ☎ *907/772–9258* ⊕ *www.pacwing.com.* **Tongass Kayak Adventures** ☎ *907/772–4600* ⊕ *www.tongasskayak.com.* **Viking Travel** ☎ *907/772–3818, 800/327–2571* ⊕ *www.alaskaferry.com.*

Visitor Information **Petersburg Visitor Information Center** ⊠ *1st and Fram Sts.* ☎ *907/772–4636* ⊕ *www.petersburg.org.*

EXPLORING

Clausen Memorial Museum. The museum's exhibits explore commercial fishing and the cannery industry, the era of fish traps, the social life of Petersburg, and Tlingit culture. Don't miss the museum shop; the 126.5-pound king salmon—the largest ever caught commercially— as well as the Tlingit dugout canoe; the Cape Decision lighthouse station lens; and *Earth, Sea and Sky,* a 3-D wall mural outside. ⊠ *203 Fram St.* ☎ *907/772–3598* ⊕ *www.*

> ### FISH AND FLOWERS
>
> Petersburg evokes Norway: tidy white buildings line the streets, bright-color leaf and flower designs (called rosemaling) decorate older homes, and row upon row of sturdy fishing vessels pack the harbor. No wonder—this community was founded by Norwegian Peter Buschmann in 1897.

clausenmuseum.net ⊠ *$3* ⊗ *May–early Sept.; Mon.–Sat. 10–5; early-Sept.–late-Dec., Tues.–Sat. 10–2.*

Eagle's Roost Park. Just north of the Petersburg Fisheries cannery, this small roadside park is a great place to spot eagles, especially at low tide. On a clear day you will also discover dramatic views of the sharp-edged Coast Range, including the 9,077-foot summit of Devil's Thumb.

Hammer Slough. Houses on high stilts and the historic Sons of Norway Hall border this creek that floods with each high tide, creating a photogenic reflecting pool.

Petersburg Marine Mammal Center. Visitors to this nonprofit research and learning center can share and gather information on marine mammal sightings, pick up reference material, and have fun with the interactive educational kiosk. ⊠ *Gjoa St. and Sing Lee Alley, behind Viking Travel* ☎ *907/772–4170 summer only* ⊕ *psgmmc.org* ⊠ *Free* ⊗ *Mid-June–Aug., Mon.–Sat. 9–5.*

Petersburg Visitor Information Center. This small office is a good source for local information, including maps and details on tours, charters, and nearby outdoor recreation opportunities. ⊠ *1st and Fram Sts.* ☎ *907/772–4636, 866/484–4700* ⊕ *www.petersburg.org* ⊗ *May–Sept., Mon.–Sat. 9–5, Sun. noon–4; Oct.–Apr., weekdays 10–2.*

Sons of Norway Hall. Built in 1912, this large, barnlike structure that stands just south of the Hammer Slough is the headquarters of an organization devoted to keeping alive the traditions and culture of Norway. The window shutters are decorated with colorful Norwegian rosemaling designs. Outside sits a replica of a Viking ship that is a featured attraction in the annual Little Norway Festival each May. On the south side of the building is the **Bojer Wikan Fisherman's Memorial,** where deceased local fishermen are honored with a bronze statue. ⊠ *23 S. Sing Lee Alley* ☎ *907/772–4575.*

OFF THE BEATEN PATH

Falls Creek Fish Ladder. Coho and pink salmon migrate upstream in late summer and early fall at this fish ladder south of town. Fish head up the ladder to get around a small falls. ✉ *Mile 10.8, Mitkof Hwy.*

Blind Slough Recreation Area. This recreation area includes a number of sites scattered along the Mitkof Highway 15–20 miles south of Petersburg. Blind River Rapids Trail is a wheelchair-accessible 1-mile boardwalk that leads to a three-sided shelter overlooking the river—one of Southeast's most popular fishing spots—before looping back through the muskeg. Not far away is a bird-viewing area where several dozen trumpeter swans spend the winter. In summer you're likely to see many ducks and other waterfowl. At Mile 18 the state-run Crystal Lake Hatchery releases thousands of king and coho salmon each year. The kings return in June and July, the coho in August and September. Nearby is a popular picnic area. Four miles south of the hatchery is a Forest Service campground. ☎ 907/772–4772.

Other popular day adventures include a kayaking trip up **Petersburg Creek** or a hike on the **Three Lakes Loop Trail.**

NORWEGIAN CRAFTS

Party House. The Party House sells objects decorated with Norwegian-style rosemaling, including plates, trays, and key chains. ✉ *14 Sing Lee Alley* ☎ *907/772–2717.*

OUTDOOR ACTIVITIES

HIKING

For an enjoyable loop hike from town, follow Dolphin Street uphill from the center of town. At the intersection with 5th Street, a boardwalk path leads 900 feet through forested wetlands to the baseball fields, where a second boardwalk takes you to 12th Street and Haugen Drive. Turn left on Haugen and follow it past the airport to **Sandy Beach Park,** where picnickers can sit under log shelters and low tide reveals remnants of ancient fish traps and a number of petroglyphs. From here you can return to town via Sandy Beach Road or hike the beach when the tide is out. Along the way is the charming **Outlook Park,** a covered observatory with binoculars to scan for marine life. A pullout at Hungry Point provides views to the Coast Range and Frederick Sound. Across the road the half-mile **Hungry Point Trail** takes you back to the baseball fields—a great spot for panoramic views of the mountains—where you can return downtown on the nature boardwalk. Plan on an hour and a half for this walk.

Raven's Roost Cabin. For something more strenuous, a 4-mile trail begins at the airport and climbs 1,600 feet in elevation to Raven's Roost Cabin. Along the way you take in a panorama that reaches from the ice-bound Coast Range to the protected waters and forested islands of the Inside Passage far below. The two-story Forest Service cabin is available for rent ($35 per night); contact the National Recreation Service. Get details on these and other hikes from the Petersburg Visitor Information Center or from the Petersburg Ranger District.

National Recreation Reservation Service ☎ *518/885–3639, 877/444–6777* ⊕ *www.recreation.gov.*

Petersburg Ranger District ✉ *12 N. Nordic Dr.* ☎ *907/772–3871* ⊕ *www.fs.fed.us/r10/tongass/districts/petersburg.*

WHERE TO EAT

$ ✕ **Coastal Cold Storage.** This busy little seafood deli in the heart of Petersburg serves daily lunch specials, including fish chowders and halibut beer bits (a local favorite), along with grilled-chicken wraps, steak sandwiches, breakfast omelets, and waffles. It's a great place for a quick bite en route to your next adventure; there isn't much seating in the shop's cramped interior. On sunny days, place your order and then grab a seat at one of the tables set up out front on the sidewalk. Live or cooked crab is available for takeout, and the shop can process your sport-caught fish. ⓢ *Average main: $10* ✉ *306 N. Nordic Dr.* ☎ *907/772–4177, 877/257–4746* ⊕ *fishbroker.tripod.com/coastalcoldstorageinc.*

SEAFOOD

$ ✕ **Helse Restaurant.** Locals flock to this modest mom-and-pop place for lunch. It's the closest thing to home cooking Petersburg has to offer, and most days it's open from 8:30 to 4, even in winter. A couple of dozen sandwiches grace the menu, as do rotating soups and homemade bread. The daily specials are a good bet, and the gyros are decent as well. Helse also doubles as an ice-cream and espresso stand. ⓢ *Average main: $7* ✉ *13 Sing Lee Alley* ☎ *907/772–3444.*

AMERICAN

$ ✕ **Papa Bear's Pizza.** Although it has a few tables, this often-crowded pizza joint primarily specializes in takeout, pizza by the slice, hamburgers, submarine sandwiches, and giant calzones. It also serves ice cream. ⓢ *Average main: $9* ✉ *301 S. Nordic Dr.* ☎ *907/772–3727* ⊕ *www. papabearspizza.com.*

PIZZA

WHERE TO STAY

For expanded hotel reviews, visit Fodors.com.

$$ ▦ **The Lucky Loon.** Sitting on a beautiful piece of waterfront property, the two-bedroom house, fitted with two double beds and two queen-size beds, feels like instant home from the moment you walk in. **Pros:** beautiful waterfront location; comfortable and nicely equipped house **Cons:** five-night minimum from May through Sept; three miles from downtown. ⓢ *Rooms from: $160* ✉ *181 Frederick Dr.* ☎ *907/772–2345* ⊕ *www.theluckyloon.com* ⤢ *2 bedrooms.*

RENTAL

$$ ▦ **Scandia House.** This hotel on Petersburg's main drag, a fixture since 1910, was rebuilt following a 1995 fire. **Pros:** some pets allowed; airport and ferry shuttle. **Cons:** fourth-floor rooms aren't accessible by elevator. **TripAdvisor:** "helpful staff," "just about the only place in town," "great location." ⓢ *Rooms from: $120* ✉ *110 Nordic Dr.* ☎ *907/772–4281, 800/722–5006* ⊕ *www.scandiahousehotel.com* ⤢ *33 rooms, 3 suites* ⓞ *Breakfast.*

HOTEL

$ ▦ **Sea Level B&B.** The views from the large picture windows at this small B&B, a home on stilts above the Wrangell Narrows, are worth the 10 or 15 minutes it takes to walk to town. **Pros:** excellent view of narrows; excellent chance of spotting a whale from the house. **Cons:** B&B is a 10- to 15-minute walk from downtown. **TripAdvisor:** "beautiful experience," "immaculate room," "amazing views." ⓢ *Rooms from:*

B&B/INN

$100 ⊠913 N. Nordic Dr. ☎907/772–3240 ⊕ www.sealevelbnb.com ⇨2 rooms ═ No credit cards ⋈ Breakfast.

$ **Tides Inn.** Petersburg's largest hotel, the Tides, is a block uphill from
HOTEL the town's main thoroughfare. **Pros:** views of the boat harbor from the
newer rooms. **Cons:** rooms in the old wing are dark and dated. **TripAdvisor:** "great location," "manager was awesome," "wonderful find."
⟨$⟩ *Rooms from: $130 ⊠307 N. 1st St. ☎907/772–4288, 800/665–8433
⊕ www.tidesinnalaska.com ⇨45 rooms ⋈ Breakfast.*

NIGHTLIFE

All bars and restaurants in Petersburg are now smoke-free.

Harbor Bar. The Harbor Bar, with ships' wheels, nautical pictures, and a
mounted red snapper, is true to the town's seafaring spirit. A separate
outside entrance leads to the bar's liquor store. *⊠310 N. Nordic Dr.
☎907/772–4526.*

Kito's Kave. Sample the brew and blasting music at Kito's Kave, a popular
hangout among rowdy local fishermen. La Fonda, a Mexican restaurant, leases space inside the bar. *⊠11 Sing Lee Alley ☎907/772–3207.*

SHOPPING

BOOKSTORE

Sing Lee Alley Books. Off an alley in a big, beautiful white house that
served as a boardinghouse to fishermen and schoolteachers, Sing Lee
Alley Books stocks books on Alaska, best sellers, cards, and gifts. *⊠11
Sing Lee Alley ☎907/772–4440.*

SEAFOOD

Northern Lights Smokeries. Outside of downtown, consider stopping in
at Northern Lights Smokeries for owner Thomas Cumps' hot-smoked
white king, red king, and sockeye salmon, or a local favorite, cold-smoked black cod. Northern Lights also ships. It's best to call ahead to
make sure he'll be around before you stop by. *☎907/772–4608 ⊕ www.
nlsmokeries.com.*

Tonka Seafoods. At Tonka Seafoods, across the street from the Sons of
Norway Hall, check out the gift shop, and sample smoked or canned
halibut and salmon. Be sure to taste the white king salmon—an especially flavorful type of Chinook that the locals swear by. Tonka will also
ship. *⊠22 Sing Lee Alley ☎907/772–3662, 888/560–3662 ⊙ Weekdays 8–6, weekends 9–5.*

SITKA

110 miles west of Petersburg.

It's hard not to like Sitka, with its eclectic blend of Native Alaskan,
Russian, and American history and its dramatic and beautiful open-ocean setting. This is one of the best Inside Passage towns to explore
on foot, with such sights as St. Michael's Cathedral, Sheldon Jackson

Museum, Castle Hill, Sitka National Historical Park, and the Alaska Raptor Center topping the town's must-see list.

Sitka was home to the Kiksádi clan of the Tlingit people for centuries prior to the 18th-century arrival of the Russians under the direction of territorial governor Alexander Baranof, who believed the region was ideal for the fur trade. The governor also coveted the Sitka site for its beauty, mild climate, and economic potential; in the island's massive timber forests he saw raw materials for shipbuilding. Its location offered trading routes as far west as Asia and as far south as California and Hawaii. In 1799 Baranof built St. Michael Archangel—a wooden fort and trading post 6 miles north of the present town.

Strong disagreements arose shortly after the settlement. The Tlingits attacked the settlers and burned their buildings in 1802. Baranof, however, was away in Kodiak at the time. He returned in 1804 with a formidable force—including shipboard cannons—and attacked the Tlingits at their fort near Indian River, site of the present-day 105-acre Sitka National Historical Park, forcing many of them north to Chichagof Island.

By 1821 the Tlingits had reached an accord with the Russians, who were happy to benefit from the tribe's hunting skills. Under Baranof and succeeding managers, the Russian-American Company and the town prospered, becoming known as the Paris of the Pacific. The community built a major shipbuilding and repair facility, sawmills, and forges, and even initiated an ice industry, shipping blocks of ice from nearby Swan Lake to the booming San Francisco market. The settlement that was the site of the 1802 conflict is now called Old Sitka. It is a state park and listed as a National Historic Landmark.

The town declined after its 1867 transfer from Russia to the United States, but it became prosperous again during World War II, when it served as a base for the U.S. effort to drive the Japanese from the Aleutian Islands. Today its most important industries are fishing, government, and tourism.

GETTING HERE AND AROUND

Sitka is a common stop on cruise routes for smaller ships and a regular stop along the **Alaska Marine Highway System. Alaska Airlines** also operates flights from Seattle and other Alaskan cities to Sitka. The best way to see the town's sights is on foot.

ESSENTIALS

Airline Contact **Alaska Airlines** ☎ 800/252–7522 ⊕ www.alaskaair.com.

Ferry Contact **Alaska Marine Highway System** ☎ 907/465–3941 or 800/642–0066 ⊕ www.dot.state.ak.us/amhs/pubs. **Sitka Ferry Terminal** ⊠ 5307 Halibut Point Rd. ☎ 907/747–8737.

Internet **Highliner Coffee Café** ⊠ 327 Seward St., in Seward Square Mall ☎ 907/747–4924 ⊕ www.highlinercoffee.com.

Medical Assistance **Sitka Community Hospital** ⊠ 209 Moller Ave. ☎ 907/747–3241 ⊕ www.sitkahospital.org.

Sitka

Pharmacy Harry Race Pharmacy ⊠ *106 Lincoln St.* ☎ *907/966–2110* ⊕ *www. whitesalaska.com/harryrace.* **White's Pharmacy** ⊠ *705 Halibut Point Rd.* ☎ *907/966–2150* ⊕ *www.whitesalaska.com/whitespharmacy.*

Visitor Information Sitka Convention and Visitors Bureau ⊠ *303 Lincoln St.* ☎ *907/747–5940* ⊕ *www.sitka.org.*

EXPLORING

TOP ATTRACTIONS

☺ **Alaska Raptor Center.** The only full-service avian hospital in Alaska, the
★ Raptor Center rehabilitates 100 to 200 birds each year. Situated just above Indian Creek, the center is a 20-minute walk from downtown. Well-versed guides provide an introduction to the rehabilitation center (including a short video), and guests are able to visit with one of these majestic birds. The Raptor Center's primary attraction is an enclosed 20,000-square-foot flight training center, built to replicate the rain forest, where injured eagles relearn survival skills, including flying and catching salmon. Visitors watch through one-way glass windows. A large deck out back faces an open-air enclosure for eagles and other raptors whose injuries prevent them from returning to the wild. Additional mews with hawks, owls, and other birds are along a rain-forest

WALKING AROUND SITKA

Most folks begin their tours of Sitka under the distinctive onion dome of St. Michael's Cathedral, right in the town center. A block behind the cathedral along Harbor Drive is **Harrigan Centennial Hall,** a low-slung convention hall that houses the smallish **Sitka Historical Society and Museum** and an information desk that opens when cruise ships are in port. A block east, along Lincoln Street, you'll find the **Russian Bishop's House,** one of the symbols of Russian rule. Continue out on Lincoln Street along the bustling boat harbor to Sheldon Jackson College, where the worthwhile **Sheldon Jackson Museum** is packed with Native cultural artifacts. Another ½ mile out along gently curving Metlakatla Street is the **Sitka National Historical Park,** where you can chat with Native artisans as they craft carvings and silver jewelry. Behind the main building a network of well-signed paths takes you through the rain forest past more than a dozen totem poles and to the site of a Tlingit fort from the battle of 1804. A signed trail crosses the Indian River (watch for spawning salmon in late summer) and heads across busy Sawmill Creek Road to the **Alaska Raptor Center,** for an up-close look at bald eagles.

Return to town along Sawmill Creek Road. On your right, you'll see the white headstones of the small Sitka National Cemetery. Back downtown, you can browse the many shops or walk along Harbor Drive and take the path to the summit of **Castle Hill,** where Russia transferred Alaska to American hands—these are the best views in town. If you follow the path down the other side of the hill, check out the impressive **Sitka State Pioneers Home,** with the statue of pioneer "Skagway Bill" Fonda. Across the street is **Totem Square,** with its tall totem pole and three ancient anchors. Adjacent to the Pioneers Home is the **Sheet'ka Kwaan Naa Kahidi** community house. Native dances take place here in summer. End your walk at the haunting (not haunted) **Russian and Lutheran cemeteries** that fill the dark woods along Marine Street a block from the blockhouse. The grave of Princess Maksoutoff, a member of the Russian royal family, is here.

Sitka has many attractions, and you can easily spend a full day exploring this culturally rich area. You can accomplish the walk in two to three hours if you do not spend much time at each stop. You can pound the pavement around town in an hour or so.

path. The gift shop sells all sorts of eagle paraphernalia, the proceeds from which fund the center's programs. ⊠ *1000 Raptor Way, off Sawmill Creek Rd.* ☎ *907/747–8662, 800/643–9425* ⊕ *www.alaskaraptor. org* ☞ *$12* ☉ *Mid-May–Sept., daily 8–4.*

★ **St. Michael's Cathedral.** This cathedral, one of Southeast Alaska's best-known national landmarks, is treasured by visitors and locals alike—so treasured that in 1966, as a fire engulfed the building, townspeople risked their lives and rushed inside to rescue the cathedral's precious Russian icons, religious objects, and vestments. Using original blueprints, an almost exact replica of onion-dome St. Michael's was completed in 1976. Today you can see what could possibly be the largest collection of Russian icons in the United States, among them the much-prized *Our Lady of Sitka* (also known as the *Sitka Madonna*) and the *Christ Pantocrator* (*Christ the World Judge*), displayed on the altar screen. ✉ *240 Lincoln St.* ☎ *907/747–8120* 🌐 *www.oca.org/parishes/oca-ak-sitsmk* 💰 *$2 requested donation* ⏱ *May–Sept., daily 8:30–4; Oct.–Apr., hrs vary.*

★ **Sheldon Jackson Museum.** Near the campus of the former **Sheldon Jackson College,** this octagonal museum, which dates from 1895, contains priceless Native Alaskan items collected by Dr. Sheldon Jackson (1834–1909), who traveled the remote regions of Alaska as an educator and missionary. This state-run museum features artifacts from every Native Alaska culture; on display are carved masks, Chilkat blankets, dogsleds, kayaks, and even the impressive helmet worn by Chief Katlean during the 1804 battle against the Russians. The museum's small but well-stocked gift shop, operated by the Friends of the Sheldon Jackson Museum, carries books, paper goods, and handicrafts created by Alaska Native artists. ■**TIP➜** Don't be shy. Open the drawers under the glass cases all around the main room of the musem. They hold on-exhibit artifacts, too. ✉ *104 College Dr.* ☎ *907/747–8981* 🌐 *www.museums. state.ak.us/sheldon_jackson/sjhome.html* 💰 *$4 mid-May–mid-Sept., $3 mid-Sept.–mid-May* ⏱ *Mid-May–mid-Sept., daily 9–5; mid-Sept.–mid-May, Tues.–Sat. 10–4.*

Fodor'sChoice
★ **Sitka National Historical Park.** The main building at this 113-acre park houses a small museum with fascinating historical exhibits and photos of Tlingit Native culture. Highlights include a brass peace hat given to the Sitka Kiksádi by Russian traders in the early 1800s and Chilkat robes. Head to the theater to watch a 12-minute video about Russian–Tlingit conflict in the 19th century. Ask a ranger to point you toward the Centennial Totem Pole, installed in honor of the park's 100th anniversary in 2011. Also here is the **Southeast Alaska Indian Cultural Center,** where Native artisans demonstrate silversmithing, weaving, wood carving, and basketry. Make sure you strike up a conversation (or two) with the artists; they're there to showcase and talk about their work as well as Tlingit cultural traditions. At the far end of the building are seven totems (some more than a century old) that have been brought indoors to protect them from decay. Behind the center a wide, 2-mile path takes you through the forest and along the shore of Sitka Sound. Scattered along the way are some of the most skillfully carved Native totem poles in Alaska. Keep going on the trail to see spawning salmon from the footbridge over Indian River. Park Service rangers lead themed walks in summer, which focus on the Russian-Tlingit conflict, the area's natural history, and the park's totem poles. ✉ *106 Metlakatla St.* ☎ *907/747–0110 visitor center* 🌐 *www.nps.gov/sitk* 💰 *$4* ⏱ *May–Sept., daily 8–5; Oct.–Apr., closed Sun.*

WORTH NOTING

Castle Hill. On this hill, Alaska was formally handed over to the United States on October 18, 1867, and the first 49-star U.S. flag was flown on January 3, 1959, signifying Alaska's statehood. To reach the hill, take the first right off Harbor Drive just before O'Connell Bridge; then go into the **Baranof Castle Hill State Historic Site** entrance. A paved path switchbacks to the top, where you can read the interpretive signs on the area's Tlingit and Russian history and take in the views of Crescent Harbor and downtown Sitka. On a clear day, look for the volcanic flanks of Mt. Edgecumbe on the horizon. ☎ *907/747–6249 DNR Sitka Ranger Station* ⊕ *www.dnr.alaska.gov/parks/aspunits/southeast/ baranofcastle.htm.*

Harbor Mountain. During World War II the U.S. Army constructed a road to the 2,000-foot level of Harbor Mountain, a perfect spot from which to watch for invading Japanese subs or ships (none were seen). This road has been improved over the years, and it is possible to drive 5 miles to a spectacular summit viewpoint across Sitka Sound. A trail climbs uphill from the parking lot, and then follows the ridge 2.5 miles to a Forest Service shelter. From there, ambitious hikers could continue downhill another 3.5 miles to Sitka via the **Gavan Hill Trail.**

Russian and Lutheran cemeteries. Most of Sitka's Russian dignitaries are buried in these sites off Marine Street, which, thanks to their wooded locations, require a bit of exploring to locate. The most distinctive (and easily accessible) grave belongs to Princess Maksoutoff (died 1862), wife of the last Russian governor and one of the most illustrious members of the Russian royal family to be buried on Alaska soil. ✉ *Marine and Seward Sts.*

Russian Bishop's House. A registered historic landmark, this house facing the harbor was constructed by the Russian–American Company for Bishop Innocent Veniaminov in 1842 and completed in 1843. Inside the house, one of the few remaining Russian-built log structures in Alaska, are exhibits on the history of Russian America, including several places where portions of the house's structure are peeled away to expose Russian building techniques. The ground level is a free museum, and Park Service rangers lead guided tours of the second floor, which houses the residential quarters and a chapel. ✉ *501 Lincoln St.* ☎ *907/747–0107 Sitka National Historical Park office* ⊕ *www.nps. gov/sitk/historyculture/russian-bishops-house.htm* ☛ *Tours $4* ☉ *May–Sept., daily 8:30–5; Oct.–Apr. by appointment.*

Sitka Historical Society and Museum. A Tlingit war canoe sits beside this brick building, formally named Harrigan Centennial Hall. Check out the museum's collection of Tlingit, Victorian-era, and Alaska-purchase historical artifacts; there's an auditorium for New Archangel Dancers performances, which take place when cruise ships are in port. ✉ *330 Harbor Dr.* ☎ *907/747–6455 museum, 907/747–5940 Visitors Bureau* ⊕ *www.sitkahistory.org* ☛ *$2* ☉ *Museum mid-May–mid-Sept., weekdays 9–4:30, weekends 10–3:30; mid-Sept.–mid-May, Tues.–Sat. 10–4.*

Sitka State Pioneers Home. Known locally as just the Pioneers Home, this large, red-roof home for elder Alaskans has an imposing 14-foot statue in front symbolizing Alaska's frontier sourdough spirit ("sourdough" generally refers to Alaska's American pioneers and prospectors); it was modeled by an authentic prospector, William "Skagway Bill" Fonda. Adjacent to the Pioneers Home is **Sitka Tribal Tours' Sheet'ka Kwaan Naa Kahidi** community house, where you can watch Native dance performances throughout the summer. ✉ *Lincoln and Katlian Sts.*

☎ *907/747–7290 for Sitka Tribal Tours reservations, 907/747–3213 for Sitka Pioneers Home* ⊕ *hss.state.ak.us/dalp/sitka.*

Totem Square. On this grassy square directly across the street from the Pioneers Home are three anchors discovered in local waters and believed to be of 19th-century British origin. Look for the double-headed eagle of czarist Russia carved into the cedar of the totem pole in the park. ⊠ *200 Katlian St.* ⊕ *www.sitka.org/play/attractions.*

Whale Park. This small waterside park sits in the trees 4 miles east of Sitka right off Sawmill Creek Road. Boardwalk paths lead to five viewing platforms and steps take you down to the rocky shoreline. A gazebo next to the parking area contains signs describing the whales that visit Silver Bay, and you can listen to their sounds from recordings and an offshore hydrophone here. ■ **TIP→** Tune your radio to FM 88.1 anywhere in Sitka to hear a broadcast of humpback whale sounds picked up by the hydrophone. ⊠ *Sawmill Creek Rd.*

4

OUTDOOR ACTIVITIES AND GUIDED TOURS

BICYCLING

Yellow Jersey Cycle Shop. If it isn't raining, rent a high-quality mountain bike from Yellow Jersey Cycle Shop and head out on the nearby dirt roads and trails. Staffers know Sitka's many mountain- and road-bike routes well. ⊠ *329 Harbor Dr.* ☎ *907/747–6317* ⊕ *www. yellowjerseycycles.com.*

BOAT AND KAYAK TOURS

Alaska Travel Adventures. Alaska Travel Adventures leads a three-hour kayaking tour in protected waters south of Sitka. The tour includes friendly guides, basic kayak instruction, and snacks at a remote cabin on the water. ☎ *800/323–5757* ⊕ *www.bestofalaskatravel.com.*

Allen Marine Tours. One of Southeast's largest and best-known tour operators, Allen Marine Tours leads different boat-based Sitka Sound tours throughout the summer, such as the Wildlife Quest tours, which are a fine opportunity to view humpback whales, sea otters, puffins, eagles, and brown bears in a spectacular setting. When seas are calm enough, Allen Marine offers a tour to the bird sanctuary at **St. Lazaria Islands National Wildlife Refuge.** ⊠ *1512 Sawmill Creek Rd.* ☎ *907/747–8100, 888/747–8101* ⊕ *www.allenmarinetours.com.*

Sitka Sound Ocean Adventures. The guide company's waterfront operation is easy to find: just look for the big blue bus it uses as its base at Crescent Harbor next to Harrigan Centennial Hall. Sitka Sound runs a variety of guided kayak trips through the mysterious and beautiful outer islands off the coast of Sitka. Experienced paddlers who want to go it on their own can rent gear from the company. Sitka Sound's guides quickly help new-to-the-area paddlers understand its wonders (and, for day trips, Sitka Sound packs a great picnic). ⊠ *Harbor Dr. at Centennial Hall* ☎ *907/752–0660* ⊕ *www.kayaksitka.com.*

BUS TOURS AND HISTORICAL WALKS

Sitka Tours. Sitka Tours meets ferries and cruise ships and leads both bus tours and historical walks. ☎ *907/747–8443.*

Tribal Tours. Tribal Tours emphasizes Sitka's rich Native culture, with bus or walking tours and dance performances at the Tribal Community House. ☎ 907/747–7290, 888/270–8687 ⊕ *www.sitkatours.com.*

FISHING

Sitka is home to a fleet of charter boats. The Sitka Convention and Visitors Bureau website (⊕ *www.sitka.org*) has descriptions of and Web links to several dozen sportfishing operators.

The Boat Company. This outfitter offers multiday wildlife-watching and fishing trips departing from Sitka and Juneau. ☎ 360/697–4242, 877/647–8268 ⊕ *www.theboatcompany.org.*

Sitka's Secrets. Operated by naturalists, Sitka's Secrets combines wildlife-viewing with fishing. ✉ *500 Lincoln St., Suite B-9* ☎ *907/747–5089* ⊕ *www.sitkasecret.com.*

FOUR-WHEELED FUN

Alaska ATV Tours. Alaska ATV Tours offers half-day tours of remote Kruzof Island aboard two-person Yamaha ATVs. Stops include Iris Meadows Estuary, a black-sand beach, and one of Kruzof's numerous salmon-laden creeks. The tour, which departs from Sitka, includes a scenic 30-minute boat transfer through the islands and channels of Sitka Sound. ☎ 907/966–2301, 877/966–2301 ⊕ *www.alaskaatvtours.com.*

HIKING AND BIRD-WATCHING

Sitka Trail Works. Get a map of local trails from Sitka Trail Works. ✉ *801 Halibut Point Rd.* ☎ *907/747–7244* ⊕ *www.sitkatrailworks.org.*

Starrigavan Recreation Area. Seven miles north of Sitka, Starrigavan Recreation Area is a peaceful, end-of-the-road place to explore the rain forest. The state ferry terminal is less than a mile from Starrigavan, and a popular Forest Service campground is also here. Several easy trails lead hikers through the area, including the ¼-mile boardwalk **Estuary Life Trail.** It circles a small estuary and includes a bird-viewing shelter and access to a nearby artesian well. The ¾-mile **Forest and Muskeg Trail** winds through a spruce-hemlock forest and traverses a muskeg, with interpretive signs along the way. Across the road is the delightful 1¼-mile loop **Mosquito Cove Trail,** which skirts the rocky shoreline to Mosquito Cove before returning through thickly forested hills. ✉ *Halibut Point Rd.* ☎ *907/747–4216.*

UNDERWATER ACTION

Sea Life Tours. This outfitter operates a semisubmersible tour vessel with large underwater windows that provide views of kelp forests, fish, crab, sea urchins, anemones, and starfish. Sea Life Tour divers with underwater cameras zoom in for close-ups that you can watch via the video monitor. ✉ *Box 132* ☎ *907/966–2301, 877/966–2301* ⊕ *www.sealifediscoverytours.com.*

WHERE TO EAT

$ ✕ **Little Tokyo.** Sitka probably isn't the first place you expect to find
JAPANESE   Japanese food, but Little Tokyo delivers great rolls and *nigiri*. It's not
fancy, but this small restaurant has a sushi bar where the chefs prepare
all the standards, plus Alaska rolls (with smoked salmon and avocado).
Udon noodle soups are popular on rainy afternoons, and bento-box
dinners—complete with katsu entrées, California rolls, tempura, pot
stickers, miso soup, and salad—hover around $10. ⑤ *Average main:*
$9 ✉ *315 Lincoln St.* ☎ *907/747–5699.*

$$$ ✕ **Ludvig's Bistro.** This remarkably creative eatery used to escape detec-
MEDITERRANEAN   tion by most tourists (much to the pleasure of Sitkans). It's now almost
Fodor's Choice   always packed with food lovers from all corners of the globe anxious
★   to try chef-owner Colette Nelson's food, so be prepared for a wait—
but rest assured that Ludvig's is worth it. The interior evokes an Ital-
ian bistro, with rich yellow walls and copper-topped tables. Seafood
(particularly king salmon and scallops) is the specialty, and organic
ingredients are used whenever possible. You'll also find Caesar salads,
vegetarian specials, Angus filet mignon, and one of the state's best wine
lists. ⑤ *Average main: $25* ✉ *256 Katlian St.* ☎ *907/966–3663* ⊕ *www.*
ludvigsbistro.com ⊗ *Closed mid-Feb.–Apr.*

$$ ✕ **Nugget Restaurant.** Travelers flying out from Sitka head here while
AMERICAN   hoping their jet will make it through the pea-soup fog outside. The set-
ting is standard, and the menu encompasses burgers (15 kinds), sandwiches, tuna melts, salads, steaks, pasta, seafood, and Friday-night
prime rib. There's a big breakfast menu, too, but the real attraction is
the range of homemade pies, which are known throughout Southeast
Alaska. ■ TIP➜ Get a slice à la mode, or buy a whole pie to take with you.
The lemon custard is a local favorite. Reservations are recommended.
⑤ *Average main: $12* ✉ *Sitka Airport Terminal* ☎ *907/966–2480.*

$$ ✕ **Van Winkle & Sons.** This restaurant's somewhat lackluster ambience
SEAFOOD   (Formica tabletops, paper napkins, vinyl swivel-chair seating) doesn't
quite match up to the gorgeous water views and upscale fare but, really,
you won't mind. One of Sitka's largest eateries, it bills itself as "Frontier
Cuisine," which translates to a seafood-heavy menu. But Van Win-
kle also serves pizzas, chicken, and duck. The create-your-own pastas
are excellent (a half order is plenty for normal-size appetites), and the
rich desserts necessitate sharing. There's no elevator to the restaurant's
second-floor location, but a stair lift assists customers with disabili-
ties. The water view is good. ⑤ *Average main: $15* ✉ *205 Harbor Dr.*
☎ *907/747–7652.*

WHERE TO STAY

For expanded hotel reviews, visit Fodors.com.

$$$ ⊞ **Alaska Ocean View Bed & Breakfast.** Carole Denkinger, who runs this
B&B/INN   cozy B&B out of the home she shares with her husband, Bill, is an
★   extremely personable host who enjoys talking about the area and prides
herself on never serving anyone the same breakfast twice. **Pros:** large,
varied breakfasts. **Cons:** only three rooms. **TripAdvisor:** "comfortable,"
"very accommodating," "lap of luxury." ⑤ *Rooms from: $150* ✉ *1101*

Edgecumbe Dr. ☎ *907/747–8310, 888/811–6870* ⊕ *www.sitka-alaska-lodging.com* ⤳ *3 rooms* ⦿ *Breakfast.*

$ **Alaska Swan Lake Bed & Breakfast.** This is one of the best B&Bs in
B&B/INN town, with a quiet, lakeside setting, attractively appointed rooms with
☾ private baths, and friendly owners. **Pros:** quiet, convenient location.
Cons: bathrooms are small. ⑤ *Rooms from: $100* ✉ *206½ Lakeview
Dr.* ☎ *907/747–5746* ⊕ *www.alaskaswanlakebnb.com* ⤳ *4 rooms*
⦿ *Breakfast.*

$$$$ **Baranof Wilderness Lodge.** This cozy fishing lodge is nestled in Warm
ALL-INCLUSIVE Springs Bay, 20 air miles from Sitka on the wild east side of Baranof
Island. **Pros:** rate is all-inclusive from Sitka. **Cons:** rate is expensive in
comparison to similar accommodations. **TripAdvisor:** "nothing better,"
"we all loved it," "an incredible Alaskan experience." ⑤ *Rooms from:
$5050* ☎ *907/738–3597, 800/613–6551* ⊕ *www.flyfishalaska.com* ⤳ *1
room, 7 cabins* ▭ *No credit cards* ⊘ *Closed Oct.–May* ⦿ *All-inclusive.*

$$ **Fairweather Vacation Rentals.** These cozy rental apartments are located
RENTAL downtown close to the harbor. **Pros:** accommodations are private; group
has the entire property; laundry facilities are one block away. **Cons:** few
amenities. ⑤ *Rooms from: $139* ✉ *308 Monastery St.* ☎ *907/747–8601*
⊕ *www.fairweatherdreams.com* ⤳ *3 apartments (1 one-bedroom, 2
studios).*

$$$ **Shee Atiká Totem Square Inn.** On Totem Square in downtown Sitka,
HOTEL this inn is one of the town's better-run outfits. **Pros:** convenient loca-
tion for fishermen; complimentary airport shuttle service, Wi-Fi, and
continental breakfast. **Cons:** rooms without harbor view overlook a
particularly unattractive parking lot. **TripAdvisor:** "nice property,"
"comfy beds," "great location." ⑤ *Rooms from: $204* ✉ *201 Katlian
St.* ☎ *907/747–3693, 866/300–1353* ⊕ *www.totemsquare.com* ⤳ *68
rooms* ⦿ *Breakfast.*

$ **Sitka Hotel.** This noisy but comfortable, old-fashioned downtown
HOTEL hotel was built in 1939. **Pros:** good views from most rooms; decent
price. **Cons:** noisy location; sparse amenities. **TripAdvisor:** "quaint,"
"total immersion in local flavor," "comfortable and clean." ⑤ *Rooms
from: $105* ✉ *118 Lincoln St.* ☎ *907/747–3288, 888/757–3288* ⊕ *www.
sitkahotel.net* ⤳ *60 rooms* ⦿ *No meals.*

$$$ **Westmark Sitka.** One of Sitka's nicest hotels, the Westmark has large
HOTEL rooms, many overlooking Crescent Harbor; the best are the corner
suites. **Pros:** nice views; big rooms. **Cons:** no ferry shuttle; breakfast not
offered. **TripAdvisor:** "great staff," "just like home," "Sitka's finest."
⑤ *Rooms from: $179* ✉ *330 Seward St.* ☎ *907/747–6241, 800/544–
0970 in U.S., 800/999–2570 in Canada* ⊕ *www.westmarkhotels.com/
sitka.php* ⤳ *100 rooms, 3 suites.*

$ **White Sulphur Springs Cabin.** Like many other Forest Service cabins,
RENTAL this Tongass National Forest public-use cabin, 65 miles northwest of
Sitka, sleeps four (bring your own sleeping bags) and has bunk beds,
a woodstove, a table, and an outhouse. **Pros:** good views of Pacific
Ocean; beautiful surroundings. **Cons:** guests must bring own bedding
and cooking utensils; requires boat ride to location. ⑤ *Rooms from:
$35* ✉ *West Chichagof–Yakobi Wilderness Area* ☎ *907/747–6671 infor-
mation, 877/444–6777 reservations* ⊕ *www.recreation.gov* ⤳ *1 cabin.*

Continued on page 159

KEEPERS OF THE DEEP:
A LOOK AT ALASKA'S WHALES

It's unforgettable: a massive, barnacle-encrusted humpback breaches skyward from the placid waters of an Alaskan inlet, shattering the silence with a thundering display of grace, power, and beauty. Welcome to Alaska's coastline.

Alaska's cold, nutrient-rich waters offer a bounty of marine life that's matched by few regions on earth. Eight species of whales frequent the state's near-shore waters, some migrating thousands of miles each year to partake of Alaska's marine buffet. The state's most famous cetaceans (the scientific classification of marine mammals that includes whales, dolphins, and porpoises) are the humpback whale, the gray whale, and the orca (a.k.a. the killer whale).

(top) A breaching humpback (left) An Orca whale

BEST REGIONS TO VIEW WHALES

Whales can be viewed throughout the world; after all, they are migratory animals. But thanks to its pristine environment, diversity of cetacean species, and jaw-dropping beauty, Alaska is perhaps the planet's best whale-watching locale.

From April through October, humpbacks visit many of Alaska's coastal regions, including the Bering Sea, the Aleutian Islands, and Prince William Sound. The **Inside Passage,** though, is the best place to see them: it's home to a migratory population of up to 600 humpbacks. Good bets for whale-viewing include taking a trip on the **Alaska Marine Highway,** spending time in **Glacier Bay National Park,** or taking a day cruise out of any of Southeast's main towns. While most humpbacks return to

Mutually curious!

Hawaiian waters in the winter, some spend the whole year in Southeast Alaska.

Gray whales favor the coastal waters of the Pacific, which terminate in the Bering Sea. Their healthy population—some studies estimate that 30,000 gray whales populate the west coast of North America—make

THE HUMPBACK: Musical, Breaching Giant

Humpbacks' flukes allow them to breach so effectively that they can propel two-thirds of their massive bodies out of the water.

Known for their spectacular breaching and unique whale songs, humpbacks are captivating. Most spend their winters in the balmy waters off the Hawaiian Islands, where females, or sows, give birth. Come springtime, humpbacks set off on a 3,000-mile swim to their Alaskan feeding grounds.

Southeast Alaska is home to one of the world's only groups of bubble-net feeding humpbacks. Bubble-netting is a cooperative hunting technique in which one humpback circles below a school of baitfish while exhaling a "net" of bubbles, causing the fish to gather. Other humpbacks then feed at will from the deliciously dense group of fish.

The Song of the Humpback

All whale species communicate sonically, but the humpback is the most musical. During mating season, males emit haunting, songlike calls that can last for up to 30 minutes at a time. Most scientists attribute the songs to flirtatious, territorial, or competitive behaviors.

QUICK FACTS:

Scientific name:
Megaptera novaeangliae

Length: Up to 50 ft.

Weight: Up to 90,000 pounds (45 tons)

Coloring: Dark blue to black, with barnacles and knobby, lighter-colored flippers

Life span: 30 to 40 years

Reproduction: One calf every 2 to 3 years; calves are generally 12 feet long at birth, weighing up to 2,000 pounds (1 ton)

them relatively easy to spot in the spring and early summer months, especially around **Sitka** and **Kodiak Island** and south of the **Kenai Peninsula**, where numerous whale-watching cruises depart from Seward into **Resurrection Bay.**

Orcas populate nearly all of Alaska's coastal regions. They're most commonly viewed in the **Inside Passage** and **Prince William Sound,** where they reside year-round. A jaunt on the Alaska Marine Highway is one option, but so is a kayaking or day-cruising trip out of **Whittier** to Prince William Sound.

When embarking on a whale-watching excursion, don't forget rain gear, a camera, and binoculars!

Whale Size Chart

The Humpback
50 ft long / 45 tons

The Orca
30 ft long / 9 tons

The Gray
50 ft long / 45 tons

Human
6 ft tall / 0.085 tons

* 1 meter per square

4

IN FOCUS KEEPERS OF THE DEEP

THE GRAY WHALE: Migrating Leviathan

Though the average lifespan of a gray whale is 50 years, one individual was reported to reach 77 years of age—a real old-timer.

While frequenting Alaska during the long days of summer, gray whales tend to stay close to the coastline. They endure the longest migration of any mammal on earth—some travel 14,000 mi each way between Alaska's Bering Sea and their mating grounds in sunny Baja California.

Gray whales are bottom-feeders that stir up sediment on the sea floor, then use their baleen—a comblike collection of long, stiff hairs inside their mouths—to filter out sediment and trap small crustaceans and tube worms.

Their predilection for near-shore regions, coupled with their easygoing demeanor—some "friendly" gray whales have even been known to approach small tour boats—cements their spot on the short list of Alaska's favorite cetacean celebrities. (Gray whales aren't always in such amicable spirits: whalers dubbed mother gray whales "devilfish" for the fierce manner in which they protected their young.)

QUICK FACTS:

Scientific name:
Eschrichtius robustus

Length: Up to 50 ft.

Weight: Up to 90,000 pounds (45 tons)

Coloring: Gray and white, usually splotched with lighter growths and barnacles

Life span: 50 years

Reproduction: One calf every 2 years; calves are generally 15 feet long at birth, weighing up to 1,500 pounds (3/4 ton)

AN AGE-OLD CONNECTION

Nearly every major Native group in Alaska has relied on whales for some portion of its diet. The Inupiaq and Yup'ik counted on whales for blubber, oil, meat, and intestines to survive. Aleuts used whale bones to build their semisubterranean homes. Even the Tlingit, for whom food was perennially abundant, considered a beached whale a bounty.

Subsistence whaling lives on in Alaska: although gray-whale hunting was banned in 1996, the Eskimo Whaling Commission permits the state's Native populations to harvest 50 bowhead whales every year.

Other Alaskan whale species:
Bowhead, northern right, minke, fin, and beluga whales also inhabit Alaskan waters.

barnacles

BARNACLES These ragged squatters of the sea live on several species of whales, including humpbacks and gray whales. They're conspicuously absent from smaller marine mammals, such as orcas, dolphins, and porpoises. The reason? Speed. Scientists theorize that barnacles are only able to colonize the slowest-swimming cetacean species, leaving the faster swimmers free from their unwanted drag.

THE ORCA: Conspicuous, Curious Cetacean

Why the name killer whale? Perhaps for this animal's skilled and fearsome hunting techniques, which are sometimes used on other, often larger, cetaceans.

Perhaps the most recognizable of all the region's marine mammals, orcas (also called killer whales) are playful, inquisitive, and intelligent whales that reside in Alaskan waters year-round. Orcas travel in multigenerational family groups known as pods, which practice cooperative hunting techniques.

Orcas are smaller than grays and humpbacks, and their 17-month gestation period is the longest of any cetacean. They are identified by their white-and-black markings, as well as by the knifelike shape of their dorsal fins, which, in the case of mature males, can reach 6 feet in height.

Pods generally adhere to one of three common classifications: **residents,** which occupy inshore waters and feed primarily on fish; **transients,** which occupy larger ranges and hunt sea lions, squid, sharks, fish, and whales; and **offshores,** about which little is known.

QUICK FACTS:

Scientific name:
Orcinus orca

Length: Up to 30 ft.

Weight: Up to 18,000 pounds (9 tons)

Coloring: Smooth, shiny black skin with white eye patches and chin and white belly markings

Life span: 30 to 50 years

Reproduction: One calf every 3 to 5 years; calves are generally 6 feet long at birth, weighing up to 400 pounds (0.2 ton)

NIGHTLIFE AND THE ARTS

BARS

Pioneer Bar. As far as the locals are concerned, a spot in one of the limited green-and-white-vinyl booths at Pioneer Bar, across from the harbor, is a fine destination. It's vintage Alaska, with hundreds of pictures of local fishing boats, rough-hewn locals clad in Carhartts and XtraTuf boots, occasional live music, and pool tables. Regulars, mostly local fishermen, swear by the submarine sandwiches and hot dogs. ⊠ *212 Katlian St.* ☎ *907/747–3456.*

DANCE

★ **New Archangel Dancers of Sitka.** The New Archangel Dancers of Sitka is an all-female troupe of local Sitka women dedicated to preserving Alaska's Russian history and has performed since 1969. Seasonal performances showcase authentic dances from Russia and the surrounding regions. Tickets are $10 and are sold a half-hour before performances. Performances are 30 minutes long and take place in Harrigan Centennial Hall. ⊠ *208 Smith St.* ⊕ *www.newarchangeldancers.com.*

Sheet'ka Kwaan Naa Kahidi Dancers. The dancers perform Tlingit dances in full Native regalia at the Sheet'ka Kwaan Naa Kahidi community house on Katlian Street. The dance schedule is listed on the board at Harrigan Centennial Hall. ⊠ *204 Katlian St.* ☎ *907/747–7290, 888/270–8687* ⊕ *www.sitkatours.com/dance.html.*

FESTIVALS

Sitka Summer Music Festival. Southeast Alaska's major chamber-music festival is the annual Sitka Summer Music Festival, a three-week June celebration of concerts and special events that attracts musicians from as far away as Europe and Asia. Most performances are held in Harrigan Centennial Hall. ⊠ *104 Jeff Davis St.* ☎ *907/277–4852, 907/747–6774* ⊕ *www.sitkamusicfestival.org.*

Sitka WhaleFest. The festival is held around town in early November, when the whales are plentiful (as many as 80) and tourists are not. ⊠ *834 Lincoln St., Suite 22* ☎ *907/747–7964* ⊕ *www.sitkawhalefest.org.*

SHOPPING

ART GALLERIES

Fairweather Gallery and Gifts. This shop sells tops, dresses, and other clothing featuring hand-painted and printed Alaska-inspired designs, as well works by local artists. ⊠ *209 Lincoln St.* ☎ *907/747–8677* ⊕ *www.fairweatherprints.com.*

Fishermen's Eye Fine Art Gallery. This tasteful downtown gallery prides itself on its vibrant collection of made-in-Sitka art, including silver jewelry, Native masks, and carved bowls. ⊠ *239 Lincoln St.* ☎ *907/747–6080* ⊕ *www.fishermenseye.com.*

Sitka Rose Gallery. Housed within a Victorian-style 1895 home next to the Bishop's House, Sitka Rose Gallery is the town's most charming shop, and features Alaskan paintings, sculptures, Native art, and jewelry. ⊠ *419 Lincoln St.* ☎ *907/747–3030, 888/236–1536* ⊕ *www. sitkarosegallery.com.*

BOOKSTORE

Old Harbor Books. View an impressive collection of Alaska titles and speak with knowledgeable staff at Old Harbor Books. ⊠ *201 Lincoln St.* ☎ *907/747–8808* ⊕ *www.oldharborbooks.net.*

Backdoor Café. Directly behind the bookstore is a cozy left-wing hangout called the Backdoor Café, with excellent espresso and fresh-baked pastries. ⊠ *104 Barracks St.* ☎ *907/747–8856.*

GIFTS

Fresh Fish Company. This company sells and ships fresh locally caught salmon, halibut, and shrimp. ⊠ *411 DeGroff St.* ☎ *907/747–5565, 888/747–5565 outside Alaska* ⊕ *www.akfreshfishinc.com.*

WinterSong Soap Company. Behind the Sitka Rose Gallery, WinterSong Soap Company sells colorful and scented soaps that are handcrafted on the premises. ⊠ *321 Lincoln St.* ☎ *907/747–8949, 888/819–8949* ⊕ *www.wintersongsoap.com.*

JUNEAU

100 miles northeast of Sitka.

Juneau, Alaska's capital and third-largest city, is on the North American mainland but can't be reached by road. The city owes its origins to two colorful sourdoughs (Alaskan pioneers)—Joe Juneau and Richard Harris—and to a Tlingit chief named Kowee, who led the two men to rich reserves of gold at Snow Slide Gulch, the drainage of Gold Creek around which the town was eventually built. That was in 1880, and shortly thereafter a modest stampede resulted in the formation of a mining camp, which quickly grew to become the Alaska district government capital in 1906. The city may well have continued under its original appellation—Harrisburg, after Richard Harris—were it not for Joe Juneau's political jockeying at a miner's meeting in 1881.

For some 60 years after Juneau's founding gold was the mainstay of the economy. In its heyday the AJ (for Alaska Juneau) Gold Mine was the biggest low-grade ore mine in the world. It was not until World War II, when the government decided it needed Juneau's manpower for the war effort, that the AJ and other mines in the area ceased operations. After the war mining failed to start up again, and government became the city's principal employer. Juneau's mines leave a rich legacy, though: before it closed, the AJ Gold Mine alone produced more than $80 million in gold.

Perhaps because of its colorful history, Juneau is full of contrasts. Its dramatic hillside location and historic downtown buildings provide a frontier feeling, but the city's cosmopolitan nature comes through in fine museums, noteworthy restaurants, and a literate and outdoorsy populace. Here you can enjoy the Mt. Roberts Tramway, plenty of densely forested wilderness areas, quiet bays for sea kayaking, and even a famous drive-up glacier.

Along with the Alaska State Museum and Mt. Roberts Tramway, make time for a tour to Mendenhall Glacier and the Macaulay Salmon Hatchery. Douglas (which at one point was a bigger outpost than Juneau) is across the Gastineau Channel to the west. For goings-on, pick up the *Juneau Empire* (⊕ *www.juneauempire.com*), which keeps tabs on state politics, business, sports, and local news.

GETTING HERE AND AROUND

Juneau is an obligatory stop on the Inside Passage cruise and ferry circuit. Hence, the town has an overabundance of visitors in midsummer. **Alaska Airlines** also flies here. Downtown Juneau is compact enough so that most of its main attractions are within walking distance of one another. Note, however, that the city is very hilly, so your legs will get a real workout. Look for the 20 signs around downtown that detail Juneau's fascinating history.

ESSENTIALS

Airline Contact **Alaska Airlines** ☎ *800/252–7522* ⊕ *www.alaskaair.com.*

Internet **Heritage Coffee Company** ✉ *174 S. Franklin St.* ☎ *907/586–1087* ⊕ *www.heritagecoffee.com* ✉ *216 2nd St.* ☎ *907/586–1752.* **Juneau Public Library** ✉ *292 Marine Way* ☎ *907/586–5249* ⊕ *www.juneau.org/library.*

Medical Assistance **Bartlett Regional Hospital** ✉ *3260 Hospital Dr.* ☎ *907/586–2611* ⊕ *www.bartletthospital.org.*

Pharmacy **Juneau Drug Co.** ✉ *202 Front St.* ☎ *907/586–1233* ✉ *631 W. Willoughby Ave.* ☎ *907/586–2012.* **Ron's Apothecary Shoppe** ✉ *9101 Mendenhall Mall Rd., in Mendenhall Mall next to Super Bear market* ☎ *907/789–0458* ⊕ *www.ronsapothecary.com.*

Post Office and Shipping **U.S. Postal Service** ✉ *709 W. 9th St.* ☎ *907/586–7987* ⊕ *www.usps.gov* ✉ *9491 Vintage Blvd.* ✉ *145 S. Franklin* ☎ *907/586–8335.* **edEx** ✉ *9203 Bonnett Way* ☎ *800/463–3339* ⊕ *www.fedex.com.* **UPS** ✉ *1900 Renshaw Way* ☎ *800/742–5877* ⊕ *www.ups.com.*

Visitor Information **Alaska Department of Fish & Game** ☎ *907/465–4180 sportfishing seasons and regulations, 907/465–2376 license information* ⊕ *www.adfg.alaska.gov.* **Alaska Division of Parks** ✉ *400 Willoughby Ave.* ☎ *907/465–4563* ⊕ *www.alaskastateparks.org.* **Juneau Convention and Visitors Bureau** ✉ *800 Glacier Ave., Suite 201* ☎ *907/586–2201, 888/581–2201* ⊕ *www.traveljuneau.com.*

EXPLORING

TOP ATTRACTIONS

★ **Alaska State Museum.** This is one of Alaska's finest museums. Those interested in Native cultures will enjoy examining the 38-foot walrus-hide *umiak* (an open, skin-covered Inupiaq boat). Natural-history exhibits include preserved brown bears and a two-story-high eagle-nesting tree. Russian-American and gold-rush displays and contemporary art complete the collection. ■**TIP**➜ Be sure to visit the gift shop (run by the Friends of the Alaska State Museum) and its extraordinary selection of Native art, including baskets, carvings, and masks. ✉ *395 Whittier St.*

☎ 907/465–2901 ⊕ *www.museums.state.ak.us* ☞ *$7 mid-May–mid-Sept., $3 mid-Sept.–mid-May* ☉ *Mid-May–mid-Sept., daily 8:30–5:30; mid-Sept.–mid-May, Tues.–Sat. 10–4.*

★ **Mt. Roberts Tramway.** One of Southeast Alaska's most popular tourist
☺ attractions, this tram whisks you from the cruise terminal 1,800 feet
up the side of Mt. Roberts. After the six-minute ride you can take in a
film on the history and legends of the Tlingits, visit the nature center,
go for an alpine walk on hiking trails (including the 5-mile round-trip
hike to Mt. Roberts's 3,819-foot summit), purchase Native crafts, or
enjoy a meal while savoring mountain views. A local company leads
guided wilderness hikes from the summit, and the bar serves locally
brewed beers. ☎ 907/463–3412, 888/461–8726 ⊕ *www.goldbelttours.
com/mount-roberts-tramway* ☞ *$29* ☉ *May–Sept., Mon. 12–9, Tues.–
Sun. 8 am–9 pm.*

South Franklin Street. The buildings on South Franklin Street (and neighboring Front Street), among the oldest and most inviting structures in
the city, house curio and crafts shops, snack shops, and a salmon shop.
Many reflect the architecture of the 1920s and '30s. When the small
Alaskan Hotel opened in 1913, Juneau was home to 30 saloons; the
Alaskan gives today's visitors the most authentic glimpse of the town's
whiskey-rich history. The barroom's massive, mirrored oak back bar is

WALKING AROUND JUNEAU

The most common starting spot is **Marine Park,** situated right along the cruise-ship dock. For an introduction to Alaska's human and natural history, head to the engaging **Alaska State Museum.** From here, circle back along Willoughby Avenue to the **State Office Building.** Catch the elevator to the eighth-floor atrium, which features an observation deck with vistas across the Gastineau Channel. The snug but cheery **Juneau-Douglas City Museum,** a local treasure that's slightly off the beaten path, sits a short distance away at 4th and Main streets. The looming, banklike building across the street is the **Alaska State Capitol.** For a far more attractive example of governmental architecture, walk past the **Governor's Mansion,** a few minutes away on Calhoun Street. If you have the time and energy, you may want to continue along Calhoun, across the Gold Creek Bridge, and then down along 12th Street to the quiet **Evergreen Cemetery,** where town fathers Joe Juneau and Richard Harris, as well as Chief Kowee, are buried.

Back in downtown, peruse the historic buildings and busy shops of downtown Juneau, particularly those along **South Franklin Street.** Check out the Alaskan Hotel, the Alaska Steam Laundry Building, and the Senate Building before dipping inside the terminally crowded **Red Dog Saloon** at the intersection of South Franklin Street and Admiralty Way. Try a microbrew, and then continue down the street to the **Mt. Roberts Tramway,** a popular way to reach alpine country for a hike overlooking Juneau and the Gastineau Channel.

To cover downtown Juneau's many interesting sights, you should allow at least three or four hours for exploring. Add at least another hour if you're a museum fan, or if you plan to ride the Mt. Roberts Tramway.

accented by Tiffany lights and panels. Topped by a wood-shingled turret, the 1901 **Alaska Steam Laundry Building** now houses a coffeehouse and other stores. The **Senate Building,** another of South Franklin's treasured landmarks, is across the street. ⊠ *South Franklin St.*

WORTH NOTING

Alaska State Capitol. Completed in 1931 and remodeled in 2006, this rather unassuming building houses the governor's office and hosts state legislature meetings in winter, placing it at the epicenter of Alaska's increasingly animated political discourse. Historical photos line the upstairs walls. Feel free to stroll right in. ■TIP➔ **You can pick up a self-guided tour brochure as you enter.** Complimentary guided tours available daily mid-May through mid-Sept. ⊠ *Corner of Seward and 4th Sts.* ☎ *907/465–4648* ⊕ *w3.legis.state.ak.us/misc/capitol.php.*

Evergreen Cemetery. Many Juneau pioneers, including Joe Juneau and Richard Harris, are buried here. Juneau (1836–99), a Canadian by birth, died in Dawson City, Yukon, but his body was returned to the city that bears his name. Harris (1833–1907), whose name can be found on downtown's Harris Street, died here. A meandering gravel path leads through the graveyard, and at the end of it is the monument commemorating the cremation spot of Chief Kowee. ⊠ *Martin and Seater Sts..*

Governor's Mansion. Completed in 1912, this stately colonial-style home overlooks downtown Juneau. With 14,400 square feet, 6 bedrooms, and 10 bathrooms, it's no miner's cabin. Out front is a totem pole that tells three tales: the history of man, the cause of ocean tides, and the origin of Alaska's ubiquitous mosquitoes. Unfortunately, tours of the residence are not permitted. ⊠ *716 Calhoun Ave..*

Ⓒ **Juneau-Douglas City Museum.** Among the exhibits interpreting local mining and Tlingit history are an Assay Lab diorama, a reconstructed Tlingit fish trap and video of excavation, historic photos, and pioneer artifacts, including a century-old store and kitchen. Digital story kiosks highlight Alaska's government, civil rights in Alaska, Alaska's quest for statehood, and cultures of Juneau. Youngsters will appreciate the hands-on room, where they can try on clothes similar to ones worn by the miners or look at gold-rush stereoscopes. Guided historic walking tours are offered May through September. ⊠ *114 4th St.* ☎ *907/586-3572* ⊕ *www.juneau.org/parksrec/museum* ☕ *$6 May–Sept., free Oct.–Apr.* ☻ *May and June, weekdays 9–6; July–Sept., weekdays 9–6, weekends 10–5; Oct.–Apr., Tues.–Sat. 10–4.*

OFF THE
BEATEN
PATH

Last Chance Mining Museum. A 1½-mile hike or taxi ride behind town, this small museum is housed in the former compressor building of Juneau's historic AJ Gold Mine. The collection includes old mining tools, railcars, minerals, and a 3-D map of the ore body. If you have time, and didn't arrive on foot, meander down **Basin Road** back toward town. Unlike most of Juneau, Basin Road is flat and relatively quiet. The surrounding country is steep and wooded, with trails leading in all directions, including one to the summit of Mt. Juneau. At the base of the Perseverance Trail, not far from the museum, you can see the boarded-up opening to an old mining tunnel; even from a safe distance you can feel a chilly breeze wafting through the cracks. ⊠ *1001 Basin Rd.* ☎ *907/586–5338* ⊕ *www.traveljuneau.com/cms/d/juneau_museums. php* ☕ *$4* ☻ *Mid-May–mid-Sept., daily 9:30–12:30 and 3:30–6:30.*

Marine Park. On the dock where the cruise ships "tie up" is a little urban oasis with benches, shade trees, and shelter. It's a great place to enjoy an outdoor meal from one of Juneau's street vendors, and on Friday evenings in summer it features live performances by Juneau musicians. A visitor kiosk is staffed according to cruise-ship schedules. ⊠ *Marine Way* ⊕ *www.juneau.org/parkrec/facilities/downtown.php.*

Red Dog Saloon. The frontierish quarters of the Red Dog have housed an infamous Juneau watering hole since 1890. Nearly every conceivable surface in this two-story bar is cluttered with graffiti, business cards, and memorabilia, including a pistol that reputedly belonged to Wyatt Earp, who failed to reclaim the piece after checking it in at the U.S. Marshall's office on June 27, 1900. The saloon's food menu includes halibut, reindeer sausage, potato skins, burgers, and locally brewed Alaskan beers. A little atmospheric sawdust covers the floor as well. Musicians pump out ragtime piano tunes when cruise ships are docked. ⊠ *278 S. Franklin St.* ☎ *907/463–3658* ⊕ *www.reddogsaloon.com.*

St. Nicholas Russian Orthodox Church. It's the oldest Russian church in Southeast Alaska. Built in 1894 by newly baptized Orthodox Natives

Mendenhall Glacier, Juneau. Kayak along this receding glacier just 13 miles outside of the city.

and Siberian gold miners, the church was refurbished in the late 1970s and is a national historic landmark. The quaint, onion-dome white-and-blue church has services sung in Slavonic, English, and Tlingit on Saturday and Sunday. ✉ *326 5th St.* ☎ *907/586–1023* ⊕ *www. stnicholasjuneau.org.*

State Office Building. The building's sprawling eighth-floor patio, which faces the Gastineau Channel and Douglas Island, is a popular lunch destination for state workers and assorted residents. On most Fridays at noon, concerts inside the four-story atrium feature a grand old theater pipe organ, a veteran of the silent-movie era. Also here are the historic old witch totem pole; the Alaska State Library, with a fine collection of historical photos; and computers with public Internet access. If you're having trouble finding the building, just ask for directions to the "S.O.B."—the locals are fond of acronyms. ✉ *4th and Calhoun Sts.*

Wickersham State Historical Site. At the top of the hill behind the capitol, on a rise sometimes known as "Chicken Ridge," stands the former residence of James Wickersham, pioneer judge, delegate to Congress, prolific author, and gutsy outdoorsman. The white New England–style home, constructed in 1898, contains memorabilia from the judge's travels throughout Alaska—from rare Native basketry and ivory carvings to historic photos and a Chickering grand piano that came "'round the Horn" to Alaska in the 1870s. The tour provides a glimpse into the life of this dynamic man. ✉ *213 7th St.* ☎ *907/586–9001* ⊕ *www. dnr.alaska.gov/parks/units/wickrshm.htm* ▣ *Free* ☉ *Mid-May–Sept., Sun.–Fri. 10–4; Sat. by appointment.*

OUTDOOR ACTIVITIES AND GUIDED TOURS

BIKING

Driftwood Lodge. Drop by the Juneau Convention & Visitors Bureau kiosk at Marine Park for details on local trails open to bikes. Nearby is Driftwood Lodge, which has basic bikes for rent. ⊠ *435 Willoughby Ave.* ☎ *907/586–2280* ⊕ *www.driftwoodalaska.com.*

BOATING, CANOEING, AND KAYAKING

Above & Beyond Alaska. In the Juneau area, Above & Beyond Alaska guides day and overnight camping, ice climbing, Mendenhall Glacier trips, and sea-kayaking trips. ⊠ *Auke Bay* ☎ *907/364–2333* ⊕ *www. beyondak.com.*

★ **Adventure Bound Alaska.** All-day trips to Sawyer Glacier within Tracy Arm in summer are available from Adventure Bound Alaska. ⊠ *76 Egan Dr.* ☎ *907/463–2509, 800/228–3875* ⊕ *www.adventureboundalaska.com.*

Alaska Boat and Kayak Rental. Rent kayaks, canoes, and camping equipment at the Auke Bay boat harbor 12 miles north of Juneau. The company also provides water-taxi services for kayakers looking to access remote paddling terrain. ⊠ *11521 Glacier Hwy.* ☎ *907/789–6886* ⊕ *www.juneaukayak.com.*

Alaska Discovery. Alaska Discovery, operated by Mountain Travel Sobek, leads 9- and 12-day trips down the Tatshenshini and Alsek rivers. ☎ *510/594–6000, 800/586–1911.*

Alaska Travel Adventures. Alaska Travel Adventures leads Mendenhall River floats and numerous other tours throughout the Juneau area. ☎ *800/323–5757, 907/789–0052 outside Alaska* ⊕ *www. bestofalaskatravel.com.*

Allen Marine Tours. Family-owned Allen Marine Tours offers catamaran trips to Tracy Arm fjord, whale-watching adventures out of Auke Bay, and several land-and-water combination tours. ⊠ *Juneau* ☎ *907/789–0081, 888/289–0081* ⊕ *www.allenmarinetours.com.*

Juneau Steamboat Company. Scenic tours of the Gastineau Channel aboard an authentic wood-fired steam launch—similar to those used around Juneau in the late 1800s and early 1900s—come with entertaining narration about the historic mines of the area. ⊠ *3328 Fritz Cove Rd.* ☎ *907/723–0372* ⊕ *www.juneausteamboat.com.*

CLIMBING GYM

Rock Dump. If it's pouring down rain—and in Juneau, it often is—head south of town to the Rock Dump. The Dump has climbing walls for all abilities from beginner to expert; day passes are $13. ⊠ *1310 Eastaugh Way* ☎ *907/586–4982* ⊕ *www.rockdump.com.*

CROSS-COUNTRY SKIING

Foggy Mountain Shop. Find groomed cross-country ski trails near the Eaglecrest Ski Area and at Mendenhall Campground in the winter. You can rent skis and get advice about touring the trails and ridges around town from Foggy Mountain Shop. The shop also outfits hikers and climbers in summer. ⊠ *134 N. Franklin St.* ☎ *907/586–6780* ⊕ *www. foggymountainshop.com.*

Parks and Recreation Department. In the winter, the Parks and Recreation Department sponsors a group ski and snowshoe outing each Wednesday and Saturday when there's sufficient snow. Hikes are also offered in the summer. ✉ *155 S. Seward St.* ☎ *907/586–5226, 907/586–0428 24-hr information* ⊕ *www.juneau.org/parksrec.*

DOWNHILL SKIING

Eaglecrest. Southeast Alaska's only downhill ski area, Eaglecrest, is on Douglas Island, 30 minutes from downtown Juneau. The resort typically offers late-November to mid-April skiing and snowboarding on 620 acres of well-groomed and off-piste terrain. Amenities include four double chairlifts, cross-country trails, a beginner's platter pull, a ski school, a ski-rental shop, a cafeteria, and a tri-level day lodge. Enjoy the northern lights while you night ski from January through mid-March. ✉ *3000 Fish Creek Rd.* ☎ *907/790–2000, 907/586–5330 recorded ski information* ⊕ *www.juneau.org/eaglecrest.*

FISHING

Alaska Trophy Fishing. Sportfishing is an exceedingly popular activity in the Juneau area, and many charter boats depart from local harbors. Alaska Trophy Fishing offers tailor-made fishing vacations and charters. ☎ *907/321–5859, 866/934–7466* ⊕ *www.alaskatrophyfishing.com.*

Juneau Sportfishing & Sightseeing. Take a fishing trip aboard a luxury boat with Juneau Sportfishing & Sightseeing. ✉ *2 Marine Way* ☎ *907/586–1887* ⊕ *www.juneausportfishing.com.*

Juneau Convention and Visitors Bureau. The website and office for the Juneau Convention and Visitors Bureau has a complete list of operators and several companies that lead whale-watching trips from Juneau. ✉ *800 Glacier Ave., Suite 201* ☎ *907/586–2201, 888/581–2201* ⊕ *www.traveljuneau.com.*

FLIGHTSEEING

Several local companies operate helicopter flightseeing trips to the spectacular glaciers flowing from Juneau Icefield. Most have booths along the downtown cruise-ship dock. All include a touchdown on a glacier, providing guests of almost all ages and abilities a chance to romp on these rivers of ice. Some also lead trips that include a dogsled ride on the glacier, an increasingly popular tourist pastime. Helicopter tours in Juneau have a controversial history due to noise complaints from residents. Note that although we recommend the best companies, even some of the most experienced pilots have had accidents; always ask a carrier about its recent safety record before booking a trip.

Coastal Helicopters. These helicopters land on several glaciers within the Juneau Icefield. ✉ *8995 Yandukin Dr.* ☎ *907/789–5600, 800/789–5610* ⊕ *www.coastalhelicopters.com.*

ERA Helicopters. Flying out of Douglas, ERA Helicopters has a fully narrated one-hour trip that includes landing on the Norris or Taku glacier. ✉ *6910 N. Douglas Hwy.* ☎ *907/586–2030, 800/843–1947* ⊕ *www.eraflightseeing.com.*

NorthStar Trekking. No experience is necessary at NorthStar Trekking, which has three levels of excellent glacier hikes. The lowest level includes a one-hour interpretive walk while the highest consists of a four-hour hike that includes the chance to practice basic climbing and rope techniques. ✉ *1910 Renshaw Way* ☎ *907/790–4530* ⊕ *www.northstar trekking.com.*

Temsco Helicopters. The self-proclaimed pioneers of Alaska glacier helicopter touring, Temsco Helicopters offers glacier tours, dogsled adventures, and year-round flightseeing. ✉ *1650 Maplesden Way* ☎ *907/789–9501, 877/789–9501* ⊕ *www.temscoair.com.*

Ward Air. Take flightseeing trips to Glacier Bay, the Juneau Icefield, Tracy Arm, and Pack Creek with Ward Air. ✉ *8991 Yandukin Dr.* ☎ *907/789–9150, 800/478–9150* ⊕ *www.wardair.com.*

★ **Wings Airways and Taku Glacier Lodge.** This Juneau-based company specializes in tours of the surrounding ice fields and the Taku Flight & Feast ride, on which a salmon feast awaits you at a classic Alaskan cabin, complete with glacier views—one of the best day trips out of the state capital. ✉ *2 Marine Way, Suite 175* ☎ *907/586–6275* ⊕ *www. wingsairways.com.*

GOLD PANNING

Alaska Travel Adventures. Gold panning is fun, especially for children, and Juneau is one of Southeast's best-known gold-panning towns. Sometimes you actually discover a few flecks of the precious metal in the bottom of your pan. You can buy a pan at almost any Alaska hardware or sporting-goods store. Alaska Travel Adventures has gold-panning tours near the famous Alaska-Juneau Mine. ☎ *800/323–5757, 907/789–0052 outside Alaska* ⊕ *www.bestofalaskatravel.com.*

GOLF

Mendenhall Golf Course. Juneau's par-3, 9-hole Mendenhall Golf Course has a modest layout, but with views that any exclusive private course would die for. Club rentals are available. ✉ *2101 Industrial Blvd.* ☎ *907/789–1221* ⊕ *home.gci.net/~hakari/mendenhall_golf/golf.html.*

HIKING

Gastineau Guiding. This company leads a variety of hikes in the Juneau area. Especially popular are the walks from the top of the tram on Mt. Roberts. ✉ *1330 Eastaugh Way, Suite 2* ☎ *907/586–8231* ⊕ *www. stepintoalaska.com.*

Parks and Recreation Department. In Juneau, the Parks and Recreation Department sponsors a group hike every Wednesday morning and an additional hike on Saturday in the summer. ✉ *155 S. Seward St.*

☎ *907/586–5226, 907/586–0428*
24-hr information ⊕ *www.juneau.*
org/parkrec/hike.

U.S. Forest Service. Hikers can contact the U.S. Forest Service for trail books and maps. ✉ *8510 Mendenhall Loop Rd. (Juneau Ranger District office)* ☎ *907/586–8790.*

SIGHTSEEING AND GLACIERS

AJ Gold Mine. Former miners lead three-hour tours of the historic AJ Gold Mine south of Juneau. The tour includes a gold-panning demonstration and time in the old tunnels that lace the mountains. Mine tours depart from downtown by bus. ✉ *Sheep Creek Mine Rd.* ☎ *907/463–5017* ⊕ *www.traveljuneau.com/listings.*

Alaska Coach Tours. Alaska Coach Tours operates the Historic Juneau Trolley, providing a 45-minute tour of Alaska's capital city. ☎ *907/586–7433* ⊕ *www.alaskacoachtours.com.*

Juneau Convention and Visitors Bureau. The Juneau Convention and Visitors Bureau has a list of companies that provide tours to Mendenhall Glacier, and others that provide boat trips to Tracy Arm's Sawyer Glacier, about 50 miles southeast of town. ✉ *800 Glacier Ave., Suite 201* ☎ *907/586–2201, 888/581–2201* ⊕ *www.traveljuneau.com.*

Mighty Great Trips. The company leads guided bus tours that include a visit to Mendenhall Glacier as well as helicopter tours, river rafting, and whale-watching. ☎ *907/789–5460* ⊕ *www.mightygreattrips.com.*

WHALE-WATCHING

Alaska Whale Watching. The company offers small-group excursions (up to 12 guests) aboard a luxury yacht with an onboard naturalist as well as a whale-watching–fishing combination tour, which is popular with multigenerational groups. ☎ *907/321–5859, 888/432–6722* ⊕ *www.akwhalewatching.com.*

Juneau Sportfishing & Sightseeing. Several companies lead whale-watching trips from Juneau. Juneau Sportfishing & Sightseeing has been around for many years, and its boats carry a maximum of six passengers, providing a personalized trip. ☎ *907/586–1887* ⊕ *www.juneausportfishing.com.*

★ **Orca Enterprises (with Captain Larry).** Take whale-watching tours via jet boats designed for comfort and speed with Orca Enterprises (with Captain Larry). The operator boasts a whale-sighting success rate of 99.9% between May 1 and October 15. ✉ *495 South Franklin St.* ☎ *907/789–6801, 888/733–6722* ⊕ *www.alaskawhalewatching.com.*

Fodor's Choice **Weather Permitting Alaska.** Take small-boat luxury whale-watching trips
★ that last four hours, including van travel, with Weather Permitting Alaska. Visitors get plenty of time to view whales and to look for other animals, including orcas, bears, sea lions, eagles, and porpoises, all while enjoying dramatic scenery. There are never more than six

4

customers on a trip, making this one of the most flexible, intimate, and comprehensive whale-watches anywhere. The boat is stable and roomy. All trips include generous snacks featuring shrimp or salmon and homemade brownies along with nonalcoholic beverages. There is a money-back guarantee for whale viewing. The boat captain is a certified Wilderness First Aid Responder and is certified in swift water rescue and proficiency in survival craft. ⊠ *19400 Beardsley Way* ☏ *907/209–4221* ⊕ *www.weatherpermittingalaska.com.*

WHERE TO EAT

$ ✕ **Douglas Café.** In the heart of quiet Douglas, across the bridge and a
AMERICAN couple of miles from downtown Juneau, this family eatery has Formica tables and a menu that includes omelets, sandwiches, kids' favorites, and a bundle of different kinds of burgers, which are often cited as the best in the city. It's a good choice for those seeking an alternative to downtown Juneau's occasional midsummer crowds. $ *Average main: $11* ⊠ *916 3rd St., Douglas* ☏ *907/364–3307* ⊘ *Closed Mon.*

$$$ ✕ **Gold Creek Salmon Bake.** Trees, mountains, and the rushing water of
SEAFOOD Salmon Creek surround the comfortable, canopy-covered benches and tables at this authentic salmon bake. Fresh-caught salmon is cooked over an alder fire and served with a succulent sauce. For $42 there are all-you-can-eat salmon, pasta, and chicken along with baked beans, rice pilaf, salad bar, corn bread, and blueberry cake. Wine and beer are extra. After dinner you can pan for gold in the stream, wander up the hill to explore the remains of the Wagner gold mine, or roast marshmallows over the fire. A round-trip bus ride from downtown is included. $ *Average main: $42* ⊠ *1061 Salmon Lane Rd.* ☏ *907/789–0052, 800/323–5757* ⊘ *Closed Oct.–Apr.*

$$ ✕ **The Hangar on the Wharf.** Crowded with locals and travelers, the Han-
ECLECTIC gar occupies the building where Alaska Airlines started business. Flight-theme puns dominate the menu (i.e., "Pre-flight Snacks" and the "Plane Caesar"), but the comfortably worn wood and vintage airplane photos create a casual dining experience that outweighs the kitsch. Every seat has views of the Gastineau Channel and Douglas Island. On warm days, outdoor seating is offered. This Juneau hotspot makes a wide selection of entrées, including locally caught halibut and salmon, filet mignon, great burgers, and daily specials. The Hangar serves more than 100 beers, including a few dozen on tap. On Friday and Saturday nights jazz or rock bands take the stage. If you've have had enough salmon, try the prime rib, which the Hangar is known for. $ *Average main: $18* ⊠ *2 Marine Way, Merchants Wharf Mall* ☏ *907/586–5018* ⊕ *www.hangaronthewharf.com.*

$ ✕ **Heritage Coffee Company.** Juneau's favorite coffee shop is a down-
CAFÉ town institution, with locally roasted coffees, gelato, fresh pastries, and all sorts of specialty drinks. ■ **TIP→** The window-front bar is good for people-watching while you sip a chai latte. The same folks also operate several other coffee outposts, including the **Glacier Cafe** in Mendenhall Valley, which boasts a bigger menu that includes breakfast burritos and omelets, along with lunchtime paninis, wraps, soups, salads, and

burgers, plus various vegetarian dishes. $ *Average main: $3* ✉ *174 S. Franklin St.* ☎ *907/586–1087* ⊕ *www.heritagecoffee.com* ☾ *No dinner.*

$$
PIZZA
✗**Island Pub.** The Island Pub in Douglas has fast service, views of the Gastineau Channel, a full bar, occasional live music, and good times, making it one of the area's coolest restaurants. There are salads, sandwiches, and wraps, but the real draw is the pizza: thin, 13-inch focaccia crusts are prepared fresh daily, topped with creative ingredients, and baked in a copper wood-fired oven. Customers are encouraged to build their own pizzas, and the best of their creations end up on the menu. (An unexpected but excellent pizza topping: pine nuts.) The menu is therefore in a state of constant flux. If you've got room, try one of the chef's dessert pizzas—bizarre, but surprisingly good. $ *Average main: $10* ✉ *1102 2nd St., Douglas* ☎ *907/364–1595* ⊕ *www.theislandpub.com.*

$
VEGETARIAN
✗**Rainbow Foods.** This crunchy natural foods market is a popular lunch-break destination for downtown workers. Organic produce, coconut-milk ice cream, and vitamin supplements fill the shelves, but the real attraction is the weekday buffet, with various hot entrées, salads, soups, and deep-dish pizzas. Arrive before 11 am for the best choices. Self-serve coffee and freshly baked breads are available, along with a few inside tables. $ *Average main: $10* ✉ *224 4th St.* ☎ *907/586–6476* ⊕ *www.rainbow-foods.org.*

$
CAFÉ
✗**The Rookery Cafe.** From fresh-baked pain au chocolat to tasty calzones, the Rookery offers an array of pastries, sandwiches, and pizzas every day but Sunday, as well as coffee drinks of all varieties. With its high ceilings and large front windows, this café is among Juneau's most pleasant indoor spaces, even on a rainy day. Check out the hand-stenciled design on the walls and rotating local art while you're here; on the weekend, live acoustic music is a possibility. $ *Average main: $9* ✉ *111 Seward St., Juneau* ☎ *907/463–3013* ⊕ *www.therookerycafe.com* ☾ *Closed Sun.*

$$$
SEAFOOD
✗**Twisted Fish Company.** Juneau's liveliest downtown eatery serves creative pan-Asian seafood and Alaska classics. Housed in a log-frame waterfront building adjacent to the Taku Store and the base of the Mt. Roberts Tramway, Twisted's fish is as fresh as you'll find. Grab a seat on the deck for prime-time Gastineau Channel gazing and a bowl of Captain Ron's chowder. Inside is a dining room with a roaring river-rock hearth and flame-painted salmon, porpoises, marlin, and tuna decorating the walls. $ *Average main: $24* ✉ *550 S. Franklin St.* ☎ *907/463–5033* ⊕ *www.twistedfish.hangaronthewharf.com* ☾ *Closed Oct.–Apr.*

$$$
MEDITERRANEAN
✗**Zephyr.** One of Juneau's more upscale restaurants, Zephyr distinguishes itself by remaining faithfully Mediterranean. The Greco-Roman menu features Spanish, Greek, Italian, and Middle Eastern specialties such as hummus spread on pita toast points, lamb kebabs, and Aegean pasta with feta and sun-dried tomatoes. The restaurant's excellent beer and wine list, along with its two bars—one on the ground floor and another on the upstairs mezzanine level—make it a great place to meet friends for an aperitif. About a block away, on Franklin Street, is **Sprazzo**, run by the same owner. New in 2012, Sprazzo serves pizza, beer, and wine in an interesting, artsy space. $ *Average main: $24* ✉ *200 Seward St.* ☎ *907/780–2221* ⊕ *www.zephyrrestaurant.com.*

WHERE TO STAY

For expanded hotel reviews, visit Fodors.com.

$$$$
B&B/INN
Fodor's Choice
★

Alaska's Capital Inn. Gold-rush pioneer John Olds built this American foursquare home in 1906, and a major restoration transformed it into Juneau's most elegant B&B. **Pros:** beautiful restoration to 1906 mansion; nice antiques. **Cons:** the inn sits atop a steep—but walkable—incline from the main section of downtown; room rates are a little high. **TripAdvisor:** "great hosts," "all around winner," "outstanding inn." ⓢ *Rooms from: $289* ✉ *113 W. 5th St.* ☎ *907/586–6507, 888/588–6507* ⊕ *www.alaskacapitalinn.com* ⤴ *5 rooms, 2 suites* ⦿ *Breakfast.*

$$
HOTEL

Aspen Suites Hotel. This all-suites hotel is Juneau's newest property. **Pros:** well-equipped kitchens; complimentary Wi-Fi. **Cons:** not near downtown attractions; housekeeping is weekly, not daily. **TripAdvisor:** "comfortable," "clean accommodations," "roomy rooms and comfy beds." ⓢ *Rooms from: $159* ✉ *8400 Airport Blvd.* ☎ *907/500–7700* ⊕ *www.aspenhotelsak.com* ⤴ *78 rooms* ⦿ *No meals.*

$$
HOTEL

Driftwood Lodge. This workaday downtown motel is one of Juneau's best values, with a central location and well-maintained rooms, some of which include kitchenettes stocked with dishes, silverware, pots, and pans. **Pros:** most units are spacious; all rooms have private bathrooms. **Cons:** not handicapped-accessible; decor is spare. **TripAdvisor:** "perfect for a quick trip," "pretty good stay," "nice location." ⓢ *Rooms from: $105* ✉ *435 Willoughby Ave.* ☎ *907/586–2280, 800/544–2239* ⊕ *www.driftwoodalaska.com* ⤴ *21 rooms, 41 suites* ⦿ *No meals.*

$$
HOTEL

Frontier Suites Airport Hotel. Near the airport in Mendenhall Valley, 9 miles from Juneau, this rambling hotel is great for families. **Pros:** large rooms; full kitchens. **Cons:** long distance from downtown; not a lot of character to hotel. **TripAdvisor:** "spacious rooms," "attention to detail," "excellent service." ⓢ *Rooms from: $159* ✉ *9400 Glacier Hwy.* ☎ *907/790–6600, 800/544–2250* ⊕ *www.frontiersuites.com* ⤴ *104 rooms, 32 suites* ⦿ *No meals.*

$$$
HOTEL

Goldbelt Hotel Juneau. A high-rise by local standards, the seven-story Goldbelt is one of Juneau's better lodging places, with decent (if somewhat overpriced) rooms with basic amenities, including local coffee. **Pros:** large rooms; free Wi-Fi. **Cons:** street-side rooms are very noisy; a little pricy. **TripAdvisor:** "functional not luxurious," "convenient and friendly," "very nice staff." ⓢ *Rooms from: $184* ✉ *51 W. Egan Dr.* ☎ *907/586–6900, 888/478–6909* ⊕ *www.goldbelttours.com* ⤴ *105 rooms.*

$$$
B&B/INN

Grandma's Feather Bed. This charming Victorian-style hotel—the smallest property in the Best Western chain—is less than a mile from the airport in Mendenhall Valley. **Pros:** delicious breakfasts; deluxe suites with in-room whirlpool baths. **Cons:** outside of downtown; hotel fills quickly, so book ahead. **TripAdvisor:** "charming setting," "lovely quiet place," "comfortable and friendly." ⓢ *Rooms from: $199* ✉ *2358 Mendenhall Loop Rd.* ☎ *907/789–5566 or 888/781–5005* ⊕ *www.grandmasfeatherbed.com* ⤴ *14 rooms* ⦿ *Breakfast.*

$$$$
B&B/INN
Fodor's Choice
★
Pearson's Pond Luxury Inn and Adventure Spa. On a small pond near Mendenhall Glacier, this large, jaw-droppingly landscaped home may be Alaska's finest B&B. **Pros:** private balconies offer excellent views; guest use kayaks and bicycles. **Cons:** two-night minimum during summer season; limited convenient public transportation. **TripAdvisor:** "best way to experience Alaska," "close to nature," "fantastic and romantic." $ *Rooms from: $399* ✉ *4541 Sawa Circle* ☎ *907/789–3772* ⊕ *www.pearsonspond.com* ⬗ *5 suites* ⦿ *Breakfast.*

$$
HOTEL
Prospector Hotel. A short walk west of downtown and next door to the Alaska State Museum, this nicely appointed but visually unremarkable hotel is frequented by business travelers and legislators during the winter legislative session. **Pros:** convenient location; friendly staff. **Cons:** very lackluster exterior and lobby; rooms could use some updating. **TripAdvisor:** "wonderful service," "very nice," "good view." $ *Rooms from: $149* ✉ *375 Whittier St.* ☎ *907/586–3737, 800/331–2711 outside Alaska, 800/478–5866 in Alaska* ⊕ *www.prospectorhotel.com* ⬗ *56 rooms, 7 suites* ⦿ *No meals.*

$$$
B&B/INN
Silverbow Inn. Conveniently located in Juneau's historic downtown, the expanded Silverbow combines a downstairs bakery and café with 11 contemporary hotel rooms on the two upper levels. **Pros:** new flat-screen televisions in rooms; nice historic location. **Cons:** no laundry facilities; parking is limited. **TripAdvisor:** "unexperted eclectic," "friendly atmosphere," "a very positive experience." $ *Rooms from: $189* ✉ *120 2nd St.* ☎ *907/586–4146, 800/586–4146* ⊕ *www.silverbowinn.com* ⬗ *11 rooms* ⦿ *Breakfast.*

$
RENTAL
Fodor's Choice
★
U.S. Forest Service Cabins. Scattered throughout Tongass National Forest, these rustic cabins offer a charming and cheap escape. $ *Rooms from: $35* ✉ *Juneau Ranger District, 8510 Mendenhall Loop Rd.* ☎ *907/586–8800, 877/444–6777 reservations* ⊕ *www.recreation.gov* ⬗ *150 cabins.*

$$$
HOTEL
Westmark Baranof Hotel. The Baranof has long been Juneau's most prestigious address; it's as close to a big-city downtown boutique hotel as you're going to find in Southeast Alaska. **Pros:** elegant art deco public areas; excellent in-house hotel and bar. **Cons:** lower floors are noisy. **TripAdvisor:** "convenient location," "charming and lovely," "beautiful historic hotel." $ *Rooms from: $179* ✉ *127 N. Franklin St.* ☎ *907/586–2660, 800/544–0970* ⊕ *www.westmarkhotels.com/juneau. php* ⬗ *195 rooms and suites.*

NIGHTLIFE AND THE ARTS

BARS

Alaskan Brewing Company. If you're a beer fan, look for Alaskan Brewing Company. These tasty brews, including Alaskan Amber, Pale Ale, IPA, Stout, Alaskan Summer Ale, and Smoked Porter, are brewed and bottled in Juneau. You can visit the brewery (and get free samples of the goods) 11 to 6 daily May through September, with 20-minute tours every half hour. Between October and April tours take place Tuesday through Saturday, 11 to 5:30. ■**TIP→** This is no designer brewery—it's in Juneau's industrial area, and there is no upscale café-bar attached—but the gift shop sells T-shirts and beer paraphernalia. You can also visit the brewery's Downtown Depot, on Franklin Street; though you can't sample the beer here, you can find out more about the brewing process and purchase Alaskan Brewing Company gear—or catch a shuttle to the brewery itself for $7.50 each way. Shuttles run hourly in the summer. ✉ *219 S. Franklin St. and 5429 Shaune Dr.* ☎ *907/780–5866* ⊕ *www. alaskanbeer.com.*

Alaskan Hotel Bar. The Alaskan Hotel Bar is Juneau's most historically authentic watering hole, with flocked-velvet walls, antique chandeliers, and vintage Alaska frontier-brothel decor. The atmosphere, however, is anything but dated, and the bar's live music and open-mike night draw high-spirited crowds. ✉ *167 S. Franklin St.* ☎ *907/586–1000* ⊕ *www. thealaskanhotel.com.*

Imperial Saloon. Past visitors to Juneau may recall the Imperial Saloon as one of the downtown dives, but a major remodeling transformed it into a favorite place to drink, shoot pool, and meet singles. The divey decor hasn't all disappeared—the walls still feature mounted moose and bison heads. There's also the original pressed-tin ceiling. ✉ *241 Front St.* ☎ *907/586–1960.*

Red Dog Saloon. When the ships are in, the music at Red Dog Saloon is live and the crowd gets livelier. ✉ *278 S. Franklin St.* ☎ *907/463–3658.*

Viking Lounge. Just down Front Street is the Viking Lounge, which sells more alcohol than any other bar in Southeast Alaska. Cruise-ship workers love it for its DJ, dance floor, karaoke nights, and general rowdy vibe, and billiards enthusiasts appreciate the bar's eight pool tables. ✉ *218 Front St.* ☎ *907/586–2159.*

MUSIC FESTIVALS

Alaska Folk Festival. The annual weeklong Alaska Folk Festival is staged each April at Centennial Hall in Juneau, drawing singers, banjo masters, fiddlers, and even cloggers from all over the state and beyond. ✉ *Centennial Hall* ☎ *907/463–3316* ⊕ *www.akfolkfest.org.*

Juneau Jazz & Classics. To celebrate music from Bach to Brubeck, musicians come from all over the world to Juneau each May and are often quite well known. The 2012 festival hosted Taj Mahal, among other luminaries. ✉ *350 Whittier St., Suite 105* ☎ *907/463–3378* ⊕ *www. jazzandclassics.org.*

SYMPHONY

Juneau Symphony. Directed by Kyle Wiley Pickett, the Juneau Symphony performs classical works October through June in both high school auditoriums and local churches. ✉ *522 W. 10th St.* ☎ *907/586–4676* ⊕ *www.juneausymphony.org.*

THEATER

Perseverance Theatre. Alaska's only professional theater company, the nationally renowned Perseverance Theatre, performs a wide range of classics and new productions, regularly promoting Alaska artists and staging world premieres. The company recently began regularly staging a limited number of plays in Anchorage every season; other plays have toured more extensively, such as its all-Tlingit version of Shakespeare's

Macbeth, which traveled to the Smithsonian's National Museum of the American Indian in Washington, D.C. Perseverance's season runs from September through May, giving travelers another good reason to visit Alaska during the shoulder season. Juneau is also home to **Theatre in the Rough,** a fantastic all-volunteer theater troupe that's been staging Shakespearian works and other classics twice a year since 1991, as well as two opera companies, **Juneau Lyric Opera** and **Opera to Go.** ⊠ *914 3rd St., Douglas* ☎ *907/364–2421* ⊕ *www.perseverancetheatre.org.*

SHOPPING

ART GALLERIES

Annie Kaill's Gallery. This gallery displays a mix of playful and whimsical original prints, pottery, jewelry, and other arts and crafts from Alaska artists. If you're in town on the first Friday of any month, ask the staff for a map of the First Friday Art Walk; more than a dozen downtown galleries participate in this monthly event by hosting evening exhibit openings, most of which feature local artists. ⊠ *244 Front St.* ☎ *907/586–2880* ⊕ *www.anniekaills.com.*

Decker Gallery. In downtown Juneau, see Rie Muñoz's paintings and tapestries at Decker Gallery. ⊠ *233 S. Franklin St.* ☎ *907/463–5536 or 800/463–5536.*

Hummingbird Hollow. A surprising exception to the cheesy-airport-gift-shop epidemic, Juneau's airport gift shop, Hummingbird Hollow, is another fine place selling authentic Native art, including a diverse selection of jewelry, baskets, and Eskimo dolls. ⊠ *1873 Shell Simmons Dr.* ☎ *907/789–4672* ⊕ *www.hummingbirdhollow.net.*

Juneau Artists Gallery. The cooperatively run Juneau Artists Gallery, on the first floor of the old Senate Building at 175 South Franklin Street, sells a nice mix of watercolors, jewelry, oil and acrylic paintings, etchings, photographs, art glass, ceramics, fiber arts, and pottery from more than 20 local artists. ⊠ *175 S. Franklin St.* ☎ *907/586–9891* ⊕ *www. juneauartistsgallery.com.*

Rie Muñoz Gallery. Rie Muñoz is one of Alaska's best-known artists. She's the creator of a stylized, simple, and colorful design technique that is much copied but rarely equaled. The gallery is located in Mendenhall Valley, a convenient 10-minute walk from the airport. ⊠ *2101 N. Jordan Ave.* ☎ *907/789–7449, 800/247–3151* ⊕ *www.riemunoz.com.*

Wm. Spear Design. Located upstairs through a separate entrance next to Heritage Coffee, Wm. Spear Design is an interesting store, where this lawyer-turned-artist produces a fun and colorful collection of enameled pins and zipper pulls. ⊠ *174 S. Franklin St.* ☎ *907/586–2209* ⊕ *www. wmspear.com.*

SEAFOOD

Taku Store. At the south end of town near the cruise-ship docks and Mt. Roberts Tramway, Taku Store processes nearly 6 million pounds of fish a year, mostly salmon. ■TIP→ The smoked sockeye fillets make excellent gifts. You can view the smoking procedure through large windows and then purchase the packaged fish in the deli-style gift shop or have some shipped back home. ⊠ *550 S. Franklin St.* ☎ *907/463–5319, 800/582–5122* ⊕ *www.takustore.com.*

SIDE TRIPS FROM JUNEAU

A few miles outside this ever-expanding city are some great day trips. The area's undisputed champion of visitor attractions is Mendenhall Glacier. Admiralty Island is also popular—it has hikes through rain forest, excellent bear viewing, and secluded sea kayaking.

NATIVE CULTURE NEARBY

If you're interested in seeing how many Alaska Natives of Southeast Alaska live today, you can fly or take one of the Alaska Marine Highway's ferries (☎ *907/465–3941 or 800/642–0066*) to **Kake, Angoon,** or **Hoonah.** Hoonah's historic cannery building has been beautifully restored, and serves as part of Huna Totem Corporation's **Icy Strait Point** (⊕ *www.icystraitpoint.com*) cruise port. Hoonah and Icy Strait Point's proximity to Point Adolphus—a favorite whale spot—means that trips from here maximize whale-watching time by cutting out extra travel time. There are daily trips into the strait, but book well in advance whether you're coming via cruise or not.

Independent travelers won't find much organized touring in Kake or Angoon, but you will find hotels (advance reservations strongly suggested), and guided fishing and natural-history trips can be arranged by asking around.

Favorite Bay Lodge. In Angoon, try the all-inclusive Favorite Bay Luxury Wilderness Resort. ⊠ *Killisnoo Rd., Angoon* ☎ *907/788–3344, 866/788–3344* ⊕ *www.favoritebay.com.*

Icy Strait Lodge. In Hoonah, Icy Strait Lodge provides very comfortable on-the-water accommodations. ⊠ *Airport Rd., Hoonah* ☎ *907/945–3636.*

Keex' Kwaan Lodge. In Kake, contact the Keex' Kwaan Lodge. ⊠ *Keku Rd., Kake* ☎ *907/723–8386* ⊕ *www.kakealaska.com.*

MACAULAY SALMON HATCHERY

3 miles northwest of downtown Juneau.

Macaulay Salmon Hatchery. Watch through an underwater window as salmon fight their way up a fish ladder from mid-June to mid-October. Inside the busy hatchery, which produces almost 125 million young salmon annually, you will learn about the environmental considerations of commercial fishermen and the lives of salmon. A retail shop sells gifts and salmon products. ⊠ *2697 Channel Dr.* ☎ *907/463–4810, 877/463–2486* ⊡ *$3.25 including short tour* ☉ *Mid-May–mid-Sept., weekdays 10–6, weekends 10–5; Oct.–mid-May by appointment.*

GLACIER GARDENS RAINFOREST ADVENTURE

6½ miles northwest of Juneau.

Glacier Gardens Rainforest Adventure. Spread over 50 acres of rain forest, the family-owned Glacier Gardens has ponds, waterfalls, hiking paths, a large atrium, and gardens. The roots of fallen trees, turned upside down and buried in the ground, act as bowls to hold planters that overflow with begonias, fuchsias, and petunias. Guided tours in covered golf carts lead you along the 4 miles of paved paths, and a 580-foot-high overlook provides dramatic views of the Mendenhall wetlands wildlife refuge, Chilkat mountains, and downtown Juneau. A café and gift shop are here, and the conservatory is a popular wedding spot. Admission includes a guided tour. ■ TIP➔ The Juneau city bus, which departs from multiple locations in downtown Juneau, stops right in front of Glacier Gardens. ✉ *7600 Glacier Hwy.* ☎ *907/790–3377* ⊕ *www.glaciergardens. com* 🖃 *$24.95* ⊗ *May–Sept., daily 9–6.*

MENDENHALL GLACIER

13 miles north of Juneau.

Fodor'sChoice
★
☺

Mendenhall Glacier. Alaska's most-visited drive-up glacier spans 12 miles and is fed by the massive Juneau Icefield. Like many other Alaska glaciers, it is retreating up the valley, losing more than 100 feet a year as massive chunks of ice calve into the small lake separating Mendenhall from the **Mendenhall Visitor Center**. The center has highly interactive exhibits on the glacier, a theater and bookstore, educational exhibits, and panoramic views. It's a great place for children to learn the basics of glacier dynamics. Nature trails lead along Mendenhall Lake and into the mountains overlooking Mendenhall Glacier; the trails are marked by posts and paint stripes delineating the historic location of the glacier, providing a sharp reminder of the Mendenhall's hasty retreat. An elevated viewing platform allows visitors to look for spawning sockeye and coho salmon—and the bears that eat them—at Steep Creek, ½ mile south of the visitor center along the Moraine Ecology Trail. Several companies lead bus tours to the glacier. A glacier express bus leaves from the cruise-ship terminal and heads right out to Mendenhall Glacier; ask at the visitor information center there. ✉ *End of Glacier Spur Rd. off Mendenhall Loop Rd.* ☎ *907/789–0097* ⊕ *www.fs.fed.us/ r10/tongass/districts/mendenhall* 🖃 *Visitor center $3 May–Sept., free Oct.–Apr.* ⊗ *May–Sept., Mon. 11:30–7:30, Tues.–Sun. 8–7:30; Oct.– Apr., Thurs.–Sun. 10–4.*

SHRINE OF ST. THERESE

23 miles northwest of downtown Juneau.

Shrine of St. Therese. Built in the 1930s, this beautiful stone church and its 15 stations of the cross are the only structures on a serene tiny island accessible via a 400-foot-long pedestrian causeway. Visitors enjoy the Merciful Love Labyrinth, the black-granite Shrine Columbarium, and the floral gardens along the Good Shepherd Rosary Trail. Sunday services are held at 1:30 pm from June through August. For those wishing

4

Haines Hwy.

Klondike Hwy.

Fraser

Haines
see detail
map

Skagway
see detail
map

Glacier Bay
National Park
see detail
map

Glacier Bay
National Park
& Preserve

Shrine of
St. Therese

Gustavus

Icy
Strait

Mendenhall
Glacier

TO
YAKUTAT,
ANCHORAGE

Pelican

Hoonah

Juneau
see detail
map.

Douglas

CHICHAGOF
ISLAND

Gulf of
Alaska

Tenakee
Springs

Admiralty
Island
National
Monument

Sitka
see detail
map

Tongass
National
Forest

Angoon

Admiralty Island

BRITISH
COLUMBIA

Baranof

0   50 miles

0   50 kilometers

BARANOF
ISLAND

Frederick Sound

Kake

Chatham Strait

Stephens Passage

COAST MOUNTAINS

to explore the area for more than a few hours, the shrine offers a lodge
and four rental cabins that run the gamut from rustic to resplendent.
■TIP→ A round-trip taxi ride may cost $60 or more. ⊠ *Mile 23 Glacier
Hwy.* ☎ *907/780–6112* ⊕ *www.shrineofsainttherese.org.*

ADMIRALTY ISLAND

40 miles south of Juneau.

Admiralty Island. The island is famous for its lush old-growth rain forest
and abundant wildlife, including one of the largest concentrations of
brown bears anywhere on the planet. Native Tlingit inhabitants called
it Kootznoowoo, meaning "fortress of the bears." Ninety miles long,
with 678 miles of coastline, Admiralty—the second-largest island in
Southeast Alaska—is home to an estimated 1,600 bears, almost one
per square mile. ⊠ *Admiralty Island.*

Admiralty Island National Monument. The Forest Service's Admiralty Island
National Monument has a system of 14 public-use cabins, a canoe route
that crosses the island via a chain of lakes and trails, the world's highest density of nesting bald eagles, large concentrations of humpback
whales, and some of the region's best sea kayaking and sportfishing.
⊠ *Admiralty Island* ⊕ *www.fs.fed.us/r10/tongass/districts/admiralty.*

Fodor's Choice **Pack Creek.** More than 90% of Admiralty Island is preserved within the
★ Kootznoowoo Wilderness. Its chief attraction is Pack Creek, where you
can watch brown bears feeding on salmon. One of Alaska's premier
bear-viewing sites, Pack Creek is comanaged by the U.S. Forest Service
and the Alaska Department of Fish and Game. Permits are required
during the main viewing season, from June 1 through September 10,
and only 24 people per day are allowed to visit Pack Creek from July 5
through August 25. If you're headed to Pack Creek without a guide or
an experienced visitor, be sure to cover the basics of bear safety before
your trip. ■TIP➜ At this writing, from January 2012 onward permits will be
processed through www.recreation.gov. ⊠ *Admiralty Island* ☎ *907/586–
8800* ⊕ *www.fs.fed.us/r10/tongass/districts/admiralty* ➾ *$20–$50.*

GLACIER BAY NATIONAL PARK AND PRESERVE

60 miles northwest of Juneau.

Fodor's Choice **Glacier Bay National Park and Preserve.** Near the northern end of the
★ Inside Passage, Glacier Bay National Park and Preserve is one of America's most magnificent national parks. Visiting Glacier Bay is like stepping back into the Little Ice Age—it's one of the few places in the world
where you can approach such a variety of massive tidewater glaciers.
Sounding like cannon fire, bergs the size of 10-story office buildings
come crashing from the "snout" of a glacier, each cannon blast signifying another step in the glacier's steady retreat. The calving iceberg
sends tons of water and spray skyward, propelling mini–tidal waves
outward from the point of impact. **Johns Hopkins Glacier** calves so
often and with such volume that large cruise ships can seldom come
within 2 miles of its face.

Glacier Bay is a still-forming body of water fed by the runoff of the ice
fields, glaciers, and mountains that surround it. In the mid-18th century, ice floes so covered the bay that Captain James Cook and then
Captain George Vancouver sailed by and didn't even know it. At the
time of Vancouver's sailing in 1794, the bay was still hidden behind
and beneath a vast glacial wall of ice, which was more than 20 miles
across and in places more than 4,000 feet in depth. It extended more
than 100 miles north to its origins in the St. Elias Mountain Range,
the world's tallest coastal mountains. Since then, the face of the glacial
ice has melted and retreated with amazing speed, exposing 65 miles of
fjords, islands, and inlets.

In 1879, about a century after Vancouver's sail-by, one of the earliest
white visitors to what is now Glacier Bay National Park and Preserve
came calling. The ever-curious naturalist John Muir, who would become
one of the region's earliest proponents, was drawn by the flora and
fauna that had followed in the wake of glacial withdrawals; he was
also fascinated by the vast ice rivers that descended from the mountains
to tidewater. Today the naturalist's namesake glacier, like others in the
park, continues to retreat dramatically: the Muir Glacier's terminus is
now scores of miles farther up the bay from the small cabin he built at
its face during his time there.

DID YOU KNOW?

On the Trail of Time, see the physical signs of Mendenhall Glacier's history. Dark (old) and light (new) green vegetation meet at the highest point reached by the glacier's ice.

Glacier Bay is a marvelous laboratory for naturalists of all persuasions. Glaciologists, of course, can have a field day. Animal lovers can hope to see the rare glacial "blue" bears of the area, a variation of the black bear, which is here along with the brown bear; whales feasting on krill; mountain goats in late spring and early summer; and seals on floating icebergs. Birders can look for the more than 200 species that have already been spotted in the park, and if you're lucky, you may witness bald eagles engaging in aerobatics.

A remarkable panorama of plants unfolds from the head of the bay, which is just emerging from the ice, to the mouth, which has been ice-free for more than 200 years. In between, the primitive plants—algae, lichens, and mosses—that are the first to take hold of the bare, wet ground give way to more-complex species: flowering plants such as the magenta dwarf fireweed and the creamy dryas, which in turn merge with willows, alders, and cottonwood. As the living plants mature and die, they enrich the soil and prepare it for new species to follow. The climax of the plant community is the lush spruce-and-hemlock rain forest, rich in life and blanketing the land around **Bartlett Cove.** ⊠ *Gustavus* ☎ *907/697–2230, 907/697–2627 boating information* ⊕ *www. nps.gov/glba.*

GUSTAVUS

50 miles west of Juneau, 75 miles south of Skagway.

For airborne visitors, Gustavus is the gateway to Glacier Bay National Park and Preserve. The long, paved jet airport, built as a refueling strip during World War II, is one of the best and longest in Southeast Alaska, all the more impressive because of its limited facilities at the field. Alaska Airlines, which serves Gustavus daily in the summer, has a new terminal at the site. Smaller, light-aircraft companies that serve the community out of Juneau also have on-site shelters. A summer ferry, operated on Friday and Sunday by Aramark (☎ *907/264–4600 or 888/229–8687* ⊕ *www.visitglacierbay.com*), runs between Juneau and Bartlett Cove.

■ TIP→ Before you get too excited about visiting this remote outpost, be forewarned: Gustavus has no downtown. In fact, Gustavus is not really a town at all. Instead, it's a scattering of homes, farmsteads, a craft studio, fishing and guiding charters, an art gallery, and other tiny enterprises peopled by hospitable individualists. Visitors enjoy the unstructured outdoor activities in the area, including beach and trail hiking in the Nature Conservancy's Forelands Preserve.

OUTDOOR ACTIVITIES AND GUIDED TOURS

Glacier Bay is best experienced from the water, whether from the deck of a cruise ship, on a tour boat, or from the level of a sea kayak. National Park Service naturalists often come aboard to explain the great glaciers and to help spot bears, mountain goats, whales, porpoises, and birds.

Glacier Bay National Park and Preserve

BRITISH COLUMBIA

CANADA
UNITED STATES

ALASKA

TO MT. FAIRWEATHER

1907

Tarr Inlet

1907
1892

Russell Island

1892

1880

1892

Rendu Glacier

Carroll Glacier

Muir Glacier

Riggs Glacier

Casement Glacier

1976
1972

1960
1948

1966

1966
1892

1966

1929

1929
1949

1907

Queen Inlet

Rendu Inlet

West Arm

Inlet

East Muir Arm Inlet

1892

1907

Adams Inlet

TO JOHNS HOPKINS GLACIER

Lamplugh Glacier

Reid Glacier

1907

1892
1907
1892
1907
1919

1879

Tidal Inlet

1860

1860

1907

1860

Beartrack River

Brady Icefield

Geikie Inlet

1966

1892

Glacier Bay

DRAKE ISLAND

1857

1845

WILLOUGHBY ISLAND

Beartrack Cove

Wood Lake

Berg Bay

BEARDSLEE ISLANDS

Visitor Center/ Glacier Bay Lodge

Dundas River

Bartlett Cove

Bartlett Cove

1794

Cove

Airport

Brady Glacier

1794

1961

Palma Bay

Dixon Harbor

Graves Harbor

Taylor Bay

Dundas Bay

1750-80

Gustavus

PLEASANT ISLAND

North Passage

LEMESURIER ISLAND

Icy   Strait

INIAN ISLANDS

South Passage

N

0   10 mile
0   10 kilometer

Cross Sound

CHICHAGOF ISLAND

BOATING AND LOCAL INTEREST

Huna Totem Corporation/Aramark. Daily summertime boat tours leave from the dock at Bartlett Cove, near Glacier Bay Lodge. These eight-hour trips into Glacier Bay have a Park Service naturalist aboard a high-speed 155-passenger catamaran. A light lunch is included. Campers and sea kayakers heading up the bay ride the same boat. ✉ *179 Bartlett Cove* ☎ *907/264–4600, 888/229–8687* ⊕ *www.visitglacierbay.com.*

> **FAIRWEATHER FOLLY**
>
> It was Vancouver who gave the name **Mt. Fairweather** to the magnificent snow-clad mountain towering over the head of the bay. Legend has it that Vancouver named Fairweather on one of Southeast's most beautiful blue days—and the mountain was not seen again during the following century. Overcast, rainy weather is certainly the norm here.

FLIGHTSEEING

Air Excursions. Besides daily scheduled air service year-round to Juneau, Gustavus/Glacier Bay, Hoonah, Haines, Kake, and Skagway, Air Excursions also offers flightseeing tours and charters to other destinations in Southeast Alaska. ✉ *PO Box 16* ☎ *907/697–2375, 800/354–2479 in Alaska* ⊕ *www.airexcursions.com.*

HIKING

Glacier Bay's steep and heavily forested slopes aren't the most conducive to hiking, but there are several short hikes that begin at the Glacier Bay Lodge. Among the most popular is the **Forest Loop Trail,** a pleasant 1-mile jaunt that begins in a forest of spruce and hemlock and finishes on the beach. Also beginning at the lodge is the **Bartlett River Trail**—a 5-mile round-trip hike that borders an intertidal lagoon, culminating at the Bartlett River estuary. The **Bartlett Lake Trail,** part of a 6-mile walk that meanders through rain forest, ends at the quiet lakeshore. The entire Gustavus beachfront was set aside by the Nature Conservancy, enabling visitors to hike the shoreline for miles without getting lost. The beachfront is part of the **Alaska Coastal Wildlife Viewing Trail** (⊕ *wildlife.alaska.gov*). The spring and fall bird migrations are exceptional on Gustavus estuaries, including Dude Creek Critical Habitat Area, which provides a stopover before crossing the ice fields for sandhill cranes. Maps and wildlife-viewing information are available from the **Alaska Division of Wildlife Conservation** (⊕ *wildlife.alaska.gov*).

SEA KAYAKING

The most adventurous way to explore Glacier Bay is by paddling your own kayak through the bay's icy waters and inlets. But unless you're an expert, you're better off signing on with the guided tours.

Alaska Discovery. You can book a five-day guided expedition through Alaska Discovery. Operated by Mountain Travel Sobek, Alaska Discovery provides safe, seaworthy kayaks and tents, gear, and food. Its guides are tough, knowledgeable Alaskans, and they've spent enough time in Glacier Bay's wild country to know what's safe and what's not. ☎ *510/594–6000, 800/586–1911* ⊕ *www.mtsobek.com/trips/br/region-north-america.*

QUAKE HAPPY IN GLACIER BAY

Glacier Bay's impressive landscape is the result of plate tectonics. The region sits directly above a chaotic intersection of fault lines—credited for creating the region's stunning topography as well as wreaking some havoc more recently. On September 10, 1899, the area was rocked by a massive temblor registering 8.4 on the Richter scale. The quake, which had its epicenter in Yakutat Bay, rattled Glacier Bay so much that the entire bay was choked with icebergs.

On July 9, 1958, a tremendous earthquake—a 7.9 on the Richter scale—triggered a landslide of epic proportions in nearby Lituya Bay: 40 million cubic yards of rock tumbled into the bay, and created a tidal wave that reached 1,720 feet.

Alaska Mountain Guides. Take day kayaking trips for whale-watching at Point Adolphus, a premier humpback gathering spot, as well as multi-tiday sea-kayaking expeditions next to tidewater glaciers in Glacier Bay National Park, with Alaska Mountain Guides. ☎ 907/766–3366, 800/766–3396 ⊕ www.alaskamountainguides.com.

Glacier Bay Sea Kayaks. Kayak rentals for Glacier Bay exploring and camping can be arranged through Glacier Bay Sea Kayaks. You will be given instructions on handling the craft plus camping and routing suggestions for unescorted trips. Guided day trips are available in Bartlett Cove. The company is an official NPS concession for guided day kayak trips. ✉ Bartlett Cove ☎ 907/697–2257 ⊕ www.glacierbayseakayaks.com.

Spirit Walker Expeditions. Take one- to seven-day sea-kayaking trips from Gustavus to various parts of Icy Strait with Spirit Walker Expeditions. Trips to Glacier Bay and other remote areas of Southeast Alaska, including Ford's Terror and West Chichagof, are also offered on a limited basis. ☎ 907/697–2266, 800/529–2537 ⊕ www.seakayakalaska.com.

WHALE-WATCHING

M/V TAZ. Step aboard the M/V TAZ and check out Icy Strait and Point Adolphus, near the entrance to Glacier Bay, for awesome views of humpback whales and many other marine mammals. All tours out of Gustavus include binoculars, snacks, and hot beverages. Half-day tours and custom charters accommodating up to 23 passengers are offered, as well as "Weddings with the Whales," where you can get married while surrounded by humpbacks. ☎ 907/321–2302, 888/698–2726 ⊕ www.taz.gustavus.com.

WHERE TO STAY

For expanded hotel reviews, visit Fodors.com.

$$$
B&B/INN ⚏ **Annie Mae Lodge.** This quiet two-story lodge, one of the few Gustavus places open year-round, faces the Good River, has beautiful grounds, and is a five-minute walk from the beach. **Pros:** beautiful grounds; good views. **Cons:** property is not on the beach; no televisions in rooms. **TripAdvisor:** "nice staff," "great food," "well run and beautiful." ⑤ *Rooms from: $170* ☎ 907/697–2346, 800/478–2346 ⊕ www.anniemae.com ⇄ 11 rooms, 9 with bath ⋈ Multiple meal plans.

$$$$
B&B/INN
⬚ **Bear Track Inn.** Built of spruce logs, this inn sits on a 97-acre property facing Icy Strait. Pros: delicious meals at restaurant; a favorite with locals. Cons: high room rate; no room TVs. TripAdvisor: "a hidden treasure," "fresh food," "a fabulous lodge." $ *Rooms from: $575* ⊠ *255 Rink Creek Rd.* ☎ *907/697–3017, 888/697–2284* ⊕ *www.beartrackinn.com* ➹ *14 rooms* ☉ *Closed Oct.–Apr.* ⫯⊘*All meals.*

$$$
HOTEL
⬚ **Glacier Bay Lodge.** Within the national park, this lodge is constructed of massive timbers and blends well into the thick rain forest surrounding it on three sides. Pros: ample hiking trails nearby; good local seafood at restaurant. Cons: dining options are all on the property; location is somewhat remote. TripAdvisor: "beautiful," "wonderfully rustic," "gorgeous wilderness lodge." $ *Rooms from: $199* ⊠ *199 Bartlett Cove Rd.* ☎ *907/264–4600, 888/229–8687* ⊕ *www.visitglacierbay.com* ➹ *49 rooms* ☉ *Closed mid-Sept.–mid-May* ⫯⊘*All meals.*

$$$
B&B/INN
Fodor's Choice
★
⬚ **Gustavus Inn.** Built in 1928 and established as a hotel in 1965, this inn continues a tradition of gracious Alaska rural living. Pros: wonderful food in the dining room; nicely decorated rooms. Cons: only one dinner seating; no phones in rooms. TripAdvisor: "fantastic food," "a special place," "first rate hospitality." $ *Rooms from: $215* ⊠ *Mile 1, Gustavus Rd.* ☎ *907/697–2254, 800/649–5220* ⊕ *www.gustavusinn.com* ➹ *13 rooms, 11 with bath* ☉ *Closed mid-Sept.–mid-May* ⫯⊘*All meals.*

HAINES

75 miles north of Gustavus, 80 miles northwest of Juneau.

Haines encompasses an area that has been occupied by Tlingit peoples for centuries on the collar of the Chilkat Peninsula, a narrow strip of land that divides the Chilkat and Chilkoot inlets. Missionary S. Hall Young and famed naturalist John Muir were intent on establishing a Presbyterian mission in the area, and, with the blessing of local chiefs, they chose the site that later became Haines. It's hard to imagine a more beautiful setting—a heavily wooded peninsula with magnificent views of Portage Cove and the snowy Coast Range. Unlike most other towns in Southeast Alaska, Haines can be reached by the 152-mile Haines Highway, which connects at Haines Junction with the Alaska Highway. It's also accessible by the state ferry (☎ *907/465–3941 or 800/642–0066*) and by scheduled plane service from Juneau. The Haines ferry terminal is 4½ miles northwest of downtown, and the airport is 4 miles west.

Haines is an interesting community: its history contains equal parts enterprising gold-rush boomtown and regimented military outpost. The former is evidenced by Jack Dalton, who in the 1890s maintained a toll route from the settlement of Haines into the Yukon, charging $1 for foot passengers and $2.50 per horse. His Dalton Trail later provided access for miners during the 1897 gold rush to the Klondike.

The town's military roots are visible at Fort William Henry Seward, located at Portage Cove just south of town. For 17 years (1923–39) prior to World War II, the post, renamed Chilkoot Barracks in commemoration of the gold-rush route, was the only military base in the territory. The fort's buildings and grounds are now part of a National Historic Landmark.

Today the Haines–Fort Seward community is recognized for the Native dance and art center at Fort Seward; the Haines Public Library (which, in 2005, was named Best Small Library in the United States); as well as for the superb fishing, camping, and outdoor recreation to be found at Chilkoot Lake, Portage Cove, Mosquito Lake, and Chilkat State Park on the shores of Chilkat Inlet. Northwest of the city is the Alaska Chilkat Bald Eagle Preserve. Thousands of eagles come here each winter to feed on a late run of chum salmon, making it one of Alaska's premier bird-watching sites.

The downtown area feels as small as a postage stamp, and the town exudes a down-home friendliness. Perhaps this is because Haines sees fewer cruise ships, or maybe it's the grand landscape and ease of access to the mountains and sea. Whatever the cause, visitors should be prepared for a relative lack of souvenir and T-shirt shops compared to other ports. Local weather is drier than in much of Southeast Alaska.

Haines has adopted a no-smoking ordinance that went into effect in 2010. Smoking is banned in all businesses, including bars, restaurants, and shops. Accommodations are allowed to have smoking rooms; be sure to reserve a smoking room if it is needed.

GETTING HERE AND AROUND

Haines is connected to other towns in Southeast Alaska by the **Alaska Marine Highway,** and from here you can connect with smaller vessels serving Bush communities. It is also one of the few towns in Southeast Alaska that is accessible by road; be aware that the weather and wildlife in this area present hazards on the highway. Take the Alaska Highway to Haines Junction and then drive on southwest on the Haines Highway to the Alaska Panhandle. The town is a delightful place to explore on foot. In addition to regional connections, **Air Excursions** offers flightseeing tours of Glacier Bay. Housed a few doors up the street from the visitor center, **Mountain Flying Service** leads flightseeing trips to nearby Glacier Bay National Park. **Wings of Alaska** has scheduled service to Juneau and Skagway.

ESSENTIALS

Medical Assistance **Haines Medical Clinic** ⊠ *131 1st Ave. N, next to Convention and Visitors Bureau* ☎ *907/766–6300.*

Tour Information **Air Excursions** ☎ *907/766–3800* ⊕ *www.airexcursions. com.* **Earth Center Adventures–Fly Drake** ☎ *907/766–3679, 907/314–0675* ⊕ *www.flydrake.com.* **Mountain Flying Service** ☎ *907/766–3007, 800/954–8747* ⊕ *www.glacierbayflightseeing.com.* **Wings of Alaska** ☎ *907/789–0790, 800/789-9464.* ⊕ *www.wingsofalaska.com.*

Visitor Information **Haines Convention and Visitors Bureau** ⊠ *122 Second Ave.* ☎ *907/766–2234, 800/458–3579* ⊕ *www.haines.ak.us.*

EXPLORING

⚅ **Alaska Indian Arts.** Dedicated to the revival of Tlingit art, this nonprofit organization is housed in the former fort hospital, on the south side of the parade ground. You can watch artisans doing everything from carving totem poles to creating delicate silver jewelry. ✉ *Ft. Seward* ☎ *907/766–2160* ⊕ *www.alaskaindianarts.com* 💲 *Free* ☉ *Weekdays 9–5.*

⚅ **American Bald Eagle Foundation.** The main focuses here are bald eagles and associated fauna of the Chilkat Preserve, explored in lectures, displays, and videos. A taxidermy-heavy diorama also shows examples of local animals. Opened in summer of 2010, a raptor center features live presentations and an aviary displaying live eagles. The gift shop sells natural-history items. ✉ *113 Haines Hwy., Box 49* ☎ *907/766–3094* ⊕ *www.baldeagles.org* 💲 *$3–$10* ☉ *Summer, daily 9–5; winter daily 10–2.*

★ **Ft. William H. Seward National Historic Landmark.** Circle the sloping parade grounds of Alaska's first U.S. army post, where stately clapboard homes stand against a mountain backdrop. The Haines Convention and Visitors Bureau provides a walking-tour brochure of the fort. ✉ *Fort Seward* ⊕ *www.haines.ak.us/history.*

WALKING AROUND HAINES

A walk through downtown Haines is best started at the helpful **Haines Convention and Visitors Bureau** on 2nd and Willard streets, where you can pick up a walking-tour brochure. To learn a bit about the area's natural and cultural history, head to the **Sheldon Museum and Cultural Center** on Main Street. From here, you can see the busy docks of Portage Cove, filled with commercial fishing boats and pleasure craft. Head down the hill (turning right on Front Street) to follow the shoreline a quarter mile to Lookout Park, a fine place to take in the view on a sunny day—which, in Haines, occurs more often than you might guess. Just up the hill from here is a small cemetery with graves dating from the 1880s. From the cemetery, steps emerge on Mission Street; follow it to 2nd Avenue, where a left turn will bring you to **American Bald Eagle Foundation**, a museum and research center for these majestic birds. Another nearly third of a mile out 2nd Avenue is perhaps the most interesting sight in Haines: **Ft. William H. Seward National Historic Landmark.** As you enter the grounds, you'll pass **Hotel Halsingland**, originally the commanding officers' quarters. Circle the parade ground if you like, passing the line of officers' homes along the top, stopping in at **Alaska Indian Arts,** housed within the old fort hospital.

Haines Convention and Visitors Bureau. At this helpful tourist office you can pick up hiking- and walking-tour brochures, learn about lodging and attractions, and check out menus from local restaurants. ⊠ *122 2nd Ave. S, Box 530* ☎ *907/766–2234, 800/458–3579* ⊕ *www.haines.ak.us* ☉ *Mid-May–mid-Sept., weekdays 8–5, weekends 9–4; mid-Sept.–mid-May, weekdays 8–5.*

Hammer Museum. The owner started his collection decades ago and founded the Hammer Museum—the world's first—in 2001. Among his impressive collection of 1,800 hammers are a Roman battle hammer and 6-foot-long posting hammers used to secure advertisements to local outside walls. ⊠ *108 Main St.* ☎ *907/766–2374* ⊕ *www. hammermuseum.org* 🖾 *$3* ☉ *May–Sept., weekdays 10–5.*

Hotel Halsingland. In Ft. Seward, wander past the huge, gallant, white-columned former commanding officers' home, now a part of the hotel on Officers' Row. ⊠ *Fort Seward* ⊕ *www.hotelhalsingland.com.*

Sheldon Museum and Cultural Center. Steve Sheldon began assembling Native artifacts, items from historic Ft. Seward, and gold-rush memorabilia, such as Jack Dalton's sawed-off shotgun, in the 1880s, and started an exhibit of his finds in 1925. Today his collection is the core of the museum's impressive array of artifacts, including Chilkat blankets, a model of a Tlingit tribal house, and the original lens from the Eldred Rock lighthouse just south of Haines on the Lynn Canal. Repatriated Bear Clan items such as an 18th-century carved ceremonial Murrelet hat are on display, thanks to loans to the museum. ⊠ *11 Main St.* ☎ *907/766–2366* ⊕ *www. sheldonmuseum.org* 🖾 *$5* ☉ *Mid-May–mid-Sept., weekdays 10–4, weekends 1–4; mid-Sept.–mid-May, Mon.–Sat. 1–4.*

A SCENIC DRIVE

Haines Highway. The breathtaking Haines Highway, a National Scenic Byway, starts at Mile 0 in Haines and continues 152 miles to Haines Junction. You don't have to drive the entire length to experience its beauty, as worthwhile stops are all along the route. At about Mile 6 a delightful picnic spot is near the Chilkat River. At Mile 9.5 the view of Cathedral Peaks, part of the Chilkat Range, is magnificent. Though at Mile 9 the Alaska Chilkat Bald Eagle Preserve begins, the best viewing is between Mile 19 and Mile 21. At Mile 33 is a roadside restaurant called, aptly, **33-Mile Roadhouse**, where you fill your tank and coffee mug and grab a burger and, most importantly, a piece of pie—do not leave without trying the pie. The United States–Canada border lies at Mile 42; stop at Canadian customs and set your clock ahead one hour. ✉ *Haines Hwy.* ☎ *907/767–5510 Mile 33 Roadhouse, 907/766–2234 HCVB* ⊕ *www.haines.ak.us/highway.*

Alaska Chilkat Bald Eagle Preserve. In winter, the Alaska Chilkat Bald Eagle Preserve, on Mile 19–Mile 21 of the Haines Highway, harbors the largest concentration of bald eagles in the world. In November and December, more eagles gather outside of Haines than live in the continental United States. Thousands come to feast on the late run of salmon in the clear, ice-free waters of the Chilkat River, which is heated by underground warm springs. ✉ *Haines Hwy.* ☎ *907/766–2292* ⊕ *www.dnr.alaska.gov/parks/units/eagleprv.htm.*

OFF THE BEATEN PATH

Chilkat State Park. This park on the Chilkat Inlet has beautiful and accessible viewing of both the Davidson and Rainbow glaciers along with public campgrounds. The Seduction Point Trail, about 7 miles one way, takes hikers to the very tip of the peninsula upon which Haines sits. ✉ *Mile 7, Mud Bay Rd.* ☎ *907/766–2292* ⊕ *www.dnr.alaska.gov/parks/aspunits/southeast/chilkatsp.htm.*

Dalton City. The four-day-long **Southeast Alaska State Fair,** held the last week of July, is one of several official regional blowouts, and thanks to its homespun feel it's a must for state fair fans. In addition to a logging show and a fisherman's rodeo, the fair has live music, rides on a vintage 1920 Herschal-Spillman carousel, local culinary arts, Native dances, totemic crafts, art, and photography. ☎ *907/766–2476* ⊕ *www. seakfair.org* ⌦ *$10–$15.*

Southeast Alaska State Fairgrounds. An 1890s gold-rush town was re-created for the movie *White Fang* and moved to the Southeast Alaska State Fairgrounds, less than a mile from downtown. ✉ *Dalton City* ☎ *907/766–2476* ⊕ *www.seakfair.org.*

Haines Brewing Company. The movie-set buildings now house local businesses, including the Haines Brewing Company. ✉ *Dalton City* ☎ *907/766–3823* ⊕ *www.hainesbrewing.com.*

OUTDOOR ACTIVITIES AND GUIDED TOURS

BICYCLING

Sockeye Cycle Company. Guided mountain- and road-bike tours along the roads and trails of Haines, including the breathtaking 360-mile Golden Circle route that connects Haines and Skagway via the Yukon Territory, are Sockeye Cycle Company's specialty. The outfit also rents, services, and sells bikes. ⊠ *24 Portage St., Box 829* ☎ *907/766–2869, 877/292–4154* ⊕ *www.cyclealaska.com.*

BOATING AND FISHING

Alaska Fjordlines. Alaska Fjordlines operates a high-speed catamaran from Skagway and Haines to Juneau and back throughout the summer, stopping along the way to watch sea lions, humpbacks, and other marine mammals. One-way service is also available. ☎ *907/766–3395, 800/320–0146* ⊕ *www.alaskafjordlines.com.*

Haines Convention and Visitors Bureau. For information on numerous sportfishing charter boats in Haines, contact the Haines Convention and Visitors Bureau. ⊠ *122 Second Ave.* ☎ *907/766–2234 or 800/458–3579* ⊕ *www.haines.ak.us.*

Haines-Skagway Fast Ferry. Take a passenger catamaran ferry between Skagway and Haines provided by Haines-Skagway Fast Ferry, with special package rates for visitors who book a ride on Skagway's White Pass Summit Train. The service is offered several times a day in summer, and the trip takes 45 minutes each way. ⊠ *39 Beach Rd.* ☎ *907/766–2100, 888/766–2103* ⊕ *www.hainesskagwayfastferry.com.*

River Adventures. The jet-boat tours offered by River Adventures are a great way to experience the bald eagle preserve in majestic Chilkat River valley. ☎ *907/766–2050, 800/478–9827* ⊕ *www.jetboatalaska.com.*

HIKING

Alaska Mountain Guides. Guide service and rock-climbing school Alaska Mountain Guides leads a variety of hiking and mountaineering trips from Haines, ranging from half-day trips to 90-day expeditionary courses for hiking, sea kayaking, fly-fishing, ice climbing, rock climbing, skiing, and mountaineering. Sea-kayak rentals are also available. ☎ *907/766–3366, 800/766–3396* ⊕ *www.alaskamountainguides.com.*

Battery Point Trail. This is a fairly level path that hugs the shoreline for 1.2 miles, providing fine views across Lynn Canal. The trail begins a mile east of town, and a campsite can be found at Kelgaya Point near the end. For other hikes, pick up a copy of "Haines Is for Hikers" at the Haines Convention and Visitors Bureau. ⊠ *End of Beach Rd.* ⊕ *www. seatrails.org/com_haines/trl-battery.htm.*

NATURE AND SKI TOURS

Fodor's Choice
★ **Alaska Nature Tours.** Alaska Nature Tours conducts bird-watching and natural-history tours through the Alaska Chilkat Bald Eagle Preserve, operates brown bear–watching excursions in July and August, and leads hiking treks in summer and ski tours in winter. ⊠ *109 Second Ave.* ☎ *907/766–2876* ⊕ *www.alaskanaturetours.net.*

Southeast Alaska Backcountry Adventures. The Chilkat Valley is a powdery heli-skier's paradise, and Southeast Alaska Backcountry Adventures lifts skiers and snowboarders by helicopter and Sno-Cat. The company also offers packages that include lodging. ☎ *907/314–0445, 877/617–3418* ⊕ *www.seaba-heli.com.*

WHERE TO EAT

$$ ✕ **Bamboo Room.** Pop culture meets greasy spoon in this unassuming
AMERICAN coffee shop with red-vinyl booths, which has been in the same family for more than 50 years. The menu doesn't cater to light appetites—it includes sandwiches, burgers, fried chicken, chili, and halibut fish-and-chips, but the place really is at its best for an all-American breakfast (available until 3 pm). The adjacent bar has pool, darts, a big-screen TV, and a jukebox. ⑤ *Average main: $10* ⊠ *2nd Ave. near Main St.* ☎ *907/766–2800* ⊕ *www.bamboopioneer.net.*

$$ ✕ **Mosey's.** The fare at this Mexican restaurant just one block up from
MEXICAN the cruise-ship dock is on the spicy side—owner Martha Stewart (yes, that's her real name) travels to New Mexico each year and brings back bushels of roasted green chilies, the signature ingredient. If your taste buds can handle the kick, you'll be rewarded: the food is bursting with fresh flavors, and the atmosphere is a cheery south-of-the-border alternative to the rest of Haines's more mainstream offerings. Order lunch at the counter or sit down for table service in the evening. ⑤ *Average main: $10* ⊠ *Soap Suds Alley, Ft. Seward* ☎ *907/766–2320* ⊕ *www. moseyscantina.com* ⊗ *No dinner Tues. No lunch weekends.*

$ ✕ **Mountain Market.** Meet the locals over espresso, brewed from fresh-
AMERICAN roasted beans, and a fresh-baked pastry at this busy corner natural-foods store, deli, café, wine-and-spirits shop, de facto meeting hall, and hitching post. Mountain Market is great for lunchtime sandwiches, wraps, soups, and salads. Friday is pizza day, but come early, since it's often gone by early afternoon. ⑤ *Average main: $8* ⊠ *3rd Ave. and Haines Hwy.* ☎ *907/766–3340* ⊕ *www.mountain-market.com.*

WHERE TO STAY

For expanded hotel reviews, visit Fodors.com.

$$ ⌂ **Alaska Guardhouse.** Conveniently located near the docks, this unpre-
B&B/INN tentious B&B in the Fort Seward area used to be the area's jail. **Pros:** near the docks; good views. **Cons:** limited amenities; only three rooms. **TripAdvisor:** "relaxed and comfortable," "very nice accommodations," "fun with style." ⑤ *Rooms from: $125* ⊠ *15 Seward Dr., Fort Seward* ☎ *907/766–2566, 866/290–7445* ⊕ *www.alaskaguardhouse.com* ⟳ *3 rooms, 2 with bath* ⫽❘ *Breakfast.*

$$ ⌂ **Captain's Choice Motel.** In the summer, overflowing flower boxes sur-
HOTEL round this downtown Haines motel. **Pros:** beautiful grounds; continental breakfast includes locally made raisin bread and muffins. **Cons:** the hotel's airport shuttle is unreliable; room amenities are limited; there's a charge for Wi-Fi. **TripAdvisor:** "great view," "great place," "nicest option in Haines." ⑤ *Rooms from: $143* ⊠ *108 2nd Ave. N, Box 392*

☎ *907/766–3111, 800/478–2345* ⊕ *www.capchoice.com* ⇨ *40 rooms, 4 suites* ❍| *Breakfast.*

$ ☲ **Hotel Halsingland.** Seward's commanding officers once lived in the big
HOTEL white Victorian building that today houses this gracious hotel. **Pros:** elegant, historic property; rental cars on-site. **Cons:** small showers; small rooms. **TripAdvisor:** "quiet room with a view," "a unique hotel," "beautiful setting." ⑤ *Rooms from: $109* ⊠ *Ft. Seward* ☎ *907/766–2000, 800/542–6363* ⊕ *www.hotelhalsingland.com* ⇨ *58 rooms, 52 with bath* ⊙ *Closed mid-Nov.–Mar.*

NIGHTLIFE AND THE ARTS

NIGHTLIFE

Fogcutter Bar. Locals might rule the pool tables at Fogcutter Bar, but they always appreciate a little friendly competition. Like many bars in Southeast Alaska, the Fogcutter sells drink tokens that patrons often purchase for their friends; you'll notice folks sitting at the bar with a small stack of these tokens next to their beverage. The Fogcutter's embossed metal tokens are among Southeast's most ornate. Purchase one for a keepsake—or for later use. ⊠ *122 Main St.* ☎ *907/766–2555.*

Haines Brewing Company. This microbrewery among the Dalton City buildings at the fairgrounds sells beer by the sample glass, pint glass, or liter growlers to go. ⊠ *108 Whitefang Way* ☎ *907/766–3823* ⊕ *www. hainesbrewing.com.*

Harbor Bar. Commercial fisherfolk gather nightly at Harbor Bar, which dates from 1907. You might catch some live music here in summer, or take in one of its poker tournaments. ⊠ *Front St. at harbor* ☎ *907/766–2444.*

Pioneer Bar. Inside one of the oldest buildings in town (it was once a brothel), the Pioneer Bar has historical photographs on the walls, a large-screen television for sports, and occasional bands. ⊠ *2nd Ave. near Main St.* ☎ *907/766–3443* ⊕ *www.bamboopioneer.net.*

SHOPPING

GALLERIES AND GIFTS

A surprising number of artists live in the Haines area and sell their works in local galleries.

Birch Boy Products. Birch Boy Products produces tart and tasty birch syrup; it's sold in local gift shops. ☎ *907/767–5660* ⊕ *www.birchboy.com.*

Sea Wolf Gallery. Tresham Gregg's Sea Wolf Gallery sells wood carvings, silver jewelry, prints, and T-shirts with his Native-inspired designs. ⊠ *Ft. Seward* ☎ *907/766–2540* ⊕ *www.tresham.com.*

Wild Iris Gallery. Haines's most charming gallery, the Wild Iris Gallery, displays attractive jewelry, prints, and fashion wear created by owner Fred Shields and his daughter Melina. Other local artists are also represented. It's just up from the cruise-ship dock, and its summer gardens alone are worth the visit. ⊠ *Portage St.* ☎ *907/766–2300* ⊕ *www. haines.ak.us/artists.*

LEARN ABOUT TLINGIT CULTURE

Jilkat Kwaan Cultural Tours. Built near Klukwan, a Native village 23 miles up the road from Haines, this site offers visitors the chance to learn about the Tlingit, including their arts, language, and traditions. Visit the site's Long House, built using traditional methods; find out about traditional Native crafts, including wood carving, beading, and the distinctive Chilkat blanket; see the process for smoking salmon; and much more. A small but well-stocked gift shop sells crafts made by Klukwan locals. ⊠ *Klukwan* ☏ *907/767–5797* ⊕ *www.visitklukwan.com.*

SKAGWAY

14 miles northeast of Haines.

Located at the northern terminus of the Inside Passage, Skagway is only a one-hour ferry ride from Haines. By road, the distance is 359 miles, as you have to take the Haines Highway up to Haines Junction, Yukon, then take the Alaska Highway 100 miles south to Whitehorse, and then drive a final 100 miles south on the Klondike Highway to Skagway. North-country folk call this sightseeing route the Golden Horseshoe or Golden Circle tour, because it passes a lot of gold-rush country in addition to spectacular lake, forest, and mountain scenery.

The town is an amazingly preserved artifact from North America's biggest, most-storied gold rush. Most of the downtown district forms part of the Klondike Gold Rush National Historical Park, a unit of the national park system dedicated to commemorating and interpreting the frenzied stampede of 1897 that extended to Dawson City in Canada's Yukon.

Nearly all the historic sights are within a few blocks of the cruise-ship and ferry dock, allowing visitors to meander through the town's attractions at whatever pace they choose. Whether you're disembarking from a cruise ship, a ferry, or a dusty automobile fresh from the Golden Circle, you'll quickly discover that tourism is the lifeblood of this town. Unless you're visiting in winter or hiking into the backcountry on the Chilkoot Trail, you aren't likely to find a quiet Alaska experience around Skagway.

GETTING HERE AND AROUND

Skagway offers one of the few opportunities to drive in the region. Take the Alaska Highway to the Canadian Yukon's Whitehorse and then drive on Klondike Highway to the Alaska Panhandle. Southeast Alaska's only railroad, the **White Pass and Yukon Route,** operates several different tours departing from Skagway, Fraser, British Columbia, and on some days, Carcross, Yukon. The tracks follow the historic path over the White Pass summit—a mountain-climbing, cliff-hanging route of as far as 67½ miles each way. Bus connections are available at Fraser to Whitehorse, Yukon. While the route is primarily for visitors, some locals use the service for transportation between Skagway and Whitehorse.

ESSENTIALS

Internet Port of Call ✉ *2nd and Broadway* ☎ *907/983–2411.*

Medical Assistance Skagway Dahl Memorial Clinic ✉ *350 14th Ave., between State and Broadway* ☎ *907/983–2255* ⊕ *www.skagway.org.*

Visitor and Tour Information Skagway Convention and Visitors Bureau ☎ *907/983–2854, 888/762–1898* ⊕ *www.skagway.com.* **Klondike Gold Rush National Historical Park** ✉ *Visitor center, 2nd Ave. and Broadway* ☎ *907/983–2921* ⊕ *www.nps.gov/klgo.* **White Pass and Yukon Route** ☎ *907/983–2217, 800/343–7373* ⊕ *www.wpyr.com.*

EXPLORING

★ **Arctic Brotherhood Hall.** The Arctic Brotherhood was a fraternal organization of Alaska and Yukon pioneers. Local members of the Brotherhood built the building's (now renovated) false front out of 8,833 pieces of driftwood and flotsam gathered from local beaches. The result: one of the most unusual buildings in all of Alaska. The AB Hall now houses the

Skagway Convention and Visitors Bureau, along with public restrooms. ✉ *Broadway between 2nd and 3rd Aves., Box 1029* ☎ *907/983–2854, 888/762–1898 message only* ⊕ *www.skagway.com* ⊗ *May–Sept., daily 8–6; Oct.–Apr., weekdays 8–noon and 1–5.*

Corrington's Museum of Alaskan History. Inside a gift shop, this impressive (and free) scrimshaw museum highlights more than 40 exquisitely carved walrus tusks and other exhibits that detail Alaska's history. Dennis Corrington, a one-time Iditarod Race runner, and the founder of the museum, is often present. A bright flower garden decorates the exterior. ✉ *5th Ave. and Broadway* ☎ *907/983–2579* ⛶ *Free* ⊗ *Open when cruise ships are in port.*

Golden North Hotel. Built during the 1898 gold rush, the Golden North Hotel was—until closing in 2002—Alaska's oldest hotel. Despite the closure, the building has been lovingly maintained and still retains its gold rush–era appearance; a golden dome tops the corner cupola. Today the downstairs houses shops. ✉ *3rd Ave. and Broadway.*

★ **Klondike Gold Rush National Historical Park.** Housed in the former White Pass and Yukon Route Depot, this wonderful museum contains exhibits, photos, and artifacts from the White Pass and Chilkoot trails. It's a must-see for anyone planning on taking a White Pass train ride, driving the nearby Klondike Highway, or hiking the Chilkoot Trail. Films, ranger talks, and walking tours are offered. Special free Robert Service poetry performances by Buckwheat Donahue—a beloved local character and head of the Skagway Convention and Visitors Bureau—occasionally take place at the visitor center. ✉ *2nd Ave. at Broadway* ☎ *907/983–2921, 907/983–9224* ⊕ *www.nps.gov/klgo* ⛶ *Free* ⊗ *Visitor Center open May–Sept., weekdays 7:30–7, weekends 8–6; Museum open May–Sept., daily 7:30–6; Oct.–Apr., daily 8–5.*

Moore Cabin. Built in 1887 by Captain William Moore and his son Ben Moore, the tiny cabin was the first structure built in Skagway. An early homesteader, Captain Moore prospered from the flood of miners, constructing a dock, warehouse, and sawmill to supply them, and selling land for other ventures. Next door, the larger **Moore House** (1897–98) contains interesting exhibits on the Moore family. Both structures are maintained by the Park Service, and the main house is open daily in summer. ✉ *5th Ave. between Broadway and Spring St.* ☎ *907/983–2921* ⊕ *www.nps.gov/archeology/sites/npsites/skagway.htm* ⊗ *Memorial Day–Labor Day, daily 10–5.*

Skagway Museum. This nicely designed museum—also known as the Trail of '98 Museum—occupies the ground floor of the beautiful building that also houses Skagway City Hall. Inside, you'll find a 19th-century Tlingit canoe (one of only two like it on the West Coast), historic photos, a red-and-black sleigh, and other gold rush–era artifacts, along with a healthy collection of contemporary local art and post–gold rush history exhibits. ✉ *7th Ave. and Spring St.* ☎ *907/983–2420* ⛶ *$2* ⊗ *Mid-May–Sept., weekdays 9–5, Sat. 10–5, Sun. 1–4; Oct.–mid-May, hrs vary.*

OUTDOOR ACTIVITIES AND GUIDED TOURS

BIKING

Sockeye Cycle Company. Based in Haines, and, in summertime, in Skagway, Sockeye Cycle Company specializes in guided bike tours in the area, including a train–bike ride combo. Sockeye also rents bikes for independent explorers. ✉ *381 5th Ave.* ☎ *907/983–2851* ⊕ *www. cyclealaska.com.*

BOATING

Alaska Fjordlines. A popular day tour from Skagway and Haines to Juneau and back is operated by Alaska Fjordlines. Passengers board a high-speed catamaran at 8 am and stop along the way to watch sea lions, humpbacks, and other marine mammals. The boat gets to Juneau at 11 am, where a bus transports visitors into town and to Mendenhall Glacier, returning to the boat at 5:30 pm for the ride back to Skagway, where the boat returns at 8:15 pm. One-way service is also available. ☎ *907/766–3395, 800/320–0146* ⊕ *www.alaskafjordlines.com.*

Haines-Skagway Fast Ferry. Take a fast passenger catamaran ferry between Skagway and Haines with Haines-Skagway Fast Ferry, with service several times a day in summer. The trip is about 45 minutes each way. ✉ *39 Beach Rd.* ☎ *907/766–2100, 888/766–2103* ⊕ *www. hainesskagwayfastferry.com.*

LOCAL INTEREST BY BUS

Skagway Street Car Company. Revisit the gold-rush days in modern restorations of the bright-yellow 1920s sightseeing buses with Skagway Street Car Company. Costumed conductors lead these popular two-hour tours, but advance reservations are recommended for independent travelers, since most seats are sold aboard cruise ships. Call a week ahead in peak season to reserve a space. ✉ *270 2nd Ave.* ☎ *907/983–2908* ⊕ *www.skagwaystreetcar.com.*

OUTDOOR ADVENTURE

Alaska Excursions. Booking independently with Alaska Excursions—which leads wheeled (no snow) sled-dog tours, horseback-riding tours, and golfing day trips—can be difficult, as cruise-ship groups reserve the bulk of available slots. ✉ *5th Ave.* ☎ *907/983–4444* ⊕ *www. alaskaexcursions.com.*

Packer Expeditions. This company offers guided hikes on wilderness trails not accessible by road. One trip includes a helicopter flight, a 2-mile hike toward the Laughton Glacier, and a one-hour ride back to town on the White Pass Railroad. A longer hike on the same trail uses the train for access in both directions and includes time hiking on the glacier. ✉ *9th Ave. and State St.* ☎ *907/983–3005* ⊕ *www.packerexpeditions. com.*

Temsco Helicopters. Fly to Denver Glacier for an hour of learning about mushing and riding on a dogsled with Temsco Helicopters. ✉ *901 Terminal Way* ☎ *907/983–2900, 866/683–2900* ⊕ *www.temscoair.com.*

Continued on page 204

GOLD! GOLD! GOLD!

At the end of the 19th Century, scoundrels and starry-eyed gold seekers alike made their way from Alaska's Inside Passage to Canada's Yukon Territory, with high hopes for heavy returns.

> "There are strange things done in the midnight sun
> By the men who moil for gold...."
> —*Robert Service, "The Cremation of Sam McGee"*

Miners have moiled for gold in the Yukon for many centuries, but the Klondike Gold Rush was a particularly strange and intense period of history. Within a decade, the towns of Skagway, Dyea, and Dawson City appeared out of nowhere, mushroomed to accommodate tens of thousands of people, and just about disappeared again. At the peak of the rush, Dawson City was the largest metropolis north of San Francisco. Although only a few people found enough gold even to pay for their trip, the rush left an indelible mark on the nation's imagination.

An 1898 photograph shows bearded miners using a gold pan and sluice as they search for riches.

A GREAT STAMPEDE

Historians squabble over who first saw the glint of Yukon gold. All agree that it was a member of a family including "Skookum" Jim Mason (of the Tagish tribe), Kate and George Carmack, and Dawson Charlie, who were prospecting off the Klondike River in 1896. Over the following months, word spread and claims were quickly staked. When the first boatload of gold reached Seattle in July 1897, gold fever ignited with the *Seattle Post-Intelligencer's* headline: "GOLD! GOLD! GOLD! Sixty-Eight Rich Men On the Steamer Portland." Within six months, 100,000 people had arrived in Southeast Alaska, intent upon making their way to the untold riches.

Skagway had only a single cabin standing when the gold rush began. Three months after the first boat landed, 20,000 people swarmed its raucous hotels, saloons, gambling houses, and dance halls. By spring 1898, the town was labeled "little better than a hell on earth." When gold was discovered in Nome the next year and in Fairbanks in the early 1900s, Skagway's population dwindled to 700 souls.

(above) Rush hour on Broadway, Skagway, 1898.

A GRITTY REALITY

To reach the mining hub of Dawson City, prospectors had to choose between two risky routes from the Inside Passage. From Dyea, the Chilkoot Trail was steep and bitterly cold. The longer, bandit-ridden White Pass Trail from Skagway killed so many pack animals that it earned the nickname Dead Horse Trail. After the mountains, there were still over 500 mi to travel. For those who arrived, dreams were quickly washed away, as most promising claims had already been staked by the Klondike Kings. Many ended up working as labor. The disappointment was unbearable.

KLONDIKE KATE

The gold rush was profitable for clever entrepreneurs. Stragglers, outfitters, and outlaws took advantage of every opportunity to make a buck. Klondike Kate, a brothel keeper and dance-hall gal, had an elaborate song-and-dance routine that involved 200 yards of bright red chiffon.

TWO ENEMIES DIE IN A SKAGWAY SHOWDOWN

CON ARTIST "SOAPY" SMITH

Claim to Fame: Skagway's best-known gold-rush criminal, Soapy was the de facto leader of the town's loosely organized network of criminals and spies.

Cold-Hearted Snake: Euphemistically referred to as "colorful," he ruthlessly capitalized on the naïveté of prospectors.

Famous Scheme: Soapy charged homesick miners $5 to wire a message home in his counterfeit Telegraph Office (the wires ended in a tangled pile behind a shed).

Shot Through the Heart: In 1898, just days after he served as grand marshal of Skagway's 4th of July parade, Soapy barged in on a meeting set up by his rival, Frank Reid. There was a scuffle, and they shot each other.

Famous Last Words: When he saw Reid draw his gun, Soapy shouted, "My God, don't shoot!"

R.I.P.: Soapy's tombstone was continually stolen by vandals and souvenir seekers; today's grave marker is a simple wooden plank in Skagway's Gold Rush Cemetery.

GOOD GUY FRANK REID

Claim to Fame: Skagway surveyor and all-around good fellow, Frank Reid was known for defending the town against bad guys.

The Grid Man: A civil engineer, Reid helped to make Skagway's streets wide and gridlike.

Thorn in My Side: Reid set up a secret vigilante meeting to discuss one very thorny topic: Soapy Smith.

In Skagway's Honor: Reid killed Soapy during the shootout on the city docks, breaking up Soapy's gang and freeing the town from its grip.

Dyin' Tryin': Reid's heroics cost him his life—he died some days later from the injuries he sustained.

R.I.P.: The town built a substantial monument in Reid's memory in the Gold Rush Cemetery, which you can visit to this day; the inscription reads: "He gave his life for the honor of Skagway."

(above) Soapy Smith (front), so named for his first con, which involved selling "lucky soap," stands with five friends at his infamous saloon.

FOLLOWING THE GOLD TRAIL TODAY

KEY

↘ 2.2 mi Cumulative distance in miles from Dyea

THE HISTORIC CHILKOOT TRAIL

If you're an experienced backpacker, consider hiking the highly scenic Chilkoot Trail, the 33-mi route of the 1897–98 prospectors from Skagway into Canada. Most hikers will need four to five days. The trail is generally in good condition, with primitive campsites strategically located along the way. Expect steep slopes and wet weather, along with exhilarating vistas at the summit. Deep snow often covers the pass until late summer. The trail stretches from Dyea (just outside of Skagway) to Lake Bennett. The National Park Service maintains the American side of the pass as part of **Klondike Gold Rush National Historical Park;** the Canadian side is part of the **Chilkoot Trail National Historic Site.** A backcountry permit is required.

■**TIP→** To return to Skagway, hikers usually catch the White Pass & Yukon Route train from Lake Bennett. The fare is $95. For more information, visit www.upyr.com/chilkoottrail.html.

For more details, including backcountry permits (C$55), contact the summer-only **Chilkoot Trail Center** ☎ 907/983–9234 ⊕ www.nps.gov/klgo. Or you can call Parks Canada ☎ 800/661–0486 ⊕ www.pc.gc.ca/chilkoot.

GOLDEN DRIVES

The Golden Circle Route starts in Skagway on the Klondike Highway, then travels to Whitehorse. The route continues to Haines Junction, and then south to Haines. On the much longer Klondike Loop, you'll take Klondike Highway past Whitehorse, all the way to Dawson City, where the Klondike Highway meets the Alaska Highway. From start to finish, this segment covers 435 miles. From start to finish, this segment covers 435 miles. From there, you can continue west and then south on the Alaska Highway, past Kluane National Park, and back down to Haines, a total distance of 890 miles. If you're taking the Klondike Highway north from Skagway,

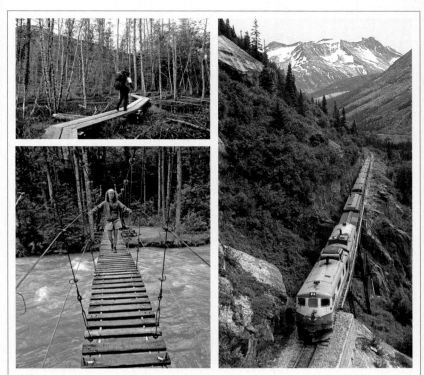

(top left) Trekking the Chilkoot Trail (right) White Pass & Yukon Route (bottom left) A bridge on Chilkoot Trail

you must stop at Canadian customs, Mile 22. If you're traveling south to Skagway, check in at U.S. Customs, Mile 6. For more on these drives, visit travelyukon.com/discover-yukon/scenic-drives.

WHITE PASS & YUKON ROUTE

You can travel the gold-rush route aboard the historic White Pass & Yukon Route (WP & YR) narrow-gauge railroad. The diesel locomotives tow vintage-style viewing cars up steep inclines, hugging the walls of precipitous cliffs with views of craggy peaks, forests, and plummeting waterfalls. It's open mid-May to late September only, and reservations are highly recommended.

■ **TIP➜** Most of the commentary is during the first half of the trip and relates to sights out of the left side of the train, so sit on this side. A "seat exchange" at the summit allows all guests a canyonside view.

Several options are available, including a fully narrated 3-hour round-trip excursion to White Pass summit (fare: $113). Sights along the way include Bridal Veil Falls, Inspiration Point, and Dead Horse Gulch. Through service to Whitehorse, Yukon (4 hours), is offered daily as well—in the form of a train trip to Fraser, where bus connections are possible on to Whitehorse (entire one-way fare to Whitehorse: $120). Also offered are the Chilkoot Trail hikers' service and a 4-hour roundtrip to Fraser Meadows on Saturday and Sunday (fare: $155).

Call ahead or check online for details and schedules. ☎ 907/983–2217 or 800/343–7373 ⊕ www.wpyr.com.

WHERE TO EAT

$ ✕ **Glacial Smoothies and Espresso.**
CAFÉ   This local hangout is the place to go for a breakfast bagel or a lunchtime soup-and-sandwich combo. Prices are steeper than at some coffee shops, but the ingredients are fresh and local, and nearly everything on the menu is made on-site. Customers can cool down with a Mango Madness or Blueberry Blues smoothie, and soft-serve ice cream in summer. $ *Average main: $7* ✉ *3rd Ave. between Main and State Sts.* ☎ *907/983–3223* ⊕ *www. glacialsmoothies.com* ⊗ *No dinner.*

$ ✕ **Skagway Pizza Station.** Housed
PIZZA   in a former gas station, this year-round restaurant is known for its comfort-food specials. The huge calzones are stuffed and served piping hot with sides of house marinara and ranch dressing—build your own or choose one of the chef's creations, like the Chicken Hawk Squawk with pineapple and jalapeños. Or do as the Skagwegians do and wash down one of the 14-inch pizzas with a pint or two of Alaskan Summer Ale. For dog-tired travelers who can't walk another block, the Pizza Station delivers for free. $ *Average main: $10* ✉ *4th Ave. between Main and State Sts.* ☎ *907/983–2200* ⊕ *pizzastation.eskagway.com.*

$$ ✕ **Starfire.** A popular spot with the locals, this Thai restaurant fills up
THAI   very quickly in the summer around dinner hour; it's best to call ahead. On warm evenings the patio offers a pleasant—and often lively—alternative to the close quarters of the dining room inside. $ *Average main: $14* ✉ *4th at Spring St.* ☎ *907/983–3663.*

$$ ✕ **Stowaway Cafe.** Always crowded, this harborside café is just a few
CAFÉ   steps from the cruise-ship dock. Seafood is the attraction—including wasabi salmon and glacé de poisson—but you can also eat steaks, chicken, or smoked ribs. "Café" is an understated description of the restaurant; this is one of Skagway's finest restaurants. While reservations are not required, they're certainly recommended. $ *Average main: $16* ✉ *205 Congress Way* ☎ *907/983–3463* ⊕ *stowaway.eskagway.com* ⊗ *Closed Oct.–Apr. No lunch.*

ALL THAT GLIMMERS

Old false-front stores, saloons, and brothels—built to separate gold-rush prospectors from their grubstakes going north or their gold pokes heading south—have been restored, repainted, and refurbished by the federal government and Skagway's citizens. The town feels a little like a Disney theme park in spots, and it's made all the more surreal by the surrounding mountains. But the scene today is not appreciably different from what the prospectors saw in the days of 1898, except that the street is now paved to make exploring easier.

WHERE TO STAY

For expanded hotel reviews, visit Fodors.com.

$$ ⌂ **Mile Zero Bed & Breakfast.** In a quiet residential area a few blocks
B&B/INN   from downtown, this comfortable B&B has spacious and well-insulated guest rooms, all with private entrances, phones, and baths. **Pros:** all rooms have televisions and phones; communal areas are comfortable

WALKING AROUND SKAGWAY

Skagway's rowdy history is memorialized at the corner of 1st Avenue and Main Street, where a marker notes the infamous 1898 gun battle between Soapy Smith and Frank Reid. From the marker, head two blocks east along 1st Avenue and turn left on Broadway into the heart of the town. Inside the old White Pass and Yukon Railroad Depot at 2nd Avenue and Broadway, you'll find the **Klondike Gold Rush National Historical Park** visitor center, one of Southeast's best museums.

The next block north on Broadway—the heart of historical Skagway—contains several of the town's best-known buildings. The two-centuries-old Red Onion Saloon remains a favorite place to imbibe under the watchful eyes of "working girl" mannequins. Next door is the **Arctic Brotherhood Hall,** the facade of which is constructed entirely of driftwood. Inside, you'll find the helpful **Skagway Convention and Visitors Bureau,** which is full of friendly faces and useful local information. The golden dome of the **Golden North Hotel,** built in 1898, sits across the street from the old Mascot Saloon. ■**TIP→** There are also public restrooms here. Keep going up Broadway for **Corrington's Museum of Alaskan History,** with its large collection of scrimshaw (carved ivory) art. A right turn on

5th Avenue brings you to the Park Service's **Moore Cabin,** Skagway's oldest structure. The beautifully restored Skagway City Hall is housed in the same granite-front building as the **Skagway Museum.** Return to Broadway and follow it to 6th Avenue, where you can see *The Days of '98 with Soapy Smith* show inside historic Eagles Hall.

If you are up for a longer walk, continue 2 miles out of town along Alaska Street to the **Gold Rush Cemetery,** where you'll find the graves of combatants Soapy Smith and Frank Reid. The cemetery is also the trailhead for the short walk to Lower Reid Falls, an enjoyable jaunt through the valley's lush forest. (A city bus takes you most of the way to the cemetery for $2 each direction.) No tour of Skagway is complete without a train ride on the famed **White Pass and Yukon Route.** Trains depart from the corner of 2nd Street and Broadway several times a day in summer.

The six blocks that compose the heart of downtown Skagway can be explored in a half hour, but budget two hours to see the Park Service's historic buildings and the Skagway Museum. (If you include the 4-mile round-trip walk to the Gold Rush Cemetery, plan on three to four hours.) Leave some time to explore Skagway's many shops, restaurants, and other attractions.

4

and clean. **Cons:** limited room amenities; not much view. **TripAdvisor:** "quiet," "big room," "wonderful place to stay." ⑤ *Rooms from: $135* ✉ *9th Ave. and Main St.* ☎ *907/983–3045* ⊕ *www.mile-zero.com* ⤳ *7 rooms* ⏐⊙⏐ *Breakfast.*

$ 🏨 **Sgt. Preston's Lodge.** This four-building lodge—which feels more like a
HOTEL   motel—occupies a former army barracks. **Pros:** convenient to the cruise-ship and ferry docks; has a handicapped-accessible room; pets allowed for a small fee. **Cons:** some rooms are shaped oddly; some rooms are

DYEA

Once a bustling town filled with miners-to-be preparing to head up the Chilkoot Trail, Dyea is quite a bit quieter these days. At its height, Dyea had 48 hotels. Now? There are a few people still living in the area, but for the most part Dyea functions as both a fascinating historic site and a stunning place of beauty. The mud flats and sky play tricks on the eyes—the land looks like it stretches on endlessly. Dyea is part of Klondike Gold Rush National Historical Park, and the National Park Service offers tours of area. Or, for those who really want to experience Dyea's quiet, consider camping here. In the town's small cemeteries, the headstones tell the stories of those who once called Dyea home.

small. TripAdvisor: "clean and convenient," "great room," "owner went all out for us." ⑤ *Rooms from: $95* ✉ *370 6th Ave., Box 538* ☎ *907/983–2521, 866/983–2521* ⊕ *sgtprestons.eskagway.com* ⟿ *40 rooms* ⦿ *No meals.*

$$
B&B/INN
⌃ **Skagway Inn Bed & Breakfast.** Each room in this family-friendly downtown Victorian inn (once a not-so-family-friendly bordello) is named after a different gold-rush gal. **Pros:** large breakfast served; nicely remodeled. **Cons:** floors are creaky; walls are thin; some rooms without private bathrooms. **TripAdvisor:** "accommodation with character," "a fun place to stay," "wonderful service." ⑤ *Rooms from: $119* ✉ *655 Broadway* ☎ *907/983–2289, 888/752–4929* ⊕ *www.skagwayinn.com* ⟿ *10 rooms, 4 with bath* ⊙ *Closed Oct.–Apr.* ⦿ *Breakfast.*

$$
B&B/INN
⌃ **White House.** This B&B is about two blocks from downtown Skagway. **Pros:** conveniently located. **Cons:** no pets allowed. **TripAdvisor:** "very quaint," "great breakfasts," "comfortable in every sense of the word." ⑤ *Rooms from: $135* ✉ *475 8th Ave.* ☎ *907/983–9000* ⊕ *www. atthewhitehouse.com* ⟿ *10 rooms* ⦿ *Breakfast.*

NIGHTLIFE AND THE ARTS

BARS

Red Onion Saloon. Whereas Skagway was once host to dozens upon dozens of watering holes in its gold-rush days, the Red Onion Saloon is pretty much the sole survivor among them. The upstairs was Skagway's first bordello, and you'll find a convivial crowd of Skagway locals and visitors among the scantily clad mannequins who represent the building's former illustrious tenants. A ragtime pianist tickles the keys in the afternoons, and local musicians strut their stuff on Thursday nights. The saloon closes up shop for winter. ✉ *205 Broadway* ☎ *907/983–2222* ⊕ *www.redonion1898.com.*

THEATER

★ ***The Days of '98 with Soapy Smith.*** Since 1927 locals have performed a show called *The Days of '98 with Soapy Smith* at Eagles Hall. You'll see cancan dancers (including Molly Fewclothes, Belle Davenport, and Squirrel Tooth Alice), learn a little local history, and watch desperado

Soapy Smith being sent to his reward. At the evening show you can enjoy a few warm-up rounds of mock gambling with Soapy's money. Performances of Robert Service poetry start a half hour before show-time. Shows run one–four times daily, mid-May through mid-September. ✉ *590 Broadway* ☎ *907/983–2545 May–mid-Sept., 808/328–9132 mid-Sept.–Apr.* ⊕ *www.thedaysof98show.com* ✉ *$20.*

SHOPPING

Alaska Artworks. For those in search of locally produced silver jewelry, watercolor prints, and other handmade crafts, the artist-owned Alaska Artworks can't be beat. ✉ *555C Broadway* ☎ *907/983–3443* ⊕ *www. inspiredartworks.com.*

Corrington's Alaskan Ivory. Corrington's Alaskan Ivory is the destination of choice for scrimshaw seekers; it has one the state's best collections of ivory art. ✉ *525 Broadway* ☎ *907/983–2579.*

Skaguay News Depot & Books. This small but quaint bookstore carries books on Alaska, magazines, children's books, maps, and gifts. Its moniker is a throwback to the town's old spelling. ✉ *264 Broadway* ☎ *907/983–3354* ⊕ *www.skagwaybooks.com.*

4

Anchorage

WORD OF MOUTH

"We spent the day visiting Kincaid Park: This is incredible, it has cross-country ski trails, wonderful hiking trails, fishing, all kinds of sports. Met some nice local people there and hiked some. Then we decided to go down to Turnagain Arm and Potter's Marsh as it is so beautiful. Ate lunch at Sack's Café, which is excellent!!!!"

—LikeToTravel

WELCOME TO ANCHORAGE

TOP REASONS TO GO

★ **Tackling a 50-pound salmon:** Anglers can cast for huge king salmon or feisty silvers while wading among reflections of skyscrapers at Ship Creek.

★ **Winter celebrations:** Beginning in late February, locals celebrate the two-week Fur Rendezvous. Events—from the blanket toss to the Running of the Reindeer, Alaska's spin on Pamplona's tradition—lead up to the start of the Iditarod Trail Sled Dog Race in early March.

★ **Shopping:** Shops and vendors at the Saturday and Sunday markets sell everything from kid-friendly tchotchkes to elegant Native Alaskan crafts and locally produced foods.

★ **Seafood:** Dining out in Anchorage means feasting on local halibut, salmon, king-crab legs, scallops, and oysters. Many fine restaurants hide in not-so-pretty strip malls.

★ **Hiking and biking:** Laced with more than 120 miles of paved urban trails, Anchorage is a paradise for hikers and bicyclists.

1 Downtown. The city's cultural center has a festive atmosphere on summer afternoons, with flowers hung from street lamps and the smell of grilled onions and reindeer hot dogs in the air along 4th Avenue. The streets are lined with art galleries and shops; the weekend markets promise good hunting for shoppers seeking souvenirs.

2 Midtown. Some 3 miles east of the airport, Midtown is a newer neighborhood with an assortment of restaurants, shopping centers, and large hotels. The city's main library branch and a major movie-theater complex are located a short walk from most hotels.

3 **Tony Knowles Coastal Trail and Kincaid Park.** An 11-mile ribbon of asphalt beginning Downtown and stretching to Kincaid Park, the popular Tony Knowles Coastal Trail traverses tidal marshes, moose-inhabited greenbelts, and bluffs overlooking the inlet, Mt. Susitna, and the distant Alaska Range. Kincaid Park offers 40 miles of trails for biking, hiking, and cross-country skiing.

4 **Spenard.** Sandwiched between the airport and Midtown, Spenard is one of Anchorage's oldest neighborhoods, yet also one of its up and comers. It is home to the Anchorage location of outdoor-gear giant REI as well as some of the city's hippest restaurants. The neighborhood has a youthful, outdoorsy vibe about it.

GETTING ORIENTED

Founded in 1915 as a railroad camp, Anchorage has grown into Alaska's largest city and main travel hub. It's connected to the state's road network by the Seward and Glenn highways and remains the headquarters for the Alaska Railroad, which runs from Seward to Fairbanks. The city is bordered to the east by the Chugach foothills, to the west by Cook Inlet, to the south by Potter Marsh, and to the north by military bases. Sled-dog races are still among the most revered events held here, moose and occasionally bears roam city bike trails, and spectacular wilderness is a short drive away.

5

Updated
by Sarah
Henning

By far Alaska's largest and most sophisticated city, Anchorage is situated in a truly spectacular location. The permanently snow-covered peaks and volcanoes of the Alaska Range lie to the west of the city while part of the craggy Chugach Range is within the eastern edge of the municipality; the Talkeetna and Kenai ranges are visible to the north and south. Two arms of Cook Inlet embrace the town's western and southern borders, and on clear days Mt. McKinley (Denali) looms on the northern horizon.

Anchorage is Alaska's medical, financial, and banking center, and home to the executive offices of most of the Native Alaskan corporations. The city has a population of roughly 292,000, accounting for approximately 40% of the people in the state. The relative affluence of this white-collar city—with a sprinkling of olive drab from nearby military bases—fosters an ever-growing range of restaurants and shops, first-rate entertainment, and sporting events.

Incorporated in 1920, Anchorage is a young city. Nearly everything has been built since the 1970s—an Anchorage home dating from the 1950s almost merits historic status. The city got its start with the construction of the federally built Alaska Railroad, completed in 1917, and traces of its railroad heritage remain today. The city's architecture is far from memorable—though it has its quirky and charming moments—but the surrounding mountains more than make up for it.

Boom and bust periods followed major events: an influx of military bases during World War II; a massive buildup of Arctic missile-warning stations during the Cold War; reconstruction following the devastating Good Friday earthquake of 1964; and in the late 1960s the biggest jackpot of all—the discovery of oil at Prudhoe Bay and the construction of the Trans-Alaska Pipeline. It is no surprise that Anchorage then positioned itself as the perfect home for the pipeline administrators and support industries, and it continues to attract a large share of the state's oil-tax dollars.

PLANNING

WHEN TO GO

Located between the coast and several mountain ranges, Anchorage is a meteorologist's nightmare. Fickle weather patterns change less by the day than by the hour. Generally, fair-weather visitors should plan trips between the last week of May and mid-August.

Of the snow-free months, May is typically the driest, while August and September are the wettest. July is the warmest month, with an average temperature of 58.4°F; May is the coolest at 46.6°F. But don't be fooled by statistics. Late-May temperatures can exceed 70°F, and "hot" July and August days sometimes break 80°F. Of course, rainy low-pressure systems from the Gulf of Alaska can skulk in at any time, bringing wet and cool weather.

With such vagaries, do as the locals do: come prepared to go with the flow. That means packing light rain jackets and layers as well as tank tops and sunblock, and allowing for some flexibility with your plans.

GETTING HERE AND AROUND

AIR TRAVEL

Ted Stevens Anchorage International Airport is 6 miles from downtown Anchorage on International Airport Road. Several carriers, including ERA, Frontier Flying Service, and PenAir, connect Anchorage with smaller Alaskan communities. Floatplane operators and helicopters serve the area from Lake Hood, which is adjacent to and part of Anchorage International Airport. A number of smaller air taxis and air-charter operations are at Merrill Field, 2 miles east of downtown on 5th Avenue.

Taxis queue up at the lower level of the airport terminals outside the baggage-claim areas. They are on a meter system; it costs about $20, not including tip, for a ride to Downtown. An Alaska Railroad station in the airport has direct service to Downtown. Most of the larger hotels provide free airport shuttle services.

Airport **Ted Stevens Anchorage International Airport** ☎ *907/266–2526* ⊕ *www.anchorageairport.com.*

BOAT TRAVEL

Most cruise ships sailing the Gulf of Alaska and the Alaska Marine ferries call in Seward, two hours by train or bus south of Anchorage. However, Holland America just started offering itineraries that dock in Anchorage.

BUS TRAVEL

The municipal People Mover bus system covers the whole Anchorage Bowl. A one-way fare is $1.75 for rides outside the Downtown area; day passes good for unlimited rides are $5. ■TIP➜ Get schedules and information from the central bus depot at 6th Avenue and G Street.

Contact **People Mover** ☎ *907/343–6543* ⊕ *www.peoplemover.org.*

CAR TRAVEL

The Glenn Highway enters Anchorage from the north and becomes 5th Avenue near Merrill Field; this route will lead you directly into Downtown. Gambell Street leads out of town to the south, becoming New Seward Highway at about 20th Avenue. South of town, it becomes the Seward Highway. If you bring your RV or rent one on arrival, know that parking an RV downtown on weekdays is challenging. There's a big parking lot on 3rd Avenue between C and E streets. Parking is usually not a problem in other parts of town. You can find an up-to-date parking map of Downtown at ⊕ *www.anchoragedowntown.org* (click on For Visitors under the About Downtown tab).

TAXI TRAVEL

If you need a taxi, call one of the cab companies for a pickup; it's not common to hail one. Prices are $2 to $3 for a pickup, plus an additional $2.50 for each mile. Allow 20 minutes for arrival of the cab during morning and evening rush hours. Alaska Yellow Cab has taxis with wheelchair lifts. In the snow-free months a network of paved trails provide good avenues for in-city travel for bicyclists and walkers.

Contact **Alaska Yellow Cab** ☎ *907/222-2222* ⊕ *www.akyellowcab.com.*

TOUR TRAVEL

Tour Anchorage and the surrounding mountains and glaciers of South Central Alaska by land or by air with one of the many sightseeing companies in the region. The Log Cabin and Visitor Information Centers have brochures for Anchorage bus tours. For a one-hour overview, hop on a trolley with **Anchorage City Trolley Tours** ($15). Alternatively, **Gray Line of Alaska** has a city tour ($54) that lasts 3½ hours.

Any air-taxi company can arrange for a flightseeing trip over Anchorage and environs. The fee is determined by the length of time you are airborne, the number of passengers, and the size of the plane. Tours of about an hour and a half generally cost around $200 per person. Three-hour flights over Mt. McKinley from **Rust's Flying Service**, including a landing on a remote lake or a stop in Talkeetna, run $385 per person.

Contacts **Anchorage City Trolley Tours** ☎ *907/276-5603, 888/917-8687* ⊕ *www.alaskatrolley.com.* **Gray Line of Alaska** ☎ *907/277-5581, 888/452-1737* ⊕ *www.graylinealaska.com.* **Rust's Flying Service** ☎ *907/243-1595, 800/544-2299* ⊕ *www.flyrusts.com.*

TRAIN TRAVEL

From mid-May through mid-September, the Alaska Railroad runs daily between Anchorage and Seward; daily between Anchorage and Fairbanks via Talkeetna and Denali National Park and Preserve; and daily between Anchorage and Whittier, Portage, Spencer Whistle Stop, and Grandview. Winter service is available once each month from Anchorage to Talkeetna and, weekly, a round-trip from Anchorage to Fairbanks and back. Call for schedule and fare information.

Contact **Alaska Railroad** ☎ *907/265-2494, 800/544-0552* ⊕ *www.akrr.com.*

HEALTH AND SAFETY

Though most areas populated by tourists are safe to wander, Anchorage is a city, so it's best just to stay aware as you walk around town. That definitely holds true if you choose to hike any local trails—even those within the city limits. Before Anchorage was a paved city, it was wild. Most locals have stories of surprise visits by a moose or bear during a morning bathrobe run to get the newspaper. Moose and other animals walk the trails, too. As you walk along, make some noise, either by singing or talking to a friend to help ward off the animals. The award for the biggest pest of all goes to the unofficial state bird, the mosquito. Bring mosquito repellent with you for all hiking excursions.

Alaska Regional Hospital ⊠ *2801 DeBarr Rd., East Anchorage* ☎ *907/276–1131* ⊕ *www.alaskaregional.com.*

Physician Referral Service ☎ *888/254–7884 Alaska Regional Hospital, 907/212–2945 Providence Alaska Medical Center.*

Police, fire, and ambulance ☎ *911.*

Providence Alaska Medical Center ⊠ *3200 Providence Dr., East Anchorage* ☎ *907/562–2211* ⊕ *www.providence.org/alaska.*

VISITOR INFORMATION

Alaska sees more than 1.5 million visitors each summer and, of that total, more than 40% spend at least one night in Anchorage. The tourist-friendly city offers a wealth of information and services to help visitors along the way. In addition to the Log Cabin and Visitor Information Center downtown, there are two visitor information centers in Ted Stevens Anchorage International Airport: one in the north terminal (open mid-May through Sept.) and one in the south terminal in the C Concourse baggage claim area (open year-round).

Alaska Department of Fish and Game ⊠ *333 Raspberry Rd., Midtown* ☎ *907/267–2218* ⊕ *www.adfg.alaska.gov.*

Alaska Public Lands Information Center ⊠ *605 W. 4th Ave., Downtown* ☎ *907/644–3661, 866/869–6887* ⊕ *www.alaskacenters.gov.*

Visit Anchorage (*ACVB*). Housed in a rustic log cabin, the center's sod roof is festooned with huge hanging baskets of flowers, and a giant jade boulder stands outside. After a stop in the cabin, step out the back door to the more spacious visitor center stocked with brochures. Ask advice from the friendly and incredibly erudite volunteers: if they don't know something, it's not worth knowing. There are also two visitor information centers in Ted Stevens Anchorage International Airport, one in the north terminal and one in the south terminal in the C Concourse baggage claim area. ⊠ *524 W. 4th Ave., Downtown* ☎ *907/276–4118, 800/478–1255 to order visitor guides* ⊕ *www.anchorage.net.*

Anchorage Downtown Partnership ⊠ *333 W. 4th Ave., Suite 317, Downtown* ☎ *907/279–5650* ⊕ *www.anchoragedowntown.org.*

Log Cabin and Visitor Information Center ⊠ *4th Ave. and F St., Downtown* ☎ *907/257–2363* ⊕ *www.anchorage.net.*

BEST BETS FOR DIFFERENT TRAVELERS

For cruise travelers:

■ Stretch your sea legs and take a walk along the Tony Knowles Coastal Trail, or venture just south of town and hike Flattop Mountain. Either way, you'll get views of Cook Inlet, Mt. Susitna, and the Alaska Range.

■ Shop at the Anchorage Market and Festival any Saturday or Sunday during the warm months for souvenirs at some of the best prices around.

For those traveling with kids:

■ The Anchorage Museum is a can't-miss spot; head to the hands-on science exhibits.

■ Watch the planes come and go at Lake Hood's seaplane base.

For those who'd like pampering and fine dining:

■ The Sheraton Anchorage Hotel and Spa features Ice Spa, one of the best places for a treatment in Anchorage (with mountain views to boot).

■ Marx Bros. Café, Downtown, has a real Alaskan atmosphere and will likely serve you one of the best meals you'll have while in Alaska.

EXPLORING ANCHORAGE

Anchorage is a pedestrian- and bike-friendly city. Downtown Anchorage's flower-lined streets are easily explored on foot, and several businesses rent bicycles. The grid plan was laid out by the Army Corps of Engineers, and streets and avenues run exactly east–west and north–south, with numbers in the first direction and letters of the alphabet or Alaska place-names (Barrow, Cordova, Denali, etc.) in the other. The only aberration is the absence of a J Street—a concession, some say, to the city's early Swedish settlers, who had difficulty pronouncing the letter. You'll need a car for longer stays, expeditions, and to reach some of the city's better restaurants without relying on taxis.

Outside Downtown, Anchorage is composed of widely scattered neighborhoods and large shopping malls clustered along busy thoroughfares. And although there's no shortage of excellent restaurants Downtown, many of the town's best places are found in cheesy strip malls. Also, you're never more than a block or two from a good espresso stand or shop.

Once you're done wandering the shops Downtown, consider heading south to Midtown. The neighborhood has some of Anchorage's best restaurants. It's also a good neighborhood to stay in if you would rather be slightly outside the main tourist fray.

The next neighborhood heading away from Downtown is South Anchorage. Until recently South Anchorage was more of a local spot, but with several new restaurants opening there's been a growing tourist presence in the area. South Anchorage also has a large mall.

Another neighborhood worth exploring is Spenard, just west of Midtown (Spenard Road is considered the dividing line). The neighborhood—which celebrates its annual Spenardi Gras every March—has an artsy hip vibe and is home to some of the city's best casual restaurants, a good farmers' market, and Anchorage's largest independent bookstore.

You'll find plenty to do year-round in Anchorage, though most visitors, particularly first-timers, might be happiest in June, July, or August, when the days are longer—up to 19 hours, 21 minutes during the summer solstice—and the temperatures warmer. If you must choose one of the shoulder seasons, choose fall. There's less chance of rain, the snow has not yet arrived on trails except in the highest mountain passes, and there's an excellent chance for warm, sunny days, cool nights, and dazzling color changes in the trees and tundra. But if you choose fall, pack a few extra layers as a just-in-case for early snow (or be prepared to visit one of Anchorage's many gear shops): the city's earliest measurable dose of snow fell on September 20, 1947.

DOWNTOWN

TOP ATTRACTIONS

Alaska Center for the Performing Arts. The distinctive stone-and-glass building overlooks an expansive park filled with brilliant flowers all summer. Look inside for upcoming events, or relax amid the blossoms on a sunny afternoon. The center—which has four theaters—is home to 10 resident performing arts companies, including Alaska Dance Theatre, Anchorage Opera, and the Anchorage Symphony Orchestra. ⊠ *621 W. 6th Ave., at G St., Downtown* 🕾 *907/263–2787, 877/278–7849 tickets* ⊕ *www.myalaskacenter.com* ✉ *Tours by appointment only.*

★ **Alaska Public Lands Information Center.** Stop here for information on all ☾ of Alaska's public lands, including national and state parks, national forests, and wildlife refuges. You can plan a hiking, sea-kayaking, bear-viewing, or fishing trip; find out about public-use cabins; learn about Alaska's plants and animals; or head to the theater for films highlighting different parts of the state. The bookstore sells maps and nature books. Guided walks to historic Downtown sights detail the role Captain James Cook played in Alaska's history. Tours depart daily throughout the summer at 11 am and 2:30 pm. ⊠ *605 W. 4th Ave., No. 105, at F St., Downtown* 🕾 *907/644–3661* ⊕ *www.alaskacenters.gov* ☾ *Mid-May–mid-Sept. daily 9–5; mid-Sept.–mid-May, weekdays 10–5.*

Fodor's Choice **Anchorage Museum.** This is no just-in-case-of-a-rainy-day attraction.
★ An extensive renovation in 2009–10 made the Anchorage Museum an
☾ essential stop for visitors. There's no better way to deepen your understanding of the state's history, people, and, thanks to an impressive collection of paintings and photographs, beauty. The post-renovation star of the museum is the Smithsonian Arctic Studies Center, featuring more than 600 objects from Alaska Native cultures, short films that teach visitors about modern-day Native life, and much more. If you have a strong interest in history, art, or culture, leave extra time for the center—though it's just one large room, you might end up staying for hours. A good follow-up: wander the galleries filled with paintings and other art that showcases Alaska landscape and history through the talents of painters and other artists. The Alaska History Gallery's dioramas and other traditional museum exhibits focus on the state's

5

Downtown

Knik Arm

W. 2nd Ave.

Eisenhower Memorial

❸

❹

W. 3rd Ave.

❺

Saturday Market

❻

W. 4th Ave.

Elderberry Park

❼❽

W. 5th Ave.

Egan Convention Center

Central Bus Depot

❾

W. 6th Ave.

L St.

K St.

I St.

F St.

E St.

D St.

C St.

B St.

A St.

❿

W. 7th Ave.

H St.

G St.

W. 8th Ave.

0   1/8 mile

0   1/8 kilometer

Delaney Park

Cook Inlet

KEY

.... Tony Knowles Coastal Trail

⊢—⊣ Rail Lines

P St.

N St.

L St.

Westchester Lagoon

W. Marston Dr.

Fish Creek

Turnagain Pkwy.

Hillcrest Dr.

Arlington Dr.

Forest Park Dr.

Spenard Rd.

Northern Lights Blvd. W.

W. 29th St.

W. 30th Ave.

W. 31st Ave.

W. 32nd Ave.

Turnagain St.

Barbara St.

Benson Blvd.

Lois Dr.

Minnesota Dr.

←TO EARTHQUAKE PARK, POINT WORONZOF

W. 34th Ave.

W. 35th Ave.

Aero Ave.

Wisconsin Dr.

McRae Dr.

Spenard Rd.

W. 40th Ave.

Northwood Dr.

Lois Dr.

Lake Hood

44th Ave.

Spenard Beach

Lake Spenard

← ⓯

⓰

TO AIRPORT

↓

Anchorage

history. Cap the visit in the Imaginarium Discovery Center. Kids and their parents—and, okay, adults without kids, too—won't want to leave the museum once they step into the 9,000-square-foot center loaded with hands-on science exhibits. There's also a planetarium. In summer the first-floor atrium is the site of free daily presentations by local artists and authors. Muse restaurant, a bright and modern spot operated by local favorite the Marx Bros. Café, serves delicious lunches, dinners, and cocktails. The gift shop is one of Anchorage's best places to buy Alaska Native art and other souvenirs. Book lovers beware (or you may spend your vacation budget all at once): the shop's book department runs the gamut from Alaska fiction to history, cookbooks, and beyond. ⊠ *625 C St., Downtown* ☎ *907/929–9201, 907/929–9200 recorded information* ⊕ *www.anchoragemuseum.org* ⊟ *$12* ☾ *May–Sept., daily 9–6; Oct.–Apr., Tues.–Sat. 10–6, Sun. noon–6.*

Fodor'sChoice
★
Tony Knowles Coastal Trail. Strollers, runners, bikers, dog walkers, and in-line skaters cram this recreation trail on sunny summer evenings, particularly around Westchester Lagoon. In winter, cross-country skiers take to it by storm. The trail begins off 2nd Avenue, west of Christensen Drive, and curls along Cook Inlet for approximately 11 miles to Kincaid Park, beyond the airport. In summer you might spot beluga whales offshore in Cook Inlet. Access points are on the waterfront at the ends of 2nd, 5th, and 9th avenues and at Westchester Lagoon.

WORTH NOTING

Alaska Railroad Historic Depot. Totem poles and a locomotive built in 1907 are outside the station, the headquarters of the Alaska Railroad since 1915. A monument in front of the depot relates the history of the railroad, which brought an influx of people into the city during the early 1900s. During February's Fur Rendezvous festival, model-train buffs set up their displays here. ⊠ *411 W. 1st Ave., Downtown* ☎ *907/265–2494, 800/544–0552* ⊕ *www.alaskarailroad.com* ☾ *Daily, depending on train schedules.*

Historic City Hall. Offices of Visit Anchorage now occupy this 1936 building. A few exhibits and historic photos are right inside the lobby. Out front, take a look at the marble sculpture dedicated to William Seward, the secretary of state who engineered the purchase of Alaska from Russia. ⊠ *524 W. 4th Ave., Downtown.*

Log Cabin and Downtown Visitor Information Center. Housed in a rustic log cabin, the center's sod roof is festooned with huge hanging baskets of flowers. Anchorage is a major stopping point for cargo jets en route to Asia, and a signpost out front marks the mileage to many international destinations. ■TIP➔ After a stop in the cabin, step out the back door to the more spacious visitor center stocked with brochures. There are also two visitor information centers in Ted Stevens Anchorage International Airport, one in the north terminal and one in the south terminal in the C Concourse baggage claim area. ⊠ *4th Ave. and F St., Downtown* ☎ *907/257–2363* ⊕ *www.anchorage.net* ☾ *June–Aug., daily 8–7; May and Sept., daily 8–6; Oct.–Apr., daily 9–4.*

Oscar Anderson House Museum. City butcher Oscar Anderson built Anchorage's first permanent frame house in 1915, at a time when most of Anchorage consisted of tents. Swedish Christmas tours are held the first two weekends of December. Guided 45-minute tours are available whenever the museum is open. ⊠ *420 M St., in Elderberry Park, Downtown* ☎ *907/274–2336* ⌐ *$3* ☾ *June–mid-Sept., weekdays noon–5; group tours (maximum 10 participants per group) must be arranged in advance.*

Resolution Park. This tiny park has a cantilevered viewing platform dominated by a monument to Captain Cook, whose explorations in 1778 led to the naming of Cook Inlet and many other geographic features in Alaska. Mt. Susitna, known as the Sleeping Lady, is the prominent low mountain to the northwest, and Mts. Spurr and Redoubt, active volcanoes, are just south of Mt. Susitna. Mt. McKinley, Mt. Foraker, and other peaks of the Alaska Range are often visible from more than 100 miles away. ⊠ *3rd Ave. at L St., Downtown.*

☾ **Ship Creek.** The creek is dammed right in Downtown, with a footbridge across the dam and access from either bank. There's a waterfall; salmon running upstream from June through August; anglers; and, above it all, downtown Anchorage. Farther upstream (follow Whitney Road and turn left on Post Road) is the newly renamed William Jack Hernandez Sport Fish Hatchery—during the runs you can see salmon in the clear, shallow water as they try to leap up the falls. ⊠ *Whitney Rd., Downtown.*

MIDTOWN

★ **Alaska Heritage Museum at Wells Fargo.** More than 900 Alaska Native artifacts are the main draw in the quiet, unassuming lobby of a large midtown bank—it's reputed to be one of the largest private collections of Native artworks in the country. Also here are paintings by Alaskan artists, a library of rare books, and a 46-troy-ounce gold nugget. ⊠ *Wells Fargo Bank, 301 W. Northern Lights Blvd., at C St., Midtown* ☎ *907/265–2834* ⊕ *www.wellsfargohistory.com/museums* ⌐ *Free* ☾ *Late May–early Sept., weekdays noon–5; early Sept.–late May, weekdays noon–4.*

GREATER ANCHORAGE

EAST ANCHORAGE

☾ **Alaska Botanical Garden.** The garden showcases perennials hardy enough to make it in South Central Alaska in several large display gardens, a pergola-enclosed herb garden, and a rock garden amid 110 acres of mixed boreal forest. There's a 1-mile nature trail loop to Campbell Creek, with views of the Chugach Range and a wildflower trail between the display gardens. Interpretive signs guide visitors and identify plants along the trail. Children can explore the garden with an activity-filled duffel bag. Docent tours are available at 1 pm daily June through August; in addition, you can schedule your own tour by appointment between June 1 and September 15. The gift shop and retail nursery are open Tuesday through Sunday late May to mid-September. ⊠ *4601 Campbell Airstrip Rd., off Tudor Rd. (park at Benny Benson School), East Anchorage* ☎ *907/770–3692* ⊕ *www.alaskabg.org* 🖾 *$7* ☉ *Daily during daylight hrs.*

Fodor's Choice
★
☼
Alaska Native Heritage Center. On a 26-acre site facing the Chugach Mountains, this facility provides an introduction to Alaska's Native peoples. The spacious Welcome House has interpretive displays, artifacts, photographs, demonstrations, Native dances, storytelling, and films, along with a café and a gift shop selling museum-quality crafts and artwork. Step outside for a stroll around the adjacent lake, where seven village exhibits represent 11 Native cultural groups through traditional structures and exhibitions. As you enter the homes in these villages, you can visit with the culture hosts, hear their stories, and experiment with some of the tools, games, and utensils used in the past. ■TIP➔ There's a free shuttle to the Heritage Center from the downtown Log Cabin and Visitor Information Center that runs several times a day in the summer. You can also hop a bus at the downtown transit center; Route 4 (Glenn Highway) will take you to the Heritage Center's front door. A Culture Pass Joint Ticket for $28.95 provides admission here and to the Anchorage Museum downtown; it's available at either location. ⊠ *8800 Heritage Center Dr.(Glenn Hwy. at Muldoon Rd.), East Anchorage* ☎ *907/330–8000, 800/315–6608* ⊕ *www.alaskanative.net* 🖾 *$24.95, $9.95 Alaska residents* ☉ *Mid-May (Mother's Day)–Sept., daily 9–5; Oct.–mid-May, Sat. 10–5.*

SOUTH ANCHORAGE

☼ **Alaska Zoo.** Roam the trails and visit with the polar bears, caribou, brown and black bears, seals, tigers, snow leopards, moose, wolves, lynx, and a large array of birds that call the Alaska Zoo home. Along with a major facility upgrade with a new entrance cabin and gift shop in 2009, the zoo has also upgraded its mission statement to concentrate on promoting the conservation of arctic and subarctic animal species. Throughout the summer, daily two-hour tours include two behind-the-scenes stops. ⊠ *4731 O'Malley Rd., 2 miles east of New Seward Hwy., South Anchorage* ☎ *907/346–3242* ⊕ *www.alaskazoo.org* 🖾 *$12* ☉ *June–Aug, daily 9–9; May and Sept., daily 9–6; Mar., Apr., and Oct., daily 10–5; Nov.–Feb., daily 10–4; winter closing hrs may vary with conditions.*

☼ **Potter Marsh.** Sandhill cranes, trumpeter swans, and other migratory birds, as well as the occasional moose or beaver, frequent this marsh about 10 miles south of Downtown on the Seward Highway. An elevated boardwalk makes viewing easy, and in summer there are salmon runs in the creek beneath the bridge. The **Potter Section House,** an old railroad service building just south of the marsh, operates as a state park office. Out front is an old engine with a rotary snowplow that was used to clear avalanches. ⊠ *Seward Hwy., South Anchorage* ☎ *907/269–8400.*

WEST ANCHORAGE

Alaska Aviation Heritage Museum. The state's unique aviation history is presented with 25 vintage aircraft—seven have been completely restored—three theaters, an observation deck along **Lake Hood,** the world's busiest seaplane base, a flight simulator, and a gift shop. Highlights include a Stearman C2B, the first plane to land on Mt. McKinley back in the early 1930s. Volunteers are working to restore a 1931 Fairchild Pilgrim aircraft and make it flyable and are eager to talk shop. A free shuttle to and from Anchorage Airport is available. ⊠ *4721 Aircraft Dr., West Anchorage* ☎ *907/248–5325* ⊕ *www.alaskaairmuseum. org* ⌕ *$10* ⊘ *May 11–Sept. 15, daily 9–5; Sept. 16–May 10, Wed.–Sat. 9–5, Sun. noon–5.*

OUTDOOR ACTIVITIES AND GUIDED TOURS

5

Few American cities feel as connected to the outdoors as Anchorage. From the in-town Tony Knowles Coastal Trail to a nearly endless supply of trails and other outdoor adventures in the Chugach National Forest and on nearby waterways, Anchorage is an outdoor-lover's playground. And that doesn't just hold true for the warmer months; a nearby ski resort offers downhill delights and there's plenty of dog mushing and ice climbing and other wintry sports to try. Up for some spectator sports instead? Anchorage doesn't disappoint: summer-league baseball, the start of the Iditarod, and a minor-league hockey team are waiting for you.

PARTICIPATORY SPORTS

BICYCLING

Anchorage has more than 120 miles of paved bicycle trails, and many streets have marked bike lanes. Although busy during the day, Downtown streets are uncrowded and safe for cyclists in the evening.

Alaskabike. Starting in Anchorage, multiday touring packages through this company explore South Central, the Interior, and nearby scenic highways. ⊠ *3900 B Woronzof Dr.* ☎ *907/538–2392, 866/683–2453* ⊕ *www.alaskabike.com.*

Alaska Pablo's Bicycle Rentals. Near the Tony Knowles Coastal Trail, this shop has rental rates beginning at $7 per hour. Discounts are available for groups of five or more. ⊠ *501 L St., Downtown* ☎ *907/250–2871* ⊕ *www.pablobicyclerentals.com* ⊘ *Daily 8–7.*

Arctic Bicycle Club. This nonprofit bicycling club organizes races and rides. ☎ *907/566–0177* ⊕ *www.arcticbike.org.*

Downtown Bicycle Rental. With an inventory of more than 100 bikes of all types, Downtown Bicycle Rental also has clip-in pedals and shoes. The minimum rental rate is $16 for three hours, which includes free lock, helmet, panniers, and map. Located five blocks from the Coastal Trail, the company also offers combo hike-and-bike trips that include a shuttle van ride to the Flattop trailhead. ⊠ *333 W. 4th Ave., Downtown* ☎ *907/279–5293* ⊕ *www.alaska-bike-rentals.com.*

Kincaid Park. At the far west end of Raspberry Road in South Anchorage the 43 miles of trails at Kincaid Park wind through 1,400 acres of mixed spruce and birch forest. Mountain bikers will find easy-to-moderate riding along with some challenging hills. Be advised that Kincaid Park is home to a sizable moose population, as well as the occasional bear, so stay alert at all times. Considered one of the best places for Nordic skiing in the United States, the park remains popular throughout the year. The Kincaid Outdoor Center—locally called Kincaid Chalet—is available for a fee for social functions such as weddings, receptions, and meetings. The park also has a climbing wall. ⌧ *9401 W. Raspberry Rd., West Anchorage* ☎ *907/343–6397.*

Lifetime Adventures. Just 30 miles north of Anchorage, Lifetime Adventures operates out of the state park campground at Eklutna Lake. Lifetime rents bikes, trailers, and kayaks. You can take the popular Paddle & Pedal package in which you paddle in one direction and pedal your way back. ☎ *800/952–8624, 907/746–4644* ⊕ *www.lifetimeadventures.net.*

Tony Knowles Coastal Trail. Bike trails in Anchorage are used by runners, cyclists, in-line skaters, and walkers. The Tony Knowles Coastal Trail begins Downtown off 2nd Avenue and is also easily accessible from Westchester Lagoon near the west end of 15th Avenue. The trail runs from the lagoon for 2 miles to Earthquake Park and then continues an additional 7 miles to Kincaid Park, where several unpaved trails provide for more adventurous biking and hiking. Those who prefer the off-road experience should pick up a copy of Mountain Bike Anchorage by Rosemary Austin.

BIRD-WATCHING

Popular bird-watching places include the Tony Knowles Coastal Trail, which provides access to Westchester Lagoon and nearby tide flats, along with Potter Marsh on the south end of Anchorage.

Audubon Society. The Anchorage chapter of the Audubon Society offers a downloadable list of the "Birds of Anchorage" on their Web site and can refer you to local birders who will advise you on the best bird-watching spots. The society also hosts bird-watching classes and field trips. ⊕ *www.anchorageaudubon.org.*

Wilderness Birding Adventures. Naturalists Lisa Moorehead and Bob Dittrick of Wilderness Birding Adventures offer backcountry birding, wildlife, and natural-history trips to remote parts of Alaska, as well as village-based, birding-focused trips to some of Alaska's birding hot spots. ☎ *907/694–7442* ⊕ *www.wildernessbirding.com.*

CANOEING AND KAYAKING

Local lakes and lagoons, such as Westchester Lagoon, Goose Lake, and Jewel Lake, have favorable conditions for canoeing and kayaking. More adventurous paddlers should head to Whittier or Seward for sea kayaking.

Alaska Rafts & Kayak. Rent or buy from a flotilla's worth of small boats, including kayaks, canoes, inflatable rafts, and one-man fishing pontoons. The store also rents float tubes. ⌧ *401 W. Tudor Rd., Midtown* ☎ *907/561–7238, 800/606–5950* ⊕ *www.alaskaraftandkayak.com.*

REI. REI sells and rents all sorts of outdoor gear, including canoes and sea kayaks. ✉ *1200 W. Northern Lights Blvd., Spenard* ☎ *907/272–4565* ⊕ *www.rei.com.*

FISHING

Nearly 30 local lakes and streams are stocked with catchable game fish. ■TIP→ You must have a valid Alaska sportfishing license to fish in the state. Fishing licenses may be purchased at any Fred Meyer or Carr's/Safeway grocery or local sporting goods store, or online at ⊕ https://www.admin.adfg.state.ak.us/buyonline. Nonresidents can buy an annual license or a 1-, 3-, 7-, or 14-day permit. A separate king salmon stamp is required to fish for the big guys. Rainbow trout, arctic char, land-locked salmon, Dolly Varden, grayling, and northern pike are among the species found in waters like Jewel Lake in South Anchorage and Mirror and Fire lakes near Eagle River. Coho salmon return to Ship Creek (downtown) in August, and king salmon are caught there between late May and early July. Campbell Creek and Bird Creek just south of town are also good spots for coho—locally called silver—salmon. Anywhere in Alaska there are fish, it's possible there are also bears, so stay aware.

Alaska Department of Fish and Game. Contact the Alaska Department of Fish and Game for licensing information. For information about Anchorage-area lakes, go to the Web site; click on Sport Fishing, the South Central portion of the "Fisheries by Area" map, and then Anchorage. ☎ *907/267–2218* ⊕ *www.adfg.alaska.gov.*

FLIGHTSEEING

This area is the state's air-travel hub. Plenty of flightseeing services operating out of city airports and floatplane bases can take you on spectacular tours of **Mt. McKinley,** the **Chugach Range, Prince William Sound, Kenai Fjords National Park,** and the **Harding Icefield.** Anchorage hosts the greatest number and variety of services, including companies operating fixed-wing aircraft, floatplanes, and helicopters.

Fodor's Choice ★ **Rust's Flying Service.** An Anchorage company in business since 1963, Rust's will take you on narrated flightseeing tours of Mt. McKinley and Denali, Columbia Glacier, and Prince William Sound, as well as on flights to the Alaska Peninsula for bear viewing. Rust's recently started offering three- and five-night fly-in hiking trips to Denali National Park and Lake Clark National Park. The company also owns Talkeetna-based **K2 Aviation.** ✉ *4525 Enstrom Circle, West Anchorage* ☎ *907/243–1595, 800/544–2299* ⊕ *www.flyrusts.com.*

CRUISE KENAI

Kenai Fjord Tours. Give your arms a rest, soak up glacier views, and spot the abundant wildlife of Kenai Fjords National Park from a cruise boat. Kenai Fjord Tours offers day packages to Kenai Fjords National Park April through September. The company offers transportation via coach and train between Anchorage and Seward. ■TIP→ Check the website for early-bird and shoulder-season special deals. ✉ *509 W. 4th Ave., Downtown* ☎ *877/777–4051, 907/777–2852* ⊕ *www.kenaifjords.com.*

5

"This picture harnesses the energy from my first hike to the top of Flat Top Mountain just outside of Anchorage. The hike is great for all skill levels." —Clay W. Padgett, Fodors.com photo contest winner

GOLF

Anchorage is Alaska's golfing capital, with several public courses. They won't compare to offerings in Phoenix or San Diego, but courses are open until 10 pm on long summer days, and at some courses the mountain views put the sights of most other courses to shame.

Anchorage Golf Course. Anchorage Golf Course has 18 holes and, as of the 2011 season, a new pro shop and bar. ⊠ *3651 O'Malley Rd., South Anchorage* ☎ *907/522–3363* ⊕ *www.anchoragegolfcourse.com* ⅄ *18 holes. 6,600 yds. Par 72. Green Fee: $37/$63* ☞ *Facilities: Driving range, putting green, pitching area, golf carts, pull carts, rental clubs, pro shop, golf academy/lessons, restaurant, bar.*

Moose Run Golf Course. Moose Run offers two 18-hole, scenic courses; the Creek Course boasts the longest layout in the state and is more challenging than the Hill Course. Moose Run has an unusual hazard: moose and bears live in the nearby woods. ■ **TIP→** Keep your eyes peeled for moose and bears, and if an animal ambles onto the green, by all means let it play through. ⊠ *27000 Arctic Valley Rd., East Anchorage, Anchorage* ☎ *907/428–0056* ⊕ *www.mooserungolfcourse.com* ⅄ *18 holes. 7,324/5,183 yds. Par 72. Green fee: $49* ☞ *Driving range, putting green, pitching area, golf carts, pull carts, rental clubs, pro shop, golf academy/lessons, restaurant.*

For information on other courses around the state, check out ⊕ *www. alaskagolflinks.com.*

ICE-SKATING

Ice-skating is a favorite wintertime activity in Anchorage, with several indoor ice arenas, outdoor hockey rinks, and local ponds opening when temperatures drop. Though Alaska's early winters and cold temperatures often allow for pond skating as early as mid-November, call the Visitor's Center or the city's parks and recreation department before stepping out onto pond ice.

Ben Boeke Ice Arena. Ben Boeke Ice Arena is a city-run indoor ice arena with open skating and skate rentals year-round. ⊠ *334 E. 16th Ave., Midtown* ☎ *907/274–5715* ⊕ *www.benboeke.com.*

Dimond Ice Chalet. An indoor ice rink at Dimond Mall, the Dimond Ice Chalet is open to the public daily. ⊠ *800 E. Dimond Blvd., South Anchorage* ☎ *907/344–1212* ⊕ *www.dimondicechalet.com.*

Westchester Lagoon. In winter, Westchester Lagoon, 1 mile south of downtown, is a favorite outdoor family (and competitive) skating area, with smooth ice, mountain views, and piles of firewood next to the warming barrels. ⊕ *www.muni.org/departments/parks.*

Other pond skating possibilities include **Cheney Lake, Goose Lake, Potter Marsh, Jewel Lake**, and **Spenard Lake**.

RAFTING

Chugach Powder Guides. Based in Girdwood, Chugach Powder Guides leads scenic floats on the Placer, Twentymile, and Portage rivers, along with white-water trips on the Talkeetna River and summer Tordrillo Mountain packages. ☎ *907/783–4354* ⊕ *www.alaskanrafting.com.*

RUNNING AND WALKING

Alaska Public Lands Information Center. ■ TIP➔ Pick up a guide to local trails before you head out. They're available at the Alaska Public Lands Information Center or area bookstores. ⊠ *605 W. 4th Ave., Downtown* ☎ *907/644–3661, 866/869-6887* ⊕ *www.alaskacenters.gov.*

Alaska Run for Women. A number of popular running events are held annually in Anchorage, including the Alaska Run for Women in early June, which raises money for the fight against breast cancer. ⊕ *www.akrfw.org.*

Heart Run. The late-April Heart Run is a fund-raiser for the American Heart Association's work to prevent heart disease. ⊕ *www.heartrun.com.*

Mayor's Marathon. Alaska's most famous running event is the Mayor's Marathon, held on the Saturday closest to summer solstice (June 21). ⊕ *www.mayorsmarathon.com.*

SKIING

★ Cross-country skiing is extremely popular in Anchorage. Locals ski on trails in town at Kincaid Park or Hillside and farther away at Girdwood Valley, Turnagain Pass, and Chugach State Park. Downhill skiing is

> TIP
>
> If you choose to travel by rail independently, the Alaska Railroad cars, which have glass-domed observation cars and onboard guides, make the trip between Anchorage and Fairbanks while hooked up to the same engines as the cruise-line cars. Alaska Railroad's website (⊕ *www.akrr.com*) has details.

5

convenient to downtown. A number of cross-country ski events are held annually in Anchorage.

Alaska Ski for Women. Held on Super Bowl Sunday in early February, Alaska Ski for Women is one of the biggest women's ski races in North America, attracting more than 1,200 skiers. Many of the skiers don crazy costumes for the event. ☎ *907/276–7609* ⊕ *www. alaskaskiforwomen.org.*

Nordic Skiing Association of Anchorage. The Nordic Skiing Association of Anchorage sponsors many other ski races and events throughout winter, from wooden-ski classics to the highly competitive Besh Cup series. ⊕ *www.anchoragenordicski.com.*

Tour of Anchorage. Biggest of all is the Tour of Anchorage, a grueling 50-km (31-mile) race in early March. If you're not up to doing 50k, there are 25k (16-mile) and 40k (25-mile) competitions as well. ⊕ *www. tourofanchorage.com.*

Alpenglow at Arctic Valley. Alpenglow at Arctic Valley is a small ski area just north of Anchorage. ⊠ *Mile 7, Arctic Valley Rd. off Glenn Hwy., just past Muldoon Exit* ☎ *907/428–1208 ski hotline* ⊕ *www.skiarctic.net.*

Hilltop Ski Area. On the eastern edge of town, Hilltop Ski Area is a favorite ski area for families. ⊠ *Abbott Rd. near Hillside Dr., East Anchorage* ☎ *907/346–2167 ski hotline* ⊕ *www.hilltopskiarea.org.*

Kincaid Park. On 1,400 acres of rolling, timbered hills and bordered on the west by Cook Inlet, Kincaid Park is a scenic treasure with maintained trails groomed for diagonal and skate-skiing. National cross-country skiing events (including U.S. Olympic team qualifying events and national masters championships) are sometimes held along the 60 km (37 miles) of interwoven trails—including 20 km (12 miles) that are lit for night skiing. The park is open year-round: for skiing in winter; and for mountain biking, hiking, and other outdoor activities in summer. The Raspberry Road gates are open 10 am–10 pm. ⊠ *Main entrance at far west end of Raspberry Rd., 9401 W. Raspberry Rd., Southwest Anchorage* ☎ *907/343–6397* ⊕ *www.muni.org/parks/ parkdistrictsw.cfm.*

Alaska Mountaineering & Hiking. The locally owned outdoors shop Alaska Mountaineering & Hiking has a highly experienced staff and plenty of cross-country skis for sale or rent. ⊠ *2633 Spenard Rd., Midtown* ☎ *907/272–1811* ⊕ *www.alaskamountaineering.com.*

REI. Ski and snowshoe sales and rentals are available from REI. ⊠ *1200 W. Northern Lights Blvd., Midtown* ☎ *907/272–4565* ⊕ *www.rei.com/ stores/16.*

SPECTATOR SPORTS

Wintertime brings hockey, dog mushing, and ski races, and long summer days provide the chance to watch a baseball game and still have time to watch the sun go down at midnight.

Sullivan Arena. Sullivan Arena is Anchorage's primary venue for large events, from ice hockey to boat shows. ⊠ *334 E. 16th Ave., Midtown* ☎ *907/566–1596.*

Mulcahy Stadium. If you're looking for baseball central in Anchorage, it's Mulcahy Stadium, where the Anchorage Bucs play. ⊠ *E. 16th Ave. at Cordova St., Midtown.*

BASEBALL

Two summer baseball teams made up of college students play at Mulcahy Stadium next to the Sullivan Arena. The games played here are intense—many players have gone on to star in Major League Baseball.

Anchorage Bucs. The Anchorage Bucs have sent many players to the majors, including standouts Wally Joyner, Jeff Kent, and Jered Weaver. ☎ *907/561–2827* ⊕ *www.anchoragebucs.com.*

Glacier Pilots. The most famous player on the Glacier Pilots was Mark McGwire, but many other pre–major leaguers have played for them over the years, including future Hall of Famer Randy Johnson and current standout Jacoby Ellsbury. ☎ *907/274–3627* ⊕ *www.glacierpilots.com.*

DOG MUSHING

Fur Rondy Festival. World-championship dog-mushing races are run in February, with three consecutive 25-mile heats through downtown Anchorage, out into the foothills, and back. People line the route with cups of coffee in hand to cheer on their favorite mushers. The three-day races are part of the annual Fur Rendezvous Festival, one of the largest winter festivals in the United States. Other attractions include a snow-sculpture competition, car races, Alaska Native blanket toss (a holdover from earlier days when dozens of people would team up to grasp a round walrus-hide blanket and launch a hunter high into the air, trampoline-style, in an effort to spot distant seals, walrus, and whales), dog weight–pulling contests (where canines of all breeds and sizes compete to see which can pull the most weight piled on a sled), a carnival, and even snowshoe softball. Fur Rondy events take place from late February to the start of the Iditarod in early March.

Fur Rondy office. Get a guide to the festival's events at the Fur Rondy office. ⊠ *400 D St., No. 200, Downtown* ☎ *907/274–1177* ⊕ *www. furrondy.net.*

Iditarod Trail Sled Dog Race. In March, mushers and their dogs compete in the 1,150-mile Iditarod Trail Sled Dog Race. The race commemorates the delivery of serum to Nome by dog mushers during the diphtheria epidemic of 1925. The serum run was the inspiration for the animated family film *Balto.* Dog teams leave downtown Anchorage and wind through the Alaska Range, across the Interior, out to the Bering Sea coast, and on to Nome. Depending on weather and trail conditions, winners can complete the race in nine days. ☎ *907/376–5155, 800/545–6874 Iditarod Trail Headquarters* ⊕ *www.iditarod.com.*

CLOSE UP

Iditarod Trail History

Since 1973, mushers and their sled-dog teams have raced more than 1,000 miles across Alaska in the Iditarod Trail Sled Dog Race, the longest sled-dog race in the world.

After a ceremonial start in downtown Anchorage on the first Saturday in March, dog teams wind through Alaska, battling almost every imaginable winter challenge. Iditarod mushers and dogs endure extreme cold, deep snow, gale-force winds, whiteouts, river overflow, and moose attacks, not to mention fraying tempers. Less than 10 days later, the front-runners in the "Last Great Race" cross under the burled-wood arch finish line in Nome, on the Bering Sea coast.

The Iditarod's origins can be traced to two events: an early-1900s long-distance race called the All-Alaska Sweepstakes and the delivery of a lifesaving serum to Nome by dog mushers during a diphtheria outbreak in 1925.

Fascinated with the trail's history, Alaskan sled-dog enthusiasts Dorothy Page and Joe Redington Sr. staged the first race in 1967 to celebrate the role of mushing in Alaska's history. Only 50 miles long and with a purse of $25,000—no small amount at that time—it attracted the best of Alaska's competitive mushers. Enthusiasm waned in 1969, however, when the available winnings fell to $1,000. Instead of giving up, Redington expanded the race.

In 1973, after three years without a race, he organized a 1,000-mile race from Anchorage to Nome, with a then-outrageous purse of $50,000. Critics scoffed, but 34 racers entered. First place went to a little-known musher named Dick Wilmarth, who finished in 20 days. Redington then billed the Iditarod as a 1,049-mile race to symbolize Alaska, the 49th state. While still the official distance, the race really covers more than 1,150 miles.

The race actually begins in Wasilla, the Iditarod's headquarters, a 50-mile drive north of Anchorage. The first few hundred miles take mushers and dogs through wooded lowlands and hills, including Moose Alley.

Teams then cross the Alaska Range and enter Interior Alaska, with Athabascan villages and gold-rush ghost towns, including Iditarod. Next, the trail follows the frozen Yukon River, then cuts over to the Bering Sea coast for the final 270-mile "sprint" to Nome. It was here, in 1985, that Libby Riddles drove her team into a blinding blizzard en route to a victory that made her the first woman to win the race. After that, Susan Butcher won the race four times, but the all-time record holder is Rick Swenson, with five victories. Lance Mackey holds the record for most consecutive wins, with his back-to-backs from 2007 to 2010. The fastest time was recorded in 2011, when Alaska native John Baker finished in 8 days, 18 hours, and 46 minutes.

Finger Lake Checkpoint. Sled dogs start the Iditarod in Anchorage and stop here, 194 miles into the 1,150-mile trek.

HOCKEY

Hockey is in the blood of any true Alaskan, and young kids crowd local ice rinks in hopes of becoming the next Scott Gomez (who, along with playing for the Montreal Canadiens, backs a namesake foundation that provides "opportunities and assistance for youth hockey in Alaska").

Alaska Aces. The Alaska Aces, 2011 ECHL Kelly Cup champions, play minor-league professional hockey in Sullivan Arena. ☎ *907/258–2237* ⊕ *www.alaskaaces.com.*

University of Alaska Anchorage. The Sullivan Arena is where several thousands of fans cheer for the University of Alaska Anchorage's Division I NCAA hockey team. ☎ *907/786–1293* ⊕ *www.goseawolves.com.*

WHERE TO EAT

Anchorage's dining scene has, to the relief of repeat visitors and, even more so, locals, been on the rise for the past several years. Established (and still highly recommended) restaurants like Jens' and Marx Bros. Café have been joined by the likes of the small-plate and wine-focused Crush Wine Bistro and Cellar and the Pacific Rim cuisine–focused Ginger. No matter the restaurant, the local catch is a frequent star. Beware: eating salmon or halibut in-state may ruin the experience for most other restaurants in the Lower 48. Anchorage also offers up plenty of worldly flavors thanks to the city's ethnic diversity. And nobody should leave Anchorage without trying the local fast-food specialty: a reindeer hot dog or sausage from the cart in front of the courthouse on 4th Avenue. Smoking is not allowed in Anchorage restaurants. *Prices in the reviews are the average cost of a main course at dinner or, if dinner is not served, at lunch. Use the coordinate (⊕ B2) at the end of each review to locate a property on the Where to Eat and Stay in Anchorage map.*

DOWNTOWN

$$$
STEAKHOUSE

✕ **Club Paris.** Alaska's oldest steak house has barely changed since opening in 1957. The restaurant, with dark wood and an old-fashioned feel, serves tender, flavorful steaks of all kinds, including a 4-inch-thick filet mignon. If you have to wait for a table, have a martini at the bar and order the hors d'oeuvres platter ($32)—a sampler of top sirloin steak, halibut chunks, cheese, and prawns that could be a meal for two. For dessert, try a slice of tart key lime or sweet-potato pie. Dinner reservations are advised. $ *Average main: $31* ⊠ *417 W. 5th Ave., Downtown* ☎ *907/277–6332* ⊕ *www.clubparisrestaurant.com* ⊘ *No lunch Sun.* ⊕ *C2.*

$$$$
EUROPEAN

✕ **Crow's Nest Restaurant.** In the Hotel Captain Cook, American and French cuisine are the order of the day, along with the best view in Anchorage—the Chugach Mountains to the east, the Alaska Range to the north, and the sprawling city of Anchorage 20 stories below. Equally impressive are the 10,000-bottle wine cellar and hefty portions. The waitstaff presents a menu of seafood, along with beef, pork, and lamb, served in an elegant setting with plenty of starched linen, brass, and teak. $ *Average main: $35* ⊠ *Hotel Captain Cook, 20th fl., 939 W. 5th Ave., Downtown* ☎ *907/343–2217* ⊕ *www.captaincook.com/ dining/crows-nest* ⊠ *Reservations essential* ⊘ *Closed Sun. and Mon. in winter. No lunch* ⊕ *A2.*

$$
ECLECTIC

✕ **Crush Wine Bistro and Cellar.** The conversation-friendly combo of sharing-friendly small plates and an extensive wine list make Crush Anchorage's go-to dining venue when you want to discuss adventures already lived or the ones to come. The restaurant could probably coast on that combo alone but, luckily, the owners aren't into coasting. They brought on chef Christopher Vane, nominated for a 2011 James Beard Award, to head up an inventive (but budget-friendly) menu that ranges from $5 plates of blue cheese–stuffed Medjool dates to $8 servings of sherried portobello-and-spinach polenta, and beyond. Though it's more fun to share, diners who prefer a plate of their own can also opt for one of the daily dinner specials. Along with a world's worth of wines, Crush serves a selection of top-flight beers and some seriously beautiful espresso drinks. Housed in a building that could easily be a setting for a 1970s-era sci-fi flick, the interior is far warmer and more inviting than its curvy porthole-ish exterior. $ *Average main: $20* ⊠ *343 W. 6th Ave., Downtown* ☎ *907/865–9198* ⊕ *www.crushak.com* ⊘ *Closed Sun.* ⊕ *C2.*

$$$
ASIAN

✕ **Ginger.** Thanks to beautifully crafted Pacific Rim dishes such as broccoli beef with wasabi-mashed peanut potatoes, Ginger was a welcome addition to the local dining scene when it opened in 2007. The menu offers dishes that will please both adventurous and more traditional diners. Ginger also keeps vegetarians happy with such dishes as grilled tofu over a cold Israeli couscous salad. Decorated in beautiful woods and warm tones, the interior perfectly complements the menu. Alaska local chef Guy Conley was nominated for a 2010 James Beard Award in the best chef/northwest category. The restaurant's new lounge is a hip place to spend happy hour: try the spicy tuna tower with a ginger mojito. Reservations are recommended. $ *Average main: $24* ⊠ *425 W. 5th Ave., Downtown* ☎ *907/929–3680* ⊕ *www.gingeralaska.com* ⊙ *No lunch weekends* ✣ *C2.*

$$
AMERICAN ✗ **Glacier BrewHouse.** The scent of hops permeates the cavernous, wood-beam BrewHouse, where a dozen or so ales, stouts, lagers, and pilsners are brewed on the premises. Locals mingle with visitors in this noisy, always-busy heart-of-town restaurant, where dinner selections range from thin-crust, 10-inch pizzas to chipotle shrimp cocktail and from barbecue pork ribs to fettuccine jambalaya and fresh seafood (in season). The bacon-laced seafood chowder is a must on cooler days. For dessert, don't miss the wood-oven-roasted apple-and-currant bread pudding (though, really, you can't go wrong with the peanut-butter pie either). You can watch the hardworking chefs in the open kitchen. The brewery sits behind a glass wall, and the same owners operate the equally popular Orso, next door. ■**TIP➔** Several large tour companies have this restaurant on their itinerary, so in summer make reservations, even for lunch. $ *Average main: $28* ⊠ *737 W. 5th Ave., Downtown* ☎ *907/274–2739* ⊕ *www.glacierbrewhouse.com* ✣ *B2.*

$$$$
EUROPEAN
Fodor's Choice
★ ✗ **Marx Bros. Cafe.** Inside a little frame house built in 1916, this nationally recognized 14-table café opened in 1979 and is still going strong. The menu changes frequently, and the wine list encompasses more than 700 international choices. For an appetizer, try the black-bean-and-duck soup or fresh Kachemak Bay oysters. The outstanding made-at-your-table Caesar salad is a superb opener for the baked halibut with a macadamia-nut crust served with coconut-curry sauce and fresh mango chutney. And if the sweet potato–and-pecan pie is on the menu, get it! $ *Average main: $36* ⊠ *627 W. 3rd Ave., Downtown* ☎ *907/278–2133* ⊕ *www.marxcafe.com* ⚇ *Reservations essential* ⊙ *Closed Sun. and Mon. No lunch* ✣ *C1.*

$
ECLECTIC ✗ **New Sagaya's City Market.** Stop at either the Downtown or Midtown New Sagaya's for quick lunches, healthy to-go food, and Kaladi Brothers espresso. The in-house bakery, L'Aroma, makes specialty breads and a wide range of snack-worthy pastries, and the international deli and grocery serves California-style pizzas, Chinese food, lasagna, rotisserie chicken, salads, and even stuffed cabbage. At the Downtown location, you can eat inside on the sheltered patio or grab an outside table on a summer afternoon. New Sagaya's has one of the best seafood counters in town, and will even box and ship your fish. The employee-owned grocery stores carry an extensive selection of Asian foodstuffs, and the produce and meat selections are excellent. $ *Average main: $8* ⊠ *900 W. 13th Ave., Downtown* ☎ *907/274–6173* ⊕ *www.newsagaya.com* $ *Average main: $8* ⊠ *3700 Old Seward Hwy., Midtown* ☎ *907/561–5173* ✣ *E2.*

$$$
ITALIAN ✗ **Orso.** Upon entering Orso ("bear" in Italian), you'll feel, to a certain degree, as though you've stepped out of Anchorage and into a Tuscan villa. Alaskan touches flavor rustic Mediterranean dishes that include traditional pastas, fresh seafood, and locally famous desserts—most

5

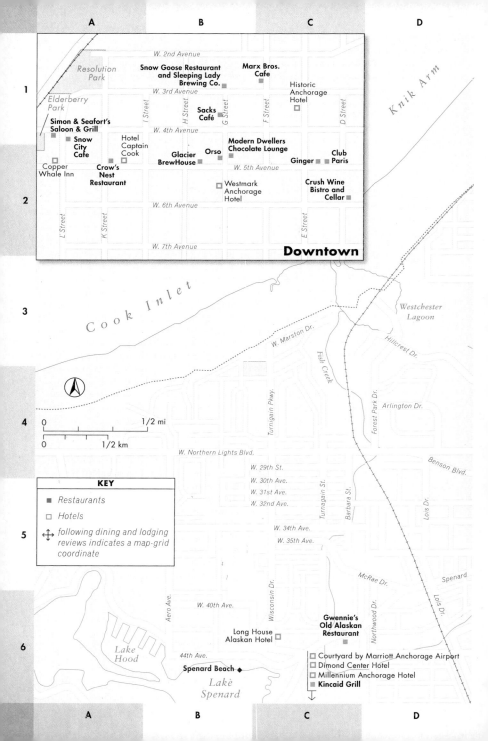

Downtown

Map Labels

W. 2nd Avenue

Resolution Park

Elderberry Park

Snow Goose Restaurant and Sleeping Lady Brewing Co.

Marx Bros. Cafe

Historic Anchorage Hotel

W. 3rd Avenue

Sacks Café

Simon & Seafort's Saloon & Grill

Snow City Cafe

Hotel Captain Cook

W. 4th Avenue

Modern Dwellers Chocolate Lounge

Club Paris

Copper Whale Inn

Crow's Nest Restaurant

Glacier BrewHouse

Orso

Ginger

W. 5th Avenue

Westmark Anchorage Hotel

Crush Wine Bistro and Cellar

W. 6th Avenue

L Street
K Street
I Street
H Street
G Street
F Street
E Street
D Street

W. 7th Avenue

Knik Arm

Cook Inlet

Westchester Lagoon

W. Marston Dr.

Fish Creek

Hillcrest Dr.

Forest Park Dr.

Arlington Dr.

Turnagain Pkwy.

Benson Blvd.

0 — 1/2 mi
0 — 1/2 km

W. Northern Lights Blvd.

W. 29th St.
W. 30th Ave.
W. 31st Ave.
W. 32nd Ave.

Turnagain St.
Barbara St.
Lois Dr.

W. 34th Ave.
W. 35th Ave.

KEY

■ Restaurants

□ Hotels

⊹ following dining and lodging reviews indicates a map-grid coordinate

McRae Dr.

Spenard

Lois Dr.

Aero Ave.

W. 40th Ave.

Wisconsin Dr.

Gwennie's Old Alaskan Restaurant

Northwood Dr.

Long House Alaskan Hotel

Lake Hood

44th Ave.

Spenard Beach ◆

Lake Spenard

□ Courtyard by Marriott Anchorage Airport
□ Dimond Center Hotel
■ Millennium Anchorage Hotel
■ Kincaid Grill

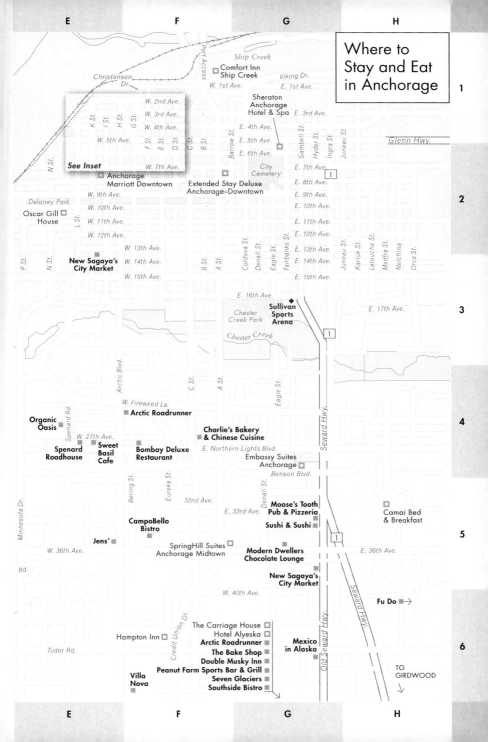

Where to
Stay and Eat
in Anchorage

"These reindeer enjoy their home at the Alaska Wildlife Conservation Center." —Amy Dawson, Fodors.com photo contest participant

notably a delicious molten chocolate cake. Be sure to ask about the daily specials. If you can't get a table at dinner (reservations are advised), you can select from the same menu at the large bar. Upstairs you'll find a cozier, quieter space. For lighter bites or drinks, consider the restaurant's daily happy hour, which features half-price appetizers and drink specials on wine, cocktails, and Glacier BrewHouse beers. Orso just put its wine list on iPads, so choosing a bottle is novel and quick. $ *Average main: $28 ⊠ 737 W. 5th Ave., at G St., Downtown ☎ 907/222–3232 ⊕ www.orsoalaska.com.*

$$$$ ✕ **Sacks Café.** This Downtown spot serves a world's worth of flavors
ECLECTIC from chicken and scallops over udon noodles to cider-brined pork ten-
★ derloin with Alaska purple potato salad. The kitchen relies on local produce when available. There's always something new to try at Sacks. When Anchorage weather turns gray, the colorful interior and art provide respite. The monthly wine flights, normally with three different selections of 3-ounce pours with information sheets on each wine, don't hurt either. Sacks cooks seafood to perfection, so ask about the daily specials, particularly the fresh king salmon and halibut. Singles congregate along a small bar, sampling wines from California, Australia, and France. The café is especially crowded during lunch, served from 11 to 2:30, and dinner begins at 5. The weekend brunch menu, one of the best Downtown, includes eggs Benedict, a Mexican scrambled egg dish called *migas,* and various salads and sandwiches. $ *Average main: $25 ⊠ 328 G St., Downtown ☎ 907/276–3546 ⊕ www.sackscafe.com* ⋐ *Reservations essential* ✛ *B1.*

$$$$
SEAFOOD

✕ **Simon & Seafort's Saloon & Grill.** Windows overlooking Cook Inlet vistas, along with the high ceilings and a classic brass-and-wood interior, have long made this an Anchorage favorite. The menu includes prime rib (aged 28 days) and other steak-house favorites, but the main attraction is fresh Alaska seafood. Try the king crab legs or the seafood linguine, and for dessert the Brandy Ice: vanilla ice cream whipped with brandy, Kahlúa, and crème de cacao. The bar is a great spot for wine, single-malt scotch, and martinis; the best tables are adjacent to tall windows facing the water. Reservations recommended. $ *Average main: $28* ✉ *420 L St., Downtown* ☎ *907/274–3502* ⊕ *www.simonandseaforts.com/page/home* ☽ *No lunch weekends* ✛ *A1.*

$
ECLECTIC
Fodor's Choice
★

✕ **Snow City Cafe.** On summer days, Snow City attracts some serious crowds—and for good reason. This modern but unassuming café, convenient to many of the downtown hotels, serves one of Anchorage's best (and reasonably priced) breakfasts. Oh, lunch, too. Service is fast in the chipper and family-friendly restaurant. The breakfast menu, served all day, features inventive spins on eggs Benedict, including one topped with king crab cakes; omelets; pancakes; and more. Snow City's lunch menu consists of hot or cold sandwiches, fresh soups, and salads, and has lots of vegetarian options. Meat eaters need look no further than the excellent meatloaf sandwich; since Snow City offers a refrigerator case filled with to-go sandwiches, the meatloaf is also a perfect picnic or hiking companion. If you're not an early riser, be prepared to wait—or make a reservation. ■**TIP**➔ Snow City now accepts reservations via phone and Web. $ *Average main: $12* ✉ *1034 W. 4th Ave., Downtown* ☎ *907/272–2489* ⊕ *www.snowcitycafe.com* ☽ *No dinner* ✛ *A1.*

$$
AMERICAN

✕ **Snow Goose Restaurant and Sleeping Lady Brewing Company.** Although you can dine indoors at this comfortable edge-of-downtown eatery, the real attraction in summer is alfresco dining on the back deck and on the rooftop. On clear days you can see Mt. McKinley on the northern horizon and the Chugach Mountains to the east. The menu emphasizes Alaskan takes on classic pub fare, including smoked salmon corn chowder and reindeer sausage–stuffed mushrooms, but the award-winning beer and the view are the best reasons to visit. To sample the specialty beers, gather around oak tables in the upstairs pub for a brewed-on-the-premises ale, India Pale Ale, stout, barley wine, or porter. Several of the beers, including the Portage Porter and 49er, an amber ale, pay homage to Alaska. The restaurant also hosts a range of events in its theater, including improv comedy nights and live music. $ *Average main: $16* ✉ *717 W. 3rd Ave., Downtown* ☎ *907/277–7727* ⊕ *www.alaskabeers.com* ✛ *B1.*

MIDTOWN

$
AMERICAN

✕ **Arctic Roadrunner.** The no-frills decor is mostly 1950s Formica, but if you prefer made-to-order burgers to industrial fast food then this is the place for you. Eat in or drive through at the Arctic Boulevard location and head to nearby Valley of the Moon Park for a sack lunch with the kids. Ultrathick milk shakes and crunchy onion rings are also on everybody's list of favorites. The South Anchorage location (5300 Old

5

Seward Hwy.) has an outdoor deck on Campbell Creek, and in mid-summer you can watch spawning salmon swim past. $ *Average main: $9* ✉ *2477 Arctic Blvd., Midtown* ☎ *907/279–7311* ▬ *No credit cards* ⊘ *Closed Sun.* $ *Average main: $9* ✉ *5300 Old Seward Hwy., South Anchorage* ☎ *907/561–1245* ✛ *F4.*

$$ ✕ **Bombay Deluxe Restaurant.** Anchorage's first Indian restaurant is

INDIAN housed in a collection of international shops at the Valhalla Center strip mall. Dinners include such spicy standards as lamb korma, chicken vindaloo, *palak paneer* (spinach and cheese), and 8 different types of Indian breads—from tandoori roti to garlic naan. The restaurant is especially popular for weekday lunch, when the big buffet provides a sampling of Indian favorites, including several vegetarian offerings. $ *Average main: $18* ✉ *555 W. Northern Lights Blvd., Midtown* ☎ *907/277–1200* ⊕ *www.bombaydeluxe.com* ✛ *F4.*

$$ ✕ **CampoBello Bistro.** Considering its location in a mall in Midtown

ITALIAN Anchorage, CampoBello has surprisingly sophisticated Italian entrées and sinful desserts. Step inside for a romantic lunch or dinner surrounded by splashes of modern art on the walls and candles on the tables. Specialties include ample servings of seafood crepes, wild-mushroom cannelloni, veal saltimbocca, homemade four-cheese ravioli, and shrimp and scallops Florentine. Service is attentive, and the wine list—particularly the Italian choices—is impressive. Dinner reservations are advised. $ *Average main: $24* ✉ *601 W. 36th Ave., Midtown* ☎ *907/563–2040* ⊕ *www.campobellobistro.com* ⊘ *Closed Sun. and Mon. No lunch Sat.* ✛ *F5.*

$ ✕ **Charlie's Bakery & Chinese Cuisine.** Tucked away in a Midtown strip

CHINESE mall, this little gem serves some of the finest authentic Chinese food in Anchorage—and at bargain prices. The atmosphere at this popular lunch spot is casual; order at the counter, take a number for your table, and wait for your meal to be delivered. Dinner is served from 5 to 8:30. Dishes like the vibrant spicy shrimp, loaded with vegetables and hot sauce, make this eatery worth a visit. $ *Average main: $12* ✉ *2729 C St., Midtown* ☎ *907/677–7777* ⊘ *Closed Sun.* ✛ *F4.*

$$$$ ✕ **Jens'.** Don't let the Midtown strip mall that houses Jens' put you

EUROPEAN off: this is one of Anchorage's best fine-dining establishments. The

★ light and airy restaurant has a playful, energetic feel; chef-owner Jens Haagen Handsen's outsized personality has a lot to do with it. Colorful paintings grace red walls, and the incredibly friendly waiters make guests feel like they're the only ones that matter. The menu changes frequently, but it usually includes Alaskan salmon, halibut, and rockfish, along with such specialties as rack of lamb, tenderloin of veal, and an "almost world-famous" pepper steak. Chef Hansen's heritage reveals itself at lunch (when the Danish specials appear) and on the dessert menu; Danish berry pudding served with cream is a delightful way to cap a meal. For a light evening meal, sample the appetizers at the wine bar, where Jens holds court. Reservations are suggested, but Jens' can usually accommodate drop-ins. $ *Average main: $32* ✉ *701 W. 36th Ave., at Arctic Blvd., Midtown* ☎ *907/561–5367* ⊕ *www. jensrestaurant.com* ⊘ *Closed Sun. and Jan. No lunch Sat., no dinner Mon.* ✛ *E5.*

$ **✗ Moose's Tooth Pub & Pizzeria.** Always the top pick when local news-
PIZZA   papers rate Anchorage pizzerias, Moose's Tooth is packed all week,
despite the ample seating (on the order of 300 guests). The reason for
the popularity is obvious: creative pizzas and handcrafted beers from
its own brewery. More than a dozen ales, ambers, porters, and stouts
are the order of the day, and homemade root beers, cream sodas, and
ginger ales are also available. You can match these brews with a seemingly endless roster of pizzas topped with standards like mushrooms
and roasted red peppers or inventive options like jalapeños, cream
cheese, halibut, or capers. If you're so inclined, check out the daily
pizza specials for some pretty exotic topping combinations, such as
southern pork barbecue and Samui shrimp. Those who prefer non-pizza
fare can choose from soups, sandwiches, and salads. $ *Average main:
$14* ⊠ *3300 Old Seward Hwy., Midtown* ☎ *907/258–2537* ⊕ *www.
moosestooth.net* ⌛ *Reservations not accepted* ✣ *G5.*

$ **✗ Sweet Basil Cafe.** Recently moved from its Downtown location to
CAFÉ   Midtown, this family-run café has hot and cold lunchtime sandwiches
on freshly baked sweet basil bread accompanied by a choice of homemade soups. Fresh pastas, salads, wraps, fish tacos, smoothies, pastries,
and light breakfasts fill out the menu, but the daily specials are often
your best bet. There's also a nice variety of dinners to go, including
wild-mushroom-and-chicken-filled crepes and a roasted-veggie-and-
goat-cheese lasagna. $ *Average main: $9* ⊠ *1021 W. Northern Lights
Blvd., Midtown* ☎ *907/274–0070* ⊕ *www.sweetbasilak.com* ☻ *Closed
Sun. No dinner* ✣ *E4.*

$$ **✗ Villa Nova.** This standby restaurant is popular for its authentic Italian
ITALIAN   cuisine including veal, lamb, chicken, steak, and seafood entrées. Ask
about the fresh catch of the day. Dim lighting, imported-tile tabletops,
and fresh flowers create a romantic ambience (though dress is casual).
The bar has domestic and imported liquors, wines, and beers, and
handcrafted desserts that change daily. $ *Average main: $20* ⊠ *5121
Arctic Blvd., Midtown* ☎ *907/561–1660* ⊕ *www.villanovaalaska.com*
⌛ *Reservations essential* ☻ *Closed Sun. and Mon.* ✣ *F6.*

SPENARD

$ **✗ Gwennie's Old Alaskan Restaurant.** Historic Alaskan photos, mounted
AMERICAN   animals, and memorabilia adorn this old family favorite just south
of the city center toward the airport. Lunch and dinners are avail-
able, but the restaurant is best known for its old-fashioned breakfasts,
available all day. Try the sourdough pancakes, reindeer sausage and
eggs, or crab omelets. Portions are very generous—a serving of fries
alone can feed a small family. Don't expect anything fancy; this is
diner food in an Alaskana-filled setting. $ *Average main: $11* ⊠ *4333
Spenard Rd., Spenard* ☎ *907/243–2090* ⊕ *www.gwenniesrestaurant.
com* ✣ *C6.*

$ **✗ Organic Oasis.** Just across the street from Chilkoot Charlie's, this popu-
CAFÉ   lar café is part eatery and part community center–event space. The menu
offers plenty of healthy (or, at least, healthy-sounding) fare, including
fresh-squeezed juices, smoothies, organic sandwiches, espresso drinks,
pizza, fresh vegan soups, and tempeh burgers. Organic's bakes its own

5

bread and buns. While vegans and vegetarian visitors to Anchorage should put a giant star on Organic's location on the city map, omnivores are not left in the cold: the menu includes buffalo burgers, chicken, salmon, and grilled Buffalo New York strip steaks. There's even organic beer and wine. There's live music many nights each week and free Wi-Fi access anytime. Service can be slow. If this place could somehow manage to acquire a more hippie vibe, it'd float to Berkeley unassisted. ⑤ *Average main: $12* ✉ *2610 Spenard Rd., Spenard* ☎ *907/277–7882* ⊕ *www.organicoasis.com* ✛ *E4*.

$$
AMERICAN

✕ **Spenard Roadhouse.** Though it pays homage to the roadhouses that dot Alaska—and the state's history—Spenard Roadhouse is by no means just a place to grab a quick meal while traveling. Settle in; order some wine, a cocktail, a house-made infused vodka, or one of the 30-plus bourbons on hand, and enjoy. The warm and inviting restaurant features art that will delight the eyes as the menu is a treat for the tastebuds. Owned by the folks behind super popular mainstays Snow City Café and Sacks Café, Spenard Roadhouse serves lunch and dinner daily and a weekend breakfast menu you'll dream about the rest of the week. The weekend breakfast "hair o'the dog" cocktails alone are worth getting out of bed for. Try the house-infused habanero Bloody Mary. Lunch and dinner menus offer plates both light and mighty hearty, from a spinach and goat cheese salad to the belly-busting bacon jam burger. (Yes, bacon jam.) Other options include pizzas, sandwiches, small plates, and seafood-laden pastas. Of course, you'll need to finish the meal off with a s'more or a slice of chocolate peanut-butter pie. Better yet: go with friends and order a few of each. Whether traveling with a pack of people or solo, service is friendly and accommodating. A perfect complement to the meal for those who need to catch up on email (or Facebook): the restaurant offers free Wi-Fi. ⑤ *Average main: $18* ✉ *1049 W. Northern Lights Blvd., Spenard* ☎ *907/770–7623* ⊕ *www.spenardroadhouse.com* ✛ *E4*.

GREATER ANCHORAGE

SOUTH ANCHORAGE

$$$$
EUROPEAN

✕ **Kincaid Grill.** This out-of-the-way restaurant provides a respite after a summertime hike or wintertime ski in nearby Kincaid Park. Chef and owner Al Levinsohn worked his way up through some of Alaska's finest restaurants, and the experience shines through in his diverse and creative menu. The upscale setting is lively, with old-time jazz spilling from the speakers and the buzz of conversation about you. Meals are artistically presented. If traveling solo, consider taking a seat at the wine bar, where you can sample a microbrew or vintages from around the globe. The menu, with a focus on Alaska regional cuisine, seafood, and game meats, changes every few weeks. Menu mainstays include filet mignon, fresh Alaskan salmon or halibut, and a rich seafood gumbo. The chocolate bourbon soufflé dessert is well worth the 15-minute wait. ⑤ *Average main: $30* ✉ *6700 Jewel Lake Rd., South Anchorage* ☎ *907/243–0507* ⊕ *www.kincaidgrill.com* ⌔ *Reservations essential* ⊙ *Closed Sun. and Mon. No lunch* ✛ *C6*.

$$ ✕ **Mexico in Alaska.** Owner Maria-Elena Ball befriends everyone, par-
MEXICAN ticularly young children, at this authentic Mexican restaurant. Favorite
☕ dishes include lime-marinated fried chicken, *chilaquiles* (tortilla casse-
role with mole sauce), and *entremesa de queso* (melted cheese, jalapeños,
and onions with homemade tortillas). A vegetarian menu is available.
The restaurant is several miles south of downtown, so you'll need to
drive or catch the city bus. ⑤ *Average main: $16 ⊠ 7305 Old Seward
Hwy., South Anchorage* ☎ *907/349–1528* ⊕ *www.mexicoinalaska.com*
⊙ *Closed Sun.* ✛ *G6.*

$ ✕ **Peanut Farm Sports Bar and Grill.** At 25,000 square feet, the mega sports
AMERICAN bar has room for athletic fans of every stripe, from hockey (of course)
to mushing and beyond. Peanut Farm has 70 TV screens, pool tables,
darts, an outdoor deck on the bank of Campbell Creek, a heated deck
overlooking the creek, and a large and varied menu. The hot wings are
the best in town, and you can slake your thirst with one of 30 draft
beers. The Farm opens at 6 for breakfast every day. ⑤ *Average main:
$15 ⊠ 5227 Old Seward Hwy., South Anchorage* ☎ *907/563–3283*
⊕ *www.wemustbenuts.com* ✛ *G6.*

$$$ ✕ **Southside Bistro.** Established in South Anchorage, the Southside
EUROPEAN (another in a long list of great Anchorage restaurants tucked away
in nondescript strip malls) quickly became a local favorite for its
artful treatments of Alaska seafood—the fresh scallop and risotto
cake is delicious, as are veal, venison, and rack of lamb. A hardwood
brick oven produces flatbreads and pizzas; cheesecakes, pastries, and
ice creams are decorated with hand-painted designs. The wine list
includes more than 100 mostly American wines, and the impressive
beer menu includes brews made locally as well as beers from the
Lower 48 and the rest of the world. If you're watching your budget,
grab a seat on the bistro side of the restaurant and order from the
bar menu—choose burgers, pizzas, appetizers, or one of our favorites,
an excellent angel-hair pasta. Reservations are highly recommended.
⑤ *Average main: $24 ⊠ 1320 Huffman Park Dr., South Anchorage*
☎ *907/348–0088* ⊕ *www.southsidebistro.com* ⊙ *Closed Sun. and
Mon.* ✛ *G6.*

WHERE TO STAY

While other cities see new hotels pop up seemingly out of nowhere,
the Anchorage hotel scene tends to stay rather consistent. Most of the
major chains have a place in town, and there are some strong indepen-
dents as well. If you're traveling without a car, consider staying Downtown, where the hotels are just steps away from shops and restaurants.
Anchorage is also home to many B&Bs. Go that route if you want to
hop right into learning about the Alaskan way of life—it's hard to find
a local who doesn't have good stories to tell. For a listing of hotels,
contact the Anchorage Convention & Visitors Bureau. Reservations
are a must for the major hotels, especially during the summer months.
*Prices in the reviews are the lowest cost of a standard double room in
high season. Use the coordinate (✛ B2) at the end of each review to
locate a property on the Where to Eat and Stay in Anchorage map.*

For expanded hotel reviews, visit Fodors.com.

DOWNTOWN

$$$$ ⌃ **Anchorage Marriott Downtown.**
HOTEL One of Anchorage's biggest lodgings, the brightly decorated Marriott appeals to business travelers, tourists, and corporate clients. **Pros:** one of the newest hotels in town; modern, up-to-date facilities. **Cons:** no free Wi-Fi; pricey valet parking; cruise-ship crowds at times in summer. **TripAdvisor:** "comfortable stay," "close to everything," "great customer service." ⑤ *Rooms from: $279* ✉ *820 W. 7th Ave., Downtown* ☎ *907/279–8000, 800/228–9290* ⊕ *www.marriott.com* ⟳ *390 rooms, 3 suites* ⓘ *No meals* ✛ *E2.*

$$ ⌃ **Comfort Inn Ship Creek.** Try catching salmon in the namesake Ship Creek gurgling past this popular family hotel, which is a short walk northeast of the Alaska Railroad Historic Depot and practically on top of the Tony Knowles Coastal Trail. **Pros:** pet-friendly; pool; free Wi-Fi. **Cons:** the walk into the downtown area is an uphill climb; rooms are a bit noisy at times. **TripAdvisor:** "great breakfast," "friendly and convenient," "excellent staff and service." ⑤ *Rooms from: $189* ✉ *111 Ship Creek Ave., Downtown* ☎ *907/277–6887, 800/424–6423* ⊕ *www.choicehotels.com/hotel/ak006* ⟳ *88 rooms, 12 suites* ⓘ *Multiple meal plans* ✛ *F1.*

$$ ⌃ **Copper Whale Inn.** A view across Cook Inlet to Sleeping Lady and
B&B/INN other mountains is a bonus at this small inn on the edge of Downtown. **Pros:** excellent breakfast; convenient downtown location; responsive and attentive staff. **Cons:** some rooms are small; some shared baths. **TripAdvisor:** "charming," "great location," "comfortable and cozy." ⑤ *Rooms from: $185* ✉ *440 L St., Downtown* ☎ *907/258–7999, 866/258–7999* ⊕ *www.copperwhale.com* ⟳ *14 rooms, 12 with bath* ⓘ *Breakfast* ✛ *A2.*

$$ ⌃ **Dimond Center Hotel.** For the price, the Dimond Center Hotel offers a
HOTEL shocking number of perks: every room has a 72-inch soaking tub, huge flat-screen TV, microwave, and mini-refrigerator—not to mention the generous breakfast buffet, with waffles and biscuits and gravy. **Pros:** free airport shuttle, Wi-Fi, and parking. **Cons:** location—it's 5 miles from downtown and surrounded by national chain stores. **TripAdvisor:** "very accommodating," "excellent service," "comfortable beds." ⑤ *Rooms from: $209* ✉ *700 E. Dimond Center Blvd., South Anchorage, Anchorage* ☎ *907/770–5000, 866/770–5002* ⊕ *www.dimondcenterhotel.com* ⟳ *109* ⓘ *Some meals* ✛ *C6.*

$$ ⌃ **Extended Stay Deluxe Anchorage—Downtown.** Undergoing a major ren-
HOTEL ovation that should be complete by February 2013, the Extended Stay Deluxe features large rooms furnished with one king or two queen

ADDITIONAL HOTEL INFO

Anchorage Alaska Bed & Breakfast Association. Find a range of accommodations on the website for Anchorage B&Bs. ⊕ *www. anchorage-bnb.com.*

Alyeska Accommodations. If you want a privately owned cabin or condo, Alyeska Accommodations can set you up. ☎ *907/783–2000, 888/783–2001* ⊕ *www. alyeskaaccommodations.com.*

beds, a writing table, 27-inch TV, DVD player, mini-refrigerator, micro-wave, and free Wi-Fi. **Pros:** very good rates available online; airport shuttle available. **Cons:** fee for laundry use; parking can be a hassle. ■ **TIP→** Parking costs $10 per day or $20 per week, so ask for the weekly rate if you'll be staying more than two days. **TripAdvisor:** "a good stay," "better than expected," "nice room." $ *Rooms from: $169* ✉ *108 E. 8th Ave., Downtown* ☎ *907/868–1605, 800/804–3724* ⊕ *www. extendedstay.com* ↰ *75 rooms, 14 suites* |○| *Multiple meal plans* ✛ *F2.*

$$$ 🏨 **Historic Anchorage Hotel.** The little building has been around since
HOTEL 1916, and experienced travelers call it the only hotel in Anchorage with
★ charm: the original sinks and tubs have been restored, and upstairs hall-ways are lined with Old Anchorage photos. **Pros:** excellent staff; new flat-screen TVs; very convenient downtown location. **Cons:** rooms are small; no airport shuttle. **TripAdvisor:** "great room," "friendly staff," "historic." $ *Rooms from: $209* ✉ *330 E St., Downtown* ☎ *907/272–4553, 800/544–0988* ⊕ *www.historicanchoragehotel.com* ↰ *16 rooms, 10 junior suites* |○| *Breakfast* ✛ *C1.*

$$$$ 🏨 **Hotel Captain Cook.** Recalling Captain Cook's voyages to Alaska and
HOTEL the South Pacific, dark teak paneling lines the hotel's interior, and a
★ nautical theme continues into the guest rooms. **Pros:** staff is very well trained and accommodating; excellent lobby bar. **Cons:** 24-hour park-ing passes cost $18. **TripAdvisor:** "great hotel service," "beautiful," "pleasant and convenient." $ *Rooms from: $280* ✉ *939 W. 5th Ave., Downtown* ☎ *907/276–6000, 800/843–1950* ⊕ *www.captaincook.com* ↰ *547 rooms, 96 suites* |○| *No meals* ✛ *A2.*

$ 🏨 **Oscar Gill House.** Originally built by Gill in the settlement of Knik
B&B/INN (north of Anchorage) in 1913, this historic home has been transformed into a comfortable B&B in a quiet neighborhood along Delaney Park Strip, with Downtown attractions a short walk away. **Pros:** great break-fast; very hospitable owners in a bit of Old Anchorage history. **Cons:** shared bath in two of the rooms; no king-size beds. **TripAdvisor:** "a historic gem," "wonderful hostess," "most charming." $ *Rooms from: $115* ✉ *1344 W. 10th Ave., Downtown* ☎ *907/279–1344* ⊕ *www. oscargill.com* ↰ *3 rooms, 1 with bath* |○| *Breakfast* ✛ *E2.*

$$$ 🏨 **Sheraton Anchorage Hotel & Spa.** A $35 million renovation has trans-
HOTEL formed the 16-story Sheraton into one of city's best hotels, with rooms that are sleek (but not sterile). **Pros:** tasteful, modern renovation; great views from the upper floors. **Cons:** fees for parking; Wi-Fi is free in common spaces but costs $9.95 per day in rooms. **TripAdvisor:** "great place to stay," "comfortable bed," "good base in Anchorage." $ *Rooms from: $229* ✉ *401 E. 6th Ave., Downtown* ☎ *907/276–8700, 800/325–3535* ⊕ *www.sheraton.com* ↰ *359 rooms, 11 suites* |○| *No meals* ✛ *G2.*

MIDTOWN

$$$ 🏨 **Courtyard by Marriott Anchorage Airport.** Business travelers pack this
HOTEL modern hotel near the airport; some rooms have a whirlpool bath and king-size bed, and all have a coffeemaker, two phones, microwave, refrigerator, and hair dryer. **Pros:** close to airport; free Wi-Fi; compli-mentary airport shuttle. **Cons:** there's a fee for breakfast; location is

5

DID YOU KNOW?

The Tongass and Chugach national forests—Alaska's only national forests—are the two largest in the United States. At 17 million acres the Tongass is three times the size of the Chugach.

noisy; not convenient for restaurants and sights. **TripAdvisor:** "clean room," "very nice and new," "outstanding customer service." ⑤ *Rooms from: $229* ✉ *4901 Spenard Rd., Midtown* ☎ *907/245–0322, 800/314–0782* ⊕ *www.marriott.com/anccy* ⤵ *148 rooms, 6 suites* †◎| *No meals* ✛ *C6.*

$$$$ **Embassy Suites Anchorage.** Opened in June 2008, this hotel, with
HOTEL its California chic–meets-Alaskana decor, is the latest addition to the Anchorage upscale hotel inventory; in addition to the long list of amenities, a hot cooked-to-order breakfast and an afternoon manager's reception featuring complimentary hors d'oeuvres and cocktails are both included. **Pros:** top-of-the-line facilities; freebies at manager's reception; great breakfast. **Cons:** neighborhood is a high-traffic area; only some rooms have a (distant) mountain view. **TripAdvisor:** "a welcoming hotel," "great breakfast," "service extraordinaire." ⑤ *Rooms from: $289* ✉ *600 E. Benson Blvd., Midtown* ☎ *907/332–7000, 800/362–2779* ⊕ *embassysuites3.hilton.com* ⤵ *169 suites* †◎| *Breakfast* ✛ *G4.*

$$$ **Hampton Inn.** Midway between the airport and Downtown, the
HOTEL Hampton has all the standard features, and a few that are better than average, such as designer furnishings, an indoor swimming pool, and a spa. **Pros:** shuttle will take you into town; great beds; excellent breakfast. **Cons:** some rooms near the pool can be noisy and smell of chlorine; basic chain-hotel ambience. **TripAdvisor:** "above and beyond on service," "very convenient," "comfy." ⑤ *Rooms from: $249* ✉ *4301 Credit Union Dr., Midtown* ☎ *907/550–7000, 800/426–7866* ⊕ *hamptoninn.hilton.com* ⤵ *97 rooms* †◎| *Breakfast* ✛ *F6.*

$ **Long House Alaskan Hotel.** It almost requires voodoo to find a hotel
HOTEL room in Anchorage in summer for less than $150: the Long House Alaskan Hotel, near the airport, fills that niche with its large, basic rooms. **Pros:** free shuttle; friendly staff; coin-operated laundry. **Cons:** no-frills rooms; no elevator to second floor; pretty basic amenities. **TripAdvisor:** "okay but very noisy," "low cost," "great hospitality." ⑤ *Rooms from: $143* ✉ *4335 Wisconsin St., Midtown* ☎ *907/243–2133, 800/243–2133* ⊕ *www.longhousehotel.com* ⤵ *54 rooms, 3 suites* †◎| *Multiple meal plans* ✛ *C6.*

$$$ **Millennium Anchorage Hotel.** Perched on the shore of Lake Spenard,
HOTEL the Millennium Anchorage Hotel is one of the city's best spots to watch planes come and go; the lobby resembles a hunting lodge with its stone fireplace, trophy heads, and mounted fish on every wall. **Pros:** close to the airport; old Alaska hunting-lodge feel; an airport shuttle is available. **Cons:** common areas getting worn; sketchy elevator; noise, both from ailing HVAC and airplanes on Lake Hood. **TripAdvisor:** "great place to stay," "beautiful view," "safe." ⑤ *Rooms from: $219* ✉ *4800 Spenard Rd., Midtown* ☎ *907/243–2300, 800/544–0553* ⊕ *www.millenniumhotels.com* ⤵ *243 rooms, 4 suites* †◎| *No meals* ✛ *C6.*

$$$ **SpringHill Suites Anchorage Midtown.** Spacious one-room suites have
HOTEL separate living and sleeping areas with either a king bed or two double beds plus a pullout sofa, microwave, mini-refrigerator, and flat-screen TV. **Pros:** complimentary parking; 24-hour airport shuttle. **Cons:** small laundry facilities for such a large hotel; most restaurants within easy walking distance are national chains. **TripAdvisor:** "pleasantly

surprised," "comfortable stay," "very helpful staff." ⑤ *Rooms from: $249* ✉ *3401 A St., Midtown* ☎ *907/562–3247, 877/729–0197* ⊕ *www. marriott.com/ancsh* ⟿ *101 suites* ❘◎❘ *Breakfast* ✛ *G5.*

GREATER ANCHORAGE

EAST ANCHORAGE

$

B&B/INN

⚜ **Camai Bed & Breakfast.** At this elegant B&B, Anchorage's oldest, two of the suites have private entries and plenty of space for families, and all suites have private baths and in-room satellite TV, DVD, and phones. **Pros:** private entries a real plus; quiet residential neighborhood; very experienced hosts. **Cons:** a relatively long way from Downtown restaurants; lack of credit-card payment option can be a bother (supposed to be coming soon). **TripAdvisor:** "friendly hosts," "wonderful place," "tasteful and tasty." ⑤ *Rooms from: $139* ✉ *3838 Westminster Way, East Anchorage* ☎ *907/333–2219* ⊕ *www.camaibnb.com* ⟿ *3 suites* ▭ *No credit cards* ❘◎❘ *Breakfast* ✛ *H5.*

5

NIGHTLIFE AND THE ARTS

NIGHTLIFE

Anchorage does not shut down when it gets dark—well, that is when it actually does get dark (it's still light at 3 am in the summer!). Bars here—and throughout Alaska—open early (in the morning) and close as late as 3 am on weekends. There's a ban on smoking in bars and bingo parlors, as well as in restaurants. The listings in the *Anchorage Daily News* entertainment section, published on Friday, and in the free weekly *Anchorage Press* (⊕ *www.anchoragepress.com*) range from concerts and theater performances to movies and a roundup of nightspots featuring live music.

DOWNTOWN

BARS AND NIGHTCLUBS

Bernie's Bungalow Lounge. Though locals say it isn't what it used to be (but, really, what is?), Bernie's Bungalow Lounge still pulls in plenty of twentysomethings looking to dance, drink, and make eyes at the cuties across the room. The best spot in the house: the outdoor patio. ✉ *626 D St., Downtown* ☎ *907/276–8808* ⊕ *www.berniesak.com.*

Club Paris. Lots of old-timers favor the dark bar of Club Paris. The Paris mural and French street lamps hanging behind the bar have lost some luster, but there's still a faithful clientele. ✉ *417 W. 5th Ave., Downtown* ☎ *907/277–6332* ⊕ *www.clubparisrestaurant.com.*

Rumrunners Old Towne Bar & Grill. Right across from Old City Hall in the center of town, Rumrunners' pub-grub menu brings the lunch crowd, but when evening comes the big dance floor gets packed as DJs spin the tunes. ✉ *415 E St., Downtown* ☎ *907/278–4493* ⊕ *www. rumrunnersak.com.*

Simon & Seafort's Saloon & Grill. A trendy place for the dressy "in" crowd, the bar at Simon & Seafort's Saloon & Grill has stunning views of Cook

ANCHORAGE CAFES

First-timers to Anchorage are often surprised by the number of places one can grab a cup of Joe around town. Yes, it's true: Anchorage residents easily rival Seattleites for their devotion to java. But, of course, some cups of coffee are better than others. Some places to start your day (or hang out between adventures):

Kaladi Brothers Coffee. A local favorite since opening its first spot in 1986, Kaladi Brothers Coffee has espresso, lattes, baked goods, and more at 10 locations around town, most with free Wi-Fi access. For a list, go to the Web site. ⊠ *621 W. 6th Ave.* ☎ *907/277–1881* ⊕ *www. kaladi.com.*

SteamDot Coffee and Espresso Lab. In South Anchorage, coffee's next wave is brewing. SteamDot Coffee and Espresso Lab treats coffee lovers to quite the coffee-brewing show at its "slow bar." This is not the place to go if you're in the mood for syrup-heavy espresso drinks. SteamDot is all about the flavor of coffee. ⊠ *10950 O'Malley Centre, Suite E* ☎ *907/344–4422* ⊕ *www. steamdot.com.*

Alaska Cake Studio. If you prefer the focus of your coffee break to be on the baked goods, pop into Alaska Cake Studio downtown. From creative cupcakes—the flavor of the month always surprises—to cookies, croissants, and, of course, cakes, sweet treats delight. ⊠ *608 W. 4th Ave.* ☎ *907/272–3995* ⊕ *www. alaskacakestudio.com.*

Inlet, a special single-malt scotch menu, and tempting cocktails. The lavender martini is particularly a palate pleaser. ⊠ *420 L St., Downtown* ☎ *907/274–3502* ⊕ *www.simonandseaforts.com.*

Snow Goose Restaurant and Sleeping Lady Brewing Company. With comedy improv and live music (check the website for the schedule), Snow Goose is a good place to unwind with a beer inside or on the airy outside deck overlooking Cook Inlet. ⊠ *717 W. 3rd Ave., Downtown* ☎ *907/277–7727* ⊕ *www.alaskabeers.com.*

GAY AND LESBIAN BARS
Anchorage's gay nightlife centers on a pair of bars, both of which attract a mixed crowd.

Mad Myrna's. There's country line dancing on Wednesday, karaoke on Thursday, and drag shows, DJs (and more karaoke) on the weekends at Mad Myrna's. ⊠ *530 E. 5th Ave., Downtown* ☎ *907/276–9762* ⊕ *www.madmyrnas.com.*

Raven. A neighborhood hangout, the Raven is where you'll meet regulars over a game of billiards or darts. ⊠ *708 E. 4th Ave., Downtown* ☎ *907/276–9672.*

LIVE MUSIC
See the "Play" section in Friday editions of the *Anchorage Daily News* for complete listings of upcoming concerts and other performances, or get the same entertainment information online at ⊕ *www.adn.com.*

Club Soraya. Fans of salsa, merengue, and other music crowd the dance floor at the downtown Club Soraya. There are dance classes several nights a week, followed by live bands. ✉ *333 W. 4th Ave., Downtown* ☎ *907/276–0670* ⊕ *www.akswing.com/clubsoraya.htm.*

Humpy's Great Alaskan Alehouse. One of Anchorage's favorite bars, Humpy's Great Alaskan Alehouse serves up rock, blues, and folk five nights a week, including open mike on Monday, along with dozens of microbrews (more than 40 beers are on tap) and surprisingly tasty

pub grub—we especially like the smoked salmon spread. Trivia buffs should head to Humpy's on Tuesday nights for the weekly pub quiz. ■ TIP→ You can grab one of Humpy's delicious halibut burgers on your way out of town—the company just opened a satellite restaurant in Terminal B of the Anchorage airport. ✉ *610 W. 6th Ave., Downtown* ☎ *907/276–2337* ⊕ *www.humpys.com.*

SPENARD

BARS AND NIGHTCLUBS

Chilkoot Charlie's. Chilkoot Charlie's, a rambling timber building with sawdust floors, multiple bars, three dance floors, loud music (rock or swing bands and DJs) nightly, two DJs every Thursday, Friday, and Saturday, and rowdy customers, is where young Alaskans go to get crazy. This legendary bar has many unusual nooks and crannies, including a room filled with Russian artifacts where vodka is the drink of choice, plus a reconstructed version of Alaska's infamous Birdhouse Bar. If you haven't been to 'Koots, you haven't seen Anchorage nightlife at its wildest. ✉ *2435 Spenard Rd., Spenard* ☎ *907/272–1010* ⊕ *www.koots.com.*

LIVE MUSIC

The Tap Root. Locals say this is one of the best places in town for live music. Folk, bluegrass, and jam bands rule the stage most nights. Beer lovers enjoy an almost overwhelming selection of 22 tap lines featuring largely local brews and a cooler with everything from Belgian Trappists to PBR tall boys. The full bar boasts 40 different bourbons and an unsurpassed whiskey menu. The chronically understaffed club serves a better-than-expected menu of sandwiches, salads, appetizers, and entrées including halibut tacos. ✉ *3300 Spenard Rd., Spenard* ☎ *907/345–0282* ⊕ *www.taprootalaska.com.*

THE ARTS

Anchorage often surprises visitors with its variety—and high quality—of cultural activities. In addition to top-name touring groups and performers, some local productions are always going on around town. These might include provocative theater, children's shows, improvisational troupes, Buddhist lectures, photography exhibits, poetry readings, and Native Alaskan dance performances. The Friday entertainment section of the *Anchorage Daily News* is packed with events and activities.

Continued on page 253

THE GLORIOUS AND RELENTLESS MIDNIGHT SUN

The side-lit afternoons seeping into late evening. The unforgettable sunsets streaking the sky with swaths of neon. The 9 PM golf tee offs and midnight baseball games. The black-out curtains and sleep masks. The bloodshot eyes. The madness of it all: Alaska's tilted life.

The light (and lack thereof) is one of Alaska's most dramatic characteristics. Long summer days goad visitors to sight-see well into the evening, while record-breaking vegetables (read: cabbages the size of coffee tables) grow in the fields. The feeble, or just plain absent, winter sun allows snow to recharge glaciers while the aurora borealis (a.k.a. the northern lights) dances above hibernating bears and humans alike.

Remember that the farther north you go in Alaska, the more pronounced the midnight sun will be. If you make it to Barrow, you'll experience nightless days in summer. Heading south means a less extreme case of the midnight sun, but often just as much revelry celebrating its presence. Summertime simply has a different feeling in Alaska—enjoy the local fairs and festivals, and the stunning mixture of persistent daylight, snow-capped mountains, and miles of vibrant wildland.

(above) A brave Midnight Sun runner (right) How does *your* garden grow?

THE MIDNIGHT SUN: HOW IT WORKS

The Earth spins on a slightly tilted axis as it rotates around the sun. The northern hemisphere is tilted toward the sun in summer and away from it in winter. So how does this explain Alaska's midnight sun? The globe's most northern areas, including much of Alaska, are tilted so far toward the sun in summer that there's continuous light.

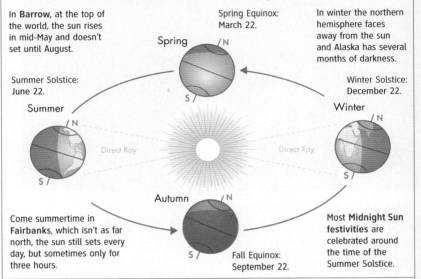

In **Barrow**, at the top of the world, the sun rises in mid-May and doesn't set until August.

Spring Equinox: March 22.

In winter the northern hemisphere faces away from the sun and Alaska has several months of darkness.

Summer Solstice: June 22.

Winter Solstice: December 22.

Come summertime in **Fairbanks**, which isn't as far north, the sun still sets every day, but sometimes only for three hours.

Most **Midnight Sun festivities** are celebrated around the time of the Summer Solstice.

Fall Equinox: September 22.

TIPS FROM AN ALASKAN

Coping with the Midnight Sun

■ Close your shades a few hours before bedtime. Bring a sleep mask or use the black-out curtains in your hotel room!

■ Bring antihistamines to soothe the mosquito bites we *promise* you'll get—the added bonus is the drowsiness.

■ You can always count sheep. Or count microbrews! Alaska has many to enjoy, including Silver Gulch, Sleeping Lady, Kodiak Brewery, and Moose's Tooth.

■ If all else fails, go out and enjoy the eerie light. Many people find that they simply need less sleep in summer.

Surviving the Polar Winter

■ Get what sunlight you can. Make sure you're up and at 'em whenever the sun is.

■ Take your vitamins, especially vitamin D, and eat plenty of fruit.

■ Some Alaskans go that extra step and visit tanning salons to boost their mood—and, of course, for a little color!

■ Fool your body into thinking the sun is out: sip your morning coffee near a lamp (preferably full-spectrum).

■ Did we mention Alaska's many excellent microbrews?

IN FOCUS

5

THE GLORIOUS AND RELENTLESS MIDNIGHT SUN

MIDNIGHT SUN REVELRY

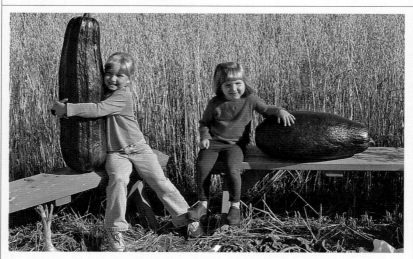

During the peak of the midnight sun season, June and early July, there's almost no end to the special activities and festivals celebrating the light. It's a good thing, too—you may have trouble falling asleep!

■ Taking place the Saturday closest to the summer solstice, the **Mayor's Marathon and Half Marathon in Anchorage** attract runners from all over the country. (⊕ www.mayorsmarathon.com)

■ The much less formal 10-km **Midnight Sun Run is held in Fairbanks** every June on the weekend closest to the summer solstice. The run starts at 10 pm. (⊕ fairbanks-alaska.com/midnight-sun-run.htm)

■ The **midnight sun baseball game in Fairbanks** is the best-known midnight sun activity in Alaska. The Alaska Goldpanners are the stars of the Alaska League, comprised of college athletes from around the country. Every summer solstice, the Goldpanners host the "high noon at midnight" classic, a tradition since 1906. The first pitch is thrown at 10:30 pm, and the entire game is played without the use of artificial lights. (They haven't worked since they were struck by lightning years ago!) (⊕ www.goldpanners.com)

■ If you'd rather steer clear of festivals and find a spot of your own, **drive out of Fairbanks** along Steese Highway or Chena Hot Springs Road for the unforgettable nighttime view.

■ Almost every Alaskan town has a special event on or near the summer solstice, but one of the best is the **Nome Midnight Sun Festival,** which celebrates 22 hours of direct sunlight with parades, barbecues, and folk music. (⊕ www.visitnomealaska.org)

■ The **Alaska State Fair** runs for 12 days before Labor Day in the town of Palmer, 40 mi northeast of Anchorage. Check out the giant midnight sun–grown vegetables on display and colorful vending booths selling an array of goods from cookies to jewelry. (⊕ www.alaskastatefair.org)

CenterTix. Purchase tickets by phone or from CenterTix's website for a wide variety of cultural events throughout South Central Alaska. ☎ *907/263–2787, 877/278–7849* ⊕ *www.centertix.net.*

Alaska Center for the Performing Arts. Four theaters comprise the Alaska Center for the Performing Arts, which is home to many local performing groups and also showcases traveling production companies. The lobby box office (open weekdays from 8 to 5) sells tickets to the productions and is a good all-around source of cultural information. ✉ *621 W. 6th Ave., at G St., Downtown* ☎ *907/263–2900* ⊕ *www.myalaskacenter.com.*

FILM

Bear Tooth Theatrepub. The popular Bear Tooth Theatrepub screens second-run films—from art house to blockbuster—for only $3.50 ($5 for reserved seating) and also serves tasty pizzas, sandwiches, burritos, salads, and Moose's Tooth beer while you watch. ■TIP➔ Once you purchase your ticket at the box office, you may need to wait in line outside while the previous movie lets out, so make sure you're in the right line—and dress for the weather. ✉ *1230 W. 27th Ave., Spenard* ☎ *907/276–4200* ⊕ *www.beartooththeatre.net.*

OPERA AND CLASSICAL MUSIC

Anchorage Opera. During its November through March season, the Anchorage Opera produces operas featuring outside singers in the lead roles and locals in supporting roles. ☎ *907/279–2557* ⊕ *www.anchorageopera.org.*

Anchorage Symphony Orchestra. October through April, the Anchorage Symphony Orchestra performs classical concerts as well as pops concerts and silent film nights. ☎ *907/274–8668* ⊕ *www.anchoragesymphony.org.*

The box office of the Alaska Center for the Performing Arts sells tickets for both.

THEATER

Alaska Center for the Performing Arts. This venue stages major theater performances and hosts the Anchorage Opera and the Anchorage Symphony Orchestra. ✉ *621 West 6th Ave..*

Anchorage Community Theatre. From September through May, the Anchorage Community Theatre offers locally produced, tried-and-true plays. ✉ *1133 E. 70th Ave., South Anchorage* ☎ *907/344–4713* ⊕ *www.actalaska.org.*

Cyrano's Off-Center Playhouse. Year-round, Cyrano's Off-Center Playhouse mounts innovative productions—including one or two world premieres by Alaska's most talented playwrights—in a cozy theater with a thrust stage. ⊠ *413 D St., Downtown* ☎ *907/274–2599* ⊕ *www. cyranos.org.*

Out North Contemporary Art House. The plays at Out North Contemporary Art House are thought-provoking and, at times, controversial. It often earns critical acclaim from local reviewers. In recent years the nonprofit has branched out to present films, art exhibits, live music, and literary events. ⊠ *3800 DeBarr Rd., East Anchorage* ☎ *907/279–8099* ⊕ *www.outnorth.org.*

University of Alaska Anchorage Theatre. Student productions from the University of Alaska Anchorage Theatre are timely and well done, and there is a good mix of classic and contemporary plays. ⊠ *3211 Providence Dr., East Anchorage* ☎ *907/786–4849* ⊕ *www.uaa.alaska.edu/ theatreanddance.*

SHOPPING

Stock up for your travels around Alaska in Anchorage, where there's no sales tax. The weekend markets are packed with Alaskan-made products of all types, and you're likely to meet local artisans.

DOWNTOWN

ART

The Anchorage **First Friday Arts Walk** is a popular monthly (and year-round) event, with dozens of galleries, coffee shops, and restaurants offering a chance to sample hors d'oeuvres while looking over the latest works by regional artists. The Anchorage Press prints a First Friday map the first Thursday of every month.

Artique. One of Alaska's oldest galleies (if not the oldest), Artique sells work such as paintings, pottery, and jewelry by prominent Alaskan artists, including painter Byron Birdsall and photographer Clark James Mishler. ⊠ *314 G St., Downtown* ☎ *907/277–1663, 800/848–1312* ⊕ *www.artiqueltd.com.*

International Gallery of Contemporary Art. Anchorage's premier fine-arts gallery, the International Gallery of Contemporary Art has changing exhibits monthly. ⊠ *427 D St., Downtown* ☎ *907/279–1116* ⊕ *www. igcaalaska.org.*

4th Avenue Market Place. Several shops selling Alaska Native art and crafts, including exquisite handwoven baskets and delicately beaded jewelry, are housed in the 4th Avenue Market Place. Don't miss Two Spirits Gallery: many artists work on-site, so it's a go-to place for anybody interested in meeting the people behind the crafts. ⊠ *411 W. 4th Ave., Downtown.*

FOOD

Fodor's Choice ★ **Anchorage Market and Festival.** On weekends throughout the summer the Anchorage Market and Festival opens for business (and loads of fun) in the parking lot at 3rd Avenue and E Street. Dozens of vendors offer Alaskan-made crafts, ethnic imports, and deliciously fattening food.

Stock up on birch candy and salmon jerky to snack on while traveling or as perfect made-in-Alaska gifts for friends back home. The open-air market runs from mid-May to mid-September on weekends from 10 to 6. ✉ *3rd Ave. between E and C Sts., Downtown* ☎ *907/272–5634* ⊕ *www.anchoragemarkets.com/main.html.*

Modern Dwellers Chocolate Lounge. Chocolate junkies can get their fix at the fun-loving Modern Dwellers Chocolate Lounge, which has locations Downtown and Midtown. Decadent traditional truffles like hazelnut are available, but don't leave without trying one of the place's many whimsical creations. Eating local takes on new depths with the Salmon Surprise truffle: bittersweet honey, black pepper ganache, and just a smidge of Alaskan smoked salmon combine for a salty-sweet melty mouthful. You may be quite popular when you get home if you bring back the "happy hour" gift set featuring a margarita truffle made with tequila and lime zest. On a cold Alaska winter day, warm up with an espresso or better yet, a cup of spicy Mayan drinking chocolate. ✉ *423 G St., Downtown, Anchorage* ☎ *907/868–1818* ⊕ *www.moderndwellers.com* ✉ *751 E. 36th Ave., Midtown, Anchorage* ☎ *907/677–9985.*

GIFTS

David Green Master Furrier. Although furs may not be to everyone's taste or ethics, a number of Alaska fur companies have stores and factories in Anchorage. One of the city's largest and best-known furriers is David Green Master Furrier. ✉ *130 W. 4th Ave., Downtown* ☎ *907/277–9595* ⊕ *www.davidgreenfurs.com.*

Oomingmak. The Native-owned cooperative Oomingmak sells items made of qiviut, the warm undercoat of musk ox. Scarves, shawls, and tunics are knitted in traditional patterns. ✉ *604 H St., Downtown* ☎ *907/272–9225, 888/360–9665* ⊕ *www.qiviut.com.*

MALLS AND DEPARTMENT STORES

Anchorage 5th Avenue Mall. Occupying a city block at 5th Avenue and A Street, Anchorage 5th Avenue Mall contains dozens of stores, including nationally known brands like JC Penney and Banana Republic, and a few local stores, such as Alaska Wild Berry Products, that are perfect for one-stop gift shopping. ✉ *320 W. 5th Ave., Downtown* ☎ *907/258–5535* ⊕ *www.simon.com.*

Nordstrom. Just across 6th Avenue, and connected by a skywalk to the 5th Avenue Mall, is Alaska's only Nordstrom. ✉ *603 D St., Downtown.*

MIDTOWN

BOOKS

Title Wave Books. Easily the largest independent bookstore in Alaska, Title Wave Books fills a 30,000-square-foot space at the other end of the REI strip mall. The shelves are filled with used titles across more than 1,600 categories and a large section of Alaska-focused books; the staff is very knowledgeable. Anyone can bring in used books and trade them for store credit. ✉ *1360 W. Northern Lights Blvd., Midtown* ☎ *907/278–9283, 888/598–9283* ⊕ *www.wavebooks.com.*

Kaladi Brothers Coffee. Kaladi Brothers Coffee, right near Title Wave Books and REI, will caffeinate you and provide free Wi-Fi access to boot. ✉ **1340 W. Northern Lights Blvd., Suite 409, Midtown** ☎ **907/277–5127** ⊕ **www.kaladi.com.**

GIFTS

Alaska Fur Exchange. In a large Midtown store, Alaska Fur Exchange sells both furs and Native artwork. ✉ *4417 Old Seward Hwy., Midtown* ☎ *907/563–3877* ⊕ *www.alaskafurexchange.com.*

SPORTS AND OUTDOOR EQUIPMENT

Mt. View Sports Center. If you're looking for brand names like Abel, Sims, Filson, Patagonia, Kimber, and Mountain Hardwear, Mt. View is your place. It is pretty much fly-fishing central in Anchorage, and you can find expert advice and guidance for your prospective fishing and hunting adventures. There's also an excellent book section that covers all sorts of outdoor activities in Alaska. ✉ *3838 Old Seward Hwy., Midtown* ☎ *907/563–8600* ⊕ *www.mtviewsports.com.*

SPENARD

GIFTS

Dos Manos. Buy souvenirs for the hipster in your life at this laid-back gallery that features individually screen-printed T-shirts, leather satchels, silver jewelry, quirky knit caps, and affordable wall art (check out Lance Lekander's retro robot prints). Most items don't say "Alaska" on them, but everything here is handmade in the state by emerging artists. ✉ *1317 W. Northern Lights, Suite 3, Spenard, Anchorage* ☎ *907/569–6800.*

SPORTS AND OUTDOOR EQUIPMENT

REI. If you get to Alaska and discover you've left some critical camping or outdoor recreation gear behind, REI rents camping, skiing, and paddling equipment. It also gives weekly seminars on season-specific outdoors subjects, and the salespeople are very knowledgeable about local conditions and activities, and the gear required to get you out and back safely. ✉ *1200 W. Northern Lights Blvd., Spenard* ☎ *907/272–4565* ⊕ *www.rei.com.*

Alaska Mountaineering & Hiking. This place is the go-to specialist for any gear having to do with, yep, mountaineering or hiking. Whether you're setting out on a series of day hikes or you're planning a serious climb, the knowledgable staff can help you choose the right equipment for the task. ✉ *2633 Spenard Rd., Spenard* ☎ *907/272–1811* ⊕ *www. alaskamountaineering.com.*

GREATER ANCHORAGE

GIFTS

Alaska Native Heritage Center. Find Native art and crafts at the Alaska Native Heritage Center gift shop. ✉ *8800 Heritage Center Dr., Glenn Hwy. at Muldoon Rd., East Anchorage* ☎ *907/330–8000, 800/315–6608* ⊕ *www.alaskanative.net.*

★ **Alaska Native Medical Center.** Several downtown shops sell quality Native Alaskan artwork, but the best buys can be found in the gift shop at the Alaska Native Medical Center, which is open weekdays 10–2 and 11–2 on the first and third Saturday of the month. It doesn't take credit cards. ✉ *4315 Diplomacy Dr., at Tudor and Bragaw Rds., East Anchorage* ☎ *907/563–2662* ⊕ *www.anmc.org.*

MALLS AND DEPARTMENT STORES

Dimond Center. The city's largest shopping mall, the Dimond Center is on the south end of town at Dimond Boulevard and Old Seward Highway. In addition to dozens of stores, including Best Buy, Gap, and Forever 21, the mall has a movie theater and an ice-skating rink. Nearby are several big-box discount stores, including Costco and Walmart. ✉ *800 E. Dimond Blvd., South Anchorage* ☎ *907/929–7108* ⊕ *www. dimondcenter.com.*

SPORTS AND OUTDOOR EQUIPMENT

Sportsman's Warehouse. This big-box outdoors store has all manner of fishing, hiking, and camping gear. Prices are lower than at most places in town, and the selection is great, but you won't find the personal attention and knowledgeable staff that the more high-end places specialize in. ✉ *8681 Old Seward Hwy., South Anchorage* ☎ *907/644–1400* ⊕ *www. sportsmanswarehouse.com.*

SIDE TRIPS FROM ANCHORAGE

GIRDWOOD

40 miles southeast of Anchorage.

A ski resort, summer vacation spot, and home to an eclectic collection of locals, the town of Girdwood sits in a deep valley and is surrounded by tall mountains on three sides as well as Turnagain Arm, one of the most photogenic sites in South Central Alaska. Originally called Glacier City (a name we're rather fond of), Girdwood got its start as a gold-mining town. The town was renamed for James Girdwood, an Irish linen merchant who had four gold claims. But the name wasn't the only thing that changed over the years; the town itself was moved 2½ miles from its original site after the 1964 earthquake.

Today Girdwood's main attraction is the Mt. Alyeska Ski Resort, the largest ski area in Alaska. Besides enjoying the obvious winter attractions, you can hike up the mountain, rent a bike, or visit several restaurants (our favorite is Seven Glaciers) and gift shops. Girdwood is wetter than Anchorage; it often rains or snows here while the sun shines to the north.

GETTING HERE AND AROUND

Though it's 40 miles from Ted Stevens Anchorage International Airport, consider adding extra time if you make the drive to Girdwood—but not because of any traffic concerns. The drive down the New Seward Highway is stunning—oh, that Turnagain Arm—and photo ops abound. Other options include a ride on the **Alaska Railroad**'s Coastal Classic or Glacier Discovery trains (☎ 907/265–2494 or 800/544–0552 ⊕ *www. alaskarailroad.com*), or reserve a spot on the Magic Bus (☎ 907/230–6773 ⊕ *www.themagicbus.com*), which runs between Anchorage and Girdwood year-round. Alyeska also runs a ski and snowboard bus from Anchorage to Girdwood weekend days throughout ski season; purchase tickets online at ⊕ *www.alyeskaresort.com*, at the Carrs/Safeway on Huffman Road, or at an Alyeska Resort ticket office. Once in town, you'll need to rely on your own car, the Alyeska Resort shuttle service, or foot power.

WHEN TO GO

Though Girdwood is best known for its winter ski activities, there's plenty to do year-round. The town's restaurants remain popular with locals—snow or no snow—and the area offers some of Anchorage's best hiking trails, fishing, and much more.

EXPLORING

Girdwood Center for Visual Arts. Though you'll go to Girdwood to ski or hike, you'll end up spending time perusing the crafts and artwork at this nonprofit co-op gallery. With pieces from more than 40 artists on display, there's plenty to look at—and you might end up taking care of any gift needs (from the trip or for the holidays) in one fell swoop. ⊠ *Olympic Mountain Loop* ☎ 907/783–3209 ⊕ *www.gcvaonline.org* ⊙ *Closed Mon. and Tues.*

OUTDOOR ACTIVITIES AND GUIDED TOURS

Alaska Backcountry Access. This outfitter zips people out of town for jetboat rides up Twentymile River, kayaking, and much more. Families with kids 6 and older might enjoy the slightly adventurous Girdwood Trekker trips, a naturalist-led day trip that includes a hike, panning for gold, and a cable hand tram trip across Glacier Creek. ⊠ *New Girdwood Townsite* ☎ 907/783–3600, 800/783–3005 ⊕ *www. akback.com.*

Alyeska Resort. Alaska's largest and best-known downhill ski resort encompasses more than 1,400 skiable acres of terrain for all skill levels. A high-speed quad lift gets you up the mountain faster. Ski rentals are available at the resort. Local ski and snowboard guides teach classes on the mountain. Boarders will dig the new super pipe, which has 18-foot walls. ☎ 907/754–7669, 800/880–3880 ⊕ *www.alyeskaresort.com.*

Chugach Powder Guides. Founded in 1997, this helicopter-ski and Sno-Cat operation focuses on backcountry skiing and snowboarding in the Chugach Range out of Girdwood and Seward; Alaska Range adventures are also featured. When you see films of extreme helicopter skiing in Alaska, it's usually these guys. ☎ 907/783–4354 ⊕ *www. chugachpowderguides.com.*

WHERE TO EAT

$ ✕ **The Bake Shop.** The atmosphere is vintage 1975 at this old-time Gird-
AMERICAN wood favorite, where you order at the counter and wait for servers to
bring your meal. Breakfasts are filling, with piles of sourdough pancakes, fluffy omelets (we heartily recommend the farmer's omelet), and
homemade pastries. Skiers and snowboarders drop by for a fast lunch
or dinner of homemade soups, sandwiches, or garden-fresh pizzas. Get
a loaf of the hearty sourdough or one of the huge cinnamon buns to go.
Dine out front in summer, surrounded by hanging baskets filled with
begonias, lobelia, and impatiens. ■TIP➔ The shop opens at 7 am every
day, making it a great option for early birds or folks who haven't adjusted
to the time change yet. ⑤ *Average main: $7* ✉ *Olympic Mountain Loop*
☎ *907/783–2831* ⊕ *www.thebakeshop.com* ▭ *No credit cards* ◷ *Sun.–
Fri. 7–7, Sat. 7–8.*

$$$ ✕ **Double Musky Inn.** Anchorage residents say eating at this award-win-
SOUTHERN ning spot is well worth the one-hour drive south to Girdwood and the
inevitable wait for dinner—you can usually find a spot at the bar, order
some halibut ceviche, and choose from the extensive martini menu or
local draft beers. It's very noisy, and the interior is completely covered
with tacky art and Mardi Gras souvenirs of all types, but the windows
frame views of huge Sitka spruce trees. The diverse menu mixes hearty
Cajun-style meals with such favorites as garlic seafood pasta, rack of
lamb, French pepper steak, and lobster kebabs. For dessert lovers, the
biggest attraction is the gooey, chocolate-rich Double Musky pie. ⑤ *Av-
erage main: $32* ✉ *Mile 0.3, Crow Creek Rd.* ☎ *907/783–2822* ⊕ *www.
doublemuskyinn.com* ⌂ *Reservations not accepted* ◷ *Closed Mon. and
late Oct.–mid-Dec. No lunch.*

$$$$ ✕ **Seven Glaciers.** A 60-passenger aerial tram (free with dinner reserva-
EUROPEAN tions, otherwise $20 round-trip) carries you to this refined yet relaxing
mountaintop Girdwood restaurant perched at the 2,300-foot level on
Mt. Alyeska. The comfortable dining room overlooks seven glaciers.
The kitchen, led by chef Jason Porter, creates an ever-changing menu
that relies, as much as possible, on local produce, seafood, and meat. À
la carte prices are high; consider the five-course chef's tasting menu ($79
per person) instead. The restaurant also caters to special diets and offers
a gluten-free menu. Both tram and restaurant are wheelchair accessible.
Reservations are recommended. ⑤ *Average main: $46* ✉ *Hotel Alyeska,
1000 Arlberg Rd.* ☎ *907/754–2237* ⊕ *www.alyeskaresort.com/dining*
◷ *Dinner only.*

WHERE TO STAY

For expanded hotel reviews, visit Fodors.com.

$ 🛏 **The Carriage House.** This Girdwood B&B is across from the Double
B&B/INN Musky restaurant and close to Alyeska Resort's downhill ski slopes.
Pros: elegant furnishings; new flat-screen TVs; very nice breakfast
spread. **Cons:** location can be a bit remote for some; restaurant traffic is
bothersome. **TripAdvisor:** "comfortable and nice," "extremely welcom-
ing," "great retreat." ⑤ *Rooms from: $125* ✉ *Mile 0.2, Crow Creek
Rd.* ☎ *907/783–9464, 888/961–9464* ⊕ *www.thecarriagehousebandb.
com* ⇨ *4 rooms* ⦿ *Breakfast.*

$$$$
HOTEL
Fodor's Choice
★

⊡ **The Hotel Alyeska.** Some rooms have views of the Chugach Mountains, and lush forests surround this large and luxurious hotel at the base of Alyeska Ski Resort in Girdwood, an hour south of Anchorage. **Pros:** great views; rooms remodeled in 2007. **Cons:** smallish rooms; service can be uneven. **TripAdvisor:** "beautiful relaxing resort," "luxury experience," "very nice." ⑤ *Rooms from: $259* ⊠ *1000 Arlberg Rd., Box 249* ☎ *907/754–1111, 800/880–3880* ⊕ *www.alyeskaresort.com/hotel* ⇨ *304 rooms, 12 suites* ⦿| *No meals.*

SHOPPING
JEWELRY
Kobuk Valley Jade Co. The Kobuk Valley Jade Co., at the base of Mt. Alyeska, sells hand-polished jade pieces as well as Native masks, baskets, and jewelry. ⊠ *Olympic Circle, Girdwood* ☎ *907/783–2764.*

South Central Alaska

INCLUDING PRINCE WILLIAM SOUND,
HOMER, AND THE KENAI PENINSULA

WORD OF MOUTH

"Homer is a cute place with plenty to do to keep you busy for a
couple of days—my favorite thing was taking a ferry to Halibut
Cove and dining at the Saltry—reservations required—it is a beautiful place."

—sunburn1944

WELCOME TO SOUTH CENTRAL ALASKA

TOP REASONS TO GO

★ **Fishing:** In summer salmon fill the rivers, which you can fish with a guide, from your own boat, or from the bank. Fishing for halibut and rockfish is also possible from charter boats out of Homer or Seward.

★ **Wildlife:** Urban moose, black and brown bears, sea lions, Dall sheep, gray whales, and bald eagles are all common in the region.

★ **Scenery:** Boasting views of volcanoes and mountains that fall right into the water, the Kenai Peninsula is a buffet for the eyes.

★ **Glaciers:** Get up close and personal with glaciers on a tour to ski, dog sled, or hike a glacier's surface, or paddle out to one.

★ **Accessibility:** With a network of roads and ferries, this region is easily accessible. No matter where you go in the region, you're only a few steps away from the wilderness.

1 Prince William Sound. Spanning 15,000 square miles, Prince William Sound is made up of remote coves, glaciers that curve right into the sea, and small islands topped with sea lions and puffins. The sound is easily accessible from Anchorage via Whittier or Valdez.

2 Kenai Peninsula. Anchorage is called "the best base camp in the world." One look at the peninsula and all the recreation available, and you'll understand why. The Kenai has world-class recreation opportunities that include

GETTING ORIENTED

South Central is the epicenter of Alaska's population and commerce. The Mat-Su Valley, just 15 miles north of Anchorage, is the fastest-growing region in America. South Central is populated for a reason: the entire region is rich with awe-inspiring natural attractions and superb recreational opportunities. Geographical features include four mountain ranges, three national parks, the country's second-largest national forest, and more glaciers, rivers, and lakes than one person could visit in a lifetime.

6

fishing, hiking, canoeing, and whale-watching.

3 Homer. Literally the end of the road, Homer is an alluring blend of commercial fishermen, artists, bohemians, and tourists. With bluffs sloping down to Kachemak Bay, it's hard to find a spot in town without a view of the ocean or mountains. Be sure to try the excellent restaurants and sip a locally brewed beer.

4 Kodiak Island. The city of Kodiak was Alaska's first capital. Not it serves as a way station for visiting

the 1.6-million-acre Kodiak National Wildlife Refuge, where spotting the enormous Kodiak brown bears is the main goal of a trip.

5 Mat-Su Valley and Beyond. Just north of Anchorage, the Matanuska-Susitna Valley is a mixture of bedroom communities, agricultural concerns, and recreation options. It's also the gateway to the Interior. Several spectacular mountain ranges converge here: the Chugach, the Talkeetna, and the Alaska, with rivers and streams full of trophy-class salmon and trout.

Updated
by Teeka A.
Ballas

There are few places in America that offer such a diverse array of natural beauty as South Central Alaska. From whales to glaciers, there is something to satiate every nature lover's appetite. Unlike those of most of Alaska, the wonders of South Central are traversable or viewable by car. There are roads to a majority of the beloved spots in the region.

Most visitors to South Central tend to begin and end their visit in Anchorage, the region's transportation hub. During the summer months this is where planes, trains, buses, and automobiles depart on a daily basis. RV rentals are also popular in Anchorage, and can be seen in droves along the Seward Highway along Cook Inlet. Most highways in South Central are two lanes and paved, but summertime traffic can be frustrating. Be wary of impatient drivers trying to get around slow-moving RVs, and always be aware of wildlife as well. Every year motorists kill hundreds of moose, and in turn there are many driver fatalities. South Central Alaska is bordered on the south and the west by ocean waters: the Gulf of Alaska, Prince William Sound, and Cook Inlet. This region is lined with a smattering of quaint port towns. From Kodiak, a commercial-fishing port, to Homer, a funky laid-back artists' colony, each town has its own personality. Inland, the remnants of mining towns continue to grow and prosper in different ways. Talkeetna, a small village on the northern edge of the region, is a starting point for many mountaineers, as it's located at the base of Mt. McKinley. Most locals refer to the 20,320-foot mountain by its original Athabascan name, Denali, which means "the High One." In the center of South Central is Alaska's farmland, the Matanuska-Susitna Valley (generally referred to as the "Mat-Su Valley," the "Matsu," or just "the Valley"). The region boasts 75-pound cabbages and gigantic award-winning rhubarb.

All of South Central is wrapped in the embrace of several mountain ranges. In a crescent shape south and east of Anchorage is the 300-mile-long Chugach Mountain Range. It bends all the way around the gulf to Valdez, where it meets the Wrangell–St. Elias National Park. The

Chugach, St. Elias, and Wrangell mountain ranges are so immense that they are often referred to, collectively, as the "mountain kingdom of North America."

The mountain peaks don't end there, however. Across Cook Inlet, easily viewed from Anchorage, is a small part of the Alaska Range known as the Pacific Ocean's great Ring of Fire, snowcapped volcanoes still known to occasionally blow off steam and lava. The Alaska Range is a narrow 400-mile-long range that embraces the highest peak in North America, Mt. McKinley.

Whether you're hoping to explore mountains or ocean, tundra, taiga, or forest, each climate zone and ecosystem is available in South Central. From the coastal rain forests around Seward and Kodiak to the rough Arctic chill of glaciers flowing off the Harding Icefield, the region offers it all.

PLANNING

WHEN TO GO

Summer is the peak season all over the state. In South Central this means it is rarely too hot or too cold, particularly along the coast, although rainfall occurs often and without warning. Long daylight hours make it possible to enjoy the beauty and the bounty of Alaska at all hours. However, if you're hoping to catch more hours of darkness, there are always the shoulder seasons. Unfortunately, the weather in spring and fall tends to be more unpredictable than in summer, with random appearances of snow and dramatic drops in temperature. Autumn starts early, with the deciduous trees beginning to show color in mid-August. Visitor services stay open until the end of September.

GETTING HERE AND AROUND
BOAT AND FERRY TRAVEL

With its glaciers, mountains, fjords, and sea mammals, the South Central coast is great to see by ferry. The ferries between Valdez and Whittier run by way of Columbia Glacier in summer, where it is not unusual to witness giant fragments of ice calving from the face of the glacier into Prince William Sound.

The **Alaska Marine Highway**, the state-run ferry operator, has scheduled service to Valdez, Cordova, Whittier, Homer, and Seldovia on the mainland; to Kodiak and Port Lions on Kodiak Island; and to the port of Dutch Harbor in the Aleutian Islands. These connect to the ferries that operate in Southeast Alaska, but the two systems connect only on once-a-month sailings. Ferries operate on two schedules; summer (May–September) sailings are considerably more frequent than fall and winter service. Check your schedules carefully: ferries do not stop at all ports every day. Reservations are required on all routes and should be made as far in advance as possible.

Alaska Marine Highway ☎ *907/465–3941, 800/642–0066* ⊕ *www. ferryalaska.com.*

BUS TRAVEL

For bus service in the region, contact Alaska Direct Bus Lines, Homer Stage Line, Park Connection Motor Coach, or Seward Bus Line.

Contacts **Alaska Direct Bus Lines** ☎ *800/770–6652* ⊕ *www. alaskadirectbusline.com.* **Homer Stage Line** ☎ *907/868–3914* ⊕ *www. stagelineinhomer.com.* **Park Connection Motor Coach** ☎ *800/266–8625* ⊕ *alaskacoach.com.* **Seward Bus Line** ☎ *907/563–0800, 888/420-7787* ⊕ *www.sewardbuslines.net.*

CAR TRAVEL

Car is definitely the way to go in South Central; the road system is more developed than in most other regions, and is also mostly paved. It also has some of the coolest driving routes that involve putting your car on a ferry. If you're renting, know that not all rental companies will let you do this (start with the larger chains, which are more likely to have a seaworthy rental policy available), so if this is part of your travel plan, aim to get your ducks in a row about two or three months in advance before the ferry-friendly rental agencies are all booked for your dates.

TRAVEL TIMES FROM ANCHORAGE

DESTINATION	TIME
Chugach State Park	20 mins–1 hr by car, depending on section of park
Cordova	1 hr to Whittier by car, then 3 hrs by ferry
Denali State Park	3 hrs by car
Glennallen	4 hrs by car
Homer	4–5 hrs by car
Kenai/Soldotna	2–3 hrs by car
Lake Clark	1–2 hrs by air taxi
Portage Glacier	50 mins by car
Seward	2–2½ hrs by car
Wrangell–St. Elias	6–8 hrs by car

TRAIN TRAVEL

Anchorage is the region's hub, connected by rail and road to major ports in South Central. To the east, you can reach McCarthy and Valdez by an indirect but scenic drive on the Glenn and Richardson highways. The Seward and Sterling highways connect to nearly every town on the Kenai Peninsula. The **Alaska Railroad Corporation** operates the Alaska Railroad, which runs 470 miles between Seward and Fairbanks via Anchorage. There's daily service between Anchorage and Fairbanks in summer, and in winter there's one round-trip per week. Service to Seward from Anchorage runs every weekend from mid-May to September.

Contacts **Alaska Railroad Corporation** ☎ *800/544-0552* ⊕ *www.akrr.com.*

HEALTH AND SAFETY

In South Central, it's important to stick to basic principles of Alaska safety: hiring a guide for anything outside your comfort zone might just prove to be the most important investment you've ever made. Follow bear safety rules; especially down the Kenai Peninsula, know that moose can be the more dangerous encounter, so use extreme respect.

MONEY MATTERS

Nothing is too surprising on the financial front here: try to bring cash if you're traveling to a small town, and even if you've prepaid for a guide's services, remember to bring a little something to tip with at the end of the day or trip.

RESTAURANTS

The best way to describe the hospitality industry in Alaska is "informal," and this applies as much to South Central as it does anywhere else. Don't worry if you still have your hiking clothes on when you go out to eat. Every kind of food is available, especially in larger towns, but options decline considerably from mid-September through April. *Prices in the reviews are the average cost of a main course at dinner or, if dinner is not served, at lunch.*

HOTELS

Accommodations in Alaska, particularly in the sparsely populated areas, can be quite rugged. You will find a lot of establishments have only shared bathrooms, and most amenities like a coffee pot, television, and Internet are scant, although the latter is beginning to find its way even into remote villages. In the most rural of places it is not entirely unheard-of to find no bathrooms in the establishment, but rather a "honey bucket" out back. If such things are important to you, it's wise to inquire in advance. *Prices in the reviews are the lowest cost of a standard double room in high season.*

PRINCE WILLIAM SOUND

Tucked into the east side of the Kenai Peninsula, the sound is a peaceful escape from the throngs of people congesting the towns and highways. Enhanced with steep fjords, green enshrouded waterfalls, and calving tidewater glaciers, Prince William Sound is a stunning arena. It has a convoluted coastline, in that it is riddled with islands, which makes it hard to discern just how vast the area is. The sound covers almost 15,000 square miles—more than 12 times the size of Rhode Island—and is home to more than 150 glaciers. The sound is vibrantly alive with all manner of marine life, including salmon, halibut, humpback and orca whales, sea otters, sea lions, and porpoises. Bald eagles are easily seen soaring above, and often brown and black bears, Sitka black-tailed deer, and gray wolves can be spotted on the shore.

Unfortunately, the *Exxon Valdez* oil spill in 1989 heavily damaged parts of the sound, and oil still washes up on shore after high tides and storms. The original spill had a devastating effect on both animal and human lives. What lasting effect this lurking oil will have on the area is still being studied and remains a topic of much debate.

BEST BETS FOR DIFFERENT TRAVELERS

For cruise travelers:

■ Get down to Homer and across Kachemak Bay to Seldovia; this area will let you experience the crowdless kayaking, small-town feel, and (if you go to Seldovia) off-road-system tranquillity your cruise may have been lacking.

For those traveling with kids:

■ Alaska SeaLife Center, in Seward, features enough hands-on displays and sea creature–viewing areas to keep both the young and young-at-heart occupied for hours.

For travelers who want to get up close and personal with wildlife:

■ Out of Seward, take a full-day cruise into Kenai Fjords National Park; this fascinating landscape is also chock-full of sea lions, birds, and other fjord-dwelling creatures.

For a comfortable retreat experience and easy access to fishing the storied waters of the Kenai:

■ Stay at the Kenai Princess Wilderness Lodge, right on the Russian River; they'll help you get set up to fish in this gorgeous location famous for huge (and delicious) salmon.

■TIP→ Bring your rain gear—Prince William Sound receives more than 150 inches of rain per year.

The sound is best explored by charter boat or guided excursion out of Whittier, Cordova, or Valdez. Even though the waters are mostly protected, open stretches are common, and the fickle Alaska weather can fool even experienced boaters. From the road system, Whittier and Valdez are your best bets for finding charter outfits.

CHUGACH STATE PARK

Bordering Anchorage to the east.

GETTING HERE AND AROUND

The Chugach forms the backdrop of Anchorage, and trailheads are accessible at the top of O'Malley, Huffman, and DeArmoun roads, south of Anchorage at Potter Valley, McHugh Creek, and Bird Ridge on the Seward Highway, and to the north of town at Arctic Valley Road (6 miles out) and Eagle River Road (13 miles out).

ESSENTIALS

Visitor Information **Park Headquarters** ⊠ Mile 115, Seward Hwy. ☎ 907/345–5014 ⊕ www.dnr.alaska.gov/parks/units/chugach.

EXPLORING

Chugach State Park. Comprising nearly a half-million acres, Chugach State Park is the third-largest state park in America. Just on the edge of Anchorage, the park is Alaska's most accessible wilderness. It has nearly 30 trails for all types of hikes and hikers. Totaling more than 150 miles, the hiking trails range from 2 miles to 30 miles long. Although the park is technically an urban park, in that it is connected to the largest city in Alaska, it is far from being a typical urban setting. Chugach State Park

Prince William Sound

is anything but tame; it's real wilderness, home to Dall sheep, mountain goats, brown bears, moose, and several packs of wolves.

Miners who sought the easiest means of traversing the mountain peaks and passes initially blazed most of the trails within the park. Today those same trails are restored every spring and maintained by park rangers and various volunteer groups. Trailheads are scattered around the park's perimeter from Eklutna Lake, 30 miles north of Anchorage, to the trailhead for the Crow Pass Trail near Girdwood, 37 miles to the south. It is free to hike in the park, whether you're there for an afternoon or a week; however, several of the more popular trailheads charge a $5 daily parking fee.

The park offers some truly intoxicating views, and depending on what perch you're looking down from, you can see across the bay to the looming white mountains of the Alaska Range, the great tides of Cook Inlet, and, on clear days, Mt. McKinley in all her glory. One of the best and most easily accessible places to try for such a view is from Flattop Mountain on the park's western edge. The peak is the most popular destination within Chugach Park. It is a 1-mile-long hike to the top, and hikers of all abilities make the trek. Be advised, however, that although you may see people hiking in flip-flops up to the peak, it is strenuous and can be very challenging. Wear sturdy hiking shoes and proper attire. The trail up can be exhausting, and the way down can be very taxing on the knees. It's always wise to hike with trekking poles; they help relieve the stress on the back and the knees. Carry water and a snack, and as always, be prepared for sudden weather changes. Every year people are rescued from this trail because they have underestimated its potential for calamity, so be prepared. ⊕ *dnr.alaska.gov/ parks/units/chugach.*

> ### CLIMB IT
>
> Every summer solstice, locals climb to the top of Flattop Mountain to celebrate the longest day of the year. If you're in town for this event, it's great fun; there's even an impromptu concert by musicians who lug their instruments to the top of the mountain. Parking spots are at a premium, so arrive early.

Eagle River Nature Center. Eagle River Road leads 12 miles into the mountains from the bedroom community of Eagle River. The Eagle River Nature Center, at the end of Eagle River Road, has wildlife displays, telescopes for wildlife spotting, and 9 miles of hiking trails within the center's perimeters, and there are volunteers to answer questions, lead hikes, and host naturalist programs throughout the year. A cabin that sleeps eight and a pair of yurts (round insulated tents) that sleep four and six are available to rent. The cost is $65 per night, and a 1.5-mile hike in is required. Amenities include woodstoves, firewood, and outdoor latrines. The center is also the trail end for the Crow Pass Trail, a 26-mile section of the Historic Iditarod Trail. ⊠ *32750 Eagle River Rd., Eagle River* ☎ *907/694–2108* ⊕ *www. ernc.org* ⊠ *Parking $5* ⊗ *May–Sept., Wed.–Sun. 10–5; Oct.–Apr., Fri.– Sun. 10–5.*

OUTDOOR ACTIVITIES AND GUIDED TOURS

The **Little Rodak Trail** is less than 1 mile long and has a viewing platform that overlooks the Eagle River valley. **Albert Loop Trail** behind the nature center has markers that coordinate with a self-guided hike along its 3-mile route; pick up a brochure at the Eagle River Nature Center.

HIKING

Several trailheads along the edge of Anchorage lead into the park and its 3,000- to 5,000-foot-tall peaks. The park's most popular day climb is **Flattop Mountain,** which towers 3,500 feet above sea level. It's reached via the Glen Alps Trailhead off Upper Huffman Road on Anchorage's Hillside. A 1-mile trail climbs 1,300 feet from the Glen Alps parking area to the top. On a bright summer day you'll encounter plenty of company. Bring along a day pack with plenty of water and energy bars, a rainproof jacket, good hiking boots, and trekking poles.

MOUNTAIN BIKING

Mountain biking has become very popular in the park, and most, but not all, trails are open to bikes; check the signs and symbols at the trailheads if in doubt. The Powerline Pass trail from the Glen Alps parking lot is wide and well maintained for bikes and offers a great view from the pass, as well as opportunities to spot moose, Dall sheep, bears, and maybe even wolves.

Sunshine Fitness and Sports. Mountain bike rentals are available here. ✉ *123 E. Fireweed La., Anchorage* ☎ *907/272–6444* ⊕ *www. sunshinefitness.com.*

CHUGACH NATIONAL FOREST

40 miles east of Anchorage.

GETTING HERE AND AROUND

The Seward Highway between Anchorage and Seward has a number of trail access points. (Check the highway for mile markers, with the distance measured from Seward.) At Mile 63.7, just south of Turnagain Pass, is the turnoff to the Johnson Pass Trail, a relatively flat trail to walk. Seven miles farther south, take the Hope Highway 18 miles to its end and find the Porcupine Campground. From there the Gull Rock Trail follows the shore of Turnagain Arm for 5 miles, offering scenic views across the arm and the chance to spot beluga whales foraging for salmon. Farther south on the Seward Highway, at Mile 23.1, the Ptarmigan Creek Trail starts at the campground and climbs 3.5 miles into the mountains, ending next to a lake surrounded by snowy peaks. Your best bet for getting around the area is by rental car.

ESSENTIALS

Visitor Information **Alaska Public Lands Information Center** ☎ *907/644– 3661, 866/869–6887* ⊕ *www.alaskacenters.gov.* **Forest Headquarters** ☎ *907/743–9500 Anchorage* ⊕ *www.fs.fed.us/r10/chugach.*

EXPLORING

Chugach National Forest. Sprawling east of Chugach State Park, Chugach National Forest encompasses nearly 6 million acres. The forest covers most of the Kenai Peninsula and parts of Prince William Sound, and is the second-largest national forest in the United States, exceeded in size only by the Tongass in Southeast Alaska.

The forest has abundant recreational opportunities: hiking, camping, backpacking, fishing, boating, mountain biking, horseback riding, hunting, and flightseeing. South Central Alaska is not the best terrain for rock climbing (aside from Mt. McKinley), as the rock is predominantly composed of hardened ocean sediments that are weak and crumbly. There are, however, some places for great bouldering, and in the wintertime ice climbing is quite popular, as are snowshoeing, skiing, snowmachining, and dog mushing.

Hiking trails offer easy access into the heart of the forest. You can spend a day hiking or looking for wildlife, or you can embark on a multiday backpacking excursion. At all but the most popular trailheads a five-minute stroll down a wooded trail can introduce you to the sights, smells, and tranquillity of backcountry Alaska.

⚠ Be prepared to be self-sufficient when entering Chugach Forest. Trailheads typically offer nothing more than a place to park and perhaps an outhouse. Running water, trail maps, and other amenities are not available. Also, be "bear aware" whenever you travel in bear country—and all of Alaska is bear country. In recent years urban and rural bear attacks have been on the rise in South Central. Try to hike in groups or pairs.

Pay attention to your surroundings, and make noise when traveling, especially in areas of reduced visibility. Bears will most likely make themselves scarce with some advance warning of your arrival. ⊕ *www. fs.usda.gov/detail/chugach/home/?cid=stelprdb5305529.*

OUTDOOR ACTIVITIES

★ **Crow Pass Trail.** Crow Pass Trail is a 26-mile-long backpacking trail that begins outside Girdwood and ends in Eagle River at the nature center. The trail is part of the Historic Iditarod Trail and is a truly great hike. The first 3 miles of this trail are the most strenuous, but after that the worst things hikers have to contend with are snow above the tree line and icy-cold river crossings. In Alaska during the summer it is wise to cross through rivers only in the morning in order to avoid the rising waters throughout the day as snow and glaciers melt under the many hours of sunshine.

In addition to offering splendid views, Crow Pass Trail winds around the front of the amazing Raven Glacier terminus. The glacier is ½ mile wide and more than 2 miles long, with many deep crevasses. You can camp anywhere along the trail, though it's important to know that camping anywhere near the glacier, even at the peak of summer, is a chilly endeavor. There is one cabin available along the trail at 3,500 feet. The cabin is above the tree line, just across from rich crystalline-blue Crystal Lake. It is almost always booked at least six months in advance. Contact forest headquarters. ⊕ *www.fs.usda.gov/detail/chugach.*

★ **Resurrection Pass Trail.** This 38-mile-long backpacking trail through the Chugach National Forest, draws hikers and backpackers for its colorful wildflowers in summer. There's also a chance to spot wildlife: moose, caribou, Dall sheep, mountain goats, black and brown bears, wolves, coyotes, and lynx all traverse the forest. Carry binoculars for the best wildlife-viewing opportunities.

The northern end of the trail starts south of the town of Hope, and follows an old mining trail through the Kenai Mountains to its end near Cooper Landing. The trail branches off at one point to the Devil's Pass trailhead along the Seward Highway. Besides cabins, the U.S. Forest Service has provided several "official" campsites along the trail, where you'll find a cleared patch of ground and a fire ring. You are free, however, to pitch your tent wherever you like. ⊕ *www.fs.usda. gov/detail/chugach.*

WHERE TO STAY

For expanded hotel reviews, visit Fodors.com.

$ ⊡ **U.S. Forest Service Cabins.** Along trails, near wilderness alpine lakes, in coastal forests, and on saltwater beaches, these rustic cabins offer retreats for the solo hiker or a group of friends. **Pros:** remote; cheap; beautiful. **Cons:** too remote for some; extremely basic; often booked months in advance for summer; mice frequent the establishment. ⑤ *Rooms from: $35* 🕾 *877/444–6777 reservations* ⊕ *www.recreation. gov* ⤳ *41 cabins.*

PORTAGE GLACIER

54 miles southeast of Anchorage.

GETTING HERE AND AROUND

Gray Line of Alaska leads summer boat tours (from mid-May to mid-September) along the face of Portage Glacier aboard the 200-passenger *Ptarmigan* for $79. The view of Portage Lake and the surrounding peaks and hanging glaciers (the high-up glaciers that terminate at the tops of cliffs) is spectacular, especially on a sunny day when the icy-blue hues of the glaciers shine through.

ESSENTIALS

Visitor and Tour Information **Begich-Boggs Visitor Center** ☎ 907/783–2326 ⊕ www.fs.fed.us/r10/chugach/chugach_pages/bbvc ⛁ $5 ⊘ early May–end of September 9 am–6 pm ⊘ Mid-Sept.–early May. **Gray Line of Alaska** ☎ 907/277–5581, 800/478–6388 ⊕ www.graylinealaska.com.

EXPLORING

Portage Glacier. Portage Glacier is one of Alaska's most frequently visited tourist destinations. A 6-mile side road off the Seward Highway leads to the Begich-Boggs Visitor Center, on the shore of Portage Lake and named after two U.S. congressmen who disappeared on a small-plane journey out of Anchorage in 1972. The center is staffed by Forest Service personnel, who can help plan your trip and explain the natural history of the area. A film on glaciers is shown hourly, and icebergs sometimes drift down to the center from Portage Glacier. Due to global climate change, Portage Glacier, like most of the glaciers in Alaska, has receded from view in recent years. ⊕ *www.fs.usda.gov/r10.*

Byron Glacier. The mountains surrounding Portage Glacier are covered with smaller glaciers. A 1-mile hike west brings you to the Byron Glacier overlook. The glacier is notable for its accessibility—it's one of the few places where you can hike onto a glacier from the road system. In summer, naturalists lead free weekly treks in search of microscopic ice worms. ⊕ *www.fs.usda.gov/r10.*

Turnagain Arm. Several hiking trails are accessible from the Seward Highway, including the steep paths up Falls Creek and Bird Ridge. Both offer spectacular views of Turnagain Arm, where explorer Captain Cook searched for the Northwest Passage. Local lore has it that the arm is so named because Cook entered it repeatedly, only to be forced to turn back by the huge tide. The tide is so powerful it sometimes rushes up the arm as a tidal bore—a wall of water that goes up an inlet. An increasingly popular, yet somewhat dangerous, sport is windsurfing the tidal bore. To view the bore tide, station yourself at one of the turnoffs along the arm about 2½ hours after low tide in Anchorage—tide books are available at sporting goods shops, grocery stores, and bookstores, or you can find tide information on the Web.

During the summer months beluga whales are frequent visitors to the arm as they patrol the muddy waters in search of salmon and hooligan, a variety of smelt. The whales travel in pods of adult and juvenile animals, the adults distinguishable by their bright white color. They're smaller than other whales that frequent Alaska's coastal waters,

reaching only 15 feet in length and weighing up to a ton. During high tide from July to August, when the surface of the water is calm, belugas are often spotted from the highway, frequently causing traffic jams as tourists and residents pull off the road for a chance to view the whales as they travel up and down the shoreline. It's an increasingly special thing to spot a beluga here; for reasons that are still unclear to scientists, South Central's beluga population has declined from 1,300 in 1980 to fewer than 375 in 2010.

Alaska Wildlife Conservation Center. Alaska Wildlife Conservation Center is a 144-acre drive-through wildlife center just before the Portage Glacier turnoff. Moose, bison, elk, caribou, Sitka black-tailed deer, musk ox, great horned owls, a brown bear, and a bald eagle, many of them orphaned in the wild, now live in the park. There are also snack and gift shops. ⊠ *Mi 79, Seward Hwy., Portage* ☎ *907/783–2025* ⊕ *www. alaskawildlife.org* ✍ *$12.50 adults, $9 children* ⊗ *Jan. and Feb., weekends only 10–5; Mar.–May 14, daily 10–6; May 15–Sept. 13, daily 8–8; Sept. 14–Dec., daily 10–5.*

Portage. Little remains of the community of Portage as a result of the 1964 earthquake. The ghost forest of dead spruce in the area was created when the land subsided by 6 to 10 feet after the quake and saltwater penetrated inland from Turnagain Arm, killing the trees. ⊕ *www. fs.usda.gov/r10.*

EN ROUTE

Indian Valley Meats. On your way to Portage, look for Indian Valley Meats. This is a popular place for Alaskans to have their game processed. There is a shop on the premises where workers sell smoked salmon and musk ox, reindeer, and buffalo sausage made on the premises. They'll also smoke, can, and package the fish you've caught and arrange for shipping. ⊠ *Huot Circle, 23 miles south of Anchorage on Seward Hwy. at Mile 104, Indian* ☎ *907/653–7511* ⊕ *www. indianvalleymeats.com.*

OUTDOOR ACTIVITIES AND GUIDED TOURS
COMBINATION TRIPS
NOVA. NOVA has been guiding residents and visitors since 1975. The company conducts river rafting, glacier hiking, fishing, and backcountry combo trips from its office in tiny Chickaloon between Palmer and Glennallen. ⊠ *Mile 76.2, Glenn Hwy., Chickaloon* ☎ *800/746–5753* ⊕ *www.novalaska.com.*

ROCK AND ICE CLIMBING
Alaska Rock Gym. For information about rock- and ice-climbing activities, check with the Alaska Rock Gym. It's got a great indoor gym, and staff can point you to where local climbers have set routes along the Seward Highway south of town that are close to Anchorage. ⊠ *4840 Fairbanks St., Anchorage* ☎ *907/562–7265* ⊕ *www.alaskarockgym.com.*

WHITTIER

60 miles southeast of Anchorage.

The entryway to Whittier is unlike any other: a 2½-mile drive atop railroad tracks through the Anton Anderson Memorial Tunnel, cut through the Chugach Mountain Range. Once on the other side of the tunnel, you enter the mysterious world of Whittier, the remnants of a military town developed in World War II. The only way to get to Whittier was by boat or train until the tunnel opened to traffic in 2000.

This quaint hamlet, nestled at the base of snow-covered peaks at the head of Passage Canal on the Kenai Peninsula, has an intriguing history. During World War II the U.S. Army constructed a port in Whittier and built the Hodge and Buckner buildings to house soldiers. These enormous monoliths are eerily reminiscent of Soviet-era communal apartment buildings. The Hodge Building (now called Begich Towers) houses almost all of Whittier's 180 year-round residents. The town averages 30 feet of snow in the winter, and in summer gets a considerable amount of rainfall. Whittier's draw is primarily fishing, but there are a number of activities to be had on Prince William Sound, including kayaking and glacier tours with some of the best glacier viewing in South Central Alaska.

Whittier is very small, and there is not much to look at in town, but the location is unbeatable. Surrounding peaks cradle alpine glaciers, and when the summer weather melts the huge winter snow load you can catch glimpses of the brilliant blue ice underneath. Sheer cliffs drop into Passage Canal and provide nesting places for flocks of black-legged kittiwakes, while sea otters and harbor seals cavort in the small-boat harbor and salmon return to spawn in nearby streams. A short boat ride out into the sound reveals tidewater glaciers, and an alert wildlife watcher can catch sight of mountain goats clinging to the mountainsides and black bears patrolling the beaches and hillsides in their constant search for food.

■TIP➜ Many companies' phones in Whittier are disconnected from October through April. If you can't get through to a number with prefix 472, check the company's website for an alternate number.

GETTING HERE AND AROUND

Unless you come in on a cruise ship, ferry, or other boat, your only way in and out of Whittier is through the tunnel. Its access, however, is limited by the railroad schedule, so it's not always possible to breeze in and out of town. ■TIP➜ For current tunnel information and schedules, check the tunnel's website. Tolls are $12 for passenger vehicles and $20 to $35 for RVs and trailers; waits of up to an hour are possible, and summer hours are from 6 am until 11 pm.

ESSENTIALS

Tunnel Information **Anton Anderson Memorial Tunnel** ⊕ *www.dot.state. ak.us/creg/whittiertunnel/index.shtml.*

OUTDOOR ACTIVITIES AND GUIDED TOURS
BOATING AND WILDLIFE VIEWING

26 Glacier Cruise. Phillips' Cruises & Tours has been running the 26 Glacier Cruise through Prince William Sound for many years. The high-speed catamaran covers 135 miles of territory in 4½ hours, leaving Whittier and visiting Port Wells, Barry Arm, and College and Harriman fjords. The boat is a very stable platform, and even visitors prone to seasickness can take this cruise with no ill effects. The heated cabin has large windows, upholstered booths, and wide aisles, and all seats are pre-reserved. There's a snack bar and a saloon on board, and wildlife encounters are commonplace. You can drive to Whittier and catch the boat at the dock, or you can arrange with the company to travel from Anchorage by rail or bus. The trip is $139 per person, plus tax, and includes a hot lunch of cod or chicken; tours are given May through September. ☎ 907/276–8023, 800/544–0529 ⊕ www.26glaciers.com.

Alaska Sea Kayakers. This outfitter supplies sea kayaks and gear for exploring Prince William Sound and also conducts guided day trips, multiday tours, instruction, and boat-assisted and boat live-aboard kayaking trips. The company practices a leave-no-trace camping ethos, and is very conscientious about avoiding bear problems. All guides are experienced Alaskan paddlers, and group sizes are kept small. Trips are May through mid-September. ☎ 907/472–2534, 877/472–2534 ⊕ www.alaskaseakayakers.com.

Lazy Otter Charters. The small fleet of boats at Lazy Otter Charters is available for private charter, sightseeing, and sea-kayak drop-offs. Groups of up to 22 people can join trips through Prince William Sound; you can also get transport to Cordova and Valdez. Customized sightseeing trips run from four or five hours to eight or nine hours. ☎ 800/587–6887 ⊕ www.lazyotter.com.

Major Marine Tours. Major Marine Tours runs a five-hour cruise from Whittier that visits two tidewater glaciers. The waters of Prince William Sound are well protected and relatively calm, making this a good option if you're inclined toward queasiness. Seabirds, waterfowl, and bald eagles are always present, and the chance to get close to the enormous walls of ice of the glaciers is not to be missed. A number of different cruises are available and range from $70 to $150 per person, and runs from mid-May to mid-September. For an additional $19 (+ tax) every cruise features a freshly prepared all-you-can-eat salmon and prime rib meal and reserved table seating for every guest inside the heated cabin. ☎ 907/274–7300, 800/764–7300 ⊕ www.majormarine.com.

Prince William Sound Glacier Cruises. From Whittier, tours with Prince William Sound Glacier Cruises travel through the sheltered bays, fjords, and canals of Prince William Sound. You can view glaciers, seabirds, and wildlife such as seals, sea lions, sea otters, whales, bears, and mountain goats. The company can arrange transportation from Anchorage to Whittier by bus or rail, or you can drive to Whittier in your own vehicle. Prices vary according to length of trip and travel options; cruises take place mid-May through mid-September. ✉ Pier 1 ☎ 877/777–4054 ⊕ www.princewilliamsound.com.

Sound Eco Adventures. Retired marine biologist Gerry Sanger runs full-day photo tours limited to 3 people in his 30-foot boat with Sound Eco Adventures from March through October. ☎ 907/242-0637 ⊕ www.soundecoadventure.com.

WHERE TO EAT

$$ ✕ **China Sea.** This restaurant offers a great array of flavors. The menu is
CHINESE filled with the standard Chinese fare, but there are a significant number of fresh, local seafood dishes that make this place a stand-out choice.

Try the excellent grilled halibut (or, for non–fish lovers, the Mongolian beef). ⑤ *Average main: $15* ✉ *Harbor* ☎ *907/472–3663* ⊘ *Closed mid-Sept.–May.*

$ ✕ **Lazy Otter Café & Gifts.** Amid the summer shops and docks this little
AMERICAN café offers warm drinks, an array of soups, sandwiches, and fresh-baked pastries, along with an Alaskan favorite: soft-serve ice cream. The busy shop only offers a couple of indoor seats, but there's outdoor seating that overlooks the harbor and is pleasant on sunny days. ⑤ *Average main: $9* ✉ *Lot 2, Whittier Harbor* ☎ *907/472–6887.*

$ ✕ **Varly's Ice Cream & Pizza.** Even though ice cream hardly seems like the
PIZZA thing you'd seek when in Alaska, hot days (and even not-so-hot days) beg for Varly's. If the weather's cold and rainy, pizza is the alternative fare. If you're not sure which way to lean, we wouldn't blame you if you opted for a little of each. The owners (of Varly's Swiftwater Seafood Café fame) take great pride in what they do, and it shows: the delicious pizza is homemade and something to write home about. It might sound frightening, but trust us when we say the Kraut—a pizza topped with sauerkraut and pepperoni (no kidding!)—is the best. ⑤ *Average main: $9* ✉ *Lot 1A Triangle Lease Area* ☎ *907/472–2547.*

$$ ✕ **Varly's Swiftwater Seafood Café.** This is a great place to get the feel of
AMERICAN Whittier. Place your order at the window and then grab a seat at the counter and wait for your food. There's outdoor seating that overlooks the small-boat harbor. Menu items include homemade chowders, hand-battered seafood, peel-and-eat shrimp, burgers, and chicken. A smoked prime rib dinner is served on Friday and Saturday nights. ⑤ *Average main: $20* ✉ *Harbor Loop* ☎ *907/472–2550* ⊘ *Closed mid-Sept.–May.*

WHERE TO STAY
For expanded hotel reviews, visit Fodors.com.

$$$ 🏨 **Inn at Whittier.** This first-class luxury hotel sits right on the water over-
HOTEL looking the harbor. **Pros:** every room has a great view. **Cons:** no kitchen
Fodor's Choice amenities. **TripAdvisor:** "old world style in dramatic setting," "really
★ good food," "helpful staff and stunning views." ⑤ *Rooms from: $175* ✉ *5a Harbor Rd.* ☎ *907/472–3200* ⊕ *www.innatwhittier.com* ⤴ *24 rooms* ❌ *Breakfast.*

$$ 🏨 **June's Whittier Condo Suites.** June's rents out 10 condominiums in
HOTEL the Begich Towers building, half with bay views, half with mountain views. **Pros:** private condos in Penthouse area of Begich Towers; lovely view. **Cons:** old building is a little rough outside. **TripAdvisor:** "very memorable," "great hospitality," "million dollar view." ⑤ *Rooms from: $155* ✉ *Begich Towers, Kenai St.* ☎ *888/472–6001* ⊕ *www. whittiersuitesonline.com* ⤴ *10 rooms* ❌ *Breakfast.*

VALDEZ

6 hrs northeast of Whittier by water, 304 miles east of Anchorage.

Valdez (pronounced val-*deez*) is the largest of the Prince William Sound communities. This year-round ice-free port was the entry point for people and goods going to the Interior during the gold rush. Today that flow has been reversed, as Valdez Harbor is the southern terminus of the Trans-Alaska Pipeline, which carries crude oil from Prudhoe Bay and surrounding oil fields nearly 800 miles to the north. This region, with its dependence on commercial fishing, is still feeling the aftereffects of the massive oil spill in 1989. Much of Valdez looks modern, because the business area was relocated and rebuilt after its destruction by the 1964 Good Friday earthquake. Even though the town is younger than the rest of developed Alaska, it's acquiring a lived-in look.

Many Alaskan communities have summer fishing derbies, but Valdez may hold the record for the number of such contests, stretching from late May into September for halibut and various runs of salmon. If you go fishing, by all means enter the appropriate derby. Every summer the newspapers run sob stories about tourists who landed possible prizewinners but couldn't share in the glory (or sizable cash rewards) because they hadn't forked over the five bucks to officially enter the contest. The **Valdez Silver Salmon Derby** is held the entire month of August. Fishing charters abound in this area of Prince William Sound, and for good reason: these fertile waters provide some of the best saltwater sportfishing in all of Alaska.

GETTING HERE AND AROUND

Valdez is road-accessible, and the 304-mile drive from Anchorage is stunning if a bit long to do in one day. The Richardson Highway portion of the drive takes you through Thompson Pass, high alpine country with 360-degree views. As you approach the town, the road descends into a steep canyon with rushing waterfalls—a popular ice-climbing destination in winter. Valdez's port is a stop on the Alaska Marine Highway, from which you can also sail to Cordova and Whittier. There's also a commercial airport.

The downtown is above the harbor, and two main avenues—Hazelet and Meals—run north–south with smaller streets branching off.

ESSENTIALS

Medical Assistance **Providence Valdez Community Hospital** ⊠ *911 Meals Ave.* ☎ *907/835–2249.*

Visitor and Tour Information **Valdez Convention and Visitors Bureau** ⊠ *200 Chenega St.* ☎ *907/835-4636* ⊕ *www.valdezalaska.org.*

EXPLORING

Valdez Museum. Stop by the Valdez Museum to learn about the lives, livelihoods, and events significant to Valdez and surrounding regions. Exhibits include a restored 1880s Gleason & Baily hand-pump fire engine, a 1907 Ahrens steam fire engine, a 19th-century saloon, information on the local native peoples, and a recently-updated exhibit on the 1989 oil spill. Every summer the museum hosts an exhibit of quilts and fiber arts made by local and regional artisans. ⊠ *217 Egan Dr.* ☎ *907/835-2764* ⊕ *www.valdezmuseum.org* ☒ *$5* ⊙ *mid-May–mid-Sept., daily 9–5.*

Historical Old Town Valdez. At a separate site, a 35- by 40-foot model of Historical Old Town Valdez depicts the original town, which was devastated by the 1964 earthquake. There's also an operating seismograph and an exhibit on local seismic activity. A Valdez History Exhibits

Pass includes admission to both the museum and the annex. ✉ *436 S. Hazlet Ave.* ⊕ *www.valdezmuseum.org.*

OFF THE BEATEN PATH

Columbia Glacier. A visit to Columbia Glacier, which flows from the surrounding Chugach Mountains, should certainly be on your Valdez agenda. Its deep aquamarine face is 5 miles across, and it calves icebergs with resounding cannonades. This glacier is one of the largest and most readily accessible of Alaska's coastal glaciers. The state ferry travels past the face of the glacier, and scheduled tours of the glaciers and the rest of the sound are available by boat and aircraft from Valdez, Cordova, and Whittier. ⊕ *www.dot.state.ak.us/amhs.*

OUTDOOR ACTIVITIES AND GUIDED TOURS

ADVENTURE

Alaska Snow Safaris. If you want a taste of backcountry snowmachining action (what snowmobiling is called in Alaska), Alaska Snow Safaris has an enormous winter playground near Valdez. From November to the end of April they'll take you into the wilderness on your machine or theirs to explore mile after mile of untouched, ungroomed snow. The trips are tailored to all levels of experience. ✉ *17435 Marcus Baker Dr., Palmer* ☎ *888/414–7669* ⊕ *www.snowmobile-alaska.com.*

Anadyr Adventures. Anadyr Adventures has 20 years' experience leading sea-kayak trips into Alaska's most spectacular wilderness, Prince William Sound. Guides will escort you on day trips, multiday camping trips, "mother ship" adventures based in a remote anchorage, or lodge-based trips for the ultimate combination of adventure by day and comfort by night. If you're already an experienced kayaker, it'll outfit you and you can travel on your own. Also available are guided hiking and glacier trips, ice caving at Valdez Glacier, soft-adventure charter-boat trips in the sound, and water-taxi service to or from anywhere on the eastern side of the sound. ☎ *907/835–2814, 800/865–2925* ⊕ *www. anadyradventures.com.*

H2O Guides. Whether you're looking for a full-on winter backcountry heli-ski excursion (in winter) or a half-day walk on a glacier, H2O Guides can hook you up. For most visitors, the day trips to Worthington Glacier State Park will suffice. It can set up any level of icy adventure you desire, from a half-day walk on the glacier to a multiday ice-climbing trip. The company is in the Mountain Sky hotel, and can arrange fishing, flightseeing, multiday, multisport, and otherwise-customized trips as well. ☎ *907/835–8418* ⊕ *www.alaskahelicopterskiing.com.*

BOATING AND WILDLIFE VIEWING

Lu-Lu Belle. Valdez-based Lu-Lu Belle leads small-group whale-watching and wildlife-viewing cruises, and sailings past the Columbia Glacier, the largest glacier in Prince William Sound. The 1 pm departure boards promptly at 12:45. ☎ *800/411–0090* ⊕ *www.lulubelletours.com.*

Stan Stephens Glacier & Wildlife Cruises. Stan Stephens Glacier & Wildlife Cruises leads Prince William Sound glacier and wildlife-viewing cruises to Columbia and Meares glaciers from mid-May through mid-September. Trips include narration on local commercial-fishing operations, as well as commentary on the Alyeska Pipeline terminal and history of defunct gold mines. ☎ *866/867–1297* ⊕ *www.stanstephenscruises.com.*

6

Anadyr Adventures. Anadyr Adventures, in business since 1989, offers an array of kayaking and glacier adventures in Prince William Sound. ☎ *907/835–2814, 800/865–2925* ⊕ *www.anadyradventures.com.*

WHERE TO EAT

$$
SEAFOOD
✗ **MacMurray's Alaska Halibut House.** At this very casual family-owned establishment you order at the counter, sit at the Formica-covered tables, and check out the photos of local fishing boats. The battered halibut is excellent—light and not greasy. Other menu items include homemade clam chowder, but if you're eating at the Halibut House, why try anything else? ⑤ *Average main: $15* ⊠ *208 Meals Ave.* ☎ *907/835–2788.*

$$
MEXICAN
✗ **Mike's Palace Ristorante.** Across from the scenic boat harbor, Mike's is a local favorite. The menu offers the world: from the standard America hamburger and Greek gyros to Mexican dishes and Italian pastas, there's a little bit of everything for every type of palate. There is an excellent selection of salads (a rarity throughout Alaska), steaks, and seafood. ⑤ *Average main: $20* ⊠ *201 N. Harbor Dr.* ☎ *907/835–2365.*

WHERE TO STAY

If you roll into town without reservations, especially if it's after hours, stop at the Valdez Convention and Visitor's Bureau on the corner of Fairbanks. It posts vacancies in bed-and-breakfasts on the window when it closes for the day.

For expanded hotel reviews, visit Fodors.com.

$$
HOTEL
🛏 **Best Western Valdez Harbor Inn.** Near the harbor, this hotel has an inlet from the sound, complete with sea otters, seals, and waterfowl right outside the lobby windows and visible from some of the rooms. **Pros:** on an inlet; very clean. **Cons:** just like any Best Western elsewhere. **TripAdvisor:** "convenient," "beautiful little town," "the place to stay." ⑤ *Rooms from: $170* ⊠ *100 Harbor Dr., Box 468* ☎ *907/835–3434, 888/222–3440* ⊕ *www.bestwesternalaska.com* ⤸ *88 rooms* ⧖ *Breakfast.*

$$$
HOTEL
🛏 **Mountain Sky Hotel and Suites.** The hotel is within easy walking distance of shops, restaurants, and the small-boat harbor—the center of summertime activity. **Pros:** has all amenities; very clean. **Cons:** not much personality. **TripAdvisor:** "amazing place," "home away from home," "great location." ⑤ *Rooms from: $180* ⊠ *100 Meals Ave.* ☎ *907/835–4445* ⊕ *www.mountainskyhotel.com* ⤸ *101 rooms* ⧖ *Breakfast.*

$$$$
RESORT
🛏 **Prince William Sound Lodge.** This fly-in lodge on a remote shore of northeastern Prince William Sound offers a wide range of vacation activities, including hiking, bird-watching, wildlife viewing, exploring nearby Alaska native villages, and the chance for some of the best silver salmon fishing in the state. **Pros:** delicious meals; incredible location. **Cons:** remote, fly-in location. **TripAdvisor:** "pristine vistas," "beautiful scenery," "all about the wildlife." ⑤ *Rooms from: $325* ⊠ *Ellamar* ☎ *907/248–0909, 907/440–0909* ⊕ *www.princewilliamsound.us* ⤸ *5 rooms* ▭ *No credit cards* ⊘ *Closed late Sept.–Apr.* ⧖ *All meals.*

CORDOVA

*6 hrs southeast of Valdez by water,
150 miles east of Anchorage by air.*

TIP

A small town with the spectacular backdrop of snowy Mt. Eccles, Cordova is the gateway to the Copper River delta—one of the great birding areas of North America. Perched on Orca Inlet in eastern Prince William Sound, Cordova began life early in the 20th century

■TIP→ Some of the more popular lodges need to be booked at least a year in advance. However, last-minute cancellations can create openings even late in the season.

as the port city for the Copper River and Northwestern Railway, which was built to serve the Kennicott Copper mines 191 miles away in the Wrangell Mountains. Since the mines and the railroad shut down in 1938, Cordova's economy has depended heavily on fishing. Attempts to develop a road along the abandoned railroad line connecting to the state highway system were dashed by the 1964 earthquake, so Cordova remains isolated. Access is limited to airplane or ferry.

GETTING HERE AND AROUND

Take the scenic ferry from either Whittier or Valdez along the **Alaska Marine Highway,** or catch a commercial flight from Anchorage. Once in town, the center is foot-friendly, but you'll want some wheels for heading down the Copper River Highway.

Though there isn't much in the way of paved road in Cordova, you can still drive the remnants of the scenic Copper River Highway, which takes you past Childs Glacier and the Million Dollar Bridge.

ESSENTIALS

Ferry Information **Alaska Marine Highway** ⊠ *6858 Glacier Hwy., Juneau* ☎ *800/642–0066* ⊕ *www.ferryalaska.com.*

Medical Assistance **Cordova Medical Center** ⊠ *602 Chase Ave.* ☎ *907/424–8000* ⊕ *www.cdvcmc.com.*

Rental Cars **Chinook Auto Rentals** ⊠ *Cordova Airport* ☎ *877/424–5279* ⊕ *www.chinookautorentals.com.*

Visitor Information **Cordova Chamber of Commerce** ⊠ *404 First St.* ☎ *907/424–7260* ⊕ *www.cordovachamber.com.*

EXPLORING

Copper River delta. Drive out of town along the Copper River Highway and visit the Copper River delta. This 700,000-acre wetland is one of North America's most spectacular vistas. The two-lane highway crosses marshes, forests, streams, lakes, and ponds that are home to countless shorebirds, waterfowl, and other bird species. Numerous terrestrial mammals including moose, wolves, lynx, mink, and beavers live here, too, and the Copper River salmon runs are world famous. When the red and king salmon hit the river in spring, there's a frantic rush to net the tasty fish and rush them off to waiting markets and restaurants all over the country.

6

The **Million Dollar Bridge**, at Mile 48, was a railroad project completed in 1910 for the Copper River and Northwestern Railway to carry copper ore to market from the mines at Kennicott. Soon after construction was completed, the nearby Childs and Miles glaciers threatened to overrun the railroad and bridge. Although the glaciers stopped short of the railroad, the copper market collapsed in 1938, making the route economically obsolete. The far span of the bridge was toppled by the Good Friday earthquake in 1964 and was not rebuilt until 2005.

From the end of the road you can view the **Childs Glacier.** Although there is no visitor center, there is a covered viewing area next to the bridge, where you can see the face of the glacier and wait for a huge chunk of ice to topple into the river. The waves produced by falling ice frequently wash migrating salmon onto the riverbank; the local brown bears have been known to patrol the river's edge looking for an easy meal, so keep your eyes peeled.

Cordova Museum. Exhibits at the Cordova Museum tell of early explorers to the area, Native culture, the Copper River and Northwestern Railway/Kennicott Mine era, and the growth of the commercial fishing industry. An informative brochure outlines a self-guided walking tour of the town's historic buildings. Evening programs and regional art exhibits such as "Fish Follies" and "Bird Flew" are sponsored by the historical society. The gift shop features a selection of local postcards, Cordova and Alaskan gifts, and local history books. ✉ *622 1st St.* ☎ *907/424–6665* ⊕ *www.cordovamuseum.org* 🗺 *$1 suggested donation* ☉ *Memorial Day–Labor Day, Mon.–Sat. 10–6; Labor Day–Memorial Day, Tues.–Fri. 10–5, Sat. 1–5.*

OUTDOOR ACTIVITIES AND GUIDED TOURS

Alaskan Wilderness Outfitting Co. Alaskan Wilderness Outfitting Co. operates an air-taxi service out of Cordova and arranges fresh- and saltwater fly-out fishing experiences, from drop-offs to guided tours with lodge accommodations. It also offers floating cabins in Prince William Sound and a full-service lodge for silver salmon on the Tsiu River. ☎ *907/424–5552* ⊕ *www.alaskawilderness.com.*

Copper River delta. Spring migration to the Copper River delta provides some of the finest avian spectacles in the world. Species include the western sandpiper, American dipper, orange-crowned warbler, and short-billed dowitcher. Trumpeter swans and dusky Canada geese can also be seen.

Copper River Delta Shorebird Festival. The Copper River Delta Shorebird Festival, held the first week of May, includes five days of workshops and guided field trips. As many as 5 million birds, mostly western sandpipers and dunlins, descend on the Copper River delta, feeding and resting on their long migration to their northern nesting grounds. This migration respite is critical for these birds, and the food they gather from the rich mudflats of the delta keeps them alive and healthy. ☎ *907/424–7260* ⊕ *www.cordovachamber.com.*

Cordova Air Service. Cordova Air Service leads aerial tours of Prince William Sound on planes with wheels or floats. ☎ *907/424–3289.*

**EN
ROUTE**

Alaganik Slough. At Mile 17 there's a turnoff to Alaganik Slough. This 5-mile road leads to a wheelchair-accessible boardwalk as well as covered viewing shelters, restrooms, and picnic areas. A dedicated bird-watcher can spend hours peering into the vegetation, seeking out interesting avian species.

WHERE TO EAT

$
AMERICAN

✕ **Ambrosia.** Pastas, hamburgers, and submarine sandwiches are served behind the storefront, but it's the hearty pizzas that have earned this place its reputation among locals. ⑤ *Average main: $15* ✉ *410 1st St.* ☎ *907/424–7175* ⊙ *Closed Nov.–Jan.*

$$$
AMERICAN

✕ **Powder House Bar & Restaurant.** On clear summer evenings you can relax on the deck overlooking Eyak Lake at this roadside bar and enjoy whatever the cook's in the mood to fix: homemade soups, sandwiches, sushi, and seasonal seafood are all possibilities. If you're lucky or skillful in your fishing endeavors, the kitchen staff will cook your catch. Steak and seasonal seafood, including shrimp, scallops, razor clams, and whatever else is fresh, are available every night. ⑤ *Average main: $25* ✉ *Mile 2.1, Copper River Hwy.* ☎ *907/424–3529.*

WHERE TO STAY

For expanded hotel reviews, visit Fodors.com.

$$
B&B/INN

▭ **Cordova Lighthouse Inn.** Two of the rooms have mountain views, but if at all possible get one of the two with harbor views for the full Alaskan fishing-village ambience, or the new large suite with the fireplace. **Pros:** in-town location; remodeled in 2008; very nice rooms. **Cons:** must climb steep stairs to access the four rooms at the top. **TripAdvisor:** "good location," "clean place to stay," "comfortable." ⑤ *Rooms from: $145* ✉ *112 Nicholoff Way, Box 2206* ☎ *907/424–7080* ⊕ *www.cordovalighthouseinn.com* ⇥ *8 rooms.*

$$
B&B/INN

▭ **Cordova Rose Lodge.** This truly unique lodge sits on a barge on the Prince William Sound breakwater. **Pros:** delicious breakfast; waterfront location. **Cons:** short walk from town; some folks might want a vehicle. ⑤ *Rooms from: $145* ✉ *1315 Whitshed, Box 1494* ☎ *907/424–7673* ⊕ *www.cordovarose.com* ⇥ *11 rooms, 2 cabins* ⊙ *Closed Oct.–Apr., or until weather is good* ❄|*Breakfast.*

$
B&B/INN

▭ **Northern Nights Inn B&B.** Commanding a dramatic view of Orca Inlet just a couple of blocks from downtown Cordova, this turn-of-the-20th-century bed-and-breakfast has roomy suites furnished with antiques. **Pros:** big, bright rooms are a great value; some rooms have full kitchens. **Cons:** only one ground-floor room for those who have trouble with stairs. **TripAdvisor:** "comfortable setting," "great room," "unique." ⑤ *Rooms from: $100* ✉ *500 3rd St., Box 1564* ☎ *907/424–5356* ⊕ *www.northernnightsinn.com* ⇥ *1 room, 3 suites.*

$$
B&B/INN

▭ **Orca Adventure Lodge.** The list of activities at the lodge goes on and on: fishing, kayaking, river rafting, hiking, bear-viewing, and flightseeing. **Pros:** spectacular views with sea otters congregating outside. **Cons:** about 2 miles from town, so some folks might want a vehicle. **TripAdvisor:** "comfortable rooms," "fantastic staff and activities," "Alaskan charm." ⑤ *Rooms from: $165* ✉ *301 Orca Rd.* ☎ *907/424–7249,*

6

866/424–6722 ⊕ *www.orcaadventurelodge.com* ↪ *23 rooms, 4 suites* ⊙ *Restaurant closed Oct.–May.*

$$ ⊡ **Reluctant Fisherman Inn.** At this waterfront hotel and restaurant you
HOTEL can watch the commercial-fishing fleet and other maritime traffic sail
by. **Pros:** perfect location in the heart of Cordova. **Cons:** Rooms can
be noisy with nightlife activity. **TripAdvisor:** "the nicest place in Cordova," "friendly," "world class food." ⑤ *Rooms from: $130* ✉ *407
Railroad Ave.* ☎ *907/424–3272* ⊕ *www.reluctantfisherman.com* ↪ *41
rooms* ⧉ *Breakfast.*

$ ⊡ **U.S. Forest Service Cabins.** The Cordova Ranger District of the
RENTAL Chugach National Forest maintains a series of 18 backcountry cabins
for rent. **Pros:** beautiful and remote. **Cons:** you must be self-sufficient
and comfortable in the wilderness. ⑤ *Rooms from: $25* ☎ *877/444–
6777* ⊕ *www.recreation.gov* ↪ *17 cabins.*

SHOPPING

Orca Book & Sound Co. Orca Book & Sound Co. is much more than a
bookstore. In addition to books, it sells music, art supplies, children's
toys, and locally produced art. The walls often double as a gallery for
local works or traveling exhibits, and the store specializes in old, rare,
out-of-print, and first-edition books, especially Alaskana. ■ **TIP➔** In the
back is an espresso-smoothie bar; the upstairs area has wireless Internet
access for a small fee. ✉ *507 1st St.* ☎ *907/424–5305* ⊙ *Closed Sun.*

KENAI PENINSULA

The Kenai Peninsula, thrusting into the Gulf of Alaska south of Anchorage, is South Central's playground, offering salmon and halibut fishing, spectacular scenery, and wildlife viewing. Commercial fishing is
important to the area's economy; five species of Pacific salmon run up
the aqua-color Kenai River every summer. Campgrounds and trailheads
for backwoods hiking are strung along the roads. Along the way you
can explore three major federal holdings on the peninsula—the western
end of the sprawling Chugach National Forest, Kenai National Wildlife
Refuge, and Kenai Fjords National Park.

HOPE

39 miles west of Portage, 87 miles south of Anchorage.

The little gold-mining community of Hope sits just across Turnagain
Arm from Anchorage. To visit, however, you must drive the 87 miles
all the way around the arm. Your reward is a quiet little community
that is accessible to but not overrun by tourists. Hope was founded by
miners in 1896, and the old log cabins and weathered frame buildings
in the town center are favorite photography subjects. You'll find lots
of gold-panning, fishing, and hiking opportunities, and the northern
trailhead for the 38-mile-long Resurrection Pass Trail is nearby. Contact
the U.S. Forest Service for information on campgrounds, cabin rentals,
and hikes in the area.

ALASKA RANGE

Eagle River

Chugach
State Park

Anchorage

Girdwood

Cook Inlet

Hope

Portage

Kenai National
Wildlife Refuge

Sterling

Seward Hwy.

Portage Glacier

Kenai

Soldotna

Clam Gulch

Lake Clark
National Park & Preserve

Cooper Landing

Sterling
Hwy.

9

Ninilchik

KENAI
PENINSULA

Seward

Nondalton

Anchor Point

Kenai Fjords
National Park

Newhalen

Iliamna
Lake

Homer

Kachemak Bay

Tutka
Bay

Halibut Cove

Seldovia

Kachemak Bay
State Park &
State Wilderness Park

Katmai
National
Park

SHUYAK IS.

Shuyak Island
State Park

AFOGNAK
ISLAND

Chugach
National
Forest

0   50miles

0   75 km

Shelikof Strait

Port Lions

Kodiak

KODIAK
ISLAND

Kodiak National
Wildlife Refuge

KEY

Ferry Lines

Kenai Peninsula
and Kodiak Island

MOUNTAIN BIKING THE KENAI PENINSULA

The Kenai Peninsula offers outstanding opportunities for mountain bikers seeking thigh-busting challenges amid extraordinary scenery. **Crescent Creek Trail** (at Mile 44.9 of Sterling Highway; drive 3 miles to the trailhead at end of gravel road); **Devil's Pass** (at Mile 39.5 of Seward Highway); **Johnson Pass** (at Miles 32.6 and 63.7 of Seward Highway); and the **Resurrection trail systems** offer miles of riding for a wide range of expertise. Cyclists here are subject to highly fickle mountain weather patterns. But remember that you're never really alone in wild Alaska: be sure to bring along bear spray and bug dope (repellent).

Department of Natural Resources. For maps and descriptions of trails, visit the state Department of Natural Resources website. ⊕ *www.dnr.state. ak.us/parks/aktrails/ats/ken-ats.htm.*

WHERE TO EAT

$$

AMERICAN

✕ **Tito's Discovery Cafe.** When the original Tito's restaurant burned down, uninsured, in 1999, the owner was faced with financial ruin. But this tiny community got together and put Tito back on his feet and rebuilt the restaurant. Tito has since passed on, but his diner still serves basic American roadhouse food, along with seafood pasta, the ubiquitous halibut, and fresh-baked pies. We highly recommend the reindeer sausage sub. ⑤ *Average main: $15* ⊠ *Mile 16.5, Hope Hwy.* ☎ *907/782–3274* ⊙ *Open May 2–Sept., Thurs.–Mon. 7–9; Tue. and Wed. 7–3.*

WHERE TO STAY

For expanded hotel reviews, visit Fodors.com.

$$$

B&B/INN

🖥 **Bowman's Bear Creek Lodge.** Of the five cabins, four are around a pond and one is down by the creek. **Pros:** great restaurant, dinners included in price; nightly campfire around the pond. **Cons:** shared bath. **TripAdvisor:** "incredible host," "charming real Alaska," "excellent restaurant." ⑤ *Rooms from: $180* ⊠ *Mile 15.9, Hope Hwy.* ☎ *907/782–3141* ⊕ *www.bowmansbearcreeklodge.com* ⊅ *5 cabins with shared bath* ⊙ *Dinner nightly 4–10.*

$

RENTAL

🖥 **Seaview Cafe & Bar.** True to its name, this rustic little establishment in the original Hope town site offers great views of the arm and the Chugach. **Pros:** charming historic location. **Cons:** cabins are rustic; food is bar food. ⑤ *Rooms from: $60* ⊠ *Main St., Box 110* ☎ *907/782–3300* ⊕ *www.seaviewcafealaska.com* ⊅ *50 tent sites, 16 RV sites with hookups ($18 with electric and $12 without), 2 cabins* ⊙ *Closed mid-Sept.–mid-May.*

SHOPPING

Sherritt Fine Art Gallery. Sherritt Fine Art Gallery This cozy gallery space exhibits Scott Sheritt's Alaska-influenced paintings, as well as those of other artists. ⊠ *2nd St.* ☎ *907/782-3436* ⊕ *www.scottsherritt.com.*

SEWARD

74 miles south of Hope, 127 miles south of Anchorage.

Fodor's Choice
★

It seems hard to believe that such beauty exists as in Seward. Surrounded on all sides by Kenai Fjords National Park, Chugach National Forest, and Resurrection Bay, Seward offers all the quaint realities of a small railroad town with the bonus of jaw-dropping scenery. This little town of fewer than 3,000 citizens was founded in 1903, when survey crews arrived at the ice-free port and began planning a railroad to the Interior. Since its inception, Seward has relied heavily on tourism and commercial fishing. It is also the launching point for excursions into Kenai Fjords National Park, where it is quite common to see marine life and calving glaciers.

GETTING HERE AND AROUND

As a cruise-ship port, Seward has several routes in and out. Arrive by boat via the Alaska Marine Highway or, from Anchorage, take a luxury Ultradome railcar, or drive the 127 miles from Anchorage. Although there's a small airport, only private planes use it. It's possible to walk around town or from the harbor to downtown, but there's also trolley service in summer.

ESSENTIALS

Medical Assistance **Providence Seward Medical Center** ⊠ *417 1st Ave.* ⊕ *907/224–5205.*

Visitor and Tour Information **Seward Visitors Bureau** ⊠ *Mile 2, Seward Hwy.* ☏ *907/224–8051* ⊕ *www.sewardak.org.*

EXPLORING

Fodor's Choice
★
☺

Alaska SeaLife Center. Spend an afternoon at the Alaska SeaLife Center, with massive cold-water tanks and outdoor viewing decks as well as interactive displays of cold-water fish, seabirds, and marine mammals, including harbor seals and a 2,000-pound sea lion. A research center as well as visitor center, it also rehabilitates injured marine wildlife and provides educational experiences for the general public. Appropriately, the center was partially funded with reparations money from the *Exxon Valdez* oil spill. Films, hands-on activities, a gift shop, and behind-the-scenes tours ($12 and up) complete the offerings. ⊠ *301 Railway Ave.* ☏ *907/224–6300, 888/378–2525* ⊕ *www.alaskasealife.org* ⊒ *$20* ☉ *Mid-May–mid-Sept., Mon.–Thurs. 9–6:30, Fri.–Sun. 8–6:30; mid-Sept.–mid-May, daily 10–5.*

★

Exit Glacier. A short walk from the parking lot along a paved path will bring you face to face with Exit Glacier *(⇨ see Kenai Fjords National Park)*, just outside Seward. Look for the marked turnoff at Mile 3.7 as you enter town or ask locals for directions. There's a small walk-in campground here, a ranger station, and access to the glacier. Exit Glacier is the most accessible part of the **Harding Icefield.** This mass of ice caps the Kenai Mountains, covering more than 1,100 square miles, and it oozes more than 40 glaciers from its edges and down the mountainsides. Reach it from Mile 3.7. The hike to the ice field from the parking lot is a 9-mile round-trip that gains 3,000 feet in elevation, so it's not for the timid or out of shape. But if you're feeling up to the task, the hike

Fishing is an important industry and popular recreational activity in Seward.

and views are breathtaking. Local wildlife includes mountain goats and bears both black and brown, so keep a sharp eye out for them. Once you reach the ice, don't travel across it unless you have the gear and experience with glacier travel. Glacier ice is notoriously deceptive—the surface can look solid and unbroken, while underneath a thin crust of snow crevasses lie in wait for the unwary. .

Seward Community Library. Seward, like Valdez, was badly damaged by the 1964 earthquake. A movie illustrating the upheaval is shown from Memorial Day until Labor Day, daily at 2 pm in the Seward Community Library. Russian icons and paintings by prominent Alaskan artists are on exhibit. ⊠ *238 5th Ave.* ☎ *907/224–4082* ⊕ *www.cityofseward.net/ library* 🎞 *Movie $3* ☉ *Mon.–Thurs. 10–8, Fri. and Sat. 10–6, Sun. 1–6.*

Seward Museum. The Seward Museum displays photographs of the quake's damage, model rooms and artifacts from the early pioneers, and historical and current information on the Seward area. ⊠ *336 3rd Ave., at Jefferson St.* ☎ *907/224–3902* 🎞 *Free, donation suggested* ☉ *Mid-May–Labor Day, Wed.–Sun., 1–5pm.*

Iditarod Trail. The first mile of the historic original Iditarod Trail runs along the beach and makes for a nice, easy stroll. There is also a great walking tour designed by the city—maps are available at the visitor bureau, the converted railcar at the corner of 3rd Avenue and Jefferson Street, or the Seward Chamber of Commerce Visitor Center at Mile 2 on the Seward Highway.

Nash Road. For a different view of the town, drive out Nash Road, around Resurrection Bay, and look down at Seward, nestled at the base of the surrounding mountains like a young bird in its nest.

Lowell Point. If you drive south from the SeaLife Center for about 10 minutes, you'll reach Lowell Point, a wooded stretch of land along the bay with great access to camping, beach walking, hiking, and kayaking; the spot is great for a day trip.

OUTDOOR ACTIVITIES AND GUIDED TOURS
For more details on Kenai Fjords, flip to the next section.

ADVENTURE AND WILDLIFE VIEWING
Exit Glacier Guides. Exit Glacier Guides offers guided tours to Exit Glacier—and not just to the moraine, where most tourists stop. The experienced guides lead travelers onto the glacier. It also offers guided hikes to viewpoints and the Harding Icefield. For those wanting to visit the glacier independently, Exit Glacier Guides runs an hourly shuttle from downtown to the glacier for $10 round-trip. ⊠ *Small-boat harbor* ☎ *907/224–5569, 907/491–0552 [Sept.–May]* ⊕ *www. exitglacierguides.com.*

BOATING
The Fish House. Operating out of Seward since 1974, this booking agency represents dozens of Resurrection Bay and Kenai Peninsula fishing charters, specializing in silver salmon and halibut, and can hook you up for half-day or full-day charters (full-day only for halibut fishing). ⊠ *Small-boat harbor* ☎ *907/224–3674, 800/257–7760* ⊕ *www.thefishhouse.net.*

Kenai Fjords Tours. Kenai Fjords Tours, part of the Native-owned Alaska Heritage Tours, is the oldest and largest company running tours through the park. From March through mid-September it leads 3.5- to 9-hour cruises, priced from $65 (Dinner Cruise) to $214 (Captain's Choice), which includes lunch. In 2007 and 2008 it added catamarans to its fleet, which are less susceptible to the rolling motion that can cause seasickness. Cruise options include exclusive visits to Fox Island, interpretive programs by National Park Service rangers, cruise and kayak combinations, glacier viewing, and opportunities to see whales, puffins, otters, and Steller sea lions. Transportation and overnight options are also available. ☎ *907/276–6249, 877/777–4051* ⊕ *www.kenaifjords.com.*

Captain's Choice Tour. Captain's Choice Tour, a part of Kenai Fjords Tours, operates smaller boats (with a maximum of 22 passengers per boat) through Kenai Fjords mid-May–August. The tour specializes in birding and photography. Breakfast and lunch are provided. ☎ *877/777–4051* ⊕ *www.kenaifjords.com.*

Major Marine Tours. Major Marine Tours conducts half-day and full-day cruises of Resurrection Bay and Kenai Fjords National Park. Park cruises are narrated by a National Park Service ranger, and meals of salmon and prime rib are an option. A custom-built catamaran runs daily from March through September. Summer cruises include a three-hour whale-watching tour and a six-hour Kenai Fjords trip, featuring narration by a national park ranger. Major Marine Tours can arrange transportation between Anchorage and Seward. ☎ *907/274–7300, 800/764–7300* ⊕ *www.majormarine.com.*

DEEP-SEA FISHING

Crackerjack Sportfishing. Crackerjack Sportfishing offers full- and half-day fishing charters as well as two- to five-day fishing expeditions in the Kenai Fjords National Park and beyond. The local captains have been guiding in Seward for more than 15 years, and offer trips year-round. ☏ *907/224–2606, 800/566–3912* ⊕ *www.crackerjackcharters.com.*

HIKING

Caines Head Trail. The Caines Head Trail allows easy, flat hiking along the coast, but a large portion of the hike is over tidal mudflats, so care must be taken to time the hike correctly—with tides here running in the 10- to 20-foot range, bad planning isn't just a case of getting your feet wet. It's officially advised that the trail be hiked only when there's a "plus 4-foot tide or greater" in summer. The trail is 4.5 miles, starting from Lowell Point, and two cabins can be rented at Derby Cove and Callisto Canyon.

Lost Lake/Primrose Trail. The Lost Lake/Primrose Trail is a 16-mile end-to-end loop through spruce forests and up into the high alpine area. The Lost Lake trailhead is near Mile 5 of the Seward Highway, and the other end is at the Primrose campground at Mile 17. The trails are steep and usually snow-covered through late June, but the views along the Lost Lake valley are worth the climb. Above the tree line you're in mountain-goat country—look for white, blocky figures perched on the precarious cliffs. The lake is a prime spot for rainbow trout fishing. As usual, be bear aware. The Dale Clemens cabin, at Mile 4.5 from the Lost Lake trailhead, has propane heat and a stunning view of Resurrection Bay. ⊕ *www.fs.usda.gov/detail/chugach.*

For a comprehensive listing of all the trails, cabins, and campgrounds in the Seward Ranger District of Chugach National Forest, check the website of the U.S. Forest Service.

Mt. Marathon Race. One of the biggest events of the year in Seward is the Mt. Marathon Race, run on July 4 since 1915. Folks come from near and far to run, and the entire town comes out to celebrate. It doesn't take the winners very long—44 minutes or so—but the route is straight up the mountain (3,022 feet) and back down to the center of town. Ambitious hikers can hit the Runner's Trail behind Providence Medical Center on Jefferson, while those who prefer a more leisurely (though still steep) climb can take the Hiker's Trail from 1st Avenue.

Seward Chamber of Commerce. For more information, contact the Seward Chamber of Commerce. ☏ *907/224–8051* ⊕ *www.sewardak.org.*

WHERE TO EAT

$$$ ╳ **Chinooks Waterfront Restaurant.** On the waterfront in the small-boat
SEAFOOD harbor, Chinooks has a dazzling selection of fresh seafood dishes, beers on tap, a great wine selection, and a stunning view from the upstairs window seats. Pasta dishes and a few beef specialties round out the menu. We recommend the seafood sauté. $ *Average main: $25* ✉ *1404 4th Ave.* ☏ *907/224–2207* ⊕ *www.chinookswaterfront.com* ☺ *Closed mid-Oct.–May.*

$$ ╳ **Christo's Palace.** Serving Greek, Italian, Mexican, and seafood meals,
ECLECTIC this ornately furnished downtown restaurant is a surprisingly elegant

hidden treasure. The nondescript facade belies the high-beamed ceilings, dark-wood accents, ornate chandeliers, and a large, gorgeous mahogany bar reputedly built in the mid-1800s and imported from San Francisco. Portions are generous, desserts are tempting, and there is a small selection of after-dinner cognacs. The baked halibut portobello is particularly good. $ *Average main: $20* ⊠ *133 4th Ave.* ☎ *907/224–5255* ⊕ *www.christospalace.com.*

$$ ✕**Le Barn Appétit.** Don't let the name fool you. This little restaurant and
FRENCH   inn are in fact in an old barn, but this is no run-of-the-mill grub. You'll find some of the finest French cuisine in Alaska. The quiche Lorraine and the crepes are worth writing home about. For dinner, the chicken cordon bleu and the stuffed pork tenderloin are perfect examples of the excellent cuisine to be found here, but you must make a reservation for dinner the day before; there's no chance of getting seated otherwise. $ *Average main: $15* ⊠ *11786 Old Exit Glacier Rd.* ☎ *907/224–8706* ⊕ *www.lebarnappetit.com* ☾ *7–4; dinner only by special reservations.*

$ ✕**Railway Cantina.** This little hole-in-the-wall in the harbor area is
MEXICAN   a local favorite. A wide selection of burritos, quesadillas, and great halibut and rockfish tacos incorporates local seafood and is supplemented by an array of hot sauces, many contributed by customers who brought them from their travels. $ *Average main: $10* ⊠ *1401 4th Ave.* ☎ *907/224–8226.*

$$ ✕**Resurrection Roadhouse.** On a sunny summer evening you'll have to
AMERICAN   fight locals for seats on the Roadhouse's deck, which overlooks the Resurrection River and the mountains surrounding it. Set off Exit Glacier/Herman Leirer Road, and part of the Seward Windsong Lodge, the Roadhouse gets warm afternoon light that goes well with multiple types of beers on tap and excellent pizzas and sweet-potato fries. ■TIP➔ The bar and restaurant have different menus—ask to see both, and then decide where to sit. $ *Average main: $15* ⊠ *Mile 0.5, Exit Glacier Rd.; 31772 Herman Leirer Rd.* ☎ *907/224–7116, 877/777–4079* ⊕ *www.sewardwindsong.com.*

WHERE TO STAY

For expanded hotel reviews, visit Fodors.com.

$$ ⬚**Alaska Paddle Inn.** A new building offers beachfront panoramic views
B&B/INN   out at Lowell Point and access to its own private beach. **Pros:** unobstructed views of Resurrection Bay; waffle irons and mix in rooms. **Cons:** 20 steps up to the High Tide room. **TripAdvisor:** "a room built around a view," "rejuvenating," "superb hospitality." $ *Rooms from: $129* ⊠ *13745 Beach Dr.* ☎ *907/362–2628* ⊕ *www.alaskapaddleinn.com* ⟿ *2 rooms* �“❘ *Breakfast.*

$$ ⬚**Breeze Inn.** Across the street from the small-boat harbor, this mod-
HOTEL   ern hotel is very convenient if you're planning an early-morning fishing trip. **Pros:** directly across from the harbor; walking distance to downtown. **Cons:** rooms are bland and chain motel–like. **TripAdvisor:** "comfortable," "very convenient," "basic and clean." $ *Rooms from: $160* ⊠ *1306 Seward Hwy.* ☎ *907/224–5237, 888/224–5237* ⊕ *www.breezeinn.com* ⟿ *100 rooms.*

$$$ ⬚**Hotel Edgewater.** The rooms at Seward's newest and snazziest
HOTEL   hotel overlook Resurrection Bay, and on clear days the panorama of

mountains, glaciers, and the bay is breathtaking. **Pros:** downtown location is convenient to the SeaLife Center, restaurants, and shops. **Cons:** it's not the cheapest waterfront lodging in town. **TripAdvisor:** "beautiful," "super helpful staff," "nice location." $ *Rooms from: $200* ⊠ *202 5th Ave.* ☎ *907/224–2700, 888/793–6800* ⊕ *www.hoteledgewater.com* ⤶ *76 rooms* ⊘ *Closed Oct.–Apr.* ᴵᴼᴵ *Breakfast.*

$$$
HOTEL
Fodor's Choice
★

☲ **Hotel Seward.** This historic downtown hotel is convenient to restaurants, shopping, and the Alaska SeaLife Center. **Pros:** cool historic building; excellent downtown location. **Cons:** no elevator in one wing. **TripAdvisor:** "very nice," "central and friendly," "pleasant hotel with local character." $ *Rooms from: $200* ⊠ *221 5th Ave.* ☎ *907/224–2378, 800/655–8785* ⊕ *www.hotelsewardalaska.com* ⤶ *62 rooms.*

$$$$
RENTAL

☲ **Kenai Fjords Wilderness Lodge.** An hour's boat ride from Seward, this wilderness lodge sits within a quiet, forest-lined cove on Fox Island in Resurrection Bay. **Pros:** solitude; great views; everything's included. **Cons:** its location makes it pricey. **TripAdvisor:** "beautiful remote island location," "fantastic experience," "awesome beachfront cabins." $ *Rooms from: $320* ⊠ *Fox Island* ☎ *907/224–8068, 877/777–4053* ⊕ *www.kenaifjordslodge.com* ⤶ *8 cabins* ⊘ *Closed Sept.–May* ᴵᴼᴵ *All meals.*

$$
RENTAL

☲ **Miller's Landing.** This sprawling waterfront complex offers cabins, campsites for tents ($26) and RVs ($36), water-taxi service to remote sites, sea-kayak and boat and motor rentals, and a booking service for area B&Bs, fishing trips, dogsled rides, hiking expeditions, sailing tours, and wildlife cruises. **Pros:** one-stop shopping for all your travel needs; a great location. **Cons:** some cabins are very, very basic; the campground can be overcrowded. **TripAdvisor:** "beautiful location," "great people," "nice cabins." $ *Rooms from: $50* ⊠ *Lowell Point Rd., Box 81* ☎ *907/224–5739, 866/541–5739* ⊕ *www.millerslandingak.com* ⤶ *13 cabins, 3 rooms, 29 tent sites, 31 RV sites with hookups.*

$$$$
HOTEL

☲ **Seward Windsong Lodge.** In a forested setting near the bank of the Resurrection River, the Seward Windsong has rooms and deluxe balcony suites decorated in warm plaids, pine furniture, and Alaskan prints. **Pros:** incredible views of the river valley; Resurrection Roadhouse is right next door. **Cons:** outside of town, so you'll want a car, though a complimentary shuttle service is offered. $ *Rooms from: $255* ⊠ *Mile 0.5, Exit Glacier Rd., about 2 miles north of Seward* ☎ *907/265–4501, 888/959–9590* ⊕ *www.sewardwindsong.com* ⤶ *180 rooms, 16 suites.*

$$
B&B/INN

☲ **Stoney Creek Inn.** Sandwiched between two streams—one glacial, the other salmon-spawning—this B&B about 6 miles out of Seward offers a quiet respite from the summer buzz. **Pros:** quiet location a perfect distance from town. **Cons:** far enough from town that you'll want a car. **TripAdvisor:** "charming," "comfortable," "fabulous spa." $ *Rooms from: $145* ⊠ *33422 Stoney Creek Ave.* ☎ *907/224–3940* ⊕ *www. stoneycreekinn.net* ⤶ *5 rooms* ᴵᴼᴵ *Breakfast.*

$$
B&B/INN
Fodor's Choice
★

☲ **Teddy's Inn the Woods Bed & Breakfast.** This lovely bed-and-breakfast is nestled in the woods across from Kenai Lake, surrounded by mountains and hiking trails. **Pros:** The setting is superb; basketball courts on the property. **Cons:** You have to go up a flight of stairs. **TripAdvisor:** "absolutely wonderful," "missed this place seconds after I left," "a

6

Kenai jewel." ⑤ *Rooms from: $120* ✉ *29792 Seward Hwy(Mile 23)* ☎ *907/288–3126* ⊕ *www.seward.net/teddys/* ⤴ *1 cabin (3 twin beds, 1 queen)* ⊟ *No credit cards* ⑩ *Breakfast.*

$$ ⌂ **Van Gilder Hotel.** Built in 1916 and listed on the National Register of
HOTEL   Historic Places, the Van Gilder is an elegant building steeped in local history. **Pros:** oldest hotel in Seward; decor is entertaining. **Cons:** shared kitchen; a little on the rustic side. **TripAdvisor:** "great choice," "old time feel," "excellent location." ⑤ *Rooms from: $149* ✉ *308 Adams St.* ☎ *800/478-0400* ⊕ *www.vangilderhotel.com* ⤴ *20 rooms, 4 suites* ⑩ *Breakfast.*

SHOPPING

☾   **Ranting Raven.** The Ranting Raven is a combination gift shop, bakery, and lunch spot, adorned with raven murals on the side of the building. You can indulge in fresh-baked goods, espresso drinks, and daily lunch specials such as quiche, focaccia, and homemade soups while perusing the packed shelves of local artwork, native crafts, and jewelry. ✉ *238 4th Ave.* ☎ *907/224–2228.*

Resurrect Art Coffeehouse. Resurrect Art Coffeehouse is a darling coffeehouse and gallery-gift shop. It is housed in a 1932 church, and the ambience and views from the old choir loft are reason enough to stop by. Local art is showcased, and it's a good place to find Alaskan gifts that aren't mass-produced. ✉ *320 3rd Ave.* ☎ *907/224–7161* ⊕ *www.resurrectart.com.*

KENAI FJORDS NATIONAL PARK

125 miles south of Anchorage.

GETTING HERE AND AROUND

The only land route to the park is via Herman Leirer (Exit Glacier) Road, which ends at Exit Glacier. Boats leaving Seward for half-day tours and beyond are ample. Beyond that, access is limited, unless you charter a boat or airplane, or arrange for a tour with one of the local companies. If you take a day trip on a tour boat out of Seward, it's highly likely you'll see frolicking sea otters, crowds of Steller sea lions lazing on the rocky shelves along the shore, a porpoise or two, bald eagles, and tens of thousands of seabirds. Humpback whales and orcas are sighted occasionally, and mountain goats mull about the seaside cliffs. The park's coastal fjords are a favorite of sea kayakers, who can camp or stay in reserved public-use cabins.

One of the park's chief attractions is Exit Glacier, which can be reached only by the one road that passes into Kenai Fjords. Trails inside the park lead to an overlook of the vast Harding Icefield.

Before venturing out into the far reaches of the park, gather as much data as possible from the locals concerning the weather, tides, and dangerous beaches. Once you leave Seward, you're a long way from help. Backcountry travelers should also be aware that some of the park's coastline has been claimed by local Native organizations and is now private property. Check with park headquarters to avoid trespassing on Native land.

ESSENTIALS

Visitor Information Kenai Fjords Park Office. Kenai Fjords Park Office ☎ *907/224–7500* ⊕ *www.nps.gov/kefj.*

★ **Kenai Fjords National Park.** Photogenic Seward is the gateway to the 670,000-acre Kenai Fjords National Park. This is spectacular coastal parkland incised with sheer, dark, slate cliffs rising from the sea, ribboned with white waterfalls, and tufted with deep-green spruce. Kenai Fjords presents a rare opportunity for an up-close view of blue tidewater glaciers as well as some remarkable ocean wildlife.

OUTDOOR ACTIVITIES AND GUIDED TOURS

BOATING

Major Marine Tours. Major Marine Tours runs ranger-led boat tours through the park, with both half- and full-day excursions available. ☎ *907/274–7300, 800/764–7300* ⊕ *www.majormarine.com.*

COMBO TOURS

Exit Glacier Guides. Exit Glacier Guides provides a $10 shuttle from town to Exit Glacier, and offers guided hikes to the glacier and Harding Icefield. ⊠ *411 Port Ave., Seward* ☎ *907/224–5569, 907/491–0552* ⊕ *www.exitglacierguides.com.*

Kenai Fjord Tours. Kenai Fjord Tours leads day trips into Kenai Fjords National Park. It also conducts combination train–cruise–motor coach trips from Anchorage. ☎ *800/478–8068.*

WHERE TO STAY

For expanded hotel reviews, visit Fodors.com.

$ 🏠 **National Park Service Cabins.** The Kenai Fjords National Park manages four cabins, including three along the coast, favored by sea kayakers and for summer use only. **Pros:** you'll get all the nature you want. **Cons:** a few are accessible by boat or floatplane only. ⑤ *Rooms from: $50* ⊠ *1212 4th Ave.* ☎ *907/224–7500 to reserve winter cabin, 907/271–2737 in Anchorage for summer rentals* ⊕ *www.nps.gov/kefj/index.htm* ⤳ *4 cabins.*

COOPER LANDING

100 miles south of Anchorage.

Centrally located on the Kenai Peninsula, Cooper Landing is within striking distance of some of Alaska's most popular fishing locations. Here the Russian River flows into the Kenai River, and spectacular fishing opportunities abound. Solid lines of traffic head south from Anchorage every summer weekend, and the confluence of the two rivers gets so crowded with enthusiastic anglers that the pursuit of salmon is often referred to as "combat fishing." However, a short walk upstream will separate you from the crowds and afford a chance to enjoy these gorgeous blue rivers.

The Russian River supports two runs of red (sockeye) salmon every summer, and it's the most popular fishery in the state. The Kenai River is famous for its runs of king (Chinook), red, pink, and silver (coho) salmon, as well as large rainbow trout and Dolly Varden char. A number

Continued on page 302

ALASKA'S GLACIERS
NOTORIOUS LANDSCAPE ARCHITECTS

(opposite) Facing the Taku Glacier challenge outside of Juneau. (top) River of ice

Glaciers—those massive, blue-hued tongues of ice that issue forth from Alaska's mountain ranges—perfectly embody the harsh climate, unforgiving terrain, and haunting beauty that make this state one of the world's wildest places. Alaska is home to roughly 100,000 glaciers, which cover almost 5% of the state's land.

FROZEN GIANTS

A glacier occurs where annual snowfall exceeds annual snowmelt. Snow accumulates over thousands of years, forming massive sheets of compacted ice. (Southeast Alaska's **Taku Glacier,** popular with flightseeing devotees, is one of Earth's meatiest: some sections measure over 4,500 feet thick.) Under the pressure of its own weight, the glacier succumbs to gravity and begins to flow downhill. This movement results in sprawling masses of rippled ice (Alaska's **Bering Glacier,** at 127 miles, is North America's longest). When glaciers reach the tidewaters of the coast, icebergs calve, or break off from the glacier's face, plunging dramatically into the sea.

6

IN FOCUS ALASKA'S GLACIERS

THE RAPIDLY RETREATING GLACIERS IN KENAI FJORDS NATIONAL PARK

Harding Icefield

Exit Glacier

Harding Icefield Trail

Interpretive shelter

Nature Trail

Exit Creek

Ranger Station

KENAI NATIONAL WILDLIFE REFUGE

Lowell Glacier

Exit Glacier see detail map at left

Exit Glacier Rd.

Seward Highway

Phoenix Peak 5,155ft

6

○ **Seward**

Killey Glacier

Icefield

KENAI FJORDS NATIONAL PARK

Skee Glacier

Bear Glacier

Callisto Peak 3,223ft ▲

Resurrection Bay

Fox Island

Truuli Glacier

Chernof Glacier

Chernof Glacier

Harding

Aialik Glacier **2006**

Addison Glacier

Pedersen Glacier

Holgate Glacier **2006**

Hokate Arm

Bulldog Cove

Hive Island

Harding Gateway

Rugged Island

KENAI

MOUNTAINS

Northwestern Glacier

2006

(Highest point in park) 6,450ft ▲

Northwestern Arm

AIALIK PENINSULA

Cheval Island

McCarty Glacier

2006

HARRIS PENINSULA

Aialik Bay

Dinglestadt Glacier

Kachemak Glacier

Glacier

McCarty Fjord

1900

Harris Bay

Dora Passage

Granite Passage

Harbor Island

Chat Island Alaska Maritime National Wildlife Refuge

Natoa Island

1942

Yasuna Arm

Sandy Bay

Granite Island

Matushka Island

Gulf of Alaska

1926

1905

Thunder Bay

Cloudy Mountain 1,810ft ▲

Black Bay

Black Mountain 2,028ft ▲

West Arm

McArthur Pass

Nuka Bay

Pye Islands

Alaska Maritime National Wildlife Refuge

0 ____ 5 mi
0 ____ 5 km

An overwhelming majority of the world's glaciers are melting at a startling clip. Alaska's climate has steadily warmed over the past three decades, dramatically increasing glacial retreat. One fact is clear: many of the state's icy icons will soon melt away. For now, though, Alaska's glaciers remain as captivating as ever. Our favorite spots for glacier viewing include **Glacier Bay National Park** in Southeast and **Portage, Columbia, Aialik** and **Exit** glaciers in South Central.

ICY BLUE HIKES & THUNDEROUS BOATING EXCURSIONS

Glaciers enchant us with their size and astonishing power to shape the landscape. But let's face it: nothing rivals the sheer excitement of watching a bus-size block of ice burst from a glacier's face, creating an unholy thunderclap that resounds across an isolated Alaskan bay.

Most frequently undertaken with a seasoned guide, **glacier trekking** is becoming increasingly popular. Many guides transport visitors to and from glaciers (in some cases by helicopter or small plane), and provide ski excursions, dogsled tours, or guided hikes on the glacier's surface. Striding through the surreal landscape of a glacier, ice crunching underfoot, can be an otherworldly experience. Whether you're whooping it up on a dogsled tour, learning the fundamentals of glacier travel, or simply poking about on a massive field of ice, you're sure to gain an acute appreciation for the massive scale of the state's natural environment.

You can also experience glaciers **via boat**, such as the Alaska Marine Highway, a cruise ship, a small chartered boat, or even your own bobbing kayak. Our favorite out of Seward is the ride with Kenai Fjords Tours. Don't be discouraged by rainy weather. Glaciers often appear even bluer on overcast days. When piloting your own vessel, be sure to keep your distance from the glacier's face.

Taking in the sights at Mendenhall Glacier

DID YOU KNOW?

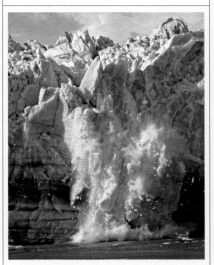

What do glaciers and cows have in common? They both *calve*. While bovine calving refers to actual calf-birth, the word is also used to describe a tidewater glacier's stunning habit of rupturing icebergs from its terminus. When glacier ice meets the sea, steady tidal movement and warmer temperatures cause these frequent, booming deposits.

GLACIER-VIEWING TIPS

- The most important rule of thumb is never to venture onto a glacier without proper training or the help of a guide.

- Not surprisingly, glaciers have a cooling effect on their surroundings, so wear layers and bring gloves and rain gear.

- Glaciers can powerfully reflect sunlight, even on cloudy days. Sunscreen, sunglasses, and a brimmed hat are essential.

- Warm, thick-soled waterproof footwear is a must. Crampons are highly recommended.

- Don't forget to bring a camera and binoculars (preferably waterproof).

6

IN FOCUS ALASKA'S GLACIERS

of nearby freshwater lakes, accessible only by hiking trail, also provide excellent fishing for rainbow trout and Dolly Varden.

Don't let the presence of dozens if not hundreds of fellow anglers lull you into a sense of complacency: in recent years the amount of brown bear activity at the Russian River has increased noticeably. This needn't deter you from enjoying yourself, though. Be aware of the posted signs warning of recent bear sightings, observe the local "rules of the road" about fishing and disposing of carcasses, and keep your senses tuned.

Cooper Landing serves as a trailhead for the 38-mile-long Resurrection Pass Trail, which connects to the village of Hope and the Russian Lakes/Resurrection River trails, which run south to Exit Glacier near Seward. The town's central location also affords easy access to saltwater recreation in Seward and Homer.

GETTING HERE AND AROUND
Follow the line of traffic flowing south out of Anchorage on the Seward Highway every Friday; take a right at the "Y" onto the Sterling Highway and soon you'll be there—just don't blink or you'll miss it! Look for the lodges and tackle shops that spring up from the wilderness, dotting either side of the highway. Cooper Landing does not operate a commercial airport.

OUTDOOR ACTIVITIES AND GUIDED TOURS
FISHING
Most lodges in Cooper Landing cater to the fishing crowd; ask when you make your reservation.

Alaska Troutfitters. For fly-fishing for trout and salmon, Alaska Troutfitters accommodates every level of fisherperson, from rank amateur to seasoned veteran. The company conducts a school covering everything from casting technique to fishing entomology and can arrange package deals with instruction, fishing, transportation, and accommodations. ☎ 907/595–1212 ⊕ www.aktroutfitters.com.

Alaska Wildland Adventures. From the lodge in Cooper Landing south of Anchorage, these folks provide fishing adventures on the upper and lower Kenai River. ☎ 907/783–2928, 800/334–8730 ⊕ www.alaskawildland.com.

HORSEBACK RIDING
Alaska Horsemen Trail Adventures. This Cooper Landing–based company offers multiday pack trips into the Kenai Mountains via Crescent Lake, Resurrection, and other area trail systems. ☎ 907/595–1806, 800/595–1806 ⊕ www.alaskahorsemen.com.

MULTISPORT
Alaska River Adventures. These Cooper Landing–based guides take small groups fishing throughout the region, with self-professed "well-seasoned old pros." In addition, they hold rare permits that allow them to offer trips into low-traversed areas. For those who want to experience the tranquil setting of Cooper Landing without having to go fish, they also offer "paddle and saddle" and scenic river-rafting day

trips, as well as a gold-panning trip that introduces you to prospecting. ☎ 907/595–2000, 888/836–9027 ⊕ *www.alaskariveradventures.com.*

WHERE TO EAT

$ ✕ **Sunrise Inn.** On the shore of Kenai Lake, this cheerful little restau-
AMERICAN rant dishes up homemade soups, chowders, and salsas. The eclectic and very reasonably priced menu includes wraps and vegetarian items. Daily specials made from scratch and hand-grated french fries feature prominently in what the owners describe as a "backwoods bistro." There's a spotting scope in the parking lot for spying on the Dall sheep and mountain goats in the surrounding peaks. The bar hosts live music on Saturday in summer, and there's a great deck for when the weather's warm. $ *Average main: $10* ⊠ *Mile 45, Sterling Hwy.* ☎ 907/595–1222 ⊕ *www.alaskasunriseinn.com.*

WHERE TO STAY

For expanded hotel reviews, visit Fodors.com.

$$$ ☵ **Alaska Wildland Adventures' Kenai Riverside Lodge.** This collection of
B&B/INN buildings on the bank of the Kenai River offers a "roughing it in authen-
tic comfort" all-inclusive package with renovated cabins that have private baths. **Pros:** beautiful wooded location; great adventure and expedition packages. **Cons:** cabins are a bit small. **TripAdvisor:** "fish-ing trip of a lifetime," "great raft trip," "enjoyed the salmon fishing." $ *Rooms from: $180* ⊠ *Mile 50.1, 16520 Sterling Hwy.* ☎ 907/595–1279, 800/478–4100 ⊕ *www.alaskasportfish.com* ⇱ *8 cabins* ⊙ *Closed Oct.–mid-May.*

$$ ☵ **Eagle Landing Resort.** Cabins come in three variations—regular, deluxe,
B&B/INN and riverfront, all with private baths, heat, and kitchens. **Pros:** accom-
modations fit any budget; great views; fantastic kitchens. **Cons:** some staircases are steep (although most cabins also have bedrooms down-stairs); some upstairs rooms are only semiprivate. $ *Rooms from: $159* ⊠ *Mile 48.1, Sterling Hwy., Box 748* ☎ 907/595–1213, 866/595–1213 ⊕ *www.eaglelandingresort.net* ⇱ *12 cabins.*

$$$$ ☵ **Great Alaska Adventure Lodge.** Midway between Seward and Homer,
B&B/INN this lodge lives up to its name. **Pros:** all-inclusive; right along the Sterling
★ Highway. **Cons:** right on the Sterling Highway. **TripAdvisor:** "great time and setting," "great Alaskan adventure," "incredible fishing." $ *Rooms from: $1195* ☎ *Mile 82.5, 33881 Sterling Hwy., Sterling* ☎ 907/262–4515, 800/544–2261, 360/697–6454 in winter ⊕ *www.greatalaska.com* ⇱ *25 rooms* ⊙ *Closed Oct.–mid-May.*

$$$ ☵ **Gwin's Lodge.** Gwin's is the epicenter of much of the activity on the
B&B/INN peninsula. **Pros:** get everything you need in one place. **Cons:** some cabins
are actually trailers with a log facade. $ *Rooms from: $200* ⊠ *Mile 52, Sterling Hwy.* ☎ 907/595–1266 ⊕ *www.gwinslodge.com* ⇱ *17 rooms* ⊙ *Restaurant closed Oct.–Mar.*

$$ ☵ **The Inn at Tern Lake.** Although the address is technically in Moose
B&B/INN Pass, the Inn at Tern Lake sits right between Cooper Landing and
Moose Pass, a few miles south of the "Y" where the Sterling Highway branches off the Seward. **Pros:** babbling springs and terns on the lake complete the Alaska experience. **Cons:** its unique location also means it's a bit far from any amenities. **TripAdvisor:** "the most luxurious

accommodations," "a little spot of heaven," "exceptionally lovely place." ⑤ *Rooms from: $150* ⊠ *Mile 36, Seward Hwy.* ☎ *907/288–3667* ⊕ *www.ternlakeinn.com* ⤴ *4 rooms* ⦿| *Breakfast.*

$$$
HOTEL
Fodor's Choice
★

⚇ **Kenai Princess Wilderness Lodge.** "Elegantly rustic" might best describe this sprawling complex approximately 45 miles from Seward, on a bluff overlooking the Kenai River. **Pros:** cozy rooms have fireplaces and manage to escape a corporate feel. **Cons:** rooms don't have views of the river, even though the lodge sits right on top of it. **TripAdvisor:** "great place to get away from it all," "the best," "a great local's getaway." ⑤ *Rooms from: $190* ⊠ *Mile 47.7, Sterling Hwy* ☎ *907/595–1425, 800/426–0500* ⊕ *www.princesslodges.com/kenai_lodge.cfm* ⤴ *86 rooms* ⊘ *Closed mid-Sept.–May.*

KENAI NATIONAL WILDLIFE REFUGE

95 miles northwest of Kenai Fjords National Park, 150 miles southwest of Anchorage.

GETTING HERE AND AROUND

■ TIP→ You must paddle into the refuge; access is generally by canoe. Road access to the canoe trailheads is off the Swanson River Road at Mile 83.4 of the Sterling Highway. Other than canoeing, the only way to get into the far reaches of the refuge is by airplane. Floatplane services in Soldotna, where the refuge is headquartered, can fly you into the backcountry. The refuge office maintains lists of transporters, air taxis, canoe rentals, and big-game guides that are permitted to operate on refuge lands. To reach the main visitor center–refuge office on Ski Hill Road, turn south on Funny River Road in Soldotna just west of the Kenai River Bridge, and follow the signs.

ESSENTIALS

Visitor Information Kenai National Wildlife Refuge Visitor Center ⊠ *Ski Hill Rd., Soldotna* ☎ *907/262–7021* ⊕ *fws.gov/refuges/profiles/index.cfm?id=74525.*

Kenai National Wildlife Refuge. Its nearly 2 million acres include a portion of the Harding Icefield as well as two large and scenic lakes, Skilak and Tustumena. The refuge is not only the finest moose habitat in the region, but its waterways are great for canoeing and kayaking. The refuge maintains two visitor centers. The main center, in Soldotna, has wildlife dioramas, free films and information, and a bookstore and gift shop. There's also a seasonal "contact" center at Mile 57.8 of the Sterling Highway, open from mid-June to mid-August.

Wildlife is plentiful even by Alaskan standards: the refuge was originally established to protect the Kenai moose. Although caribou seldom appear near the road, Dall sheep and mountain goats live on the peaks near Cooper Landing, and black and brown bears, wolves, coyotes, lynx, beavers, and lots of birds reside here as well.

The refuge also contains a canoe trail system through the Swan Lake and Swanson River areas. Covering more than 140 miles on 100 lakes and the Swanson River, this route is an underused portion of the refuge that escapes the notice of most visitors and residents alike. This series of lakes linked by overland portages offers fantastic access to the remote backcountry, well away from what passes for civilization in the subarctic. The fishing improves exponentially with distance from the road system, and opportunities for undisturbed wildlife viewing are nearly unlimited.

> **MOOSE ALERT**
>
> Moose are the most commonly seen large animals in the refuge—it was originally named the Kenai National Moose Range.

OUTDOOR ACTIVITIES AND GUIDED TOURS

BIKING

Alaska Backcountry Bike Tours. Guided day and multiday hiking-mountain biking combo trips are a great way to get into the Kenai NWR wilderness. Contact Alaska Backcountry Bike Tours to set something up. ✉ *132, W. Arctic Ave., Palmer* ☎ *907/7465018* ⊕ *www. mountainbikealaska.com.*

CANOEING

The best way to experience the refuge's backcountry is by canoe. The **Swan Lake Canoe System** and the **Swanson River Canoe System** are accessed from the road system at the turnoff at Mile 83.4 of the Sterling Highway. Several loop trips enable visitors to fish, hike, and camp away from the road system and motorized boat traffic. Fishing for trout, salmon, and Dolly Varden is excellent, and the series of lakes and portages offer access to more than 100 miles of waterways. The Kenai National Wildlife Refuge Visitor Center has a list of canoeing outfitters.

HIKING

Hiking trails branch off from the Sterling Highway and the Skilak Lake Loop. Degree of difficulty ranges from easy half-mile walks to strenuous climbs to mountain lakes. Bring topographic maps, water, food, insect repellent, and bear awareness. You won't find toilets, water fountains, or signposts. Remember: brown and black bears are numerous on the Kenai Peninsula.

WHERE TO STAY

For expanded hotel reviews, visit Fodors.com.

$$$$
ALL-INCLUSIVE 🏨 **Kenai Backcountry Lodge.** A trip to the Kenai Backcountry Lodge involves much more than driving up to the door and booking a room—in fact, that's not even an option. **Pros:** gets you to the backcountry without roughing it too much. **Cons:** shared bathrooms. ⑤ *Rooms from: $525* ☎ *800/334–8730* ⊕ *www.alaskawildland.com/ kenaibackcountrylodge.htm* ⇆ *4 log cabins, 6 tent cabins* ⊘ *Closed Sept.–May.*

$
RENTAL 🏨 **USFWS Cabins.** These cabins are in remote areas of the refuge accessible only by air or boat. **Pros:** the true experience of being off the grid. **Cons:** making a reservation is no easy feat; no amenities. ⑤ *Rooms from: $35* ☎ *907/262–7021, 877/285–5628* ⊕ *kenai.fws.gov/ visitorseducators/cabin/reserve.htm* ⇆ *11 cabins.*

KENAI AND SOLDOTNA

116 miles northwest of Seward, 148 miles southwest of Anchorage.

The towns of Kenai and Soldotna are mentioned almost interchangeably due to their proximity. Soldotna, with its strategic location on the peninsula's northwest coast, is the commercial and sportfishing hub of the Kenai Peninsula. Along with its sister city, Kenai, whose onion-dome Holy Assumption Russian Orthodox Church highlights the city's old town, it is home to Cook Inlet oil-field workers and their families. Soldotna's commercial center stretches along the Sterling Highway, making this a stopping point for those traveling up and down the peninsula. The town of Kenai lies near the end of the road that branches off the Sterling Highway in Soldotna. Near Kenai is Captain Cook State Recreation Area, one of the least-visited state parks on the road system. This portion of the peninsula is level and forested, with numerous lakes and streams pocking and crisscrossing the area. Trumpeter swans return here in spring, and sightings of moose are common.

GETTING HERE AND AROUND

As you're driving either north or south on the Sterling Highway from Cooper Landing or Homer, you'll know you've hit Soldotna when you're suddenly stuck in traffic in between strip malls. Kenai is 11 miles up the Kenai Spur Highway, which originates in central Soldotna. Commercial flights are available to Kenai from Anchorage.

ESSENTIALS

Medical Assistance **Central Peninsula General Hospital** ✉ *250 Hospital Pl.* ☎ *907/714–4404.*

Visitor Information **Kenai Visitor and Convention Bureau** ✉ *11471 Kenai Spur Hwy., Kenai* ☎ *907/283–1991.*

EXPLORING

☾ **Clam Gulch.** In addition to fishing, clam digging is also popular at Clam Gulch, 24 miles south of Soldotna on the Sterling Highway. This is a favorite of local children, who love any excuse to dig in the muddy, sloppy goo. Ask locals on the beach how to find the giant razor clams (recognized by their dimples in the sand). Ask for advice on how to clean the clams—cleaning is pretty labor intensive, and it's easy to get into a clam-digging frenzy when the conditions are favorable, only to regret your efforts when cleaning time arrives. The clam digging is best when tides are minus 4 or 5 feet. ■TIP➔ A sportfishing license, available at grocery stores, sporting-goods shops, and drugstores, is required for clam diggers 16 years old and over.

OUTDOOR ACTIVITIES AND GUIDED TOURS
FISHING

Anglers from around the world come for the salmon-choked streams and rivers, most notably the Kenai River and its companion, the Russian River. Knowledgeable fishery professionals figure it's only a matter of time before someone with sportfishing gear catches a 100-pounder. There are two runs of kings up the Kenai every summer. The first run starts in mid-May and tapers off in early July, and the second run is from early July until the season ends on July 31. Generally speaking, the first run has more fish, but they tend to be smaller than second-run fish. Smaller, of course, has a whole different meaning when it comes to these fish. Fifty- and 60-pounders are unremarkable here, and 40-pound fish are routinely tossed back as being "too small." The limit is one king kept per day, five

> **DID YOU KNOW?**
>
> The Kenai River is home to the world's largest king salmon. In 1985 a local resident, Les Anderson, caught a 97-pound, 4-ounce fish. That record still stands.

per season, no more than two of which can be from the Kenai. In addition to a fishing license, you must obtain a special Alaska king salmon license stamp and a harvest record. These can be purchased on the Alaska Department of Fish and Game website (⊕ *www.adfg.alaska. gov*), or check with your guide, as most guides sell them. The river also supports two runs of red (sockeye) salmon every year, as well as runs of silver (coho) and pink (humpback) salmon. Rainbow trout of near-mythic proportions inhabit the river, as do Dolly Varden char.

■**TIP➔** Fishing pressure is heavy, so don't expect a wilderness experience, especially in the lower river near Soldotna.

Farther up the river, between Kenai Lake in Cooper Landing and Skilak Lake, motorboats are banned, so a more idyllic experience can be had. Scores of guide services ply the river, and if you're inexperienced at the game, consider hiring a guide for a half-day or full-day trip. Deep-sea fishing for salmon and halibut out of Deep Creek is challenging Homer's position as the preeminent fishing destination on the southern Kenai Peninsula. This fishery is unusual in that tractors launch boats off the beach and into the Cook Inlet surf. The local campground and RV lot is packed on summer weekends.

Area phone books list some 300 fishing charters and guides, all of whom stay busy during the hectic summer fishing season.

Alaska Wildland Adventures. Head down the Kenai River and learn about the surroundings and wildlife with these guides. One of the oldest and largest outfitters on the peninsula, it has trips to suit anyone. ☏ *800/478–4100* ⊕ *www.alaskarivertrips.com.*

Hi Lo Charters. Hi Lo Charters is a family-operated outfit that's been in business for more than 20 years. It's a full-service guide outfitter that specializes in hooking king salmon. ☏ *907/283–9691* ⊕ *www. hilofishing.com.*

Sports Den. The Sports Den arranges fishing trips on the river, on the saltwater, or to a remote fly-in location for salmon, trout, or halibut. ☏ *907/262–7491* ⊕ *www.alaskasportsden.com.*

MULTISPORT

Alaska Canoe & Campground. This region is known for its outstanding kayaking, canoeing, and fishing. Alaska Canoe & Campground outfits cabins, offers instruction, and shuttles to put-in and take-out points. They also outfit for fishing adventures. ☏ *907/262–2331* ⊕ *www.alaska canoetrips.com.*

WHERE TO EAT

$$
AMERICAN
✕ **The Duck Inn.** With pizzas, burgers, chicken, steaks, and seafood, there's something for everyone. Portions are generous, and the prices are reasonable. Locally caught halibut is a specialty, prepared in enough different ways to stave off halibut overload. There's also lots of artwork featuring ducks. $ *Average main: $15* ✉ *43187 Kalifornsky Beach Rd.* ☎ *907/262–2656.*

$
AMERICAN
✕ **Sal's Klondike Diner.** In Sterling, between Cooper Landing and Soldotna, Sal's has a true diner atmosphere. It's open 24 hours, and the portions are large; there's even a sign on the wall that says, "If you're still hungry, tell us." Burgers, sandwiches, fish-and-chips, halibut, salmon, and some steaks are available, along with homemade bread and pies baked every day. You can buy loaves of sourdough, white, or wheat bread. It's a favorite spot for locals. $ *Average main: $10* ✉ *44619 Sterling Hwy., Sterling* ☎ *907/262–2220.*

$
AMERICAN
✕ **St. Elias Brewing Company.** Everything at St. Elias is homemade: the ever-rotating beers, the stone-fired rustic pizza, the sandwiches, and the desserts. The calzones are to die for and the Mt. Redoubt chocolate cake with a molten center is simply divine. This is a great place to check out the locals; the patrons are just as friendly as the staff. $ *Average main: $12* ✉ *434 Sharkathmi Ave., Sterling* ☎ *907/260–7837* ⊕ *www. steliasbrewingco.com.*

WHERE TO STAY

For expanded hotel reviews, visit Fodors.com.

$$
HOTEL
⛺ **Aspen Hotel Soldotna.** The Soldotna hostelry sits on a bluff overlooking the Kenai River, and if you get a river-view room you'll have a front-row seat for the fishing action during salmon runs. **Pros:** hot tub; swimming pool; river frontage. **Cons:** bland, corporate feel. **TripAdvisor:** "great little hotel," "very comfortable," "clean." $ *Rooms from: $169* ✉ *326 Binkley Circle* ☎ *907/260–7736, 888/308–7848* ⊕ *www.aspenhotelsak. com* ⇆ *63 rooms* ⦿ *Breakfast.*

$$
HOTEL
⛺ **Best Western King Salmon Motel.** This Best Western has large rooms, including some with kitchenettes. **Pros:** meticulously cleaned. **Cons:** surrounded by strip malls. **TripAdvisor:** "great breakfast," "spacious room," "very clean." $ *Rooms from: $149* ✉ *35546-A Kenai Spur Hwy.* ☎ *907/262–5857, 888/262–5857* ⊕ *www.bestwestern.com* ⇆ *49 rooms.*

HOMER

77 miles south of Soldotna, 226 miles southwest of Anchorage.

At the southern end of the Sterling Highway lies the city of Homer, at the base of a narrow spit that juts 4 miles into beautiful Kachemak Bay. Glaciers and snowcapped mountains form a dramatic backdrop across the water.

Founded in the late 1800s as a gold-prospecting camp, this community was later used as coal-mining headquarters. Chunks of coal are still common along local beaches; they wash into the bay from nearby slopes where the coal seams are exposed. Today the town of Homer is an eclectic community with most of the tacky tourist paraphernalia relegated to

GOOD ALASKAN READS

Travelers at Fodors.com weigh in on the best reads to inspire you before your trip to Alaska and to introduce you to a bit of the history and culture of the state:

"I enjoyed Peter Jenkins' *Looking For Alaska*. He spent time in several towns. One interesting part was about people who live miles from a main road so a trip to town might be a 60-mile snowmobile trip. The Pratt Museum in Homer has a short video about homesteading in the 50s." —dfrostnh

"I enjoyed the novel *Alaska* by James Michener." —Connie

"*Coming into the Country* by John Mcphee is my favorite. *Last Light Breaking: Living Among Alaska's Inupiat Eskimos* by Nick Jans—he lived in a small village (Ambler, I think) teaching at a native school and exploring in his spare time, and writes beautifully. He also writes a popular monthly column for *Alaska Magazine*." —Bill_H

"My choice would also be *Coming into the Country*—pushing 30 years old but still as evocative. And now for something completely different,

have a go at Michael Chabon's amazing *The Yiddish Policemen's Union*, a mystery set in an alternate-history Southeast Alaska populated by Jews following the collapse of Israel in the War of Independence. Fabulous read." —Gardyloo

"*Good Time Girls*, by Lael Morgan—the true account of the 'ladies of the night' who migrated to the Klondike (Dawson City) and on to Fairbanks. Lots of photos and interesting stories. If you like mysteries, anything by Sitka resident John Straley, Alaska's 'Novelist Laureate' for 2007. *The Last Run: the True Story of Rescue and Redemption on Alaska's Seas*, by Todd Lewan, is a gripping and very readable account of a rescue by the Coast Guard. You'll learn a lot about Southeast Alaska, the life of a fisherman, and helicopters. Amazing." —enzian

"*Drop City* by T.C. Boyle is on the list of 1,001 books you must read before you die. It's about the clash/interaction of a hippie community and the Alaskan residents. Interesting reading and provided interesting color on life in the interior." —keymom

the Spit (though do note the Spit has plenty else to recommend it, not the least of which is the 360-degree view of the surrounding mountains); the rest of the town is full of local merchants and artisans. The community is an interesting mix of fishermen, actors, artists, and writers. Much of the commercial fishing centers on halibut, and the popular Homer Jackpot Halibut Derby is often won by enormous fish weighing more than 300 pounds. The local architecture includes everything from dwellings that are little more than assemblages of driftwood to steel commercial buildings and magnificent homes on the hillside overlooking the surrounding bay, mountains, forests, and glaciers.

GETTING HERE AND AROUND

The Sterling Highway ends in Homer, and the drive in is beautiful. Once there, you'll see signs on your left for Pioneer Avenue, Homer's commercial district. On the right is the historic town center, and if you keep to the road you'll hit the spit. Homer also operates a commercial airport, with flights daily to and from Anchorage, Seldovia, and elsewhere. If you're traveling on the Marine Highway system, ferries to Kodiak and beyond dock several times a week in summer.

ESSENTIALS

Medical Assistance **South Peninsula Hospital** ⊠ *4300 Bartlett St.* ☎ *907/235–8101, 866/235-0369* ⊕ *www.sphosp.com.*

Visitor Information **Homer Chamber of Commerce** ⊠ *201 Sterling Hwy.* ☎ *907/235–7740* ⊕ *www.homeralaska.org.*

EXPLORING

Visitor Information Center. Start your visit with a stop at the Homer Chamber of Commerce's Visitor Information Center, where racks are filled with brochures from local businesses and attractions. ⊠ *201 Sterling Hwy.* ☎ *907/235–7740* ⊕ *www.homeralaska.org* � *Memorial Day–Labor Day, weekdays 9–7, weekends 10–6; early Sept.–late May, weekdays 9–5.*

Halibut Cove. Directly across from the end of Homer Spit is Halibut Cove, a small artists' community. Spend a relaxing afternoon or evening meandering along the boardwalk and visiting galleries. The cove is lovely, especially during salmon runs, when fish leap and splash in the clear water. Several lodges are on this side of the bay, on pristine coves away from summer crowds. The *Danny J* ferries people across from Homer Spit, with a stop at the rookery at Gull Island and two or three hours to walk around Halibut Cove, for $50 apiece. The ferry makes two trips daily: the first leaves Homer at noon and returns at 5 pm, and the second leaves at 5 pm and returns at 10 pm. Central Charters and the Saltry Restaurant handle all bookings. *(⇨ See Outdoor Activities and Guided Tours and Where to Eat below.)* ☎ *907/266-2424, 907/399-2683* ⊕ *www.halibut-cove-alaska.com/ferry.htm.*

Fodor's Choice ★ ☺ **Homer Spit.** Protruding into Kachemak Bay, Homer Spit provides a sandy focal point for visitors and locals. A paved path stretches most of the 4 miles and is great for biking or walking. A commercial-fishing-boat harbor at the end of the path has restaurants, hotels, charter-fishing businesses, sea-kayaking outfitters, art galleries, and on-the-beach camping spots. Fly a kite, walk the beaches, drop a line in the Fishing Hole, or just wander through the shops looking for something interesting; this is one of Alaska's favorite summertime destinations.

★ ☺ **Islands and Ocean Center.** Islands and Ocean Center provides a wonderful introduction to the Alaska Maritime National Wildlife Refuge. The refuge covers some 3.5 million acres spread across some 2,500 Alaskan islands, from Prince of Wales Island in the south to Barrow in the north. Opened in 2003, this 37,000-square-foot facility with towering windows facing Kachemak Bay is a must-see for anyone interested in wild places—and it's free! A film takes visitors along on a voyage of the Fish and Wildlife Service's research ship, the MV *Tiglax.* Interactive exhibits detail the birds and marine mammals of the refuge (the largest seabird refuge in America), and one room even re-creates the noisy sounds and pungent smells of a bird rookery. In summer, guided bird-watching treks and beach walks are offered. ☒ *95 Sterling Hwy.* ☎ *907/235–6961* ⊕ *www.islandsandocean.org* ☐ *Free* ☉ *Memorial Day–Labor Day, daily 9–6; Labor Day–Sept. 30, Tues.–Sun. 10–5; Oct.–May, Tues.–Sat. noon–5; May–Memorial Day, daily 10–5.*

Kachemak Bay. Kachemak Bay abounds with wildlife, including a large population of puffins and eagles. Tour operators take you past bird rookeries or across the bay to gravel beaches for clam digging. Most fishing charters include an opportunity to view whales, seals, porpoises, and birds close up. At the end of the day, walk along the docks on Homer Spit and watch commercial fishing boats and charter boats unload their catch.

Kachemak Bay State Park. Across Kachemak Bay from Homer Spit lies 400,000-acre Kachemak Bay State Park, one of the largest coastal parks in America. *Flip ahead to the next section of this chapter for more information about this park.* The park encompasses a line of snowcapped mountains and several large glaciers; the prominent one visible from the spit is called Grewingk Glacier. One of the most popular trails leads 2 miles, ending at the lake in front of Grewingk Glacier. Several state park cabins can be rented for $50–$65 a night, and a number of luxurious private lodges occupy remote coves. ☎ *907/235-7024* ⊕ *www.alaskastateparks.org.*

Mako's Water Taxi. Park access is primarily by water taxi from the spit; contact Mako's Water Taxi ☎ *907/235-9055* ⊕ *www.makoswatertaxi.com.*

★ **Pratt Museum.** The Pratt Museum is an art gallery and natural history museum rolled into one. In addition to a monthly showcase of an Alaskan artist, it has a saltwater aquarium, an exhibit on the 1989 *Exxon Valdez* oil spill, botanical gardens, nature trails, a gift shop, and pioneer, Russian, and Alaska Native displays. You can spy on wildlife with robotic video cameras set up on a seabird rookery and at the McNeil River Bear Sanctuary. A refurbished homestead cabin and outdoor summer exhibits are along the trail out back. ☒ *Bartlett St. off Pioneer Ave.* ☎ *907/235-8635* ⊕ *www.prattmuseum.org* ☐ *$8* ☉ *Mid-May–mid-Sept., daily 10–6; mid-Sept.–mid-May, Tues.–Sun. noon–5* ☉ *Closed January.*

BEAR WATCH

Emerald Air Service. Homer is a favorite departure point for viewing Alaska's famous brown bears in Katmai National Park. Emerald Air Service is one of several companies offering all-day and custom photography trips starting around $650 per person. ☎ *907/235–4160, 877/235–9600* ⊕ *www.emeraldairservice.com.*

Hallo Bay Wilderness. Hallo Bay Wilderness offers guided close-range viewing without the crowds. Day trips are offered, but it's the two- to seven-day stays at this comfortable coastal location that provide the ultimate in world-class bear- and wildlife-viewing. ☎ *907/235–2237, 888/535–2237* ⊕ *www.hallobay.com.*

OUTDOOR ACTIVITIES AND GUIDED TOURS

BOATING AND FISHING

Homer is a major commercial fishing port (especially for halibut) and a popular destination for sport anglers in search of giant halibut or feisty king and silver salmon.

Fishing Hole. Near the end of the Spit, Homer's famous Fishing Hole is a small bight stocked with king and silver salmon smolt (baby fish) by the Alaska Department of Fish and Game. The salmon then head out to sea, returning several years later to the Fishing Hole, where they are easy targets for wall-to-wall bank-side anglers throughout summer. The Fishing Hole isn't anything like casting for salmon along a remote stream, but your chances are good and you don't need to drop $800 for a flight into the wilderness. Fishing licenses and rental poles are available from fishing-supply stores on the Spit.

Quite a few companies offer charter fishing in summer, from about $250 to $350 per person per day, including bait and tackle. The pricing is usually based on how many different types of fish you're fishing for.

Central Charters & Tours. Central Charters & Tours can arrange fishing trips in outer Kachemak Bay and Lower Cook Inlet—areas known for excellent halibut fishing. Boat sizes vary considerably; some have a six-person limit, whereas others can take up to 16 passengers. They can also arrange non-fishing tours. ✉ *4241 Homer Spit Rd.* ☎ *907/235–7847* ⊕ *www.centralcharter.com.*

Homer Ocean Charters. Homer Ocean Charters on the Spit sets up fishing and sightseeing trips, as well as sea kayaking and water-taxi services and remote-cabin rentals. Some of its most popular cruises go to the famous **Otter Cove Resort.** ☎ *800/426–6212* ⊕ *www.homerocean.com.*

Inlet Charters. Also try Inlet Charters for fishing charters, water-taxi services, sea-kayaking, and wildlife cruises. ☎ *800/770–6216* ⊕ *www.halibutcharters.com.*

Homer Jackpot Halibut Derby. Anyone heading out on a halibut charter is advised to buy a $10 ticket for the Homer Jackpot Halibut Derby; first prize for the largest halibut is more than $40,000. ☎ *907/235–7740* ⊕ *www.homerhalibutderby.com.*

SEA KAYAKING

Across the Bay Tent & Breakfast. For something more unusual, book an overnight trip to Kasitsna Bay through the beautiful Across the Bay Tent & Breakfast. Grounds are gorgeous, facilities are basic, and guests can take kayak tours, rent a mountain bike, or just hang out on the shore and participate in workshops on topics like fish-skin basketry, wildlife photography, and permaculture design. ☎ *907/235–3633, 907/345– 2571 Sept.–May* ⊕ *www.tentandbreakfastalaska.com.*

True North Kayak Adventures. Several local companies offer guided sea-kayaking trips to protected coves within Kachemak Bay State Park and nearby islands. True North Kayak Adventures has a range of such adventures, including a six-hour paddle to Elephant Rock for $130 and an all-day boat and kayak trip to Yukon Island for $150 (both trips include round-trip water taxi to the island base camp, guide, all kayak equipment, and bakery lunch). ☎ *907/235–0708* ⊕ *www. truenorthkayak.com.*

WHERE TO EAT

$$$
ECLECTIC

✕ **Café Cups.** It's hard to miss this place as you drive down Pioneer Avenue—look for the huge namesake cups on the building's facade. A longtime Homer favorite, this café serves dinners that make the most of the locally abundant seafood, complemented by a terrific wine list. The menu includes hand-cut steaks, a "twisted fettuccine" that blends seafood, raspberries, and chipotle in an Alfredo cream sauce. Be sure to make a reservation, as this place gets quite busy during the summer months. ■ **TIP→** Locals know to ignore the menu and just ask to hear the day's specials. Vegetarian options are also offered, and singles mix at the hand-carved wine bar. ⑤ *Average main: $25* ✉ *162 W. Pioneer Ave.* ☎ *907/235–8330* ⊕ *www.cafecups.com* ⌖ *Reservations essential* ☉ *Closed Sun. and Mon.*

$$
SEAFOOD

✕ **Captain Pattie's Seafood Restaurant.** A favorite with hard-to-please locals, Captain Pattie's offers a wide array of fresh local seafood, along with beachfront views of Kachemak Bay. The appetizer menu alone is worth the wait, which can be considerable during the summer rush. The clam chowder is excellent, and the staff is friendly and efficient. There's a good wine selection, and local beer on tap. If you get lucky on your fishing excursion, the restaurant will cook your catch to your liking. Try the great desserts, too. ⑤ *Average main: $20* ✉ *4241 Homer Spit Rd.* ☎ *907/235–5135* ☉ *Closed Oct.–Mar.*

$$
MEDITERRANEAN

✕ **Fat Olives Restaurant.** Pumpkin-color walls, light streaming through tall front windows, and a playful collection of Italian posters add to the appeal of this fine Tuscany-inspired bistro. The menu encompasses enticing appetizers, salads, sandwiches, calzones, and pizzas throughout the day, along with oven-roasted chicken, fresh seafood, pork loin, and other fare in the evening. If you're in a hurry, just get a giant slice of the thin-crust cheese pizza to go for $5. You can order meals at the bar, where there is a great wine selection, and there's always something decadent for dessert. $ *Average main: $15* ✉ *276 Olson La.* ☎ *907/235–8488.*

$$
CAFÉ
☺
✕ **Fresh Sourdough Express Bakery & Café.** This place was the first certified green restaurant in Alaska, and proud of it. It features regional, organic ingredients, baked goods made with hand-ground grain, and fresh seafood in season. You can get box lunches for your all-day fishing or sightseeing trips—even order them online for next-day pickup. There's a small gift shop and a play area outside for kids. $ *Average main: $15* ✉ *1316 Ocean Dr.* ☎ *907/235–7571* ⊕ *www.freshsourdoughexpress. com* ☾ *Closed Nov.–Mar.*

$
ECLECTIC
✕ **Fritz Creek General Store.** Directly across the road from the Homestead Restaurant is this old-fashioned country store, gas station, liquor store, post office, video-rental shop, and deli. The latter is the primary reason for stopping at Fritz's. The food is amazingly good, from the hot and fattening turkey sandwiches to incredible freshly baked breads and pastries, pizza by the slice, veggie burritos, tamales, and ribs to go. Pull up a chair at a table crafted from an old cable spool and join the back-to-the-land crowd as they drink espresso, talk Alaskan politics, and pet the cats. $ *Average main: $6* ✉ *55770 E. End Rd.(Mile 8.2)* ☎ *907/235–6753.*

$$$
EUROPEAN
Fodor's Choice
★
✕ **Homestead Restaurant.** This former log roadhouse 8 miles from town is a favorite of locals who appreciate artfully presented food served amid contemporary art. The Homestead specializes in seasonal fish and shellfish prepared with garlic, citrus fruits, or spicy ethnic sauces, as well as steak, rack of lamb, and prime rib. Epic views of the bay, mountains, and hanging glaciers are yours for the looking. Homestead has an extensive wine list and locally brewed beer on tap. $ *Average main: $20* ✉ *Mile 8.2, E. End Rd.* ☎ *907/235–8723* ⊕ *www.homesteadrestaurant. net* ⟲ *Reservations essential* ☾ *Dinner seating begins at 5pm* ☾ *Closed Nov.–Mar. 8.*

$$
SEAFOOD
Fodor's Choice
★
✕ **Saltry Restaurant.** On a hill overlooking Halibut Cove, this is a wonderful place to soak up a summer afternoon. Local seafood is the main attraction, prepared as everything from curries and pastas to sushi. They also serve fresh-baked bread, and their salads are made of freshly harvested greens from their gardens. The restaurant is small, and although the tables aren't exactly crowded together, it's definitely intimate. When weather permits, get a table on the deck. Dinner seatings are at 6 and 7:30; before or after dinner you can stroll around the boardwalks at Halibut Cove and visit the art galleries or just relax on the dock. Sea otters often play just offshore. Reservations are essential for the ferry ($30 round-trip), which leaves Homer Spit at 5 pm. A noon ferry ($50) will take you to the Saltry for lunch (¢–$), stopping along the way for wildlife-viewing. $ *Average main: $25* ✉ *9 W. Ismilof Rd.* ☎ *907/399– 2683* ⊕ *www.thesaltry.com* ⟲ *Reservations essential* ☾ *Closed Labor Day–Memorial Day.*

$
CAFÉ
✕ **Two Sisters Bakery.** This very popular café is a short walk from both Bishops Beach and the Islands and Ocean Center. In addition to fresh breads and pastries, Two Sisters specializes in deliciously healthful lunches, such as vegetarian focaccia sandwiches, homemade soups, quiche, and salads. Sit on the wraparound porch on a summer

afternoon, or take your espresso and scone down to the beach to watch the waves roll in. ■**TIP➔** Upstairs are three comfortable guest rooms ($), all with private baths. Your latte and Danish pastry breakfast is served in the café. $ *Average main: $5* ✉ *233 E. Bunnell Ave.* ☎ *907/235–2280* ⊕ *www.twosistersbakery.net.*

WHERE TO STAY

For expanded hotel reviews, visit Fodors.com.

$$$$
HOTEL

⛺ **Alaskan Suites.** These modern log cabins offer million-dollar views from a hilltop on the west side of Homer. **Pros:** crow's-nest views; highway location with no highway noise. **Cons:** not within walking distance of anything. **TripAdvisor:** "beautiful cabins," "fantastic views," "most beautiful place to stay." $ *Rooms from: $265* ✉ *3255 Sterling Hwy.* ☎ *907/235–1972, 888/239–1972* ⊕ *www.alaskansuites.com* ↘ *5 cabins.*

$
B&B/INN

⛺ **Driftwood Inn.** The Driftwood seeks to accommodate all travelers, with an RV park, two deluxe lodges, a cottage, and a historic inn. **Pros:** accommodation for every budget. **Cons:** the ship's quarters are tight. **TripAdvisor:** "unique," "beautiful," "awesome cottage." $ *Rooms from: $95* ✉ *135 W. Bunnell Ave.* ☎ *907/235–8019, 800/478–8019* ⊕ *www.thedriftwoodinn.com* ↘ *22 rooms, 14 with bath; 1 cottage.*

$$
HOTEL

⛺ **Land's End Resort and Lodges.** This sprawling complex at the end of Homer Spit has wide-open views of the bay. **Pros:** the Spit-end location puts you 5 miles out into the bay. **Cons:** you might be disappointed if you get a room without a view. **TripAdvisor:** "great location," "nice place to crash and enjoy," "gorgeous views." $ *Rooms from: $160* ✉ *4786 Homer Spit Rd.* ☎ *907/235–0400, 800/478–0400* ⊕ *www.lands-end-resort.com* ↘ *108 rooms, 24 2-room suites, 34 lodges.*

$
B&B/INN

⛺ **Old Town Bed & Breakfast.** Bright and cozy, the Old Town B&B is housed in the oldest commercial building in Homer. **Pros:** warm and inviting, breakfast is divine. **Cons:** some rooms have shared baths. **TripAdvisor:** "historic and memorable," "cute," "completely charming accommodations." $ *Rooms from: $110* ✉ *106 W. Bunnell St., in Old Inlet Trading Post* ☎ *907/235–7558* ⊕ *www.oldtownbedandbreakfast.com* ↘ *3 rooms, 1 with bath* ⦙○⦙ *Breakfast.*

$$$$
RESORT

⛺ **Tutka Bay Wilderness Lodge.** On a small cove 9 miles by boat (the trip is included in the price) from Homer Spit, this luxurious small resort is adjacent to Kachemak Bay State Park. **Pros:** location, location, location. **Cons:** because of its location, it's a bit pricey. **TripAdvisor:** "delightful staff," "beautiful setting," "perfect in every way." $ *Rooms from: $885* ☎ *907/235–3905, 800/606–3909* ⊕ *www.tutkabaylodge.com* ↘ *4 cabins, 2 suites* ⦙○⦙ *All meals.*

NIGHTLIFE

★ **Alice's Champagne Palace.** Dance to lively bands on weekends at Alice's Champagne Palace. The bar attracts nationally known singer-songwriters on a regular basis. ✉ *195 E. Pioneer Ave.* ☎ *907/235–6909.*

Pier One Theater. The members of Pier One Theater perform plays on weekends throughout the summer. Find them in the old barnlike building on the Spit. ☎ 907/235–7333 ⊕ *www.pieronetheatre.org.*

Salty Dawg Saloon. The Spit's infamous Salty Dawg Saloon is a tumble-down lighthouse of sorts, sure to be frequented by a carousing fisher-man or two, along with half the tourists in town. ✉ *4380 Homer Spit Rd.* ☎ *907/235–6718* ⊕ *www.saltydogsaloon.com.*

SHOPPING

ART AND GIFTS

A variety of art by the town's residents can be found in the galleries on and around Pioneer Avenue.

Bunnell Street Gallery. The Bunnell Street Gallery showcases and sells innovative contemporary art, all of it produced in Alaska. The gallery, which occupies the first floor of a historic trading post, also hosts work-shops, lectures, musical performances, and other community events. ✉ *106 W. Bunnell St., on corner of Main St.* ☎ *907/235–2662* ⊕ *www. bunnellstreetgallery.org.*

Pratt Museum. The gift shop at the Pratt Museum stocks natural-history books, locally crafted or inspired jewelry, note cards, and gifts for chil-dren. ✉ *3779 Bartlett St., off Pioneer Ave.* ☎ *907/235–8635* ⊕ *www. prattmuseum.org.*

Ptarmigan Arts. Ptarmigan Arts is a cooperative gallery with photo-graphs, paintings, pottery, jewelry, woodworking, and other pieces by local artisans. ✉ *471 E. Pioneer Ave.* ☎ *907/235–5345* ⊕ *www. ptarmiganarts.com.*

CLOTHING

Homer's Jeans. Homer's Jeans offers name-brand outdoor wear in addition to more utilitarian gear. Buy your cute shoes or your hiking boots here. ✉ *564 E. Pioneer Ave., Suite 1* ☎ *907/235–6234* ⊕ *www. homersjeans.com.*

Nomar. Nomar creates Polarfleece garments and other rugged Alaskan outerwear, plus duffels, rain gear, and children's clothing. The com-pany manufactures equipment and clothing for commercial fisher-men. ✉ *104 E. Pioneer Ave.* ☎ *907/235–8363, 800/478–8364* ⊕ *www. nomaralaska.com.*

FOOD

Alaska Wild Berry Products. Alaska Wild Berry Products sells chocolate-covered candies, jams, jellies, sauces, and syrups made from wild berries handpicked on the Kenai Peninsula, as well as Alaska-theme gifts and clothing. Drop by for free samples of the chocolates. ✉ *528 E. Pioneer Ave.* ☎ *907/235–8858* ⊕ *www.alaskawildberryproducts.com.*

Coal Point Trading Company. Homer is famous for its halibut, salmon, and Kachemak Bay oysters. For fresh fish, head to Coal Point Trading Company. Coal Point can also package and ship fish that you catch. ✉ *4306 Homer Spit Rd.* ☎ *907/235–3877, 800/325–3877* ⊕ *www. welovefish.com.*

Fritz Creek Store. Fritz Creek Store sells fresh, homemade food in an old log building. ✉ *Mile 8.2, E. End Rd.* ☎ *907/235–6753.*

Two Sisters Bakery. Enjoy fresh-baked bread as well as coffee, muffins, soup, and pizza at Two Sisters Bakery. ✉ *233 E. Bunnell Ave.* ☎ *907/235–2280.*

SIDE TRIPS FROM HOMER

KACHEMAK BAY STATE PARK AND STATE WILDERNESS PARK

10 miles southeast of Homer.

GETTING HERE AND AROUND

Kachemak Bay State Park and State Wilderness Park are accessible by boat or bush plane.

ESSENTIALS

Visitor Information Kenai State Parks Office ☎ 907/262–5581, 907/235–7024 ⊕ www.dnr.alaska.gov/parks/units/kbay/kbay.htm.

EXPLORING

Kachemak Bay State Park and State Wilderness Park. Kachemak Bay State Park and State Wilderness Park protects more than 350,000 acres of coast, mountains, glaciers, forests, and wildlife on the lower Kenai Peninsula. Recreational opportunities include boating, sea kayaking, fishing, hiking, and beachcombing. Facilities are minimal, but include 20 primitive campsites, five public-use cabins, and a system of trails accessible from Kachemak Bay.

WHERE TO STAY

For expanded hotel reviews, visit Fodors.com.

$
RENTAL

Alaska State Parks Cabins. Three public-use cabins are within Kachemak Bay's Halibut Cove Lagoon area, another is near Tutka Bay Lagoon, and a fifth is at China Poot Lake. **Pros:** solitude; views. **Cons:** remote locations with no amenities. ⑤ *Rooms from: $50* ☎ *907/262–5581* ⊕ *www.dnr.alaska.gov/parks/cabins/kenai.htm* ⌁ *5 cabins* ▭ *No credit cards.*

$$$$
RESORT
★

Kachemak Bay Wilderness Lodge. Across Kachemak Bay from Homer, this luxurious lodge provides wildlife-viewing opportunities and panoramic mountain and bay vistas in an intimate setting for up to 14 guests. **Pros:** extraordinary facility in a stunning location; sauna and outdoor hot tub. **Cons:** its remote location makes the lodge fairly pricey. ⑤ *Rooms from: $1750* ☎ *907/235–8910* ⊕ *www.alaskawildernesslodge. com* ⌁ *4 cabins, 1 room in lodge* ⊙ *Closed Oct.–Apr.* ⦿ *All meals.*

SELDOVIA

16 miles south of Homer.

The town of Seldovia is another off-the-road-system settlement on the south side of Kachemak Bay that retains the charm of an earlier Alaska. The town's Russian bloodline shows in its onion-dome church and its

CAMPING ON KACHEMAK BAY

Homer is a gateway to some truly remote destinations, as well as a few that are only seemingly remote. After a day or two of the bustling commerce of Homer, an overnight camping trip just across the bay may be just what it takes to feel like you're really experiencing Alaska.

Alaska State Parks Campsites. Twenty primitive, free campsites with pit toilets and fire rings are scattered along the shores of Kachemak Bay across from Homer and are accessible by boat (water taxis operate here daily in summer). The sites are available on a first-come, first-served basis, and camping is allowed nearly everywhere in the park, not restricted to developed sites. ☎ 907/235–7024 or 907/262–5581 ⊕ www.dnr.alaska.gov/parks/units/kbay/kbay.htm.

name, which means "herring bay." For many years this was the primary fishing town on the bay, but today the focus is on tourism. The town was heavily damaged in the 1964 earthquake, but a few stretches of old boardwalk survive and houses stand on stilts along Seldovia Slough. Seldovia has several restaurants and lodging places, plus a small museum and a hilltop Russian Orthodox church. The area abounds with hiking, mountain-biking, and sea-kayaking options.

GETTING HERE AND AROUND

Access is via the Alaska Marine Highway ferry (twice weekly from Homer), aboard a water taxi ($40–$50), or by air from Homer ($65).

WHERE TO STAY

For expanded hotel reviews, visit Fodors.com.

$
B&B/INN
🏕 **Across the Bay Tent & Breakfast Adventure Co.** A step up the comfort ladder from camping, this beachfront establishment is reachable via water taxi from Homer. **Pros:** friendly owners; excellent food; beautiful grounds. **Cons:** although comfortable, you're still sleeping in a tent. **TripAdvisor:** "yummy food," "relaxing adventure in a beautiful setting," "lovely owners." ⑤ *Rooms from: $75* ⊠ *Mile 8, Jakalof Bay Rd., 8 miles east of Seldovia* ☎ *907/235–3633 in summer, 907/345–2571 in winter* ⊕ *www.tentandbreakfastalaska.com* ⤵ *6 tents* ☉ *Closed Labor Day–Memorial Day* ⑤ *Rooms from: $75* ☎ *907/235.*

$
HOTEL
🏕 **Seldovia Boardwalk Hotel.** This hotel with a fabulous view of the harbor has immaculate modern rooms, half of which face the water. **Pros:** in-town location. **Cons:** few on-site amenities. ⑤ *Rooms from: $100* ⊠ *Main St.* ☎ *907/234–7816* ⊕ *www.theseldoviaboardwalkhotel.com* ⤵ *14 rooms* ⛾ *Breakfast.*

KODIAK ISLAND

Russian explorers discovered Kodiak Island in 1763, and the city of Kodiak served as Alaska's first capital until 1804, when the government was moved to Sitka. Situated as it is in the northwestern Gulf of Alaska, Kodiak has been subjected to several natural disasters. In 1912 a volcanic eruption on the nearby Alaska Peninsula covered the town site in knee-deep drifts of ash and pumice. The 1964 earthquake and resulting tsunami destroyed the island's large fishing fleet and smashed Kodiak's low-lying downtown area.

KODIAK

Updated by
Lisa Hupp

248 miles southwest of Anchorage by air.

Today commercial fishing is king in Kodiak. Despite its small population—about 13,500 people scattered among the several islands in the Kodiak group—the city is among the busiest fishing ports in the United States. The harbor is also an important supply point for small communities on the Aleutian Islands and the Alaska Peninsula.

Visitors to the island tend to follow one of two agendas: either immediately fly out to a remote lodge for fishing, kayaking, or bear viewing; or stay in town and access whatever pursuits they can reach from the limited road system. If the former is too pricey an option, consider combining the two: driving the road system to see what can be seen inexpensively, then adding a fly-out or charter-boat excursion to a remote lodge or wilderness access point.

Floatplane and boat charters are available from Kodiak to numerous remote attractions. Chief among these areas is the 1.6-million-acre Kodiak National Wildlife Refuge *(see full section below)*, lying partly on Kodiak Island and partly on Afognak Island to the north, where spotting the enormous Kodiak brown bears is the main goal of a trip. Seeing the bears, which weigh a pound at birth but up to 1,500 pounds when fully grown, is worth the trip to this rugged country. The bears are spotted easily in July and August, feeding along salmon-spawning streams. Chartered flightseeing trips go to the area, and exaggerated tales of encounters with these impressive beasts are frequently heard.

GETTING HERE AND AROUND

Access to the island is via the Alaska Marine Highway (which makes several stops a week) or by plane. A few roads stretch out of town, perfect for a day of sightseeing. The action, however, is in town. Kodiak is the entry point for Kodiak National Wildlife Refuge.

Your first stop in exploring the island should be the Kodiak Island Convention & Visitors Bureau. Here you can pick up brochures, pamphlets, and lists of all the visitor services on Kodiak and the surrounding islands, and get help with planning your adventures. If you want to strike out and hike the local trails, there's an informative *Hiking and Birding Guide* published by the Kodiak Audubon Society.

ESSENTIALS

Medical Assistance **Providence Kodiak Island Medical Center** ⊠ *1915 E. Rezanof Dr.* ☎ *907/486–3281.*

Visitor Information **Kodiak Island Convention & Visitors Bureau** ⊠ *100 Marine Way, Suite 200* ☎ *907/486–4782, 800/789–4782* ⊕ *www.kodiak.org.*

EXPLORING

★ **Alutiiq Museum and Archaeological Repository.** The Alutiiq Museum and Archaeological Repository is home to one of the largest collections of Alaska Native materials in the world, and contains archaeological and ethnographic items dating back 7,500 years. The museum displays only a fraction of its more than 150,000 artifacts, including harpoons, masks, dolls, stone tools, seal-gut parkas, grass baskets, and pottery fragments. The museum store sells Native arts and educational materials. ✉ *215 Mission Rd., Suite 101* ☎ *907/486–7004* ⊕ *www.alutiiqmuseum.org* 🍴 *$5* ⊙ *May–Aug., Mon.–Sat. 9–5, Sun. by appointment; Sept.–April, Tues.–Fri. 9–5, Sat. noon–4.*

> **LOCAL BREW**
>
> **Kodiak Island Brewing Co.** The Kodiak Island Brewing Co. sells fresh-brewed, unfiltered beer in liters, growlers, pigs, and kegs, so you can stock up for your wilderness expedition and avoid beer withdrawal. Brewer Ben Millstein will also give you a tour of the facility on request. It's open noon–7 daily; drop on by for a couple of pints in the tasting room. ✉ *117 Lower Mill Bay Rd.* ☎ *907/486–2537* ⊕ *www. kodiakbrewery.com.*

Baranov Museum. The Baranov Museum presents artifacts from the area's Russian past. On the National Register of Historic Places, the building was built in 1808 by Alexander Baranov to warehouse precious sea-otter pelts. W.J. Erskine made it his home in 1911. On display are samovars, a collection of intricate native basketry, and other relics from the early Native Koniags and the later Russian settlers. A collection of 40 albums of archival photography portrays various aspects of the island's history. Contact the museum for a calendar of events. ✉ *101 Marine Way* ☎ *907/486–5920* ⊕ *www.baranovmuseum.org* 🍴 *$5* ⊙ *June–Aug., Mon.–Sat. 10–4; Sept.–May, Tues.–Sat. 10–3.*

↻ **Fort Abercrombie State Historical Park.** As part of America's North Pacific defense in World War II, Kodiak was the site of an important naval station, now occupied by the Coast Guard fleet that patrols the surrounding fishing grounds. Part of the old military installation has been incorporated into Fort Abercrombie State Historical Park, 3½ miles north of Kodiak on Rezanof Drive. Self-guided tours take you past concrete bunkers and gun emplacements, and a network of trails wind through moss-draped spruce forest. There's a spectacular scenic overlook, great for bird- and whale-watching, and a volunteer-run military history museum inside a bunker; call the park for museum hours. ✉ *Mile 3.7, Rezanof Dr.* ☎ *907/486–6339* ⊕ *www.dnr.alaska.gov/ parks/units/kodiak/ftaber.htm* 🚫 *No credit cards.*

Holy Resurrection Russian Orthodox Church. The ornate Holy Resurrection Russian Orthodox Church is a visual feast, both inside and out. The cross-shape building is topped by two onion-shape blue domes, and the interior contains brass candelabra, distinctive chandeliers, and numerous icons representing Orthodox saints. Three different churches have stood on this site since 1794. Built in 1945, the present structure is on the National Register of Historic Places. ✉ *385 Kasheva-*

roff Rd. ☎ *907/486–3854 parish priest* ✉ *Donations accepted* ⊙ *By appointment.*

☼ **Kodiak National Wildlife Refuge Visitor Center.** Whether you're spending time in the Kodiak National Wildlife Refuge itself, make sure you stop by the new Kodiak National Wildlife Refuge Visitor Center (located a block from the downtown ferry dock). Wander through exhibits about Refuge flora and fauna, attend an interpretive talk, and marvel at the complete 36-foot hanging skeleton of a male gray whale on the second floor. ✉ *402 Center Ave.* ☎ *907/487–2626* ⊕ *kodiak.fws.gov.*

OUTDOOR ACTIVITIES AND GUIDED TOURS

Kodiak Adventures Unlimited. Kodiak Adventures Unlimited books charter and tour operators for all of Kodiak. Find their summer kiosk in St. Paul Harbor across from Wells Fargo. ✉ *105 Marine Way* ☎ *907/486–8766, 907/539–8767* ⊕ *www.kodiakadventuresunlimited.com.*

Memory Makers Tour and Guide Service. Memory Makers Tour and Guide Service specializes in angling day trips on the local Kodiak road system; guide Dake Schmidt's knowledge and passion for fishing the 15 local rivers are a real find for those not flying off to remote lodges. Fishing gear, lunch, and a comfy van provided, with sightseeing, wildlife-viewing, and photography tours also available. ✉ *1523 B Mission Road* ☎ *907/486–7000* ⊕ *www.memorymakersinak.com.*

WHERE TO EAT

$$
AMERICAN

✕ **Henry's Great Alaskan Restaurant.** Henry's is a big, boisterous, friendly place at the plaza near the small-boat harbor. The menu is equally big, ranging from fresh local seafood and barbecue to pastas and even some Cajun dishes. Dinner specials, a long list of appetizers, salads, rack of lamb, and a tasty dessert list round out the choices. $ *Average main: $18* ✉ *512 E. Marine Way* ☎ *907/486–8844* ⊕ *www.henryskodiak.com* ⊙ *Closed Sun. Oct.–Apr.*

$
CAFÉ

✕ **Java Flats.** This great coffee shop represents the true essence of Kodiak life. Fantastic breakfast burritos, vegetarian sandwiches, and excellent coffee make this the perfect place to stock up on provisions before embarking on exciting bear-watching and salmon-fishing adventures. $ *Average main: $9* ✉ *11206 W. Rezanof Dr.* ☎ *907/487–2622* ⊕ *www. javaflats.com* ⊙ *No dinner. Closed Mon.*

$
CAFÉ

✕ **Mill Bay Coffee & Pastries.** Serving breakfast, lunches and fabulous pastries, this charming little shop is well worth a visit. The coffee is freshly roasted on-site every other day. Inside, elegant antique furnishings are complemented by local artwork and handicrafts. $ *Average main: $7* ✉ *3833 Rezanof Dr. E* ☎ *907/486–4411* ⊕ *www.millbaycoffee.com* ⊙ *No dinner. Closed Tues.*

$$
SEAFOOD

✕ **Old Powerhouse Restaurant.** This converted powerhouse facility allows a close-up view of Near Island and the channel connecting the boat harbors with the Gulf of Alaska. Enjoy fresh sushi and sashimi while watching the procession of fishing boats gliding past on their way to catch or deliver your next meal. Keep your eyes peeled for sea otters, seals, sea lions, and eagles, too. The menu also features tempura, *yakisoba* (fried noodles), and rice specials. $ *Average main: $18* ✉ *516 E. Marine Way* ☎ *907/481–1088* ⊙ *Closed Mon. No lunch Sun.*

WHERE TO STAY

For expanded hotel reviews, visit Fodors.com.

$$
B&B/INN
⌂ **A Channel View Bed & Breakfast.** Owned and operated by a fifth-generation Kodiak Alaskan, this emerald-isle favorite has sea views and is conveniently located less than 1 mile from downtown Kodiak. **Pros:** channel views; very hospitable owners. **Cons:** slightly inconvenient if you don't have a car and aren't keen on a 20-minute walk into town (but Mary and Ron can help you call a cab). **TripAdvisor:** "incredible scenery," "wonderful hosts," "spacious and fun." $ *Rooms from: $130* ⊠ *1010 Stellar Way* ☎ *907/486–2470* ⊕ *www.kodiakchannelview.com* ☞ *4 rooms* �◯ *Breakfast.*

$$
HOTEL
⌂ **Best Western Kodiak Inn.** Rooms here have soothing floral decor, and some overlook the harbor. **Pros:** downtown location. **Cons:** harbor-view rooms are on the street; quieter rooms are in the back. **TripAdvisor:** "all you need in a motel," "great location," "convenient and friendly." $ *Rooms from: $179* ⊠ *236 W. Rezanof Dr.* ☎ *907/486–5712, 888/563–4254* ⊕ *www.kodiakinn.com* ☞ *82 rooms* �◯ *Breakfast.*

$$
B&B/INN
⌂ **Cliff House B&B.** Perched on Kodiak's rocky coastline, this newly-built custom house hosts a suite of 3 rooms with common sitting area, private entrance, shared bath, and kitchen facilities complete with homemade granola and a "bottomless cookie jar." **Pros:** excellent views; we repeat: bottomless cookie jar; cozy library for rainy-day relaxation. **Cons:** shared bath for some rooms. $ *Rooms from: $125* ⊠ *1223 W Kouskov* ☎ *907/486–5079* ⊕ *www.kodiak-alaska-dinner-cruises.com/kodiak-bed-breakfast.html* ☞ *4 rooms, 2 baths* ⓞ *Breakfast.*

$$
HOTEL
★
⌂ **Comfort Inn Kodiak.** This recently remodeled hotel is a five-minute walk from the main terminal at the airport, about 4½ miles from downtown (but free airport transportation is provided). **Pros:** fish for salmon in the river out back. **Cons:** a bit out of town, so you might want a vehicle. **TripAdvisor:** "a comfortable stay," "excellent service," "great breakfast." $ *Rooms from: $180* ⊠ *1395 Airport Way* ☎ *907/487–2700, 800/544–2202* ⊕ *www.comfortinn.com/hotel-kodiak-alaska-AK025?promo=gglocal* ☞ *50 rooms* ⓞ *Breakfast.*

$
B&B/INN
⌂ **Hilltop B&B.** This spacious, split-level home features 7 bedrooms and 3.5 bathrooms, with a private entrance, kitchenette, deck with BBQ grill, and plenty of parking space. **Pros:** wood-burning stove, close to grocery shopping. **Cons:** away from downtown, so rental car advisable. $ *Rooms from: $125* ⊠ *993 Hilltop St.* ☎ *907/539–2325* ⊕ *www.kodiakhilltopbnb.com* ☞ *7 rooms.*

KODIAK NATIONAL WILDLIFE REFUGE

50 miles south of Katmai National Park, 300 miles southwest of Anchorage.

GETTING HERE AND AROUND

The refuge is on Kodiak Island and is therefore accessible only by boat or plane. The Alaska Marine Highway stops at the town of Kodiak several times a week in the summer months. From there the Visitor's Bureau can provide lists of the numerous guides, outfitters, and air taxis that service the refuge.

ESSENTIALS

Visitor Information Kodiak National Wildlife Refuge ✉ *1390 Buskin River Rd., MS 559* ☎ *907/487–2600, 888/408–3514* ⊕ *kodiak.fws.gov.*

EXPLORING

Kodiak National Wildlife Refuge. The 1.9-million-acre Kodiak National Wildlife Refuge lies mostly on Kodiak Island and neighboring Afognak and Uganik islands, in the Gulf of Alaska. All are part of the Kodiak Archipelago, separated from Alaska's mainland by the stormy Shelikof Strait. Within the refuge are rugged mountains, tundra meadows and lowlands, thickly forested hills that are enough different shades of green to make a leprechaun cry, plus lakes, marshes, and hundreds of miles of pristine coastland. No place in the refuge is more than 15 miles from the ocean. The weather here is generally wet and cool, and storms born in the North Pacific often bring heavy rains.

Dozens of species of birds flock to the refuge each spring and summer, including Aleutian terns, horned puffins, black oystercatchers, ravens, ptarmigan, and chickadees. At least 600 pairs of bald eagles live on the islands, building the world's largest bird nests on shoreline cliffs and in tall trees. Seeing the Kodiak brown bears alone is worth the trip to this rugged country. When they emerge from their dens in spring, the bears chow down on some skunk cabbage to wake their stomachs up, have a few extra salads of sedges and grasses, and then feast on the endless supply of fish when salmon return. About the time they start thinking about hibernating again the berries are ripe (they may eat 2,000 or more berries a day). Kodiak brown bears, the biggest brown bears anywhere, sometimes topping out at more than 1,500 pounds, share the refuge with only a few other land mammals: red foxes, river otters, short-tailed weasels, and tundra voles.

Six species of Pacific salmon—chums, kings, pinks, silvers, sockeyes, and steelhead—return to Kodiak's waters from May to October. Other resident species include rainbow trout, Dolly Varden (an anadromous trout waiting for promotion to salmon), and arctic char. The abundance of fish and bears makes the refuge popular with anglers, hunters, and wildlife-watchers.

SPORTS, THE OUTDOORS, AND GUIDED TOURS

BEAR VIEWING AND SPORTFISHING

Rohrer Bear Camp. Rohrer Bear Camp guides both bear viewers and visitors who come to Kodiak seeking the island's abundant sportfishing opportunities. ☎ *907/486–5835* ⊕ *www.sportfishingkodiak.com.*

WHERE TO STAY

For expanded hotel reviews, visit Fodors.com.

$ ▦ **Kodiak Refuge Public-Use Cabins.** Some of the Refuge's lesser-known wonders are the fantastic cabins that it has scattered all over Alaska. **Pros:** true Alaska wilderness, all to yourself. **Cons:** the chance of getting weathered in for a couple of days means a loose schedule is a necessity; less likely is getting picked for the lottery. ⑤ *Rooms from: $30* ✉ *1390 Buskin River Rd.* ☎ *907/487–2600* ⊕ *www.recreation.gov* ⌫ *Reservations essential* ⤳ *8 cabins.*

MAT-SU VALLEY AND BEYOND

Giant homegrown vegetables and the headquarters of the best-known dogsled race in the world are among the most prominent attractions of the Matanuska-Susitna (Mat-Su) Valley. The valley, lying an hour north of Anchorage by road, draws its name from its two largest rivers, the Matanuska and the Susitna, and is bisected by the Parks and Glenn highways. Major cities are Wasilla (on the Parks Highway) and Palmer (on the Glenn Highway). To the east the Glenn Highway connects to the Richardson Highway by way of several high mountain passes sandwiched between the Chugach Mountains to the south and the Talkeetnas to the north. ■TIP→ At Mile 103 of the Glenn Highway you can view the massive Matanuska Glacier from the road.

LAKE CLARK NATIONAL PARK AND PRESERVE

100 miles southwest of Anchorage by air.

GETTING HERE AND AROUND

There's no road access to the park, so all visits are via small plane. There are no roads within the park, nor are any groceries or camping supplies available. Most people fly into Port Alsworth, where lodging and supplies are available; while you're there sign in at the visitor center.

ESSENTIALS

Visitor Information **Lake Clark Administrative Headquarters.** Lake Clark Administrative Headquarters ☎ 907/644–3626 ✉ *Park visitor center: 1 Park Pl., Port Alsworth* ☎ 907/781–2218 ⊕ www.nps.gov/lacl.

EXPLORING

Lake Clark National Park and Preserve. When the weather is good, an idyllic choice beyond the Mat-Su Valley is the 3.4-million-acre Lake Clark National Park and Preserve, on the Alaska Peninsula and a short flight from Anchorage or Kenai and Soldotna. The parklands stretch from the coast to the heights of two grand volcanoes: Mt. Iliamna and Mt. Redoubt (which made headlines in 2009 when it erupted, sending ash floating over the region), both topping out above 10,000 feet. The country in between holds glaciers, waterfalls, and turquoise-tinted lakes. The 50-mile-long Lake Clark, filled by runoff waters from the mountains that surround it, is an important spawning ground for thousands of red (sockeye) salmon.

The river-running is superb in this park. You can make your way through dark forests of spruce and balsam poplars or hike over the high, easy-to-travel tundra. The animal life is profuse: look for bears, moose, Dall sheep, wolves, wolverines, foxes, beavers, and mink on land; seals, sea otters, and white (or beluga) whales offshore. Wildflowers embroider the meadows and tundra in spring, and wild roses bloom in the shadows of the forests. Plan your trip to Lake Clark for the end of June or early July, when the insects may be less plentiful. Or consider late August or early September, when the tundra glows with fall colors.

Mat-Su Valley and Beyond

KEY

Ferry Lines

50 miles

75 km

YUKON

Beaver Creek

CANADA

U.S.A.

Mt. Logan

Mt. St. Elias

Northway

Nabesna

Kennicott

McCarthy

Wrangell–St. Elias National Park and Preserve

WRANGELL MOUNTAINS

Tok

Slana

Chistochina

Gakona

Glennallen

Copper Center

Chitina

Chitina River

Copper River

CHUGACH MOUNTAINS

Gulf of Alaska

Cape St. Elias

Paxson

Richardson Hwy.

Valdez

Cordova

Columbia Glacier

Chugach National Forest

Prince William Sound

MONTAGUE ISLAND

Denali Hwy. (closed in winter)

Cantwell

Glenn Hwy.

Matanuska R.

Sutton

Independence Mine State Historical Park

Palmer

Chugach State Park

Girdwood

Portage

Whittier

Chenega Bay

Seward

Resurrection Bay

Talkeetna

ALASKA RR

Hatcher Pass Rd.

Wasilla

Willow

Eagle River

Anchorage

Hope

Cooper Landing

Kenai Fjords National Park

George Parks Hwy.

Denali National Park and Preserve

Denali (Mt. McKinley)

Denali State Park

Petersville

Trapper Creek

ALASKA RANGE

Seward Hwy.

Kenai National Wildlife Refuge

Sterling

Kenai

Soldotna

Sterling Hwy.

Cook Inlet

KENAI PENINSULA

Clam Gulch

Ninilchik

Anchor Point

Homer

Kachemak Bay

Lake Clark National Park and Preserve

Nondalton

Newhalen

Iliamna Lake

ALASKA

SPORTS AND THE OUTDOORS

Castle Mountain Outfitters. Based in Chickaloon, north of Anchorage in Matanuska Valley, this outfitter conducts a variety of trips ranging from guided hour-long horseback rides to one-week expeditions. ☎ *907/745–6427* ⊕ *www.mtaonline.net/~cmoride/index.html.*

WHERE TO STAY

For expanded hotel reviews, visit Fodors.com.

$$$
B&B/INN
☐ **Farm Lodge.** Near park headquarters in Port Alsworth, the farm was built as a homestead back in the 1940s and has been a lodge since 1977. **Pros:** at the headquarters of Lake Clark National Park; renowned flight service; family-friendly. **Cons:** removed from road system. ⑤ *Rooms from: $185* ☎ *888/440–2281 Lake Clark, 800/668-7761 Anchorage* ⊕ *www.lakeclarkair.com/farm_lodge.html* ⇨ *13 rooms* ⫯❍⫯ *All meals.*

PALMER

40 miles northeast of Anchorage.

With mountain-ringed farms, Palmer is charming and photogenic. This is the place to search for 100-pound cabbages and fresh farm cheese. Historic buildings are scattered throughout the Matanuska-Susitna Valley (often just referred to as the "Mat-Su Valley" or simply "the Valley"); in 1935 the federal government relocated about 200 farm families from the Depression-ridden Midwest to the Mat-Su Valley. Now it has developed into the state's major agricultural region. Good growing conditions of rich soil combined with long hours of summer sunlight result in some huge vegetables.

GETTING HERE AND AROUND

The Glenn Highway heads north out of Anchorage and right through Palmer. The Chugach Range lines both sides of Palmer's valley, and if you continue past the town you'll find yourself smack in the middle of the mountains.

ESSENTIALS

Medical Assistance **Mat-Su Regional Medical Center** ⊠ *2500 S. Woodworth Loop* ☎ *907/861–6000* ⊕ *www.matsuregional.com.*

Visitor Information **Mat-Su Convention & Visitors Bureau** ⊠ *7744 E. Visitors View Ct.* ☎ *907/746–5000* ⊕ *www.alaskavisit.com.* **Palmer Chamber of Commerce** ⊠ *723 S. Valley Way* ☎ *907/745–2880* ⊕ *www.palmerchamber.org.*

EXPLORING

★ **Independence Mine.** Gold mining was an early mainstay of the Mat-Su Valley's economy. You can tour the long-dormant Independence Mine on the Hatcher Pass Road, a loop that in summer connects the Parks Highway just north of Willow to the Glenn Highway near Palmer. The road to Independence Mine from the Palmer side was paved in the summer of 2003. The remainder of the roadway to Willow is gravel. In the 1940s as many as 200 workers were employed by the mine. Today it is a 271-acre state park and a cross-country ski area in winter. Only the wooden buildings remain; one of them, the red-roof manager's house, is now used as a visitor center. Guided tours are given on weekdays at

"The Hatcher Pass road was paved a little way off Highway 3, then became a narrow gravel road, which led to the abandoned Independence Mine. The scenery was awesome." —Tom Wells, Fodors.com photo contest participant.

1:30 and 3:30. ✉ *Independence Mine State Historical Park, 19 miles from Glenn Hwy. on Hatcher Pass Rd.* ☎ *907/745–3975* ⊕ *www.dnr. alaska.gov/parks/units/indmine.htm* ✉ *$5 tours* ☉ *Visitor center early June–Labor Day, daily 11–7; grounds year-round. Guided tours start June 20, daily at 1 and 3. There is a day-use parking fee and a separate tour fee.*

☾ **Musk Ox Farm.** Fifty or so animals roam at the Musk Ox Farm, which conducts 30-minute guided tours from May to September. There's a hands-on museum and a gift shop featuring hand-knitted items made from the cashmere-like underfur (qiviut) combed from the musk ox. The scarves, caps, and more are made by Oomingmak, an Alaskan Native collective. ✉ *Mile 50.1, Glenn Hwy.* ☎ *907/745–4151* ⊕ *www. muskoxfarm.org* ✉ *$9* ☉ *May–Sept., daily 10–6; Oct.–Apr., by appointment only.*

☾ **Pyrah's Pioneer Peak Farm.** On a sunny day the town of Palmer looks like a Swiss calendar photo, with its old barns and log houses silhouetted against craggy Pioneer Peak. On nearby farms (on the Bodenburg Loop off the old Palmer Highway) you can pay to pick your own raspberries and other fruits and vegetables. The peak picking time at Pyrah's Pioneer Peak Farm, which cultivates 35 kinds of fruits and vegetables, occurs around mid-July. ✉ *Mile 2.6, Bodenburg Loop* ☎ *907/745–4511* ⊕ *www.pppfarm.net.*

WHERE TO STAY

For expanded hotel reviews, visit Fodors.com.

$ **Colony Inn.** All guest rooms in
B&B/INN this lovingly restored historic building are tastefully decorated with antiques and quilts. **Pros:** quiet; charming; centrally located. **Cons:** front desk a five-minute walk away at Valley Hotel; rooms are small. **TripAdvisor:** "historic location," "a unique space," "lots of character." $ *Rooms from: $110* ⊠ *325 E. Elmwood Ave.* ☎ *907/745–3330* ↙ *12 rooms.*

$ **Hatcher Pass Lodge.** This lodge has
B&B/INN spectacular views and can serve as a base camp for hiking, berry-picking, and—in fall and winter—skiing. **Pros:** views and nature right out your door. **Cons:** no kitchens and a bit far from town, so dining options are limited. **TripAdvisor:** "amazing view," "the real Alaska," "delightful escape." $ *Rooms from: $100* ⊠ *Mile 17, Hatcher Pass Rd., Box 763* ☎ *907/745–5897, 907/745–1200* ⊕ *www.hatcherpasslodge.com* ↙ *3 rooms, 9 cabins with shared showers.*

MEGA STATE FAIR

Alaska State Fair. Giant vegetables (a 105-pound cabbage, a 300-plus-pound summer squash that took four people to carry) are big attractions at Palmer's Alaska State Fair. Shop for Alaskan-made gifts and crafts, and whoop it up with midway rides, livestock and 4-H shows, bake-offs, home-preserved produce contests, food, and live music. The fair runs 12 days, ending on Labor Day. Admission is $9–$11. ⊠ *Mi 40.2, Glenn Hwy.* ☎ *907/745–4827, 800/850–3247* ⊕ *www.alaskastatefair.org.*

WASILLA

42 miles north of Anchorage, 10 miles west of Palmer.

Wasilla made national news in 2008 when Sarah Palin, the former governor of the state and resident and former mayor of the town, was picked to be the Republican vice presidential candidate. Wasilla is one of the valley's original pioneer communities, and over time has served as a supply center for farmers, gold miners, and mushers. Today fast-food restaurants and strip malls line the Parks Highway. ■ **TIP→** It's the best place for stocking up if you're heading north to Talkeetna or Denali. Rolling hills and more scenic vistas can be found by wandering the area's back roads.

GETTING HERE AND AROUND

Wasilla is accessible by car. Going north along the Glenn Highway, turn off just before Palmer and head west. Not far from there you'll come across the sleepy town of Wasilla. It's not known for glamour or beauty, but strolling through town you'll find some quaint shops and quiet streets that make for great, character-rich photographs.

ESSENTIALS

Visitor Information Wasilla Chamber of Commerce ⊠ *415 E. Railroad Ave.* ☎ *907/376–1299* ⊕ *www.wasillachamber.org.*

EXPLORING

Iditarod Trail Headquarters. The Iditarod Trail Headquarters displays dogsleds, mushers' clothing, and trail gear, and you can catch video highlights of past races. The gift shop sells Iditarod items. Dog-sled rides are available year-round; in summer rides on wheels are available for $10. ⊠ *Mile 2.2, Knik Rd.* ☎ *907/376–5155* ⊕ *www.iditarod.com* ◨ *Free* ◔ *Mid-May–mid-Sept., daily 8–7; mid-Sept.–mid-May, weekdays 8–5 (during week of Fur Rondy, open daily).*

Museum of Alaska Transportation and Industry. On a 20-acre site, the Museum of Alaska Transportation and Industry exhibits some of the machines that helped develop Alaska, from dogsleds to jet aircraft and everything in between. The Don Sheldon Building houses aviation artifacts as well as antique autos, trains, and photographic displays. There is also a snowmachine (Alaskan for snowmobile) exhibit. ⊠ *From Parks Hwy., turn south onto Neuser Rd. at Mile 47, follow road ¾ mile to end* ☎ *907/376–1211* ⊕ *www.museumofalaska.org* ◨ *$8* ◔ *May–Sept., daily 10–5; Sept.–May, Tues. 10–2.*

WHERE TO EAT

$ ✕ **Cadillac Café.** Hearty fare fills the menu at this diner-style café, including homemade pies; big, juicy burgers; exotic pizzas turned out of a
AMERICAN
stone, wood-fired oven; and Southwestern-style Mexican food. The owner describes the decor as "Alaska minimalist," but the booths are plush and comfortable, and hand-rubbed wood is evident. Breakfast is served only on weekends. ⑤ *Average main: $10* ⊠ *Mile 49, Parks Hwy. at Pittman St., in the Tesoro Bldg.* ☎ *907/357–5533.*

$$ ✕ **Evangelo's Restaurant.** The food is good and the servings are ample at
ITALIAN
this spacious local favorite on the Parks Highway. Try the garlic-sautéed shrimp in a white-wine butter sauce or a mammoth calzone. The pizzas are loaded with goodies, and a salad bar provides a fresh selection. ⑤ *Average main: $15* ⊠ *Mile 40, Parks Hwy.* ☎ *907/376–1212.*

WHERE TO STAY

For expanded hotel reviews, visit Fodors.com.

$$ ⛺ **Best Western Lake Lucille Inn.** This well-maintained resort on Lake
HOTEL
Lucille provides easy access to several recreational activities, including boating in summer and ice-skating and snowmobiling in winter. **Pros:** beautiful lakefront property. **Cons:** the sound of powerboats whizzing by. **TripAdvisor:** "nice accommodation," "beautiful view," "good room." ⑤ *Rooms from: $170* ⊠ *1300 W. Lake Lucille Dr., Mile 43.5, Parks Hwy.* ☎ *907/373–1776, 800/528–1234* ⊕ *www.bestwesternlakelucilleinn.com* ⤴ *50 rooms, 4 suites* ⧈ *Breakfast.*

$ ⛺ **Pioneer Ridge Bed and Breakfast Inn.** Each of the spacious, log-parti-
B&B/INN
tioned rooms in the converted old Fairview Dairy barn and award-win-
★
ning inn is decorated according to a theme. **Pros:** cozy and warm; views you can't stop staring at. **Cons:** not handicapped-friendly—although it's only one story, the hotel has many steps. **TripAdvisor:** "welcoming retreat," "the best," "rustic elegance." ⑤ *Rooms from: $99* ⊠ *2221 Yukon Circle, HC31, Box 5083K* ☎ *907/376–7472, 800/478–7472* ⊕ *www.pioneerridge.com* ⤴ *1 suite; 1 cabin; 4 rooms with private*

6

baths; 1 room with separate, unshared bath ⊘ *Closed Sept.–May* ⏏ *Breakfast.*

TALKEETNA

56 miles north of Wasilla, 112 miles north of Anchorage.

Talkeetna lies at the end of a spur road near Mile 99 of the Parks Highway. The town maintains a Wild West vibe with a small, unpaved downtown area surrounding a central green. Lucky is the traveler who gets a few sunny days—Denali looms over the town, begging you to take dramatic photos. Mountaineers congregate here to begin their assaults on Mt. McKinley in Denali National Park; those just off the mountain are recognizable by their tanned faces with sunglasses lines. The Denali mountain rangers have their climbing headquarters here, as do most glacier pilots who fly climbing parties to the mountain. A carved pole at the town cemetery honors deceased mountaineers.

EXPLORING

Talkeetna Historical Society Museum. The Talkeetna Historical Society Museum, across from the Fairview Inn, explores the history of Mt. McKinley climbs. The museum has a scale model of Mt. McKinley and features information on the history of climbing attempts on the continent's highest peak. A Talkeetna walking-tour map points out sites of historical interest. ✉ *Mile 14.5, Talkeetna Spur and D St.* ☎ *907/733–2487* ⊕ *www.talkeetnahistoricalsociety.org* ⚏ *$3* ⊘ *May 15–Sept. 15, daily 10–6.*

OUTDOOR ACTIVITIES AND GUIDED TOURS
BOATING, FLOATING, AND FISHING

Mahay's Riverboat Service. Mahay's Riverboat Service conducts scenic jet-boat tours and guided fishing charters on the Susitna and Talkeetna rivers. ☎ *907/733–2223, 800/736–2210* ⊕ *www.mahaysriverboat.com.*

Tri-River Charters. Tri-River Charters operates fishing trips out of Talkeetna and on the nearby Deshka River, and can provide all the necessary tackle and gear. ☎ *907/733–2400* ⊕ *www.tririvercharters.com.*

FLIGHTSEEING

Talkeetna Aero Services. Take a twin-engine aerial tour of the mountain. It's the only service that actually flies over the summit of McKinley (weather allowing). ☎ *907/683-2899 Denali, 888/733-2899* ⊕ *www.talkeetnaaero.com.*

Talkeetna Air Taxi. Check out McKinley and environs, then swoop down to a glacier to test your boots. Maybe even land on one ☎ *907/733–2218, 800/533–2219* ⊕ *www.talkeetnaair.com.*

HIKING

Alaska Mountaineering School. Whether it's on mountaineering expeditions to McKinley or less extreme treks into the Alaska Range, this Talkeetna company takes the time to train you before heading out to glacier trek or hit the pristine backcountry. ☎ *907/733–1016* ⊕ *www.climbalaska.org.*

WHERE TO STAY

For expanded hotel reviews, visit Fodors.com.

$ · B&B/INN — ⌂ **Swiss-Alaska Inn.** Family-run since 1976, this rustic-style property is well known among those who come to fish in the Talkeetna, Susitna, and Chulitna rivers. **Pros:** very quiet. **Cons:** about a half-mile from town, so some folks might want a car. **TripAdvisor:** "top notch fishing experience," "the trip of a lifetime," "very professional guide service." Ⓢ *Rooms from: $100 ✉ East Talkeetna, by boat launch* ☎ *907/733-2424* ⊕ *www.swissalaska.com* ⤳ *20 rooms.*

$$$$ · HOTEL · ★ — ⌂ **Talkeetna Alaskan Lodge.** This luxury hotel has excellent views of Mt. **Pros:** the restaurant is the place to watch the sun set while you also gaze at Mt. McKinley. **Cons:** large and lacking personality. **TripAdvisor:** "fun and unique," "beautiful resort," "great service." Ⓢ *Rooms from: $279 ✉ Mile 12.5, Talkeetna Spur Rd.* ☎ *888/959-9590, 907/733-9500* ⊕ *www.talkeetnalodge.com* ⤳ *212 rooms, 3 suites.*

$ · B&B/INN · ★ — ⌂ **Talkeetna Roadhouse.** This circa-1917 log roadhouse has a common sitting area and rooms in a variety of sizes, including a hostel-style bunk room with four beds ($21) and two rustic cabins ($99–$147). **Pros:** this is true, down-home Alaska at its best. **Cons:** shared bath. **TripAdvisor:** "heart and soul of Talkeetna," "wonderful Alaskan experience," "great breakfast." Ⓢ *Rooms from: $57 ✉ 13550 E. Main St., Box 604* ☎ *907/733-1351* ⊕ *www.talkeetnaroadhouse.com* ⤳ *5 rooms, 2 cabins, share 5 baths.*

SMALL-TOWN FLAVOR

Talkeetna is a must-visit if you're driving between Anchorage and Denali or Fairbanks. A true small town, Talkeetna has a genuine roadhouse (with delicious homemade berry pies), quirky locals, and a pebbly shore along the Susitna with fantastic views of Mt. McKinley on a clear day. If you do come through town, be sure to check out the **West Rib Pub and Grill** (☎ 907/733-3354), which is in the back of historic Nagley's Store on Main Street (a mini-museum of sorts). Grab a seat out back and wash down the delicious chili, burgers, and fries with a local microbrew.

6

DENALI STATE PARK

34 miles north of Talkeetna, 132 miles north of Anchorage.

GETTING HERE AND AROUND

The George Parks Highway bisects Denali State Park and offers not only a majestic view of year-round snow-covered mountaintops, but also a mad array of wildlife. The highway is paved, but after the breakup of winter ice it tends to be riddled with potholes. It's always wise when driving in Alaska to have at least one good spare tire.

ESSENTIALS

Visitor Information **Alaska State Parks, Mat-Su Area Office.** Alaska State Parks, Mat-Su Area Office ☎ *907/745-3975.*

The First to Summit Mt. McKinley

Between 1903 and 1912 eight expeditions walked the slopes of 20,320-foot Mt. McKinley. But none had reached the absolute top of North America's highest peak. Thus the stage was set for Hudson Stuck, a self-described American amateur mountaineer.

Stuck came to Alaska in 1904, drawn not by mountains but by a missionary calling. As the Episcopal Church's archdeacon for the Yukon River region, he visited Native villages year-round. His passion for climbing was unexpectedly rekindled in 1906, when he saw from afar the "glorious, broad, massive uplift" of McKinley, the "father of mountains."

Five years after that wondrous view, Stuck pledged to reach McKinley's summit—or at least try. For his climbing party he picked three Alaskans experienced in snow and ice travel, though not in mountaineering: Harry Karstens, a well-known explorer and backcountry guide who would later become the first superintendent of Mt. McKinley National Park; Robert Tatum, Stuck's missionary assistant; and Walter Harper, part Native, who served as Stuck's interpreter.

Assisted by two sled-dog teams, the group began its expedition on St. Patrick's Day, 1913, at Nenana, a village 90 miles northeast of McKinley. A month later they began their actual ascent of the great peak's northern side, via the Muldrow Glacier. The glacier's surface proved to be a maze of crevasses, some of them wide chasms with no apparent bottom. Carefully working their way up-glacier, the climbers established a camp at 11,500 feet. From there the team chopped a staircase up several miles—and 3,000 vertical feet—of rock, snow, and ice.

Their progress was delayed several times by high winds, heavy snow, and near-zero visibility.

By May 30 the climbers had reached the top of the ridge (later named in Karstens' honor) and moved into a high glacial basin. Despite temperatures ranging from subzero to 21°F, they kept warm at night by sleeping on sheep and caribou skins and covering themselves with down quilts, camel's-hair blankets, and a wolf robe.

On June 6 the team established its high camp at 18,000 feet. The following morning was bright, cloudless, and windy. Three of the climbers suffered headaches and stomach pains, but given the clear weather everyone agreed to make an attempt. They left camp at 5 am and by 1:30 pm stood within a few yards of McKinley's summit. Harper, who had been leading all day, was the first to reach the top, soon followed by the others. After catching their breath, the teammates shook hands, said a prayer of thanks, made some scientific measurements, and reveled in their magnificent surroundings.

In his classic book *The Ascent of Denali*, Hudson Stuck later reflected, "There was no pride of conquest, no trace of that exultation of victory some enjoy upon the first ascent of a lofty peak, no gloating over good fortune that had hoisted us a few hundred feet higher than others who had struggled and been discomfited. Rather, was the feeling that a privileged communion with the high places of the earth had been granted."

EXPLORING

Denali State Park. Overshadowed by the larger and more charismatic Denali National Park and Preserve, "Little Denali," or Denali State Park, offers excellent access, beautiful views of Mt. McKinley, scenic campgrounds, and prime wilderness hiking and backpacking opportunities within a few miles of the road system. Between the Talkeetna Mountains and the Alaska Range, Denali State Park combines wooded lowlands and forested foothills topped by alpine tundra.

OUTDOOR ACTIVITIES

Curry-Kesugi Ridge. The park's chief attraction, other than views of McKinley, is the 35-mile-long Curry-Kesugi Ridge, which forms a rugged spine through the heart of the park that is ideal backpacking terrain. The initial climb to get to the ridge is strenuous, but once you get up high, it's mostly gentle up-and-down terrain. The trail runs from the Troublesome Creek trailhead at Mile 137.3 to the Little Coal Creek trailhead at Mile 163.9. The Byers Lake campground at Mile 147 has a trailhead for a spur trail that intersects the Kesugi Ridge trail, offering an alternative to hiking the entire trail. Views of Mt. McKinley and the Alaska Range from the ridge trail are stunning. ■TIP➔ This is a bear-intensive area, especially the Troublesome Creek area in late summer when the salmon runs are in full force.

Denali Backcountry Lodge. For lovers of outdoor activities like naturalist hikes and mountain biking, Denali Backcountry Lodge offers the complete wilderness package. ☎ 877/223-6254 ⊕ www.denalilodge.com.

Peters Hills. Another destination favored by backcountry travelers is the Peters Hills, accessible from Petersville Road in Trapper Creek. Denali State Park borders the hills, and primitive trails and campgrounds are used year-round. It's especially popular with snowmachiners in winter and mountain bikers in summer.

WHERE TO STAY

For expanded hotel reviews, visit Fodors.com.

$ ☷ **Alaska State Parks Cabins.** Three public-use cabins are in Denali State Park, along the shores of Byers Lake. **Pros:** more accessible than most wilderness cabins. **Cons:** very basic; no running water or electricity. ⑤ *Rooms from: $45* ☎ *907/269–8400* ⊕ *dnr.alaska.gov/parks/cabins/matsu.htm* ⤳ *3 cabins* ⊟ *No credit cards.*

$$ ☷ **McKinley Princess Wilderness Lodge.** When the sky is clear and Mt.
HOTEL McKinley is visible, this lodge has excellent views of North America's highest peak, especially from the lobby, which has a large stone fireplace. **Pros:** clean; with everything you might need. **Cons:** huge; somewhat bland. **TripAdvisor:** "beautiful setting," "nice views," "pleasant and attractive." ⑤ *Rooms from: $149* ⊠ *Mile 133, Parks Hwy., Trapper Creek* ☎ *907/733-2900, 800/426-0500* ⊕ *www.princesslodges.com* ⤳ *460 rooms, 4 suites* ⊘ *Closed mid-Sept.–mid-May.*

6

GLENNALLEN

187 miles northeast of Anchorage.

This community of a few more than 500 residents is the gateway to Wrangell–St. Elias National Park and Preserve. It's 124 miles from Glennallen to McCarthy, the last 58 miles on unpaved gravel. It is also the service center for the Copper River Basin and is a fly-in base for several wilderness outfitters.

GETTING HERE AND AROUND

The Glenn Highway from Anchorage to Glennallen is relatively well maintained all year round. The town's main street, however, is sand and gravel.

ESSENTIALS

Medical Assistance **Crossroads Medical Center** ⊠ *Mile 187.5, Glenn Hwy.* ☎ *907/822–3203* ⊕ *www.crossroadmc.com.*

Visitor Information **Bureau of Land Management** ☎ *907/822–3217* ⊕ *www. glennallen.ak.blm.gov.*

WHERE TO STAY

For expanded hotel reviews, visit Fodors.com.

$$
\begin{array}{l}
\text{\$\$}\\
\text{HOTEL}
\end{array}
$$

$$ **Caribou Hotel.** Mauve and sea-green rooms fill this modern hotel. **Pros:** several rooms have hot tubs. **Cons:** some rooms have shared bath. **TripAdvisor:** "helpful staff," "good location," "good accommodation." ⑤ *Rooms from: $149* ⊠ *Mile 186.5, Glenn Hwy.* ☎ *907/822–3302, 800/478–3302* ⊕ *www.caribouhotel.com* ↩ *83 rooms, 63 with bath; 3 suites; 2 cabins.*

WRANGELL–ST. ELIAS NATIONAL PARK AND PRESERVE

77 miles southeast of Glennallen, 264 miles east of Anchorage.

GETTING HERE AND AROUND

The park is accessible from Alaska's highway system, via one of two gravel roads. The unpaved Nabesna Road leaves the Glenn Highway–Tok Cutoff at the village of Slana and takes you 45 miles into the park's northern foothills. The better-known route is McCarthy Road, which stretches 60 miles as it follows an old railroad bed from Chitina to the Kennicott River. ⚠ Before setting out on McCarthy Road, make sure both you and your car are prepared. Your car should be equipped with a working jack and a properly inflated spare tire, or else potholes, old railroad ties, and occasional railroad spikes may leave you stranded. At the end of the road you must park and cross the river via a footbridge.

Limited services are available in the end-of-the-road town of McCarthy. Facilities include guest lodges, a B&B, and a restaurant. There's no gas station or post office.

ESSENTIALS

Visitor Information **Wrangell–St. Elias Parks Office.** Wrangell–St. Elias Parks Office ⊠ *Mile 106.8, Richardson Hwy.* ☎ *907/822–5234* ⊕ *www.nps.gov/wrst.*

EXPLORING

★ **Kennicott Mine.** The nearby abandoned Kennicott Mine is one of the park's main visitor attractions. The open pit mine is reminiscent of ancient Greek amphitheatres, and the abandoned structures are as impressive as the mountains they stand against.

Malaspina Glacier. The park's coastal mountains are frequently wreathed in snow-filled clouds, their massive height making a giant wall that contains the great storms brewed in the Gulf of Alaska. As a consequence, they bear some of the continent's largest ice fields, with more than 100 glaciers radiating from them. One of these, the Malaspina Glacier, is 1,500 square miles—larger than the state of Rhode Island. This tidewater glacier has an incredible pattern of black-and-white stripes made by the other glaciers that coalesced to form it. ■TIP→ Look for Malaspina Glacier on the coast north of Yakutat if you fly between Juneau and Anchorage.

Mt. St. Elias. The white-iced spire of Mt. St. Elias, in the St. Elias Range, reaches more than 18,000 feet. It's the fourth-tallest mountain on the North American continent and the crown of the planet's highest coastal range.

Wrangell–St. Elias National Park and Preserve. In a land of many grand and spectacularly beautiful mountains, those in the 9.2-million-acre Wrangell–St. Elias National Park and Preserve are possibly the finest of them all. This extraordinarily compact cluster of immense peaks belongs to four different mountain ranges. Rising through many ecozones, the Wrangell–St. Elias Park and Preserve is largely undeveloped wilderness parkland on a grand scale. The area is perfect mountain-biking and primitive-hiking terrain, and the rivers invite rafting for those with expedition experience. The mountains attract climbers from around the world; most of them fly in from Glennallen or Yakutat.

Wrangells. Covering a 100-mile by 70-mile area, the Wrangells tower above the 2,500-foot-high Copper River Plateau, and the peaks of Mts. Jarvis, Drum, Blackburn, Sanford, and Wrangell rise 15,000 feet to 16,000 feet from sea level.

OUTDOOR ACTIVITIES AND GUIDED TOURS
ADVENTURE TOURS

St. Elias Alpine Guides. Based in the town of McCarthy and operating for over three decades, this guide outfit gives introductory mountaineering lessons, leads excursions ranging from half-day glacier walks to month-long backpacking trips, and is the only company contracted by the Park Service to conduct guided tours of historic Kennicott buildings. If you'd rather raft than hike, its Copper Oar rafting outfit (⊕ *www.copperoar. com*) has river trips into the heart of the wilderness. ☎ *907/345–9048, 888/933–5427* ⊕ *www.steliasguides.com.*

WHERE TO STAY

For expanded hotel reviews, visit Fodors.com.

$$ 🏨 **Copper River Princess Wilderness Lodge.** At the gateway to the park, HOTEL this lodge has views of the Wrangell–St. Elias mountain range and the Copper and Klutina rivers. **Pros:** luxurious lodge in the wilderness.

ECOTOURISM IN ALASKA

Ecotourists aim to travel responsibly. Typically, ecotourism is on a smaller scale and involves more education than traditional tourism; often you are led by guides who know the local natural history and cultures. Itineraries allow you a closer connection to the areas explored. As one Alaska guide says, "Slow down, take a deep breath, feel where you are." The **International Ecotourism Society** (⊕ www.ecotourism.org) is a great resource.

When contacting outfitters, learn about the guides, the nature of the activities they offer, and the area you want to explore. Also be sure to determine how well the guides know the area and how long the company has been in operation. Make it a point to ask for references.

Alaska Travel Industry Association. A state-produced *Alaska Vacation Planner* (which also contains information on ecotourism) can be obtained from the Alaska Travel Industry Association. ☎ *907/929–2842, 800/862–5275 to order vacation planners ⊕ www.travelalaska. com.*

Alaska Wilderness Recreation and Tourism Association. The Alaska Wilderness Recreation and Tourism Association can provide information on many businesses and activities across the state. ☎ *907/258-3171 ⊕ www.awrta.org.*

Cons: little else nearby in the way of amenities. **TripAdvisor:** "rustic lodge," "very comfortable room," "a super place to relax and rejuvenate." ⑤ *Rooms from: $139* ⊠ *Brenwick Craig Rd., Mile 102, Richardson Hwy., Copper Center* ☎ *800/426–0500 reservations* ⊕ *www. princesslodges.com* ⌁ *85 rooms* ⊗ *Closed mid-Sept.–mid-May.*

$$$ ⌕ **Kennicott Glacier Lodge.** Artifacts and photos of the era when mining
HOTEL   was the main order of business in the ghost town of Kennicott adorn
★   the small rooms in this modern wood lodge. **Pros:** lots of character; delicious food. **Cons:** some rooms have shared bath. **TripAdvisor:** "way off the beaten path," "superlatives fall short," "pristine." ⑤ *Rooms from: $205* ⊠ *5 miles from McCarthy* ☎ *907/258-2350, 800/582–5128* ⊕ *www.kennicottlodge.com* ⌁ *35 rooms, 10 with bath* ⊗ *Closed mid-Sept.–mid-May.*

$$$$ ⌕ **Ultima Thule Outfitters.** This remote fly-in-only lodge on the Chitina
RESORT   River in Wrangell–St. Elias National Park and Preserve provides a won-
★   derful chance to experience an "air-safari adventure." **Pros:** adventure and comfort at their best. **Cons:** four-night minimum means it will be an expensive venture. ⑤ *Rooms from: $1700* ☎ *907/688–1200* ⊕ *www. ultimathulelodge.com* ⌁ *6 cabins* ⊟ *No credit cards* ⏐⊙⏐ *All meals* ⑤ *Rooms from: $1700* ⊕ *www.ultimathulelodge.com.*

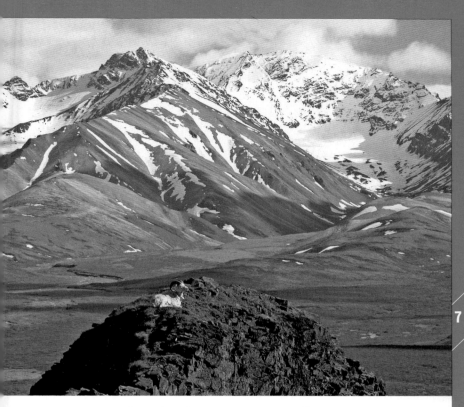

Denali National Park and Preserve

WORD OF MOUTH

"What a view! This Dall sheep was catching some rays, surveying his magnificent kingdom in Denali National Park."
—Chris Marlow, Photo Contest Winner

WELCOME TO DENALI NATIONAL PARK AND PRESERVE

TOP REASONS TO GO

★ **Backcountry hiking:** Getting off the road system and into the park's managed units allows for a true wilderness experience, limited only by time and the strength of your legs. For on-trail hiking try Savage River or Mt. Healy Overlook Trail.

★ **Denali flightseeing:** Soar over river valleys and up glaciers to the slopes of Denali to see the continent's wildest scenery. Some tours also offer landings on Ruth Glacier.

★ **Sled-dog demonstrations:** Watch half-hour demonstrations at the nation's oldest working dogsled kennel. Since the 1920s, sled dogs have been hauling rangers and workers to Denali's interior.

★ **Rafting trip:** Experience Denali through wild rapids or serene flat water.

★ **Bus to Wonder Lake:** It takes all day, but your chances of spotting wildlife are excellent. And from Wonder Lake the view of the massive slopes of Mt. McKinley—Denali—is something you'll never forget.

1 The Entrance. Just outside the park you'll find a strip of hotels, restaurants, and shops; just inside the park are the official visitor's center, the least scenic campsites in Denali, and a level of chaos that does not reflect the park's amazing beauty. Just put all this at your back as soon as you can.

2 Eielson Visitor Center. Deep in the heart of the park, near a favored caribou trail, Eielson offers great mountain views and sweeping vistas of glaciated landscape. If you can't make it to Wonder Lake, at least make it here.

3 The Mountain. Call it Mt. McKinley or Denali or just "the Mountain." It's the highest spot on the continent, a double-edged peak that draws more than 1,000 climbers a year; fewer than half make it to the top. But that's okay: it's easy enough to enjoy the view from below.

4 Wonder Lake. The end of the road for most vehicles, the lake is a full day's ride on one of the park buses. For your time, when the weather allows, you get the best view of the mountain anywhere in the park. And even when the mountain is hiding in the clouds, this is one of the prettiest stretches of landscape in the world.

KEY

┝━━┥	Rail Line
┄┄┄	Trail
▲	Campground
▦	Lodge
⛱	Picnic Area
🚶	Ranger Station
🍴	Restaurant
🚌	Free shuttle bus

SNOHOMISH HILLS

DENALI NATIONAL PRESERVE

Castle Rocks 2079ft ▲

DENALI NATIONAL P.

COTTONWOOD HILLS

SLOW FORK HILLS

Heart Mtn 6500ft ▲

A L A S K A

Mt Russell 11670ft ▲

Mount Dall 8756ft ▲

DENALI NATIONAL PRESERVE

0   10 miles
0   10 kilometers

DENALI NATIONAL PARK

KANTISHNA HILLS

Sanctuary River (mile 22)

Healy

Mount Margaret 5059ft

Park Entrance & Headquarters

Teklanika (mile 29)

Denali Park Road

Savage River (mile 13)

Lagoon

WYOMING HILLS

Sable Mtn 6002ft

Igloo Creek (mile 34)

Kankone Peak 4987ft

Polychrome Mtn 5790ft

Sable Pass

Fang Mtn 6736ft

Kantishna

Toklat (mile 53)

Polychrome Pass

Highway Pass

Panorama Mountain 5778ft

Thorofare Pass

Stony Dome 4700ft

Mount Pendleton 7840ft

Cantwell

Denali Highway

8

Wonder Lake (mile 85)

Eielson Visitor Center (mile 66)

Wilderness area boundary

RANGE

Wilderness area boundary

3

ARK WILDERNESS

Red Mtn 7165ft

Mt Brooks 11940ft

Muldrow Glacier

Mt Mather 12123ft

Mt Koven 12210 ft

Mt Silverthrone 13220ft

Mt Eldridge 10433ft

Eldridge Glacier

North Peak 19470ft

MT McKINLEY (DENALI)

Kahiltna Dome 12525ft

South Peak 20320ft

Explorers Peak 8540ft

Mt Crosson 12800ft

Mt Hunter 14573ft

Mooses Tooth 10335ft

Denali Viewpoint North

Mt Foraker 17400ft

Chulitna

Avalanche Spire 10105ft

Mt Goldie 6315ft

Tokositna Glacier

Ruth Glacier

Tokosha Mountains

George Parks Highway

DENALI STATE PARK

The Alaska Railroad

Denali Viewpoint South

DUTCH HILLS

PETERS HILLS

Mount Kliskon 3943ft

3

Fairview Mountain 3266ft

Petersville Road

Talkeetna

Trapper Creek

7

GETTING ORIENTED

Denali National Park is located 120 miles south of Fairbanks and 240 miles north of Anchorage on the George Parks Highway. More than 6 million acres of wilderness, Denali National Park and Preserve is the heart of Alaska: the biggest mountains, the wildest rivers, and so much wildlife you'll probably end up frying your camera trying to catch it all. Founded in 1917 as Mt. McKinley National Park (despite the fact that the park's then borders went right across the mountain), government caught up with thousands of years of Native tradition and renamed the park Denali in 1980. One road in, the tallest mountain on the continent, and endless possibilities await you.

Updated
by Edward
Readicker–
Henderson

Denali National Park and Preserve is Alaska's most visited attraction for a reason: the most accessible of Alaska's national parks and one of only three connected to the state's highway system, the 6-million-acre wilderness offers views of mountains so big they seem like a wall on the horizon; endless wildlife, from cinnamon-color Toklat grizzlies to herds of caribou, to moose with antlers the size of coffee tables; glaciers with forests growing on them; autumn tundra the color of a kid's breakfast cereal.

The keystone of the park is Mt. McKinley: more commonly called by its Athabascan name, *Denali,* meaning "the High One," or often referred to by Alaskans simply as "the Mountain," the peak measures in at 20,320 feet, the highest point on the continent. Denali is also the tallest mountain in the world—yes, Mt. Everest is higher, but it sits on the Tibetan plateau, like it was standing on a chair to rise above Denali, which starts barely above sea level.

Unfortunately for visitors on a tight schedule, Denali, like big mountains everywhere, makes its own weather systems, and the simple truth is that the mountain really, really likes clouds: the peaks are wreathed in clouds an average of two out of three days in summer. You can increase your odds of glimpsing Denali's peak by venturing into the heart of the park or staying at a wilderness lodge at the western park boundary. Or get really ambitious: more than 1,000 adventurers climb the mountain's slopes each summer. On average, of those who take the most common route, the West Buttress, just over half make it to the peak. The rest turn back, gasping for breath in the thin air.

Although the mountain is the biggest attraction, you don't need to see it—much less climb it—to appreciate the park; in fact, few people who visit Denali National Park and Preserve will come any closer than 35 miles to the mountain's slopes—and most visitors won't even get that close.

Because even if the mountain is shy, a trip along the park's Denali Park Road offers sights you won't forget: an opportunity to see grizzly bears, wolves, caribou, moose, and Dall sheep—the "big five" of Alaskan animals. And don't miss the soaring golden eagles, clucking ptarmigans, and chattering ground squirrels. If you prefer to take in the scenery without glass between you and the wild, you can bike or hike along the park road. Or see it all from an eagle's point of view: flightseeing is one of the best ways to gain a full appreciation of the park, especially the wild spires of the Great Gorge along the flanks of Mt. McKinley.

No matter how you come to the park—staying on the bus, flying over the peaks in a small plane, or hiking across the tussocks of the tundra on a route that takes you days away from the nearest person, exploring Denali offers rich rewards: wilderness solitude, a sense of discovery, amazing wildlife encounters, and a chance to truly appreciate the scale, the mystery, and the grandeur of this landscape.

GEOLOGY AND TERRAIN

The most prominent geological feature of the park is the Alaska Range, a 600-mile-long crescent of mountains that separates South Central Alaska from the Interior. Mt. Hunter (14,573 feet), Mt. Foraker (17,400 feet), and Mt. McKinley (20,320 feet) are the mammoths of the group. Glaciers flow from the entire Alaska Range.

Another, smaller group of mountains—the Outer Range, north of Denali's park road—is a mix of volcanics and heavily metamorphosed sediments. Though not as breathtaking as the Alaska Range, the Outer Range is popular with hikers and backpackers because its summits and ridges are not as technically difficult to reach.

Several of Denali's most spectacular landforms are deep in the park, but are still visible from the park road. The multicolor volcanic rocks at Cathedral Mountain and Polychrome Pass reflect the vivid hues of the American Southwest. The braided channels of glacially fed streams such as the Teklanika, Toklat, and McKinley rivers serve as highway routes for both animals and hikers. The debris- and tundra-covered ice of the Muldrow Glacier, one of the largest glaciers to flow out of Denali National Park's high mountains, is visible from Eielson Visitor Center, at Mile 66 of the park road. Wonder Lake, a dark and narrow kettle pond that's a remnant from Alaska's ice ages, lies at Mile 85, just a few miles from the former gold-boom camp of Kantishna.

DENALI PLANNER

WHEN TO GO

Denali's main season is mid-May into early September. About 90% of the people come in these months, and with good reason: warmish weather, long days, and all the facilities open. Shoulder seasons—early May and late September—can be incredibly beautiful in the park, with few people around; plus, you can often drive your own car a fair way down the park road, since the buses don't run. In winter the only way into the park is on ski or snowshoe or by dogsled. You'll have the place almost entirely to yourself—most of the businesses at the park entrance are closed—and if you're comfortable in deep snow and freezing weather, there is no better time to see Denali.

TIMING

You can do a bus tour of the park in a single day. Allow for all day, and try to go at least as far as Eielson Visitor Center. If you can, go out to Wonder Lake. A few buses go a few miles farther to Kantishna, but the views from Wonder Lake are better; there's no reason to go those last miles unless you're staying at one of the inholding lodges.

If you have more than a single day, the best thing to do is camp in the park. The longer you stay deeper in the park, the better chance you'll have of seeing Mt. McKinley, which, on average, is only visible one day out of three. Again, Wonder Lake is the spot of choice.

It's also easy to fill a day around the park entrance, taking rafting trips on the Nenana River or going on some of the short hikes near the visitor center.

No matter how much time you have, plan ahead. Bus and campsite reservations are available for the summer season beginning December 1. ■TIP→ Reserve tickets for buses ahead of time; call the numbers provided here or log on to ⊕ www.reservedenali.com. Although you can often just walk up and get on something, it may not be the experience you're after. Advance planning makes for the best trips.

GETTING HERE AND AROUND

BUS TRAVEL

Only one road penetrates Denali's expansive wilderness: the 92-mile Denali Park Road, which winds from the park entrance to Wonder Lake (as far as the regular buses go) and on the inholding of Kantishna, the historic mining district in the heart of the park, where there are a couple of private lodges. The first 15 miles of the road are paved and open to all vehicles, but beyond the checkpoint at Savage River access is limited to tour buses, special permit holders, and the community members of Kantishna. To get around the park, you need to get on one of the buses (⇨ see Transportation chart in this chapter) or start hiking. Campers with permits for the Teklanika campground can drive to and back out from their campsites at Mile 29, but they cannot tour the park road in their vehicles.

CAR TRAVEL

The park is 120 miles south of Fairbanks, or 240 miles north of Anchorage, on the George Parks Highway, which is the most common access route.

There is a second, seldom-used road to the park: the Denali Highway leads from Paxon, which is accessible from the Richardson Highway (which connects Fairbanks and Valdez) to Cantwell, coming out just south of the park entrance. This 134-mile road is mostly unpaved, with few services. Only people with high-clearance cars should try it. The Denali Highway is closed in winter.

MOUNTAIN BIKE TRAVEL

Mountain bikes are allowed anywhere on the park road, although you should check with officials before pedaling out; you need to know if there has been a wolf kill or a lot of bear sightings by the road that might limit access.

TRAIN TRAVEL

For those who don't want to drive, Denali National Park is a regular stop on the Alaska Railroad's Anchorage–Fairbanks route. The railway sells packages that combine train travel with hotels and trips into the park. There are great views along the way, after the first hour or so outside of Anchorage, and the train is a lovely, comfortable way to travel. The final approach to the park is much prettier by train than via car.

HEALTH AND SAFETY

Even if you're not hiking, carry durable rain gear made of a breathable material, and dress in layers. Good, sturdy, broken-in hiking boots, a hat, and warm gloves are a must, as are polypropylene long underwear and layers of wool or fleece for hikers. Avoid cotton. Bring insect repellent, binoculars, and a camera. Park water isn't safe to drink, and past the park entrance there's no food except what you bring in yourself—and don't forget to get a mandatory bear-proof container for it from the park headquarters.

PARK ESSENTIALS

PARK FEES AND PERMITS

Admission to Denali is $10 per person (or $15 for motorcycles).

PARK HOURS

The park never closes. There may not be anybody around to accept the admission fee in deep winter, but the gates are always open.

CELL-PHONE RECEPTION

Don't count on cell-phone reception past the first mile or two beyond the visitor center.

RESTAURANTS

For eating inside the park, your only option is what you carry in—and don't forget the bear-proof food container (available at the visitor center). Just outside the park entrance, in summer, there are dozens of restaurants to choose from. In winter, do what the few year-rounders do: get your groceries in Fairbanks or Anchorage. Really. *Prices in the reviews are the average cost of a main course at dinner or, if dinner is not served, at lunch.*

HOTELS

There are plenty of options right outside the park entrance, but don't expect to find anything open in winter. *Prices in the reviews are the lowest cost of a standard double room in high season.*

TOURS

Don't be alarmed by the crowded park entrance; that gets left behind very quickly. After the chaos of private businesses that line the George Parks Highway and the throngs at the visitor center, there's pretty much nothing else in the park but wilderness. From the bus you'll have the opportunity to see Denali's wildlife in natural settings, as the animals are habituated to the road and vehicles, and go about their daily routine with little bother. In fact, the animals really like the road: it's easier for them to walk along it than to work through the tundra and tussocks.

Bus trips take time. The maximum speed limit is 35 mph, and the buses don't hit that very often. Add in rest stops, wildlife sightings, and slow-downs for passing, and it's an 8- to 11-hour day to reach the heart of the park and the best Denali views from Miles 62–85. Buses run from May 20–September 13, although if you're running up close against one of those dates, call to make sure. *All prices listed below are for adults, and include the $10 park admission fee, unless otherwise noted.* ■TIP➔ If you decide to tour the park by bus, you have two choices: a sightseeing bus tour offered by a park concessionaire or a ride on the shuttle bus. The differences between the two are significant.

Tour buses. Tour buses offer a guided introduction to the park. Advance reservations are required for the tour buses and are recommended for the park shuttles. Reservations for the following season become available on December 1, so if you have only a small window to see Denali, plan far ahead. If you're not organized enough to think six months or more out, you can usually get on the bus of your choice with less than a week's notice—and you can almost always get on a shuttle bus within a day or two—but try not to count on that. Work as far ahead as you can to avoid disappointment.

Rides through the park include a five-hour Natural History Tour ($76.50) a six- to eight-hour Tundra Wilderness Tour ($123.25), and an 11- to 12-hour Kantishna Experience ($169). These prices do not include the park entrance fee, but kids are half price. Trips are fully narrated by the driver-guides and include a snack or box lunch and hot drinks. Although the Natural History Tour lasts five hours, it goes only 17 miles into the park (2 miles beyond the private-vehicle turnaround), emphasizing Denali's human and natural history. Do not take this tour if you want the best wildlife- or Mt. McKinley–viewing opportunities. You might see a moose or two but not much else. The Tundra Wilderness Tour is a great way to go for a fun, thorough introduction to the park, but if it leaves you wanting more, the Kantishna Experience travels the entire length of the road, features an interpretive guide and ranger, lunch, and some walking. Note, though, that none of the tours allows you to leave the bus without the group or to travel independently through the park. ☎ 800/622–7275, 907/272–7275 *in Alaska or outside U.S.* ⊕ *www.reservedenali.com.*

Shuttle buses. The park's own shuttle buses don't include a formal interpretive program or food and drink. ■TIP➔ They're less expensive, and you can get off the bus and take a hike or just stop and sightsee almost anywhere you like, then catch another bus along the road. Most of the drivers are well versed in the park's features and will point out plant, animal, and geological sights. The shuttles are less formal than the tour buses, and generally less comfortable (converted school buses). They do stop to watch and photograph wildlife, but with a schedule to keep, time is sometimes limited. Shuttle-bus round-trip fares are $26.75 to

Continued on page 349

THE HIGH ONE

In the heart of mainland Alaska, within 6-million-acre Denali National Park & Preserve, the continent's most majestic peak rises into the heavens. Officially known as **Mount McKinley,** this 20,320-foot massif of ice, snow, and rock is most commonly referred to by its native name of Denali, or "the High One." Some simply call it "The Mountain." One thing is certain: It's a giant among giants, and the most dominant feature in a land of extremes and superlatives.

Those who have walked McKinley's slopes know it to be a wild, desolate place. As the highest peak in North America, McKinley is a target of mountaineers who aspire to ascend the "seven summits"—the tallest mountains on each continent. A foreboding and mysterious place, it was terra incognita—unclimbed and unknown to most people—as recently as the late 1890s. Among Athabascan tribes, however, the mountain was a revered landmark; many generations regarded it as a holy place and a point of reference.

NAMING TERRA INCOGNITA

Linguists have identified at least eight native Alaskan names for the mountain, including Deenaalee, Doleyka, Traleika, and Dghelay Ka'a. The essence of all the names is "the High One" or "Big Mountain." The first recorded sighting of Mt. McKinley by a foreign explorer was in 1794, when Captain George Vancouver spotted it in the distance. More than a century later, after a summer of gold-seeking, Ivy Leaguer William Dickey reported his experiences in the *New York Sun*. His most significant news was of a massive peak, which he dubbed "Mt. McKinley," after Republican William McKinley of Ohio. Mountaineer Hudson Stuck, who led the first mountaineering team to McKinley's summit, was just one in a long line of Alaskans to protest this name. In Stuck's view, the moniker was an affront to both the mountain and Alaska's native people. For these very reasons, a vast majority of Alaskans call the continent's highest peak by its original name, Denali.

Mount McKinley Facts & Figures

■ The mountain's vertical rise is the highest in the world. This means that at 18,000 feet over the lowlands (which are some 2,000 feet above sea level), McKinley's vertical rise is even greater than Mt. Everest, at 29,035-feet (which rises 12,000 feet above the Tibetan plateau, some 17,000 feet above sea).

Halfway to the summit, McKinley's weather is equivalent to that of the North Pole in severity. In summer, night temperatures may reach -40° F.

11,000' Camp ▲

Route proceeds behind ridge

Kahiltna Pass 10,320'

West Buttress Route

Kahiltna Glacier

Climbers begin expeditions by flying to the Kahiltna Glacier Base Camp at 7,200 ft.

THE WEST BUTTRESS ROUTE

■ The safest route to the summit is the West Buttress. Eighty to 90% of climbers attempting to ascend the peak take this route, with only about half reaching the top.

■ More than 30 people—including some world-class mountaineers—have been killed on the West Buttress.

■ From base camp to high camp, climbers must trek

some 16 miles and 10,000 vertical feet—a trip that takes two to three weeks.

■ The most technically challenging stretch is the ascent to 18,200-foot Denali

■ In addition to coping with severe weather, climbers face avalanches, open crevasses, hypothermia, frostbite, and high-altitude illnesses. Nearly 100 people have died on the mountain and hundreds more have been seriously injured.

■ McKinley's awesome height and its subarctic location make it one of the coldest mountains on Earth, if not the coldest.

■ Primarily made of granite, McKinley undergoes continual shifting and uplift thanks to plate tectonics (the Pacific plate pushing against the North American Plate); it grows about 1 mm per year.

South Summit
20,320′

North Summit
19,470′

Mount McKinley

Denali Pass
18,200′

South Buttress

Cassin Ridge

Northwest Buttress

High Camp
17,200′

West Buttress

Ridge Camp
16,200′

West Rib

14,200′ Camp

Windy Corner Camp
13,000′

The high camp is at 17,200 feet; teams often find themselves stuck here waiting out storms and high winds. From high camp it takes another 8 to 12 hours of physically demanding climbing to reach the summit.

This very steep and treacherous headwall is navigated with a fixed line (meaning climbers are hooked together). Dangerous and exhilarating!

Pass; climbers must cross a steep snow-covered slope then a shallow bowl called the Football Field.

■ Then, still roped together, climbers ascend an 800-foot snow-and-ice wall to reach the "top of the continent" itself.

Fearless climbers facing the icy challenge at 16,400 feet on the West Buttress Route.

EARLY MILESTONES

Climbing Mt. McKinley in the early 1900s

■ In **1903**, two different expeditions made the first attempts to climb Mt. McKinley. The highest point reached? 11,000 feet. Over the next decade, other expeditions would try, and fail, to reach the top.

■ Finally, in **1913**, a team led by Hudson Stuck reached the summit. The first person to the top was Walter Harper, a native Alaskan.

■ After the Stuck party's success in **1913**, no attempts were made to climb the mountain until **1932**. That year, for the first time, a pilot landed a small plane on one of the mountain's massive glaciers. Another first: a party climbed both the 20,320-foot South Peak and 19,470-foot North Peak. More tragically, the first deaths occurred on the mountain.

■ Alaskans Dave Johnston, Art Davidson, and Ray Genet completed the first winter ascent of McKinley in February **1967**. Japanese climber Naomi Uemura completed the first solo ascent of McKinley in **1970**.

A FLIGHT TO REMEMBER

Talkeetna is the home of the popular Denali Flyers. Pilots take you on a variety of air tours into the Alaska Range in small, ski-equipped planes. Flights usually include a passage through the Ruth Glacier's Great Gorge, which is bordered by breathtaking granite spires. Leaving the gorge, you'll enter immense glacial basins of the Don Sheldon Amphitheater (named in honor of the first Denali Flyer). Most trips also include flights past McKinley's southern flanks and show glimpses of its climbing routes. Longer tours circle the mountain, passing among the perennially ice-capped upper slopes, saw-toothed ridges, and vertical rock faces. Flights generally range from 30 minutes to 3 hours and cost $150 to $350 per person.

SHELDON AIR SERVICE is the new incarnation of Hudson Air Service; in 2010 the Talkeetna-based stalwart changed hands and name. The Denali Grand Tour is 90 minutes and costs $280 per person. A glacier landing adds 45 minutes to your flight and costs an additional $75.

☎ *907/733–2321 or 800/478–2321*
⊕ *www.sheldonairservice.com*

K2 AVIATION specializes in flightseeing and glacier landings in the Alaska Range. Prices range from $195 (for a 1-hour flightsee) to $365 (for a 120-minute flightsee with a glacier landing).

☎ *907/733–2291 or 800/764–2291*
⊕ *www.flyk2.com*

TALKEETNA AIR TAXI conducts a breathtaking exploration flight close to massive Mt. McKinley, as well as glacier landings. See Ruth Glacier and the South Face ($195); the base camp ($240); or the Grand Denali Tour ($285). For glacier landings add $75.

☎ *907/733–2218 or 800/533–2219*
⊕ *www.talkeetnaair.com*

BUS	EXPERIENCE	ROUTE	FREQUENCY	COST
Riley Creek Loop	Like taking a bus downtown	Among buildings at park entrance	Continuous	Free
Savage River Shuttle	An easy way to see the wooded areas near the park entrance; good chance of moose	First 14 miles of park road	Hourly in summer	Free
Natural History Tour	Much like the Savage River Shuttle, but with a narrator and a more comfortable bus	First 17 miles of park road	Twice a day	$76.50 adults; $33.25 under 14
Tundra Wilderness Tour	From the park entrance to the Toklat River, from a heavily forested area to tundra, and the chance of mountain views. Fully narrated.	First 53 miles of park road to the Toklat River rest area	Twice a day	$123.25 adults; $56.75 under 14
Kantishna Experience	The grand tour of Denali: from forest to tundra beyond Wonder Lake. Best views of the mountain. Fully narrated.	To the end of the park road	Daily	$169 adults; $79.50 under 14
The Shuttle Bus	The park's own bus: get on and off wherever you want, stay on as long as you feel like paying for. No formal narration, but most of the drivers like to talk and know the park well. This is the most flexible option.	To the end of the park road	Depends on how far out the particular bus goes: every half hour as far as Eielson, every hour to Wonder Lake, four times a day to Kantishna	Round-trip: $26.75 to Toklat, $34 to Eielson, $46 to Wonder Lake, $50 to Kantishna; kids half price
Camper Bus	Transport to all campgrounds inside the park. Like the shuttle bus, no formal narration, but the drivers like to talk and know their stuff.	To Wonder Lake, with stops at all campgrounds along the way	Several times a day	$34; $17 under 18

the Toklat River at Mile 53; $34.00 to Eielson Visitor Center at Mile 66; and $46.00 to Wonder Lake at Mile 85. They also run a shuttle to Kantishna, for $50.00; the trip takes about 13 hours. Kids 14 and under ride free on the shuttles; 15- to 17-year-olds pay ½ adult fare on all shuttle buses. Obviously, the farther out you're going, the earlier in the day you'll need to be starting; the last bus for Wonder Lake leaves at 10:15 am; the last one for Toklat, at 5 pm. Check with the park for the current schedule.

If you decide to get off the shuttle bus and explore the tundra, just tell the driver ahead of time where you'd like to get out. Some areas are closed to hiking, so check with the rangers at the visitor center before you decide where to go. Some areas are closed permanently, such as Sable Pass, which is heavily traveled by bears; others close as conditions warrant, such as when there's been a wolf kill nearby.

When it's time to catch a ride back, just stand next to the road and wait; it's seldom more than 30 minutes or so between buses. The drivers stop if there is room on board. However, during the mid- and late-summer peak season, an hour or more may pass between stopping buses, as they are more likely to be full. Be prepared to split up if you are in a big group in order to fit on crowded buses during peak times. ☎ 800/622–7275, 907/272–7275 ⊕ www.reservedenali.com.

Camper buses. These buses serve permitted backpackers and those staying in campgrounds along the road. Seats in the back of the bus are removed for gear storage and there is no formal narration, although the bus drivers aren't likely to let you miss anything important. The $34.00 pass includes transportation anywhere down the road as far as Wonder Lake for the length of the backpacker's stay. Tell the driver ahead of time where you'd like to get out. ☎ 800/622–7275, 907/272–7275 ⊕ www.reservedenali.com.

VISITOR INFORMATION
PARK CONTACT INFORMATION
Denali National Park Headquarters ☎ 907/683–2294 *information,* 907/272–7275, 800/622–7275 *reservations* ⊕ www.reservedenali.com ⊘ All but Riley Creek (no visitor facilities) closed mid-Sept.–late May.

VISITOR CENTERS
Denali Visitor Center. Open from mid-May to mid-September, the Denali Visitor Center exhibits beautiful displays about the park's natural and cultural history, and holds regular showings of *Heartbeats of Denali* in the Karstens Theater. In addition, the center offers a wide variety of interpretive programs and a chance to browse the nearby Denali

DENALI'S DINOSAURS

On June 27, 2005, a geologist discovered the track of a theropod, or a three-toed carnivorous dinosaur, in 65- to 70-million-year-old Cretaceous sedimentary rock, just 35 miles west of the park entrance. This is the first hard evidence of dinosaurs in the Interior of Alaska. While the initial discoveries were made by geologists, subsequent finds were uncovered by participants in a teacher workshop with the Murie Science and Learning Center.

Bookstore, a great source for wildlife guides, birding guides, and picture books; send some to relatives to make them jealous of your trip. While the park itself is open year-round with limited vehicle access, everything is up and running from mid-May through mid-September. ☎ *907/683–2294* ⊕ *www.nps.gov/dena.*

Eielson Visitor Center. At Mile 66 on the Park Road is the Eielson Visitor Center, the park's pride and joy. LEED certified as a green building, Eielson offers amazing views of the mountain, the glaciers, and what happens to a landscape when glaciers go away. Inside is the usual interpretive material. Starting around the beginning of June, the center offers a daily guided walk at 1 pm, an easy 45-minute exploration of the landscape. Another hike each day takes on a little rougher terrain. Guided hikes vary from day to day to minimize the impact on the surroundings. Guided snowshoe walks are also offered January–March on Saturday and Sunday, weather permitting. ⊠ *Mile 66 on Park Rd.* ⊕ *www.nps.gov/dena/planyourvisit/the-eielson-visitor-center.htm* ⊙ *June–mid-Sept. 9-7.*

Murie Science and Learning Center. Next to the Denali Visitor Center, Murie Science and Learning Center is the foundation of the park's science-based education programs, and also serves as the winter visitor center when the Denali Visitor Center is closed. This center has basic but good displays, and is a good option when the main visitor center is closed. ⊠ *Mile 1.5, Park Rd.* ☎ *907/683–1269* ⊕ *www.muriesllc.org.*

Wilderness Access Center. The Wilderness Access Center near the park's entrance at Mile 237.3, George Parks Highway, is where you can handle reservations for roadside camping and bus trips into the park. A smaller building nearby is the **Backcountry Information Center,** for those visitors who want to travel and stay overnight in the wilderness. The Backcountry Information Center has backcountry permits and hiking information, including current data on animal sightings (remember the whole park is bear territory), river-crossing conditions, weather, and closed areas. The center is closed in winter (mid-September through mid-May). ■ TIP➔ Free permits are required for overnight backpacking trips, but you won't need one for day hiking. ⊠ *Mile 1, Park Rd.* ☎ *907/683–9274.*

EXPLORING

It's important to reserve tickets for buses ahead of time; call the numbers provided here or log on to ⊕ *www.reservedenali.com.*

With a landmass larger than Massachusetts, Denali National Park and Preserve has too much area for even the most dedicated vacationer to explore in one go. When planning your trip, consider whether you want to strike out on your own as a backcountry traveler or to stay at a lodge nearby and enjoy Denali as a day hiker with the help of a tour or shuttle bus. Either option requires some advance planning, for bus tickets or backcountry permits. But either option also offers a magnificent experience.

PLANTS AND WILDLIFE IN DENALI

Thirty-seven species of mammals reside in the park, from wolves and bears to little brown bats and pygmy shrews that weigh a fraction of an ounce. The park also has a surprisingly large avian population in summer, with 167 identified species. Most of the birds migrate in fall, leaving only two dozen year-round resident species, including ravens, boreal chickadees, and hawk owls. Some of the summer birds travel thousands of miles to nest and breed in subarctic valleys, hills, and ponds. The northern wheatear migrates from southern Asia, warblers arrive from Central and South America, and the arctic tern annually travels 24,000 miles while commuting between the Arctic and Antarctica.

The most sought-after species among visitors are the large mammals: grizzlies, wolves, Dall sheep, moose, and caribou. All inhabit the forest or tundra landscape that surrounds Denali Park Road. You can expect to see Dall sheep finding their way across high meadows, grizzlies and caribou frequenting stream bottoms and tundra, moose in the forested areas both near the park entrance and deep in the park, and the occasional wolf or fox that may dart across the road.

Vegetation in the park consists largely of taiga and tundra. Taiga is coniferous forest in moist areas below a tree line of 2,700 feet and consists mainly of white and black spruce trees. Due to the layer of permafrost that lies just under the surface of the land, the trees have shallow root systems. This means they are very susceptible to wind and weather conditions, and it's not at all unusual to see entire sections of forest, usually black spruce, leaning to one side, or leaning every which way like a bunch of jackstraws. Called a "drunken forest," the lean comes from trees trying to make their home in permafrost that thaws, freezes, and thaws again, shifting the soil right under the roots. Ground cover in the taiga forest includes dwarf birch, blueberry, and willow shrubs.

The rest of the landmass not covered by ice and snow is carpeted by tundra, consisting of a variety of delicate plants such as lichens, berries, bright wildflowers, and woody plants. This complex carpet of low-lying vegetation generates brilliant color, especially in August, when the fall weather begins. Take a really close look at tundra: it's like being a giant and looking down on a forest, it's all so perfect and detailed and tiny. A single square foot of tundra can hold 40 or 50 different species. The park as a whole contains more than 650 species of flowering plant, plus who knows how many mosses, fungi, and lichen. While you're busy watching for moose and bears, don't forget to check out the plants.

OUTDOOR ACTIVITIES AND GUIDED TOURS

MULTISPORT OUTFITTERS

Fodor's Choice
★

Denali Outdoor Center. One of the oldest operators in Glitter Gulch (the area right in front of the park entrance), Denali Outdoor Center can take you rafting in Class IV rapids, kayaking, put you on a mountain bike, and then get you a cabin so you can sack out and recover from your day. Prices for white-water rafting start at $87; bike rentals cost $25 for six hours, tours cost $50. Lakefront cabins on Otto Lake run $92 per night, or just stay at the campground for $8. ✉ *Mile 0.5, Otto Lake Rd., off Mile 247 Parks Hwy., Healy* ☎ *907/683–1925, 888/303–1925* ⊕ *www.denalioutdoorcenter.com.*

Denali Park Resorts. This outfitter provides one-stop shopping for lodging, activities, and more. It can set you up with pretty much any trip in the Denali region, from rafting to fly-fishing. For $100, a guide can take you on a mellow wilderness raft trip 13 miles down the Nenana—or on a river trip that hits Class III and IV rapids. Or choose from a variety of guided hikes, with one suitable for just about any level of fitness. Take an easy guided bike ride for $30, or rent a bike and hit the trails yourself. It also runs both the McKinley Chalet Resort and the McKinley Village Lodge, with more than 500 rooms in all. The lodge and resort frequently fill up with tour groups so it's best to plan ahead if you want to stay here. ✉ *Mile 238.5 Parks Hwy., at the entrance to Denali National Park* ☎ *907/276–7234, 800/276–7234* ⊕ *www. denaliparkresorts.com.*

FLIGHTSEEING

A flightseeing tour of the park is one of the best ways to get a sense of the Alaska Range's size and scope. Flightseeing is also the best way to get close-up views of Mt. McKinley and its neighboring giants, and maybe even stand on a glacier, all without the hassle of days of hiking and lugging food and gear.

Most Denali flightseeing is done out of Talkeetna, a small end-of-the-road town between Anchorage and Denali, and the operators will offer several tours, including a quick fly-by, a summit tour, a glacier landing—something for everybody. We suggest you take the longest, most detailed tour you can afford, so you don't go back home wishing you'd had a chance to see more. (⇨ *See "The High One" in this chapter for more information.)*

HIKING

You can have one of North America's premier hiking and wilderness experiences in Denali with the proper planning: know your goals; consult park staff before setting out to learn Leave No Trace and bear etiquette; carry proper clothing, food, and water; and don't try to cover too much ground in too short a time.

Most of Denali is trail-less wilderness, so you have to make your own way across the landscape. Distances in the wide-open tundra can be

MOOSE AND BEAR SAFETY

Enjoy moose from a distance! Weighing 1,000 pounds or more, they can get pretty mean despite their harmless appearance; in fact, every year moose injure more people than any other large wild animal on the planet aside from hippos. Never get between a moose and its calf. If you encounter a moose at close range acting aggressively, leave the area immediately and quickly. If it decides to charge, either stand behind a tree or stand still with your arms raised but not waving and fingers spread to convince the moose that you are the bigger animal. Remember: moose can kick with either their front *or* back hooves. Tactics are a bit more clear-cut for one of Denali's other major megafauna: never run from a bear—food runs, so you may trigger its predatory chase instincts and encourage the bear to respond to you as prey. This is a bad thing. Keep in mind that a surprised bear is an unhappy bear, so make some noise as you hike to let them know you're coming. If you see a bear, back up slowly in the direction you came from, and wait for the animal to move on. Do not even think of getting anywhere near a bear cub as its mother is surely somewhere nearby and she will not be amused by your interest in her baby. If a bear makes a move towards you, stand next to your hiking partners and hold your jackets open, so you look as large as possible. Talk in a low, calm voice. The bear standing up is not a threat maneuver; that's just him trying to get a better look at you; threat is turning sideways to show you just how big he really is. But truly, the bear has pretty much no interest in messing with you: you're just something distracting them from their daily business of survival, so a little caution and a large dose of common sense should assure you a safe trip in the park. A don't-miss summary of bear-safety tips is available at the Denali Visitor Center. ⇨ *For more information, see "Welcome to Bear Country" in Chapter 9.*

deceiving; what looks like a 2-mile walk may in fact be 6 miles or more. Main lesson: be conservative in route planning. Also deceiving is the tundra; though it looks like a smooth carpet from a distance, it may have bogs and thickets of willow, and the tussocks can drive you insane as you try to avoid twisting your ankles into pretzels. You won't walk through the park at the speed you're used to hiking most places in the Lower 48. Besides the distractions of drop-dead gorgeous landscape, the territory is simply rougher and more varied here than most places down south. Plus it's a good idea to plan for animal delays here. Remember, moose, bear, caribou—pretty much anything with fur—have the right of way.

A big draw for more experienced hikers and backpackers are the foothills and ridges accessible from the park road. As long as you don't go deep into the Alaska Range, it's possible to reach some summits and high ridges without technical climbing expertise. Stamina and physical fitness are required, though. Once up high, hikers find easy walking and sweeping views of braided rivers, tundra benches and foothills, and ice-capped mountains.

NATURE TRAILS AND SHORT WALKS

The park offers plenty of options for those who prefer to stay on marked and groomed pathways. The entrance area has more than a half-dozen forest and tundra trails. These range from easy to challenging, so there's something suitable for all ages and hiking abilities. Some, like the **Taiga Loop Trail** and **McKinley Station Loop Trail**, are less than 1½ miles; others, like the **Rock Creek Trail** and **Triple Lakes Trail**, are several miles round-trip, with an altitude gain of hundreds of feet. Along these paths you may see beavers working on their lodges in Horseshoe Lake; red squirrels chattering in trees; red foxes hunting for rodents; sheep grazing on tundra; golden eagles gliding over alpine ridges; and moose feeding on willow.

The **Savage River Trail,** farthest from the park entrance and as far as private vehicles are allowed, offers a 1¾-mile round-trip hike along a raging river and under rocky cliffs. Be on the lookout for caribou, Dall sheep, foxes, and marmots.

The only relatively long, marked trail for hiking in the park, **Mt. Healy Overlook Trail,** is accessible from the entrance area; it gains 1,700 feet in 2.5 miles and takes about four hours round-trip, with outstanding views of the Nenana River below and the Alaska Range, including the upper slopes of Mt. McKinley.

GUIDED HIKES

In addition to exploring the park on your own, you can take free ranger-guided discovery hikes and learn more about the park's natural and human history. Rangers lead daily hikes throughout summer. Inquire at the visitor center. You can also tour with privately operated outfitters like Denali Park Resorts.

Denali Park Resorts. Privately operated, three- to four-hour, 4-mile-round-trip guided hikes are available through Denali Park Resorts. ⊠ *Mile 238.5, Parks Hwy., at the entrance to Denali National Park* ☎ *907/276–7234, 800/276–7234* ⊕ *www.denaliparkresorts.com.*

KAYAKING AND RAFTING

Several privately owned raft and tour companies operate along the Parks Highway near the entrance to Denali, and they schedule daily rafting, both in the fairly placid areas on the Nenana and through the 10-mile-long Nenana River canyon, which has stretches of Class IV–V rapids—enough to make you think you're on a very wet roller coaster. The Nenana is Alaska's most accessible white water, and if you don't mind getting a little chilly, a river trip is not just a lot of fun, it's a fantastic way to see a different side of the landscape.

TOURS AND OUTFITTERS

Alaska Raft Adventures. Book 1½- to 2-hour-long white-water and scenic raft trips along Nenana River through Denali Park Resorts *(⇨ Multisport Outfitters)* with Alaska Raft Adventures. White-water trips give you two options: do the work and paddle yourself (though it's not a lot of work as there's a good current); or sit back and let the guide do the work. ⊠ *Denali Park Resorts, Mile 238.5 Parks Hwy.* ☎ *800/276–7234* ⊕ *www.deffaliraft.com.*

★ **Denali Outdoor Center.** This tour operator has a respected reputation among locals for its scenic rafting trips on the Nenana River and splash-filled trips down the Nenana River canyon's rapids where no river experience is necessary. One of the most challenging trips is a two-hour paddle in inflatable kayaks, called Duckies. They are easy to get out of, stable, and self-bailing, but if you're not used to paddling yourself, you're going to have sore arms. The company also teaches white-water kayaking. All gear is provided, including full dry suits, something you'll appreciate in the splash. Budget travelers can rent canoes or kayaks on Otto Lake for $8 an hour. Camping sites ($8 by the lake), rental cabins ($92) with Wi-Fi in the laundry-shower room, and mountain-bike tours and rentals are also available. Plus, there's a free local shuttle from hotels, lodges, the Alaska Railroad depot, the Denali visitor center, and Otto Lake. There are two locations, the Healy office on Otto Lake Road and the Canyon office on Parks Highway. ⊠ *Mile 0.5 Otto Lake Rd. for main office, Mile 238.9, Parks Hwy.* ☎ *907/683–1925, 888/303–1925* ⊕ *www.denalioutdoorcenter.com.*

Denali Raft Adventures. This outfitter launches its rafts several times daily on two- and four-hour scenic and white-water trips on the Nenana River. Gore-Tex dry suits are provided. Guests under the age of 18 must have a release waiver signed by a parent or guardian. Contact the company for copies before the trip. Courtesy pick-up at hotels and the train depot is available witin a seven-mile radius of their location. ⊠ *Mile 238.6, Parks Hwy.* ☎ *907/683–2234, 888/683–2234* ⊕ *www.denaliraft.com.*

MOUNTAIN BIKING

Mountain biking is allowed on the park's dirt road, and no permit is required for day trips. The first 15 miles of the road are paved. Beyond the Savage River checkpoint the road is dirt and gravel, and during the day the road is busy with the park buses, which can leave bikers choking on dust. The road can get really sloppy in the rain, too. The best time to bike is late evening, when the midnight sun is shining and buses have stopped shuttling passengers for the day. When biking on the road, you need to be aware of your surroundings and observe park rules if you decide to leave the road. Off-road riding is forbidden, and some sensitive wildlife areas are closed to hiking. The Sable Pass area is always closed to off-road excursions on foot because of the high bear population, and other sites are posted due to denning activity or recent signs of carcass scavenging. Check current conditions at the visitor center before heading out. **Denali Outdoor Center** *(⇨ Multisport Outfitters)* rents mountain bikes by the hour, half day, or full day. They also conduct guided 2- to 2½-hour tours on trails near the Otto Lake center, which come complete with bike, helmet, water bottle, and shuttle service.

MOUNTAINEERING

Alaska Mountaineering School. This outfitter leads backpacking trips in wilderness areas near Talkeetna and elsewhere in the state, including the Brooks Range, and glacier treks that can include overnighting on the ice. It also conducts mountaineering courses that run from 6 to 12 days, expeditions to Mt. McKinley (figure on at least three weeks; prices from $6,000) and other peaks in the Alaska Range, and climbs for all levels of expertise. A novice course, which should be enough to get you comfortable in the mountains, will run a bit over $2,000. While you're in Talkeetna, check out its mountain and gear shop on F Street. ⊠ *13765 3rd St., Talkeetna* ☎ *907/733–1016* ⊕ *www.climbalaska.org.*

Mountain Trip. This operator has been guiding climbing expeditions on Mt. McKinley and other Alaska Range peaks since 1973, making it the most senior of the guide companies to operate on the High One. Though the company emphasizes climber safety, most McKinley expeditions reach the summit. Novice to experienced trip levels are offered, and this is the place to call if you're really serious about doing the mountains. Their trips include a Northwest Buttress trip on Denali, which is very rarely attempted, as well as trips around the world. First-class operation, safety first. ☎ *866/886–8747, 970/369–1153* ⊕ *www.mountaintrip.com.*

WINTER SPORTS

Snowshoers and skiers generally arrive with their own gear and park or camp at the Riley Creek Campground at the park entrance. Dog mushing can also be done with your own team, or you can contact one of the park concessionaires that run day or multiday trips.

TOURS AND OUTFITTERS

Denali Dog Sled Adventures. This operation offers one- to four-hour trips, including an "Into the Wild" trip with sites from Jon Krakauer's book; they also run up to 10-day excursions. Rooms at the EarthSong Lodge—cabins with nice views—start at $155. ⊠ *Mile 4, Stampede Rd., Healy* ☎ *907/683–2863* ⊕ *www.earthsonglodge.com.*

Denali West Lodge. Run by Tonya Schlentner, a 1,000-mile Yukon Quest finisher (the Quest is considered a much tougher race than the Iditarod), this fly-in lodge, fueled by alternative energy, offers multiday dog-mushing expeditions from the end of February to March. The lodge is located near the western boundary of Denali National Park, on the shores of Lake Minchumina. ☎ *907/674–3112* ⊕ *www.denaliwest.com.*

THE STAMPEDE TRAIL

One of Healy's greatest attractions is the **Stampede Trail**, perhaps most famous to today's traveler for being where Christopher McCandless of *Into the Wild* fame met his end (and where people who seem to want to replicate it have caused endless problems for Healy's rescue services). On the Stampede Trail you can enter Denali by snowmobile, dogsled, cross-country skis, or mountain bike.

This wide, well-traveled path leads all the way to Kantishna, 90 miles inside the park. To get here, take the George Parks Highway 2 miles north of Healy to Mile 251.1, where Stampede Road intersects the highway. Eight miles west on Stampede Road is a parking lot and the start of the trail.

WHERE TO EAT

IN THE PARK

$
CAFÉ
✕ **Canyon Market & Café.** The "only grocery store in Denali" (there's a general store as well, with some groceries) sells fresh fruit, box lunches, and espresso. It has a deli counter, free Wi-Fi, and indoor and outdoor seating. Inside is also Sled Dog Liquor. ⑤ *Average main: $11* ⊠ *Mile 238.4, Parks Hwy.* ☎ 907/683–7467 ⊕ *www.canyonmarketcafe.com* ⊙ *Open limited hrs in Apr., daily May through Sept.*

$
AMERICAN
✕ **The Great Alaska Fish & Chip Company.** Stop in for fried halibut, cod, great salad bar, and beer on tap. Or go for the corn fritters, calamari, or ⅓-lb., hand-pressed burger with some sweet-potato fries. Recently expanded, it all got so popular. ⑤ *Average main: $13* ⊠ *Mile 238, Parks Hwy.* ☎ 907/683–3474 ⊕ *www.alaskafishandchip.com* ⊙ *Mid-May–mid-Sept.*

$$
AMERICAN
✕ **McKinley Creekside Cafe.** This restaurant serves breakfast, lunch, and dinner. Skip right to dessert for one of the famous bakery goods such as "monster" cinnamon rolls and strawberry-rhubarb coffee cake, which are made fresh daily on-site. Or for something more substantial, try the "homestyle goodness" specialties, like the meatloaf, chicken potpie, half-pound hand-formed hamburgers, fish-and-chips, or signature baked halibut. For a hearty, prehike breakfast, try the meat loaf and egg. ■ **TIP→** At the beginning of each season the café hosts a chili cook-off party for the community with live bluegrass music and $2.50 beers. ⑤ *Average main: $18* ⊠ *Mile 238.5, Parks Hwy.* ☎ 907/683–2277 ⊕ *www.mckinleycabins.com* ⊙ *Mid-May–mid-Sept.*

$$
AMERICAN
✕ **Prospector's Historic Pizzeria and Ale House.** Built to have an old-time saloon feel, this restaurant serves handcrafted pizza, salad, soup, pastas, grinder sandwiches, and 49 beers on tap. There's a $10 light-lunch special. This family-owned restaurant makes for a nice refueling stop; the family also runs the Perch and the Perch Resort. ⑤ *Average main: $20* ⊠ *Mile 238.9, Parks Hwy.* ☎ 907/683–7437 ⊕ *www.prospectorspizza.com* ⊙ *Closed Oct.–Apr.*

OUTSIDE THE PARK

ALONG THE GEORGE PARKS HIGHWAY

$$
AMERICAN
Fodor's Choice
★

✕ **229 Parks Restaurant and Tavern.** Even if this hot spot didn't serve amazing food, the graceful timber-frame design, inviting atmosphere, and elaborate elm etchings would be enough to draw in crowds. But chef and owner Laura Cole directs a scratch kitchen that serves local produce; grass-fed, free-range meat; homemade ice cream and breads; and delectable imports. With its own vegetable gardens and sourcing from small, nearby producers, this is as organic and local as you can get without doing the hunting and gathering yourself. Menus change daily, according to availability. From handmade pappardelle pasta with reindeer sausage and leeks to wild-caught Alaskan weather-vane scallops with crisped prosciutto, Laura knows how to make food come to life. The restaurant takes reservations and may be the only place in Denali that can book up entirely, so plan ahead. $ *Average main:* $15 ✉ *Mile 229.7, Parks Hwy.* ☎ *907/683–2567* ⊕ *www.229parks. com* ⚑ *Reservations essential* ☾ *No lunch; May–Oct. 1 closed Mon.; mid-Sept.–mid-May closed weekdays.*

$
AMERICAN

✕ **The Denali Doghouse.** It's all about the dog at this casual, dog-decorated and hotdog-theme joint. The local owners put love back into the fast-food burger and hotdog fare. All quarter-pound burger patties are hand pressed, fries and onion rings fresh and hand cut. Specialties include bacon, cheese, kraut, slaw, and chili-cheese hot dogs. The Doghouse is a good choice for a quick but filling lunch or dinner in the Glitter Gulch area. $ *Average main: $7* ✉ *Mile 238.6, Parks Hwy., Boardwalk* ☎ *907/683–3647* ⊕ *www.denalidoghouse.com* ☾ *Closed mid-Sept.–mid-May.*

$$
SEAFOOD

✕ **McKinley/Denali Salmon Bake.** Fresh Alaska salmon and seafood bought directly from fishermen top the menu at this rustic spot. It also serves steaks, burgers, and chicken, as well as other breakfast, lunch, and dinner specialties. It's a hot spot with live music and Monday-night poker. Twenty-four-hour shuttle service is provided to area hotels, the park entrance, and Healy, and 12 cabins (8 tent cabins) with shared bath are for rent starting at $74. $ *Average main: $18* ✉ *Mile 238.5, Parks Hwy.* ☎ *907/683–2733* ⊕ *www.denaliparksalmonbake.com* ☾ *Closed late Sept.–early May.*

$$
PIZZA

✕ **Panorama Pizza Pub.** This friendly eatery serves hand-tossed brick-oven pizzas, along with soups and sandwiches for dinner, and fine Alaskan microbrews. There's live music Wednesday through Saturday nights, 5 pm–midnight. Cabin rentals, with creek-side and mountain views, are available May–September (starting at $85, with breakfast included), as is complimentary shuttle service for overnighters. There's also free Wi-Fi. $ *Average main: $16* ✉ *Mile 224, Parks Hwy.* ☎ *907/683–2623* ⊕ *www.panoramapizzapub.com.*

$$$$
AMERICAN

✕ **The Perch.** The bay windows of this fine-dining restaurant, 13 miles south of the park entrance atop a forested hillside, offer a panoramic view of the surrounding Alaska Range foothills. The Perch serves breakfast and dinner, featuring home-baked breads and desserts along with steak and seafood; don't miss the all-you-can-eat wild Alaska salmon dinner. $ *Average main: $30* ✉ *Mile 224, Parks Hwy.* ☎ *888/322–2523*

7

⊕ www.denaliperchresort.com
☽ Closed mid-Sept.–mid-Apr.

HEALY

$$$
AMERICAN

✕ **Black Diamond Grill.** For a casual and family-oriented atmosphere, dine with a view at this off-the-beaten-path local hangout. The menu features hand-pressed burgers, New York steaks, crab cakes, penne pasta, salads with local and organic greens, and homemade foods, plus fresh baked goodies. To make a day of it, try the ATV tours, horse-drawn carriage rides that end with a barbecue meal at a scenic pavilion, a game of golf (9-hole or mini varieties available), or the fishing at nearby Otto Lake. ⑤ *Average main: $25* ✉ *Mile 1, Otto Lake Rd., off Mile 247, Parks Hwy.* ☎ *907/683–4653* *⊕ www.blackdiamondtourco.com* *☽ Closed mid-Sept.–mid-May.*

$$
AMERICAN

✕ **Totem Inn.** Travelers from the George Parks Highway, Healy, and Denali come here not so much for the lodging (which is modest at best) as for standard American food at reasonable prices. Steaks, sandwiches, and homemade pizzas are served year-round, while breakfast is served all day. An attached pub and game room allow for swapping stories with the locals, and the free Wi-Fi and Kinect games will help you catch up with the world, or ignore it. Take advantage of the fitness center if you're not getting enough exercise on Denali's trails or a sauna if you are. And, of course, this is the only place around where you can try to ride "The Griz"—a mechanical bull shaped like a grizzly bear. The kitchen is open daily, year-round, 7 am–10 pm. ⑤ *Average main: $20* ✉ *Mile 248.7, Parks Hwy.* ☎ *907/683–6500* *⊕ www.thetoteminn.com.*

RUTH GLACIER

Even the shortest flightseeing trips usually include a passage through the Great Gorge of the **Ruth Glacier**, one of the major glaciers flowing off Denali's south side. Bordered by gray granite walls and gigantic spires, this spectacular chasm is North America's deepest gorge. Leaving the area, flightseers enter the immense, mountain-encircled glacial basins of Ruth Glacier's Don Sheldon Amphitheater. Among the enclosing peaks are some of the range's most rugged and descriptively named peaks, including Moose's Tooth and Rooster Comb. Truly, it's one of the most beautiful places on the planet.

WHERE TO STAY

For expanded hotel reviews, visit Fodors.com.

IN THE PARK

If you can afford the price tag, it's worth it to book your stay at a wilderness lodge within Denali, like Camp Denali and North Face Lodge or the Kantishna Roadhouse.

Alaskans call Mt. McKinley by its original name, Denali, which means "the High One."

$$$$
RESORT
ALL-INCLUSIVE
Fodor's Choice
★

🔲 **Camp Denali and North Face Lodge.** The legendary, family-owned-and-operated Camp Denali and North Face Lodge both offer stunning views of Mt. McKinley and active learning experiences deep within Denali National Park, at Mile 89 on the park road, past where most of the park buses stop at Wonder Lake. **Pros:** only in-park lodge with a view of Denali; access to canoes; strong emphasis on learning; attention to detail; dedicated staff. **Cons:** credit cards not accepted; rates start at $1,545 per person; alcohol is BYOB; not advisable for families with children under eight; Camp Denali cabins lack private baths (but you can't beat the view from the outhouse). **TripAdvisor:** "incredible view," "pretty good food," "best way to experience Denali." ⑤ *Rooms from: $1545* ✉ *Mile 89, Denali Park Rd.* ☎ *907/683–2290* ⊕ *www.campdenali.com* ⚲ *18 cabins (Camp Denali) with shared shower, 15 rooms (North Face Lodge)* ▬ *No credit cards* ☉ *Closed mid-Sept.–early June* ⊙| *All-inclusive.*

$$$$
RESORT
ALL-INCLUSIVE

🔲 **Kantishna Roadhouse.** Run by the Athabascan Doyon Tourism, this establishment at Mile 95 on the Park Road offers an enriching wilderness getaway. **Pros:** guided hikes with naturalists; all rooms have private baths; home to the only saloon in the Denali backcountry; transport from the train station is provided. **Cons:** no connection to the outside world besides a phone booth; lacks a direct view of Denali. **TripAdvisor:** "peace and quiet in beautiful surroundings," "super hospitality," "wonderful remote location." ⑤ *Rooms from: $450* ✉ *Mile 95, Denali Park Rd.* ☎ *800/942–7420* ⊕ *www.kantishnaroadhouse.com* ⚲ *32 rooms* ☉ *Closed mid-Sept.–early June* ⊙| *All-inclusive.*

$$
HOTEL

🔲 **McKinley Creekside Cabins & Creekside Café.** This nice spot sits on 10 acres along Carlo Creek. **Pros:** great location by the water. **Cons:** no

CLOSE UP

Tent and RV Camping in Denali

If you want to camp in the park, either in a tent or an RV, there are five campgrounds, with varying levels of access and facilities. Two of the campgrounds—Riley Creek (near the park entrance, essentially no scenery at all) and Savage River (Mile 13; on a very clear day, you might be able to see the mountain from here, but not much of it)—have spaces that accommodate tents, RVs, and campers. Visitors with private vehicles can also drive to the Teklanika campsite (Mile 29; check for rules about minimum stays, which help keep traffic down), but they must first obtain park-road travel permits; in recent years no tent camping has been allowed at Teklanika, but visitors should check with park staff for updates. Morino Backpacker Campground (Mile 1.9, about the same as Riley Creek, but tents only), Sanctuary River (Mile 22, the smallest campground in the park, ideal if you want to be alone but can't backpack), Igloo Creek (Mile 43, comparable to Sanctuary River), and Wonder Lake (Mile 85, the cream of the crop in Denali camping—best views of the mountain and

great easy hikes) have tent spaces only. The camper buses offer the only access to these sites.

Visitors to the Sanctuary and Igloo Creek campsites should come prepared: both campgrounds lack treated drinking water. All campgrounds have vault toilets and food lockers. Individual sites are beyond sight of the park road, though within easy walking distance.

Fees for individual sites range from $16 to $28 per night. Campsites can be reserved in advance several ways: online, through the Denali National Park website (⊕ www.reservedenali. com); by faxing a reservation form (form available at ⊕ www.nps.gov/ dena ☎ 907/264–4684); by calling the reservation service (☎ 800/622–7275 or 907/272–7275); or by email to ✉ reservedenali@aramark.com. Reservations can also be made in person at the park. It's best to visit Denali's website before making reservations, both to see the reservation form and to learn whether any changes in the reservation system have been made.

TV may lead to withdrawal symptoms in some. **TripAdvisor:** "awesome family place," "great cabin experience," "nice place to chill between Denali adventures." ⑤ *Rooms from: $169* ✉ *Mile 238.5, Parks Hwy.* ☎ *888/533–6254* ⊕ *www.mckinleycabins.com* ⤵ *32 cabins* ⊗ *Mid-May–mid-Sept.*

$ ⌂ **Mountain House.** For the true Denali wilderness experience, book an
B&B/INN   overnight here. **Pros:** the single best view from a bed anywhere near
Denali National Park. **Cons:** the final hike up, carrying your food and gear. ⑤ *Rooms from: $135* ☎ *907/733–1016* ⊕ *www.climbalaska. org/mountain-house.html* ⤵ *1 house* ⊗ *Closed mid-July–mid-March.* ⑪ *No meals.*

OUTSIDE THE PARK

ALONG THE GEORGE PARKS HIGHWAY

Hotels, motels, RV parks, camp-grounds, and some restaurants are clustered along the highway near the park entrance, which is at Mile 237.3. You can judge distance from the park by mileage markers; numbers increase northward and decrease southward.

$$$$
RESORT

📺 **Denali Princess Wilderness Lodge.** This humongous lodge lies along the Parks Highway in the Glitter Gulch community a mile north of the park entrance. **Pros:** most gran-diose lodge in Denali; gym and gift shop on-site. **Cons:** with more than 600 rooms, too big to feel intimate; killer views from the right parts of the lodge, though. **TripAdvisor:** "good accommodation," "great food," "beautiful location." ⑤ *Rooms from: $299* ✉ *Mile 238.5, Parks Hwy., 1 mile north of park entrance* ☎ *907/683–2282, 800/426–0500 reser-vations* ⊕ *www.princesslodges.com* ⤳ *656 rooms* ☾ *Closed mid-Sept.– mid-May* ⦿ *No meals.*

$$
HOTEL

📺 **Denali River Cabins and Cedars Lodge.** The cabins, clustered along the glacially fed Nenana River, are next to McKinley Village Lodge, 7 miles south of the park entrance. **Pros:** river views and Finnish sauna; pro-pane grills available. **Cons:** cabins crowded together; property situated near other resorts. **TripAdvisor:** "cabins are nice," "rustic," "perfect people." ⑤ *Rooms from: $159* ✉ *Mile 231.1, Parks Hwy.* ☎ *800/230–7275, 907/374–3041 year-round, 907/683–8000 June 1–Sept. 15* ⊕ *www.seedenali.com* ⤳ *48 rooms, 54 cabins* ☾ *Closed mid-Sept.–late May* ⦿ *Breakfast.*

HEALY

$$$
B&B/INN

📺 **Denali Dome Home.** A 7,200-square-foot modified geodesic dome houses this year-round B&B. **Pros:** thoughtful and knowledgeable owners; unique architecture; attention to detail; DVD and VCR collection. **Cons:** anyone with dog allergies should beware of two Scottish terriers; anyone squeamish about animal hides should be warned that the house is decorated with a few prize trophies. **TripAd-visor:** "wonderful lodging," "very comfortable," "Alaskan hospital-ity at its best." ⑤ *Rooms from: $175* ✉ *137 Healy Spur Rd., Healy* ☎ *907/683–1239, 800/683–1239* ⊕ *www.denalidomehome.com* ⤳ *7 rooms* ⦿ *Breakfast.*

$$
B&B/INN
★

📺 **EarthSong Lodge.** Above the tree line at the edge of Denali National Park, EarthSong has views of open tundra backed by peaks of the Alaska Range. **Pros:** each cabin has unique character, as well as hypo-allergenic bedding in a totally smoke-free environment; the owners offer a wealth of knowledge. **Cons:** a 17-mile drive from the park entrance; some people might not like the "shoes off" policy in the cabins, but it really does help keep things cleaner. **TripAdvisor:** "quaint and com-fortable," "a real taste of Alaska," "such a special place." ⑤ *Rooms*

7

from: $155 ✉ *Mile 4, Stampede Rd., Healy* ☎ *907/683–2863* ⊕ *www. earthsonglodge.com* ↵ *12 cabins* ⦶ *No meals.*

$$
HOTEL
▦ **Motel Nord Haven.** Five wooded acres protect this motel from the road, providing a secluded feeling that other accommodations along the George Parks Highway lack. **Pros:** reading and puzzle area with comfy couches; meeting–dining room with large deck and fireplace; one of the least expensive options in the area. **Cons:** lacks character; no stovetops in kitchenettes. **TripAdvisor:** "big rooms and wonderful location," "this is why I love Alaska," "comfortable and quiet." ⑤ *Rooms from: $142* ✉ *Mile 249.5, Parks Hwy., Healy* ☎ *907/683–4500, 800/683–4501* ⊕ *www.motelnordhaven.com* ↵ *28 rooms* ⦶ *No meals.*

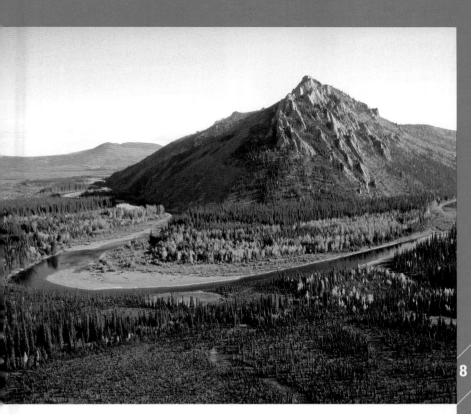

The Interior

WITH FAIRBANKS AND THE YUKON

WORD OF MOUTH

"Riverboat Discovery: I waited 20 years to do it 'cause I thought it was too 'touristy.' But we did it and EVERYONE had a great time. Kids loved it. The Binkley family does a great job."

—zoom907

WELCOME TO THE INTERIOR

TOP REASONS TO GO

★ **Gold-rush heritage:** The frontier spirit of the richest gold rush in Alaska remains alive in Fairbanks. From exploring dredges to panning for gold, chances to participate in the past abound.

★ **Stern-wheeler cruises:** The riverboat *Discovery* is an authentic stern-wheeler that cruises the Chena and Tanana rivers, which served as highways long before there were roads.

★ **The gateway to the Arctic:** Fairbanks is an essential point for connections to northern Alaska—vast land of the midnight sun and the northern lights.

★ **Dog mushing:** The Interior is Alaska's prime mushing spot. Many people live here just so they can spend every free winter moment running sled dogs.

★ **The U of A:** Fairbanks is home to Alaska's main university campus. This means the best museums, endless cultural events, and all the other perks of a college town. Just one that gets to −50°F in the winter.

1 **Fairbanks.** With an area population of about 85,000, Fairbanks is Alaska's northern capital: home to the main campus of the University of Alaska and an important point along the Trans-Alaska oil pipeline. This rough-edged town has a symphony orchestra, Alaska's largest library, and a vibrant local arts scene, including one of the best museums in the state.

2 **North of Fairbanks.** The Alaska wilderness is right at Fairbanks's door, with hundreds of miles of subarctic wilderness to explore. Hiking, canoeing, dog mushing, skiing, hot-spring soaking, and fishing are part of daily life. A few roads and isolated villages are the extent of civilization here.

THE BUSH

Coldfoot

BROOKS

Bettles

Prospect Camp

Kanuti National Wildlife Refuge

Dalton Hwy.

Five-Mile Camp

Rampart

River

Tanana

Yukon

Eureka

Elliott

Tofty

Manley Hot Springs

Tanana River

Denali National Park & Preserve

ALASKA RANGE

3 Fortymile Country and the Yukon. Fortymile Country yielded some of the first gold discoveries in the state, and today mining operations can be seen along the Taylor Highway. Over the border is Dawson City, the Canadian Klondike Gold Rush boomtown. The Yukon offers countless outdoor activities, such as paddling, climbing, backpacking, and cycling, as well as the best music festival you'll find north of the border and west of the Rockies.

GETTING ORIENTED

Interior Alaska is the central part of the state, a vast and broad plateau bordered by the Alaska Range to the south and the Brooks Range to the north. The Yukon River and its many tributaries, including the Tanana River, are dominant features of the landscape. There are few roads, so most of the villages scattered around the Interior are reachable only by aircraft. Fairbanks is the major town in the Interior and serves as the transportation hub for northern and central Alaska, and is the last place to buy supplies before heading into the Bush.

8

Updated
by Edward
Readicker-
Henderson

Alaska's Interior remains the last frontier, even for the Last Frontier state. The northern lights sparkle above a vast, mostly uninhabited landscape that promises adventure for those who choose to traverse it. Come here for wildlife-rich, pristine land and hardy locals, a rich and quirky history, gold panning, nonstop daylight in the summer, or ice-sculpting competitions under the northern lights in winter. Outdoors enthusiasts can enjoy hiking, rafting, fishing, skiing, and dogsledding. And don't forget to top off the experience with a soak in the hot springs.

The geology of the Interior played a key role in human history at the turn of the 20th century. The image of early-1900s Alaska, set to the harsh tunes of countless honky-tonk saloons and the clanging of pans, is rooted around the Interior's goldfields. Gold fever struck in Circle and Eagle in the 1890s, spread into Canada's Yukon Territory in the big Klondike Gold Rush of 1898, headed as far west as the beaches of Nome in 1900, then came back to Alaska's Interior when Fairbanks hit pay dirt in 1903. Through it all, the broad, swift Yukon River was the rush's main highway. Flowing almost 2,300 miles from Canada to the Bering Sea, just below the Arctic Circle, it carried prospectors across the north in search of instant fortune.

Although Fairbanks has grown into a small, bustling city with some serious attractions, many towns and communities in the Interior seem little changed from the gold-rush days. While soaking in the water of the Chena Hot Springs Resort you can almost hear the whispers of gold seekers exaggerating their finds and claims, ever alert for the newest strike. When early missionaries set up schools in the Bush, the Native Alaskan peoples were herded to these regional centers for schooling and "salvation," but that stopped long ago, and today Interior Alaska's Native villages are thriving, with their own schools and a particularly

Alaskan blend of modern life and tradition. Fort Yukon, on the Arctic Circle, is the largest Athabascan village in the state.

Alaska's current gold rush—the pipeline carrying (a little less each year) black gold from the oil fields in Prudhoe Bay south to the port of Valdez—snakes its way through the Interior. The Richardson Highway, which started as a gold stampeders' trail, parallels the Trans-Alaska Pipeline on its route south of Fairbanks. And gold still glitters in the Interior: Fairbanks, the site of the largest gold production in Alaska in pre–World War II days, is home to the Fort Knox Gold Mine, which has approximately doubled Alaska's gold production. Throughout the region, as the price of gold continues to climb to record highs on an almost daily basis, hundreds of tiny mines—from one-man operations to full-scale works—are starting up again, proving that what Robert Service wrote more than a hundred years ago still holds true: "There are strange things done in the midnight sun/by the men who moil for gold."

PLANNING

WHEN TO GO

June and July bring near-constant sun (nothing quite like walking out of a restaurant at 11 pm into broad daylight), sometimes punctuated by afternoon cloudbursts. In winter it gets so cold (–30°F or below) that boiling water flung out a window can land as ice particles.

Like most of Alaska, many of the Interior's main attractions are seasonal, May into mid-September. A trip in May avoids the rush, but it can snow in Fairbanks in spring. Late August brings fall colors, ripe berries, active wildlife, and the start of northern lights season, with marvelous shows, if you hit the right night. Winter-sports fans should come in March, when the sun's back but there's still plenty of snow.

TRAVEL TIMES FROM FAIRBANKS

DESTINATION	TIME
Anchorage	7 hrs by car; 1 hr by air
Barrow	1½ hrs by air
Dawson City	14 hrs by car
Denali	2 hrs by car
Juneau	3¾ hrs by air
Nome	2 hrs by air
Prudhoe Bay	1½ hrs by air
Seattle	3½ hrs by air
Seward	9½ hrs by car
Skagway	15 hrs by car
Whitehorse	12 hrs by car

GETTING HERE AND AROUND

AIR TRAVEL

Beyond the highways are many Native villages reached by small airplanes making daily connections out of Fairbanks, which is the regional hub and the thriving commercial center of the Interior.

CAR TRAVEL

Interior Alaska is sandwiched between two monumental mountain ranges: the Brooks Range to the north and the Alaska Range to the south. In such a vast wilderness many of the region's residents define their area by a limited network of two-lane highways. You really need a car in the Interior, even if you're based in Fairbanks.

Fairbanks is a sprawling city. Things are too spread out for walking; public transportation is good but service is limited. Hotels run shuttle buses to and from the airport, and you can get around by taxi, but that's going to add up fast. Save yourself some frustration and just rent a car.

The Steese Highway, the Dalton Highway, and the Taylor Highway (which is closed in winter) are well-maintained gravel roads. However, summer rain can make them slick and dangerous. ■TIP➔ Rental-car companies have varying policies on whether they allow travel on gravel roads, so check in advance.

The George Parks Highway runs south to Denali National Park and Preserve and on to Anchorage, the state's largest city, 360 miles away on the coast. The Richardson Highway extends to the southeast to Delta Junction before turning south to Valdez, which is 368 miles from Fairbanks.

Two major routes lead north. You can take the Elliott Highway to the Dalton Highway, following the Trans-Alaska Pipeline to its origins at Prudhoe Bay on Alaska's North Slope (you can't drive all the way to the end, but you can get close). Alternatively, explore the Steese Highway to its termination at the Yukon River and the town of Circle.

TOURS

Especially if you're interested in getting out into the wilderness or out to one of the villages, we recommend a tour—it's far less stressful, particularly if you'd otherwise be faced with tasks that you've never undertaken before, things like driving remote unpaved roads without knowing how to change a tire or, worse, wandering the backcountry with limited previous Alaska experience.

TOUR CONTACTS

Go North Alaska Adventure Travel Center ☎ 907/479–7272, 866/236–7272 ⊕ www.gonorth-alaska.com. **Northern Alaska Tour Company** ☎ 907/474–8600, 800/474–8600 ⊕ www.northernalaska.com. **Trans Arctic Circle Treks Ltd.** ☎ 907/479–5451, 800/336–8735 ⊕ www.arctictreks.com.

CUSTOM SIGHTSEEING

Alaska/Yukon Trails ☎ 907/479–2277, 800/770–7275 ⊕ www.alaskashuttle.com.

RIVER TRIPS
Sternwheeler *Tanana Chief* ✉ *1020 Hoselton Rd., Fairbanks* ☎ *907/452–8687*
⊕ *www.sternwheelerak.com.* **Riverboat *Discovery*** ✉ *1975 Discovery Dr., near Fairbanks International Airport, Fairbanks* ☎ *907/479–6673, 866/479–6673* ⊕ *www.riverboatdiscovery.com.*

SEA AND LAND TOURS
Denali Park Resorts ☎ *907/276–7234, 800/276–7234* ⊕ *www. denaliparkresorts.com.* **Northern Alaska Tour Company** ☎ *907/474–8600* ⊕ *www.northernalaska.com.* **Trans Arctic Circle Treks Ltd.** ☎ *907/479–5451, 800/336–8735* ⊕ *www.arctictreks.com.*

RESTAURANTS

Even in the most elegant establishments Alaskans sometimes sport sweats or Carhartts. Most restaurants fly in fresh salmon and halibut from the coast. Meat-and-potatoes main courses and the occasional pasta dish fill menus, but most restaurants offer palatable vegetarian choices, too. The food isn't the only thing full of local flavor: walls are usually decked out in some combination of snowshoes, caribou and bear hides, the state flag, and historic photos. *Prices in the reviews are the average cost of a main course at dinner or, if dinner is not served, at lunch.*

HOTELS

You won't find ultra-luxury hotels, but you can find a range of bed-and-breakfasts, rustic-chic lodges, and national chains, as well as local spots that will please even the most discriminating travelers. For interaction with Alaskans, choose a B&B, as they're usually local-owned; proprietors tend to be eager to provide travel tips or an unforgettable story. The cheapest options are tents or RVs, and there is no shortage of campgrounds here. *Prices in the reviews are the lowest cost of a standard double room in high season.*

HEALTH AND SAFETY

The Interior really only has two health concerns: hypothermia, and mosquito-induced insanity. To prevent going insane when you're being attacked by a cloud of mosquitoes—and they grow them big in the interior—DEET, and lots of it, is your best bet. And don't wear blue. Mosquitoes really like blue.

Hypothermia, the lowering of the body's core temperature, is an ever-present threat in Alaska's wilderness. Wear layers of warm clothing when the weather is cool or wet; this includes a good wind- and water-proof parka or shell, warm hat and gloves, and waterproof or water-resistant boots. Heed the advice of locals who will tell you, "cotton kills." It does nothing to move moisture away from your skin, and can speed the onset of hypothermia. Any time you're in the wilderness, eat regularly to maintain energy, and stay hydrated.

Early symptoms of hypothermia are shivering, accelerated heartbeat, and goose bumps; this may be followed by clumsiness, slurred speech, disorientation, and unconsciousness. In the extreme, hypothermia can result in death. If you notice any of these symptoms in yourself or anyone in your group, stop, add layers of clothing, light a fire or camp

8

BEST BETS FOR DIFFERENT TRAVELERS

For those traveling with kids:

■ Pioneer Park in Fairbanks

■ Riverboat Discovery in Fairbanks

■ Beringia Centre in Whitehorse

For travelers who want to immerse themselves in the landscape but aren't so keen on roughing it:

■ Soak up Chena Hot Springs (if you're traveling in winter or the shoulder season, you might also see the northern lights)

■ Take a Klondike River float trip, from Dawson

■ Take an organized trip up the Dalton Highway, the northernmost highway in the country (bonus: great views of the Brooks Range, the tundra, and beyond)

For those who want to experience an Interior few tourists see:

■ Chicken and Eagle in Fortymile Country

■ Dawson in the winter—come when it's a checkpoint for the Yukon Quest, but be ready for temperatures cold enough to make car tires explode

For those who want to experience Alaskan culture:

■ Eskimo Olympics in Fairbanks

■ Dawson City Music Festival

stove, and warm up; a cup of tea or any hot fluid also helps. Avoid alcohol, which speeds hypothermia and impairs judgment. If your clothes are wet, change immediately. Be sure to put on a warm hat (most of the body's heat is lost through the head) and gloves. If there are only two of you, stay together: a person with hypothermia should never be left alone. Keep an eye on your traveling companions; frequently people won't recognize the symptoms in themselves until it's too late. For the person it's happening to, except for the shivering, hypothermia is really kind of peaceful, so watch out for each other and stay dry and safe.

MONEY MATTERS

ATMs are widely available in all the cities, and most of the towns; if you move out to the villages, though, take cash and don't expect to find much in the way of banking services.

FAIRBANKS

At first glance Fairbanks appears to be little more than a sprawling conglomeration of strip malls, chain stores, and other evidence of suburbia (or, as a local writer once put it, "su-brrr-bia"). But look beyond the obvious in the Interior's biggest town and you'll discover why thousands insist that this is the best place to live in Alaska.

The hardy Alaskans who refuse to leave during the cold and dark winters share a strong camaraderie. To live here, you really have to want to live here, which gives the whole city a relaxed, happy vibe. The fight to stave off cabin fever leads to creative festivals, from winter solstice celebrations to midnight baseball in summer. And isn't there something marvelous about people who, if their car breaks down and it's cold enough to freeze the tires and make them explode, still know what to do? It takes a special kind of confidence to live here, and that adds to the town's attractions.

Many of the old homes and commercial buildings trace their history to the city's early days, especially in the downtown area, with its narrow, winding streets following the contours of the Chena River. Even if each year brings more chain stores, the beautiful hillsides and river valleys remain. And of course there is Fairbanks's fall, winter, and spring bonus: being able to see the aurora, or northern lights, an average of 243 nights a year.

These magic lights were a common sight to the Native Alaskans who lived and traveled through Interior Alaska for thousands of years. But outsiders started coming to Fairbanks for the view all because of one guy's bad day: In 1901 E.T. Barnette, a merchant traveling upstream, was forced to leave the boat with all of his trading goods at a wooded spot in the middle of nowhere along the Chena River because the water was too shallow to pass. But while awaiting passage farther east, Barnette's luck took a turn for the wonderful when an Italian prospector discovered gold 12 miles north of Barnette's settlement the next summer. The resulting gold rush created customers for his stockpile of goods and led to the birth of Fairbanks, which for a brief time became the largest and wealthiest settlement in Alaska.

The city's nickname, the Golden Heart, reflects Fairbanks's gold-rush history and its location: it's the gateway to the Far North—the Arctic and the Bering Coast—and to Canada's Yukon Territory.

As you walk the streets of Fairbanks today, it takes a good imagination to envision the rough-and-tumble gold-mining camp that first took shape along the Chena River in the early 1900s. Although a few older neighborhoods have weathered log cabins, the rest is a Western hodgepodge that reflects the urge to build whatever one wants, wherever one wants—a trait that has long been a community standard (and sometimes leads to really interesting roof angles as the house sinks in permafrost).

The city is making some real efforts to preserve what's left of its gold-rush past, most notably in the 44-acre Pioneer Park, where dozens of cabins and many other relics were moved out of the path of progress. Downtown Fairbanks began to deteriorate in the 1970s, before and after the boom associated with the building of the Trans-Alaska Pipeline. But the downward spiral ended long ago and most of downtown has been rebuilt.

For details on all local attractions, historical and otherwise, stop by the downtown Fairbanks Convention and Visitors Bureau in the Morris Thompson Cultural and Visitors Center—the new pride of downtown, with a fantastic museum inside that will introduce you to the region's wonders. We also highly recommend a trip to the campus of the University of Alaska Fairbanks, where the University of Alaska Museum of the North got a makeover in 2006; the building is full of soothing, swooping lines that evoke glaciers, mountains, and sea life, and contains one of the best collections of material from around the state that you'll see anywhere.

GETTING HERE AND AROUND

Delta offers seasonal nonstop service from Fairbanks to the Lower 48. Alaska Airlines and ERA Alaska fly the Anchorage–Fairbanks route. There are hotel shuttles, rental cars, and taxis available at the Fairbanks airport.

FAIRBANKS GOLD

The gold strike by Felix Pedro in 1902 is commemorated annually in late July with the celebration of Golden Days, marked by a parade and several days of gold rush–inspired activities.

As for ground transportation, the Alaska Park Connection provides regularly scheduled shuttle service between Seward, Anchorage, and Denali National Park from mid-May to mid-September. Denali Overland Transportation serves Anchorage, Talkeetna, and Denali National Park with charter bus and van service. Alaska/Yukon Trails runs between Fairbanks, Denali, Anchorage, Talkeetna, Whitehorse, and Dawson City.

Between late May and early September, Alaska Railroad's daily passenger service runs between Seward, Anchorage, and Fairbanks, with stops at Talkeetna and Denali National Park and Preserve. Standard trains have dining, lounge, and dome cars, plus the only outdoor viewing platform of its kind. Holland America and Princess offer luxurious travel packages as well.

Make the **Morris Thompson Cultural and Visitors Center** your first stop in Fairbanks, where you can plan your whole trip, from a quick visit to a local attraction or a backcountry adventure. This center is also home to the **Fairbanks Convention and Visitors Bureau** and the **Alaska Public Lands Information Center.** While you're here, browse the free exhibits on Interior Alaska's environment and people, as well as the recently opened, fantastic displays of both gold rush and Native history. In the summer, the center hosts Alaska Native art, music, storytelling, and dance. Don't forget to enjoy the free films, use the Wi-Fi and Internet access, or peruse the literature at the Alaska Geographic Bookstore.

ESSENTIALS

Airline Contacts **Alaska Airlines** ☎ *800/252–7522* ⊕ *www.alaskaair.com.* **ERA Alaska** ☎ *907/266–8394, 800/866–8394* ⊕ *www.flyera.com.*

City Bus **Fairbanks MACS Bus System** ☎ *907/459–1011* ⊕ *www.co.fairbanks. ak.us/transportation* ⊑ *$1.50/ride or $3/day.*

Commuter Buses **Alaska/Yukon Trails** ☎ *800/770–7275* ⊕ *www. alaskashuttle.com.*

Internet **College Coffeehouse** ✉ *3677 College Rd., Unit 4* ☎ *907/374–0468* ⊕ *www.collegecoffeehousefairbanks.com.* **Fairbanks Convention and Visitors Bureau** ✉ *101 Dunkel St., Suite 111* ☎ *907/456–5774, 800/327–5774* ⊕ *www. explorefairbanks.com.* **Noel Wien Library** ✉ *1215 Cowles St.* ☎ *907/459–1020* ⊕ *www.fnsblibrary.org.*

Medical Assistance **Fairbanks Memorial Hospital** ✉ *1650 Cowles St.* ☎ *907/452-8181* ⊕ *www.bannerhealth.com.* **Fairbanks Urgent Care Center** ✉ *1867 Airport Way, Suite 130B* ☎ *907/452-2178.* **Tanana Valley Clinic** ✉ *1001 Noble St.* ☎ *907/459-3500* ⊕ *www.tvcclinic.com.*

Post Offices and Shipping **U.S. Postal Service** ✉ *315 Barnette St.* ☎ *907/452-3323* ⊕ *www.usps.com* ✉ *4025 Geist Rd.* ☎ *907/479-6021.* **FedEx** ✉ *418 3rd St., 5A* ☎ *907/456-7348, 800/463-3339* ⊕ *www.fedex.com.*

Rail **Alaska Railroad** ☎ *907/458-6025, 800/544-0552* ⊕ *www.alaskarailroad. com.* **Holland America Tours/Gray Line of Alaska** ☎ *800/544-2206* ⊕ *www. graylinealaska.com.* **Princess Tours** ☎ *800/426-0500* ⊕ *www.princesslodges.com.*

Rental Cars **Budget Rent-A-Car** ☎ *907/474-0855, 800/474-0855 in Alaska* ⊕ *www.budget.com.* **Dollar Rent A Car** ☎ *907/451-4360, 800/800-4000* ⊕ *www.dollar.com.* **Hertz** ☎ *907/452-4444, 800/654-3131* ⊕ *www.hertz.com.*

Visitor and Tour Information **Alaska Department of Fish and Game** ✉ *1300 College Rd.* ☎ *907/459-7207* ⊕ *www.adfg.alaska.gov.* **Alaska Public Lands Information Center** ✉ *101 Dunkel St., Downtown* ☎ *907/459-3730* ⊕ *www. alaskacenters.gov/fairbanks.cfm.* **Fairbanks Convention and Visitors Bureau** ✉ *101 Dunkel St., Downtown* ☎ *907/456-5774, 800/327-5774 recording* ⊕ *www.explorefairbanks.com.* **Morris Thompson Cultural and Visitors Center** ✉ *101 Dunkel St.* ☎ *907/459-3700* ⊕ *www.morristhompsoncenter.org* ✐ *Free* ☉ *Summer, daily 8–9; winter, daily 8–5.*

TOURS

Gray Line of Alaska. Gray Line of Alaska runs scenic and informative trips through the Fairbanks area, including a four-hour Discover the Gold sightseeing tour of the *Gold Dredge Number 8,* a stern-wheeler cruise, and a lunch of miner's stew for $114. ☎ *800/544-2206* ⊕ *www. graylinealaska.com.*

EXPLORING

TOP ATTRACTIONS

★ **Fairbanks Ice Museum.** You'd think that the last thing Fairbanksans would want to hang on to through the too-brief summer is a reminder of the brutal winters. However, the folks at the Ice Museum do just that. Sculptors work behind glass in large freezers where they create intricate sculptures from ice. About 25 sculptures are usually on display. Billed as "the coolest show in town," the Ice Showcase, a large glass-wall display, is kept at 20°F. *Freeze Frame* is a large-screen film demonstrating the techniques of ice sculpture. The museum is in the historic Lacey Street Theater, on the corner of 2nd Avenue and Lacey Street. ✉ *500 2nd Ave., Downtown* ☎ *907/451-8222* ⊕ *www.icemuseum.com* ✐ *$12* ☉ *May–Sept., daily 10–9.*

"Fountainhead" Antique Automobile Museum. Located on the property of the Wedgewood Resort, this museum features automobiles from 1898 to 1938—all of which run, the curators taking them out on the roads regularly. The museum also has the first car ever made in Alaska, built in Skagway out of sheet metal and old boat parts, all to impress a girl (didn't work). Alongside the cars are displays of vintage clothing and historical photographs. Widely considered one of the best auto museums in the world, and incredibly interesting, even if you're not interested in old cars. ✉ *212 Wedgewood Dr.* ☎ *907/450–2100* ⊕ *fountainhead museum.com* ✆ *$8; $4 for guests of Wedgewood Resort, Sophie Station Suites, or Bridgewater Hotel* ⏱ *Mid-May–mid-Sept., Sun.–Thurs. 11–10, Fri. and Sat. 11–6; mid-Sept.– mid-May, Sun. noon–6.*

★ **Georgeson Botanical Garden of the Agricultural and Forestry Experiment Station Farm.** When most people think of Alaska vegetation, they conjure up images of flat, treeless tundra, so the amazing variety of native and cultivated flowers on exhibit here is often unexpected. This is where researchers at the University of Alaska Fairbanks study Interior Alaska's unique, short, but intense midnight-sun growing season. The results are spectacular. The grounds feature about 1,000 perennials. The nonstop daylight brings out rich and vibrant colors. The best times to visit are from mid-June to late August. ✉ *117 W. Tanana Dr.* ⚓ *West end of campus, 4 miles west of downtown* ☎ *907/474–6921* ⊕ *www.georgesonbg. org* ✆ *$2* ⏱ *May–Sept., daily 8–8; tours Fri. at 2.*

★ **Large Animal Research Station.** Out on the fringes of the University of
ⓒ Alaska campus is a 134-acre home to about 50 musk ox, 45 caribou, and 40 domestic reindeer (those last two are actually the same animal from most standpoints; they can interbreed, and the main difference comes down to the fact that reindeer, having been domesticated, are lazier and fatter than caribou). Resident and visiting scientists study these large ungulates to better understand their physiologies and how they adapt to Arctic conditions. The station also serves as a valuable outreach program. Most people have little chance to see these animals in their natural habitats, especially the musk ox. Once nearly eradicated from Alaska, these shaggy, prehistoric-looking beasts are marvels of adaptive physiques and behaviors. Their qiviut, the delicate musk ox undercoat of hair that is so soft it makes cashmere feel like steel wool, is combed out (without harming the animals) and made into yarn for scarves, hats, and gloves. The station has this unprocessed wool and yarn for sale to help fund the care of the animals. On tours you visit the pens for a close-up look at the animals and their young, while learning about the biology and ecology of the animals from a naturalist. The tours are a very good deal, and the best way to learn about the animals, but you can also just come by any time of day, and usually see musk ox from the parking lot; they sometimes come quite close to the fence. ✉ *Yankovich Rd. off Ballaine Rd., behind University of Alaska Fairbanks* ☎ *907/474–5724 tour information* ⊕ *www.uaf.edu/research/ lars* ✆ *Tours $10* ⏱ *Free general viewing year-round. June 1–Aug. 30, 45-min tours beginning at 10, noon, and 2, Tues.–Sat.*

★ **Pioneer Park.** The 44-acre park is along the Chena River near downtown
ⓒ Fairbanks, and has several museums, an art gallery, theater, civic center, Native village, large children's playground, miniature-golf course, antique merry-go-round, and restaurants. The park also has a re-created gold-rush town with historic buildings saved from urban renewal, log-cabin gift shops, and **Mining Valley,** an outdoor museum of mining artifacts surrounding an indoor-outdoor Alaska Salmon Bake restaurant. The 227-foot stern-wheeler *Nenana* is the second-largest wooden

DID YOU KNOW?

The University of Alaska Museum of the North is pure Alaska inside and out: the exterior was inspired by the state's alpine ridges, glaciers, Yukon River, and the northern lights, while the interior houses thousands of years of Alaskan art, culture, and nature. Don't miss Blue Babe, the 36,000-year-old steppe bison. Also inside, one of the best gift shops in the city.

vessel in existence and a national historic landmark. A diorama inside the stern-wheeler details the course the riverboat took on the Yukon and Tanana rivers around the turn of the 20th century. The **Crooked Creek and Whiskey Island Railroad,** a narrow-gauge train, circles the park. The newest addition to the park is a museum housing the first locomotive in Fairbanks, which has been restored to its 1905 condition and is run on special occasions. This is one of the best places in Fairbanks to bring kids and let them run off some energy. ■ TIP➜ No-frills (dry) RV camping is available for $12 a night in the west end of the large parking lot on Airport Way. ✉ *2300 Airport Way(Airport Way and Peger Rd.)* ☎ *907/459–1087* ⊕ *www.fnsb.us/pioneerpark* ✉ *Free* ☉ *Park 24 hrs; museum and shops Memorial Day–Labor Day, daily noon–8.*

> ### GARDENS FOR GIANTS
>
> Interior Alaska gets an extra-large helping of sunlight between May and August. The growing season is short in days, but every day counts because the sun is rarely out of sight. The long daylight hours create intense, vivid colors in flowers, while allowing vegetables to grow to gargantuan dimensions. Cabbages that top 50 pounds and zucchini with telephone-pole-size diameters are common.

Fodor'sChoice ★ **University of Alaska Museum of the North.** This museum has some of the most distinctive architecture in the state, with sweeping curves and graceful lines that evoke glaciers, mountains, and a fluke of a diving whale. Inside, two-story viewing windows look out on the Alaska Range and the Tanana Valley. Otto, the 8-foot, 9-inch brown bear, greets visitors to the entrance of the Gallery of Alaska, also featuring Blue Babe, a mummified steppe bison that lived 36,000 years ago during the Pleistocene epoch. The museum has several "please touch" items, including the molars of a mammoth and a mastodon, a gray whale skull, and a 5,495-pound copper nugget. Also in the gallery is a fantastic collection of Native clothes, tools, boats, and more from around the state, offering a chance to see how different groups came to terms with climatic extremes; other dioramas show the state's animals and how they interact. And don't miss the treasured Rose Berry Alaska Art Gallery, representing 2,000 years of Alaska's art, from ancient to modern, or the year-round special exhibits. In the Place Where You Go to Listen, ever-changing light and sound, composed by the real-time movements of the sun, moon, aurora, and seismic activity, create a mesmerizing effect. This is one of the best museums in Alaska, and a can't-miss stop. The gift shop also has one of the better selections of Alaskana in town. ✉ *University of Alaska Fairbanks, 907 Yukon Dr.* ☎ *907/474–7505* ⊕ *www.uaf.edu/museum* ✉ *$10 general admission and additional charges for 30-min summer auditorium shows* ☉ *Mid-May–mid-Sept., daily 9–7; mid-Sept.–mid-May, Mon.–Sat. 9–5.*

WORTH NOTING

Alaska Range Overlook. Much of the north side of the Alaska Range is visible from this overlook, a favorite spot for time-lapse photography of the midwinter sun just peeking over the southern horizon on a low arc. The three major peaks, called the Three Sisters, are nearly

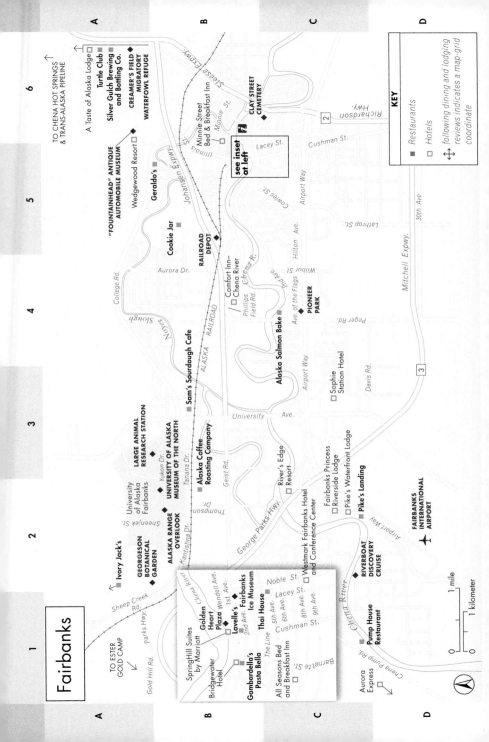

Fairbanks

TO CHENA HOT SPRINGS & TRANS-ALASKA PIPELINE

TO ESTER GOLD CAMP

Gold Hill Rd.

Sheep Creek Rd.

Parks Hwy.

Ivory Jack's

GEORGESON BOTANICAL GARDEN

University of Alaska Fairbanks

Sheenjek St.

ALASKA RANGE OVERLOOK

Kantishna Dr.

Thompson Dr.

LARGE ANIMAL RESEARCH STATION

UNIVERSITY OF ALASKA MUSEUM OF THE NORTH

Yukon Dr.

Tanana Dr.

Alaska Coffee Roasting Company

Sam's Sourdough Cafe

College Rd.

Noyes Slough

Aurora Dr.

"FOUNTAINHEAD" ANTIQUE AUTOMOBILE MUSEUM

Wedgewood Resort

Geraldo's

Cookie Jar

RAILROAD DEPOT

ALASKA RAILROAD

Johansen Expwy.

Illinois St.

Minnie St.

A Taste of Alaska Lodge
Turtle Club
Silver Gulch Brewing and Bottling Co.
CREAMER'S FIELD MIGRATORY WATERFOWL REFUGE

Steese Expwy.

Minnie Street Bed & Breakfast Inn

CLAY STREET CEMETERY

see inset at left

Lacey St.

Cushman St.

Richardson Hwy.

2

KEY

■ Restaurants
□ Hotels
✢ following dining and lodging reviews indicates a map-grid coordinate

Comfort Inn– Chena River

Chena R.

Phillips Field Rd.

2nd Ave.

Wilbur St.

Ave. of the Flags

PIONEER PARK

Cowles St.

Airport Way

Hilton Ave.

Lathrop St.

Mitchell Expwy.

30th Ave.

Alaska Salmon Bake

Sophie Station Hotel

Airport Way

Davis Rd.

Peger Rd.

3

University Ave.

Geist Rd.

George Parks Hwy.

River's Edge Resort

Fairbanks Princess Riverside Lodge

Pike's Waterfront Lodge

Pike's Landing

FAIRBANKS INTERNATIONAL AIRPORT

Airport Way

RIVERBOAT DISCOVERY CRUISE

Chena River

Westmark Fairbanks Hotel and Conference Center

Chena Pump Rd.

Pump House Restaurant

Aurora Express

0   1 mile
0   1 kilometer

Inset

Chena River

Wendell Ave.

Noble St.

1st Ave.

SpringHill Suites by Marriott

Golden Heart Plaza

Lavelle's

Fairbanks Ice Museum

2nd Ave.

Thai House

Lacey St.

5th Ave.

6th Ave.

8th Ave.

9th Ave.

Cushman St.

The Line

Barnette St.

Bridgewater Hotel

Gambardella's Pasta Bella

All Seasons Bed and Breakfast Inn

always distinguishable on a clear day. From your left are **Mt. Hayes,** 13,832 feet; **Mt. Hess,** 11,940 feet; and **Mt. Deborah,** 12,339 feet. Much farther to the right, toward the southwest, hulks **Mt. McKinley,** the highest peak in North America. On some seemingly clear days it's not visible at all. At other times the base is easy to see but the peak is lost in cloud cover. ■ TIP➔ Look for the parking area just east of University of Alaska Museum. ⊠ *West Ridge, University of Alaska Fairbanks campus, Yukon Dr.*

Creamer's Field Migratory Waterfowl Refuge. Thousands of migrating ducks, geese, and sandhill cranes stop here in spring as they head north to nesting grounds, and in late summer as they head south before the cold hits. It's amazing to watch them gather in huge flocks, with constant take-offs and landings, yet no one ever running into anyone else. This is also a great place to view songbirds and moose. Five miles of nature trails lead through fields, forest, and wetlands, and are open year-round. Don't miss the daily one- to two-hour naturalist walks. Now on the National Register of Historic Places, Creamer's Dairy was the northernmost dairy in North America from 1910 to 1966. The farmhouse is an interpretive center and gift shop open daily 9:30 am–5 pm mid-May to mid-September and Saturday noon–4 pm the rest of the year. Call for listings of year-round events. ⊠ *1300 College Rd.* ☎ *907/459–7307, 907/452–5162* ⊕ *www.creamersfield.org* ☉ *Walks June–Aug., Mon., Tues., Thurs., and Fri. at 10 am; Wed. at 10 am and 7 pm. Additional scheduled on request.*

Golden Heart Plaza. This riverside park is the hub of downtown celebrations, including free evening concerts in the park. The plaza is dominated by the towering statue of the Unknown First Family, encircled by plaques containing the names of 4,500 local families who contributed to the building of the plaza.

▌OFF THE
BEATEN
PATH

Trans-Alaska Pipeline. Just north of Fairbanks you can see and touch the famous Trans-Alaska Pipeline. This 48-inch-diameter pipe travels 800 miles from the oil fields on the North Slope of the Brooks Range over three mountain ranges and over more than 500 rivers and streams to the terminal in Valdez. There the crude oil is pumped onto tanker ships and transported to oil refineries in the Lower 48 states. Since the pipeline began operations in 1977, more than 15 billion barrels of North Slope crude have been pumped. Currently the pipe is carrying about 600,000 barrels per day (a number that's decreasing a bit, year by year). The parking lot is right off the Steese Highway. ⊠ *Mile 8.4, Steese Hwy.* ▧ *Free.*

OUTDOOR ACTIVITIES AND GUIDED TOURS

ADVENTURE TOURS

Northern Alaska Tour Company. Northern Alaska Tour Company leads year-round half- and full-day excursions to the Arctic Circle and the Yukon River and two- and three-day fly-drive tours to Prudhoe Bay, Barrow, and the Brooks Range. It also has winter aurora-watching trips. ☎ *907/474–8600, 800/474–1986* ⊕ *www.northernalaska.com.*

BASEBALL

★ **Alaska Goldpanners.** Scores of baseball players, including Tom Seaver, Dave Winfield, and Jason Giambi, have passed through Fairbanks on their way to the major leagues. The Interior is home to the Alaska Goldpanners, a member of the Alaska Baseball League, a string of amateur baseball organizations throughout the state. Players are recruited from college teams nationwide, and the summer season (mid-June–late July) generates top-caliber competition. Home games are played at Growden Field, along Lower 2nd Avenue at Wilbur Street, not far from Pioneer Park. The baseball park hosts the **Midnight Sun Baseball Game,** a Fairbanks tradition (2013 is the 108th year) in which the Goldpanners play baseball at midnight of the summer solstice without benefit of artificial lights. This is thrilling (and possibly chilly) to watch on a clear, sunny night when the daylight never ends. ☎ *907/451–0095* ⊕ *www. goldpanners.com.*

BICYCLING

Bicyclists in Fairbanks use the paved paths from the University of Alaska campus around Farmers Loop to the Steese Highway. Another path follows Geist and Chena Pump roads into downtown Fairbanks. Be warned that many of the trails are in rough shape and suffer from lack of maintenance. A shorter, less strenuous route is the bike path between downtown and Pioneer Park along the south side of the Chena River. Maps showing all the bike paths are available at the Fairbanks Convention and Visitors Bureau. Mountain bikers can test their skills in summer on the ski trails of the University of Alaska Fairbanks and the Birch Hill Recreation Area or on many of the trails and dirt roads around Fairbanks.

Alaska Public Lands Information Center. Stop by the Alaska Public Lands Information Center for mountain-biking information. ✉ *101 Dunkel St., #110* ☎ *907/459–3730* ⊕ *www.alaskacenters.gov.*

BOATING

For relaxing boating in or near Fairbanks, use Chena River access points at Nordale Road east of the city, at the Cushman and Wendell Street bridges near downtown, in Pioneer Park above the Peger River Bridge, at the state campground, and at the University Avenue Bridge.

The Tanana River, with a current that is fast and often shallow, is ideally suited for riverboats. On this river and others in the Yukon River drainage, Alaskans use long, wide, flat-bottom boats powered by one or two large outboard engines. The boats include a lift to raise the engine a few inches, allowing passage through the shallows; lately, it's more common just to get a jet boat, which doesn't have a propeller, and so can go into much shallower waters. Arrangements for riverboat charters can be made in almost any river community. Ask at the Fairbanks Convention and Visitors Bureau.

TOURS AND OUTFITTERS

Fodor's Choice **Alaska Outdoor Rentals and Guides.** Alaska Outdoor Rentals and Guides
★ rents gear and arranges pick-ups and drop-offs for the Class I waters of the lower Chena River (the only real challenge for canoeists on the lower river is watching out for powerboats), as well as other local

rivers. ✉ *Pioneer Park Boat Dock, along Chena River next to Peger Rd.* ☎ *907/457–2453* ⊕ *www.akbike.com.*

Sternwheeler *Tanana* **Chief.** Sternwheeler *Tanana Chief* provides nightly dinner cruises on the Chena River aboard the stern-wheeler *Tanana Chief,* a replica of the riverboats that once plied Interior rivers. The dinner cruise costs $49.95 and boards at 6:30 pm. Day cruises run $24.95, with no food. ✉ *1020 Hoselton Rd.* ☎ *907/452–8687* ⊕ *www. tananachiefak.com.*

Fodor's Choice ★ **Riverboat** *Discovery.* The city's riverboat history and the Interior's cultural heritage are relived each summer aboard the Riverboat *Discovery,* a 3½-hour narrated trip by stern-wheeler along the Chena and Tanana rivers to a rustic Native village on the Tanana River. The cruise provides a glimpse of the lifestyle of the dog mushers, subsistence fishermen, traders, and Native Alaskans who populate the Yukon River drainage. Sights along the way include operating fish wheels, a bush airfield, floatplanes, a smokehouse and cache, log cabins, and dog kennels once tended by the late Susan Butcher, the first person to win the Iditarod four times. The Binkley family, with four generations of river pilots, has run the great rivers of the north for more than 100 years. Cruises are $54.95 and run twice daily (at 8:45 am and 2 pm) mid-May to mid-September. ✉ *1975 Discovery Dr.* ☎ *907/479–6673, 866/479–6673* ⊕ *www.riverboatdiscovery.com.*

CURLING

Hundreds of Fairbanksans participate each year in curling, a game in which people with brooms play a giant version of shuffleboard on ice. Curlers have an almost fanatical devotion to their sport, and they're eager to explain its finer points to the uninitiated.

Fairbanks Curling Club. The Fairbanks Curling Club hosts an annual Yukon Title *bonspiel* (match) on the first weekend of November and an international bonspiel on the first weekend of April. The club season runs from early October through the middle of April. ✉ *1962 2nd Ave.* ☎ *907/452–2875* ⊕ *www.curlfairbanks.org.*

DOG MUSHING

Throughout Alaska, sprint races, freight hauling, and long-distance endurance runs are held in late February and March, during the season when longer days afford enjoyment of the remaining winter snow. Men and women often compete in the same classes in the major races. For children, various racing classes are based on age, starting with the one-dog category for the youngest. The Interior sees a constant string of sled-dog races from November to March, which culminates in the **North American Open Sled-Dog Championship,** attracting international competition to Fairbanks.

Alaska Dog Mushers Association. In Fairbanks many of the sprint races are organized by the Alaska Dog Mushers Association, one of the oldest organizations of its kind in Alaska, and held at its Jeff Studdert Sled Dog Racegrounds at Mile 4, Farmers Loop. ☎ *907/457–6874* ⊕ *www. sleddog.org.*

Paws for Adventure Sled Dog Tours. Offering a mix of trips, Paws for Adventure Sled Dog Tours is a good choice. The most adventurous can embark on multiday trips, but other options include a mushing school or a short sled ride. ☎ *907/378–3630* ⊕ *www.pawsforadventure.com* ⊙ *Oct.–Apr., weather permitting.*

★ **Sun Dog Express Dog Sled Tours.** If you want to experience dog mushing for yourself, Sun Dog Express Dog Sled Tours, with more than 20 years of experience, offers summer and winter tours (weather permitting), demonstrations, and instruction, in addition to a three-day mushing camp. ☎ *907/479–6983* ⊕ *www.mosquitonet.com/~sleddog.*

Yukon Quest International Sled-Dog Race. The Yukon Quest International Sled-Dog Race is an endurance race held in February that covers more than 1,000 miles between Fairbanks and Whitehorse, Yukon Territory (the starting point alternates between the two each year), via Dawson and the Yukon River. Considered much tougher and, among mushers, more prestigious than the more famous Iditarod, the Quest goes through more remote lands, with fewer checkpoints. You can get more details from the visitor center in either city or by checking in with the Fairbanks Yukon Quest office, located in the log cabin at 550 1st Avenue. ✉ *550 1st Ave.* ☎ *907/452–7954* ⊕ *www.yukonquest.com.*

FISHING

Although a few fish can be caught right in town from the Chena River, the best thing for an avid fishermen to do is hop on a plane or riverboat to get to the best areas for angling. Fishing trips include air charters to Lake Minchumina (an hour's flight from Fairbanks), known for good pike fishing and a rare view of the north sides of Mt. McKinley and Mt. Foraker. Another charter trip by riverboat or floatplane will take you pike fishing in the Minto Flats, west of Fairbanks off the Tanana River, where the mouth of the Chatanika River spreads through miles of marsh and sloughs.

Salmon run up the Tanana River most of the summer, but they're not usually caught on hook-and-line gear. Residents take them from the river with gill nets and fish wheels, using special commercial and subsistence permits. Check the "Outdoors" section in the Friday *Fairbanks Daily News–Miner* for weekly updates on fishing in the Interior.

■ **TIP→** You can purchase fishing licenses (good for one day or longer; $20 and up for nonresidents) at many sporting-goods stores and online at ⊕ www.admin.adfg.state.ak.us/license.

Arctic Grayling Guide Service. Arctic Grayling Guide Service offers guided and unguided fishing trips via jet boat to a remote fishing spot 60 miles south of Fairbanks to fish for grayling and salmon (May–October). Cabins are available. They've been around forever, a good bet for the serious angler. ☎ *907/479–0479, 907/322–8004* ⊕ *www.wildernessfishing.com.*

GOLD PANNING

Alaskan Prospectors. The gold information center for Interior Alaska, Alaskan Prospectors is the oldest mining and prospecting supply store in the state, also featured on the Travel Channel. Stop here for gold pans and books or videos, or to visit the rocks and minerals museum.

8

MONUMENTAL FORCES

Over the last 100 million years, a collage of microtectonic plates of igneous and sedimentary rocks collided with and attached itself to the North American continent. The original rocks of these microplates are up to 800 million years old. During these collisions active volcanoes peppered the plates with patches of hard, granitic rock. This tough rock underlies much of the Alaska Range, helping the peaks withstand millions of years of erosion by wind, weather, rivers, and glaciers.

Pressure along the 1,300-mile-long Denali Fault causes uplift throughout the Alaska Range, which continues to rise as fast, in geologic terms, as 1 millimeter per year. Mt. McKinley, at 20,320 feet, the highest peak in North America, was pushed to its towering height by movement along this fault. Today large glaciers pour from the valleys, remnants of the last Ice Age's extensive glaciation, which ended 6,000–7,000 years ago.

Because of the way the ice carved the landscape out as it disappeared, the region is full of thousands upon thousands of lakes and rivers, as well as broad alluvial fans of glacial outwash.

The central part of the Interior was never glaciated; it was, in fact, part of Beringia, a vast, ice-free zone that stretched from the Mackenzie River in the Yukon to as far as the Lena River in Russia, the continents connected by the Bering Land Bridge—which was really more of a subcontinent than a bridge, since it covered as much as 600 miles north to south. Beringia was home to steppe bison (like Blue Babe at the UAF Museum), mammoths, camels, a couple of different kinds of saber-toothed cats, and American lions, as well as horses not much bigger than collies. Beringia disappeared as the ice around it melted, climate change making an entire world disappear.

The Brooks Range was formed by compression generated from a spreading ridge in the Arctic Ocean. The forces stacked and folded Paleozoic and early Mesozoic rock against the northernmost part of the North American continent. Because it is drier and doesn't receive enough moisture to feed glaciers, the Brooks Range to the north was never extensively glaciated.

Employees have valuable advice for the neophyte gold bug. ⊠ *504 College Rd.* ☎ *907/452-7398.*

Gold Dredge 8 and El Dorado Gold Mine. Gold Dredge 8 offers a two-hour tour of a seasonal mining operation, all from the comfort of a narrow-gauge railroad. Miners demonstrate classic and modern techniques, and at the end, you get to try your own luck panning for gold. They've also brought over a lot of the historic elements from the old El Dorado Gold Mine, so it's a pretty complete look at how Fairbanks got rich. ⊠ *1603 North Old Steese Highway* ☎ *907/479-6673, 866/479-6673* ⊕ *www.golddredge8.com* 💵 *$35.*

GOLF

Chena Bend. Chena Bend, a well-maintained army course open to civilians, is an 18-hole spread on nearby Ft. Wainwright. ☎ *907/353-6223.*

Fairbanks Golf Course. The 9-hole course at the Fairbanks Golf Course straddles Farmers Loop just north of the university. Summertime midnight golf with a 3 am tee time is considered normal at this course. Come on, that'll give you something to brag about at home, right? Watch for ravens stealing balls, though. ☎ 907/479–6555.

North Star Golf Club. The 18-hole course at the North Star Golf Club is on the Old Steese Highway, 0.7 mile past Chena Hot Springs Road. It is the northernmost course in the United States, and perhaps the only one where you are encouraged to mark your scorecard with a tally of the wildlife you see. Book tee times online during the mid-May–September open season, or give a call. ☎ 907/457–4653 ⊕ www.northstargolf.com.

HIKING

Creamer's Field Migratory Waterfowl Refuge (⇨ see Exploring Fairbanks) has three nature trails within its 1,800 acres on the edge of Fairbanks. The longest trail is 2 miles, and one is wheelchair accessible.

RIVERBOAT RACING

Fairbanks Outboard Association. A summer highlight is riverboat racing sanctioned by the Fairbanks Outboard Association. These specially built 24-foot racing boats are powered by 50-horsepower engines and reach speeds of 75 mph. Weekend races in summer and fall begin and end either at the Chena Pump Campgrounds or at Pike's Landing, just off Airport Way near Fairbanks International Airport. ⊕ www. yukon800.com.

Roland Lord Memorial Race. The Roland Lord Memorial Race, from Fairbanks to Nenana and back, is held in early August.

SKIING
CROSS-COUNTRY

The Interior has some of the best weather and terrain in the nation for cross-country skiing, especially in late fall and early spring. Among the developed trails in the Fairbanks area, the ones at the **Birch Hill Recreation Area,** on the city's north side, and at the **University of Alaska Fairbanks** are lighted to extend their use into winter nights. Cross-country ski racing is a staple at several courses on winter weekends. The season stretches from October to late March or early April. Other developed trails can be found at **Chena Hot Springs Resort, White Mountains National Recreation Area,** the **Chena Lakes Recreation Area,** and the **Two Rivers Recreation Area.**

Alaska Public Lands Information Center. For more information on cross-country skiing, check with the Alaska Public Lands Information Center. Fairbanks is laced with trails, and you could spend all winter out there and never see the same thing twice. ☎ 907/459–3730.

DOWNHILL

Birch Hill. In Ft. Wainwright, Birch Hill has a chairlift and beginner and intermediate runs; it's open November through March, Friday through Sunday. ☎ 907/353–7053.

Mt. Aurora Skiland. On the Steese Highway about 20 miles from Fairbanks at Cleary Summit, Mt. Aurora Skiland has a chairlift, rentals, more than 20 runs ranked intermediate to expert, and a 1,100-foot vertical drop. There's lodging in an old gold-camp bunkhouse and aurora viewing. It's

8

open weekends from December to mid-April, if there's enough snow. ☎ *907/456–7669, 907/389–2314 for office* ⊕ *www.skiland.org.*

Moose Mountain. This mountain, off Murphy Dome Road, has 42 runs from two summits for intermediate to advanced skiiers, all accessed by a bus lift system. It's open November through March on weekends, plus school and government holidays. ☎ *907/479–4732, 907/459–8132 for ski report* ⊕ *www.shredthemoose.com.*

WHERE TO EAT

Use the coordinate (✛ B2) at the end of each review to locate a property on the Fairbanks map.

$ ✕**Alaska Coffee Roasting Company.** Fuel up with the university folk, where
CAFÉ green coffee beans from around the world are roasted and blended. The scratch kitchen also offers flatbread, perfect for one or two, and pastries and desserts like tiramisu, scones, and cheesecake. With its inviting hardwood floors, Tuscan wood oven, and tasteful artwork, this hangout is so popular that a line often curls out the door. ⑤ *Average main: $8* ✉ *4001 Geist Rd., Suite 2, University West* ☎ *907/457–5282* ⊕ *www. alaskacoffeeroasting.com* ✛ *B2.*

$$$ ✕**Alaska Salmon Bake.** Salmon cooked over an open fire with a lemon-
SEAFOOD and-brown-sugar sauce is a favorite at this indoor-outdoor restaurant in
★ Pioneer Park's Mining Valley. Halibut, cod, prime rib, a salad bar, and dessert are also available at the nightly all-you-can-eat dinner. ⑤ *Average main: $31* ✉ *Airport Way and Peger Rd., Pioneer Park* ☎ *907/452–7274, 800/354–7274* ⊕ *www.akvisit.com/salmon.html* ☾ *Dinner only, mid-May–mid-Sept.* ✛ *C4.*

$$ ✕**Cookie Jar.** Tucked away in a nondescript neighborhood on a street
AMERICAN not found on most Fairbanks maps, this restaurant is worth tracking
★ down. The open space features lots of cookie jars, along with plants and artwork. Spanning breakfast, lunch, and dinner, the huge menu includes scads of homemade items, an extensive kids' menu, and vegetarian selections. Entrées range from steak and shrimp to coq au vin. For dessert, try the homemade pies or cookies to match anything your grandma ever baked. Weekend breakfasts are especially popular, so allow extra time. Take Danby Street off the Johansen Expressway; the restaurant is behind Kendall Motors. ⑤ *Average main: $15* ✉ *1006 Cadillac Ct., Aurora* ☎ *907/479–8319* ⊕ *www.cookiejarfairbanks.com* ✛ *B5.*

$$$ ✕**Gambardella's Pasta Bella.** Locals crowd the family-run Italian restau-
ITALIAN rant, which has earned a reputation as one of the best in town. The menu includes salads, pasta, pizza, vegetarian entrées, and submarine sandwiches on homemade bread. Its specialties are lasagna, which the *Seattle Times* aptly described as "the mother of all lasagnas," and the tiramisu. The two-story restaurant has outdoor seating on a balcony and at street level. It feels as close to a romantic back-alley restaurant in Italy as you can get in Interior Alaska. ⑤ *Average main: $21* ✉ *706 2nd Ave., Downtown* ☎ *907/456–3417* ⊕ *www.gambardellas.com* ☾ *No lunch Sun.* ✛ *B1.*

$$$ ✕**Geraldo's.** The sign outside will likely contain a plug for the virtues of
ITALIAN garlic. Rightly so, for no one in Fairbanks puts fresh chopped garlic to

better use than Geraldo's, which has gourmet pizza, seafood, pasta, and veal dishes. A painting of Don Corleone hangs on the wall, and Frank Sinatra and Dean Martin provide background music for this cozy and often crowded spot. ⑤ *Average main: $25* ☒ *701 College Rd., Lemeta* ☎ *907/452–2299* ✛ *B5.*

$$$ ✕ **Ivory Jack's.** Jack "Ivory" O'Brien used to deal Alaskan ivory and
AMERICAN whalebone out of this small restaurant tucked into the gold-rich hills of the Goldstream Valley on the outskirts of Fairbanks. Crab-stuffed mushrooms are a specialty of this large, open, and airy bar-restaurant. You can choose from more than 15 appetizers as well as burgers, pizza, and entrées such as halibut Dijon and Alaskan king crab. ⑤ *Average main: $30* ☒ *2581 Goldstream Rd., Goldstream* ☎ *907/455–6666* ⊕ *www.ivoryjacks.alaskansavvy.com* ✛ *A1.*

$$$$ ✕ **Lavelle's Bistro.** With offerings ranging from rack of lamb and lobster
AMERICAN cakes to halibut and New York steaks, this impressive restaurant has won a loyal local following. Lavelle's features an extensive 3,000-bottle wine cellar, and holds regular wine tastings and other events that give the restaurant sophistication far removed from the frontier image cultivated elsewhere in Fairbanks. This is one of the few places where Fairbanksans dress up for dinner. ⑤ *Average main: $30* ☒ *SpringHill Suites, 575 1st Ave., Downtown* ☎ *907/450–0555* ⊕ *www.lavellesbistro.com* ⊙ *No lunch Sept. 15–May 15* ✛ *B1.*

$$$ ✕ **Pike's Landing.** Enjoy lunch on a huge outside deck (it seats 420) over-
AMERICAN looking the Chena River, or inside in the elegant dining room of an
★ extended log cabin. The meals cost up to $47 for steak and lobster and rank with the best in the Interior. For a dinner in the $12 range, relax in the sports bar and catch a view of the river. The palate-pleasing Sunday brunch has an irresistible dessert table. ⑤ *Average main: $25* ☒ *4438 Airport Way* ☎ *907/479–7113* ⊕ *www.pikeslodge.com* ✛ *C2.*

$$$$ ✕ **Pump House Restaurant.** Alongside the Chena River, this mining pump
AMERICAN station–turned–restaurant claims it's the northernmost oyster bar in the
★ world, and also turns out house specialties such as Alaskan wild game and seafood chowder. Listed on the National Register of Historic Places, this pump house, circa 1930s, now houses and utilizes antiques up to 150 years old. The furnishings and floor are made of rich, polished wood, the pool table dates from 1898, and an Alaskan grizzly bear in a glass case stands sentry next to the hostess station. Wednesday night is karaoke night in the bar. In summer, enjoy the midnight sun on the deck out back by the Chena River. Ask locals where to go for a nice night out, this is probably where they'll send you. ⑤ *Average main: $30* ☒ *796 Chena Pump Rd.* ☎ *907/479–8452* ⊕ *www.pumphouse. com* ⊙ *No lunch mid-Sept.–June 1* ✛ *C1.*

$$ ✕ **Sam's Sourdough Cafe.** Although Sam's serves meals all day, Fairbank-
AMERICAN sans know it as the best breakfast place in town. Sourdough recipes are
★ a kind of minor religion in Alaska, and Sam's serves an extensive menu of sourdough specialties, including hotcakes and French toast, as well as standard meat-and-eggs options, all at reasonable prices. On weekends get here early or be prepared for a wait. The address says Cameron Street, but it's really fronted on University, just over the railroad tracks. ⑤ *Average main: $12* ☒ *3702 Cameron St.* ☎ *907/479–0523* ✛ *B3.*

8

$$ ✕ **Silver Gulch Brewing and Bottling Co.** You'll find some unique souvenirs
AMERICAN   and an interesting collection of Fairbanks citizens at North America's
northernmost brewery. Founded in 1998, Silver Gulch is probably best
known for its pilsner and lager brews, carried throughout the state. The
brewery is in the Fox Roadhouse building. A preserved section of the
old roadhouse's exterior still stands in the second floor of the restaurant.
This hot spot is 10 miles north of Fairbanks on the Old Steese Highway,
across from the Howling Dog Saloon. After your brewery tour (make
sure to call ahead to arrange it), satisfy your hunger with I.P.A.–bat-
tered fish-and-chips or fresh Alaskan seafood, or enjoy a brew while
sitting in the outdoor beer garden. ⑤ *Average main: $15* ✉ *2195 Old
Steese Hwy., Fox* ☎ *907/452–2739* ⊕ *www.silvergulch.com* ⊘ *No lunch
weekdays* ☞ *Free brewery tours available in summer* ✛ *A6.*

$$ ✕ **Thai House.** Fairbanks is not known for a wide selection of interna-
THAI   tional cuisine, but Thai food is an exception, and the Thai House is
★   among the best of the bunch. The prices are astounding, the staff dress
in elaborate Thai silks, and the atmosphere is elegant with hardwood
floors and Thai decor on the walls. The restaurant has a loyal following
because the food is authentic. ⑤ *Average main: $11* ✉ *412 5th Ave.,
Downtown* ☎ *907/452–6123* ✛ *C2.*

$$$ ✕ **Turtle Club.** Don't go to this windowless and nondescript dining room
AMERICAN   expecting great variety. Do go if you are hungry for prime rib, lobster,
prawns, or king crab and have a big appetite. There's a good salad bar,
the service is prompt, and every order comes with homemade bread.
The "Turtle Cut" serving of prime rib, advertised as a "medium por-
tion," weighs a pound. Many of the patrons make this a regular stop
on Friday and Saturday nights, so call ahead for reservations. It's worth
the 10-mile drive north of Fairbanks. ⑤ *Average main: $28* ✉ *Mile
10, Old Steese Hwy., Fox* ☎ *907/457–3883* ⊕ *www.alaskanturtle.com.*

WHERE TO STAY

*Use the coordinate (✛ B2) at the end of each review to locate a property
on the Fairbanks map.*

For expanded hotel reviews, visit Fodors.com.

$$$ ⌂ **A Taste of Alaska Lodge.** The Eberhardt family's lodge is 20 minutes
B&B/INN   from Fairbanks, yet far enough away to make you feel like you're on
a wilderness retreat. **Pros:** great view; eclectic collections; quiet location. **Cons:** not close to town. **TripAdvisor:** "scenic," "very Alaskan,"
"a little bit of heaven." ⑤ *Rooms from: $185* ✉ *551 Eberhardt Rd.,
Two Rivers* ☎ *907/488–7855* ⊕ *www.atasteofalaska.com* ⇗ *8 rooms
in lodge, 2 in log house, 1 in annex* ⎢⊙⎢ *Breakfast* ✛ *A6.*

$$$ ⌂ **All Seasons Bed and Breakfast Inn.** In a quiet residential neighborhood
B&B/INN   within walking distance of downtown, this nicely furnished inn pro-
vides relaxation and privacy. **Pros:** close to downtown; clean rooms;
trip planning help available. **Cons:** lacks an Alaskan ambience. **Tri-
pAdvisor:** "wonderful company," "great breakfast," "cozy and quiet."
⑤ *Rooms from: $179* ✉ *763 7th Ave., Downtown* ☎ *907/451–6649*
⊕ *www.allseasonsinn.com* ⇗ *8 rooms* ⎢⊙⎢ *Breakfast* ✛ *C1.*

$$
B&B/INN

⌕ **Aurora Express.** It's off the beaten path, but this B&B is unforgettable, especially for railroad buffs. **Pros:** most unique lodging in the area; sweeping views of the valley. **Cons:** far from town; phone and TV in common area only; no kids under 12. **TripAdvisor:** "unique experience with awesome hosts," "what a hoot," "quirky and clean." ⑤ *Rooms from: $160* ✉ *1550 Chena Ridge Rd.* ☎ *907/474–0949, 800/221–0073* ⊕ *www.fairbanksalaskabedandbreakfast.com* ↝ *7 rooms* ☾ *Closed early Sept.–end of May* ⧉ *Breakfast* ✛ *D1.*

$$
HOTEL

⌕ **Bridgewater Hotel.** In the heart of downtown Fairbanks, just above the Chena River, this hotel has gone through a number of incarnations and is now a thoroughly modern, European-style hotel. **Pros:** good location; weekend specials available; downtown hotel with the most character. **Cons:** small and modest rooms; no kitchen or refrigerators; restaurant serves breakfast only. **TripAdvisor:** "well located," "very welcoming staff," "best customer service experience ever." ⑤ *Rooms from: $145* ✉ *723 1st Ave., Downtown* ☎ *907/452–6661, 800/528–4916* ⊕ *www. fountainheadhotels.com/bridgewater/bridgewater.htm* ↝ *93 rooms* ☾ *Closed mid-Sept.–mid-May* ⧉ *Breakfast* ✛ *B1.*

$$$
RESORT

⌕ **Fairbanks Princess Riverside Lodge.** An expansive wooden deck facing the Chena River draws a crowd at this luxury lodge in summer. **Pros:** grandiose halls and lounge; next to the Chena River; large gym to work off the steam. **Cons:** caters to large tours; basic rooms, kitchenettes and refrigerators available on request only. **TripAdvisor:** "very comfortable," "lovely friendly place to stay," "a travel back in time." ⑤ *Rooms from: $199* ✉ *4477 Pikes Landing Rd.* ☎ *907/455–4477, 800/426–0500* ⊕ *www.princesslodges.com* ↝ *326 rooms* ✛ *C2.*

$$
B&B/INN

⌕ **Minnie Street Bed & Breakfast Inn.** Martha Stewart would approve of this B&B. **Pros:** luxurious decor; massage available; variety of room styles. **Cons:** not directly downtown; no pets allowed. **TripAdvisor:** "cozy," "perfect place," "beautiful rooms and gardens." ⑤ *Rooms from: $149* ✉ *345 Minnie St., Downtown* ☎ *907/456–1802, 888/456–1849* ⊕ *www.minniestreetbandb.com* ↝ *12 rooms, 3 suites, 1 standalone house* ⧉ *Breakfast* ✛ *B6.*

$$$$
HOTEL

⌕ **Pike's Waterfront Lodge.** Log columns and beams support the high ceiling in the lobby of this hotel and conference center on the banks of the Chena River. **Pros:** located on the banks of the Chena River; Pike's Landing next door is a hot spot; close to the airport. **Cons:** small gym; cabins are a walk from the restaurant. **TripAdvisor:** "the most guest-friendly place," "great location and service," "nice cabin." ⑤ *Rooms from: $235* ✉ *1850 Hoselton Rd.* ☎ *907/456–4500, 877/774–2400* ⊕ *www.pikeslodge.com* ↝ *180 rooms, 28 cabins* ⧉ *Breakfast* ✛ *C2.*

$$
HOTEL

⌕ **River's Edge Resort.** If you want the privacy of a cottage, a bit of elbow room, and the amenities of a luxury hotel, you can find it along the banks of the Chena River at the River's Edge Resort. **Pros:** prime location along the Chena River; private cabins. **Cons:** no kitchenettes; ½-mile walking distance of nearby shop or bar. **TripAdvisor:** "quaint," "clean and comfortable cottages," "relaxing spot on the river." ⑤ *Rooms from: $125* ✉ *4200 Boat St., University West* ☎ *907/474–0286, 800/770–3343* ⊕ *www.riversedge.net* ↝ *86 cottages, 8 lodge suites* ☾ *Closed mid-Sept.–mid-May* ✛ *C2.*

8

WINTER IN FAIRBANKS

The temperature gets down to –40°F every winter in Fairbanks, but school is almost never canceled, no matter how cold it gets. In recent years, in fact, the only times schools have closed were when rare winter warm spells created icy conditions on the roads that made it too hazardous for bus travel. Young Alaskans are so hardy that outdoor recess takes place down to –20°F.

The weather is a great unifying factor among Fairbanks residents.

Winter conditions freeze the pipes of university presidents as well as laborers. After a night of 40 below it's common to see cars bumping along as if the tires were flat; the bottoms of the tires freeze flat, and it takes a quarter mile or so before they warm up and return to round. It's a pretty sure thing, if you live in Fairbanks, that your car has an electric plug hanging out front between the headlights—they need to be plugged in for heat during winter in order to keep running.

$$$
HOTEL
★

⚕ **Sophie Station Hotel.** Its quiet location and helpful staff make this spacious hotel near the airport one of Fairbanks's best. **Pros:** complimentary newspaper upon arrival; walking distance to grocery stores; equipped with full kitchens. **Cons:** average interior decor; no DVD players or VCRs. **TripAdvisor:** "nice and spacious," "large room," "comfortable." ⑤ *Rooms from: $219* ✉ *1717 University Ave.* ☎ *907/479–3650, 800/528–4916* ⊕ *www.fountainheadhotels.com* ⮐ *149 suites* ✛ *C3.*

$$$$
HOTEL

⚕ **SpringHill Suites by Marriott.** At the center of what was once the heart of the commercial district, the SpringHill Suites has 140 comfortable suites, each with a microwave, refrigerator, living-room furniture, and well-lighted work areas. **Pros:** comfortable in-room desk areas; a pool to relax in; home to one of Fairbanks's favorite restaurants. **Cons:** small lounge; no DVD players or VCRs; moderate-size gym. **TripAdvisor:** "fine place to lay your head," "fantastic service," "all considered, great choice." ⑤ *Rooms from: $229* ✉ *575 1st Ave., Downtown* ☎ *907/451–6552, 800/314-0858* ⊕ *www.marriott.com/faish* ⮐ *140 suites* ⦿| *Breakfast* ✛ *B1.*

$$
RESORT
Fodor's Choice
★

⚕ **Wedgewood Resort.** Both wild and cultivated flowers adorn the landscaped grounds of the Wedgewood Resort, which borders on Creamer's Field Migratory Waterfowl Refuge. **Pros:** courteous staff; 4 miles of trails through 76 acres of wildlife sanctuary; antique automobile museum; elegant banquet halls; airport shuttle. **Cons:** a bit far from most of Fairbanks's other attractions. **TripAdvisor:** "lots to do and see," "excellent choice," "great place to stay." ⑤ *Rooms from: $175* ✉ *212 Wedgewood Dr.* ☎ *907/456–3642, 800/528–4916* ⊕ *www. fountainheadhotels.com* ⮐ *297 suites* ✛ *A5.*

NIGHTLIFE AND THE ARTS

Check the "Kaleidoscope" section in the Thursday *Fairbanks Daily News–Miner* for current nightspots, plays, concerts, and art shows.

THE ARTS

Festivals are a big part of life in Fairbanks, the months of February and March bringing the most revelry.

FESTIVALS

JULY **Fairbanks Summer Arts Festival.** Alaska's premier cultural gathering, the Fairbanks Summer Arts Festival takes place over two weeks in late July on the University of Alaska Fairbanks Campus. The festivities, which grew from a small jazz festival, now attract visitors worldwide for music, dance, literary arts, healing arts, visual arts, American roots music. They even have classes and cooking on theatre and culinary arts. Visitors are encouraged to participate in one- or two-week classes and mini-workshops. ☎ *907/474–8869* ⊕ *www.fsaf.org.*

Golden Days. This is the annual celebration of Fairbanks's gold-rush past. Several days of events are capped by a street fair and big parade through the city in late July. ☎ *907/452–1105* ⊕ *www.fairbankschamber.org.*

AUGUST **Tanana Valley State Fair.** Interior Alaska's largest annual gathering, it fills a week in early August with attractions such as giant vegetables and the handiwork of local artisans. If you've ever really, seriously wondered what a 50-pound cabbage looks like, this might be your best chance to find out. ✉ *1800 College Rd., Aurora* ⊕ *www.tananavalleyfair.org.*

FEBRUARY **Yukon Quest.** The early-February Yukon Quest calls itself the "toughest sled dog race in the world," passing through historic early-gold-rush territory. In odd-numbered years the 1,000-mile race starts in Whitehorse and in even-numbered years it starts in Fairbanks. ☎ *907/452–7954* ⊕ *www.yukonquest.com.*

World Ice Art Championships and U.S. National Championships. The World Ice Art Championships and U.S. National Championships in late February to late March draw ice artists from around the world for an ice-sculpting competition extravaganza. ☎ *907/388-6388* ⊕ *www.icealaska.com.*

NIGHTLIFE

SALOONS

★ **Blue Loon.** The Blue Loon, between Ester and Fairbanks, presents year-round entertainment and great grill food. Movies are nightly at 5:30 and 8. Catch national touring bands, comedy, outdoor summer concerts, DJ dancing late nights on weekends, and much more, including free Wi-Fi. ✉ *Mile 353.5, Parks Hwy.* ☎ *907/457–5666* ⊕ *www.theblueloon.com.*

★ **Midnight Mine.** Don't be alarmed by the exterior of the Midnight Mine. It's a friendly neighborhood bar with darts, foosball, a pool table, and a big-screen TV, and it's within walking distance of downtown. Cleo the dog is likely to greet you as you come in—be sure to ask to see her trick. It'll cost you a buck, but it's worth it. ✉ *308 Wendell St.* ☎ *907/456–5348.*

Palace Theatre. The *Golden Heart Revue* at the Palace Theatre is a musical-comedy show about the founding and building of Fairbanks. It begins at 8:15 nightly from mid-May to mid-September. ✉ *Pioneer Park, Airport Way and Peger Rd.* ☎ *907/456–5960, 800/354–7274* ⊕ *www.akvisit.com.*

8

Celestial Rays of Light: Aurora Borealis

The light show often begins simply, as a pale yellow-green luminous band that arches across Alaska's night sky. Sometimes the band will quickly fade and disappear. Other nights, however, it may begin to waver, flicker, and pulsate. Or the quiescent band may explode and fill the sky with curtains of celestial light that ripple wildly above the northern landscape. Growing more intense, these dancing lights take on other colors: pink, red, blue, or purple. At times they appear to be heavenly flames, leaping across the sky, or perhaps they're exploding fireworks, or cannon fire.

The Fairbanks area is one of the best places in the world to see the aurora borealis—commonly called the northern lights. Here they may appear more than 200 nights per year; they're much less common in Anchorage, partly because of urban glare.

As you watch these dazzling lights swirling from horizon to horizon, it is easy to imagine why many Northern cultures, including Alaska's Native peoples, created myths to explain auroral displays. What start out as patches, arcs, or bands can be magically transformed into vaporous, humanlike figures. Some of Alaska's Native groups have traditionally believed the lights to be spirits of their ancestors. According to one belief, the spirits are celebrating with dance and drumming; another says they're playing games. Yet another tradition says the lights are torches, carried by spirits who lead the souls of recently deceased people to life in the afterworld.

During Alaska's gold-rush era some non-Native stampeders supposed the aurora to be reflections of ore deposits. Even renowned wilderness explorer John Muir allowed the northern lights to spark his imagination. Once, while traveling through Southeast Alaska in 1890, Muir stayed up all night to watch a gigantic, glowing auroral bridge and bands of "restless electric auroral fairies" who danced to music "too fine for mortal ears."

Scientists have a more technical explanation for these heavenly apparitions. The aurora borealis is an atmospheric phenomenon that's tied to explosive events on the sun's surface, known as solar flares. Those flares produce a stream of charged particles, the "solar wind," which shoots off into space. When such a wind intersects with Earth's magnetic field, most of the particles are deflected; some, however, are sent into the upper atmosphere, where they collide with gas molecules such as nitrogen and oxygen. The resulting reactions produce glowing colors. The aurora is most commonly a pale green, but its borders are sometimes tinged with pink, purple, or blue. Especially rare is the all-red aurora, which appears when charged solar particles collide with oxygen molecules from 50 to 200 miles above Earth's surface.

■TIP→ Alaska's long hours of daylight hide the aurora in summer, so the best viewing is from September through March. Scientists at the University of Alaska Geophysical Institute give a daily forecast from late fall to spring of when the lights will be the most intense at ⊕ *www.gedds. alaska.edu/auroraforecast* and in the *Fairbanks Daily News-Miner.*

SEEING THE NORTHERN LIGHTS
Aurora Borealis Lodge. The Aurora Borealis Lodge has late-night tours to a log lodge on Cleary Summit, with big picture windows to see the sky. The $75–$85 tour includes hot drinks and transportation from Fairbanks. With independent transportation, admission is $25 per person. Four spacious rooms in the two-story building are also available for overnight accommodation (call ahead in the summer season), each with large, north-facing windows, WI-FI private bath, and kitchen. Aurora tours run from August 20 to April 1. If space is available, snowshoe tours are $95 for four hours, with transportation. Rooms range from $199-224 per night, with discounts for longer stays. ⊠ *Mile 20.5, Steese Hwy., Cleary Summit* ☎ *907/389–2812* ⊕ *www.aurora cabin.com.*

Chena Hot Springs Resort. About 60 miles northeast of Fairbanks, the Chena Hot Springs Resort treats guests to a Sno-Cat ride to a yurt with a 360-degree panoramic vista of nothing but wilderness. Open every day of the year. ⊠ *End of Chena Hot Springs Rd., Chena Hot Springs* ☎ *907/451– 8104* ⊕ *www.chenahotsprings.com.*

Mount Aurora Skiland. Visitors fill the two warm mountaintop lodges at Mount Aurora Skiland after 10 pm on winter nights. Images from an aurora Web cam are shown on a large-screen TV. Admission is $30 and includes hot drinks. ⊠ *Mile 20.5, Steese Hwy., Cleary Summit* ☎ *907/389–2314* ⊕ *www.skiland.org.*

Northern Alaska Tour Company. Northern Alaska Tour Company has a variety of single or multiday winter aurora tours going north to the Arctic Circle and the Brooks Range. ☎ *907/474–8600, 800/474–1986* ⊕ *www.northernalaska.com.*

8

Senator's Saloon. The Senator's Saloon at the Pump House Restaurant, is the place to hear easy-listening music alongside the Chena River on a warm summer evening. ✉ *796 Chena Pump Rd.* ☎ *907/479–8452* ⊕ *www.pumphouse.com.*

SHOPPING

CRAFTS

Alaska Rag Company. Known for handwoven rugs, the Alaska Rag Company carries the work of many local artists. ✉ *603 Lacey St., Downtown* ☎ *907/451–4401* ⊕ *www.alaskaragco.com.*

Beads and Things. Beads and Things sells Native handicrafts from around the state. ✉ *537 2nd Ave., Downtown* ☎ *907/456–2323.*

Great Alaskan Bowl Company. The Great Alaskan Bowl Company sells lathe-turned bowls made out of Alaskan birch. Open every day of the year, except New Year's, Thanksgiving, and Christmas, this is the big one-stop shop for pretty much any kind of Alaskan thing you need—more than 70 vendors are selling out of the place. They have on the spot engraving, plenty of Alaskan goodies to sample, and they'll ship just about anything. They also have a summer-only second location in Denali, at mile 238.6. ✉ *4630 Old Airport Rd.* ☎ *907/474–9663* ⊕ *www.woodbowl.com.*

A Weaver's Yarn. A Weaver's Yarn has musk-ox qiviut to spin. This is undoubtedly the softest stuff imaginable. ✉ *1810 Alaska Way, College* ☎ *907/374–1995* ⊕ *www.aweaversyarn.com.*

JEWELRY

Judie Gumm Designs. In her small, eponymous shop Judie Gumm Designs Ms. Gumm fashions stunning (and moderately priced) silver and gold designs best described as sculptural interpretations of Northern images. Ester is 6 miles south of Fairbanks off the George Parks Highway. ✉ *3600 Main St., Ester* ☎ *907/479–4568* ⊕ *www.judiegumm.com.*

Larson's Fine Jewelers. Larson's Fine Jewelers has been making Alaskan gold-nugget jewelry and other contemporary designs for six decades. ✉ *405 Noble St., Downtown* ☎ *907/456–4141.*

Taylor's Gold-N-Stones. Taylor's Gold-N-Stones uses gemstones mined in Alaska and creates unique gold designs. ✉ *3578-B Airport Way, University Avenue* ☎ *907/456–8369, 800/306–3589.*

OUTERWEAR AND OUTDOOR GEAR

Apocalypse Design. Apocalypse Design makes its own specialized cold-weather clothing for dog mushers and other winter adventurers. Travelers from colder areas of the Lower 48 will appreciate the double-layer fleece mittens, among other items. ✉ *201 Minnie St.* ☎ *907/451–7555, 877/521–7555* ⊕ *www.akgear.com.*

Beaver Sports. Beaver Sports is equipped with a fine selection of quality backpacking, biking, paddling, and skiing gear; a big part of Beaver Sports is community involvement, from supporting high school sports teams to facilitating midnight-sun runs. ✉ *3480 College Rd., College* ☎ *907/479–2494* ⊕ *www.beaversports.com.*

NATIVE ALASKA BY BUSH PLANE

From Fairbanks you can catch a ride on regularly scheduled mail planes to small, predominantly Athabascan villages along the Yukon River or to Eskimo settlements on the Arctic coast. All of the smaller air services operate the mail runs on varying schedules. If you want to visit a particular village, or just have the desire to see a bit of Native Alaska village life, contact any one of the services. Do be aware that not all villages are interested in tourism; some are more prepared than others, and in a few, you're just going to be a nuisance. And what's happening where can change fast, with season, with hunting conditions, with weather. Get up-to-date local information before heading out.

Era Alaska. Era Alaska has an extensive roster of scheduled flights to many of the bush villages in northwest Alaska, the Interior, and the North Slope of the Brooks Range. It is one of the largest, most trusted bush flight services in the state. ☎ 907/266-8394, 800/866-8394 in Alaska ⊕ www.flyera.com.

Warbelow's Air Ventures. Warbelow's Air Ventures serves approximately a dozen villages. ☎ 907/474-0518, 800/478-0812 ⊕ www.warbelows.com.

Wright Air Service. Wright Air Service flies from its Fairbanks base to Interior and Brooks Range villages. ☎ 907/474-0502, 800/478-0502 in Alaska ⊕ www.wrightairservice.com.

SIDE TRIP: NENANA

56 road miles southwest of Fairbanks, 75 miles north of Denali National Park, 304 miles north of Anchorage on the George Parks Highway.

For a break from the buzz of the George Parks Highway, take a detour in Nenana (pronounced like banana), a year-round town of approximately 500 people, on the banks of the Tanana River and under the shadow of Toghotthele Hill or, in Athabascan, the "mountain that parallels the river." The downtown avenue seems stuck in time, a relic of the early Alaska Railroad construction heyday from 1915 to 1923.

Nenana has several claims to fame: home to the world's second-largest single-span bridge, 700 feet long; the site where President Warren Harding drove the golden spike into Alaska's railroad to commemorate its completion (and possibly where he caught the case of pneumonia that killed him); and the start of the 1925 serum run to Nome. It's also home to the Nenana Ice classic, where Alaskans annually bet on the date and time of the river's spring breakup. Ongoing since 1917, the jackpot sometimes climbs over $300,000.

NENANA WALKING TOUR

To get your blood flowing, start with a short walking tour at 5th Street, where you can talk with the staff at the Nenana Visitor Center. Continue north down A Street, past old storefronts, like Coghill's General Store dating from 1916, to the Alaska Railroad Depot, home of the Alaska Railroad Museum, which was built in 1923 and is now on the National Register of Historic Places. It's a fascinating stop, with a lot more inside than just train stuff. One block more along Front Street, peek into

St. Mark's Episcopal Church, built upriver in 1905; note its beautiful handcrafted altar and Athabascan moose-hide beadwork inside. Finish the tour along the river at the Alfred Starr Nenana Cultural Center, where you'll find authentic gifts by local artists from within 50 miles of Nenana, or browse the exhibits highlighting history and Athabascan culture of the area.

WHERE TO EAT

$ ✕ **Rough Woods Inn & Cafe.** One of the only places to eat and rent a AMERICAN very basic room is the Rough Woods Inn & Cafe. This establishment offers roadside food from fresh, deep-fried halibut to Angus charbroiled New York steak, and even breakfast, which is served all day. ⑤ *Average main: $12 ⊠ 2nd and A Sts., Nenana ☎ 907/832–5299 ⊕ www. roughwoodsinn.biz.*

NORTH OF FAIRBANKS

When you drive north of Fairbanks you enter territory where people are few and far between. Away from the thin line of the highways spread hundreds of thousands of square miles with few signs of human habitation. Accordingly, driving in the north country involves both nail-biting and jaw-dropping experiences. You might pick up hitchhikers carrying a moose and the smell of having camped for a month. You might see the swirl of musk oxen running from the noise of your car. And you might—probably will—set a personal record for how many cracks your windshield gets in a single day.

On the roads heading east, northeast, and northwest of Fairbanks, the going gets tougher the farther you drive. However, the gravel and other assorted surfaces are worth the trouble of navigating; these roads open up long slivers of the Alaskan wilderness. And since Alaska is so big, the more country you cover, the better your understanding of the place—and the better your chances of understanding the history of each unique road from the stories shared by the people you meet. ■ TIP→ Road conditions can be rough, and if you break down, help may be a long way off, so be sure to check your fuel and spare tire before you go. And if you're driving your own car, windshield replacement insurance is the smartest money you'll spend on the trip. You will be making a claim. No question.

Follow the Chena Hot Springs Road to its end and you'll find a natural hot spring that is among the best in the state. The Steese Highway connects to historic goldfields in Central and Circle, while the Elliott Highway leads northwest and, before shifting to the southwest, connects to the roughly north–south Dalton Highway (built to assist construction of the Trans-Alaska Pipeline System). All three roads provide access to countless starting points for hiking, skiing, camping, fishing, canoeing, and other outdoor-oriented adventures.

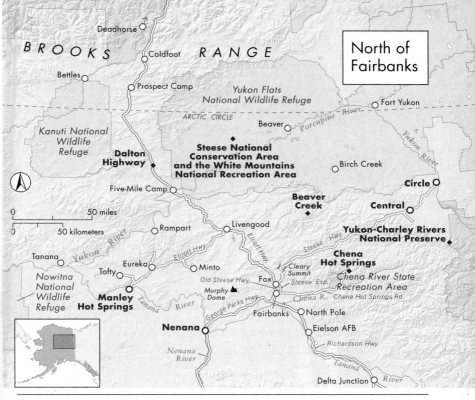

CHENA HOT SPRINGS

62 miles northeast of Fairbanks.

EXPLORING

Chena Hot Springs. The 57-mile paved Chena Hot Springs Road, which starts 5 miles outside Fairbanks, leads to Chena Hot Springs, a favorite playground of many Fairbanks residents. The road passes several attractions, including Chena River State Recreation Area and Chena Hot Springs Resort. If you're heading to the resort, don't skip the hiking, fishing, camping, and canoeing along the way. ■ TIP→ The chances of spotting a moose are excellent if you keep a sharp eye on the roadside.

From Mile 26 to Mile 51 the road passes through the **Chena River State Recreation Area,** a diverse wilderness of nearly 400 square miles. You can also stop for a picnic, take a hike for an hour or an extended backpacking trip, fish for the beautiful yet gullible arctic grayling, or rent a rustic backcountry cabin to savor a truly wild Alaskan adventure. Grayling fishing in the Chena River is catch-and-release, single-hook, artificial lure only. There are several stocked lakes along the road affording catch-and-keep fishing for rainbow trout, which are well suited for the frying pan.

CAMPING OFF CHENA HOT SPRINGS ROAD

The best rooms with views anywhere north of Fairbanks are in good campgrounds with a good, four-season tent. Don't forget the DEET, never, ever take food into your tent (do you really want your shelter to smell like a candy wrapper to bears?) and be prepared to spend the night in the real Alaska, under the stars, listening to the wolves howl.

Red Squirrel Campground. If you want to combine easy fishing access with your camping, the grassy Red Squirrel State Campground at Mile Marker 42.8 is your top choice: it's got a pond stocked with grayling. ⊠ *Mile 42.8, Chena Hot Springs Rd.*

Rosehip Campground. At Mile 27 you'll find these campgrounds; they're very basic but have the essentials for family camping. There's a trail that leads down to the river, which makes it a good put-in and take-out spot for paddlers. ⊠ *Mile 27, Chena Hot Springs Rd.*

Tors Trail Campground. Campers at Mile 39.5 are adjacent to the Granite Tors trailhead, a 15-mile loop into the high country. Also across from the campground you'll find a parking area (free for campers) and picnic spot near the river. There are no flush toilets here. ⊠ *Mile 39.5, Chena Hot Springs Rd.*

OUTDOOR ACTIVITIES AND GUIDED TOURS

DOGSLEDDING

Chena Dog Sled Adventures. Chena Dog Sled Adventures provides winter visitors a chance to drive a dog team or ride in a sled. Ice fishing and snowshoeing are also available. Call ahead for reservations, directions, and accommodations. ⊠ *Box 16037, Two Rivers* 🕾 *907/488–5845* ⊕ *www.ptialaska.net/~sleddogs.*

HIKING

Granite Tors Trail. The Granite Tors Trail, a 15-mile loop, can be done in a day, and offers a view of the upper Chena Valley and an opportunity to see dramatic "tors" (fingers of rock protruding through grassy meadow) that are reminiscent of the *moai* monuments of Easter Island. The trail is steep, but the views at the top make the climb worthwhile. Although the Interior landscapes lack the impressive mountain views of other parts of the state, the enormous expanse of rolling hills and seemingly endless tracts of forest are every bit as awe-inspiring. However, since there are no mountains here to collect snow and contribute to the water table, water sources along the way are unreliable. ■TIP➔ Bring a couple of quarts of water per person, plus mosquito repellent. Hiking uphill on a hot summer day is dehydrating. Also, weather is fickle here, and a bright, sunny morning can easily turn into an overcast, rainy, and windy afternoon. Come with adequate clothing, including rain gear, no matter how promising the skies look in the morning. A shorter hike is the 3.5-mile Angel Rocks Trail, near the eastern boundary of the area.

PADDLING

Chena River State Recreation Area. The Chena River State Recreation Area has numerous well-marked river-access points (the Chena Hot Springs Road parallels the Chena River, and canoeists use several put-in points along the way). The lower sections of the river area are placid, but the

CLOSE UP

Renewable Energy

Don't feel guilty about leaving on the lights at Chena Hot Springs Resort; most of the energy is geothermal. Since July 2006 the resort has been utilizing the 165°F springwater to power three turbines. This feat shocked geothermal experts who claimed that water temperatures must be at least 220°F. This free source of power allows the resort to run greenhouses through the –40°F winters. The daily 2 pm free Renewable Energy tours end at these productive greenhouses, where row upon row of lettuce, up to 25 heads a day, and five varieties of tomatoes thrive off a hydroponic, or soil-free, system. Order a salad for dinner and taste the special flavor of local, fresh-picked greens.

area above the third bridge, at Mile 44.1, can be hazardous for inexperienced boaters.

Alaska Wilderness Enterprises. Wilderness Enterprises has guided fishing for arctic grayling and scenic float trips on the Chena River. Half-day and full-day trips are available. When the temperatures drop, try your hand at ice fishing. Prices start around $175/day. ☎ 907/488–7517 ⊕ *www.wildernessenterprises.com.*

WHERE TO EAT

$$$
SEAFOOD
★

✕ **Two Rivers Lodge.** Fairbanksans are known to make the 40-mile round-trip for the delicious dinners here, including prime rib, frequent crab specials, and other Alaskan seafood dishes. Don't be discouraged by the building's outward appearance—rustic logs belie the menu's elegance. For a study in Alaskan-style contrasts, stop in the Trapline Lounge first for a predinner refreshment. $ *Average main: $25* ⊠ *Mile 16, Chena Hot Springs Rd.* ☎ 907/488–6815 ⊕ *www.tworiverslodge. com* ⊗ *No lunch.*

WHERE TO STAY

For expanded hotel reviews, visit Fodors.com.

$$$
RESORT
Fodor'sChoice
★

⚇ **Chena Hot Springs Resort.** People come in droves to soak in the hot springs—in the hot tubs, the indoor family swimming pool, or the outdoor natural-rock lake (ages 18-plus). **Pros:** it's 95% powered by geothermal energy; there's an activity for every taste. **Cons:** Wi-Fi comes with a daily usage fee at the Aurora Cafe; there are only eight TV channels. **TripAdvisor:** "rustic location," "just super," "lots of stuff to do." $ *Rooms from: $189* ⊠ *Mile 56.5, Chena Hot Springs Rd.* ☎ 907/451–8104 ⊕ *www.chenahotsprings.com* ⊅ *80 rooms.*

$
RENTAL

⚇ **Department of Natural Resources Cabins.** Used by adventurers with extensive backcountry experience, these cabins have woodstoves, bunks, and tools for cutting wood. **Pros:** wilderness is at your doorstep. **Cons:** only amenities are the ones you bring along. $ *Rooms from: $25* ⊠ *Mile 32 to 50, Chena Hot Springs Rd., Chena River State Rec-*

8

reation Area ☎ *907/451–2705* ⊕ *www.dnr.alaska.gov* ⌖ *Reservations essential* ⌁ *5 cabins.*

CENTRAL AND CIRCLE

From Fairbanks: 128 miles northeast on the Steese Hwy. to Central, 162 miles on Steese to Circle.

Steese Highway. The Steese Highway follows the Chatanika River and several other creeks along the southern part of the White Mountains. It eventually climbs into weatherworn alpine mountains, peaking at Eagle Summit (3,624 feet), about 100 miles from Fairbanks, and drops back down into forested creek beds en route to Central. At Central you can drive the 30-plus miles on a winding gravel road to Circle, a small town on the Yukon River. The highway is paved to Mile 44 and usually in good shape. A possible exception is in winter, when Eagle Summit is sometimes closed due to drifting snow.

OUTDOOR ACTIVITIES AND GUIDED TOURS

Tour companies are scarce in the area. Outdoor activities are generally do-it-yourself.

PADDLING

Chatanika River. The Chatanika River, a choice spot for canoeists and kayakers, is still fairly close to Fairbanks. The most northerly **access point** is at Cripple Creek campground, near Mile 60, Steese Highway. Other commonly used access points are at Long Creek (Mile 45, Steese Highway); at the state campground, where the Chatanika River crosses the Steese Highway at Mile 39; and at the state's Whitefish Campground, where the river crosses the Elliott Highway at Mile 11. The stream flows into the Minto Flats below this point, and river access is more difficult.

Water in the Chatanika River may or may not be clear, depending on mining activities along its upper tributaries. In times of very low water, the upper Chatanika River is shallow and difficult to navigate. ⚠ Avoid the river in times of high water, especially after heavy rains, because of the danger of sweepers, floating debris, and hidden gravel bars.

Alaska Public Lands Information Center. Contact the Alaska Public Lands Information Center for the status of the river. ☎ *907/459–3730.*

WHERE TO STAY

For expanded hotel reviews, visit Fodors.com.

$$
⌖ Chatanika Lodge. Rocket scientists from the nearby Poker Flat
B&B/INN Research Range gather at this cedar lodge, as do mushers (staff can arrange dogsled rides), snowmachiners, and local families. **Pros:** a local favorite; Alaskan character. **Cons:** long drive from Fairbanks; shared bathrooms. **TripAdvisor:** "another fun stop," "one of the best lodges in Alaska," "worth the scenic drive." ⑤ *Rooms from: $80* ⌖ *Mile 28.5, 5760 Steese Hwy.* ☎ *907/389–2164* ⊕ *www.chatanikalodgealaska.com* ⌁ *10 rooms with shared bath.*

STEESE AND WHITE MOUNTAINS

30 miles north of Fairbanks via Elliott Hwy.

The Steese and White Mountains are readily accessible, just a quick jaunt up the Elliott Highway. But once you're here, you'll have a few hundred thousand acres pretty much to yourself, with opportunities for everything from a short hike to a monthlong expedition.

EXPLORING

Beaver Creek. Rising out of the White Mountains National Recreation Area, Beaver Creek makes its easy way north. If you have enough time, it's possible to run its entire length to the Yukon, totaling 360 river miles if done from road to road. If you make a shorter run, you will have to arrange a take-out via small plane. A lot of people make the trip in five or six days, starting from Nome Creek and taking out at Victoria Creek. Contact Alaska Outdoor Rentals and Guides *(⇨ see Cruising and Canoeing Tours under Outdoor Activities and Guided Tours in Fairbanks)* to schedule a trip. Don't try this on your own unless you're an expert in a canoe.

Birch Creek. In the Steese National Conservation Area you can take a four- to five-day or 126-mile float trip on the lively, clear-water Birch Creek, a challenge with its several rapids; Mile 94 of the Steese Highway is the access point. Along the way you should see plenty of moose, caribou, and dozens of species of birds. This stream winds its way north through the historic mining country of the Circle District. The first take-out point is the Steese Highway Bridge, 25 miles from Circle. Most people exit here to avoid the increasingly winding river and low water. From there Birch Creek meanders on to the Yukon River well below the town. Fairbanks outfitter Alaska Outdoor Rentals and Guides arranges these trips.

Steese National Conservation Area and the White Mountains National Recreation Area. For those who want to immerse themselves in nature for several days at a time, the Steese National Conservation Area and the White Mountains National Recreation Area have opportunities for backcountry hiking and paddling. Both areas have road-accessible entry points, but you cannot drive into the Steese Conservation Area. The White Mountains Recreation Area has limited camping facilities from June to November; reservations are not accepted. ☎ *907/474–2200 Bureau of Land Management [BLM].*

WHERE TO STAY

For expanded hotel reviews, visit Fodors.com.

$
RENTAL

Public-Use Cabins. The Bureau of Land Management runs 11 public-use cabins in the White Mountains National Recreation Area and one road-accessible cabin on the Elliot Highway, with 300 miles of interconnecting trails. **Pros:** remote locations allow for an intimate experience with the land. **Cons:** permits required; geared for winter use; no place to take a hot bath. ⑤ *Rooms from: $25* ✉ *Fairbanks District Office of BLM, 1150 University Ave., Fairbanks* ☎ *907/474–2251, 800/437–7021* ⊕ *www.blm.gov/ak* ⤳ *12 cabins.*

8

YUKON–CHARLEY RIVERS NATIONAL PRESERVE

20 miles north of Eagle, 100 miles east of Fairbanks.

GETTING HERE AND AROUND

If you've driven out to Eagle, you might as well go beyond: Yukon–Charley Rivers is one of the most untouched, unspoiled, unvisited parts of Alaska. Hire a charter to get you onto the river, or just drop the canoe in the water and start paddling.

EXPLORING

Yukon–Charley Rivers National Preserve. The 126-mile stretch of the Yukon River running between the small towns of Eagle and Circle—former gold-rush metropolises—is protected in the 2.5-million-acre Yukon–Charley Rivers National Preserve. In the pristine Charley River watershed a crystalline white-water stream flows out of the Yukon-Tanana uplands, allowing for excellent river running for expert rafters.

In great contrast to the Charley River, the Yukon River is a powerful stream, dark with mud and glacial silt. The only bridge built across it in Alaska carries the Trans-Alaska Pipeline, north of Fairbanks. The river surges deep, slow, and through this stretch, generally pretty flat, and to travel on it in a small boat is a humbling and magnificent experience. You can drive from Fairbanks to Eagle (via the Taylor Highway off the Alaska Highway) and to Circle (via the Steese Highway), and from either of these arrange for a ground-transportation shuttle back to your starting city at the end of your Yukon River trip. Weeklong float trips down the river from Eagle to Circle, 150 miles away, are possible. ■ TIP→ Note that there are no developed campgrounds or other visitor facilities within the preserve itself, though low-impact backcountry camping is permitted. ⊠ *National Park Service, 4175 Geist Rd., Fairbanks* ☎ *907/457–5752* ⊕ *www.nps.gov/yuch.*

National Park Service. For information, contact the National Park Service in Eagle. ☎ *907/547–2233.*

OUTDOOR ACTIVITIES AND GUIDED TOURS

HIKING

Alaska Public Lands Information Center. The Alaska Public Lands Information Center has detailed information about the trails in the Yukon–Charley Rivers National Preserve. ☎ *907/459–3730.*

Circle-Fairbanks Historic Trail. The Circle-Fairbanks Historic Trail stretches 58 miles from the vicinity of Cleary Summit to Twelve-Mile Summit. This route, which is not for novices, follows the old summer trail used by gold miners; in winter they generally used the frozen Chatanika River to make this journey. The trail has been roughly marked and cleared, but there are no facilities and water is often scarce. Most of the trail is on state land, but it does cross valid mining claims that must be respected. Although you'll find rock cairns and mileposts while hiking, no well-defined tread exists, so it's easy to become disoriented. ■ TIP→ The State Department of Natural Resources strongly recommends that backpackers on this trail equip themselves with the following USGS topographical maps: Livengood (A-1), Circle (A-6), Circle (A-5), and Circle (B-4).

Pinnell Mountain National Recreation Trail. The Bureau of Land Management maintains the Pinnell Mountain National Recreation Trail, connecting Twelve-Mile Summit and Eagle Summit on the Steese Highway. This 27-mile-long trail passes through alpine meadows and along mountain ridges, all above the tree line. It has two emergency shelters with water catchment systems, although no dependable water supply is available in the immediate vicinity. Most hikers spend three days making the trip.

RAFTING
Rafting trips on the Charley River are for experts only. With access via a small plane, you can put in a raft at the headwaters of the river and travel 88 miles down this exhilarating, bouncing waterway. Contact the National Park Service *(⇨ see above)*. The river here is too rough for kayaks and open canoes.

WINTER SPORTS
Once past Mile 20 of the Steese Highway you enter a countryside that seems to have changed little in 100 years, even though you're only an hour from downtown Fairbanks. Mountains loom in the distance, and in winter a solid snowpack of 4 to 5 feet makes the area great for snowshoeing, backcountry skiing, and snowmachine riding.

MANLEY HOT SPRINGS

From Fairbanks: 73 miles north on Elliott Hwy. to Livengood, then 79 miles west on Elliott Hwy. to Manley.

EXPLORING
Manley Hot Springs. The Elliott Highway, which starts in Fox, takes you to the Tanana River and the small community of Manley Hot Springs. A colorful, close-knit, end-of-the-road-type place, this town was a trading center for placer miners who worked the nearby creeks. Residents maintain a small public campground across from the Manley Roadhouse. Northern pike are caught in the nearby slough, and a dirt road leads to the Tanana River with its summer runs of salmon. The Manley Hot Springs Resort has closed, but the hot springs are only a short walk from the campground. The highway is paved for 28 miles outside Fairbanks. If you travel here over land, take a moment to reflect on how year-round access to Manley Hot Springs only became available as recently as 1982, when the state decided to start plowing the Elliott highway in winter.

OUTDOOR ACTIVITIES
HIKING
Summit Trail. The BLM maintains the moderately difficult 20-mile Summit Trail, from the Elliott Highway, near Wickersham Dome, north into the White Mountains National Recreation Area. This nonmotorized trail can be explored as a day hike or in an overnight backpacking trip. It quickly rises into alpine country with 360-degree vistas that include abundant wildflowers and bird-watching in summer, blueberry picking in fall. This is not a loop trail, but ends at Beaver Creek. Be sure to bring

8

water, as sometimes the sources are scarce, and take advantage of the rest shelter at Mile 8. You'll find the parking lot at Mile 28.

THE DALTON HIGHWAY

GETTING HERE AND AROUND

Drive north out of Fairbanks and keep your compass needle pointed to the pole. That will get you to the Dalton, America's northernmost road.

EXPLORING

Dalton Highway. Plenty of hardy, adventurous visitors are choosing to "do the Dalton," a 414-mile gravel highway that connects Interior Alaska to the oil fields at Prudhoe Bay on the Beaufort Sea. Alaska's northernmost highway, the Dalton was built in the mid-1970s so that trucks could haul supplies to Prudhoe and Trans-Alaska Pipeline construction camps in Alaska's northern reaches.

The pipeline is the main attraction for many who make it up this way: stretching 800 miles across the 49th state from Prudhoe Bay to Valdez, it's both an engineering marvel and a reminder of Alaska's economic dependence on oil production. It carries crude oil across three mountain ranges, 34 major rivers—including the Yukon—and hundreds of smaller creeks. It crosses permafrost regions and three major fault lines, too; half of the pipeline runs aboveground and is held aloft by 78,000 vertical supports that proved their ability to withstand sudden, violent ground shifts as recently as 2002 in a 7.9 magnitude quake along the Denali Fault.

Thousands of 18-wheelers still drive the formerly private Dalton each year, but since 1994 they've shared it with sightseers, anglers, and other travelers. That doesn't mean the Dalton is an easy drive. The road is narrow, often winding, and has several steep grades. Sections may be heavily potholed, and its coarse gravel is easily kicked up into headlights and windshields by fast-moving trucks. If you drive the Dalton in your own car, make sure you have windshield replacement insurance, because you positively will be making a claim when you get home. There are few visitor facilities along the way, and almost nowhere to get help if something goes wrong. And with tow-truck charges of up to $5 per mile (both coming and going), a vehicle breakdown can cost hundreds of dollars even before repairs. Thus, before setting out, check everything you can in your car to make sure it's all working properly, and know how to change tires. Public access ends at **Deadhorse,** just shy of the Arctic coast. This town exists mainly to service the oil fields of Prudhoe Bay.

Unless you're an experienced outdoors person, areas off the Dalton Highway are best explored on a guided adventure tour. The only lodging options are down-at-the-heels motels or wilderness camping.

Coldfoot. At Coldfoot, more than 250 miles north of Fairbanks, the **Arctic Interagency Visitor Center** (☎ 907/678–5209) provides information on road and backcountry conditions, along with recent wildlife spottings. A picnic area and a large, colorful sign mark the spot where the road crosses the Arctic Circle.

8

⚠ There are no services between Coldfoot and Prudhoe Bay, a distance of nearly 250 miles.

OUTDOOR ACTIVITIES AND GUIDED TOURS

Although this is not a prime fishing area, fish, mostly grayling, populate the streams along the Dalton. You'll do better the farther you hike from the road, where less-motivated fishermen are weeded out. Lakes along the road contain grayling, and some have lake trout and arctic char. The Alaska Department of Fish and Game's pamphlet "Sport Fishing along the Dalton Highway" is available at the Alaska Public Lands Information Center (⇨ *Fairbanks Essentials, above*).

Alaskan Arctic Turtle Tours. Alaskan Arctic Turtle Tours specializes in Dalton Highway–area trips, with tours in 15-passenger vans. They also can do smaller groups, down to 2-4, or even groups as big as 55 in a full-sized bus. Driving the Dalton yourself is a major pain in the butt and hard on the car; if you're not feeling up to it, this is a great alternative. ☎ *907/457–1798* ⊕ *www.wildalaska.info*.

Coyote Air. Coyote Air is a family-run bush-plane service that specializes in scenic flights, backcountry trip support, and fall hunting trips in the Brooks Range. ⊠ *Mile 175, Dalton Hwy., Coldfoot* ☎ *907/678–5995, 800/252–0603 mid-May–mid-Sept., 907/479–5995 in winter* ⊕ *www. flycoyote.com*.

Marina Air Fly-In Fishing. Marina Air Fly-In Fishing has fly-in trips to remote lakes for northern pike, rainbow trout, grayling, and silver salmon. Overnight packages with a cabin are $300. ⊠ *1195 Shypoke Dr., Fairbanks* ☎ *907/479–5684* ⊕ *www.akpikefishing.com*.

Northern Alaska Tour Company. Northern Alaska Tour Company is the most established Dalton Highway tour company. It has numerous trips to the Arctic Circle and beyond, some with fly-drive options that operate year-round. ☎ *907/474–8600, 800/474–1986* ⊕ *www. northernalaska.com*.

WHERE TO STAY

For expanded hotel reviews, visit Fodors.com.

Here are the most accessible options for the trip north. *For details on options in Prudhoe Bay or Deadhorse, see Prudhoe Bay.*

$$ ⊞ **Coldfoot Camp.** Fuel, tire repairs, and towing are available here. **Pros:**
HOTEL guided outdoor activities available. **Cons:** basic rooms; greasy road food. **TripAdvisor:** "in the most amazing place," "comfortable," "rustic and clean." ⑤ *Rooms from: $219* ⊠ *Mile 175, Dalton Hwy., Coldfoot* ☎ *866/474–3400* ⊕ *www.coldfootcamp.com* ⤳ *106 rooms*.

$$ ⊞ **Yukon River Camp.** The motel is basic and clean, built from surplus
HOTEL pipeline-worker housing. **Pros:** tire-repair shop. **Cons:** no private bath. ⑤ *Rooms from: $199* ⊠ *Mile 56, Dalton Hwy.* ☎ *907/474–3557* ⊕ *www.yukonrivercamp.com* ⤳ *42 rooms without private baths* ☾ *Closed Oct.–Apr.* ⊺⊙⫾ *No meals.*

Continued on page 414

NATIVE HANDICRAFTS

Intricate Aleut baskets, Athabascan birch-bark wonders, Inupiaq ivory carvings, and towering Tlingit totems are just some of the eye-opening crafts you'll encounter as you explore the 49th state. Alaska's native peoples—who live across 570,000 square miles of tundra, boreal forest, arctic plains, and coastal rain forest—are undeniably hardy, and their unique artistic traditions are just as resilient and enduring.

TIPS ON CHOOSING AN AUTHENTIC ITEM

1 The Federal Trade Commission has enacted strict regulations to combat the sale of falsely marketed goods; it's illegal for anything made by non-native Alaskans to be labeled as "Indian," "Native American," or "Alaska Native."

2 Some authentic goods are marked by a silver hand symbol or are labeled as an "Authentic Native Handicraft from Alaska."

3 The "Made in Alaska" label, often accompanied by an image of a polar bear with cub, denotes that the handicraft was made in the state.

4 Be sure to ask for written proof of authenticity with your purchase, as well as the artist's name. You can also request the artist's permit number, which may be available.

5 The Alaska State Council on the Arts, in Anchorage, is a great resource if you have additional questions or want to confirm a permit number. Call 907/269–6610 or 888/278–7424 in Alaska.

6 Materials should be legal. For example, only some feathers, such as ptarmigan and pheasant feathers, comply with the Migratory Bird Act. Only Native artisans are permitted to carve new walrus ivory. The seller should be able to answer your questions about material and technique.

THE NATIVE PEOPLE OF ALASKA

There are many opportunities to see the making of traditional crafts in native environments, including the Southeast Alaska Indian Cultural Center in Sitka and Anchorage's Alaska Native Heritage Center.

After chatting with the artisans, pop into the gift shops to peruse the handmade items. Also check out prominent galleries and museum shops.

RUSSIA

Inupiaq

Athabascan

CANADA

Yup'ik,
Cup'ik

Eyak, Tlingit,
Haida, Tsimshian

Aleut,
Alutiiq

NORTHWEST COAST INDIANS: TLINGIT, HAIDA & TSIMSHIAN

Scattered throughout Southeast Alaska's rain forests, these highly social tribes traditionally benefited from the region's mild climate and abundant salmon, which afforded them a rare luxury: leisure time. They put this time to good use by cultivating highly detailed crafts, including ceremonial masks, elaborate woven robes, and, most famously, totem poles.

(left) A wagging tongue at the Juneau-Douglas City Museum
(right) A Tlingit totem reaches for the skies in Ketchikan

TOWERING TOTEM POLES
Throughout the Inside Passage's braided channels and forested islands, Native peoples use the wood of the abundant cedar trees to carve totem poles, which illustrate history, pay reverence, commemorate

a potlatch, or cast shame on a misbehaving person.

Every totem pole tells a story with a series of animal and human figures arranged vertically. Traditionally the totem poles of this area feature ravens, eagles, killer whales, wolves, bears, frogs, the mythic thunderbird, and the likenesses of ancestors.

K'alyaan Totem Pole

Carved in 1999, the K'alyaan totem pole is a tribute to the Tlingits who lost their lives in the 1804 Battle of Sitka between invading Russians and Tlingit warriors. Tommy Joseph, a venerated Tlingit artist from Sitka, and an apprentice spent three months carving the pole from a 35-ft western red cedar. It now stands at the very site of the skirmish, in Sitka National ßHistorical Park.

Woodworm: The woodworm—a Tlingit clan symbol—is a wood-boring beetle that leaves a distinctive mark on timber.

Beaver: Sporting a fearsome pair of front teeth, this beaver symbol cradles a child in its arms, signifying the strength of Tlingit family bonds.

Frog: This animal represents the Kik.sádi Clan, which was very instrumental in organizing the Tlingit's revolt against the Russian trespassers. Here, the frog holds a raven helmet—a tribute to the Kik.sádi warrior who wore a similar headpiece into battle.

Raven: Atop the pole sits the striking raven, the emblem of one of the two moieties (large multi-clan groups) of Tlingit culture.

Sockeye Salmon (above) and Dog/Chum Salmon (below): These two symbols signify the contributions of the Sockeye and Dog Salmon Clans to the 1804 battle. They also illustrate the symbolic connection to the tribe's traditional food sources.

IN FOCUS NATIVE HANDICRAFTS

8

Tools and Materials

As do most modern carvers, Joseph used a steel adz to carve the cedar. Prior to European contact—and the accompanying introduction of metal tools—Tlingit artists carved with jade adzes. Totem poles are traditionally decorated with paint made from salmon-liver oil, charcoal, and iron and copper oxides.

ALEUT & ALUTIIQ

The Aleut inhabit the Alaska Peninsula and the windswept Aleutian Islands. Historically they lived and died by the sea, surviving on a diet of seals, sea lions, whales, and walruses, which they hunted in the tumultuous waters of the Gulf of Alaska and the Bering Sea. Hunters pursued their prey in *Sugpiaq*, kayaklike boats made of seal skin stretched over a driftwood frame.

WATERPROOF *KAMLEIKAS*

The Aleut prize seal intestine for its remarkable waterproof properties; they use it to create sturdy cloaks, shelter walls, and boat hulls. To make their famous cloaks, called *kamleikas*, intestine is washed, soaked in salt water, and arduously scraped clean. It is then stretched and dried before being stitched into hooded, waterproof pullovers.

FINE BASKETRY

Owing to the region's profusion of wild rye grass, Aleutian women are some of the planet's most skilled weavers, capable of creating baskets with more than 2,500 fibers per square inch. They also create hats, socks, mittens, and multipurpose mats. A long, sharpened thumbnail is their only tool.

ATHABASCANS

Inhabiting Alaska's rugged interior for 8,000 to 20,000 years, Athabascans followed a seasonally nomadic hunter-gatherer lifestyle, subsisting off of caribou, moose, bear, and snowshoe hare. They populate areas from the Brooks Range to Cook Inlet, a vast expanse that encompasses five significant rivers: the Tanana, the Kuskwin, the Copper, the Susitna, and the Yukon.

BIRCH BARK: WATERPROOF WONDER

Aside from annual salmon runs, the Athabascans had no access to marine mammals—or to the intestines that made for such effective boat hulls and garments. They turned to the region's birch, the bark of which was used to create canoes. Also common were birch-bark baskets and baby carriers.

FUNCTIONAL & ORNAMENTED PIECES

Much like that of the neighboring Eskimos, Athabascan craftwork traditionally served functional purposes. But tools, weapons, and clothing were often highly decorated with colorful embroidery and shells. Athabascans are especially well known for ornamenting their caribou-skin clothing with porcupine quills and animal hair—both of which were later replaced by imported western beads.

INUPIAQ, YUP'IK & CUP'IK

Residing in Alaska's remote northern and northwestern regions, these groups are often collectively known as Eskimos or Inupiaq. They winter in coastal villages, relying on migrating marine mammals for sustenance, and spend summers at inland fish amps. Ongoing artistic traditions include ceremonial mask carving, ivory carving (not to be confused with scrimshaw), sewn skin garments, basket weaving, and soapstone carvings.

Thanks to the sheer volume of ivory art in Alaska's marketplace, you're bound to find a piece of ivory that fits your fancy—regardless of whether you prefer traditional ivory carvings, scrimshaw, or a piece that blends both artistic traditions.

IVORY CARVING

While in Alaska, you'll likely see carved ivory pieces, scrimshaw, and some fake ivory carvings (generally plastic). Ivory carving has been an Eskimo art form for thousands of years. After harvesting ivory from migrating walrus herds in the Bering Sea, artisans age tusks for up to one year before shaping it with adzes and bow drills.

KEEP IN MIND

The Marine Mammal Protection Act states that only native peoples are allowed to harvest fresh walrus ivory, which is legal to buy after it's been carved by a native person. How can you tell if a piece is real and made by a native artisan? Real ivory is likely to be pricey; be suspect of anything too cheaply priced. It should also be hard (plastic will be softer) and cool to the touch. Keep an eye out for mastery of carving technique, and be sure to ask questions when you've found a piece you're interested in buying.

WHAT IS SCRIMSHAW?

The invention of scrimshaw is attributed to 18th-century American whalers who etched the surfaces of whale bone and scrap ivory. The etchings were filled with ink, bringing the designs into stark relief.

More recently the line between traditional Eskimo ivory carving and scrimshaw has become somewhat blurred, with many native artisans incorporating both techniques.

TIPS

Ivory carving is a highly specialized native craft that is closely regulated. As it is a by-product of subsistence hunting, all meat and skin from a walrus hunt is used.

Ivory from extinct mammoths and mastodons (usually found buried underground or washed up on beaches) is also legal to buy in Alaska; many native groups keep large stores of it, as well as antique walrus tusk, for craft purposes. Many of the older pieces have a caramelized color.

FORTYMILE COUNTRY

A trip through the Fortymile Country up the Taylor Highway will take you back in time more than a century—when gold was the lure that drew hardy travelers to Interior Alaska. It's one of the few places to see active mining without leaving the road system. In addition, remote wilderness experiences and float trips abound.

Taylor Highway. The 160-mile Taylor Highway runs north from the Alaska Highway at Tetlin Junction, 12 miles east of Tok. It's a narrow rough-gravel road that winds along mountain ridges and through valleys of the Fortymile River. The road passes the tiny community of Chicken and ends in Eagle at the Yukon River. This is one of only three places in Alaska where the Yukon River can be reached by road. A cutoff just south of Eagle connects to the Canadian Top of the World Highway leading to Dawson City in the Yukon Territory, which is the route many Alaskans take to Dawson City—far more scenic, and shorter, than the alternative of taking the Alcan to Whitehorse and then turning north, but it's another of those places where it's good to check your insurance policy's attitude towards towing and windshield replacement. ⚠ The highway is not plowed in winter, so it is snowed shut from fall to spring. Watch for road equipment. If you're roughing it, know that in addition to the lodging listed below, the Alaska Bureau of Land Management also maintains three first-come, first-served campsites (as all BLM campsites are) on the Taylor Highway between Tetlin Junction and Eagle at Miles 48.5, 82, and 160.

> ## TIPS FOR DRIVING THE DALTON HIGHWAY
>
> ■ Slow down and move to the side of the road for trucks.
>
> ■ Always leave your headlights on.
>
> ■ Yield on one-lane bridges.
>
> ■ Pull to the side of the road when stopping for pictures.
>
> ■ Carry at least one spare tire.
>
> ■ Consider bringing extra gas.
>
> ■ Purchase a citizens band (CB) radio.
>
> Note: Not all car-rental companies allow their vehicles on this highway; check in advance.

EN ROUTE If you're headed to Fortymile Country from Fairbanks, you'll drive along the historic Richardson Highway, once a pack-train (think mules with bags) trail and dogsled route for mail carriers and gold miners in the Interior. As quirky places to turn off a highway go, North Pole and Delta Junction are up there with the best of them.

NORTH POLE

It may be a featureless suburb of Fairbanks, but you'd have to be a Scrooge not to admit that this town's year-round acknowledgement of the December holiday season is at least a little bit fun to take in.

Knotty Shop. The Knotty Shop has a large selection of Alaskan handicrafts as well as a mounted wildlife display and a yard full of spruce-burl sculptures, including a 6-foot mosquito and other wooden animals that

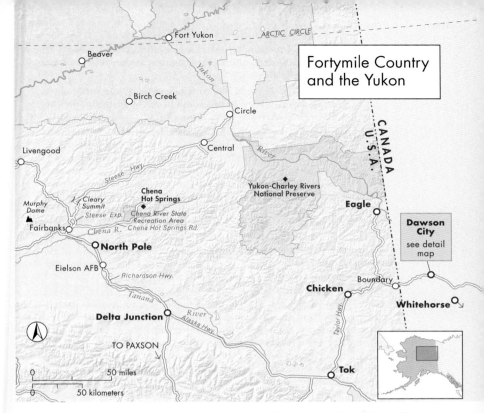

Fortymile Country and the Yukon

photographers find hard to resist. Get served soft drinks, coffee, and ice cream over a spruce-burl counter. Burls are actually caused by parasites in the living tree, and they create beautiful patterns in the wood. ⊠ *Mi 332, 6565 Richardson Hwy., 32 miles south of Fairbanks, Tok* ☎ *907/488–3014* ⊕ *www.alaskaknottyshop.com.*

Santa Claus House Gift Shop. If you stop in North Pole, don't skip the Santa Claus House Gift Shop. Look for the giant Santa statue and the Christmas mural on the side of the building. You'll find toys, gifts, and Alaskan handicrafts; Santa is often on duty to talk to children. And yes, you can get your mail sent with a genuine North Pole postmark. ⊠ *101 St. Nicholas Dr., Tok* ☎ *907/488–2200, 800/588–4078* ⊕ *www. santaclaushouse.com.*

DELTA JUNCTION

A good 100 miles southeast of Fairbanks, Delta is not only a handy stop on the Richardson Highway but is also the official western terminus of the Alaska Highway (when the Alcan was built, although Fairbanks was the ultimate destination, there was already a road from Fairbanks down to Delta). It's no surprise, then, that in summer Delta becomes a bustling rest stop for road-weary travelers. On top of this, it's the largest agricultural center in Alaska, boasting a local farmers' market, meat-and-sausage company, and dairy. Delta is also known for its access to good fishing and its proximity to the Delta Bison Range. Don't expect to see the elusive 500-strong bison herd, though, as they roam free and generally avoid people.

Buffalo Center Drive-In. If you'd like to try local dairy and meat, check out the Buffalo Center Drive-In just south of the Sullivan Roadhouse. ☎ 907/895–4055 ⊙ *May–late Aug., daily 11–10.*

Delta Chamber of Commerce. At the actual junction of the Alaska and Richardson highways, stop in the Delta Chamber of Commerce for more information on the area. This is also where you can get your "I Drove the Alaska Highway" certificates–technically, the Alcan ends here, in Delta, since there was already an extant road this far from Fairbanks. It's also worth the stop to see the chunk of pipeline outside, just to get an idea of what's carrying all that oil across the state. ⊠ *2855 Alaska Highway, Ste. 1B* ☎ *907/895–5068, 877/895–5068* ⊕ *www. deltachamber.org.*

Across the street are the **Sullivan Roadhouse Historical Museum** and the **Highway's End Farmer's Market,** open on Wednesday and Saturday mid-May to early September, 10 am–3 pm.

Rika's Roadhouse. Historic landmark Rika's Roadhouse, part of Big Delta State Historical Park, is a good detour for the free tours of the beautifully restored and meticulously maintained grounds, gardens, and historic buildings. Roadhouses were once stretched out at pretty regular intervals in the north, providing everything a traveler might need. You can use your imagination for what that must have been like in the old days. But Rika's is far and away the prettiest, best preserved of what's left, and it's a great place to get out, stretch and snack on some of their wonderful baked goods. ⊠ *Mile 275, Richardson Hwy., Tok* ☎ *907/895–4201* ⊕ *www.rikas.com.*

TOK

12 miles west of Tetlin Junction, 175 miles southwest of Dawson City.

Loggers, miners, old sourdoughs (Alaskan for "colorful local curmudgeons"), and hunting guides who live and work along Tok's streams or in the millions of acres of spruce forest nearby come here for supplies, at the junction of the Glenn Highway and the Alaska Highway. Each summer the city, with a resident population of fewer than 1,500, becomes temporary home to thousands of travelers, including adventurers journeying up the Alaska Highway from the Lower 48.

After crossing into Alaska from the Yukon Territory on the Alaska Highway, the first vestiges of what passes for civilization in the Far North are found in the town of Tok. Here you'll find a visitor center (one of the biggest in Alaska, since it serves as a center for roads branching across the state), food, fuel, hotels, and a couple of restaurants, and the need to make a decision.

Staying on the Alaska Highway and heading roughly west will take you into the Interior and to Fairbanks, whereas heading south on the Tok Cutoff will aim you toward South Central Alaska and the population center of Anchorage. Or you can make a huge loop tour, covering

ALASKA HIGHWAY HISTORY

It's hard to overestimate the importance of the Alaska Highway in the state's history. Before World War II there was no road connection between the Alaskan Interior and the rest of North America. Alaska's population center was in the coastal towns of the Southeast panhandle region, and most of the state's commerce was conducted along its waterways. Access to the Interior was via riverboat until 1923, when the railroad connection from Seward through Anchorage and into Fairbanks was completed.

The onset of World War II changed everything. An overland route to the state was deemed a matter vital to national security, to supply war material to the campaign in the Aleutians, and to fend off a potential invasion by Japan. In a feat of amazing engineering and construction prowess (and hubris—the United States started construction in Canada without bothering to ask the Canadian government if it was okay with them), the 1,500-mile-long route was carved out of the wilderness in eight months in 1942. The original road was crude but effective (the first truck to travel it made a blazing average speed of 15 mph), and has been undergoing constant maintenance and upgrading ever since. Today the highway is easily traversed by every form of highway vehicle imaginable, from bicycles and motorcycles to the biggest, lumbering RVs, known not so affectionately by locals as "road barns."

most of the paved highway in the state, taking in much of the terrific variety of landscapes and terrain that the 49th state has to offer. Head down the Tok Cutoff to the Richardson Highway (no one in Alaska uses the highway route numbers, and if you try to, you'll most likely just get blank stares), and then keep going south to Valdez. From there, catch the ferry to Whittier, Cordova, or Seward, explore the Kenai and Anchorage, then head north on the Seward Highway to the parks, to Denali, Fairbanks, and beyond. Loop back to Tok and you've seen most of what can be seen from the road system.

Tetlin National Wildlife Refuge. The Tetlin National Wildlife Refuge parallels the Alaska Highway for the first 65 highway miles after leaving Canada and offers two basic and seasonal campgrounds at Mileposts 1,249 and 1,256, or take a break from driving at Mile 1,240 and hike 1 mile over a raised-plank boardwalk to Hidden Lake. This 700,000-acre refuge has most of the charismatic megafauna that visitors travel to Alaska to see, including black and grizzly bears, moose, Dall sheep, wolves, caribou, and tons of birds. The visitor center at Mile 1,229 has a large deck with spotting scopes, and inside are maps, wildlife exhibits, books, and interpretive information, as well as a board with information on current road conditions. ⊠ *Mile 1,229, Alaska Hwy.* ☎ *907/883–5312* ⊕ *tetlin.fws.gov* ⊴ *Free* ☽ *Closed mid-Sept.–mid-May.*

Tok Main Street Visitors Center. To help with your planning, stop in at the Tok Main Street Visitors Center, which has travel information covering the entire state, as well as wildlife and natural-history exhibits. The staff is quite helpful. This is one of the largest info centers in all of Alaska–no matter what direction you want to go from Tok, you'll find something here to help you along the way. ✉ *Mile 1,314, Alaska Hwy.* ☎ *907/883–5775* ⊕ *www.tok alaskainfo.com.*

ESSENTIALS

Medical Assistance Public Health Clinic ✉ *Mile 1,314, Alaska Hwy.* ☎ *907/883–4101.*

WHERE TO EAT

$$$
AMERICAN
✕ **Fast Eddy's Restaurant.** It's much better than the name would indicate: the chef makes his own noodles for chicken noodle soup, and the homemade hoagies and pizza are a welcome relief from the roadhouse hamburgers served by most Alaska Highway restaurants. It's open late, but the soup is usually gone by 5. ⑤ *Average main: $25* ✉ *Mile 1,313.3, Alaska Hwy.* ☎ *907/883–4411.*

WHERE TO STAY

For expanded hotel reviews, visit Fodors.com.

$$
B&B/INN
▥ **Cleft of the Rock Bed & Breakfast.** With options for larger families and couples, this B&B offers either picturesque private cabins or comfortable rooms. **Pros:** cabins with all the comforts of home; on-site basketball courts; close to town. **Cons:** no guided activities; no airconditioning. **TripAdvisor:** "comfortable little cabin," "friendly hosts and great breakfast," "pleasantly secluded with good hospitality." ⑤ *Rooms from: $135* ✉ *Box 245, 0.5 Sundog Trail, off Mile 1,316.5 of Alaska Hwy.* ☎ *907/883–4219* ⊕ *www.cleftoftherock.net* ⟿ *5 cabins, 3 rooms* ⊙ *Cabins closed end Sept.–mid-May, rooms open year-round* ⑩ *Breakfast.*

$
RENTAL
▥ **Gateway Salmon Bake RV Park.** Behind the Gateway Salmon Bake are a full-service RV park and a very clean shower facility if you need to hose off the road dust from the long drive. ⑤ *Rooms from: $26* ✉ *Mile 1,313.1, Alaska Hwy.* ☎ *907/883–5578* ⊙ *Closed Sept.–mid-May.*

$$
HOTEL
▥ **Westmark Tok.** Made up of a series of interconnected buildings, the hotel has been updated and has decent accommodations for this remote part of Alaska. **Pros:** satellite TV; margaritas to get lost in; some pets allowed. **Cons:** not for those looking for lots of in-room character; frequently booked up with tour groups. **TripAdvisor:** "rustic," "very nice stay," "good stopover." ⑤ *Rooms from: $120* ✉ *Junction of Alaska and Glenn Hwys.* ☎ *907/883–5174, 800/544–0970* ⊕ *www. westmarkhotels.com* ⟿ *97 rooms* ⊙ *Closed mid-Sept.–mid-May.*

BORDER CROSSING

Crossing into Interior Alaska from the Lower 48 or from the ferry terminals in the Southeast requires border crossings into Canada and then into Alaska. Be very certain of all the requirements for crossing an international border before you travel, including restrictions on pets and firearms and the need for adequate personal identification for every member of the party. Know that even citizens of Canada and the United States traveling between Alaska and Canada are now required to have a passport.

SHOPPING

Burnt Paw. The Burnt Paw sells Alaska jade, gold, Native crafts, quality apparel, and even sled-dog puppies. On display is a sled-dog and equipment exhibit. There are also log cabin B&B rentals with traditional sod roofs. This is the place to be for the best breakfast in Tok. ✉ *Mile 1,314.3, Alaska Hwy.* ☏ *907/883–4121* ⊕ *www.burntpaw cabins.com.*

Naabia Niign. In Northway, south of Tok, Naabia Niign is a Native-owned crafts gallery with an excellent selection of authentic, locally made birch baskets, beadwork items, fur moccasins, and gloves. The friendly staff also operate a general store, gas station, bar, and RV park. ✉ *Mile 1,264, Alaska Hwy.* ☏ *907/778–2234.*

ON THE DEFENSIVE

Ft. Greely, which is 5 miles south of Tok toward Valdez, contains a growing number of underground silos with missiles that are part of the Ballistic Missile Defense System. The missiles are connected to tracking stations elsewhere and would be launched to try to shoot down enemy missiles in space if the United States were ever so attacked.

CHICKEN

78 miles north of Tok, 109 miles west of Dawson City.

Chicken was, and still is, the heart of the southern Fortymile Mining District, and many of these works are visible along the highway. Chicken (the story goes: they wanted to name the town "Ptarmigan," but nobody knew how to spell that), the second town in Alaska to be incorporated (Skagway was the first), has only a handful of permanent residents, mostly miners and trappers, creating an authentic frontier atmosphere. Do not encroach on private property, as miners rarely have a sense of humor about trespassing. Overland travel to Dawson City winds along a gravel road. Some drivers love it, some white-knuckle it. The road still closes for the entire winter, but in February and March snowmachiners hold a "poker run" on the road from Tok to Dawson City (⊕ *www.alaskatrailblazers.com*). Chicken only has three businesses in town, but what it lacks in infrastructure, it makes up for in atmosphere.

Get a feel for the past on a gold-mining adventure, where finder's keepers is the name of the game (in 2008 one participant walked away with a 1.4-ounce nugget), or tour the historic Pedro Dredge at 9 am and 1 pm daily at the Chicken Gold Camp & Outpost. The Gold Camp also provides meals, drinks, cabins, a campground–RV park, showers, free Wi-Fi, firewood, and espresso, as well as kayaking and other activities. Bluegrass lovers will appreciate the Chickenstock Music Festival on the second weekend in June.

Downtown Chicken, the longest-running business in town, has classic wooden porches and provides multiple services: the Chicken Creek Cafe; a saloon; liquor store; emporium with gifts and odds and ends; free Wi-Fi; and overnight parking, rental cabins, and wall tents, along

8

with gas and diesel service. Wild Alaskan baked salmon is available for lunch and dinner.

All in one establishment, you'll find Chicken Creek RV Park & Cabins, the Historic Town of Chicken, and the Goldpanner Gift Shop, which offers free Wi-Fi and an ATM. The RV park has gas and diesel, cabins, hostel rooms, and camping sites. Activities include gold panning and daily tours of Tisha's Schoolhouse at 9 am and 2 pm.

OUTDOOR ACTIVITIES AND GUIDED TOURS
CANOEING
Fortymile River. The beautiful Fortymile River offers everything from a 38-mile run to a lengthy journey to the Yukon and then down to Eagle. Its waters range from easy Class I to serious Class IV (possibly Class V) stretches. Only experienced canoeists should attempt boating on this river, and rapids should be scouted beforehand. Several access points can be found off the Taylor Highway.

Canoe Alaska. Since 1980 Canoe Alaska has conducted guided canoe and raft trips on Interior Alaska rivers. Trips (mid-May–Labor Day) range from two to eight days on rivers that vary in difficulty and remoteness. Evening interpretive tours in the *Arctic Voyageur*, a replica of a 34-foot voyageur canoe, are offered on a lake. Multiday *Voyageur* trips, canoe instruction, and rentals to qualified paddlers are also available. ☎ *907/883–2628* ⊕ *www.canoealaska.net.*

EAGLE

95 miles north of Chicken, 144 miles northwest of Dawson City. Road closed in winter.

Eagle was once a seat of government and commerce for the Interior. An Army post, Ft. Egbert, operated here until 1911, and territorial judge and noted Alaska historian James Wickersham had his headquarters in Eagle until Fairbanks began to grow from its gold strike. The population peaked at 1,700 in 1898. Today there are fewer than 200 residents. Although the majority of the population is gone, the town still retains its frontier and gold-rush character.

The Yukon River has shaped Eagle in more ways than just geographically. In earlier times it provided a vital mode of transportation. Today vacationers use Eagle as a jumping-off point for self-planned journeys through the Yukon–Charley Rivers National Preserve. Eagle was devastated by a flood in 2009; fortunately most historical structures were left undamaged.

Eagle Historical Society. The Eagle Historical Society has a two- to three-hour walking tour ($7) that visits six museum buildings while regaling participants with tales of the famous people (including Arctic explorer Roald Amundsen and aviation pioneer Billy Mitchell) who have passed through this historic Yukon River border town. One daily tour begins at the courthouse at 9 am from Memorial Day to Labor Day; special tours are available with advance notice. For the extra-curious traveler, there is an extensive archive and photo collection with staff available to help dig into the late 1800s at the office on 3rd and Chamberlain streets.

In addition, the Museum Store offers locally made items and oriented books. Eagle is a place unlike any other in the North. If you've gone to the trouble to get here, plan to spend some time and look around. ⊠ *1st and Berry St.* ☎ *907/547–2325* ⊕ *www.eagleak.org.*

National Park Service and BLM Visitor Center. The National Park Service and BLM Visitor Center is the headquarters for the 2.5-million-acre Yukon–Charley Rivers National Preserve. Informal interpretive programs, talks, and videos are available. Peruse the reference library, maps, and books for sale. It's located off 1st Avenue by the airstrip and the Yukon River, and is open Memorial Day to Labor Day. If you're even thinking of heading into the wilderness, stop here first. ⊠ *100 Front St.* ☎ *907/547–2233* ⊕ *www.nps.gov/yuch.*

YUKON TERRITORY

Gold! The happy, shining promise of gold is what called Canada's Yukon Territory to the world's attention with the Klondike Gold Rush of 1897–98. Maybe as many as 100,000 people set off for the confluence of the Yukon and Klondike rivers, on the promise of gold nuggets the size of basketballs just waiting to be picked up. In the end, roughly a dozen of them went home rich, but they all went home rich in memories and stories that are still being told.

Though the international border divides Alaska from Yukon Territory, the Yukon River tends to unify the region. Early prospectors, miners, traders, and camp followers moved readily up and down the river with little regard to national boundaries. An earlier Alaska strike preceded the Klondike find by years, yet Circle was all but abandoned in the stampede to the creeks around Dawson City. Later gold discoveries in the Alaskan Fortymile Country, Nome, and Fairbanks reversed that flow across the border into Alaska.

DAWSON CITY

109 miles east of Chicken.

Dawson City, one of the most beautiful, coolest towns in the north, is the prime specimen of a Yukon gold-rush town. Since the first swell of hopeful migrants more than 100 years ago, many of the original buildings have disappeared, victims of fire, flood, and weathering. But plenty remain, and it's easy to step back in time, going to a performance at the Palace Theatre, originally built in 1899, or stepping into a shop whose building originally went up to serve stampeders. In modern Dawson City street paving seems erratic at best, and the place maintains a serious frontier vibe. But it's also a center for the arts—the Dawson City Music Festival, held each summer, is one of the biggest in Canada, as the whole town turns into one big party and all kinds of music echoes under the midnight sun—and as the last touch of civilization before the deep wild, hikers share tables with hardcore miners at the local restaurants.

In the years leading up to the turn of the 20th century Dawson was transformed from a First Nations camp into the largest, most refined city north of Seattle and west of Winnipeg. It had grand buildings with running water, telephones, and electricity. In 1899 the city's population numbered almost 30,000—a jump of about 29,900 over the previous few years—which all but overwhelmed the Tr'ondëk Hwëch'in, the First Nations Hän-speaking people that inhabited the area. Their chief, a man named Isaac, who is still revered as the savior of the culture, packed his people up and moved them from the confluence, where they had hunted and fished for thousands of years, to the village of Moosehide a few miles downstream. The town he left behind grew into a place where a fresh egg could cost the equivalent of a day's salary down south, and where one of the most profitable jobs was panning gold dust out of the sawdust scattered on saloon floors.

> ### DAWSON CITY MUSIC FESTIVAL
>
> The Dawson City Music Festival, held every July, is the town's biggest party: at venues across town, from a big tent near the museum to inside the beautiful Palace Theatre, musicians from around Canada and around the world get together to jam. The entire town turns out, every hotel room is full, every camping spot taken, and there is no better time to be in Dawson. ⊕ *www.dcmf.com*

Today Dawson City is home to about 1,800 people, 400 or so of whom are of First Nation descent. The city itself is now a National Historic Site of Canada. Besides being one of the coolest, funkiest towns in the north, Dawson also serves as a base from which to explore the Tombstone Territorial Park located on the Dempster Highway, a region sometimes referred to as the "Patagonia of the northern hemisphere": a natural wonderland, with plants and animals found nowhere else, living in the spaces between high, steep mountain ranges.

GETTING HERE AND AROUND

The Alaska Highway starts in Dawson Creek, British Columbia, and goes almost 1,500 miles to Fairbanks. Drivers traveling north and southbound on the Alaska Highway can make a loop with the Taylor Highway route. This adds 100 miles to the trip, but is worth it. Part with the Alaska Highway at Tetlin Junction and wind through the Fortymile Country past the little communities of Chicken and Jack Wade Camp into Canada. The border is open from 8 am to 8 pm in summer. The Canadian section of the Taylor Highway is called Top of the World Highway, and with most of it on a ridgeline between two huge valleys, it really does feel like the top of the world, opening broad views of range after range of tundra-covered mountains stretching in every direction. Join back with the Alaska Highway at Whitehorse.

Numerous bus companies offer package tours or simple shuttle services *(➪ see Whitehorse Essentials, below)*. Regular air service to Dawson flies from Fairbanks in summer. **Air North, Yukon's Airline,** based in Whitehorse, offers direct air service from Whitehorse to Dawson City in summer.

ESSENTIALS

Airline Information **Air North, Yukon's Airline** ☎ 800/661–0407 ⊕ www.flyairnorth.com.

Emergency Assistance **Royal Canadian Mounted Police** ☎ 867/993–2677, 867/993–5555 for emergencies ⊕ www.rcmp.ca.

Internet **Tasty Byte Internet Cafe** ✉ 1076 Front St., Dawson City, Yukon, Canada ☎ 867/993–6100.

Medical Assistance **Dawson Health Center** ✉ 530 Church St., Dawson City, Yukon, Canada ☎ 867/993–4444.

Visitor and Tour Information **Klondike Visitors Association** ✉ 1102 Front St., Dawson City, Yukon, Canada ☎ 867/993–5575 ⊕ www.dawsoncity.ca ☉ Year-round. **Visitor Information Centre** ✉ 1102 Front St., Dawson City, Yukon, Canada ☎ 867/993–5566 ☉ Early May–late Sept.

EXPLORING

Dänojà Zho Cultural Centre. Dänojà Zho Cultural Centre creates an inviting atmosphere in which to explore the Tr'ondëk Hwëch'in First Nation heritage. For countless generations this group of Hän-speaking people lived in the Yukon River drainage of western Yukon and eastern Alaska. This specific language group settled around the mouth of the Klondike

River. Through seasonal displays, tours, cultural activities, films, and performances, learn about the traditional and contemporary life of "the people of the river." The gift shop celebrates fine First Nations art, offering unique First Nations clothing, beaded footwear, music, and books. The displays are kind of sparse, but it's good to stop in and see what the gold rush was like for the people who were here first and saw there was more value to a good caribou hunt than a bunch of shiny stuff in the ground. ⊠ *1131 Front St., across from Visitor Information Centre, Dawson City, Yukon, Canada* ☎ *867/993-6768* ⊕ *www.trondekheritage.com* ⊠ *$6* ⊘ *May– Sept., Mon.–Sat. 10–6.*

Dawson City Museum. The Dawson City Museum, housing the Yukon's largest collection, presents exhibits focusing on the gold rush, but also includes the geology and prehistory of the Klondike, as well as of the First Nations. Downstairs offers excellent displays of gold rush material; it might surprise you just how luxurious Dawson managed to be for the lucky few. Upstairs are more household goods, which most people skim through, but don't miss the piece of mammoth meat on the stairway landing. Not many places where you'll see that. Four restored locomotives and other railway cars and gear from the Klondike Mines Railway are housed in an adjacent building, which tends to open at odd hours. The museum also features a library and archives, helpful for visitor's hoping to find their gold rush ancestors. Daily programs include justice in the Klondike before the arrival of the NWMP, and "Camp Cheechacko," which gives you a chance to test your skills with a rocker box, finding out if you could have made it as a miner. During the summer season, the museum features costumed interpreters, and don't miss "City of Gold," a fascinating documentary on the region, narrated by Pierre Berton, perhaps Canada's foremost historian of the gold rush and Yukon. ⊠ *Territorial Administration Bldg., 5th Ave., Dawson City, Yukon, Canada* ☎ *867/993-5291* ⊕ *www.dawsonmuseum.ca* ⊠ *C$9* ⊘ *Mid-May– Labor Day, daily 10–6; call ahead for winter visits.*

Diamond Tooth Gerties Gambling Hall. Diamond Tooth Gerties Gambling Hall, for adults 19 and over only, presents nightly live entertainment and high-energy performances, including cancan, seven days a week from May until late September. It is also the only authentic, legal gambling establishment operating in all of the North and the oldest in Canada, although it's mostly just slots and a few table games. Yes, there really was a Diamond Tooth Gertie—Gertie Lovejoy, a prominent

WALKING DAWSON CITY

Dawson City is small enough that you can walk end to end in about twenty minutes—if you stop and spend five of those watching the river flow by. The Visitor Information Centre has an excellent walking map of town, and following it is one of the best things you can do while here. A lot of the old buildings have displays in the windows showing what they once were—bank, blacksmith, etc. A couple of older buildings have also been filled with historic photos and information. Walking tours—in English, French, and Dutch—leave regularly from the VIC.

dance-hall queen who had a diamond between her two front teeth. ✉ *Queen and 4th Sts., Dawson City, Yukon, Canada* ☎ *867/993–5575* ⊕ *www.dawsoncity.ca* 🔖 *C$10.*

Gold Dredge Number 4. Parks Canada leads tours of Gold Dredge Number 4, a wooden-hull gold dredge along Bonanza Creek, about 20 minutes outside town. The one-hour walking tour takes you into what's billed as "the largest wooden hulled, bucket line gold dredge in North America." When it was in operation the dredge ate rivers whole, spitting out gravel and keeping gold for itself. (To get an idea of how much area the dredge affected, think of the economics of this: hauling this enormous piece of machinery this far into the middle of nowhere, at a time when gold was worth less than $20 per ounce, and still making money.) Tours also include a short film about the site and the relocation of the dredge. Nearby you can visit working gold mines or pan for gold yourself in Bonanza Creek, where the Klondike Visitors Association offers a free claim for visitors. Be sure to bring your own supplies (almost every gift shop in town sells gold pans). Exit the Klondike Highway at Km Marker 74. ✉ *Mile 8, Bonanza Creek Rd., Dawson City, Yukon, Canada* ☎ *867/993–7200* ⊕ *www.pc.gc.ca* 🔖 *C$6.30* ☽ *End May–mid-Sept., daily 10–4; restoration work continues on dredge, so please confirm ahead.*

Jack London Museum. Literally a stone's throw from Robert Service's cabin, this reproduction of London's home from 1897 to 1898 is constructed with half of the wood from his original wilderness home that was found south of Dawson in the 1930s. The other half was sent to Oakland, California, where a similar structure sits at Jack London Square. The small museum contains photos, documents, and letters from London's life and the gold-rush era. Half-hour talks are given twice daily during peak season. ✉ *8th Ave. and Firth St., Dawson City, Yukon, Canada* ☎ *867/993–5575* 🔖 *C$5* ☽ *May–Sept., daily interpretation presentations.*

Robert Service Cabin. Scholars still argue the precise details of the lives of writers Robert Service (1874–1958) and Jack London (1876–1916) in Dawson City, but no one disputes that between Service's poems and London's short stories the two did more than anyone else to popularize and romanticize the Yukon. Service lived in his Dawson cabin from 1909 to 1912. The Robert Service Cabin is open for visitors June through mid-September, and holds multiple daily readings, including an evening program. ✉ *8th Ave. and Hanson St., Dawson City, Yukon, Canada* ☎ *867/993–7237* 🔖 *C$6.*

OUTDOOR ACTIVITIES AND GUIDED TOURS
BOATING

Klondike River Float Trip. The Klondike River Float Trip offers a chance to relax on a Class I river. You can put in at the Dempster Highway Bridge or Rock Creek. The journey ends when the Klondike spits you into the Yukon River at Dawson. Don't forget to take advantage of photo ops along the way. Other options include a guided 3½-hour float trip for $75 or a 3½-hour jeep tour for $95. Pick-up is at Westmark Dawson

8

City. ✉ *Dawson City, Yukon, Canada* ☎ *867/993–5599, 800/544–2206* ⊕ *www.graylineyukon.com.*

HIKING

Tombstone Territorial Park. Tombstone Territorial Park, located 1½ hours north of Dawson City and bisected by the Dempster Highway, is a 2,200-square-km (850-square-mile) area dubbed the "Patagonia of the northern hemisphere." Here you'll find some of the best hiking and views of granite peaks in the Yukon. The unique geology and geography of this wilderness supports a vast array of wildlife and vegetation. The park maintains four day-use trails at Km Markers 58, 72, 75, and 78, along with one campground and a new interpretation center at Km Marker 71.4, with good displays and great views of the mountains. It's worth stopping in to see how animals make it through the winter here. Throughout the park, backcountry mountaineering and wildlife-viewing options are endless. The new Visitor Center is a great place to get a handle on everything the park has to offer. You can book flightseeing trips over the jagged Tombstones from Dawson City. ✉ *Box 600, Dawson City, Dawson City, Yukon, Canada* ☎ *867/993–6850 in Dawson City, 867/667–5648 in Whitehorse, 866/617–2757 toll-free* ⊕ *www.yukonparks.ca* ☉ *Interpretation center open late May–mid-Sept.*

WHERE TO STAY

For expanded hotel reviews, visit Fodors.com.

$$$
B&B/INN
★
🍴 **Bombay Peggy's.** Named and fashioned after one of the last of Dawson's legal madams, Peggy's is done in elaborate Victorian gold-rush style, with heavy, plush draperies and rich color schemes. **Pros:** little imagination is needed to step back in time thanks to elaborate refurbishing; nice touches like fresh croissants and the "Sherry Hour." **Cons:** no elevator; not all rooms have air-conditioning. **TripAdvisor:** "swanky and fun," "luxury in Dawson," "quaint inn with a history." ⑤ *Rooms from: C$175* ✉ *2nd Ave. and Princess St., Dawson City, Yukon, Canada* ☎ *867/993–6969* ⊕ *www.bombaypeggys.com* ⤴ *3 rooms, 6 suites* 🍴 *Breakfast.*

$$
HOTEL
🍴 **Downtown Hotel.** A large collection of local artwork, including mushing scenes and antiques, adds to the hotel's early-1900s decorations. **Pros:** courtyard of the annex building has a hot tub; in the heart of downtown. **Cons:** not all rooms have air-conditioning. **TripAdvisor:** "great for Dawson," "first impressions are everything," "treated like a prince." ⑤ *Rooms from: C$123* ✉ *2nd Ave. and Queen St., Dawson City, Yukon, Canada* ☎ *867/993–5346, 800/661–0514 reservations* ⊕ *www.downtownhotel.ca* ⤴ *59 rooms, 5 suites.*

$$
HOTEL
🍴 **Eldorado Hotel.** The pioneer-style front to this hotel may be misleading, as the modern rooms, some with kitchenettes, are outfitted with decidedly non-1898 amenities such as cable TV. **Pros:** in-hotel bar and restaurant; top off the evening with a drink at the Sluice Box Lounge. **Cons:** no elevator. **TripAdvisor:** "clean and convenient," "far west feel with all the comforts of home," "fantastic location." ⑤ *Rooms from: C$150* ✉ *3rd Ave. and Princess St., Dawson City, Yukon, Canada* ☎ *867/993–5451, 800/764–3536 from Alaska and Canada* ⊕ *www.eldoradohotel.ca* ⤴ *46 rooms, 16 suites.*

$$ ☒ **Triple J Hotel.** Log cabins with kitchenettes, a central hotel, and a
HOTEL   detached annex make up this clean, quiet compound next to Diamond
Tooth Gerties. **Pros:** coffeemakers and coffee in every room; coin-oper-
ated laundry facilities. **Cons:** some rooms could use a face-lift; no DVD
or VCR. **TripAdvisor:** "nice cabins and good food," "budget hotel,"
"extremely noisy." ⑤ *Rooms from: C$142* ✉ *5th Ave. and Queen
St., Dawson City, Yukon, Canada* ☎ *867/993–5323, 800/764–3555*
⊕ *www.triplejhotel.com* ⤺ *27 rooms, 22 cabins.*

$$ ☒ **Westmark Dawson City.** This downtown two-story hotel is built around
HOTEL   a central courtyard and is convenient to the sights. **Pros:** good loca-
tion; laundry facilities; gold-rush ambience. **Cons:** no elevator; not all
rooms have air-conditioning. **TripAdvisor:** "large room with a view,"
"good location," "step back in time." ⑤ *Rooms from: C$154* ✉ *5th
Ave. and Harper St., Dawson City, Yukon, Canada* ☎ *867/993–5542,
800/544–0970 reservations* ⊕ *www.westmarkhotels.com* ⤺ *177 rooms*
⊘ *Closed mid-Sept.–mid-May.*

WHITEHORSE

337 miles southeast of Dawson City, 600 miles southeast of Fairbanks.

Near the White Horse Rapids of the Yukon River, Whitehorse began
as an encampment in the late 1890s, a logical layover for gold rush-
ers heading north along the Chilkoot Trail toward Dawson. The next
great population boom came during World War II with the building of
the Alcan—the Alaska-Canada Highway. Today this city of more than
22,000 residents is Yukon's center of commerce (only Walmart and Tim
Horton's for hundreds of miles), communication, and transportation,
and the seat of the territorial government.

Besides being a great starting point for explorations of other areas of the
Yukon, the town has plenty of diversions and recreational opportunities. You can spend a day exploring its museums and cultural displays—
research the Yukon's mining and development history, look into the
backgrounds of the town's founders, learn about its indigenous First
Nations people, and gain an appreciation of the Yukon Territory from
prehistoric times up to the present.

GETTING HERE AND AROUND

Air Canada flies in summer from Anchorage through Vancouver to
Whitehorse. **Air North, Yukon's Airline** (yes, that's really the name), based
in Whitehorse, offers direct, seasonal air service between Alaska and
Canada, flying regular runs from Fairbanks (summer only), Dawson
City, and Whitehorse.

To take in all the scenery along the way, you can drive yourself up
the Alcan Highway, or let someone else do the driving on a bus tour.
Alaska Direct Bus travels to Anchorage and Fairbanks year-round.
Alaska/Yukon Trails provides tours from Whitehorse to Dawson City
to Fairbanks. MGM Bus Services offers service from Inuvik to Whitehorse year-round when weather permits; charter trips are available.
There are multiple rental-car companies, buses, and taxis in Whitehorse; Whitehorse Transit has a city bus circuit that will get you where
you need to go.

8

ESSENTIALS
Airline Contacts Air Canada ☎ *888/247–2262* ⊕ *www.aircanada.com.* **Air North, Yukon's Airline** ☎ *800/661–0407, 876-668-228* ⊕ *www.flyairnorth.com.*

Bus Contacts Alaska/Yukon Trails ☎ *800/770–7275* ⊕ *www.alaskashuttle. com.* **Atlin Express** ☎ *866/651-7575* ⊕ *www.atlinexpress.ca.* **MGM Bus Services** ☎ *867/777–4295, 867/678–0129.*

City Bus Whitehorse Transit ⊠ *139 Tlingit St., Whitehorse, Yukon, Canada* ☎ *867/668–8394* ⊕ *www.whitehorse.ca* ☒ *C$2.50.*

Currency Exchange Bank of Montreal ⊠ *111 Main St., Whitehorse, Yukon, Canada* ☎ *867/393–8160.* **Scotiabank** ⊠ *212 Main St., Whitehorse, Yukon, Canada* ☎ *867/667–6231.*

Emergency Assistance Royal Canadian Mounted Police ☎ *867/667–5555.*

Internet Whitehorse Public Library. Whitehorse Public Library has free 60-minute Internet use, first come, first served. ⊠ *1171 First Ave, Downtown, Whitehorse, Yukon, Canada* ☎ *867/667–5239* ⊕ *www.ypl.gov.yk.ca.*

Medical Assistance Medicine Chest Pharmacy ⊠ *406 Lambert St., Whitehorse, Yukon, Canada* ☎ *867/668–7000.* **Second Avenue Walk-In Clinic** ⊠ *2131 2nd Ave, Suite 102, Whitehorse, Yukon, Canada* ☎ *867/667–6119.* **Whitehorse General Hospital** ⊠ *5 Hospital Rd., Whitehorse, Yukon, Canada* ☎ *867/393–8700* ⊕ *www.whitehorsehospital.ca.*

Post Office Canada Post ⊠ *300 Range Rd., Whitehorse, Yukon, Canada* ☎ *867/668-2195.*

Rental Cars Budget Rent-A-Car ☎ *867/667–6200, 800/268–8900.* **Whitehorse Subaru** ☎ *867/393–6550* ⊕ *www.whitehorsesubaru.com.*

Taxis 5th Avenue Taxi, Yellow Cab, Whitehorse Taxi, Northstar Taxi, and Golden Cab ☎ *867/667–4111.* **Yukon Taxi Service** ☎ *867/667–6677.*

Visitor and Tour Information City Hall ⊠ *2121 2nd Ave., Whitehorse, Yukon Territory, Canada* ☎ *867/668–8687* ⊕ *www.visitwhitehorse.com.* **Yukon Visitor Information Centre** ⊠ *100 Hanson St., Whitehorse, Yukon Territory, Canada* ☎ *867/667–3084, 800/661–0494* ⊕ *www.travelyukon.com* ☉ *Mid-May–mid-Sept., daily 8–8; mid-Sept.–mid-May, weekdays 8:30–5, Sat. 10–2.*

EXPLORING
Canyon City Archaeological Dig. The Canyon City Archaeological Dig provides a glimpse into the past of the local First Nations people. Long before the area was developed by Western civilizations, the First Nations people used the Miles Canyon area as a seasonal fish camp. The Yukon Conservation Society conducts free tours of the area twice a day on weekdays in summer; it also leads two-hour hikes Tuesday through Saturday in July and August. All the hikes are free and provide a great way to see the surrounding countryside with local naturalists. The society office houses a bookstore on Yukon history and wilderness and sells souvenirs, maps, and posters. ⊠ *302 Hawkins St., Whitehorse, Yukon, Canada* ☎ *867/668–5678* ⊕ *www.yukonconservation. org* ☒ *Free* ☉ *Tours July–late Aug., weekdays at 10 and 2.*

MacBride Museum of Yukon History. From gold-rush fever to the birth of Whitehorse, the MacBride Museum of Yukon History offers a comprehensive view of the colorful characters and groundbreaking events that shaped the territory. Follow the Yukon River through the history of Whitehorse in the Gold to Government exhibition. The museum also boasts a unique collection of wildlife, geology, historic artifacts, and photographs, alongside fine First Nations beadwork. The gold-rush displays are particularly telling of just what people went through to find a little glint of color. Outdoor artifacts include the cabin of Sam McGee, who was immortalized in Robert Service's famous poem "The Cremation of Sam McGee." MacBride also offers guided tours and a chance to try your hand at one of the Yukon's oldest professions—gold panning. ⊠ *1124 1st Ave., and Wood St., Whitehorse, Yukon, Canada* ☎ *867/667–2709* ⊕ *www.macbridemuseum.com* ⊠ *C$10* ⊗ *Mid-May–Aug., daily 9:30–4; Sept.–mid-May, Tues.–Sat. 10–4 or by appointment.*

Miles Canyon. Miles Canyon, a 10-minute drive south of Whitehorse, is both scenic and historic. Although the dam below it makes the canyon seem relatively tame, it was this perilous stretch of the Yukon River that determined the location of Whitehorse as the starting point for river travel north. In 1897 Jack London won the admiration—and cash—of fellow stampeders headed north to the Klondike goldfields because of his steady hand as pilot of hand-hewn wooden boats here. You can hike on trails along the canyon or take a two-hour cruise aboard the MV *Schwatka* and experience the canyon from the waters of Lake Schwatka. This lake was created by the dam built in 1958, putting an end to the infamous White Horse Rapids. ⊠ *68 Miles Canyon Rd., 1 mile from Whitehorse city center, Whitehorse, Yukon, Canada* ☎ *867/668–4716* ⊕ *www.yukonrivercruises.com* ⊗ *Cruises depart daily early June–mid-Sept.*

★ **SS *Klondike*.** The SS *Klondike*, a national historic site, is dry-docked on the bank of the Yukon River in central Whitehorse's Rotary Park, just a minute from downtown. The 210-foot stern-wheeler was built in 1929, sank in 1936, and was rebuilt in 1937. In the days when the Yukon River was the transportation link between Whitehorse and Dawson City, the SS *Klondike* was the largest boat plying the river. Riverboats were as much a way of life here as on the Mississippi of Mark Twain, and the tour of the Klondike is a fascinating way to see how the boats were adapted to the north; as an added bonus, in the old days they were also one of the few places where First Nations men could get paying jobs, so there's a rich Native history to the riverboats as well. You can't really understand the scale of the goldrush without touring a riverboat; really, it's one of the best things you can do in Whitehorse. ⊠ *Robert Service Way and 2nd Ave., Whitehorse, Yukon, Canada* ☎ *867/667–4511 mid-May–mid-Sept., 867/667–3910 rest of year* ⊕ *www.pc.gc.ca/lhn-nhs/yt/ssklondike/index.aspx* ⊠ *C$6* ⊗ *Mid-May–mid-Sept., daily 9:30–5.*

Takhini Hot Springs. At Takhini Hot Springs, off the Klondike Highway, there is swimming in the hot spring–warmed water (suits and towels are for rent), horseback riding, areas for camping with tent and RV sites, picnicking, an outdoor climbing wall, and a licensed (beer and wine) restaurant. Admission prices fluctuate; usually admission is around C$10. ⊠ *Km 10, Takhini Hot Springs Rd., 17 mile north of Whitehorse, Whitehorse, Yukon, Canada* ☎ *867/456–8000* ⊕ *www. takhinihotsprings.com* ⊙ *May–Sept., daily 8 am–10 pm; call for winter hrs.*

Waterfront Walkway. The Waterfront Walkway along the Yukon River will take you past a few points of interest. Your walk starts on the path along the river just east of the MacBride Museum entrance on 1st Avenue. Traveling upstream (south), you'll go by the old White Pass and Yukon Route Building on Main Street. It's a good way to get an overview of the old town site, and just stretch your legs if you've been driving all day. ⊠ *Whitehorse, Yukon, Canada.*

Whitehorse Rapids Dam and Fish Ladder. If you're in Whitehorse in late summer, it's possible to see Chinook (king) salmon. They hold one of nature's great endurance records: the longest fish migration in the world, which is more than 2,000 miles from the Bering Sea to Whitehorse. The Whitehorse Rapids Dam and Fish Ladder (founded 1958–59) has interpretive exhibits, talks by local First Nations elders, display tanks of freshwater fish and salmon fry, and a platform for viewing the fish ladder. The best time to visit is August, when between 150 and 2,100 salmon (average count is 800) use the ladder to bypass the dam. ⊠ *End of Nisutlin Dr., Whitehorse, Yukon, Canada* ☎ *867/633–5965* ⊕ *www.yukonenergy.ca* ▭ *$3 suggested donation* ⊙ *June–Aug., daily; hrs vary, so call ahead.*

Yukon Beringia Interpretive Centre. Near the Whitehorse Airport is the Yukon Beringia Interpretive Centre, which presents the story of the Yukon during the last Ice Age. Beringia is the name given to the large subcontinental landmass of eastern Siberia and Interior Alaska and the Yukon, which stayed ice-free and were linked by the Bering Land Bridge during the latest Ice Age. Although Whitehorse itself was glaciated, Dawson City, farther north, was right in the center of it, and miners still turn up mammoth bones today. Large dioramas depict the lives of animals in Ice Age Beringia, and there are replicas of skeletons and a 26,000-year-old horsehide; horses weren't as big back then. ⊠ *Mile 886, Alaska Hwy., Whitehorse, Yukon, Canada* ☎ *867/667–8855* ⊕ *www. beringia.com* ▭ *C$6* ⊙ *May–Sept., daily 9–6; Sept.–May, Sat. 1–5.*

Yukon Permanent Art Collection. The lobby of the Yukon Government Building displays the Yukon Permanent Art Collection, featuring traditional and contemporary works by Yukon artists, including a 24-panel mural by artist David MacLagan depicting the historical evolution of the Yukon. In addition to the collection on the premises, the brochure *Art Adventures on Yukon Time,* available at visitor reception centers throughout the Yukon, guides you to artists' studios as well as galleries, festivals, and public art locations. ⊠ *2071 2nd Ave., Whitehorse, Yukon, Canada* ☎ *867/667–5811* ▭ *Free* ⊙ *Weekdays 8:30–5.*

Yukon Transportation Museum. The Yukon Transportation Museum, next door to the Yukon Beringia Interpretive Centre, takes a great look at the planes, trains, trucks, and snowmachines that opened the North. Even if you're not interested in big machines, it's a pretty cool place to see the adaptations that transport in the north has required. ✉ *Mile 886, Alaska Hwy., Whitehorse, Yukon, Canada* ☎ *867/668–4792* ⊕ *www. goytm.ca* ✉ *C$6.*

Yukon Wildlife Preserve. The Yukon Wildlife Preserve provides a fail-safe way of photographing rarely spotted animals in a natural setting. Animals roaming freely here include elk, caribou, mountain goats, musk oxen, bison, mule deer, and Dall and Stone sheep. ✉ *HAPAY, 2nd Ave. at Steele St., Whitehorse, Yukon, Canada* ☎ *867/668–3225* ⊕ *www. graylinealaska.com* ✉ *C$30* ⊙ *Tours mid-May–mid-Sept., daily.*

OUTDOOR ACTIVITIES AND GUIDED TOURS
HIKING
Kluane National Park and Reserve. The Kluane National Park and Reserve, about 170 km (100 miles) west of Whitehorse, has millions of acres for hiking. This is a completely roadless wilderness, with so many mountains over 14,000 feet that they haven't even bothered to name most of them, along with hundreds of glaciers. Together with the neighboring Wrangell–St. Elias National Park in Alaska and a couple smaller parks, this is the largest protected wilderness on the entire continent. The Visitor Center has a few short guided hikes, and it's easy to book flightseeing into the park in Haines Junction. ✉ *Visitor Center, 119 Logan St., Haines Junction, Yukon, Canada* ☎ *867/634–7207.*

Yukon Conservation Society. The Yukon Conservation Society leads natural and historical hikes from July through August of varying lengths and difficulty. ✉ *Whitehorse, Yukon, Canada* ☎ *867/668–5678* ⊕ *www. yukonconsevation.org.*

SLED-DOG RACING
Yukon Quest International Sled-Dog Race. Whitehorse and Fairbanks organize the Yukon Quest International Sled-Dog Race in February. The race's starting line alternates yearly between the two cities. This is one of the longest and toughest races in the north—a thousand miles, and considered by mushers to be much harder than the Iditarod, as the terrain is rougher and the checkpoints fewer. ✉ *Whitehorse, Yukon, Canada* ☎ *867/668–4711* ⊕ *www.yukonquest.com.*

WHERE TO EAT
$$$$
EUROPEAN
✕ **The Cellar Steakhouse and Wine Bar.** In the Edgewater Hotel in downtown Whitehorse, this intimate two-room spot—down some stairs, as the name implies—is touted by the locals as the place to go for special occasions. The front room is less formal, with a bar and TV, while the back room, separated by an etched-glass partition, is quieter. The menu offers seafood and meat dishes, complemented by a decent wine list. ⑤ *Average main: C$30* ✉ *101 Main St., Whitehorse, Yukon, Canada* ☎ *867/667–2572.*

$
CAFÉ
★
✕ **Chocolate Claim.** Choose from fresh-baked breads and pastries, homemade soups and sandwiches, salads, and quiches at this charming café and deli. Artwork—ranging from paintings and pottery to rugs and quilts by local artists—displays change monthy, and it's all for sale. On sunny days you can sit outside. Friday happy hour is from 5:15 to 6:45 pm, with live music. ⑤ *Average main: C$10* ✉ *305 Strickland St.,*

8

Whitehorse, Yukon, Canada ☎ *867/667–2202* ⊕ *www.chocolateclaim. com* ☺ *Closed Sun.*

$$$ ✕ **Klondike Rib & Salmon BBQ.** If you're in the mood for something com-
AMERICAN   pletely different, this is the place. It's known not just for its wild-game
Fodor's Choice   dishes such as musk ox, caribou, and bison, but also for its halibut,
★   salmon, Arctic char, and killer ribs. It's open for lunch, but the famous
rib dishes are served only at dinner. Due to its popularity, there's almost
always a line, but it's worth the wait—for the best food in town, yes,
but also for the chance to dine in the oldest operating building in White-
horse. $ *Average main: C$25* ✉ *2116 2nd Ave., Whitehorse, Yukon,
Canada* ☎ *867/667–7554* ☺ *Closed mid-Sept.–mid-May.*

WHERE TO STAY
For expanded hotel reviews, visit Fodors.com.

$$ ⌕ **Edgewater Hotel.** On a quiet end of Main Street, this corner hotel, first
HOTEL   built during the 1898 gold rush, is in its third incarnation (the first two
burned down). **Pros:** rich history; borders the Yukon River. **Cons:** small
lobby and hallways to rooms; no continental breakfast. **TripAdvisor:**
"best place to stay in Whitehorse," "great location," "great little hotel."
$ *Rooms from: C$149* ✉ *101 Main St., Whitehorse, Yukon, Canada*
☎ *867/667–2572, 877/484–3334* ⊕ *www.edgewateryukon.com* ⤴ *32
rooms, 4 suites.*

$$ ⌕ **High Country Inn.** At this downtown inn you'll find tastefully
B&B/INN   appointed modern rooms. **Pros:** stay connected with Wi-Fi; try locally
brewed beers at the saloon. **Cons:** not all rooms have air-condition-
ing; standard rooms are minimally decorated, and some of them are
really small. **TripAdvisor:** "lovely room," "very helpful," "staff is the
best." $ *Rooms from: C$170* ✉ *4051 Fourth Ave., Whitehorse, Yukon,
Canada* ☎ *867/667–4471, 800/554–4471* ⊕ *www.highcountryinn.yk.ca*
⤴ *84 rooms, 24 suites.*

$$ ⌕ **Westmark Whitehorse Hotel and Conference Center.** You can catch a
HOTEL   nightly Klondike vaudeville show, the *Frantic Follies*, in summer at
this full-service hotel in the heart of downtown, the largest hotel in the
Yukon. **Pros:** laundry facilities; some pets allowed; breakfast buffet
available in the summer season. **Cons:** not the place to go to escape the
action; no air-conditioning. **TripAdvisor:** "very friendly staff," "safe
location," "would stay again." $ *Rooms from: C$149* ✉ *201 Wood St.,
Whitehorse, Yukon, Canada* ☎ *867/393–9700, 800/544–0970 reservations* ⊕ *www.westmarkhotels.com* ⤴ *180 rooms, 8 suites.*

The Bush

INCLUDING NOME, BARROW, PRUDHOE
BAY, AND THE ALEUTIAN ISLANDS

WORD OF MOUTH

"One thing I enjoyed on one of my trips was a plane trip out of
Fairbanks up to Prudhoe Bay—we stopped at two Eskimo villages
along the way—and visited with them and they put on a little show
for us—also, by doing this you could really comprehend the vastness of Alaska—also, seeing wild life from the air."

—Ronko

WELCOME TO THE BUSH

TOP REASONS TO GO

★ **Spend time in the company of bears:** The Alaska Peninsula has the world's largest concentrations of brown bears, which congregate near salmon runs each year.

★ **Learn about Native culture:** Native communities celebrate and support their cultural traditions. Come to the Bush for everything from blanket tossing to arts-and-crafts exhibits.

★ **Go fishing:** You'll see 100-pound salmon, 8-pound trout, and be the only one on your block to know what sheefish tastes like.

★ **Experience the Land of the Midnight Sun:** Only north of the Arctic Circle is the sun above the horizon 24 hours a day; in Barrow the sun doesn't set from mid-May to August.

★ **Get outside like never before:** Want the world to yourself? Bush Alaska includes millions of acres of remote parklands and wildlife refuges, including the least visited national park in the United States.

1 Southwest. This broad area ranges from the northern shores of the Shelikof Strait to the Yukon-Kuskokwim Delta. It's Alaska's least developed region; small Native villages are scattered across a wilderness rich in fish and wildlife.

2 Northwest and the Arctic. This region runs from the Seward Peninsula to Alaska's northernmost mountain chain, the Brooks Range, and the vast plain of the North Slope. Home to the Porcupine caribou herd and the Alaska National Wildlife Refuge, the Arctic is a balancing act of pristine wilderness, oil development, and villages where whale meat is still a vital part of the daily diet.

Point Hope
Point Hope
Noatak National Preserve
Cape Krusenstern National Monument
Bering Land Bridge National Preserve
Cape Espenberg
Kotzebue
RUSSIA
Wales
SEWARD PENINSULA
Taylor
Bering Strait
Teller
Council
Nome
Saint Lawrence Island
Norton Sound
Unalakleet
St. Michael
YUKON DELTA
Scammon Bay
Yukon
Hooper Bay
Yukon Delta National Wildlife Refuge
Bethel
Nunivak Island
Togiak National Wildlife Refuge
Kuskokwim Bay
Platinum
Togiak
Cape Newenham
Dillingham
St. Paul Island
PRIBILOF ISLANDS
Saint George Island
Wood–Tikchik State Park
Bristol Bay
Port Heiden
3
Port Moller
Chignik
Alaska Peninsula National Wildlife Refuge
ALASKA PENINSULA
Unimak Island
ALEUTIANS ISLANDS
Dutch Harbor/ Unalaska
Nikolski

0   100 mi
0   100 km

GETTING ORIENTED

As much a lifestyle as a place, "the Bush" generally refers to all of mainland Alaska that lies beyond the road system, plus the western islands. And that really means about 90% of the state. Geographically, though, the Bush encompasses all of western Alaska, from the North Pacific to the Beaufort Sea; that part of Alaska's mainland lying north of the Arctic Circle; and a good chunk of the Interior. Figure it this way: if your cell phone works, you're probably not really in the Bush.

9

3 Alaska Peninsula, Pribilof Islands, and Aleutian Island Chain. Considered part of the Southwest, the Aleutians are closer to Japan than to San Francisco. Even more remote are the Pribilof Islands; they're the northern edge of Aleut settlement and the seasonal home of hundreds of thousands of seals and breeding birds, some seen nowhere else in North America. It's a birder's paradise.

Updated by
Lisa Hupp

Often when an Alaskan talks about going out to the Bush, they mean anywhere off the grid, which is most of Alaska. However, there's another area that Alaskans call the Bush, which refers to those wild and lonely expanses of territory beyond cities, towns, highways, and railroad corridors, stretching from the Kodiak Archipelago, Alaska Peninsula, and Aleutian Islands in the south through the Yukon-Kuskokwim Delta and Seward Peninsula and into the northern High Arctic. It's just a matter of understanding context.

For the sake of this guide, the Bush refers to this territory. The Bush extends over two-thirds of Alaska, where caribou outnumber people and where the summer sun really does shine at midnight; in fact, at the state's northern edge it remains in the sky for several weeks in June and July, disappearing altogether for weeks in winter. The Bush is a land that knows the soft footsteps of the Eskimos and the Aleuts, the scratchings of those who searched (and still search) for oil and gold, and the ghosts of almost-forgotten battlefields of World War II.

If you visit the Arctic plains in summer, you'll see an array of bright wildflowers growing from a sponge of rich green tundra dotted with pools of melting snow. Willow trees barely an inch tall might be a hundred years old, and sometimes berry bushes have berries bigger than the bush they grow on. In the long, dark Arctic winter, a painter's-blue kind of twilight rises from the ice and snowscapes at midday, but the moon can be bright enough to read by, and on a clear night you will have a new appreciation for the depth of the heavens. Spring and fall are fleeting moments when the tundra awakens from its winter slumber or turns briefly brilliant with autumn colors.

The Brooks Range, which stretches east–west across the state from nearly the sea to the Canadian border, separates the Arctic from the rest of the state. The Brooks is actually a superchain, including several mountain systems, from pale, softly rounded limestone mountains in the east and west to the towering granite spires of the Arrigetch Peaks in the heart of the range. Large portions of the Brooks Range's middle and western sections are protected within Gates of the Arctic National Park and the neighboring Noatak National Preserve; its eastern reaches lie within the Arctic National Wildlife Refuge.

North of the Brooks Range a great apron of land called the North Slope tilts gently toward the Beaufort Sea and the Arctic Ocean. The vast sweep of this frozen tundra brightens each summer with yellow Arctic poppies, bright red bearberry, and dozens of other wildflower species that pepper endless stretches of landscape. Beneath the surface, permanently frozen ground known as permafrost has shifted and shaped this land for centuries, fragmenting it into giant polygons that make a fascinating pattern when viewed from the sky. This same permafrost, due to global climate change, is melting rapidly, radically changing not only the lives of humans, but also the annual migrations of numerous different animals, as well as the very composition of the atmosphere.

At the very edge of this wilderness, where land meets sea, Prudhoe Bay, America's largest oil field, was discovered in 1968. At its peak, more than 2 million barrels a day of North Slope crude from Prudhoe and neighboring basins flowed south via the 800-mile pipeline to the port of Valdez, on Prince William Sound in South Central Alaska. Today the flow has diminished to around 600,000 barrels per day, a number that decreases slightly every year.

The rivers that drain the Brooks Range include the Kongakut, Kobuk, and Sheenjek, names that reflect the native peoples who have lived here for thousands of years, ever since their ancestors crossed the Bering Land Bridge. The great Noatak River defies the Arctic's north–south drainage pattern and runs east–west, making a right-angle turn before emptying into Kotzebue (*kots*-eh-bew) Sound. Perched on this sound is the colorful Eskimo (technically, Inupiaq; the term "Eskimo" is falling out of favor, being replaced by local and more specific terms) town of Kotzebue, the largest Native settlement in the state and the jumping-off point for much of the surrounding area. Native ceremonial dances are demonstrated at Kotzebue's Living Museum of the Arctic, as is the Eskimo blanket toss, a traditional activity dating to prehistoric times, when hunters were bounced high in the air so they could scan the horizon for seals.

STOMPING GROUNDS

Great herds of caribou—including the western herd with more than a half million animals, and the Porcupine herd with around a hundred thousand—move slowly across the tundra, feeding and fattening for the next winter and attempting to stay clear of wolves and grizzlies. In the Arctic Ocean's Beaufort Sea, polar bears, stained a light gold from the oil of seals they have killed, pose like monarchs on ice floes. One of Alaska's premier wildlands, the Arctic National Wildlife Refuge protects mountain and tundra landscape important to caribou, polar bears, grizzlies, wolves, and musk ox.

9

BEST BETS FOR DIFFERENT TRAVELERS

For an easy adventure in the wild:

■ Take a tour with Nome Discovery Tours. See leftover artifacts from the gold rush, explore the tundra, and maybe even see some musk ox.

■ Ride the Alaska Marine Highway to Dutch Harbor. Bring your birding scope. This will get you talking with locals better than any cruise can.

For serious animal watching:

■ Head to Brooks Camp or Hallo Bay to see bears.

■ Make your way to the Pribilof Islands for birds and Northern fur seals.

To get deep into the middle of nowhere:

■ Take a guided trip into the Brooks Range and Gates of the Arctic National Park.

■ Travel with Arctic Treks deep into the Alaska National Wildlife Refuge.

If you want major bragging rights:

■ Visit Barrow, the northernmost city on the continent, and probably the only town where you can find whale spears in the hardware store.

Another coastal community, this one first settled by prospectors, is the former gold-rush boomtown of Nome, where you can still pan for riches. In early spring Nome celebrates the appearance of the sun with a golf tournament where the "greens" are painted on the ice of the Bering Sea coast. Nome also serves as the end of the Iditarod Trail Sled Dog Race, which begins in Anchorage the first Saturday in March and finishes about 10 days later, when the fastest dog teams make their way up Front Street to the cheers of locals and visitors alike.

Southwest Alaska includes the biologically productive wetlands of the Yukon-Kuskokwim Delta, where the state's greatest river meets the wild ocean. Sloughs, ponds, marshes, mud, streams, and puddles in these flat regions near sea level can slow water travel to a standstill. The delta is one of the most important migratory flyways for birds in North America, and the waters teem with life. Farther south, Bristol Bay is the site of some of the largest salmon runs in the world. Nearby Wood-Tikchik State Park (the nation's largest, at more than 1.6 million acres) encompasses huge lake systems and vast stretches of untouched wilderness where moose with antlers the size of end tables browse their way through the glaciated landscape. And on the upper reaches of the Alaska Peninsula the brown bears of Katmai rule a vast national park dominated by dramatic volcanic scenery. Also in the Southwest, the lower Alaska Peninsula and the Aleutian (pronounced ah-*loo*-shun) Islands reach well into the Pacific Ocean toward Japan. This chain beckoned Russian explorers to Alaska in the 18th century, as they tried to turn the islands' sea otter population into furs to trade with China for tea. Along the islands, weathered onion-dome Russian Orthodox churches in Aleut villages brace against fierce Pacific winds.

Dutch Harbor, the largest town in the Aleutians and a former U.S. Navy base pounded by Japanese bombs in 1942, is one of America's busiest commercial fishing ports. Deep-sea trawlers and factory ships venture from here into the stormy North Pacific Ocean and the Bering Sea for harvests of bottom fish, crab, and other catches. Unalaska, an ancient Aleut village, is Dutch Harbor's neighbor and home to one of the oldest and most beautiful Russian Orthodox churches in Alaska. North of the Aleutian chain, in the Bering Sea, the remote volcanic islands of the Pribilofs support immense populations of birds and sea mammals, as well as two small Aleut communities, St. George and St. Paul.

Alaskans who live in towns use the Bush as an escape valve, a place to get away. And those who've made the Bush their home are practically heroes to the rest of the state; they're the people who are bold enough to do what the majority of urban Alaskans wish they could do. Bush Alaskans have a deep affection for their raw land that is difficult to explain to strangers. They talk of living with complete independence, "close to nature." A cliché, perhaps, until you realize that these Alaskans reside in the Bush all year long, adapting to brutal winter weather and isolation, preferring to live off the road system. They know a store-bought hamburger will never taste as good as fresh moose meat, and whatever they're missing by not having a TV can't possibly be as interesting as the view out the cabin window. They have accepted the Bush for what it is: dramatic, unforgiving, and glorious.

EXPLORING THE BUSH

Philosophically speaking, the Bush is more a lifestyle than a location. It brings a new definition to "roughing it"; after you experience the Bush, you come to understand that the term "rural" only applies in the Lower 48, where there's always an urban hub nearby to bail you out. But if a village or town store in the Bush runs out of something, it won't be in stock again until the next delivery—whether it be by boat or by plane—which can take anywhere from a week to a month, maybe even not until the next spring after the ice thaws; hopefully the store didn't just run out of toilet paper! People who live in the boonies know transportation schedules like the backs of their hands, and they know that if they don't show up at the store within hours of the supply boat or plane's arrival, the odds of getting any fresh milk or vegetables are about zero.

Technically, the Bush is more or less any place in mainland Alaska that can't be reached by road. To outsiders the Bush represents three distinct destinations. The southwestern part of the Bush, the Yukon Delta region and Bethel down to the Shelikof Strait, is the preferred territory for sportsmen and those looking to spot big animals. The Aleutian and Pribilof islands and the Alaska Peninsula attract birders and history buffs. And the northern part of the Bush, from Nome to Point Barrow, is for those who see north as a direction to go. A lot of people may say they're traveling to the far north for the Native culture, for a chance to see the beauty of tundra, but really, most of them are doing it for bragging rights.

Of course, just going to Alaska is cause enough to boast, and each region has its own distinct draw. Kodiak and Katmai are great for grizzly viewing and birding, Nome is not only the best place for gold-rush

9

history, but is also known for its large and small wildlife as well as bird-watching in summer. No matter where you go, that distinct Alaskan culture—created by the simple fact that the only people who live here are people who genuinely want to live here—is abundant, distinct, and welcoming.

A tour of the Bush's southwestern region can begin in Bethel, an important outpost on the Yukon-Kuskokwim Delta and surrounded by the Yukon Delta National Wildlife Refuge; off the mainland coast is the undeveloped wilderness of Nunivak Island.

The Alaska Peninsula juts out between the Pacific Ocean and the Bering Sea; here are the Becharof and Alaska Peninsula National Wildlife refuges, as well as the prime bear-viewing area of Katmai National Park and Preserve. To the northeast of the Alaska Peninsula is the Kodiak Archipelago, where you'll find Kodiak National Wildlife Refuge and Shuyak Island State Park.

The Aleutian Islands start where the peninsula ends, and sweep southwest toward Japan. The Pribilof Islands—windswept, grassy, whale bones scattered on the beaches—lie north of the Aleutians, 200 miles off Alaska's west coast. Head north along the Bering Sea coast and you come to Nome, just below the Arctic Circle and the Bering Land Bridge National Preserve. Kotzebue, just above the circle, is a coastal Inupiaq town surrounded by sea and tundra and a jumping-off place for several parklands: Kobuk Valley, Noatak, Cape Krusenstern, and Gates of the Arctic (though the last is more easily reached from the inland village of Bettles). Barrow, another Inupiaq community, sits at the very top of the state, and is the northernmost town in the United States. Follow the Arctic coastline eastward and you reach Deadhorse, on Prudhoe Bay, the custodian to the region's important oil and gas reserves. East of Prudhoe Bay is the embattled Arctic National Wildlife Refuge, the nation's last great chance to truly show that wilderness matters.

PLANNING

WHEN TO GO
The best time to visit is June through August, when the weather is mildest (though you should still anticipate cool, wet, and sometimes stormy weather), daylight hours are longest, and the wildlife is most abundant. Because summer is so short, though, things happen fast, and seasonal activities may need to be crammed into just a couple of weeks.

Go birding in May and August, when migrants come through. The peak wildflower season is usually short, particularly in the Arctic, when most flowers may not blossom until mid-June and then go to seed by late July.

Salmon runs vary from region to region, so it's best to do your homework before choosing dates. For the most part, though, you're looking at July and August, which is also when the tundra starts turning from its summer hues to autumnal colors. The best times for bear-viewing coincide with salmon runs.

GETTING HERE AND AROUND

It's nearly impossible to travel to or around the Bush without taking an air taxi. Still, a few areas are accessible by car or boat.

AIR TRAVEL

Alaska Airlines flies within the state to most major communities. Peninsula Airways serves the communities on the Alaskan Peninsula, the Aleutian and Pribilof islands, and parts of the Interior and northwest.

Bush-based carriers such as Bering Air also offer flightseeing tours and, weather and politics permitting, specially arranged charter flights to the Provid'eniya Airport in the Chukotka Region, on the Siberian coast across the Bering Strait. Currently, it is mandatory for Americans to obtain a visa, invitation, and permission to go to Russia in advance of travel—this can take time, so plan ahead. Frontier Flying Service serves the Interior and the Bering and Arctic coasts. Wright Air Service flies throughout the Interior and Arctic Alaska.

Information about certified air-taxi operations is available from the Federal Aviation Administration. Individual parks and Alaska Public Lands Information centers can also supply lists of reputable air-taxi services. Make your reservations in advance, and always plan for the unexpected; weather can delay a scheduled pickup for days.

Air Contacts **Alaska Airlines** ☎ 800/252–7522 ⊕ www.alaskaair.com. **Alaska Public Lands Information Center** ☎ 907/644–3661, 866/869–6887 ⊕ www. alaskacenters.gov. **Bering Air** ☎ 907/443–5464 in Alaska, 800/478–5422, 907/443–8988 Russian desk ⊕ www.beringair.com. **Federal Aviation Administration** ☎ 907/271–5438 ⊕ www.faa.gov. **Frontier Flying Service** ☎ 907/266–8394 in Anchorage, 800/866–8394 for reservations ⊕ www.flyera.com. **Peninsula Airways** ☎ 907/771–2640, 800/448–4226 ⊕ www.penair.com. **Wright Air Service** ☎ 907/474–0502, 800/478–0502 ⊕ www.wrightairservice.com.

BOAT TRAVEL

In the Aleutians, the Alaska Marine Highway, the state's amazing ferry system, makes one trip a month between Kodiak and Dutch Harbor/Unalaska from April through October.

Boat Contacts **Alaska State Ferry** ☎ 800/642–0066 ⊕ www.dot.state.ak.us/amhs.

CAR TRAVEL

The Dalton Highway connects with the state's highway system and traverses the Arctic, but it only leads to the oil fields of Prudhoe Bay.

HEALTH AND SAFETY

When traveling in the Bush, you should never head out without a decent first-aid kit; you can be a very long way from help out here. The main concern, though, is hypothermia. Watch out for each other. The only other prevalent hazard is bugs—until you've experienced it, it's hard to understand just how thick the mosquitoes and other things that bite can get. Bring plenty of DEET.

9

MONEY MATTERS

Many small villages don't have bank offices, so visitors should bring cash. Most places within the larger Bush communities accept major credit cards, but don't take that for granted. Always be sure to confirm in advance what sort of payment tour companies, hotels, and restaurants accept. Hub communities that do have bank services are Nome, Bethel, Kotzebue, and Barrow.

TOURS

Package tours are the most common way of traveling to Bush communities, where making your flight connections and having a room to sleep in at the end of the line are no small feats. During peak season—late May through Labor Day—planes, state ferries, hotels, and sportfishing lodges are often crowded with travelers on organized tours; to create a trip on your own can sometimes mean making reservations a year in advance for the really popular destinations. But the Bush is also large enough that there's always somewhere to go, and wherever you end up the odds are it will be amazing and like nothing you've ever seen before.

The type of tour you choose will determine how you get there. On air tours—the only way to get to most Bush communities—you will fly to and from your destination, getting there relatively quickly and enjoying an aerial perspective of the Arctic en route. Tours to Arctic towns and villages are usually short—one, two, or three days—so it's easy to combine these with visits to other regions.

The Bush is home to many Alaska Native groups, quite a few of which are active in tourism. Often, local Native corporations act as your hosts—running the tours, hotels, and attractions. Nome Tour and Marketing in Nome (book through Alaska Airlines Vacations) provides ground transportation, accommodations, and other services for visitors. The NANA Regional Corporation provides ground transportation and accommodations in Kotzebue as well as at Prudhoe Bay, in conjunction with bus tours. If you visit Barrow and stay at the Top of the World Hotel, Tundra Tours (book through Alaska Airlines Vacations), another Native operation, will be your host.

The Northern Alaska Tour Company conducts highly regarded ecotours to the Arctic Circle, the Brooks Range, and Prudhoe Bay that emphasize natural and cultural history, wildlife, and geology. Groups are limited to 25 people on Arctic day tours and to 10 people on Prudhoe Bay overnight trips. Some tours are completely ground-based; others include a mix of ground and air travel.

Contacts Alaska Airlines Vacations ☎ *866/500-5511* ⊕ *www.alaskaair.com.* **NANA Regional Corporation** ☎ *907/442-3301* ⊕ *www.nana.com.* **Northern Alaska Tour Company** ☎ *907/474-8600, 800/474-1986* ⊕ *www.northernalaska. com.* **Tundra Tours** ☎ *907/852-3900* ⊕ *www.tundratoursinc.com.*

RESTAURANTS

The dining options are few when traveling around Alaska's Bush; smaller communities may have one or two eateries, if any at all. On the bright side, you won't need to worry about reservations. If they're open, they'll let you in, and you'll likely be surprised at the variety available: in addition to Alaskan seafood, game, and locally grown vegetables, Mexican and Asian fare are standard, even in the state's remotest corners. All food prices, including at grocery shops, will reflect large transportation charges, so be prepared to pay. *Prices in the reviews are the average cost of a main course at dinner or, if dinner is not served, at lunch.*

HOTELS

Lodging choices in the Bush are also limited. Some communities have a single hotel; the smallest have none. Others have a mix of hotels and bed-and-breakfasts. As a rule, rooms are simply furnished. You may have to share bathroom or kitchen facilities. Rooms go fast during the summer season, so book as far ahead as possible. And it never hurts to carry a tent as backup so you'll never be without a place to stay. *Prices in the reviews are the lowest cost of a standard double room in high season.*

TAKE TO THE SKIES

Roads in the Bush are few, so airplanes—from jetliners to small bush planes—are the lifelines. Throughout Alaska you'll hear about the legendary pilots of the far north—Noel and Sig Wien, Bob Reeve, Ben Eielson, Harold Gillam, Joe Crosson, Jack Jefford, and others—who won their wings in the early years. They are Alaska's counterparts to the cowboy heroes of the Wild West. And just as in the Wild West, the adventure came with risk: the Bush is where America's favorite humorist, Will Rogers, died in a crash with famed aviator Wiley Post in 1935.

VISITOR INFORMATION
GETTING OUTSIDE

The Bush presents some of the world's best opportunities to participate in backcountry adventures, from canoeing to wildlife-viewing. The following organizations can help you get in touch with your inner explorer.

Contacts Alaska Department of Fish and Game ✉ *1255 W. 8th St., Juneau* ☏ *907/465-4190 hunting and wildlife-related information, 907/465–4180 sportfishing seasons and regulations, 907/465–2376 licenses* ⊕ *www.adfg. alaska.gov.* **Alaska State Parks Information** ✉ *550 W. 7th Ave., Suite 1260, Anchorage* ☏ *907/269–8400* ⊕ *www.dnr.alaska.gov/parks.* **Anchorage Alaska Public Lands Information Center** ✉ *605 W. 4th Ave., Suite 105, Anchorage* ☏ *907/644–3661 in Alaska, 866/869–6887* ⊕ *www.alaskacenters.gov.* **Fairbanks Alaska Public Lands Information Center** ✉ *Morris Thompson Visitor Center, 101 Dunkel St., Suite 110, Fairbanks* ☏ *907/459–3730, 866/869–6887* ⊕ *www.alaskacenters.gov/fairbanks.* **U.S. Fish and Wildlife Service** ✉ *1011 E. Tudor Rd., Anchorage* ☏ *907/786–3309* ⊕ *alaska.fws.gov.*

9

SOUTHWEST

The Southwest region, below the Arctic Circle, encompasses some of Alaska's most remote, inaccessible, and rugged land- and seascapes. Reaching from the Kodiak Archipelago to the Yukon-Kuskokwim Delta, this area contains the world's densest brown bear population and the world's greatest salmon runs. Given all this richness, it's no surprise to learn that Southwest Alaska has some of Alaska's premier parklands

Southwest

and refuges, from Katmai National Park to Aniakchak National Monument and the Kodiak National Wildlife Refuge. Here, too, are dozens of rural communities, most of them small Native villages whose residents continue to engage in a subsistence lifestyle augmented by modern conveniences and, frequently, satellite- and computer-delivered schools.

BETHEL

400 miles west of Anchorage.

Spread out on the tundra along the Kuskokwim River, Bethel is a frontier town of about 5,800 residents, originally established by Moravian missionaries in the late 1800s. One of rural Alaska's most important trading centers, it's a hub for 56 native villages in a region roughly the size of the state of Oregon. The Yup'ik Eskimo language and culture are still predominant in this regional center.

The surrounding lowland tundra is a rich green in summer and turns fiery shades of red, orange, and yellow in autumn, when plants burst with blueberries, cranberries, blackberries, and salmonberries. Salmon, arctic grayling, and Dolly Varden (a species of seagoing trout that some biologists continually try to promote to salmon) fill the area's many lakes, ponds, and streams, providing excellent fishing just a few miles outside town. Pretty much everyone in Bethel has smoked, dried, and frozen fish aplenty. The wetlands are also important breeding grounds for more than 60 species of birds, from shrikes to warblers. The town is also the northernmost freshwater port for oceangoing vessels. Among its businesses are radio and television stations, a theater, credit union, auto repair shop, car-rental agency, beauty-barber shop, DVD rental store, newspaper, two colleges (including a tribal college), and the largest Alaska Native Health Service field hospital in the state, which is contracted to the tribally owned Yukon-Kuskokwim Health Corporation.

> **TOUR-SHY?**
>
> So you've heard that organized tours are the best way to go but still cringe at the thought of not doing it yourself. What's a traveler to do? Fear not: these resources can help you troubleshoot your own Bush itinerary.
>
> **Alaska Travel Industry Association** ⊠ *2600 Cordova St., Suite 201, Anchorage* ☎ *907/929-2200, 800/862-5275 for vacation planner* ⊕ *www.travelalaska.com.*
>
> **Southwest Alaska Municipal Conference** ⊠ *3300 Arctic Blvd., Suite 203, Anchorage* ☎ *907/562-7380* ⊕ *www.swamc.org.*

Each year on the last weekend in March Bethel hosts a regional celebration called the Cama-i Dance Festival (in Yup'ik, *cama-i* means "hello"), a great time to experience Native culture. Held in the local high school's gym, which is filled to capacity for the three-day event, this festival of food, dance, music, and crafts draws dance groups from dozens of outlying villages.

GETTING HERE AND AROUND
To get to Bethel, take a flight on Alaska Airlines, Frontier, or Era. Once you're there, the town itself is walkable.

ESSENTIALS
Banking **Alaska USA Federal Credit Union** ⊠ *AC Company Bldg., 135 Ridgecrest Dr.* ☎ *800/525-9094* ⊕ *www.alaskausa.org.* **First National Bank Alaska** ⊠ *700 Front St.* ☎ *907/543-7650* ⊕ *www.fnbalaska.com.* **Wells Fargo** ⊠ *460 Ridgecrest Dr.* ☎ *907/543-3875* ⊠ *830 River St.* ☎ *800/869-3557* ⊕ *www.wellsfargo.com.*

Emergencies **Police** ☎ *907/543-3781 in Bethel.* **State troopers** ☎ *907/543-2294.*

Mail **USPS** ⊠ *1484 Chief Eddie Hoffman Hwy.* ☎ *907/543-2525.*

Visitor Information **Cama-i Dance Festival** ⊕ *www.bethelarts.com.*

EXPLORING
★ **Yupiit Piciryarait (the people's way of living) Museum.** The Yupiit Piciryarait (the people's way of living) Museum emphasizes cultural education through Native elders, while also showcasing artifacts and artwork of three Native cultures: Dene Athabascan, Cup'ik, and Yup'ik. In its galleries you'll find historic and prehistoric treasures: masks, statues, and carvings in ivory, baleen, and whalebone. The permanent collection features past and present clothing styles plus numerous implements and tools used in traditional

subsistence lifestyles of the people inhabiting the Yukon-Kuskokwim region. ⊠ *420 Chief Eddie Hoffman Hwy.* ☎ *907/543–1819* ⊕ *www.yp museum.org* ➧ *Free* ☉ *Tues.–Sat. noon–4.*

WHERE TO EAT AND STAY

For expanded hotel reviews, visit Fodors.com.

$$$
ECLECTIC ✕ **Shogun.** This rural café-style restaurant specializes in Chinese food, sushi, and authentic Mexican cuisine, with daily lunch and dinner specials. It also serves Italian dishes and American pub fare. ⑤ *Average main: $20* ⊠ *320 Tundra St.* ☎ *907/543–2272.*

$$
B&B/INN 🏨 **Allanivik Hotel.** Three detached buildings make up this inn, which provides a quiet stay and insightful tips from the Bush-savvy owners. **Pros:** great, knowledgeable staff. **Cons:** many rooms share baths. ⑤ *Rooms from: $172* ⊠ *1220 Hoffman Hwy.* ☎ *907/543–4305* ⊕ *www.allanivik. com* ➥ *30 rooms, 14 with bath.*

$$
B&B/INN 🏨 **Bentley's Porter House B&B.** Hospitality is never in short supply at this two-story B&B in downtown Bethel. **Pros:** river views; very safe and quiet. **Cons:** not for those who want to stay up late making noise; not all rooms have baths. ⑤ *Rooms from: $174* ⊠ *624 1st Ave.* ☎ *907/543–3552* ⊕ *www.bentleysbnb.com* ➥ *35 rooms, 10 with bath* ⚫ *Breakfast.*

OFF THE BEATEN PATH
Nunivak Island. Due west of Bethel, and separated from the Yukon-Kuskokwim Delta by the Etolin Strait, Nunivak Island is an important wildlife refuge. Part of the **Yukon Delta National Wildlife Refuge,** this site is noted for its large herd of reindeer, a transplanted herd of musk ox, and the Eskimo settlement of Mekoryuk.

U.S. Fish and Wildlife Service. For information on the island, contact the U.S. Fish and Wildlife Service in Bethel. ☎ *907/543–3151* ⊕ *yukondelta.fws.gov.*

Bethel Chamber of Commerce. Visitors should check with Bethel Chamber of Commerce about transport and accommodations, which are limited and far from deluxe. ☎ *907/543–2911* ⊕ *www.bethel akchamber.org.*

YUKON DELTA NATIONAL WILDLIFE REFUGE

Surrounds Bethel.

GETTING HERE AND AROUND

There are no roads to or in the refuge. The best way to enter the area is to take a commercial flight to Bethel and then fly into the refuge by air taxi. If you only want to see the smallest edge of the refuge, or are a very strong hiker, it is also possible to walk in by driving 2 miles down Chief Eddie Hoffman State Highway, the only paved road in town, to the Refuge Office and Visitors Center at the end of the road.

TAKE NOTE

Many Bush communities have voted to be dry areas in order to fight alcohol-abuse problems affecting Alaska's Native peoples. Sale and possession of alcohol is prohibited in dry communities. Enforcement is strict, and bootlegging is a felony. Nome remains wet, with numerous lively saloons, and usually a line at the liquor store.

ESSENTIALS
Visitor Information **Refuge Manager**
☎ *907/543-3151* ⊕ *yukondelta.fws.gov.*

EXPLORING
Yukon Delta National Wildlife Refuge. Yukon Delta National Wildlife Refuge, at 20 million acres, is the nation's largest wildlife refuge; nearly one-third of the area is water in the form of lakes, sloughs, bogs, creeks, and rivers—including the **Yukon** and **Kuskokwim** rivers, Alaska's largest. Both are broad and slow by the time they get this close to the sea, and they carry huge amounts of sediment; over the millennia the sediments have formed an immense delta that serves as critical breeding and rearing grounds for an estimated 100 million shorebirds and waterfowl.

NESTING GROUNDS

More than 100 species of birds nest here in the Yukon Delta NWR, traveling from nearly every state and province in North America and from every continent that borders the Pacific Ocean. Many of North America's cackling Canada geese and more than half the continent's population of black brant (Pacific brant goose) are born here. Other birds making the annual pilgrimage to the Yukon Delta refuge include emperor geese, huge tundra swans, gulls, jaegers, cranes, loons, snipe, sandpipers, and the rare bristle-thigh curlew.

Of course, not all of the refuge is wetlands. North of the Yukon River are the Nulato Hills, site of the 1.3-million-acre **Andreafsky Wilderness area,** which includes both forks of the Andreafsky River, one of Alaska's specially designated Wild and Scenic Rivers. Rainbow trout, arctic char, and grayling flourish in upland rivers and creeks; pike, sheefish, and burbot thrive in lowland waters. These abundant waters are also spawning grounds for five species of Pacific salmon. Black and grizzly bears, moose, beavers, mink, and Arctic foxes also call this refuge home. Occasionally, wolves venture into the delta's flats from neighboring uplands.

Given the abundance of fish and wildlife, it's not surprising that the delta holds special importance to surrounding residents. The Yup'ik have lived here for thousands of years; despite modern encroachment, they continue to practice many features of their centuries-old subsistence lifestyle. Access is by boat or aircraft only, and, as in most of Alaska's other remote wildlands, visitor facilities are minimal. Refuge staff can provide tips on recreational opportunities and guides and outfitters who operate in the refuge.

OUTDOOR ACTIVITIES AND GUIDED TOURS
Opportunities for wildlife-watching abound at the Yukon Delta refuge. With so many lakes, ponds, streams, and wetlands, the big thing to do is get in a boat, or hang out on the shore, and watch all the waterfowl. The refuge is also a great place for sportfishing, especially for rainbow trout, salmon, char, pike, grayling, and sheefish. Flat-water paddlers will never run out of water to try, although camping can be a bit marshy and DEET-dependent. Or try hiking and river floating in the uplands of the Andreafsky Wilderness area. You are a long way from help when you're in the refuge; know what you're doing.

9

Kuskokwim Wilderness Adventures. Local expert Jim McDonald leads camping, fishing, birding, photo trips, and more. ☎ 907/543–3900 ⊕ *www.kuskofish.com.*

WOOD-TIKCHIK STATE PARK

150 miles southeast of Bethel, 300 miles southwest of Anchorage.

GETTING HERE AND AROUND

Like most of the Bush, there is no road access into Wood-Tikchik State Park. The only way in is either by air taxi or by boat. In the summer months it's not uncommon to see kayakers navigating their way through the river systems, their point of origin in the town of Dillingham or farther away via the waters of Bristol Bay. Kayaking the river system is suggested only for experienced kayakers who have very good navigational skills, as it is quite easy to get lost in the labyrinth of mosquito-infested waters.

ESSENTIALS

Visitor Information **Walrus Island State Game Sanctuary** ☎ 907/267–2257 ⊕ *www.wildlife.alaska.gov.* **Wood-Tikchik State Park** ☎ 907/842–2641 ⊕ *www.alaskastateparks.org* ☎ 907/269–8400.

EXPLORING

Wood-Tikchik State Park. In the Bristol Bay region, Wood-Tikchik State Park—the nation's largest state park—is a water-based wildland despite its inland setting. Two separate groups of large, idyllic, interconnected lakes, some up to 45 miles long, dominate the park. Grizzlies, caribou, porcupines (people who live in the Bush will tell you they taste like squirrels), eagles, and loons abound in the park's forests and tundra, but Wood-Tikchik is best known for its fish. The park's lakes and streams are critical spawning habitat for five species of Pacific salmon; they also support healthy populations of rainbow trout, arctic char, arctic grayling, and northern pike. And where there are fish, there are fishermen: Wood-Tikchik is kind of a Holy Grail locale for serious anglers; all that water is perfect for canoes and kayaks, too.

Managed as a wild area, Wood-Tikchik has no maintained trails and few visitor amenities. ■TIP→ Most of its campsites are primitive, and anyone planning to explore the park should be experienced in backcountry travel and camping.

Besides the many large lakes and streams that fill its 1.6 million acres, the park's landscape includes rugged mountains, glaciers, and vast expanses of tundra. Think of it as a kind of CliffsNotes to the best of Alaskan scenery.

OUTDOOR ACTIVITIES AND GUIDED TOURS

Because it is largely a water-based region, it's easiest to explore Wood-Tikchik by boat, whether that's canoe, kayak, or raft. The most popular fly-in float trip is the 90-mile journey from Lake Kulik to Aleknagik, a Yup'ik Eskimo village. Most people doing this trip arrange for drop-off and pickup services with local guides in Dillingham. The lakes are large enough to behave like small inland seas in stormy weather, so boaters need to be cautious when winds are high; always be prepared for bad weather, know proper emergency procedures, and don't ever go out unless somebody knows where you're headed. The water systems also present some of the world's best sportfishing opportunities for salmon and rainbow trout; anglers come from around the world to stay at wilderness fishing lodges here. Hiking is difficult because of dense brush, except for the upper-most part of the park, where tundra makes on-land travel easier.

Tikchik Narrows Lodge. Tikchik Nar-rows Lodge is owned and managed by Bud Hodson, who has been a guide in the region for more than 25 years. The lodge caters primarily to sportfishing enthusiasts who are also looking for comfortable housing and scrumptious gourmet-style meals at night—and who can afford $7,400 for a week's stay, which includes guided fishing trips throughout the region via the lodge's float-plane fleet. The lodge rents kayaks and rafts and provides an air-taxi service into the park's most remote corners. ☎ 907/243–8450 ⊕ *www. tikchiklodge.com.*

KATMAI NATIONAL PARK AND PRESERVE

100 miles southeast of Wood-Tikchik, 290 miles southwest of Anchorage.

★ Katmai is the most famous of Alaska's remote parks for two simple rea-sons: bears and volcanoes. Although Katmai sees only a fraction of the number of visitors to Denali National Park, its name echoes with just as much mythical force. Remote and expensive (even by Alaska travel standards) to get to, Katmai is true wilderness Alaska, with limited visi-tor facilities (except for a few nice wilderness lodges)—but that's reason enough to go and have Alaska to yourself. These 4 million acres offer up plenty of opportunities for wildlife-viewing and an extraordinary perspective on the awesome power of volcanoes—still active through-out the park, echoes of the 1912 eruption sequence that was one of the most powerful ever recorded, covering more than 46,000 square miles with ash. Today in this wild, remote area at the northern end of the Alaska Peninsula, moose and almost 30 other species of mammals, including foxes, lynx, and wolves, share the landscape with bears fishing for salmon from stream banks and rivers and along the coast. At the immensely popular **Brooks Falls and Camp** you can see brown bears when the salmon are running in July and September. No special permits are required, though there is a $10 day-use fee at Brooks. Bears are com-mon along the park's outer coast, where they graze on sedge flats, dig clams and sculpin on the beach at low tide (quite a sight!), and fish for salmon. But even on slow bear days it's a beautiful place to be. Ducks

9

fill the park's rivers, lakes, and outer coast, arguing over nesting space with huge whistling swans, loons, grebes, gulls, and shorebirds. Bald eagles perch on rocky pinnacles by the sea. More than 40 species of songbirds call the region home during the short spring and summer, and if you fall back into big-mammal mood, Steller sea lions and a couple of species of seals hang out on rock outcroppings.

From Brooks Lodge a daily tour bus with a naturalist aboard makes the 23-mile trip through the park to the **Valley Overlook.** Hikers can walk the 1.5-mile trail for a closer look at the pumice-covered valley floor. (Some consider the return climb strenuous.)

Brooks River. The Katmai area is one of Alaska's premier sportfishing regions. You can fish for rainbow trout and salmon at the Brooks River, though seasonal closures have been put in place to prevent conflicts with bears, and only fly-fishing is permitted; check locally for the latest information. For those who would like to venture farther into the park, seek out the two other backcountry lodges, **Grosvenor** and **Kulik,** or contact fishing-guide services based in King Salmon. A short walk up the Brooks River brings you to Brooks Falls. Viewing platforms here overlook a 6-foot-high cascade where salmon leap to try and make it upstream, past the bears, to spawn. One platform is right at the falls; the other is a short way below it (an access trail and boardwalk are separated from the river to avoid confrontations with bears). ☎ 907/246–3305 ⊕ www.nps.gov/katm.

No roads lead to Katmai National Park. To get to it, at the base of the Alaska Peninsula, it's easiest to arrange a flight from Anchorage, where you can take in the amazing scenery along Cook Inlet, rimmed by the lofty, snowy peaks of the Alaska Range (check out ⊕ www.alaskaair. com for fares and schedules). They land at **King Salmon,** near fish-famous Bristol Bay, where passengers transfer to smaller floatplanes for the 20-minute hop to **Naknek Lake** and Brooks Camp. Travel to Brooks from King Salmon is also possible by boat. You are required to check in at the park ranger station, next to Brooks Lodge (⇨ see below), for a mandatory bear safety talk (for the safety of both you and the bears).

Fodor'sChoice
★
McNeil River State Game Sanctuary. At the northern end of the Alaska Peninsula, 200 miles southwest of Anchorage, McNeil River State Game Sanctuary was established in 1967 to protect the world's largest gathering of brown bears. Since then, it has earned a reputation as the finest bear-viewing locale in North America, and likely the world—the standard by which all others are measured. The main focus is **McNeil Falls,** where bears come to feed on chum salmon returning to spawn. All those *National Geographic* films you've seen of bears fishing? Odds are this is the spot. During the peak of the chum run (July to mid-August) dozens of brown bears congregate at the falls playing who can slap the most fish out of the water. When the salmon are running thickest, the bears only eat the fattiest parts of the fish—brains, roe, and skin—which means the leftovers are a smorgasbord for other animals; even the plant life depends on nutrients from bear leftovers. As many as 70 bears, including cubs, have been observed along the river in a single day. More than 100 bears have been identified within a single season.

"[W]hen the salmon [move] upstream in Katmai N.P.'s Brooks River, dozens of brown bears with their cubs gather to feast. This one ran up a nearby tree to escape with his catch." —Jose Vigano, Fodors.com photo contest winner

Not just the sheer number of bears makes McNeil special; over the years several bears have become highly accustomed to human presence. They will play, eat, nap, and nurse cubs within 15 to 20 feet of the falls viewing pad, sometimes closer—which will let you learn firsthand that bears smell like very wet dogs. Do not think the bears are tame; they are still wild animals and the sanctuary staff makes sure that visitors behave in a nonthreatening, nonintrusive way.

To that end, no more than 10 people a day, always accompanied by one or two state biologists, are allowed to visit bear-viewing sites from June 7 through August 25. Because demand is so high, an annual drawing is held in mid-March to determine permit winners. ■TIP→ Applications must be received by March 1 to be eligible. Nearly all visitors fly into McNeil Sanctuary on floatplanes. Most arrange for air-taxi flights out of Homer, on the Kenai Peninsula. Once you are in the sanctuary, all travel is on foot. ⊠ *Alaska Department of Fish and Game, Division of Wildlife Conservation, 333 Raspberry Rd., Anchorage* ☎ *907/267–2253* ⊕ *www.adfg.state.ak.us.*

OUTDOOR ACTIVITIES AND GUIDED TOURS

The Katmai region offers an abundance of recreational opportunities, including sportfishing, bear viewing, hiking through the Valley of Ten Thousand Smokes, running the wild and scenic Alagnak River and other clear-water streams, flightseeing, exploring the outer coast, and backpacking through remote and seldom-visited backcountry wilderness.

FLIGHTSEEING AND WILDLIFE VIEWING

Katmai Air Services. This company can arrange flightseeing tours of the park and also does charter flights to Brooks Camp. ☎ *907/246–3079 in King Salmon, summer only, 800/544–0551 in Anchorage* ⊕ *www. katmailand.com.*

Katmailand. Contact this company for bear-viewing and fishing packages to Katmai National Park, as well as trips to Katmai's Valley of Ten Thousand Smokes. ✉ *4125 Aircraft Dr., Anchorage* ☎ *907/243–5448, 800/544–0551* ⊕ *www.katmailand.com.*

Lifetime Adventures. This outfitter organizes a variety of customized trips for small groups (eight people or fewer), including bear-watching, river kayaking, mountain biking, and hiking in the Valley of Ten Thousand Smokes. ☎ *800/952–8624* ⊕ *www.lifetimeadventures.net.*

Northwind Aviation. Located in Homer, Northwind Aviation offers charter flights to Katmai's outer coast and McNeil River. ✉ *1184 Lakeshore Dr., Homer* ☎ *907/235–7482* ⊕ *www.northwindak.com.*

RIVER RUNNING AND SPORTFISHING

Ouzel Expeditions. This outfitter guides fishing and river-running trips down the Wild and Scenic Alagnak River and American Creek, which flows through Katmai National Park and is widely known as a rainbow-trout heaven. ☎ *907/783–2216; 800/825–8196* ⊕ *www.ouzel.com.*

WHERE TO STAY

All five lodges listed here are on inholdings (privately owned land inside a protected area) within Katmai National Park. Three are inland; Katmai Wilderness Lodge and Hallo Bay Bear Lodge are on the remote outer coast.

For expanded hotel reviews, visit Fodors.com.

$$$$
B&B/INN
Fodor'sChoice
★

Brooks Lodge. Initially a fishing camp, this lodge has been in operation since 1950. **Pros:** private facilities; bear-viewing at Brooks Falls. **Cons:** fly-fishing only in Brooks River, unless you're a bear. **TripAdvisor:** "a magical place," "amazing wildlife," "a home in the wilderness." ⑤ *Rooms from: $1345* ☎ *907/243–5448, 800/544–0551* ⊕ *www. katmailand.com/lodging/brooks.html* ⤴ *16 cabins* ⊙ *Closed Sept.–May* ⅏ *All meals.*

$$$$
B&B/INN

Grosvenor Lodge. Once you've arrived at this remote Katmai National Park lodge, reachable only by floatplane, you have access by motorboat to numerous rivers and streams filled with sport fish. **Pros:** great fishing; accessible to two spawning streams. **Cons:** bathhouse is outside the cabin; absolute seclusion—but isn't that why you picked the place? ⑤ *Rooms from: $1800* ☎ *907/243–5448, 800/544–0551* ⊕ *www. katmailand.com/lodging/grosvenor.html* ⤴ *3 cabins with shared baths* ⊙ *Closed Sept.–May* ⅏ *All meals.*

$$$$
RESORT

Hallo Bay Bear Lodge. Located at the northern end of the bay, Hallo Bay Bear Lodge is an ecofriendly camp that has been running bear-viewing trips for 22 years. Guests stay in rustic yet comfortable heated platform tents or heated cabins and enjoy gourmet meals in an enclosed kitchen. **Pros:** truly wild bear viewing; ecofriendly; gourmet meals. **Cons:** rustic; expensive. ⑤ *Rooms from: $1800* ☎ *888/535–2237* ⊕ *www.hallobay. com* ⊙ *Closed Oct.–mid-May.*

Continued on page 457

WELCOME TO BEAR COUNTRY

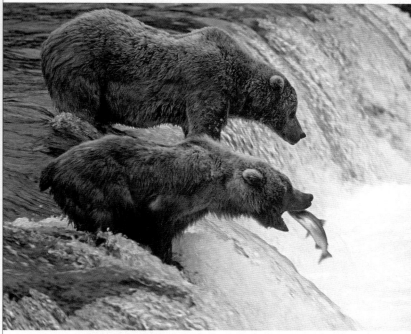

(top) Grizzly bears fishing in Katmai National Park (bottom) Polar bear

An 800–pound brown bear plows through the shallows of Pack Creek on Southeast Alaska's Admiralty Island, adroitly flipping a 20-pound salmon out of the current like an NFL lineman snapping a football. This bear, which stands over 8 feet tall when perched on his hind legs, can devour 50 pounds of food every day. And, when sprinting, he can reach speeds of 35 miles per hour. Governmentally speaking, Alaska is a democracy. But in the wilderness, the state is a monarchy—and the bear the undisputed king.

KING OF THE WILDERNESS

A GOOD HOME

Thanks to its vast stretches of wilderness, Alaska is the only state that is home to healthy populations of all three North American ursine species. Polar bears (*Ursus maritimus*) don't venture south of the state's chilly Arctic coastline, while black bears (*Ursus americanus*) and brown bears (*Ursus arctos*; also known as grizzlies) live throughout the state's many refuges and parks. Bear populations are plentiful here: the Alaska Department of Fish and Game estimates that Alaska is home to roughly 100,000 black bears and 25,000 to 38,000 brown bears.

Watching a bear gorge on salmon from a chilly creek or seeing a mother bear wandering the shoreline in the early morning, her two cubs trailing behind her is an unforgettable sight. Sure it's a matter of luck and timing. But sightings like this are a gift from the Alaskan landscape. However, as illustrated by *Grizzly Man*—a 2005 documentary by Werner Herzog about the troubled life and tragic death of Alaska bear activist Timothy Treadwell—Alaska's bears are wild, unpredictable creatures that should *never* be underestimated.

Polar Bear

SAFE PLACES TO VIEW BEARS

Bear-viewing in Alaska has become an increasingly popular tourist activity—and one that is safely enjoyed by thousands of visitors using expert outdoor tour guides every year at such locations as Denali National Park & Preserve (⇨ Ch. 7), Kodiak Island (⇨ Ch. 6), Katmai National Park's McNeil River State Game Sanctuary (⇨ Ch. 9), Admiralty Island's Pack Creek (⇨ Ch. 4), Anan Creek Wildlife Observatory (⇨ Ch. 4), and Fish Creek Wildlife Observation Site (⇨ Ch. 4).

Keep in mind that your best bet is to hire an experienced guide and always to check in with rangers at the refuges or parks you plan to visit. It's never certain that you'll see a bear, though your chances increase dramatically if you're visiting one of the aforementioned premier viewing areas during

Strolling black bear

BEAR OF THE NORTHERN REACHES

Along Alaska's icy northern coast roams the most majestic of all ursine species: the polar bear. Massive in stature (males can reach 1,700 pounds and 11 feet in height), polar bears are also cunning predators that prey chiefly on seals. With relatively short average life spans (15 to 20 years) and one of the slowest reproductive rates of any mammal on earth—females give birth to two cubs every two to five years—polar bear populations are especially vulnerable to human intrusion and, most recently, the continuing retreat of polar sea ice. These bears are worthy of the utmost respect: exercise special caution when traveling along the coastline, as they are known to be aggressive toward humans.

A Kodiak mama bear is followed by two young cubs.

summer salmon runs on a guided tour or if you're traveling in Alaska's more remote backcountry regions. If it's the latter, the chances of an aggressive bear encounter are real but remote.

You should be very well prepared and well versed in safe travel and camping techniques, which include using bear-resistant food containers; never traveling alone; steering clear of forested areas, berry patches, and salmon runs; checking in with park rangers to find out about potential bear zones; and making noise to warn bears that humans are present.

BLACK VERSUS BROWN

Despite their given names, black and brown bears range in color from pure black to nearly blond. Size is the defining characteristic: male brown bears on Kodiak Island—home to the largest brown bear subspecies on Earth—can reach 1,500 pounds and stand 10 feet tall. Male black bears, by comparison, rarely exceed 500 pounds or stand taller than 6 feet. Brown bears have longer claws, longer faces, and a distinct shoulder hump. Brown bears are also more protective of their territory and less intimidated by human intrusion.

Black and brown bears feed on a diverse diet, the staples being salmon, berries, roots, carrion, and the occasional deer, moose, or caribou. Both species hibernate in winter, although bears in the southern coastal regions spend less time hibernating. In the wild, brown and black bears live for 20 to 30 years. Mature female brown and black bears produce a litter of one to four cubs every two years. And thanks to state and federal protections, Alaska's bear populations are holding steady.

THE SOFT SIDE OF TEDDY

Question: How did the bear—one of nature's largest, most fearsome creatures—become such a popular stuffed animal?

Answer: Because Theodore "Teddy" Roosevelt, former U.S. president, avid hunter, and all-around tough guy, refused to shoot a bear while hunting in Mississippi in 1902. Hence "Teddy's bear" was born. If Roosevelt were alive today, there's only one place he'd surely want to visit to see his beloved bears: Alaska.

A playful brown bear

THE BEAR FACTS: TIPS FOR STAYING SAFE

AVOID SURPRISE

Whenever possible, travel in open country, during daylight hours, and in groups. Make constant noise—talking or singing is preferable to carrying "bear bells"—and leave your dog at home. Most attacks occur when a bear is surprised at close quarters or feels threatened.

CAMP WITH CARE

Pitch your tent away from trails, streams with spawning salmon, berry patches, and other food sources. Avoid areas that have a rotten smell or where scavengers have gathered; these may indicate the presence of a nearby food cache, which a bear will aggressively defend.

BE BEAR AWARE

Keep your eyes open for signs of bears: fresh tracks, scat, matted vegetation, or partially consumed salmon.

ISOLATE YOUR FOOD SUPPLIES

Since bears are practically walking noses, it's imperative that you cook meals at least 100 yards from your tents and that you store food and other odorous items away from campsites (*never* in your tent). Hang food between trees or store it in bear-resistant food containers. Thoroughly clean your cooking area and utensils after each use. Store garbage in airtight containers—or burn it—and pack up the remains.

IF YOU ENCOUNTER A BEAR IN THE WILD

1 IDENTIFY YOURSELF. Talk to the bear in a steady, monotone voice. Don't yell. As for running: don't do it. Running has been known to trigger a bear's predatory instincts, and a bear can easily outrun you (remember, brown bears can run as fast as 35 mph). Back away slowly, and give the bear an escape route. Don't ever get between a mother and her cubs.

A grizzly bear strolls Katmai National Park's tidal flats.

2 BIGGER IS BETTER. To increase your apparent size, raise your arms above your head wave them slowly. With two or more people, it helps to stand side by side. In a forested area it may be appropriate to climb a tree, but remember that black bears and young grizzlies are agile tree climbers.

3 AS A LAST RESORT, PLAY DEAD. If a bear charges and makes contact with you, fall to the ground, curl into a ball with your hands behind your neck, and remain passive. If you are wearing a pack, leave it on. Once a bear no longer feels threatened, it will usually end its attack. Wait for the bear to leave before you move. If such an attack persists for more than a few minutes—in other words, if the bear seems intent on actually harming you further—there's only one option: fight back with all of your might. Keep in mind that such worst-case scenarios are exceedingly rare.

$$$$
B&B/INN
★

Katmai Wilderness Lodge. Built on land owned by the Russian Orthodox Church, this rustic lodge straddles the rugged outer coast of Katmai National Park, along the shores of Kukak Bay. **Pros:** private rooms; hot showers; flush toilets. **Cons:** no place to do your shopping. $ *Rooms from: $2150* ☎ *800/488–8767, 907/486-8767 in Alaska* ⊕ *www.katmai-wilderness. com* ⇆ *7 cabins* ⊗ *Closed Oct.– mid-May* ⎟⊙⎟ *All meals.*

$$$$
B&B/INN

Kulik Lodge. Positioned along the gin-clear Kulik River, between Nonvianuk and Kulik lakes, this remote wilderness lodge is reachable only by floatplane. **Pros:** great rainbow-trout fishing; modern facilities. **Cons:** BYOT—bring your own tackle. **TripAdvisor:** "great fishing lodge," "best experience of my life," "exceptional." $ *Rooms from: $2116* ☎ *907/243–5448, 800/544–0551* ⊕ *www.katmailand.com/lodging/kulik.html* ⇆ *12 cabins* ⊗ *Closed Sept.–May* ⎟⊙⎟ *All meals.*

CAMPGROUNDS IN KATMAI

Brooks Campground. This National Park Service campground is a short walk from Brooks Lodge, where campers can pay to eat and shower. Designated cooking and eating shelters, latrines, well water, and a storage cache to protect food from the ever-present brown bears are available. Reservations are required. ☎ *907/246– 3305 information; 877/444–6777 reservations* ⊕ *www.recreation. gov.*

SHUYAK ISLAND STATE PARK

54 miles north of Kodiak Island.

GETTING HERE AND AROUND
On Shuyak Island there are no amenities, groceries, or roads. It is accessible by air or water only. Because it's not as popular a destination as some of the other islands, it's recommended for those who wish to arrive by air to book a flight well in advance (as there are fewer flights out to choose from). It is a popular destination for kayakers. For guided kayaking trips or other expeditions to the island, the best place to start is on Kodiak Island (⇨ *see Kodiak Island in Chapter 6*).

ESSENTIALS
Visitor Information Alaska State Parks, Kodiak District Office ✉ *1400 Abercrombie Dr., Kodiak* ☎ *907/486–6339* ⊕ *www.alaskastateparks.org.*

EXPLORING
Shuyak Island State Park. The 46,000-acre Shuyak Island State Park is one of the most remote and overlooked units in the state parks system. Located at the northern end of the Kodiak Archipelago, it is accessible only by plane or boat. Its rugged outer coastline is balanced by a more protected system of interconnected bays, channels, and passages that make the park a favorite with sea kayakers. It also has excellent wildlife-viewing, especially of seabirds and sea mammals, and top-notch sportfishing for salmon. Wildlife ranges from Sitka black-tailed deer and brown bears to sea otters, sea lions, bald eagles, puffins, and whales.

9

BELCHING GIANTS

Some evidence suggests that Alaskans inhabited Katmai's eastern edge for at least 9,000 years up to 1912. But on the morning of June 1 of that year everything changed. After five days of violent earthquakes, the 2,700-foot **Novarupta** blew its top, erupting steadily for the next 60 hours. Rivers of white-hot ash poured into the valley. A foot of ash fell on Kodiak Island, 100 miles away, and in all more than 46,000 square miles of territory ended up under at least an inch of ash, winds carrying yet more ash to eastern Canada and as far as Texas. While Novarupta was belching away, another explosion occurred 6 miles east. The mountaintop peak of **Mt. Katmai** collapsed, creating a chasm almost 3 miles long and 2 miles wide. The molten andesite that held up Mt. Katmai rushed through newly created fissures to Novarupta and was spewed out. Over 2½ days, more than 7 cubic miles of volcanic material were ejected, and the green valley lay under 700 feet of ash. Miraculously, the people who called this remote region home made it out safely; no one was killed.

By 1916 things had cooled off sufficiently to allow scientists to explore the area. A National Geographic expedition led by Dr. Robert F. Griggs reached the valley and found it full of steaming fumaroles (holes in the volcanic terrain that fume smoke), creating a moonlike landscape. The report on what Griggs dubbed the **Valley of Ten Thousand Smokes** inspired Congress in 1918 to declare the valley and the surrounding wilderness a national monument. Steam spouted in thousands of fountains from the smothered streams and springs beneath the ash and gave the valley its name. Although the steam has virtually stopped, an eerie sense of earth forces at work remains, and several nearby volcanoes still smolder, or even threaten to blow every couple of years. Anchorage's airport will sometimes get shut down by smoke or ash from the peninsula's active volcanoes.

The Native peoples never returned to their traditional village sites, though many now live in nearby communities. They are joined by sightseers, anglers, hikers, and other outdoors enthusiasts who migrate to the Katmai region each summer. Fish and wildlife are plentiful, and a few "smokes" still drift through the volcano-sculpted valley.

The park has four public-use cabins but no developed campgrounds; limited hiking trails pass through old-growth coastal rain forest.

OUTDOOR ACTIVITIES AND GUIDED TOURS

There are no guided kayaking tours on this island, so those new to the region or the sport should take advantage of tour companies and guides located near the major hubs on Kodiak or the Kenai Peninsula. For more experienced kayakers, a limited number of sea kayaks may be reserved in advance from Sea Hawk Air charter company in Kodiak. The kayaks are located in front of the Big Bay Ranger Station on Shuyak Island and can be picked up when you fly in.

Sea Hawk Air. This company offers floatplane charters, scenic flights and bear-viewing, custom hunting and fishing trips, and Shuyak kayak rentals. ⊠ *506 Trident Way, Kodiak* ☎ *907/486–8282* ⊕ *www.seahawk air.com.*

WHERE TO STAY

For expanded hotel reviews, visit Fodors.com.

$ **⏣ Alaska State Parks Cabins.** Alaska State Parks maintains four public-
RENTAL use cabins on Shuyak Island. **Pros:** scenery that can't be beat; bucket
showers available. **Cons:** during the off-season inclement weather can
pose potential problems for seaplane pick-ups at the end of your stay.
TripAdvisor: "beautiful views," "great cabin," "super clean and quiet."
⑤ *Rooms from: $75* ⊠ *Alaska State Parks, Kodiak District Office, 1400
Abercrombie Dr., Kodiak* ☎ *907/486–6339, 907/269–8400 DNR*
⊕ *dnr.alaska.gov/parks/units/kodiak/shuyak.htm* ⇆ *4 cabins.*

ALEUTIAN ISLANDS, ALASKA PENINSULA, AND PRIBILOF ISLANDS

From the Alaska Peninsula down through the Aleutian chain, this area
also includes many islands within the Bering Sea, among them the
Pribilof Islands, as well as the Bristol Bay watershed. Altogether, this
is a place of enormous biological richness. It harbors many of North
America's largest breeding populations of seabirds and waterfowl and
a vast fur-seal population. This whole region offers wildlife so diverse
and rarefied that is often compared to its counterpart in the southern
hemisphere: the Galapagos Islands.

ANIAKCHAK NATIONAL MONUMENT AND PRESERVE

100 miles southwest of Katmai National Park.

GETTING HERE AND AROUND

Aniakchak National Monument and Preserve is expensive to reach,
even by remote Alaska standards. The only easy access is by air, usually
from the town of King Salmon. Thus, few people visit this spectacular
place—and those who do are likely to have the caldera all to themselves.
Needless to say, come here and you get permanent bragging rights about
what you did on your Alaska vacation.

ESSENTIALS

Visitor Information **Aniakchak National Monument and Preserve**
☎ *907/246–3305* ⊕ *www.nps.gov/ania.*

EXPLORING

Aniakchak National Monument and Preserve. Aniakchak National Monument and Preserve, 586,000 acres of protected land, was established by
Congress in 1980 to mark the significance of Aniakchak, an extraordinary living volcano that rises to the south of Katmai. Towering more
than 4,400 feet above the landscape, the volcano also has one of the
largest calderas in the world, with a diameter averaging 6 miles across
and 2,500 feet deep; **Surprise Lake** lies within it. Although Aniakchak
last erupted in 1931, the explosion that formed the enormous crater
occurred before history was written. Because the area is not glaciated,

geologists place the blowup after the last Ice Age. It was literally a world-shaking event. The Park Service calls it "one of the least visited units of the National Park system"—maybe a handful of people a year make it out here.

Aniakchak is wild and forbidding country, with a climate that brews mist, clouds, and serious winds much of the year; the caldera is so big that it can entirely create its own local weather patterns, and it really seems to like the bad stuff. Although the **Aniakchak River** (which drains Surprise Lake) is floatable, it has stretches of Class III and IV white water navigable only by expert river runners, and you must travel through open ocean waters to reach the nearest community, Chignik Bay (or get picked up by plane, along the coast). In other words, this is not something for the unprepared to try, unless you're seriously into hypothermia and have an up-to-date will. An alternate way to enjoy Aniakchak is to wait for a clear day and fly to it in a small plane that will land you on the caldera floor or on Surprise Lake. But be aware that there are no trails, campgrounds, ranger stations, or other visitor facilities here, and it is bear country; you must be prepared to be self-sufficient. Aniakchak is the world in the raw.

OUTDOOR ACTIVITIES AND GUIDED TOURS

FLIGHTSEEING

Branch River Air. Located in King Salmon, Branch River Air offers charter flights and flightseeing, and will also arrange fishing and bear-viewing trips. ☎ 907/246–3437 June–Sept., 907/248–3539 Oct.–May ⊕ www.branchriverair.com.

RIVER RUNNING

Ouzel Expeditions. This outfitter guides river-running trips down the Aniakchak River. Trips begin at Surprise Lake, within the caldera, and end at the coast, and feature white-water rafting and fishing for salmon, char, and rainbow trout. ☎ 907/783–2216, 800/825–8196 ⊕ www.ouzel.com.

BECHAROF AND ALASKA PENINSULA NATIONAL WILDLIFE REFUGES

★ *Adjacent to Aniakchak National Monument and Preserve, 250 miles to 450 miles southwest of Anchorage.*

GETTING HERE AND AROUND

No visitor facilities are available here, and access is only by boat or plane. Most visitors begin their trips in King Salmon and use guides or outfitters.

ESSENTIALS

Visitor Information **Becharof National Wildlife Refuge** ☎ 907/246–4250, 907/246–3339 ⊕ becharof.fws.gov.

EXPLORING

The Becharof and Alaska Peninsula National Wildlife Refuges. The Becharof and Alaska Peninsula National Wildlife Refuges stretch along the southern edge of the Alaska Peninsula. These two refuges encompass nearly 6 million acres of towering mountains, glacial lakes, broad tundra valleys, and coastal fjords. Volcanoes dominate the landscape; there are 14 in all, of which 9 are considered active. **Mt. Veniaminov**—named after Alaska's greatest Russian Orthodox bishop—last erupted in 1993. Other evidence of volcanic activity includes **Gas Rocks,** where gases continually seep through cracks in granitic rocks, and **Ukrinek Maars,** a crater that bears the marks of a violent eruption in 1977.

Aside from the rugged volcanic landscapes, which are reason enough to come, the two refuges are best known for Garden of Eden–quality wildlife. More than 220 species of resident and migratory wildlife use the refuges, including 30 land mammals such as moose and otter; 11 marine mammals, including several kinds of whales; and nearly three-dozen species of fish, with the five main types of salmon. Look up for nearly 150 species of birds, from the bald eagle doing its perfect impersonation of life after taxidermy high in the tree, to Alaska's trickster, the raven, as well as enough waterbirds to keep a hard-core twitcher at the binoculars for a week. Just put the binocs down from time to time to keep an eye out for the brown bears that live in every corner of the refuges.

Becharof Lake, at 35 miles long and up to 15 miles wide, is the second-largest lake in Alaska (behind Lake Iliamna). Fed by two rivers and 14 major creeks, it serves as a nursery to the world's second-biggest run of sockeye salmon. **Ugashik Lakes** are known for their salmon and trophy grayling. The world-record grayling, nearly 5 pounds (most grayling weigh a pound or less), was caught at Ugashik Narrows in 1981.

Remote and rugged, with the peninsula's usual unpredictable weather, the Becharof and Alaska Peninsula refuges draw mostly anglers and hunters; however, backpackers, river runners, and mountain climbers also occasionally visit.

ALEUTIAN ISLANDS

The Aleutians begin 540 miles southwest of Anchorage and stretch more than 1,400 miles.

It is easier to get to the Aleutian Islands than the Pribilof Islands or Alaska Peninsula, because there's a regular ferry service that runs out this way.

Separating the North Pacific Ocean from the Bering Sea, the Aleutian Islands are not a single sequence of islands. Actually, they're a superchain, made of up eight smaller island groups—the Andreanof, Delarof, Fox, Four Mountain, Near, Rat, Shumagin, and Sanak islands. In all, this adds up to more than 275 islands, stretching from the Alaska Peninsula in a southwesterly arc toward Japan. The islands are volcanic in origin, treeless, and alternate between towering (and frequently smoking) volcanic cones, and high tablelands. Separating the islands is some of the wildest, deepest water anywhere: on the Pacific side of the chain the water can be more than 25,000 feet deep, and the north side's Bering Canyon is twice as long as the Grand Canyon, as well as twice as deep, bottoming out at 10,600 feet below the water's surface. The Aleutian Islands and surrounding coastal waters make up one of the most biologically rich areas in Alaska, harboring abundant seabird, marine mammal, and fish populations—and the fish feed the ships of one of the world's busiest fishing fleets.

Before the Russians arrived in the mid-1700s, the islands were dotted with Aleut villages, a total population of perhaps 3,000 people; within a hundred years, that number had dropped to maybe 200 through disease and war. Today's Native communities include **Nikolski**, on Umnak Island; **Atka**, on Atka Island; and **Cold Bay**, at the peninsula's tip. Like everybody in the Aleutians, the descendants of the

The Alaska Marine Highway System, that is. This much-loved form of Alaskan transport is best known for its routes along the Inside Passage. In summer these ferries also depart from Homer, in South Central, and pass by Kodiak on the three-plus-day trip to Dutch Harbor. It's an unforgettable way to see the Southwest's dramatic landscape (📞 800/642–0066 ⊕ www.dot.state.ak.us/amhs).

original inhabitants mostly work at commercial fishing or in canneries and as expert guides for those who hunt and fish. The settlements are quite small, and accommodations are scarce.

Visitors aren't allowed on Shemya Island, which has a remote U.S. Air Force base, without special permission. Because of downsizing, the military has closed its Adak operation, and the base's infrastructure provides the core infrastructure for what now is a small coastal community and commercial fishing port.

Unalaska/Dutch Harbor. These twin towns midway out the chain are by far the most populous destinations in the Aleutian Islands. Although they're sometimes called "the Crossroads of the Aleutians," even by Alaska standards people who live here are living remote. Usually referred to simply as "Dutch" (or, by people who spend winter here, "the gulag"), the towns are connected by a bridge that spans a narrow channel between Unalaska and Amaknak islands. (Locals playfully call the span the "Bridge to the Other Side.") Despite the often-harsh weather—this region is known as the "Cradle of Storms" for good reason—the Aleut people and their ancestors have occupied these islands and others in the Aleutians for thousands of years. Today Dutch is the region's tourism center, as well as one of the busiest fishing ports in the world. Scattered around both islands are reminders of history: the Japanese bombed Dutch Harbor during World War II (unexploded ordnance may still be out there, so don't handle any odd metal objects you see while hiking), and you can still explore concrete bunkers, gun batteries, and a partially sunken ship left over from the war.

It's worth the trip out to Dutch on the ferry just for the scenery along the way, but when travelers finally reach the islands they discover a surprisingly gentle landscape of tawny, rolling hills sheltering a town that is built for work, not beauty. Which is not to say the town lacks pretty things. The most dramatic attraction in Dutch is the Holy Ascension Russian Orthodox Church, a perfect blue, onion-dome chapel right on the edge of the water, the best Russian church left in Alaska. The extant buildings date to the 1890s, although there has been a church on the site since 1808. Inside is a collection of Russian icons and artworks that is not to be missed, certainly the most impressive in the Americas. These are not museum pieces; they have been used regularly, and it shows.

Next to the church is the Bishop's House, which is undergoing continuing restoration. A walk in the graveyard between the two buildings shows the full history of the area: Aleuts, sailors, and, always oriented to face the church, the graves of the Orthodox parishioners.

Easy walking distance from the ferry terminal is the Aleutian World War II National Historic Area Visitor Center, on the edge of the airport. The Aleutians saw heavy fighting through much of the war—some outer islands were occupied by Japanese forces for years—and the museum does a nice job of presenting the history of the conflict. At the peak of the war, more than 60,000 servicemen were stationed out here.

The Aleut take on the islands is offered at the Museum of the Aleutians, behind the grocery store, about a 15-minute walk from the ferry. Small, but quite remarkable, displays include original drawings from Captain Cook's third voyage, a traditional gut parka, and more. A don't-miss stop.

Don't worry about opening hours: if the ferry is in, the town's attractions will be open.

For facilities, the towns have hotels and restaurants that rival those on Alaska's mainland, plus guided adventure tours, many geared toward birders.

Unalaska–Dutch Harbor Convention and Visitors Bureau. If you need help planning your stay, contact the Unalaska–Dutch Harbor Convention and Visitors Bureau for a little extra guidance. ☎ *907/581–2612, 877/581–2612* ⊕ *www.unalaska.info.*

OUTDOOR ACTIVITIES AND GUIDED TOURS

OUTDOOR ADVENTURING

Aleutian Adventure Sports. Since 1994 AAS owner Jeff Hancock has offered an Aleutian resident's outdoor experience, and is the only year-round outfitter operating in the chain. Services include guided hiking, camping, sea kayaking and mountaineering, as well as marine charters for guided birding and water-taxi. For the intrepid adventurer, gear rentals for mountain bikes, camping gear, and sea kayaks are also available. ☎ *907/581–4489* ⊕ *www.aleutianadventure.com.*

WHERE TO EAT AND STAY

For expanded hotel reviews, visit Fodors.com.

$$$

HOTEL

★

Grand Aleutian Hotel. The airy three-story atrium lobby with a large stone fireplace conjures images of a Swiss chalet, while each carpeted, brightly lighted room is decorated with Alaskan artwork and has a view overlooking the water. **Pros:** bay-view rooms; masseuse on call. **Cons:** a bit generic; once you're inside, you could be almost anywhere. **TripAdvisor:** "beautiful," "bright and clean," "exceptional wildlife." $ *Rooms from: $184* ⊠ *498 Salmon Way, Box 921169, Dutch Harbor* ☎ *866/581–3844, 907/581–3844* ⊕ *www.grandaleutian.com* ⤴ *112 rooms, 2 suites.*

$$
B&B/INN
⊞ **Unisea Inn of the Grand Aleutian Hotel.** This inn is the little sister of the Grand Aleutian Hotel, built to accommodate travelers on a budget. **Pros:** what passes for budget prices in the Aleutians; cozy. **Cons:** not as grand as the Grand Aleutian; views not as great either. **TripAdvisor:** "work in progress," "budget," "love their sports bar." ⓢ *Rooms from: $119* ⊠ *185 Gilman Rd., Box 921169, Dutch Harbor* ☎ *866/581–3844 reservations* ⤴ *22 rooms.*

PRIBILOF ISLANDS

200 miles north of the Aleutian Islands, 800 miles southwest of Anchorage.

GETTING HERE AND AROUND

For most travelers it is much easier and more efficient to sign up for package tours that arrange air travel from Anchorage, lodging, ground transportation on the islands, and guided activities. It can be nearly, if not completely, impossible to arrange such things after you arrive. Guest accommodations in the Pribilofs are very limited, with lodgings only on St. George and St. Paul. The best way to hop between islands is by air on Peninsula Airways, but both islands are notorious fog magnets; you should never plan on getting out quite as scheduled.

ESSENTIALS

Airline Contacts **Peninsula Airways** ☎ 907/771–2640 ⊕ www.penair.com.

Emergency Contacts **St. George Traditional Clinic** ☎ 907/859–2254. **St. Paul Health Clinic/APIA** ⊠ 1990 Polovina Tpke. ☎ 907/546–2310, 911.

Mail **U.S. Post Office** ⊠ 2000 Polovina Tpke. ☎ 907/546–2270.

EXPLORING

Pribilof Islands. The Pribilof Islands are a misty, fog-bound breeding ground of seabirds and northern fur seals. Rising out of the surging waters of the Bering Sea, the Pribilofs consist of five islets, a tiny, green, treeless oasis with rippling belts of lush grass contrasting with volcanic rocks. In early summer seals come home from far Pacific waters to mate, and the larger islands, St. Paul and St. George, are overwhelmed with frenzied activity. The seals' barks and growls can roll out several miles to sea.

Although St. Paul and St. George are less than 50 miles apart, the island group itself is a 1,600-mile round-trip from Anchorage, over the massive snowy peaks of the Alaska Peninsula and north of the rocky islands of the Aleutian chain.

About the only visitors to the Pribilofs are commercial fishermen—this is where many of the "Deadliest Catch" boats call their home port—or those who've come to see wildlife. Together, St. Paul and St. George islands are seasonal homes to hundreds of thousands of fur seals (about 80% of them on St. Paul) and nearly 250 species of birds. Some birds migrate here from as far away as Argentina, whereas others are year-round residents. Most spectacular of all is the islands' seabird population: each summer more than 2 million seabirds gather at traditional Pribilof nesting grounds; about 90% of them breed on St. George.

Fodor's Choice
★

St. Paul Island. The largest northern fur-seal herd in the world and more than 180 varieties of birds await nature lovers on St. Paul Island. In town you can visit with local residents; about 500 descendants of Aleut-Russians live here now in the shadow of the old but beautifully-cared-for Russian Orthodox church and amid the vestiges of Aleut culture. The local museum shows how the island was once essentially a factory, as the U.S. government controlled sealing, and therefore, the only jobs on the island.

DID YOU KNOW?

Of special interest to birders are the rare vagrant birds of native Asian species, such as the Siberian rubythroat and Eurasian skylark, sometimes blown here by strong winds. But just for day-to-day birding, come here, see a red-legged kittiwake, and make birders back home scream in envy.

St. George Island. Though it is home to nearly 2 million nesting seabirds, St. George Island is rarely visited because no organized tours visit here, and accommodations are limited. Even people who live on St. Paul try to avoid going to St. George because it's so easy to get weathered in there.

OUTDOOR ACTIVITIES AND GUIDED TOURS

The Pribilofs are considered a birders' paradise for good reason: species that are seldom, if ever, seen elsewhere in North America frequently show up here, including an array of "Asian vagrants" blown here by westerly winds. Birders can expect to find all manner of shorebirds, waterfowl, and seabirds, including puffins, murres, red- and black-legged kittiwakes, plovers—the list goes on and on. Tour guides are usually hired for their birding skills, but will also show visitors the best places to view seals (well, the seals are kind of hard to miss, since a lot of the adolescent males hang out near the roads) and maybe the occasional whale.

9

BIRDING AND SEAL WATCHING

Tanadgusix Village Corporation of St. Paul Island. This is the place to contact for St. Paul Island tour information. ✉ *615 E. 82nd Ave., Anchorage* ☎ *907/762–8429, 877/424–5637* ⊕ *www.alaskabirding.com.*

Wilderness Birding Adventures. The owners of Wilderness Birding Adventures run intermittent trips in the Pribilofs; elsewhere in the state, they combine birding, hiking, and river rafting in their wilderness adventures. ☎ *907/694–7442* ⊕ *www.wildernessbirding.com.*

WHERE TO STAY

For expanded hotel reviews, visit Fodors.com.

$$
HOTEL

King Eider Hotel. This newly built, sprawling addition to the airport offers comfortable, dormitory style lodging at the remote reaches of civilization. **Pros:** clean, very well cared for, and the only game in town. **Cons:** pretty bare-bones rooms for the price; a lot of rooms share just a couple of baths. **TripAdvisor:** "overall a great experience," "on the edge of the world," "excellent location." ⑤ *Rooms from: $125* ✉ *523 Tolstoi St.* ☎ *907/546–2477, 907/278–2312, 877/424–5637 to make tour reservations* ⊕ *www.alaskabirding.com* ⤳ *20 rooms, 2 shared baths.*

$$
B&B/INN

⊞ **St. George Tanaq Hotel.** A national historic landmark, St. George Island's only hotel is a small, rustic building with a dark-wood interior and a mix of modern and vintage furniture. **Pros:** National Historic Landmark flavor; can hear the seals from your room. **Cons:** come ready for every weather condition possible, all at once; seals keep light sleepers awake. **TripAdvisor:** "felt like home," "good size rooms," "it is okay." ⑤ *Rooms from: $169* ⊠ *Downtown* ☎ *907/859–2255* ⊕ *www. stgeorgetanaq.com* ⇲ *10 rooms share 5 baths.*

NORTHWEST AND THE ARCTIC

This is a largely roadless region of long, dark, sunless winters and short, bright summers, when the sun provides nearly three months of perpetual daylight in places like Barrow. The round-the-clock sunshine lasts for only a few days farther south, but the extended twilight hours turn the midnights bright. The Northwest and Arctic are the land of Eskimos and huge caribou herds and polar bears, a place where people still lead subsistence lifestyles and where the Native cultural traditions live on. This region is also a place of gold rushes past and America's largest oil field, as well as a region with many of Alaska's most remote parklands—not to mention one of the country's grandest refuges, the Arctic National Wildlife Refuge.

NOME

540 miles northwest of Anchorage.

More than a century has passed since a great stampede for gold put a speck of wilderness now called Nome on the Alaska map, but gold mining and noisy saloons are still mainstays here. This frontier community on the icy Bering Sea once boasted 20,000 people during the gold stampede in the 1890s, but now has only 3,500 year-round residents. At first glance the town may come off as a collection of ramshackle houses and low-slung commercial buildings—like a vintage gold-mining camp; or, because of the spooky, abandoned, monolithic microwave towers from World War II that sit atop Anvil Mountain, the set for an Arctic horror movie—but only a couple of streets back you'll find tidy, modern homes and charming, hospitable shopkeepers. In fact, Nome is one of Alaska's greatest places, very much itself, the kind of town where the grocery store sells ATVs next to the meat counter.

Just 165 miles from the coast of Siberia, Nome is considerably closer to Russia than to either Anchorage or Fairbanks. And though you'll find 300 miles of local road system well worth exploring, to get to Nome you must either fly or mush a team of sled dogs.

For centuries before Nome gained fame as a gold-rush town, nomadic Inupiaq Eskimos seasonally inhabited the area in hunting and fishing camps; an archaeological site south of town has the remains of some round pit houses that prove the locals didn't much like corners. The gold stampede—far, far richer than the more famous Klondike strike—occurred in the 1890s and was over relatively soon, even though gold is still mined by both prospectors and open-pit mining productions.

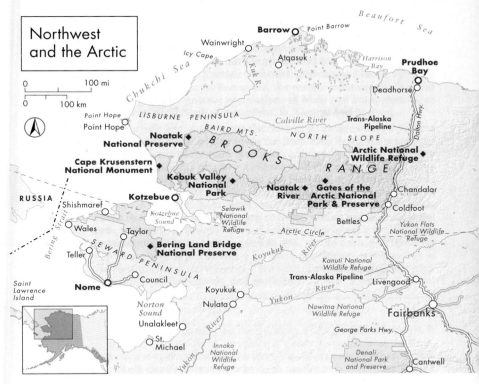

Barrow ○ · Point Barrow
Wainwright ○
Icy Cape ○
Atqasuk ○
Harrison Bay
Prudhoe Bay ○
Deadhorse ○
Beaufort Sea
Chukchi Sea
Kuk R.
Colville River
NORTH SLOPE
Trans-Alaska Pipeline
Dalton Hwy.
Point Hope ○
Point Hope
LISBURNE PENINSULA
BAIRD MTS.
B R O O K S
Arctic National Wildlife Refuge ◆
R A N G E
Noatak National Preserve ◆
Cape Krusenstern National Monument ◆
Kobuk Valley National Park ◆
Noatak River ◆
Gates of the Arctic National Park & Preserve
Chandalar ○
Coldfoot ○
RUSSIA
Kotzebue ○
Selawik National Wildlife Refuge
Bettles ○
Yukon Flats National Wildlife Refuge
Shishmaref ○
Kotzebue Sound
Arctic Circle
Wales ○
Taylor ○
Bering Land Bridge National Preserve ◆
Koyukuk River
Kanuti National Wildlife Refuge
Trans-Alaska Pipeline
Livengood ○
Teller ○
S E W A R D P E N I N S U L A
Bering Strait
Nome ○
Council ○
Norton Sound
Koyukuk ○
Nulata ○
Yukon River
Nowitna National Wildlife Refuge
Fairbanks
Saint Lawrence Island
Unalakleet ○
St. Michael ○
Innoko National Wildlife Refuge
George Parks Hwy.
Denali National Park and Preserve
Cantwell ○
Yukon River

What Nome is best known for, however, is the Iditarod Trail. Even though parts of the historic trail from Nome to Anchorage were long used as routes for the Native Eskimos and Athabascans, the full trail gained fame in 1925, when Nome was hit with an outbreak of diphtheria. There was no remedy in town, so the serum was ferried by the Alaska Railroad to Nenana, 250 miles from Anchorage, and then a 20-dog sled team ran it the remaining 674 miles in −50°Fahrenheit temperatures over five days and seven hours; Nome was saved. In 1973, in honor of the original Iditarod (a word derived from the Athabascan word *haiditarod*, meaning "a far, distant place"), an annual race for dog mushers was started. The race begins in Anchorage and traverses snow and tundra for 1,049 miles, to commemorate Alaska's being the 49th state (the actual distance is give or take a few miles, of course; dog sleds don't come with odometers). Thousands of people converge in Nome to watch the dogs and mushers come over the finish line in March. Still more visitors come to Nome in the summer months to take advantage of the beautiful effulgent colors of wildflowers and green grass, its wildlife viewing and birding, and its marvelous end-of-the-world vibe.

Though at first there doesn't seem to be much to this town on the edge of the Bering Sea, there are many relics of the past in and around the area. There are 44 abandoned gold dredges, enormous constructions of steel that are scattered from the outskirts of town to the surrounding miles of tundra beyond. Just east of town on the road out to Council, a quiet summer fishing village inhabited by many locals during the summer, you'll stumble across not only fantastic marshlands for birding, but also the Last Train to Nowhere—a railway built to haul gold that was never finished—quietly rusting away. In the opposite direction, northeast of Nome on the road to Taylor, you'll come to the Pilgrim Hot Springs, the site of an old settlement including the former Our Lady of Lourdes chapel and orphanage for Eskimo children during the 1918 influenza epidemic. And directly north of Nome is the beautiful Native village of Teller, a subsistence village in Grantley Harbor, which may have one of the most perfect locations in the world, set on a buttonhook spit in a sheltered bay. Teller made the world news in 1926, when Roald Amundsen landed his zeppelin Norge here after the first successful flight over the north pole.

The roads to these destinations are unpaved but traversable, and mostly in good shape. From the road you might see herds of reindeer (they like to use the road themselves, since it's easier than running in tundra), musk oxen, grizzly bears, and moose, and a slew of different birds like the long-tailed jaegers, yellow wagtails, and the bristle-thighed curlew, rarely seen in North America.

GETTING HERE AND AROUND

Alaska Airlines Vacations packages air tours to Barrow and Nome. Local arrangements are taken care of by ground operators. The Alaska Travel Industry Association can give tips on air travel and flightseeing opportunities throughout the Bush. From Nome visitors can access Serpentine Hot Springs, in the Bering Land Bridge National Preserve, by charter plane. These hot springs are well maintained despite their location.

If you're set on doing your own driving, head to Stampede Ventures, which rents cars and vans of various types. ■TIP➔ Be sure to fill up with gas in Nome, as there are no services once you leave town. And even if the gauge says the tank is full when you rent it, be sure to fill 'er up anyway—sometimes the gauges lie.

ESSENTIALS

Airline and Visitor Contacts **Alaska Airlines Vacations** ☎ 866/500-5511 ⊕ www.alaskaair.com. **Alaska Travel Industry Association** ⊠ 2600 Cordova St., Suite 201, Anchorage ☎ 907/929-2200, 800/862-5275 for vacation planner ⊕ www.travelalaska.com. **Nome Convention and Visitors Bureau** ⊠ 301 Front St. ☎ 907/443-6555 ⊕ www.visitnomealaska.com.

Banking **Credit Union 1** ⊠ 406 Warren Pl. ☎ 800/478-2222 ⊕ www.cu1. org. **Wells Fargo** ⊠ 109A Front St. ☎ 907/443-2223, 800/869-3557 ⊕ www. wellsfargo.com.

Emergency **Norton Sound Regional Hospital** ☎ 907/443-3311 ⊕ www.nortonsoundhealth.org. **Police** ☎ 907/443-5262. **State troopers** ☎ 907/443-2835.

Internet **City Library** ⊠ 223 Front St. ☎ 907/443-6628 ⊕ www.nomealaska.org.

Mail **USPS** ⌖ *113 E. Front St.* ☎ *907/443–2401.*

Vehicle Rental Stampede Vehicle Rentals ☎ *907/443–3838, 800/354–4606* ⊕ *www.aurorainnome.com.*

EXPLORING

Anvil Mountain. In the summer months, when the sun stays up late, take an evening drive to the top of Anvil Mountain, near Nome, for a panoramic view of the old gold town and the Bering Sea. Be sure to carry mosquito repellent.

Carrie M. McClain Memorial Museum. Nome's Carrie M. McClain Memorial Museum showcases the history of the Nome gold rush, from the "Lucky Swedes'" discovery in 1898 to Wyatt Earp's arrival in 1899 and the stampede of thousands of people into Nome in 1900. The museum also has exhibits about the Bering Strait Inupiaq Eskimos, plus displays on the Nome Kennel Club and its All-Alaska Sweepstakes. However, the highlight of the museum is the historical photo collection: thousands of pictures from the early days make it a perfect place to lose yourself on a rainy day. ⌖ *223 Front St.* ☎ *907/443–6630* ⌖ *Free* ☉ *June–early Sept., daily 10–5:30; early Sept.–May, Tues.–Fri. 1–5.*

Nome Convention and Visitors Bureau. For exploring downtown, stop at the Nome Convention and Visitors Bureau for a historic walking-tour map, a city map, and information on local activities from flight-seeing to bird-watching. ⌖ *301 Front St.* ☎ *907/443–6555* ⊕ *www. visitnomealaska.com.*

OUTDOOR ACTIVITIES AND GUIDED TOURS

LOCAL TOURS

Alaska Airlines Vacations. Alaska Airlines Vacations arranges trips to Nome (such as the "Day in Nome" and "Adventure in Nome" packages), including air travel, hotels, and local tours. ☎ *866/500–5511* ⊕ *www.alaskavacationsalaska.com.*

Nome Discovery Tours. Visitors seeking to learn more about Nome and the surrounding region can join former Broadway showman Richard Beneville, flat-out one of Alaska's most entertaining guides, who emphasizes Nome's gold-rush and Inupiaq history of the region in his Nome Discovery Tours. If you only have one day in town, spend it with Richard. ☎ *907/443–2814.*

Northern Alaska Tour Company. This tour company arranges one-day cultural tours to Nome via Fairbanks or Anchorage. ☎ *800/474–1986, 907/474–8600* ⊕ *www.northernalaska.com.*

SLED-DOG RACING

Iditarod Trail Sled Dog Race. The famed Iditarod Trail Sled Dog Race—the Olympics of sled-dog racing—reaches its culmination in Nome in mid-March. Racers start in Anchorage for a trip of nine days to two weeks (the record, set in 2011, is an astounding eight days, 18 hours, 46 minutes, 39 seconds). The arrival of the mushers heralds a winter carnival.

Iditarod Trail Committee. For dates, starting times, and other information, contact the Iditarod Trail Committee. ☎ *907/376–5155* ⊕ *www.iditarod.com.*

WHERE TO EAT

$$
STEAKHOUSE
Fodor's Choice
★
☺
✕**Airport Pizza.** This family-friendly pizza joint isn't like any other. Not only does it make some of the best food in town with a menu boasting great pizza and toppings, but it also features Tex-Mex, sandwiches, and a full breakfast menu. What's given this restaurant national attention is its delivery service: not only in town, but also to the surrounding Bush villages. Call up, order a pizza, and it'll be put on the next plane out, no extra charge. There are 11 beers on tap (many of which are microbrews), an extensive wine selection, and live music on the weekends. It also has a drive-thru coffee shop. ⑤ *Average main: $18* ✉ *406 Bering St.* ☎ *907/443–7992, 877/749–9270.*

$$
PIZZA
✕**Milano's Pizzeria.** This Front Street restaurant has a casual atmosphere and offers dine-in service as well as takeout. Besides pizzas with a wide assortment of toppings, there's Japanese, Korean, and Italian food. One side of the restaurant has Italian decor and the other has Japanese. Sit on the side that suits your palate. ⑤ *Average main: $20* ✉ *110 W. Front St.* ☎ *907/443–2924.*

$
AMERICAN
✕**Subway.** Nome's only fast-food restaurant has probably the nicest view you'll ever see from a fast-food chain. Overlooking the Bering Sea through large vista windows, this eatery adjoins the only movie theater in town. When the foreign surroundings and harsh weather start to get you down, a little bit of familiarity can go a long way. Nothing surprising on this menu. ⑤ *Average main: $8* ✉ *135 E. Front St.* ☎ *907/443–8100.*

WHERE TO STAY

For expanded hotel reviews, visit Fodors.com.

$$
HOTEL
Fodor's Choice
★
⊡**Aurora Inn & Suites.** Located right in the historic district and in walking distance of shops, eateries, and watering holes, the inn offers clean, modern rooms. **Pros:** refreshingly clean; friendly service; sauna. **Cons:** proximity to the bars means it can get a little rowdy outside; most rooms don't have a view. **TripAdvisor:** "nice rooms," "it is what it is," "best place to stay in Nome." ⑤ *Rooms from: $155* ✉ *302 E. Front St.* ☎ *907/443–3838, 800/354–4606* ⊕ *www.aurorainnnome.com* ⤵ *54 rooms.*

$
HOTEL
⊡**Nome Nugget Inn.** The architecture and decor of the Nugget Inn combine every cliché of the Victorian gold-rush era. **Pros:** cool atmosphere in the public areas; great location. **Cons:** a little less cool in the rooms. **TripAdvisor:** "super friendly," "comfortable accommodation," "caring owners." ⑤ *Rooms from: $110* ✉ *315 Front St.* ☎ *907/443–4189, 877/443–2323* ⊕ *www.nomenuggetinnhotel.com* ⤵ *47 rooms.*

SHOPPING

Nome is one of the best places to buy ivory, because many of the Eskimo carvers from outlying villages come to Nome first to sell their wares to dealers.

Arctic Trading Post. Peruse the extensive stock of authentic Eskimo ivory carvings and other Alaskan artwork, jewelry, and books at Arctic Trading Post, and maybe grab a coffee; this is the place most locals stop for their morning cup of joe. ✉ *302 Front St.* ☎ *907/443–2686.*

RICHES OF THE PAST

The region's golden years began in 1898, when three prospectors—known as the Lucky Swedes—struck rich deposits on Anvil Creek, about 4 miles from what became Nome. Their discovery was followed by the formation of the Cape Nome Mining District. The following summer even more gold was found on the beaches of Nome, a place where no one ever would have expected to find gold—placer gold is usually lying on bedrock, but here thousands of winter melts had washed it down to the sea.

Word spread quickly to the south, right about the same time everybody was discovering all the good spots for gold in the Klondike were staked. When the Bering Sea ice parted the next spring, ships from Puget Sound (in the Seattle area) arrived in Nome with eager stampeders, and miners who struck out in the Klondike arrived via the Yukon River to try again in Nome. An estimated 15,000 people landed in Nome between June and October 1900, bringing the area's population to more than 20,000. Dozens of gold dredges were hauled into the region to extract the metal from Seward Peninsula sands and gravels; more than 40 are still standing, though no longer operating (if you explore them, be sure to call out regularly, as warning to any bears that might have taken shelter inside). Among the gold-rush luminaries were Wyatt Earp, the old gunfighter from the O.K. Corral, who mined the gold of Nome the easy way: by opening a posh saloon and serving drinks to thirsty diggers. Also in Nome were Tex Rickard, the boxing promoter, who operated another Nome saloon (money made there later helped him build the third incarnation of Madison Square Garden, and helped him found the New York Rangers hockey team); and Rex Beach, whose first novel, *The Spoilers,* was based on the true story of government officials stealing gold from the hardworking miners (it was a best seller, letting even people warm and cozy down south experience the stampede).

The city of Nome was incorporated in 1901, which means it is now Alaska's oldest first-class city, with the oldest continuously operating school district. But the community's heyday lasted less than a decade; by the early 1920s the bulk of the region's gold had been mined, and only 820 or so people continued to live in Nome.

Although the city's boom times ended long ago, gold mining has continued to the present; depending on the economy, the size of the mines (and the number of offshore minidredges) fluctuates. Visitors are welcome to try their own luck; you can pick up a gold pan at one of Nome's stores and sift through the beach sands along a 2-mile stretch of shoreline east of Nome. Visitors can also contact the **Nome Convention and Visitors Bureau** for information on tours that feature gold panning.

9

Chukotka-Alaska. Stop here to browse for both Native Alaskan and Russian artwork and handicrafts, as well as books, beads, and furs. ⊠ *514 Lomen* ☎ *907/443–4128.*

Maruskiyas of Nome. This shop specializes in authentic Native Alaskan artwork and handicrafts, including ivory, baleen, and jade sculptures, jewelry, dolls, and masks. ⊠ *895 Front St.* ☎ *907/443–2955* ⊕ *www.maruskiyas.com.*

BERING LAND BRIDGE NATIONAL PRESERVE

100 miles north of Nome.

GETTING HERE AND AROUND

The Bering Land Bridge National Preserve is pretty much exactly like it was when people first came to this continent from Asia: it has no trails, campgrounds, or other visitor facilities. Access is largely by air taxi, although there is a road leading from Nome that passes within possible hiking distance.

ESSENTIALS

Air Taxi Contacts **Bering Air** ☎ *907/443–5464* ⊕ *www.beringair.com.* **Northwestern Aviation, Inc.** ☎ *907/442–3525* ⊕ *www.alaskaonyourown.com.*

Visitor Information **National Park Service** ☎ *907/443–2522* ⊕ *www.nps.gov/bela.*

EXPLORING

Bering Land Bridge National Preserve. The frozen ash and lava of the 2.8-million-acre Bering Land Bridge National Preserve lie between Nome and Kotzebue, immediately south of the Arctic Circle, one of the most remote parks in the world. The Lost Jim lava flow is the northernmost flow of major size in the United States, and the paired *maars* (clear volcanic lakes) are a geological rarity.

Of equal interest are the paleontological features of this preserve. Sealed into the permafrost are flora and fauna—bits of twigs and leaves, tiny insects, small mammals, even the fossilized remains of woolly mammoths—that flourished here when the Bering Land Bridge linked North America to what is now Russia. "Bridge" is something of a misnomer; essentially, the Bering Sea was dry at the time, and the intercontinental connection was as much as 600 miles wide at places. Early peoples wandered through this treeless landscape, perhaps following the musk ox, whose descendants still occupy this terrain, or the mammoths and steppe bison, who are both long gone. Flowering plants thrive in this seemingly barren region, about 250 species in all, and tens of thousands of migrating birds can be seen in season. More than 100 species, including ducks, geese, swans, sandhill cranes, and various shorebirds and songbirds, come here from around the world each spring.

KOTZEBUE

170 miles northeast of Nome.

Kotzebue is Alaska's largest Eskimo community, home to more than 3,000 people. Most of the residents of this coastal village are Inupiaq, whose ancestors have had ties to the region for thousands of years. For most of that time the Inupiaq lived in seasonal camps, following caribou, moose, and other wildlife across the landscape. They also depended on whales, seals, fish, and the wide variety of berries and other plants the rich tundra landscape offers. Besides being talented hunters, the Inupiaq were—and still are—skilled craftsmen and artists, known for their rugged gear, ceremonial parkas, dolls, caribou-skin masks, birch-bark baskets, and whalebone and walrus-ivory carvings.

WELCOME TO KOTZEBUE

Comprising clusters of weather-bleached little houses and a few public buildings on the gravelly shore of Kotzebue Sound, this village provides a glimpse of how Alaska's Eskimos live today. It was an ancient Eskimo trading center; now it is an example of the modern spirit nudging Alaska Natives into the state's mainstream culture without leaving their traditions behind.

Built on a 3-mile-long spit of land that juts into Kotzebue Sound, this village lies 33 miles above the Arctic Circle, on Alaska's northwest coast. Before Europeans arrived in the region, the Inupiaq name for this locale was Kikiktagruk; that was changed to Kotzebue after German explorer Otto von Kotzebue passed through in 1818 while sailing for Russia. Kotzebue is the region's economic and political hub and headquarters for both the Northwest Arctic Borough and the NANA Regional Corporation, one of the 13 regional Native corporations formed when Congress settled the Alaskan Natives' aboriginal land claims in 1971. The region's other Eskimo villages have populations of anywhere from 90 to 700 residents.

Just as their ancestors did, modern Inupiaq depend heavily on subsistence hunting and fishing. Some residents also fish commercially. This region of the state has few employment opportunities outside of the government and the Native corporation, but in Kotzebue, the biggest private employer is the Red Dog Mine. Located on NANA land, Red Dog has the world's largest deposit of zinc, and is expected to produce ore for at least 50 years. Local government here, as in many Bush villages, is a blend of tribal government and a more modern borough system. Other facilities and programs include the Maniilaq Health Center and the Northwest Arctic District Correspondence Program.

Kotzebue has long, cold winters and short, cool summers. The average low temperature in January is –12°F, and midsummer highs rarely reach the 70s. "We have four seasons—June, July, August, and winter," a tour guide jests. But don't worry about the sometimes chilly weather—the local sightseeing company has snug, bright loaner parkas for visitors on package tours. And there's plenty of light in which to take in the village and surrounding landscape: the sun doesn't set for 36 days from June into July. One of summer's highlights is the annual

Northwest Native Trade Fair; held each year after the July 4 celebration, it features traditional Native games, seal-hook-throwing contests, and an Eskimo buggy race.

GETTING HERE AND AROUND

As with pretty much everywhere else in the Bush, your main mode of transportation into Kotzebue will be via airplane. **Alaska Airlines** offers regular flights between Anchorage and Kotzebue. Check the website for more details. The main air-taxi services serve Kotzebue, and there's a daily flight from Anchorage. Cabs will take you anywhere in town for $5 flat, plus $5 per stop.

ESSENTIALS

Airline Information **Alaska Airlines** ⊕ www.alaskaair.com.

Banking **Wells Fargo** ✉ 360 Lagoon St. ☎ 907/442–3258, 800/869–3557 ⊕ www.wellsfargo.com.

Emergency **Maniilaq Health Center** ✉ 436 5th Ave ☎ 800/431–3321, 907/442–3321 ⊕ www.maniilaq.org. **Police** ☎ 907/442–3351 ⊕ www. kotzpdweb.tripod.com. **State troopers** ☎ 907/442–3222 in Kotzebue.

Internet Access **Chukchi Consortium Library** ✉ 604 3rd St. ☎ 907/442–2410.

Mail **USPS** ✉ 333 Shore Ave. ☎ 907/442–3291.

Visitor Information **NANA Regional Corporation** (Northwest Alaska Native Association). ☎ 907/442–3301, 800/478–3301 ⊕ www.nana.com. **Northwest Arctic Borough** ☎ 907/442–2500, 800/478–1110 in Alaska.

EXPLORING

Brooks Range. North and east of Kotzebue is the Brooks Range, one of Alaska's great mountain ranges. Stretching across the state, much of the range is protected by Gates of the Arctic National Park and Preserve and the Arctic National Wildlife Refuge.

Permafrost. If you're hiking the wildflower-carpeted tundra around Kotzebue, you are entering a living museum dedicated to permafrost, the permanently frozen ground that lies just a few inches below the spongy tundra. Even Kotzebue's 6,000-foot airport runway is built on permafrost—with a 6-inch insulating layer between the frozen ground and the airfield surface to ensure that landings are smooth.

Wilderness areas. Although most people come to Kotzebue on day trips or overnight package tours, for those with time to linger, the town also serves as a gateway for three exceptional national wilderness areas: Cape Krusenstern National Monument, Kobuk Valley National Park, and Noatak National Preserve.

WHERE TO EAT AND STAY

For expanded hotel reviews, visit Fodors.com.

$$
ECLECTIC ✗ **Bayside Restaurant.** One of the few restaurants in Kotzebue, the Bayside is the best place in town for breakfast, and it features a selection of American, Italian, and Chinese food for lunch and dinner. $ *Average main: $16* ✉ 303 Shore Ave. ☎ 907/442–3600.

$$$$ 🖵 **Nullagvik Hotel.** Recently constructed to replace the old Nullagvik, this
HOTEL new hotel provides comfort and class with spacious, modern rooms full
of amenities and a third-floor observation lounge overlooking the Chukchi Sea. **Pros:** great views; comfortable rooms. **Cons:** the best lodging in
town comes at a price. **TripAdvisor:** "beyond words," "beautiful new
property," "unbelievable comfort." ⑤ *Rooms from: $259* ✉ *306 Shore
Ave.* ☎ *907/442–3331* ⊕ *www.nullagvik.com* ⤴ *78 rooms* ⧄ *No meals.*

CAPE KRUSENSTERN NATIONAL MONUMENT

10 miles north of Kotzebue.

Cape Krusenstern National Monument. Just north of Kotzebue, the 560,000-
acre Cape Krusenstern National Monument has important cultural and
archaeological value. This is coastal parkland, with an extraordinary
series of beach ridges built up by storms over a period of at least 5,000
years. Almost every ridge—more than 100 in all—contains artifacts of
different human occupants, representing every known Arctic Eskimo
culture in North America. The present Eskimo occupants, whose culture
dates back some 1,400 years, use the fish, seals, caribou, and birds of
this region for food and raw materials much as their ancestors did. They
are also closely involved in the archaeological digs in the park that are
unearthing part of their own history.

Cape Krusenstern is a starkly beautiful Arctic land shaped by ice, wind,
and sea. Its low, rolling, gray-white hills covered by light-green tundra attract hikers and backpackers, and kayakers sometimes paddle
its coastline. The monument is a marvelous living museum. ■ **TIP→ It's
possible to camp in the park, but be mindful, as are the Native people when
they pitch their white canvas tents for summer fishing, that the shoreline is
subject to fierce winds. Both grizzlies and polar bears patrol the beaches in
search of food, so clean camping is a must.**

Check with the National Park Service in Kotzebue about hiring a local
guide to the monument, which has no visitor facilities; it's accessible
by air taxi and by boat from Kotzebue. ☎ *907/442–3890* ⊕ *www.nps.
gov/cakr.*

KOBUK VALLEY NATIONAL PARK

65 miles east of Kotzebue.

Kobuk Valley National Park. Kobuk Valley National Park lies entirely
north of the Arctic Circle, along the southern edge of the Brooks Range.
Its 1.14 million acres contain remarkable inland deserts and the **Great
Kobuk Sand Dunes** that stand up to 100 feet high and cover 25 square
miles. These are home to interesting relict (remnants of otherwise
extinct) flora. The park is bisected by the west-flowing **Kobuk River,** a
347-mile-long stream born in the foothills of the western Brooks Range.
The Kobuk, whose native name means "big river," has been a major
transportation and trade route for centuries. Besides the Kobuk, this
park contains two smaller streams that provide delightful river running:
the Ambler and the Salmon. These brilliantly clear rivers are accessible

by wheeled plane, and each provides a good week's worth of pleasure (if the weather cooperates).

Another place of special interest is the **Onion Portage.** Human occupation here dates back 12,500 years, back to a time when Asia and North America were still connected by the Bering Land Bridge, and the region is rich in archaeological history; herds of caribou that fed the Woodland Eskimo centuries ago are still hunted at Onion Portage by present-day Eskimo residents of the region.

Like most other remote Alaska parks, Kobuk Valley National Park is undeveloped wilderness with no visitor facilities. If you come prepared, it can be a good place for backpacking and river trips. In nearby Kotzebue the National Park Service has a visitor center where staff can provide tips for travel into the park. The villages of Kobuk and Kiana both provide immediate take-off points and have air service. ☎ *907/442–3890* ⊕ *www.nps.gov/kova.*

NOATAK NATIONAL PRESERVE

20 miles northeast of Kotzebue.

Noatak River. Adjacent to Gates of the Arctic National Park and Preserve, the 6.5-million-acre Noatak National Preserve encompasses much of the basin of the Noatak River. This is the largest mountain-ringed river basin in the United States; part of it is designated by the National Park Service as a Wild and Scenic River. Along its 425-mile course this river carves out the "Grand Canyon of the Noatak," and serves as a migration route between arctic and subarctic ecosystems. Its importance to wildlife and plants has resulted in this parkland's designation as an International Biosphere Reserve.

The Noatak River also serves as a natural highway for humans, and offers particular pleasures to river runners, with inviting tundra to camp on and the Poktovik Mountains and the Igichuk Hills nearby for good hiking. Birding can be exceptional: horned grebes, gyrfalcons, golden eagles, parasitic jaegers, owls, terns, and loons are among the species you may see. You may also spot grizzly bears, Dall sheep, wolves, caribou, or lynx, as well as the occasional musk ox. The most frequently run part of the river, ending at Lake Machurak, is mostly an easy Class I–III paddle, worth the trip just for the chance to hunt freshwater snail shells as delicate as origami along the shores of the take-out lake (where the river trip ends). The mountains around the river make for excellent hiking, and along the way the geology goes wild a couple of times, including with a massive pingo—kind of a glacial bubble. As with other parks and preserves in this northwest corner of Alaska, no visitor facilities are available and you are expected to be self-sufficient. Do not neglect the bear precautions. Most trips on the Noatak use the inland town of Bettles as a gateway. ☎ *907/442–3890* ⊕ *www.nps.gov/noat.*

9

GATES OF THE ARCTIC NATIONAL PARK AND PRESERVE

180 miles east of Kotzebue.

★ **Gates of the Arctic National Park and Preserve.** Gates of the Arctic National Park and Preserve is entirely north of the Arctic Circle, in the center of the Brooks Range; at 8.2 million acres, it's the size of four Yellowstones. This is parkland on a scale suitable to the country.

It includes the **Endicott Mountains** to the east and the **Schwatka Mountains** to the southwest, with the staggeringly sharp and dramatic **Arrigetch Peaks** in between. To the north lies a sampling of the Arctic foothills, with their colorful tilted sediments and pale green tundra. Lovely lakes are cupped in the mountains and in the tundra.

This landscape, the ultimate wilderness, captured the heart of Arctic explorer and conservationist Robert Marshall in the 1930s. Accompanied by local residents, Marshall explored much of the region now included within Gates and named many of its features, including Frigid Crag and Boreal Mountain, two peaks on either side of the North Fork Koyukuk River. These were the original "gates" for which the park is named.

Wildlife known to inhabit the park includes barren-ground caribou, grizzlies, wolves, musk oxen, moose, Dall sheep, wolverines, and smaller mammals and birds. The communities of Bettles and Anaktuvuk Pass are access points for Gates of the Arctic, which has no developed trails, campgrounds, or other visitor facilities (though there is a wilderness lodge on private land within the park). You can fly into Bettles commercially and charter an air taxi into the park or hike directly out of Anaktuvuk Pass. The Park Service has rangers stationed in both Bettles and Anaktuvuk Pass; they can provide information for those entering the wilderness, including the mandatory orientation films and bear-proof canisters for food storage. ☎ *907/692–5494 in Bettles, 907/661–3520 in Anaktuvuk Pass (this station is sometimes unmanned)* ⊕ *www.nps.gov/gaar.*

OUTDOOR ACTIVITIES AND GUIDED TOURS

Arctic Treks. This outfitter guides wilderness hikes and backpacking expeditions, sometimes combined with river trips, in both Gates of the Arctic and the Arctic National Wildlife Refuge, with new trips into the farthest west reaches of the Brooks Range and the North Slope. ☎ *907/455–6502* ⊕ *www.arctictreksadventures.com.*

WHERE TO STAY

For expanded hotel reviews, visit Fodors.com.

$$$$
B&B/INN
★

Peace of Selby Wilderness. On Selby and Narvak lakes within Gates of the Arctic National Park, Peace of Selby is perfectly situated for wilderness adventures. **Pros:** endless activity options. **Cons:** small, so reservations and planning are a must. ⑤ *Rooms from: $500* ☎ *907/672–3206* ⊕ *www.alaskawilderness.net* ↪ *1 room in lodge, 4 cabins* ▭ No

A hiker stands atop a rocky summit at the Arctic National Wildlife Refuge.

credit cards ⊘ *Closed end-Sept.–mid-June, except for specially arranged expeditions Mar. and Apr.* ⦵ *All meals.*

BARROW

330 miles northeast of Kotzebue.

The northernmost community in the United States, Barrow sits 1,300 miles south of the North Pole. The village is 10 miles south of the Beaufort Sea and Point Barrow, from which it takes its name. Point Barrow, in turn, was named in 1825 by British captain Frederick William Beechey, who'd been ordered by the British Navy to map the continent's northern coastline. Beechey wished to honor Sir John Barrow, a member of the British Admiralty and a major force in arctic exploration. The region's Inupiaq Eskimos knew the site as Ukpeagvik, or "place where owls are hunted." Even today, many snowy owls nest in the tundra outside Barrow each summer, though they're not hunted as they once were: they are now protected by federal law.

About 4,000 people inhabit Barrow today, making it easily the largest community on the North Slope. Nearly two-thirds of the residents are Inupiaq Eskimos. Though they remain deeply rooted in their Inupiaq heritage, Barrow's residents have adopted a modern lifestyle. Homes are heated by natural gas taken from nearby gas fields, and the community is served by most modern conveniences, including a public radio station and cable TV and Internet access. The community recreation center has a gymnasium, racquetball courts, weight room, and sauna, and hosts a variety of social events, from dances to basketball tournaments. In

BARROW'S RICHNESS

Barrow is truly the land of the midnight sun. From mid-May until August the sun doesn't set for more than 80 days. (Conversely, the sun disappears during the dead of winter from November through January—this is called the polar winter.) Despite the season's unending daylight, summertime temperatures can be brisk—you should even be prepared for snow flurries. Nevertheless, midsummer temperatures can occasionally reach the 60s and low 70s. Despite the region's abundant wetlands, Barrow—and the North Slope in general—has a desert climate, with annual precipitation averaging less than 10 inches.

Archaeological evidence from more than a dozen nearby ancient "dwelling mounds" suggests that people have inhabited this area for at least the past 1,500 years. A highlight of those mounds is **Mound 44**, where the 500-year-old frozen body of an

Eskimo was discovered. Scientists have been studying her remains to learn more about Eskimo life and culture before encounters with outsiders. Described as members of the **Birnirk culture,** these early residents depended heavily on marine mammals, a tradition that continues to this day. Combining modern technology with traditional knowledge, Barrow's whaling crews annually hunt for the bowhead whales that migrate through Arctic waters each spring and fall. If the whalers are successful in their springtime hunts, they share *muktuk*—whale meat (to the uninitiated, it tastes kind of like really greasy tuna mixed with steak)—with other members of the village and celebrate their good fortune with a festival called **Nalukataq.** Besides whales, residents depend on harvests of seals, walrus, caribou, waterfowl, grayling, and whitefish.

Barrow, as in much of Bush Alaska, basketball is the favored sport, played year-round by people of all ages.

Barrow is the economic and administrative center of the **North Slope Borough,** which encompasses more than 88,000 square miles, making it the world's largest municipal government (in terms of area). The village is also headquarters of the **Arctic Slope Regional Corporation,** formed in 1971 through the Alaska Native Claims Settlement Act (ANCSA), as well as the Ukpeagvik Inupiat Corporation, which economically and politically represents the community of Barrow. Several village councils are also headquartered in the town.

GETTING HERE AND AROUND

Alaska Airlines Vacations packages air tours to Barrow and Nome. Local arrangements are taken care of by Native ground operators. The Alaska Travel Industry Association can give tips on air travel and flightseeing opportunities throughout the Bush.

ESSENTIALS

Contacts **Alaska Airlines Vacations** ☎ 866/500–5511 ⊕ *www. alaskavacationsalaska.com.* **Alaska Travel Industry Association** ✉ *2600 Cordova St., Suite 201, Anchorage* ☎ *907/929–2200, 800/862–5275 for vacation* *planner* ⊕ *www.travelalaska.com.* **City of Barrow** 🖨 *907/852-5211* ⊕ *www. cityofbarrow.org.*

Banking Wells Fargo ✉ *1078 Kiogak St.* ☎ *907/852-6200, 800/869-3557* ⊕ *www.wellsfargo.com.*

Emergency Police ☎ *907/852-6111.* **Samuel Simmonds Memorial Hospital** ✉ *1296 Agvik St.* ☎ *907/852-4611* ⊕ *www.arcticslope.org.* **State troopers** ☎ *907/852-3783* ⊕ *www.dps.state.ak.us/ast.*

Internet Tuzzy Library ✉ *5421 N. Star St.* ☎ *800/478-6916* 🖨 *907/852-4050* ⊕ *www.tuzzy.org.*

Mail USPS ✉ *3080 Eben Hobson St.* ☎ *907/852-6800.*

EXPLORING

Non-Natives established a presence at Barrow in the early 1880s, when the U.S. Army built a research station here. Drawn to the area by the Beaufort Sea's abundant whales, commercial whalers established the **Cape Smythe Whaling and Trading Station** in 1893; a cabin from that operation still stands, and is the oldest frame building in Alaska's Arctic. The station is now listed on the National Register of Historic Places (as are the Birnirk dwelling mounds).

By the early 1900s both a Presbyterian church and U.S. post office had been established. Recalling those days, an Inupiat elder named Alfred Hopson once recounted that the famed Norwegian explorer Vilhjalmur Stefansson used the church as a base for studies of local residents, including measurements of their head sizes. From then on, Stefansson was known locally as the "head measurer." Oil and gas exploration later brought more whites from the Lower 48 to the area; even more came as schools and other government agencies took root in the region. Hopson, too, played a role in the area's development, as he funneled millions of dollars in tax revenues into road building, sanitation and water services, and heath-care services.

Barrow has opened its annual springtime whale festival to outsiders, and there are several historic sites, including a military installation, points of Native cultural importance, and a famous crash site. The Barrow airport is where you'll find the **Will Rogers and Wiley Post Monument,** marking the 1935 crash of the American humorist and his pilot 15 miles south of town.

Drawn by both cultural and natural attractions, visitors to Barrow usually arrive on a one- or two-day tour with Alaska Airlines, the only national carrier serving the area. Packages include a bus tour of the town's dusty roads and major sights. ■TIP➔ Though Barrow's residents invite visitors to attend their annual whale festival in spring, summer is the ideal time to survey the town and its historic sites.

OUTDOOR ACTIVITIES AND GUIDED TOURS

Alaska Airlines Vacations. From mid-May through September you can take an Alaska Airlines Vacations package from Anchorage or Fairbanks to "the top of the world" and get a chance to learn about the natural and cultural history of the area. ☎ *866/500-5511* ⊕ *www. alaskavacationsalaska.com.*

VISITING IN WINTER

Although many people think visiting Alaska in winter is insane, there are plenty of good reasons for doing so. It just takes a bit of an adventurous spirit and proper clothing.

The northern lights (aurora borealis) are active all year long, but it has to get dark before you can enjoy them. On a clear night these shimmering curtains of color in the sky are absolutely breathtaking: rippling reds and greens and blues that seem to make the entire sky come alive. Weather and solar activity have to cooperate in order to make the aurora performances happen, but when they do, the results are astounding. ■TIP➜ To check out aurora borealis activity, look up the forecast at ⊕ www.gedds.alaska.edu/AuroraForecast.

There are almost no insects in the winter months; if you've visited in summer and been subjected to the mosquitoes, no-see-ums, and white socks, this alone might entice you.

For a real Alaska winter experience, dog mushing is the ultimate. Spectators can watch sprint and long-distance races all over the state, capped off by the Yukon Quest and Iditarod races in February and March. There are numerous outfits in the Interior and South Central that will train you to mush your own team. Fodor's discusses dog mushing and surrounding competitions with the expectation and hope that all the animals are treated with care and respect. And if you hang out with serious mushers, you'll see that their animals are more pampered than the average Park Avenue poodle.

Tundra Tours. Year-round tours are organized through Tundra Tours. Offered from mid-September through mid-May, the winter tours feature visits to a traditional hunting camp, the whaling station, the Distant Early Warning System site, and opportunities to visit Point Barrow and watch northern lights. The summer program is highlighted by visits to local historic sites and opportunities to witness traditional cultural activities such as Eskimo dances, sewing demonstrations, and the blanket toss. In both winter and summer, visitors can purchase locally made Inupiaq arts and crafts. ☎ 907/852–3900 ⊕ www.tundratoursinc.com.

WHERE TO EAT AND STAY
For expanded hotel reviews, visit Fodors.com.

$$$
MEXICAN
★
✕ **Pepe's North of the Border.** The warmth of Pepe's will make you forget that you're in the middle of the Arctic tundra in the most famous restaurant north of Fairbanks. Murals depicting Mexican village scenes highlight the Mission-style decor, and an extensive selection of Mexican dishes, from soft tacos to burritos and flautas, makes this restaurant a favorite of locals and visitors alike. The restaurant's menu is also spiced up with dishes that feature Alaskan seafood and, at the high end of things, steak and lobster. Dinner at Pepe's is surprisingly refined for being on the very fringe of civilization. $ *Average main: $28* ⊠ *1204 Agvik St., next to Top of the World Hotel* ☎ *907/852–8200.*

$$
B&B/INN
🛏 **Barrow Airport Inn.** As the name suggests, this modern and well-appointed property is convenient to the airport (it's only two blocks away). **Pros:** convenient; clean; in walking distance of eateries. **Cons:**

must like the odd bit of airplane noise; no restaurant on premises. **TripAdvisor:** "more than I expected," "friendly people," "so very nice." $ *Rooms from: $135* ⊠ *1815 Momeganna St.* ☎ *907/852–2525, 800/375–2527 in Alaska* ⤳ *16 rooms* ❍ *Breakfast.*

$$$ ⚿ **Top of the World Hotel.** Built in 1974, this refurbished hotel on the
HOTEL   shore of the Arctic Ocean has just about every imaginable modern con-
★   venience, including cable TV and Internet access. **Pros:** every modern convenience, next door to restaurant, quick walk to the beach. **Cons:** no elevators (which means you're taking the stairs to the top of the world); a little worn in some places. **TripAdvisor:** "pretty darn good," "a fine place to stay," "very accommodating." $ *Rooms from: $235* ⊠ *1200 Agviq St.* ☎ *907/852–3900* ⊕ *www.tundratoursinc.com* ⤳ *44 rooms.*

SHOPPING

Stuaqpak (*"Big Store"*). The AC Value Center, or, as it's known locally, Stuaqpak, is the largest store in town. Though it mainly sells groceries, the store also stocks Eskimo crafts made by locals, including furs, parkas, mukluks, and ceremonial masks. ⊠ *4725 Ahkovak St.* ☎ *907/852–6711* ⊕ *www.alaskacommercial.com.*

PRUDHOE BAY

250 miles southeast of Barrow.

Most towns have museums that chronicle local history and achievements. Deadhorse is the town anchoring life along Prudhoe Bay, but it could also serve as a museum dedicated to humankind's hunt for energy and its ability to adapt to harsh conditions to capture that energy.

The costly, much-publicized Arctic oil and gas project is complex and varied. Visitors can survey oil wells, stations, and oil-company residential complexes—small cities themselves—and might get the chance to spot caribou and wildflowers.

GETTING HERE AND AROUND

In the past, individual travelers rarely turned up in Deadhorse and Prudhoe Bay. But now that the Dalton Highway has been opened as far north as Deadhorse, adventurous independent travelers are finding their way north. Still, rather than driving solo on a couple of hundred miles of gravel road filled with semis going faster than you knew semis could go, most people traveling to Deadhorse come on a tour with one of Alaska's airlines or bus-tour operators. A guided tour is recommended to really explore the area, and is necessary to cross the oil fields to get to the Arctic Ocean. You'll find no restaurants around the oil fields, though meals can sometimes be arranged through the Prudhoe Bay Hotel; unless you have official business, though, you're not likely to be invited to linger.

ESSENTIALS

Contacts Alaska Airline Vacations ☎ *866/500-5511* ⊕ *www. alaskavacationsalaska.com.*

WHERE TO STAY

For expanded hotel reviews, visit Fodors.com.

$$ 　　 ⊡ **Prudhoe Bay Hotel.** Located near the end of the road at Deadhorse, this
B&B/INN 　hotel is primarily intended for the workers employed in the Prudhoe
Bay oil-field complex, but tourists are also welcome. **Pros:** convenient;
a great view of icy flats and the occasional polar bear. **Cons:** sharing a
bathroom with someone who just got off a 24-hour oil-rig shift; has
bare necessities only. **TripAdvisor:** "perfect for the end of the road," "a
diamond in the rough," "great way of staying far up north." ⑤ *Rooms
from: $110* ☎ *907/659–2449* ⊕ *www.prudhoebayhotel.com* ↩ *270
beds, shared bath* ⧈ *No meals.*

ARCTIC NATIONAL WILDLIFE REFUGE

70 miles southeast of Prudhoe Bay.

Arctic National Wildlife Refuge. The 19-million-acre Arctic National Wild-
life Refuge (ANWR), lying wholly above the Arctic Circle, is adminis-
tered by the U.S. Fish and Wildlife Service and contains one of the few
protected Arctic coastal lands in the United States, as well as millions of
acres of mountains and alpine tundra in the easternmost portion of the
Brooks Range. This protected region is an area of much dispute, as it is
believed to harbor billions of barrels of oil (statistically, hardly a drop
in what the country uses). It is sure to be a hot topic for years to come.

The refuge's coastal areas also serve as critical denning grounds for
polar bears, which spend much of their year on the Arctic Ocean's
pack ice. Other residents here are grizzly bears, Dall sheep, wolves,
musk ox, and dozens of varieties of birds, from snowy owls to geese
and tiny songbirds. The refuge's northern areas host legions of breeding
waterfowl and shorebirds each summer. As in many of Alaska's more
remote parks and refuges, there are no roads here, and no developed
trails, campgrounds, or other visitor facilities. This is a place to experi-
ence true wilderness—and to walk with care, for the plants are fragile
and the ground can be soft and wet in summer. Footprints in tundra
can last a hundred years. You can expect snow to sift over the land
in almost any season, and should anticipate subfreezing temperatures
even in summer, particularly in the mountains. Many of the refuge's
clear-flowing rivers are runnable, and tundra lakes are suitable for base
camps (a Kaktovik or Fort Yukon air taxi can drop you off and pick
you up). The hiking is worth it; upon scrambling up a ridge, you'll look
out on wilderness that seems to stretch forever. ✉ *Refuge Manager,
Arctic National Wildlife Refuge, 101 12th Ave., Room 236, Fairbanks*
☎ *907/456–0250, 800/362–4546* ⊕ *arctic.fws.gov.*

Porcupine Caribou Herd. ANWR is the home of one of the greatest
remaining groups of caribou in the world, the Porcupine Caribou Herd.
The herd, its numbers exceeding 120,000, is unmindful of interna-
tional boundaries and migrates back and forth across Arctic lands into
Canada's adjacent Vuntut and Ivvavik National Parks, flowing like a
wide river across the expansive coastal plain, through U-shape valleys
and alpine meadows, and over high mountain passes.

OUTDOOR ACTIVITIES AND GUIDED TOURS

Arctic Treks. Guided wilderness hikes and backpacking expeditions in both Gates of the Arctic and the Arctic National Wildlife Refuge are available through Arctic Treks. ☎ *907/455–6502* ⊕ *www. arctictreksadventures.com.*

Wilderness Birding Adventures. The owners of Wilderness Birding Adventures are both experienced river runners and expert birders. ☎ *907/694–7442* ⊕ *www.wildernessbirding.com.*

BROOKS RANGE

For those who love vast wilderness landscapes, few places can match the Brooks Range, the "backbone of the Arctic Wilderness"; Alaska's most northerly mountain chain, it stretches east–west across the state above the Arctic Circle. Fortunately, most of this ultimate wilderness is protected by national parklands and the Arctic National Wildlife Refuge. However, it is also a place of great controversy between environmentalists and proponents of oil drilling.

As it stands, you can still go days, and even weeks, without seeing another person. The Brooks are the homeland of grizzlies, wolves, Dall sheep, caribou, moose, musk oxen, and golden eagles. They are also the homeland of Athabascan Indians and Inupiaq and Nunamiut Eskimos, who have lived here for centuries, traveling the mountain pathways and paddling great rivers like the Noatak.

Arctic Treks. Guided wilderness hikes and backpacking expeditions, sometimes combined with river trips, are available through Arctic Treks in both Gates of the Arctic and the Arctic National Wildlife Refuge. ☎ *907/455–6502* ⊕ *www.arctictreksadventures.com.*

9

Travel Smart Alaska

WORD OF MOUTH

"When and where you see wildlife in Alaska seems to have to do with luck. I have known people who have seen lots, and then some who have seen little, on both the Kenai and Denali."

—Barblab

"Before you get into any bookings, map out your entire itinerary and what activities are going to fill your areas. Do not underestimate time and distances necessary."

— BudgetQueen

GETTING HERE AND AROUND

▌ AIR TRAVEL

Alaska Airlines is the state's flagship carrier, with year-round service from its Seattle hub to Anchorage, Fairbanks, Juneau, Ketchikan, and Sitka. The airline and its subsidiary, Horizon Air, also fly to many other North American cities from Seattle. In addition, Alaska Airlines offers year-round flights between Anchorage and Hawaii.

Other airlines that fly to and from the Lower 48 include **American, Delta, Frontier, United,** and **US Airways.** Note, however, that few offer nonstop flights and many of those that do offer such flights do so only seasonally (primarily in the summer months).

The average travel time (nonstop flights only) from Seattle to Anchorage is 3½ hours. Travel times from other destinations depend on your connection, because you'll probably need to route through other cities. Many of the low-fare flights out of Anchorage depart around 1 am, so be sure you're at the airport on the correct day when flying just after midnight.

Major Airlines Alaska Airlines ☎ 800/252–7522 ⊕ www.alaskaair.com. **American Airlines** ☎ 800/433–7300 ⊕ www.aa.com. **Delta Airlines** ☎ 800/221–1212 ⊕ www.delta.com. **Frontier Airlines** ☎ 800/432–1359 ⊕ www.frontierairlines.com. **United Airlines** ☎ 800/864–8331 for U.S. reservations, 800/538–2929 for international reservations ⊕ www.united.com. **US Airways** ☎ 800/428–4322 ⊕ www.usairways.com.

AIRPORTS

Anchorage's Ted Stevens International Airport is Alaska's main hub. There are also major airports ("major" meaning that they serve jets as well as bush planes) in Fairbanks, Juneau, and Ketchikan. The Fairbanks airport is the largest of the three; Juneau and Ketchikan have few facilities and gates. Sixteen other airports throughout the state also serve jet planes.

Unless you're flying from the West Coast or manage to get a nonstop flight, chances are you'll spend some time in Seattle's international airport, Seattle-Tacoma (known locally as Sea-Tac), waiting for a connection. And Vancouver, Canada, is often the starting point for Alaskan cruises that make their first stop in Ketchikan, Alaska's southernmost town.

You won't find much in terms of entertainment in Ted Stevens, Sea-Tac, or Vancouver's airport, so if you have really long layovers at any of the three, consider taking a taxi into the city. Ted Stevens is only 6 miles from downtown Anchorage; Seattle's downtown area is 14 miles from the airport, and if you don't get stuck in the city's notorious rush-hour traffic you can get there in 20 minutes. It can take 30 to 45 minutes to get to downtown Vancouver from the airport.

There are no departure taxes for travel within the United States. Vancouver's airport does have a departure tax of C$5 for flights within British Columbia and the Yukon or C$10 to U.S. destinations, payable at automatic ticket machines or staffed booths before you board.

Airlines and Airports Airline and Airport Links.com ⊕ www.airlineandairportlinks.com.

Airline Security Issues Transportation Security Administration ☎ 866/289–9673 ⊕ www.tsa.gov.

Airport Information Fairbanks International Airport (FAI). ☎ 907/474–2500 ⊕ www.dot.state.ak.us/faiiap. **Juneau International Airport** (JNU). ⊕ www.juneau.org/airport. **Ketchikan Airport** (KTN). ☎ 907/225–6800 ⊕ www.borough.ketchikan.ak.us/airport/airport.htm. **Seattle-Tacoma International Airport** (SEA). ☎ 206/787–3000 ⊕ www.portseattle.org/seatac. **Ted Stevens Anchorage International Airport** (ANC). ☎ 907/266–2437 South Terminal, 907/266–2657 North Terminal ⊕ dot.alaska.gov/anc/index.shtml. **Vancouver**

International Airport (YVR). ☎ 604/207-7077 ⊕ www.yvr.ca.

WITHIN ALASKA

Air travel within Alaska is quite expensive, particularly to Bush destinations where flying is the only option. A round-trip flight between Anchorage and Dutch Harbor typically costs more than $900. Flights from Anchorage to Fairbanks or Juneau are a little more forgiving; at this writing, one-way flights run about $130 and $175, respectively.

AIR TAXIS

The workhorse planes of the north are the Beavers, most of which were built in the 1950s and are still flying. The cost of an air-taxi flight between towns or back-country locations depends on distance and the type of plane used, whether the plane is on floats, the number of people in your group, the length of the flight in each direction (including the time the pilot flies back after dropping you off), and the destination. Typical hourly rates are approximately $600–$800 for a Beaver, with room for up to six people and gear; or $400–$600 for a Cessna 185, with room for three people and gear. Expect to pay more the farther you are from Anchorage.

SMALL PLANES

Many scheduled flights to Bush communities are on small planes that seat 6 to 15 passengers. These planes have played a legendary part in the state's history: bush pilots helped explore Alaska and have been responsible for many dramatic rescue missions. That said, small craft have their inconveniences. They can only transport a limited amount of gear, so plan to leave your large, hard-sided suitcases behind. Small, soft duffels make more sense, and are easier for the pilot to stash in cramped cargo spaces.

Small planes also can't fly in poor weather, which could mean delays counted in days, not hours. And even on good days turbulence might leave you white-knuckled and green in the face. Fortunately, most flights are uneventful, with the scenery below—rather than a rough ride—making them memorable.

Contact **Bering Air** for flights from Nome or Kotzebue to smaller communities of the Far North; **Era Alaska** for flights from Anchorage to Cordova, Homer, Iliamna, Kenai, Kodiak, Valdez, and 17 western Alaska villages; and **Frontier Flying Service, Inc.** (a part of Era Alaska) for flights from Anchorage to Fairbanks, Bethel, and many Bush villages.

Try **Warbelow's Air Ventures** and **Larry's Flying Service** for flights out of Fairbanks to Interior destinations. **Peninsula Airways (PenAir)**, based in Anchorage, covers southwestern Alaska, including Aniak, Dillingham, Dutch Harbor, McGrath, King Salmon, Sand Point, St. George, and St. Paul. **Wings of Alaska** serves several Southeast Alaska towns, including Gustavus, Haines, Juneau, and Skagway. **Grant Aviation** flies from Anchorage to Homer and Kenai as well as Bethel, Dillingham, Emmonak, and St. Mary's.

Carriers Bering Air ☎ 907/443-5464, 800/478-5422 Nome and Unalakleet reservations, 907/442-3943, 800/478-3943 Kotzebue reservations ⊕ www.beringair.com. **Era Alaska** ☎ 907/266-8394, 800/866-8394 ⊕ www.flyera.com. **Frontier Flying Service** ☎ 907/450-7200 Fairbanks, 907/266-8934 Anchorage, 800/866-8394 Outside Anchorage only ⊕ www.frontierflying.com. **Grant Aviation** ☎ 888/359-4726 ⊕ www.flygrant.com. **Larry's Flying Service** ☎ 907/474-9169. **PenAir** ☎ 907/771-2640, 800/448-4226 ⊕ www.penair.com. **Warbelow's Air Ventures** ☎ 907/474-0518, 888/459-6250 ⊕ www.warbelows.com. **Wings of Alaska** ☎ 907/789-0790, 800/789-9464 ⊕ www.wingsofalaska.com.

▌ BOAT TRAVEL

If you're looking for a casual alternative to a luxury cruise, travel as Alaskans do, aboard the ferries of the **Alaska Marine Highway System**. These vessels may not have the same facilities as the big cruise ships, but they do meander through some beautiful regions. In summer you won't be completely without entertainment. Forest Service naturalists ride larger ferries, providing a running commentary on sights, and select routes also have an Arts-on-Board Program, which presents educators and entertainers.

Most long-haul ferries have cabins with private bathrooms. You'll need to reserve these accommodations in advance or settle for a reclining seat on the aft deck. Most ships also have cheap or free showers as well as spaces where you can roll out sleeping bags or even pitch tents. All long-haul ferries have cafeterias with hot meal service (not included in the fare), along with concession stands and vending machines. Some larger boats even have cocktail lounges.

RESERVATIONS AND FARES

You can make reservations by phone or online and have tickets mailed to you or arrange to pick them up from the ferry office at your starting point. Book as far in advance as possible for summertime travel, especially if you have a vehicle. You should also book ahead for the Bellingham–Ketchikan journey.

You can pay for ferry travel with cash, credit card (American Express, Discover, MasterCard, or Visa), cashier's check, money order, certified check, or personal check from an Alaskan bank.

The Bellingham–Ketchikan route costs roughly $240 one way in summer. Shorter trips cost anywhere from $30 to $190 one way. Note that there are surcharges for vehicles (including motorcycles), bicycles, and kayaks. Renting cabins will also increase the fare significantly.

ALASKAPASS

The **AlaskaPass** offers rental-car usage and unlimited travel on ferry and rail lines in Alaska, along with rental-car usage and ferry travel in British Columbia and the Yukon. Passes are available for 15 consecutive days of travel ($879), as well as for eight days of travel in a 12-day period ($749) or 12 days of travel in a 21-day period ($899). There's an $85 booking fee. Most travelers book their entire itinerary in advance; if you don't have a car, there's usually room on ferries for those without prebookings.

Information Alaska Marine Highway ☎ *907/465–3941, 800/642–0066* ⊕ *www. ferryalaska.com.* **AlaskaPass** ☎ *800/248–7598, 206/463–6550* ⊕ *www.alaskapass. com.* **BC Ferries** ☎ *888/223–3779* ⊕ *www. bcferries.com.* **Inter-Island Ferry Authority** ☎ *907/755–4848 Ketchikan Terminal, 907/530–4848 Hollis Terminal, 866/308–4848* ⊕ *www.interislandferry.com.*

ROUTES

The Inside Passage route, which stretches from Bellingham, Washington (or Prince Rupert, British Columbia), all the way up to Skagway and Haines, is the most popular route, mimicking that of most major cruise lines. The Bellingham–Ketchikan trip, the longest leg, takes roughly 37 hours. (The trip from Prince Rupert to Ketchikan takes six hours; BC Ferries provide service from Vancouver to Prince Rupert.) Other trips along the Inside Passage take from three to eight hours.

Sporadic summer service across the Gulf of Alaska from either Prince Rupert, Ketchikan, or Juneau links the Southeast with South Central Alaska destinations (trips usually end in Whittier, about 60 miles south of Anchorage). There's further service to limited ports in South Central Alaska as well as connecting service to the Southwest from Whittier and Homer to Kodiak and Port Lions, respectively. Southwest ferries can take you all the way to Dutch Harbor.

Two high-speed catamarans can cut travel time in half. The MV *Fairweather* is based in Juneau and serves Petersburg and Sitka. In summer the MV *Chenega,* based in Cordova, serves Prince William Sound, with stops in Valdez and Whittier. In fall and winter its route changes, serving either the same route as the *Fairweather* or Ketchikan to Juneau via Wrangell and Petersburg.

The Inter-Island Ferry Authority connects Southeast Alaska's Prince of Wales Island with the towns of Ketchikan, Wrangell, and Petersburg.

Note that although major ports like Juneau and Ketchikan will likely have daily departures, service to smaller towns is much more sporadic—one departure per week in some cases.

▌ BUS TRAVEL

Traveling by bus in Alaska can be more economical than traveling by train or by air, but don't count on it being your main mode of travel. Always confirm your trip via phone, as schedules often change at the last minute.

Greyhound Canada Transportation Corp. serves Vancouver, with service as far north as Whitehorse in the Canadian Yukon. Two companies provide onward bus service into South Central and Interior Alaska from Whitehorse. **Alaska Direct Bus Lines** operates year-round van service connecting Anchorage and Fairbanks with Glennallen, Delta Junction, Skagway, and Tok in Alaska, along with Whitehorse in the Yukon. **Alaska/Yukon Trails** provides year-round bus service between Anchorage and Fairbanks, plus seasonal service connecting Fairbanks with Dawson City in the Yukon.

Denali Overland Transportation has frequent van service in summer between Anchorage, Talkeetna, and Denali National Park and Preserve. The **Alaska Park Connection** has summertime bus service between Seward and Anchorage, continuing north to Denali. **Homer Stage Line** provides year-round service between Anchorage and Homer, plus summertime service connecting Seward with Anchorage and Homer.

Quick Shuttle buses run between Vancouver and Seattle. **Green Tortoise** provides a casual alternative way to travel north, with funky classic buses that are popular with backpackers.

Many bus lines—particularly those heading to Denali—either require or strongly recommend reservations. Accepted forms of payment vary among bus companies, but all accept MasterCard, Visa, and traveler's checks. The AlaskaPass allows unlimited travel on ferry, rail lines, and Holland America buses (Whitehorse to Fairbanks only) in Alaska and the Yukon. (⇨ *For more information, see Boat Travel*).

Bus Information Interior Alaska Bus Line ☎ 800/770-6652 ⊕ www.alaskadirectbusline. com. **Alaska Park Connection** ☎ 800/266-8625 ⊕ www.alaskacoach.com. **Alaska/Yukon Trails** ☎ 800/770-7275 ⊕ www.alaskashuttle. com. **Denali Overland Transportation** ☎ 907/733-2384 ⊕ www.denalioverland. com. **Green Tortoise** ☎ 415/956-7500, 800/867-8647 ⊕ www.greentortoise.com. **Greyhound Canada Transportation Corp.** ☎ 800/661-8747 ⊕ www.greyhound.ca. **Stage Line** ☎ 907/235-2252 Homer, 907/868-3914 Anchorage, 907/422-7037 Seward ⊕ www. stagelineinhomer.com. **Quick Shuttle** ☎ 604/940-4428 Vancouver, 800/665-2122 ⊕ www.quickcoach.com.

FROM ANCHORAGE			
To	Time by Air	Road Miles	Time by Road
Denali	N/A	264 mi	5–6 hrs
Fairbanks	50 mins	364 mi	7–9 hrs
Homer	50 mins	223 mi	5–6 hrs
Talkeetna	20 mins	113 mi	2–3 hrs
Valdez	40 mins	302 mi	6–8 hrs

▌ CAR TRAVEL

Though journeying through Canada on the Alaska Highway can be exciting, the trek from the Lower 48 states is a long one. It's a seven-day trip from Seattle to Anchorage or Fairbanks, covering close to 2,500 miles. From Bellingham, Washington, and the Canadian ports of Prince Rupert and Stewart you can link up with ferry service along the Marine Highway to reach Southeast Alaska.

The Alaska Highway begins at Dawson Creek, British Columbia, and stretches 1,442 miles through Canada's Yukon to Delta Junction; it enters Alaska east of Tok. The two-lane highway is paved for its entire length and is open year-round. Highway services are available about every 50 to 100 miles (sometimes at shorter intervals).

The rest of the state's roads are found almost exclusively in the South Central and Interior regions. They lie mainly between Anchorage, Fairbanks, and the Canadian border. Only one highway extends north of Fairbanks, and one runs south of Anchorage to the Kenai Peninsula. These roads vary from four-lane freeways (rare) to nameless two-lane gravel roads.

If you plan extensive driving in Alaska, join an automobile club such as AAA that offers towing and other benefits. Because of the long distances involved, you should seriously consider a plan (such as AAA Plus) that extends towing benefits to 100 miles in any direction. *The Milepost,* available in bookstores or from Morris Communications, is a mile-by-mile guide to sights and services along Alaska's highways. It's indispensable.

The Alaska Department of Transportation is a great resource for road reports, animal alerts, and other advisories.

Contacts Alaska Department of Transportation ☎ *511 in Alaska, 866/282-7577 outside Alaska.* **American Automobile Association** ☎ *800/222-4357* ⊕ *www.aaa.com.* **The Milepost** ☎ *907/272-6070, 800/726-4707* ⊕ *www.themilepost.com.* **National Automobile Club.** *Membership is open to California residents only.* ☎ *800/622-2136* ⊕ *www.nationalautoclub.com.*

GASOLINE

Gas prices in the Anchorage area are usually higher than those in the Lower 48, and you can expect to pay even more in Juneau and Ketchikan, and far more in remote villages off the road network, where fuel must be flown in. Fuel prices in Canada along the Alaska Highway are also very high. Most stations are self-serve and take Visa and MasterCard; many also accept other credit cards and debit cards.

Many stations remain open until 10 pm, and in the larger towns and cities some stay open 24 hours a day. Most are also open on weekends, particularly along the main highways. In the smallest villages gas may be available only on weekdays, but these settlements typically have only a few miles of roads.

ROAD CONDITIONS

Driving in Alaska is much less rigorous than it used to be, although it still presents some unusual obstacles. Road construction sometimes creates long delays on the Canadian side of the border, so come armed with patience and a flexible schedule. Also, frost damage creates dips in the road that require slower driving.

Moose often wander onto roads and highways. If you encounter one, pull off to the side and wait for the moose to cross. Be especially vigilant when driving at dusk or at night, and keep your eyes open for other moose in the area, since a mother will often cross followed by one or two calves.

Flying gravel is a hazard along the Alaska and Dalton highways, especially in summer. A bug screen will help keep gravel and kamikaze insects off the windshield, but few travelers use them. Some travelers use clear, hard plastic guards to cover their headlights. (These are inexpensive and are available from garage or service stations along the major access routes.) Don't cover headlights with cardboard or plywood, because you'll need your lights often, even in daytime, as dust is thrown up by traffic in both directions.

Unless you plan to undertake traveling on remote highways (especially the Dalton Highway to Prudhoe Bay) you won't need any special equipment. But be sure that the equipment you do have is in working condition, from tires and spare to brakes and engine. Carrying spare fuses, spark plugs, jumper cables, a flashlight with extra batteries, a tool kit, and an extra fan belt is recommended.

If you get stuck on any kind of road, be careful about pulling off; the shoulder can be soft. In summer it stays light late, and though traffic is also light, one of Alaska's many good Samaritans is likely to stop to help and send for aid (which may be many miles away). In winter, pack emergency equipment—a shovel, tire chains, high-energy food, and extra clothing and blankets. Never head out onto unplowed roads unless you're prepared to walk back.

Cell phones are an excellent idea for travel in Alaska, particularly on the main roads. There's no ban on using cell phones in cars in Alaska, and you aren't required to use a hands-free set while driving. Check with your provider about service, though, as gaps in service, even on the road system, are the rule rather than the exception.

RULES OF THE ROAD

Alaska honors valid driver's licenses from any state or country. The speed limit on most highways is 55 mph, but much of the Parks Highway (between Wasilla and Fairbanks) and the Seward Highway (between Anchorage and Seward) is 65 mph. State troopers rigorously enforce these limits.

Unless otherwise posted, you may make a right turn on a red light *after* coming to a complete stop. Seat belts are required on all passengers, and children under age five must be in child safety seats.

State law requires that slow-moving vehicles pull off the road at the first opportunity if leading more than five cars. This is particularly true on the highway between Anchorage and Seward, where RV drivers have a bad reputation for not pulling over. Alaskans don't take kindly to being held up en route to their favorite Kenai River fishing spot.

RVS

The secret to a successful RV trip to Alaska is preparation. Expect to drive on more gravel and rougher roads than you're accustomed to. Batten down everything; tighten every nut and bolt in and out of sight, and don't leave anything to bounce around inside. Travel light, and your tires and suspension system will take less of a beating. Protect your headlights and the grille area in front of the radiator. Make sure you carry adequate insurance to cover the replacement of your windshield.

Most of Alaska's public campgrounds accommodate trailers, but hookups are available only in private RV parks. Water can be found at most stopping points, but it may be limited for trailer use. Think twice before deciding to drive an RV or pull a trailer during the spring thaw. The rough roadbed can be a trial.

RV Rentals and Tours **ABC Motorhome Rentals** ☎ 907/279-2000, 800/421-7456 ⊕ www.abcmotorhome.com. **Alaska Travel Adventures** ☎ 800/323-5757, 907/789-0052 ⊕ www.alaskarv.com. **Clippership Motorhome Rentals** ☎ 907/562-7051, 800/421-3456 ⊕ www.clippershiprv.com. **Fantasy RV Tours** ☎ 800/952-8496 ⊕ www.fantasyrvtours.com. **GoNorth RV Camper Rental** ☎ 907/479-7272, 866/236-7272 ⊕ www.gonorth-alaska.com. **Great Alaskan Holidays** ☎ 907/248-7777, 888/225-2752 ⊕ www.greatalaskanholidays.com.

RENTAL CARS

Rental cars are available in most Alaska towns. In Anchorage and other major destinations, expect to pay at least $55–$75 a day or $300 (and up) a week for an economy or compact car with automatic transmission and unlimited mileage. Some locally owned companies offer lower rates for older cars. Also, be sure to ask in advance about discounts if you have an AAA or Costco card, or are over age 50.

Rates can be substantially higher for larger vehicles, four-wheel drives, SUVs, and vans. (Although the extra space for gear and luggage might be nice, note that you don't need four-wheel drive or an SUV to navigate Alaska highways.) Rates are also higher in small towns, particularly those off the road system in Southeast Alaska or the Bush. In addition, vehicles in these remote towns are typically several years old, and some would rate as "beaters."

You must be 21 to rent a car, and rates may be higher if you're under 25. When picking up a car, non-U.S. residents will need a reservation voucher, a passport, a driver's license (written in English) and a travel policy that covers each driver. Reserve well ahead for the summer season, particularly for the popular minivans, SUVs, and motor homes. A 10% state tax is tacked on to all car rentals, and there are also local taxes.

Be advised that most rental outfits don't allow you to drive on some of the unpaved roads such as the Denali Highway, the Haul Road to Prudhoe Bay, and the McCarthy Road. If your plans include any sketchy routes, make sure your rental agreement covers those areas.

Local Agencies Arctic Rent-A-Car
☎ 888/714–4960, 907/561–2990 Anchorage, 800/478-8696, 907/479–8044 Fairbanks ⊕ www.arcticrentacar.com. **Denali Car Rental** ☎ 907/276–1230, 800/757–1230 in Anchorage ⊕ akdenalicarrental.com.

Major Agencies Alamo ☎ 877/222–9075 ⊕ www.alamo.com. **Avis** ☎ 800/331–1212 ⊕ www.avis.com. **Budget** ☎ 800/527–0700 ⊕ www.budget.com. **Hertz** ☎ 800/654–3131 ⊕ www.hertz.com. **National Car Rental** ☎ 877/222–9058 ⊕ www.nationalcar.com.

CAR-RENTAL INSURANCE
If you own a car and carry comprehensive car insurance for both collision and liability, your personal auto insurance will probably cover a rental, but read your policy's fine print to be sure. If you don't have auto insurance, then you should probably buy the collision- or loss-damage waiver (CDW or LDW) from the rental company. This eliminates your liability for damage to the car.

Some credit cards offer CDW coverage, but it's usually supplemental to your own insurance and rarely covers SUVs, minivans, luxury models, and the like. If your coverage is secondary, you may still be liable for loss-of-use costs from the car-rental company (again, read the fine print). But no credit-card insurance is valid unless you use that card for *all* transactions, from reserving to paying the final bill.

You may also be offered supplemental liability coverage; the car-rental company is required to carry a minimal level of liability coverage insuring all renters, but it's rarely enough to cover claims in a really serious accident if you're at fault.

U.S. rental companies sell CDWs and LDWs for about $15–$25 a day; supplemental liability is usually more than $10 a day. The car-rental company may offer you all sorts of other policies, but they're rarely worth the cost. Personal accident insurance, which is basic hospitalization coverage, is an especially egregious rip-off if you already have health insurance.

▋ CRUISE SHIP TRAVEL

See Chapter 2: Alaska by Cruise Ship for information about cruises and our favorite voyages.

▋ TRAIN TRAVEL

The state-owned **Alaska Railroad** has service connecting Seward, Anchorage, Denali National Park, and Fairbanks, as well as additional service connecting Anchorage and Whittier. The Alaska Railroad also offers a variety of package tours that range from one-day Denali excursions to 10-day tours, which include many excursions along the way between Anchorage and Fairbanks.

Traveling by train isn't as economical as traveling by bus, but it is a wonderful way to go; the scenery along the way is spectacular. Some cars have narration, and food is available on board in the dining car and at the café. Certain private tour companies that offer glitzy trips between Anchorage and Fairbanks hook their luxury railcars to the train. Or sign up for the railroad's Gold Star service on its regular routes—you get confirmed seating in the dome car, priority check-in, and other first-class perks, all for an additional fee, of course.

RESERVATIONS

Reservations are highly recommended for midsummer train travel. You can buy tickets over the phone using a credit card. If your reservation is a month or more ahead of time, the company will mail you the tickets; otherwise you can pick them up at the departure station.

Trains usually leave on time, so be sure to arrive at the station at least 15 minutes prior to departure to ensure that you make it aboard.

The AlaskaPass allows unlimited travel on ferry and rail lines in Alaska. (⇨ *See Boat Travel.*)

Information Alaska Railroad ☎ *907/265–2494 in Anchorage, 800/544–0552* ⊕ *www. alaskarailroad.com.* **Gray Line Alaska** ☎ *907/277–5581 in Anchorage, 907/479–9660 in Fairbanks, 888/425–1737* ⊕ *www. graylinealaska.com.* **White Pass & Yukon Route** ☎ *800/343–7373* ⊕ *www.wpyr.com.*

ROUTES

Travel aboard the Alaska Railroad is leisurely: Anchorage to Seward ($75 one way) takes four hours, Anchorage to Denali ($117–$146) takes a little more than seven hours, and Anchorage to Fairbanks ($167–$210) takes about 12 hours. The trip to Whittier takes a little more than two hours and costs $65 one way (or $80 round-trip).

For a less expensive alternative, ride one of the public dome cars, owned and operated by the railroad. Seating in the public cars is unassigned, and passengers take turns under the observation dome. The railroad's public cars are a great place to meet residents.

Except for the Seward–Anchorage leg, all service operates year-round. Trains run daily in summer; service is reduced from September to late May. Dining cars are available on all trains.

Gray Line of Alaska offers three-day packages that include luxury train travel from Anchorage to Fairbanks or vice versa. You can opt for one-way or round-trip travel. All packages include at least a day of exploring in Denali National Park.

For a scenic and historic five-hour trip between Skagway and Fraser, British Columbia, take the White Pass and Yukon Route, which follows the treacherous path taken by prospectors during the Klondike gold rush of 1897–98. (As this trip is popular with cruise-passenger excursions, advance reservations are strongly recommended.)

ESSENTIALS

■ ACCOMMODATIONS

Off-season hotel rates are often much lower, but most travelers prefer to visit Alaska in summer, when days are long and temperatures are mild. During shoulder season (May and September) travelers may find slightly lower rates, but some businesses and attractions may be closed. Camping is always an option, and, if you're willing to sleep in bunks you can check out the state's many hostels, some of which have family rooms.

BED-AND-BREAKFASTS

Nearly every Alaskan town (with the exception of most Bush villages) has at least one B&B, and dozens of choices are available in the larger cities. At last count, Anchorage had more than 175 B&Bs, including modest suburban apartments, elaborate showcase homes with dramatic vistas, and everything in between.

Reservation Services **Alaska Private Lodgings/Stay with a Friend** ☎ *907/235–2148* ⊕ *www.alaskabandb.com.* **Alaska's Mat-Su Bed & Breakfast Association** ⊕ *www.alaskabnbhosts.com.* **Anchorage Alaska Bed & Breakfast Association** ☎ *907/272–5909, 888/584–5147* ⊕ *www.anchorage-bnb.com.* **Bed & Breakfast Association of Alaska** ⊕ *www.alaskabba.com.* **Bed & Breakfast Association of Alaska, INNside Passage Chapter** ⊕ *www.accommodations-alaska.com.* **Fairbanks Association of Bed & Breakfasts** ⊕ *www.ptialaska.net/~fabb.* **Kenai Peninsula Bed & Breakfast Association** ⊕ *www.kenaipeninsulabba.com.*

HOTELS

Alaskan motels and hotels are similar in quality to those in the Lower 48 states. Most motels are independent, but you'll find the familiar chains (Best Western, Comfort Inn, Days Inn, Hampton Inn, Hilton, Holiday Inn, Marriott, Motel 6, Super 8, and Sheraton, among others) in Anchorage.

Westmark Hotels is a regional chain, owned by cruise-tour operator Holland America Westours, with hotels in Anchorage, Fairbanks, Juneau, Sitka, Skagway, Tok, and Valdez in Alaska, plus Beaver Creek, Dawson City, and Whitehorse in Canada's Yukon Territory.

Princess Tours owns a luxury hotel in Fairbanks and lodges outside Denali National Park, near Denali State Park, near Wrangell–St. Elias National Park, and on the Kenai Peninsula. All hotels listed have private bath unless otherwise noted.

WILDERNESS LODGES

To get away from it all, book a lodge with rustic accommodations in the middle of breathtaking Alaskan wilderness. Some of the most popular are in the river drainages of Bristol Bay, throughout the rugged islands of Southeast Alaska, and along the Susitna River north of Anchorage.

Some lodge stays include daily guided fishing trips as well as all meals. They can be astronomically expensive (daily rates of $250–$1,000 per person and up, plus airfare), so if you're not interested in fishing, avoid these.

Lodges in and near Denali National Park emphasize the great outdoors, and some even include wintertime dogsledding. Activities focus on hiking, rafting, flightseeing, horseback riding, and natural-history walks. For getting deep into the wilderness, these lodges are an excellent alternative to the hotels and cabins outside the park entrance.

■ EATING OUT

Alaska is best known for its seafood, particularly king salmon, halibut, king crab, and shrimp, and you'll find fine seafood on the menu in virtually any coastal Alaskan town. At the open-air (and often all-you-can-eat) salmon bakes in Juneau, Tok, Denali National Park and Preserve, and Fairbanks, you can expect excellent grilled salmon and halibut.

Anchorage has the greatest diversity of restaurants, including classy steak houses, noisy brewpubs, authentic Thai and Mexican eateries, and a wide variety of other ethnic places.

PAYING

Credit cards are widely accepted in resort restaurants and in many restaurants in major towns like Anchorage. Many small towns have only one or two eateries; some establishments may not take credit cards. (⇨ *For guidelines on tipping, see Tipping.)*

RESERVATIONS AND DRESS

During summer high season make reservations as soon as and wherever possible, especially in the Southeast. We specifically mention reservations only when they are essential or when they are not accepted. For popular restaurants, book as far ahead as you can (often 30 days), and reconfirm as soon as you arrive.

Alaska is a casual place. Cruise ships are probably the only places you'll encounter formal wear, though some of the pricier lodges may have dress codes for dinner. We mention dress only when men are required to wear a jacket or a jacket and tie.

WINES, BEER, AND SPIRITS

Alcohol is sold at liquor stores in most towns and cities along the road system, as well as in settlements along the Inside Passage. Alcoholism is a devastating problem in Native villages, and because of this many of these Bush communities are "dry" (no alcohol allowed) or "damp" (limited amounts allowed for personal use, but alcohol cannot be sold). Check the rules before flying into a Bush community with alcohol, or you might find yourself charged with illegally importing it.

Alaska's many excellent microbreweries include the Glacier BrewHouse, Silver Gulch Brewing & Bottling Co., Sleeping Lady Brewing Company, Kodiak Brewery, and the Moose's Tooth Brewing Co. The state's best-known beer, Alaskan Amber, is made by Alaskan Brewing Company in Juneau.

Anchorage is home to several popular brewpubs, and their beers are sold in local liquor stores. Homer Brewing Company in the town of Homer sells its beers in local bars or in take-away bottles. You'll also find brewpubs in Fairbanks, Haines, Skagway, and Wasilla.

▮ HOLIDAYS

In addition to the standard nationwide holidays, Alaska celebrates two statewide holidays: Alaska Day (October 18), celebrating the transfer of the state's ownership from Russia to the United States; and Seward's Day (last Monday in March), which marks the signing of the treaty that authorized the transfer. Although these are not major holidays, some businesses may be closed, particularly in Sitka.

▮ MONEY

Because of its off-the-beaten-path location, Alaska has always been an expensive travel destination. Major roads link Anchorage with Fairbanks and other cities and towns in South Central and Interior Alaska, but most other parts of the state are accessible only by air or water. This is even true of Alaska's state capital, Juneau. Costs in Anchorage and Fairbanks are only slightly higher than for Lower 48 cities, and you will find discount chain stores, but as you head to more remote parts of the state, prices escalate. In Bush communities food, lodging, and transportation costs can be far higher than in Anchorage, since nearly everything must be brought in by air.

▮ PACKING

Befitting the frontier image, dress is mostly casual day and night. Unless you're on a cruise, pack just one outfit that's appropriate for "dress-up" (though even this one set of nice togs probably won't be necessary).

FOR WINTER

Not all of Alaska has the fierce winters usually associated with the state. Winter in the Southeast and South Central coastal regions is relatively mild—Chicago and Minneapolis experience harsher weather than Juneau. But it's a different story in the Interior, where temperatures in the subzero range and biting winds keep most visitors indoors.

The best way to keep warm is to wear layers of clothing, starting with thermal underwear and socks. The outermost layer should be lightweight, windproof, rainproof, and hooded. Down jackets (and sleeping bags) and cotton clothing have the disadvantage of becoming soggy when wet; the newer synthetics (particularly wind-blocking fabrics) are the materials of choice. Footgear needs to be sturdy, and if you're going into the backcountry, be sure it's waterproof. Rubber boots are often a necessity in coastal areas, where rain is a year-round reality. When wearing snow boots, be certain they are not too tight. Restricting your circulation will only make you colder.

FOR SUMMER

Summer travelers should pack plenty of layers, too. Although Alaskan summers are mild, temperatures can vary greatly through the course of a day.

The summer months are infamous for the sometimes dense clouds of mosquitoes and other biting insects. These pests are generally the worst in Interior Alaska but can be an annoyance throughout the state. Bring mosquito repellent with DEET. Also occasionally used (but less effective) is the Avon product Skin So Soft. Mosquito coils may be of some help if you are camping or staying in remote cabins. Head nets are sold in local sporting-goods stores and are a wise purchase if you plan to spend extended time outdoors, particularly in the Interior or on Kodiak Island.

OTHER CONSIDERATIONS

Wherever you go in Alaska (and especially in the Southeast), be prepared for rain. To keep dry, pack a collapsible umbrella or bring a rain slicker, as sudden storms are common.

Always bring good UVA/UVB sunscreen with you on outings, even if the temperature is cool. Sunglasses are also essential, especially for visits to glaciers. A pair of binoculars will help you track any wildlife you encounter.

▮ PASSPORTS

U.S. citizens of all ages traveling between the United States and other countries by air need to present a valid U.S. passport.

All American citizens now need either a passport (for all modes of travel and for anywhere in the world) or a passport card (for land or sea travel only between the United States and Canada, Mexico, Bermuda, and the Caribbean).

Note that parents traveling with small children should bring photocopies of their children's birth certificates to avoid any problems.

U.S. Passport Information U.S. Department of State ☏ 877/487–2778 ⊕ travel.state.gov/ passport.

▮ SAFETY

Alaska does have a high crime rate, but that doesn't mean it's unsafe for tourists.

Women are generally safe in Alaska, but sexual assaults do occur at an alarming rate, so a little extra caution is in order when traveling alone. Common sense is enough of a safeguard in most cases: don't hike in secluded areas alone, be sure to keep your hotel room door locked, don't accept drinks from strangers, and take cabs if you're returning to your hotel late at night. Some of the middle-of-nowhere work towns can resemble frontier towns a little *too* much, and women may experience unwanted attention (catcalls and the like).

In addition to following the bear-safety rules *(listed below)*, women who are camping during their menstrual cycle should take extra care in how they dispose of feminine hygiene products—seal them tightly in plastic bags and store them in bear-proof containers.

OUTDOOR SAFETY

Alaska is big, wild, and not particularly forgiving, so travelers lacking outdoor experience need to take precautions when venturing away from the beaten path. If you lack backcountry skills or feel uncomfortable handling yourself if a bear should approach, hire a guide, go on guided group tours, or join a class at the National Outdoor Leadership School, which is based in Palmer (one hour north of Anchorage).

Education **National Outdoor Leadership School** ☎ *907/745-4047, 800/710-6657* ⊕ *www.nols.edu.*

BEARS

The sight of one of these magnificent creatures in the wild can be a highlight of your visit. By respecting bears and exercising care in bear country, neither you nor the bear should suffer from the experience. Remember that bears don't like surprises. Make your presence known by talking, singing, clapping, rattling a can full of gravel, or tying a bell to your pack, especially when terrain or vegetation obscures views. Travel with a group, which is noisier and easier for bears to detect. If possible, walk with the wind at your back so your scent will warn bears of your presence. And avoid bushy, low-visibility areas whenever possible.

Give bears the right-of-way—lots of it—especially sows with cubs. Don't camp on animal trails; they're likely to be used by bears. If you come across a carcass of an animal or detect its odor, avoid the area entirely; it's likely a bear's food cache. Store all food and garbage away from your campsite in specially designed bear-proof containers (not just airtight ones not designed with bears in mind—there's a chance bears will be able to detect and open them). The Park Service supplies these for hikers in Denali and Glacier Bay national parks and requires that backcountry travelers use them. If a bear approaches you while you are fishing, stop. If you have a fish on your line, cut your line.

If you do encounter a bear at close range, don't panic, and, above all, don't run. You can't outrun a bear, and by fleeing you could trigger a chase response from the bear. Talk in a normal voice to help identify yourself as a human. If traveling with others, stand close together to "increase your size." If the bear charges, it could be a bluff; as terrifying as this may sound, the experts advise standing your ground. If a brown bear actually touches you, then drop to the ground and play dead, flat on your stomach with your legs spread and your hands clasped behind your head. If you don't move, a brown bear will typically break off its attack once it feels the threat is gone. If you are attacked by a black bear, you are better off fighting back with rocks, sticks, or anything else you find, since black bears are more likely to attack a person as prey. Polar bears can be found in remote parts of the Arctic, but tourists are highly unlikely to encounter them in summer.

For more information on bears, ask for the brochure "Bear Facts: The Essentials for Traveling in Bear Country" from any of the Alaska Public Lands offices (⊕ *www.nps.gov/aplic*). Bear-safety information is also available on the Internet at ⊕ *www.state.ak.us/adfg.*

∎ TAXES

Alaska does not impose a state sales tax, but individual cities and boroughs have their own taxes. (Anchorage has no sales tax.) In addition to local taxes, a hotel tax is often applied to your hotel bill. Rates are variable, generally ranging 2%–6%.

You won't have to pay any departure taxes if you're flying within the United States. Vancouver's airport has a departure tax of C$5 for flights within British Columbia and the Yukon or C$10 to U.S. destinations, payable at automatic ticket machines or staffed booths before you board your flight.

▌ TIME

Nearly all of Alaska lies within the Alaska time zone, 20 hours behind Sydney, nine hours behind London, four hours behind New York City, three hours behind Chicago, and one hour behind Los Angeles and western Canada. The nearly unpopulated Aleutian Islands are in the same time zone as Hawaii, five hours behind the East Coast. Alaska observes daylight saving time and changes its clocks along with the Lower 48.

▌ TIPPING

In addition to tipping waiters and waitresses, taxi drivers, and baggage handlers, tipping others who provide personalized services is common in Alaska. Tour-bus drivers who offer a particularly informative trip generally receive a tip from passengers at the end of the tour. Fishing guides are commonly tipped around 10% by their clients, particularly if the guide helped them land a big one. In addition, gratuities may also be given to pilots following a particularly good flightseeing or bear-viewing trip; use your discretion.

▌ TOURS

For certain types of travelers, package tours in Alaska can eliminate some of the guesswork and logistics-induced headaches that often accompany a self-planned tour. For others, the grandeur of the 49th state begs to be explored without such a fixed itinerary. The choice, dear Alaska traveler, is yours.

Several cruise lines—including **Holland America, Royal Caribbean International,** and

TIPPING GUIDELINES FOR ALASKA	
Bartender	$1–$5 per round of drinks, depending on the number of drinks
Bellhop	$1–$5 per bag, depending on the level of the hotel
Coat Check	$1–$2 per item checked unless there is a fee, then nothing
Hotel Concierge	$5 or more, if he or she performs a service for you
Hotel Doorman	$1–$2 if he helps you get a cab
Hotel Maid	$1–$3 a day (either daily or at the end of your stay, in cash)
Hotel Room-Service Waiter	$1–$2 per delivery, even if a service charge has been added
Porter at Airport or Train Station	$1 per bag
Restroom Attendants	Small change or $1 in more expensive restaurants
Skycap at Airport	$1–$3 per bag checked
Taxi Driver	15%–20%, but round up the fare to the next dollar amount
Tour Guide	10% of the cost of the tour
Valet Parking Attendant	$1–$2, but only when you get your car
Waiter	15%–20%, with 20% being the norm at high-end restaurants; nothing additional if a service charge is added to the bill

Princess Cruises—offer "cruisetours" that combine the comforts of cruise-ship travel with inland forays to luxury lodges. A host of smaller tour companies offer package tours as well. Standouts include **Alaska Tours,** which offers tours in almost every corner of the state; and **Alaska Railroad Scenic Rail Tours,** which operates a variety of train-based tours between the state's iconic destinations, including Seward, Denali, and Kenai Fjords. In addition, chances are good that there's a tour operation with itineraries to match your needs and interests—whatever those may be.

Organization **United States Tour Operators Association (USTOA)** ☎ *212/599-6599* ⊕ *www.ustoa.com.*

Recommended Companies **Alaska Airlines Vacations** ☎ *800/468-2248* ⊕ *www.alaskaair. com/shopping/vacations.* **Alaska Bound** ☎ *231/439-3000, 888/252-7527* ⊕ *www. alaskabound.com.* **Alaska Railroad Scenic Rail Tours** ☎ *907/265-2494, 800/544-0552* ⊕ *www.alaskarailroad.com.* **Alaska Tour & Travel** ☎ *907/245-0200, 800/208-0200* ⊕ *www.alaskatravel.com.* **Alaska Tours** ☎ *907/277-3000, 866/317-3325* ⊕ *www. alaskatours.com.* **Alaska Wildland Adventures** ☎ *907/783-2928, 800/334-8730* ⊕ *www.alaskawildland.com.* **Gray Line of Alaska** ☎ *907/277-5581, 888/425-1737* ⊕ *www.graylinealaska.com.* **Holland America Line** ☎ *877/932-4259* ⊕ *www.hollandamerica. com.* **Homer Travel & Tours** ☎ *907/235-7751, 800/478-7751.* **Knightly Tours** ☎ *206/938-8567, 800/426-2123* ⊕ *knightlytours.com.* **Princess Cruises** ☎ *800/774-6237* ⊕ *www. princess.com.* **Royal Caribbean International** ☎ *866/562-7625* ⊕ *www.royalcaribbean. com.* **Viking Travel, Inc.** ☎ *907/772-3818, 800/327-2571* ⊕ *www.alaskaferry.com.*

SPECIAL-INTEREST TOURS
ECOTOURS
Contact **Alaska Wildland Adventures** ☎ *907/783-2928, 800/334-8730* ⊕ *www. alaskawildland.com.*

LEARNING VACATIONS
Contacts **Earthwatch Institute** ☎ *978/461-0081, 800/776-0188* ⊕ *www.earthwatch.org.* **National Audubon Society** ☎ *212/979-3000, 800/274-4201, 907/276-7034 Audubon Alaska* ⊕ *www.audubon.org.* **Natural Habitat Adventures** ☎ *303/449-3711, 800/543-8917* ⊕ *www.nathab.com.* **Nature Expeditions International** ☎ *800/869-0639, 954/693-8852* ⊕ *www.naturexp.com.* **Naturequest** ☎ *800/369-3033* ⊕ *www.naturequesttours. com.* **Sierra Club** ☎ *415/977-5500* ⊕ *www. sierraclub.org.* **Smithsonian Journeys** ☎ *877/338-8687* ⊕ *www.smithsonianjourneys. org.*

NATIVE TOURS
Contacts **Alexander's River Adventure** ☎ *907/474-3924* ⊕ *fairbanks-alaska.com/ alexander.htm.* **Cape Fox Tours** ☎ *907/225-4846* ⊕ *www.capefoxtours.com.* **Goldbelt** ☎ *888/820-2628, 907/463-3412* ⊕ *www. goldbelttours.com.* **Northern Alaska Tour Company** ☎ *907/474-8600, 800/474-1986* ⊕ *www.northernalaska.com.* **Sitka Tribal Tours** ☎ *907/747-7290, 888/270-8687* ⊕ *www. sitkatours.com.*

NATURAL HISTORY TOURS
Contacts **Camp Denali** ☎ *907/683-2290* ⊕ *www.campdenali.com.* **Great Alaska International Adventure Vacations** ☎ *800/544-2261, 907/262-4515 summer, 360/697-6454 winter* ⊕ *www.greatalaska.com.* **Hallo Bay Bear Camp** ☎ *907/235-2237, 888/535-2237* ⊕ *www.hallobay.com.*

PHOTOGRAPHY TOURS
Contacts **Alaska Photography Tours** ☎ *907/781-2208, 888/440-2281* ⊕ *www. alaskaphotographytours.com.* **Joseph Van Os Photo Safaris** ☎ *206/463-5383* ⊕ *www. photosafaris.com.* **Jividen's Naturally Wild Photo Adventures** ☎ *740/774-6243* ⊕ *www. naturallywild.net.*

▌ TRIP INSURANCE

Comprehensive trip insurance is valuable if you're booking a very expensive or complicated trip (particularly to an isolated region) or if you're booking far in advance. Comprehensive policies typically cover trip cancellation and interruption, letting you cancel or cut your trip short because of a personal emergency, illness, or, in some cases, acts of terrorism in your destination. Such policies also cover evacuation and medical care. Some also cover you for trip delays because of bad weather or mechanical problems as well as for lost or delayed baggage.

Another type of coverage to look for is financial default—that is, when your trip is disrupted because a tour operator, airline, or cruise line goes out of business. Generally you must buy this when you book your trip or shortly thereafter, and it's only available to you if your operator isn't on a list of excluded companies.

Always read the fine print of your policy to make sure that you are covered for the risks that are of most concern to you. Compare several policies to make sure you're getting the best price and range of coverage available.

Comprehensive Travel Insurers **Access America** ☎ 800/284-8300 ⊕ www. accessamerica.com. **AIG Travel Guard** ☎ 800/826-4919 ⊕ www.travelguard.com. **CSA Travel Protection** ☎ 800/348-9505 ⊕ www.csatravelprotection.com. **HTH Worldwide** ☎ 610/254-8700 ⊕ www.hthworldwide. com. **Travelex Insurance** ☎ 800/228-9792 ⊕ www.travelex-insurance.com. **Travel Insured International** ☎ 800/243-3174 ⊕ www. travelinsured.com.

Insurance Comparison Sites **Insure My Trip. com** ☎ 800/487-4722 ⊕ www.insuremytrip. com. **Square Mouth.com** ☎ 800/240-0369, 727/564-9203 ⊕ www.squaremouth.com.

■ VISITOR INFORMATION

The Alaska Travel Industry Association (a partnership between the state and private businesses) publishes the *Alaska Vacation Planner*, a free, comprehensive information source for statewide travel year-round. Alaska's regional tourism councils distribute vacation planners highlighting their local attractions.

Get details on Alaska's vast public lands from Alaska Public Lands Information centers in Ketchikan, Tok, Anchorage, and Fairbanks.

British Columbia and Yukon **Tourism British Columbia** ☎ 800/435-5622 ⊕ www. hellobc.com. **Tourism Yukon** ☎ 800/661-0494 ⊕ www.travelyukon.com.

Regional Information **Kenai Convention & Visitors Bureau** ☎ 907/283-1991 ⊕ www. visitkenai.com. **Kenai Peninsula Tourism Marketing Council** ☎ 907/262-5229, 800/535-3624 ⊕ www.kenaipeninsula.org. **Southeast**

Alaska Discovery Center ☎ 907/228-6220 ⊕ www.fs.fed.us/r10/tongass/districts/ discoverycenter. **Southwest Alaska Municipal Conference** ☎ 907/562-7380 ⊕ www. southwestalaska.com.

Statewide Information **Alaska Department of Fish and Game** ☎ 907/465-4100 Juneau ⊕ www.state.ak.us/adfg. **Alaska Division of Parks** ☎ 907/269-8400 Anchorage, 907/451-2705 Fairbanks ⊕ www.alaskastateparks. org. **Alaska Public Lands Information Centers** ☎ 866/869-6887, 907/644-3661 in Anchorage, 907/459-3730 in Fairbanks, 907/228-6220 in Ketchikan, 907/883-5667 in Tok ⊕ www.alaskacenters.gov. **Alaska Travel Industry Association** ☎ 907/929-2200, 800/862-5275 to order Alaska Vacation Planner ⊕ www.travelalaska.com.

ONLINE TRAVEL TOOLS

Alaska.com is a subsidiary of the *Anchorage Daily News* and has travel features, photo galleries, and a service that allows you to order a variety of brochures and e-newsletters. **Alaska Department of Fish and Game** has tips on wildlife viewing, news on conservation issues, and information about fishing and hunting licenses and regulations. **Alaska Geographic** has links to sites with information on the state's public lands, national parks, forests, and wildlife refuges, as well as an online bookstore, where you can find maps and books about the Alaskan experience. **Alaska Magazine** posts some of its feature stories online and maintains an extensive statewide events calendar. **Alaska Native Heritage Center** has information on Alaska's Native tribes, as well as links to other cultural and tourism websites.

Contact **Alaska.com** ⊕ www.alaska.com. **Alaska Department of Fish and Game** ⊕ www.adfg.alaska.gov. **Alaska Geographic** ⊕ www.alaskageographic.org. **Alaska Magazine** ⊕ www.alaskamagazine.com. **Alaska Native Heritage Center** ⊕ www.alaskanative. net.

INDEX

PHOTO CREDITS

1, Randall Pugh. 3, Stephen Frink Collection/Alamy. Chapter 1: Experience Alaska: 6-7, Papilio/Alamy. 8, Brian Embacher. 9 (left), Frank Lukasseck/age fotostock. 9 (right), Morales/age fotostock. 10, John W. Warden/age fotostock. 11 (left), Photodisc. 11 (right), Clark James Mishler/Aurora Photos. 12 (left), José Vigano. 12 (top center), Richard Cummins/viestiphoto.com. 12 (top right), Salvatore P. DeRicco. 12 (bottom), Marlene Edin. 13 (top left), Joshua Strong. 13 (bottom left), Alaska Stock LLC/Alamy. 13 (bottom center), Bernd Römmelt/Mauritius Images/age fotostock. 13 (right), Ron Niebrugge/Alamy. 14, SCPhotos/Alamy. 15, Anchorage Museum/Alaska Stock Images/age fotostock. 16, True North Images/ age fotostock. 17, Richard Cummins/viestiphoto.com. 18, Library of Congress Prints and Photographs Division. 19 (left), Glenbow Museum/age fotostock. 19 (right), Alaska Stock LLC/Alamy. 20, World-Foto/Alamy. 22, Photodisc. 23, Bill Terry/viestiphoto.com. 25, Stuart Westmorland/age fotostock. 36, Ron Niabruggo/Almy. 37, Workfoto/Almy. 38, Herb Christian. 39 (top), Fodor's Travel Publication. 39 (bottom), Steve Faber/Stockphoto. 40, Jeff Schultz. 41, Seymour Levy. 42, Som Vembar. Chapter 2: Alaska by Cruise Ship: 43, American Safari Cruises. 44, Jon Arnold Images Ltd/Alamy. 47, Jochen Tack/ Alamy. 48, Visual&Written SL/Alamy. Chapter 3: The Alaska Wilderness: 61, Harry Kolenbrander/ iStockphoto. 62, areeya/Shutterstoc k. 63, David Parsons/iStockphoto. 66-67, Alaska Stock / age fotostock. 68 (top), John Hyde / age fotostock. 68 (2nd from top), Frond and cone by Peter Stevenshttp:// www.flickr.com/photos/nordique/4336465454/ Attribution License. 68 (3rd from top), Walter Siegmund/Wikimedia Commons. 68 (bottom), Nancy Nehring/iStockphoto. 69 (top), Vacclav/Shutterstock. 69 (2nd from top), Young Mom by Carl Chapmanhttp://www.flickr.com/photos/carlchapman/ 3192849285/ Attribution-ShareAlike License. 69 (3rd from top), sitkablacktaileddeer by U.S. Department of Agriculturehttp://www.flickr.com/photos/usdagov/5710052397/ Attribution-ShareAlike License. 69 (bottom), Mayskyphoto/Shutterstock. 70, Wanetta Ayers/Wikimedia Commons. 71 (top), Aumiller, Larry/Wikimedia Commons. 71 (bottom), Bald Eagle, Kodiak Island, Alaska, near the Kodiak Launch Complex (KLC), Kodiak, Alaska by James Gordonhttp://www.flickr.com/photos/james_gordon_los_ angeles/5682224801/ Attribution License. 72-73, Alaska Stock / age fotostock. 74 (top), Alaskan Paper Birch by Alfred Cookhttp://www.flickr.com/photos/bottomdollar/414221300/ Attribution License. 74 (center), oksana.perkins/Shutterstock. 74 (bottom), Sten Porse/Wikimedia Commons. 75 (top), Deb Turman/Shutterstock. 75 (2nd from top), Zefram/Wikimedia Commons. 75 (3rd from top), Richard Seeley/ Shutterstock. 75 (bottom), Patrick Hermans/Shutterstock. 76, Home Stretch by Douglas Evanshttp:// www.flickr.com/photos/dougevans/5967978434/ Attribution-ShareAlike License. 77 (top), areeya/Shutterstock. 77 (bottom), Gary Whitton / Shutterstock.com. 78-79, Denali National Park backpacking 2010 by http://www.flickr.com/photos/16725630@N00/4939263540/ Attribution License. 80 (top), Tom Thulen / Alamy. 80 (2nd from top), Blueberries were everywhere on the climb up to Lost Lake by Frank Kovalchekhttp://www.flickr.com/photos/72213316@N00/3866114851/ Attribution License. 80 (3rd from top), Saxifraga oppositifolia by Joan Simonhttp://www.flickr.com/photos/simonjoan/5605279565/ Attribution-ShareAlike License. 80 (bottom), TTphoto/Shutterstock. 81 (top), Images in the Wild/iStockphoto. 81 (2nd from top), Hi-Res Version by Troyhttp://www.flickr.com/photos/arctic_troy/4914115675/ Attribution-ShareAlike License. 81 (3rd from top), Harry Kolenbrander/iStockphoto. 81 (bottom), caribou by ori0nishttp://www.flickr.com/photos/sach1tb/5918575964/ Attribution-ShareAlike License. 82, BradfordRex/Shutterstock. 83 (top), Lars Johansson/iStockphoto. 83 (bottom), Suzann Julien/Thinkstock. 84-85, Alaska Stock / age fotostock. 86 (top), Richard Fitzer/Shutterstock. 86 (center), Complementary Colors by Michael Arrighihttp://www.flickr.com/photos/arrighi/5718394863/ Attribution License. 86 (bottom), Accent Alaska.com / Alamy. 87 (top), Accent Alaska.com / Alamy. 87 (center), Andrea Leone/Shutterstock. 87 (bottom), Håkan Karlsson/iStockphoto. 88, Glacier Bay National Park, Alaska by Emmett Humehttp://www.flickr.com/photos/emmett_hume/5983178712/ Attribution-Share-Alike License. 89 (top), Sitting Pretty on Ruth Glacier by Andrei Taranchenkohttp://www.flickr.com/ photos/9702212@N03/2644607083/ Attribution License. 89 (bottom), oksana.perkins/Shutterstock. 90-91, Alaska Stock / age fotostock. 92 (top), ImageState / Alamy. 92 (2nd from top), E.R. Degginger / Alamy. 92 (3rd from top), Chocolate Lily by Dancing Nomadhttp://www.flickr.com/photos/dancingnomad3/5847101839/ Attribution-ShareAlike License. 92 (bottom), Alexander Solentsov/iStockphoto/ Thinkstock. 93 (top), IPK Photography/Shutterstock. 93 (2nd from top), Jupiterimages/Photos.com/ Thinkstock. 93 (3rd from top), Jupiterimages/Photos.com/Thinkstock. 93 (bottom), Golden Eagle about to Take Off by http://www.flickr.com/photos/dlbezaire/3666233827/ Attribution-ShareAlike License. 94, Michael Papasidero/Shutterstock. 95 (top), Vivian Fung/Shutterstock. 95 (bottom), Roman Van/ Shutterstock. 96-97, FloridaStock/Shutterstock. 98(top), Accent Alaska.com / Alamy. 98 (2nd from top), Accent Alaska.com / Alamy. 98 (3rd from top), Accent Alaska.com / Alamy. 98 (bottom), Kevin Schafer / Alamy. 99 (top), Joyce Johnsen/iStockphoto. 99 (2nd from top), Steven Russell Smith Photos/Shutterstock. 99 (3rd from top), Richard Legner/iStockphoto. 99 (bottom), Sea Otter 2 by Dave Bezairehttp://

NOTES